BUILDING ACCOUNTS OF KING HENRY III

BUILDING ACCOUNTS OF KING HENRY III

EDITED BY

H. M. COLVIN

Fellow of St. John's College
Oxford

OXFORD
AT THE CLARENDON PRESS
1971

Oxford University Press, Ely House, London W. I

GLASGOW NEW YORK TORONTO MELBOURNE WELLINGTON
CAPE TOWN SALISBURY IBADAN NAIROBI DAR ES SALAAM LUSAKA ADDIS ABABA
BOMBAY CALCUTTA MADRAS KARACHI LAHORE DACCA
KUALA LUMPUR SINGAPORE HONG KONG TOKYO

PRINTED IN GREAT BRITAIN
AT THE UNIVERSITY PRESS, OXFORD
BY VIVIAN RIDLER
PRINTER TO THE UNIVERSITY

EDITOR'S PREFACE

THOUGH architecture has always had architects among its historians, builders have rarely shown much interest in the history of their own craft. It is therefore gratifying to place on record the fact that this volume of building accounts was commissioned by a builder and published at the expense of the Trust of which he was the founder. It is to the late Mr. Norman Wates and the Wates Foundation that this book owes its existence, and as its Editor it is my first duty to express my gratitude to them for giving me the opportunity to print these documents. I much regret that it did not prove possible to publish this book before Mr. Wates's death, and wish to acknowledge the patience with which the Foundation has awaited the results of what has necessarily been a spare-time occupation, carried out in the intervals of teaching and research.

To Sir Nikolaus Pevsner, who first suggested the idea of such a publication to Mr. Wates and myself, I am grateful both for his continuing interest in its progress, and for the Foreword which he has kindly written. To Mr. L. C. Hector I owe a rather special debt. Not only has the index been his work in all but its typographical presentation (which conforms to the normal conventions of the Clarendon Press); he has also improved the text at many points, both by reading what to me seemed illegible in the original manuscripts, by correcting errors of transcription and translation, and above all by enforcing those principles of editorial consistency from which I have been only too apt to stray. For such errors and inconsistencies as remain I alone am responsible.

For assistance in the laborious task of transcribing the original documents I am indebted to Miss Coral Wicks and Mr. Angus Fowler. The architectural drawings are the work of Mr. Alan Cook. Mr. Martin Biddle kindly provided information used in drawing Figure 2. Several documents from the Muniment Room of Westminster Abbey are published by kind permission of the Dean and Chapter, and the transcripts of Crown-copyright records appear by permission of H.M. Stationery Office. The sources of the photographic plates are acknowledged in the List of Illustrations.

H. M. C.

CONTENTS

FOREWORD

BY SIR NIKOLAUS PEVSNER

THIS volume and, I hope, further volumes are due to the late Mr. Norman Wates's curiosity about the cost of medieval buildings, the methods of their construction, the transport of materials for them, and similar problems. When I first met him, we talked about such things and especially about L. F. Salzman's *Building in England down to 1540* (Clarendon Press, 1952), the one book in which one could find answers. But even that remarkable work is by no means definitive, and so Mr. Wates suggested that the Wates Foundation might help in doing something more comprehensive and more systematic, especially concerning buildings of major importance. I put it to him that the only way to obtain results would be to look round for such original building accounts as survive and then to publish them lock, stock, and barrel. He concurred at once, and so enthusiastically that in this volume we have now at long last some of the earliest building accounts in existence, those of Henry III for Dover Castle, the Great Hall of Winchester Castle, and Westminster Abbey. Portions of these had of course already been published in one form or another, but neither easily get-at-able nor complete. Moreover the editor now is Mr. Colvin, fresh from the monumental *History of the King's Works*, of which the first two volumes were published in 1963. Mr. Colvin is probably better known to laymen by his *Biographical Dictionary of English Architects, 1660–1840* (John Murray, 1954), a prodigious work, done single-handed by him to a degree of perfection which in America would be aimed at by appointing a regiment of assistants. But Mr. Colvin is a medievalist by training and much of his current work is concerned with medieval history. In preparing this volume for publication he has received much help from Mr. L. C. Hector, formerly an Assistant Keeper of the Public Records, who has contributed greatly to the accuracy of both text and translation.

That the book will be welcomed I have no doubt. May it lead to further volumes on the later accounts for Westminster Abbey, on the accounts for St. Stephen's Chapel in the Palace of Westminster, on the Exeter accounts, the Ely accounts, the Vale Royal accounts, the Durham accounts. Only when they are all available and when a comprehensive glossary has been compiled of the terms used in them and their meaning, can we hope that those who wish to see the activities of the master masons and their workmen come to life will find satisfaction.

N. P.

EDITORIAL NOTE

ALTHOUGH the aim has been to reproduce in the Latin text exactly what the medieval clerks wrote, the conversion of manuscript into print inevitably imposes some conventions on the transcriber. In the present volume the confused arrangement of some of the accounts has been mitigated by typographical adjustment and the italicization of some headings and sub-headings. With certain exceptions all abbreviated words have normally been extended whenever the extension is certain. When it is not, the medieval mark of contraction has been indicated in the usual way by an apostrophe. Certain recurrent terms of money and quantity have, however, generally been standardized, whatever the form in which they appear in the original manuscript. Thus the words *libre*, *solidi*, *denarii*, meaning pounds sterling, shillings, and pence, have been consistently printed as *li.*, *sol.*, *d.*, irrespective of the form used in the manuscript. Other abbreviations regularly used are:

cent. when it is not clear whether the word intended is *centum* or the appropriate inflexion of *centena* (*centenum*).
dim. for all inflexions of *dimidius*.
mill. when it is not clear whether the word intended is *mille*, or the appropriate inflexion of *millia*, *millenarium*, etc.
quart. when it is not clear whether the word intended is the appropriate inflexion of *quarterium*, *quarterius*, *quart(e)rona*, etc., or the vernacular *quart(e)ron*.

In using the figures printed in the translation the reader must be warned of the possibility that in some cases the figure C represents not 100, but the 'long hundred' of 120. There is no evidence to suggest that long hundreds were used in the Dover or Winchester accounts: on the contrary these accounts from time to time afford evidence that C was equivalent to 100. At Westminster, on the other hand, there is one clear case of the use of the long hundred (pp. 229, 237), and its use may be suspected, though it cannot be proved, throughout the three 1259 accounts (Nos. 7, 8, and 9). In the case of these three accounts, at least, any calculation involving items such as boards, tiles, laths, and nails, which were habitually bought by the hundred or thousand, should take into account the possibility that the figures printed in the translation should be increased by 20 per cent.

LIST OF ILLUSTRATIONS

FIGURES

PLATES

(*at end*)

INTRODUCTION

It is well known that England is unique in the wealth of her medieval public records, and it is therefore not surprising that among them there should be some of the earliest building accounts in Western Europe. Records of royal expenditure on building are, indeed, extant from the reign of Henry II (1154–89) onwards, but these are for the most part summary enrolments only, and the earliest detailed accounts for major building operations in England are those printed in this volume. They date from the reign of Henry III (1216–72), a king whose political ineptitude did not prevent him from being one of the greatest patrons of architecture, sculpture, and painting in our history. On the Continent the only building records of comparable antiquity to have survived as a series appear to be those of Charles of Anjou as King of Sicily (1266–85), printed in 1912–26 by Sthamer.[1] Though many important texts relating to building in medieval France were collected together by Mortet and Deschamps in their invaluable *Recueil de textes relatifs à l'histoire de l'architecture en France au Moyen Age* (Paris, 1911–29), very few building accounts are to be found among them, and none comparable to the series printed below. Imperfect though they are, it would indeed appear that the accounts for the building of Westminster Abbey are unique as an administrative record of the construction of a major church of the High Gothic period.[2] Though some, but by no means all, of the Westminster accounts were printed in the nineteenth century, none of them were published in a form that was either satisfactory to the scholar or easily intelligible to the layman.[3] As for the still earlier

[1] E. Sthamer, *Dokumente zur Geschichte der Kastellbauten Kaiser Frederichs II. und Karls I. von Anjou*, 2 vols., Leipzig 1912–26, forming vols ii and iii of *Die Bauten der Hohenstaufen in Unteritalien* published by the Königl. Preussiches Historisches Institut at Rome.

[2] Reference should, however, be made here to the account for works at Vale Royal Abbey, Cheshire, in 1277–80, printed in *The Ledger Book of Vale Royal Abbey* (Lancs. & Cheshire Record Soc. 1914), and studied by D. Knoop and G. P. Jones in *Ars Quatuor Coronatorum* xliv (1931), pp. 5–47. See also *History of the King's Works*, ed. Colvin, i (1963), pp. 248–57.

[3] The Westminster account for 1253 (below, No. 6) was printed by Gilbert Scott as an appendix to his *Gleanings from Westminster Abbey* (1863). A

accounts for works at Dover and Winchester castles, none of these has ever been printed, and it is only recently that one of them has been identified.[1] These are not the only building accounts that survive from the reign of Henry III,[2] but they are by far the most important, and between them they fully illustrate the process of account of which they are the record. They also throw a good deal of light on the employment of labour and the economics of building in thirteenth-century England. As evidence of building technology they are less informative than could be wished: anyone who hopes to learn from them the secrets of the Gothic masons will be disappointed, for there is nothing here to tell him about the setting out of a chevet, or the construction of a high vault. But, as the index shows, many technical building terms are to be found in these pages, and whether one is interested in words as such or in the tools and processes that they represent, it is to these accounts that one must repeatedly turn for their earliest known occurrence.

In the edition that follows, an English translation has been provided for the benefit of those who do not read Latin. Translating documents of this kind is a hazardous enterprise, and no two persons, however expert, would probably produce an identical text. While hoping that his version will prove acceptable, the present editor can only hope that too much reliance will not be placed upon it. Whenever possible the opportunity has been taken to give the modern forms of personal and place-names occurring in the texts. The counties in which places named lie will be found in the index.

Nearly all the documents here printed are more or less damaged, and large portions of some of them are almost obliterated. Though the formal Exchequer hand in which the enrolments are written is easily decipherable, several of the preliminary accounts were casually written on odd scraps of parchment in a far from orderly fashion. The task of transcription has therefore been arduous, and frequent recourse has been had to the ultra-violet lamp in order to decipher passages that are all but illegible. In the case of one of the Dover accounts (No. 2) a transcript made in the nineteenth

translation of the 1259 account (No. 7) was published in F. Devon's *Issues of the Exchequer* (1837). A portion of No. 3 was printed by J. G. Noppen in *Antiquaries Journal* xxviii (1949), p. 147.

[1] Winchester, No. 2.

[2] Two accounts for minor works at Marlborough Castle in 1237–9 were edited by Miss S. B. Challenger (now Mrs. R. L. Storey) for the Wiltshire Archaeological Society's Records Branch, vol. xii (1956).

century by R. C. Hussey[1] has been helpful in making out some passages that were then more easily legible than they are now. Although some errors have no doubt been committed, it is hoped that the text printed below is comparable in accuracy with that of other public records of the period published early in the nineteenth century by the Record Commission and more recently by Her Majesty's Stationery Office.

The purpose of this edition is to make these, the earliest English building accounts, generally available to architectural and economic historians rather than to exploit their contents in a lengthy introduction. The notes which follow are therefore intended as a guide to the reader rather than as anything in the nature of an exhaustive analysis of the documents.

THE PROCESS OF ACCOUNT

All the principal documents printed below were products of the highly organized administrative system which had developed in England in the course of the twelfth century. Its two most important departments were a secretariate, the Chancery, and an accounting body, the Exchequer. From the Chancery issued those precepts, known as writs, which authorized the expenditure of money for building or for any other purpose desired by the king or his ministers. From the reign of John onwards copies of such writs were made for reference, and are preserved today among the Public Records. As they are accessible in print, it has not been thought necessary to print below the many writs relating to works at Dover, Winchester, and Westminster throughout the reign of Henry III, but only to provide a selection of those relating more or less directly to the surviving accounts. The accounts themselves all form part of the records of the Exchequer,[2] whose responsibility it was to ensure that every royal official accounted for the money that had been entrusted to him. The ultimate record of such an audit was a highly condensed statement of receipt and expenditure which was enrolled on the Great Roll of the Exchequer known as the

1 Bodleian Library, MS. Top. Gen. c. 20.

2 Though two of them (Winchester, No. 2 and Westminster, No. 12) have by some accident found their way into the miscellanea of the Chancery.

Pipe Roll (Dover, No. 4, Winchester, No. 4, Westminster, No. 15). But before closing an account the Barons of the Exchequer demanded both authority for, and proof of, the expenditure incurred. Authority for it was of course provided by the Chancery writs. Proof of it had in the past been furnished by the sworn testimony of 'law-worthy' men—men, that is, whose word would be acceptable in a court of law—who were required to come to the Exchequer and declare on oath that the accountant had, to their knowledge, spent the money in the way he claimed. Instances of this procedure will be found below (pp. 21, 93). But this archaic method of audit was scarcely appropriate to complex and prolonged building operations of the kind represented by this volume, and the special commissioners (known as 'keepers of the works') to whom the works at Dover, Winchester, and Westminster were entrusted were all expected to submit written evidence of their outlay. In order to do so they were obliged to keep a running record of their disbursements, which could periodically be summarized for submission to the Exchequer. Thus at Winchester we have fragments of a weekly record of the wages paid to masons, carpenters, and labourers in 1222 (No. 2), a statement of expenditure from 1222 to 1224 (No. 3) incorporating the weekly totals furnished by the previous document, and the final enrolment (No. 4) summarizing in half a dozen lines the contents of No. 3 and of several other comparable rolls now lost. In the Dover documents the process of condensation is less clearly exemplified, but in the case of Westminster we again have the nominal rolls of workmen, various statements, more or less condensed, of expenditure over longer or shorter periods, and finally the Exchequer enrolments. The last, it will be noted, do not begin until 1264, nearly twenty years after the commencement of the works in 1245. The explanation of this anomaly is that when Henry III began building at Westminster he set up a special board or 'exchequer' to audit the accounts of the keepers of the works (cf. writ no. xxv) and it was not until 1266 that the Exchequer succeeded in asserting its rights as the ultimate place of account.[1]

Although the enrolments give the total audited expenditure of the respective keepers of the works they do not necessarily represent the total cost of the buildings in question, for (as the writs

[1] For further details see *History of the King's Works* i, pp. 130–57.

show) sheriffs and other royal officials might be ordered to supply timber, lead, and other building materials which were to be obtained in their own districts, and for this expenditure they would account separately at the Exchequer. Moreover, as much timber and some stone came from royal works and quarries, no payment was made for its capital value, but only for its felling or extraction and for its transport to the building site.

THE BUILDINGS

All three of the building operations documented in this volume have recently been described at some length elsewhere,[1] and only a brief summary is therefore required here.

Both at Dover and at Winchester the purpose of the works was to make good damage incurred during the warfare at the end of the previous reign. Both castles had been besieged by the French forces commanded by the future Louis VIII of France, and their restoration was one of the major tasks of the regency which governed the kingdom during Henry III's minority. At Winchester the reconstruction included the building of a new and magnificent great hall which still survives (Fig. 2), and many references to this building will be found in the accounts. At Dover, whose heroic defence by Hubert de Burgh had saved the kingdom for the infant Henry, a great programme of fortification was undertaken in order to render the castle as nearly impregnable as possible. The main gateway upon which the French had directed their attack was filled up with a beaked tower specially designed to deflect missiles fired from the level ground in front, and its place was taken by a new gatehouse of improved design in a more commanding situation on the west side of the castle. At the same time the outer curtain begun by Henry II and John was extended towards the cliff in order to complete the double line of fortifications which made Dover one of the most advanced examples of military architecture in Europe (Fig. 1). The breaching of the wall to build 'the new gate', the laying of its foundations, and the erection of the 'pilers' of its drawbridge are all specifically mentioned in the

[1] *History of the King's Works*, vols. i and ii (1963), with references to further literature on all these buildings.

accounts. An unusual feature of the defences was a series of underground passages from which the garrison could issue unseen in order to take their enemies in the rear. These too are referred to in the accounts printed below.

Dover and Winchester were both works of Henry's minority,[1] and (although he visited Dover in 1227) he was too young to be personally responsible for such major works of defence. Though the writs were, of course, written in his name, they were all issued by authority of two members of the regency council, Hubert de Burgh and Peter des Roches, Bishop of Winchester. Westminster Abbey, on the other hand, was the great artistic achievement of his majority, upon which he lavished all the enthusiasm of a royal connoisseur. The work began in 1245 and was still in progress at the time of the king's death in 1272. Henry had, however, lived long enough to see the body of St. Edward translated to the new shrine which was the religious and artistic climax of the new church, and by 1272 the whole of the eastern arm, the crossing, and five of the twelve bays of the nave were finished (Fig. 4). Between 1245 and 1272 three successive master-masons were in charge of the works: first Master Henry 'de Reyns', to whom the design of the whole must be attributed, then Masters John of Gloucester (1253–60) and Robert of Beverley (1260–72). Each was in turn one of the keepers of the works who were responsible for the financial side of the operation. As the enrolled accounts make clear, the keepers of the abbey works were at the same time keepers of the works at the neighbouring palace of Westminster. Though Henry's major works here had been completed before 1245, further repairs and alterations were called for from time to time, and a full record of those carried out in 1259 has survived (Nos. 7–9). Attention may also be drawn to an account for 1265 which shows Master Walter of Durham, the king's painter, at work in the palace with six other artists.

For the student of medieval building the most valuable of the Westminster accounts is No. 6, which gives the total number of workmen of different trades employed week by week throughout the greater part of the year 1253. For the convenience of readers a tabulated analysis of this account, previously published in *The*

[1] One later account for works at Winchester is also printed in this volume (No. 5).

Week	*White cutters*	*Marblers*	*Layers*	*Carpenters*	*Polishers*	*Smiths*	*Glaziers*	*Plumbers*	*Labourers*	*Total*
1 Feb.–18 April (11 weeks)	74	45	24	4	13	20	15		131	326
28 April–4 May	39	14	20	32	13	19	14	4	150	305
5–12 May	39	15	26	32	13	19	14	4	176	338
12–18 May	39	15	26	32	15	17	14	6	200	364
19–25 May	41	16	31	32	15	17	13	6	213	384
26 May–1 June	41	16	31	32	15	17	13	6	213	384
2–8 June	41	16	35	33	15	18	13	6	213	390
9–15 June										
16–22 June	42	18	28	33	15	17	14	4	220	391
23–9 June	53	49	28	33	15	17	14	4	220	433
30 June–6 July	56	49	28	23	15	17	14	4	220	426
7–13 July	60	49	14	21	15	17	13	4	215	408
14–20 July	60	49	14	16	15	17	6	4	215	396
21–7 July	66	49	14	16	15	17	6	4	140	327
28 July–3 Aug.	68	49	14	16	15	16	6	4	133	321
4–10 Aug.	78	49	14	16	15	16	6	4	135	333
11–17 Aug.	68	49	14	16	15	16	2		138	318
18–24 Aug.	68	49	14	16	15	16	2		138	318
25–31 Aug.	49	31	13	13	15	18	2		91	232
1–7 Sept.	49	31	13	13	15	18	2		91	232
8–14 Sept.	49	15	13	13	15	18	2		91	216
15–21 Sept.	56	15	23	13	15	18	2		108	250
22–8 Sept.	58	14	26	13	15	18	3		120	267
29 Sept.–5 Oct.	60	14	31	14	15	18	3		155	310
6–12 Oct.	42	14	31	14	15	18	3		155	292
13–19 Oct.	58	16	33	15	16	18	3	1	158	318
20–6 Oct.	58	15	34	14	15	18	2	1	157	314
27 Oct.–2 Nov.	58	15	34	14	15	18	2		140	296
3–9 Nov.	58	11	11	14	16	18	2		140	270
10–16 Nov.	34	7	5	9		13	2		30	100
17–23 Nov.	35	7	5	9		13	2		35	106
24–30 Nov.	35	7	4	9		13	2	2	37	109
1–6 Dec.	35	7	4	9		13	2	2	37	109

History of the King's Works, has been reprinted here with some corrections.[1]

In view of the French characteristics of the abbey church it is interesting to find, in an undated memorandum (No. 11), unequivocal evidence of the employment of masons from across the

[1] The significance of this table as evidence of the manpower involved in major medieval building operations is considered by H. Thomas Johnson in 'Cathedral Building and the Medieval Economy' in *Explorations in Entrepreneurial History*, Spring 1967.

Channel. For whatever nationality may be assigned to Master Henry 'de Reyns',[1] there can be no doubt that Matthew and Henry de Rems came from Rheims, and that Richard Norman and Richard of Caen were of Norman origin. It would, however, be unwise to exaggerate their significance as a link between French and English Gothic, for none of them was a master, and all four of them are bracketed together as masons who had failed to complete their allotted tasks.

WAGES AND CONDITIONS OF EMPLOYMENT

On this subject the accounts here printed furnish abundant information. In the thirteenth century it does not appear to have been the normal practice, at any rate in England,[2] to enter into contracts for the execution of entire structures. Most of the work at Dover, Winchester, and Westminster was accordingly paid for by the day. Relatively small jobs were, however, put out to task for a fixed sum agreed in advance. Thus, at Dover, masons were engaged to cut freestone by task at rates varying from 12*s.* to 13*s.* 4*d.* per 100 feet. At Westminster such payments were distinguished from the daily wage-roll by being included with the purchases of materials. Here we find evidence of some more substantial tasks: in 1249 Master Aubrey was engaged on a task in the cloister worth £30 (p. 219) and the entrance to the chapter-house was being built by the same method (p. 227). It is understandable that a skilled operation such as roofing a building with lead should be performed on a task-work basis (p. 381), but some quite trivial and unskilled jobs were also included under the heading of *Tasche*. Thus at Westminster in 1259 even the carriage of sand and stone was sometimes performed by task, and the employment of a man to take delivery of building-materials on feast-days was similarly recorded (p. 353). In fact the same men might be paid by the day one week and as task-workers

[1] Though 'Reyns' was a contemporary English spelling of 'Reims', it was also the normal thirteenth-century form of Rayne in Essex. Unfortunately only one document (W.A.M. 17358) is known in which Henry is given this toponymic.

[2] Task-work was extensively employed by Philip Augustus of France for his great programme of fortification on the French frontiers in the early years of the thirteenth century (V. Mortet et P. Deschamps, *Recueil de textes relatifs à l'histoire de l'architecture en France au Moyen Age* ii, 1929, pp. 214–20), but in England there is little evidence of extensive masonry contracts before the fourteenth century.

the next. At Dover in 1221 four masons were regularly paid for cutting stone at 12*s.* a hundred feet, but in one fortnight in August they were paid 4*d.* a day for 9 days, *quia incisio defuit de tassca*, which appears to mean 'because the cutting fell short of the task'. It may be presumed either that absenteeism interfered with the performance of the agreed task or that there was a shortage of stone to cut. One of the Westminster documents mentions masons who had failed to complete their allotted tasks. It goes on to give figures for what the same masons would receive at day rates for work begun on a task-work basis, and concludes with a computation which might be instructive if its exact significance could be understood.

When in 1256 Master John of Gloucester, the king's mason, and Master Alexander, his carpenter, were appointed 'chief masters of the king's works', one of their functions appears to have been to encourage the more general use of task-work in appropriate circumstances.[1] Thus two years later we find that it was by their advice that a master-mason contracted to rebuild one of the towers at Winchester Castle for £110, and that a carpenter undertook for 10 marks to saw and convert into planks twenty oaks which the newly elected Bishop of Winchester had presented to the king (pp. 159, 183). These may well be the earliest English building-contracts of which a written text has survived, and everything suggests that they represented an innovation in the practice of the royal works.

The well-known index of building wages compiled by Phelps Brown and Hopkins begins in 1264–1300.[2] The accounts here printed should make it possible to extend it back to 1220–7.[3] In using the figures for this purpose account must, however, be taken of the seasonal variation in wages due to the shorter length of the working day in winter. There is every reason to suppose that in the twelfth, as in the fifteenth, century, the working day began at dawn and ended at 7 p.m. in summer or at dusk in winter.[4] With meal-breaks this gave a maximum working day of 10½ hours in summer,

[1] *History of the King's Works*, i, pp. 107–8.

[2] E. H. Phelps Brown and Sheila V. Hopkins, 'Seven Centuries of Building Wages', *Economica* (1955), reprinted in *Essays in Economic History*, ed. E. M. Carus-Wilson, ii (1962).

[3] See the table at the end of this section.

[4] L. F. Salzman, *Building in England down to 1540* (1952), pp. 61–4.

falling to 7 or 8 hours in winter. This reduction in productivity was often matched by a corresponding reduction in wages. Thus at Winchester in 1222 the leading masons were receiving 4*d.* a day in September, approximately $3\frac{1}{4}$*d.* a day in October, and $2\frac{1}{2}$*d.* a day in November, while the remuneration of the lower-paid masons showed a corresponding diminution. In 1253 the clerk at Westminster noted that it was usual to reduce the wages of the freemasons during the first week of November (p. 281). At Dover, on the other hand, there appears to have been no significant change in the wages paid throughout the year, either in 1220–1 or in 1227.

Another factor which must be borne in mind when considering the wages of medieval English workmen is the observance of feast-days and holidays. The normal working week was of six days. But it was frequently interrupted by the festivals of the Church whose calendar marked the progress of the workman's year. The great feasts, Easter, Whitsun, and Christmas, were universally observed as holidays, but the observance of every recognized saint's day would have constituted an intolerable interruption of work and a corresponding loss of wages. A compromise was accordingly established, whereby feast-days were allocated alternately to the employer and to the workmen. In 1328 this was explicitly stated in the following terms:

> when any workmen, of whatever rank or craft they be, have been engaged on the king's works continuously for a fortnight or three weeks, a month, or more, and two or more feast days happen to occur within such time, exclusive of Sundays, the king always has one feast day, beginning with the first, and the workmen the other; so that the workmen shall receive from the king for every alternate feast day their wages full and complete, although they do not work on it, just as they would for a working day.[1]

Instructions to the keepers of the works at Bristol Castle in 1251[2] show that this custom was already in force at that date, and it can be seen in operation at Westminster in 1253, 1259, 1265, and 1270 (below, pp. 237, etc.). This system of alternate holidays with pay does not affect the calculation of daily wage-rates, but it does mean that productivity was less than the weekly pay-roll might at first sight suggest. Thus at Westminster in 1253 there were 12 paid

[1] Op. cit., p. 66. [2] Ibid.

holidays in the course of the 42 working weeks for which accounts survive and in 1259 the masons and carpenters enjoyed 11 days off in 32 working weeks between May and December. In addition the whole of Easter week and part at least of Whitsun week was a holiday, and it appears to have been normal for no work to be done during the fortnight after Christmas. If we attempt to reconstruct an average workman's year in the thirteenth century we may therefore envisage 3 to 4 weeks holiday without pay (2 at Christmas, 1 at Easter, and 4 to 7 days at Whitsun), plus a number of individual days off with pay which might amount to the equivalent of another fortnight's holiday. But the extent to which saints' days were observed as holidays and the practice of paying or not paying wages in respect of such days differed from one building operation to another, and the arrangements in force at Westminster in the reign of Henry III were not necessarily of universal application.[1]

The mason, carpenter, or labourer who continued in regular employment at one building site throughout a whole calendar year was, however, the exception rather than the rule. Building has always been to some extent a seasonal occupation, and even when work continued during the winter it was generally on a small scale. It was, therefore, common practice to reduce the number of workmen on a site during the winter months, and this reduction is reflected in the weekly totals at, for instance, Winchester. At Westminster in 1253 it was 'to pay the wages of those leaving' that the clerk received £66. 13*s.* 4*d.* from the Exchequer on 12 November (p. 217). Many workmen could therefore anticipate temporary redundancy during the winter. But absenteeism (to adopt another modern term) was also prevalent. From marginal notes in the Westminster accounts it is possible to follow the movements of individual workmen, whose arrivals and departures were carefully noted by the clerk in order to calculate the wages due to them. The frequency with which men arrived, departed, or returned is remarkable. What determined these comings and goings it is impossible to say: ill health, other employment, the need to return to a distant family, or to some by-occupation such as farming, may all have played their part. But it is clear that in the thirteenth, as in later centuries, there was considerable mobility among building

[1] For the practice elsewhere, see D. Knoop and G. P. Jones, *The Mediaeval Mason* (3rd ed., 1967), pp. 106–7.

workmen, and this is borne out by the toponymics of the individuals, which show that many of them had come from distant parts of the country to work at Dover, Winchester, or Westminster. It should perhaps be added that there is little evidence, at Westminster or elsewhere, of the compulsory recruitment of masons for the king's works before the fourteenth century, though workmen were impressed for military purposes by John, Henry III, and Edward I. But a payment at Winchester to a chaplain 'to carry writs for masons' (p. 137) may indicate that impressment was resorted to in the exceptional circumstances of Henry III's minority. The presence at Westminster of two French and two Norman masons has already been noted. Another Norman mason, Gillot of Caen, was employed at Westminster in 1270 (p. 407).

Money wage-rates of building craftsman and labourer, in southern England in the thirteenth century, expressed in pence per day

	Craftsman	*Labourer*
1220–7	From 2 to 4	From 1½ to 2 (women 1)
1237–9[1]	From 2 to 5	From 1½ to 2 (women 1)
1253–9	From 4 to 6	From 1½ to 2½

BUILDING MATERIALS

The building materials mentioned in the accounts include stone, flint, lime, chalk (presumably the sort known as 'clunch'), sand, Purbeck marble, various kinds of timber, tiles, stone slates, shingles, thatch, iron, lead, and glass. Stone quarried at Folkestone was the principal material used at Dover. For the reconstruction of Winchester Castle quarries were worked at Selborne (Hants), Haslebury (Somerset), and the Isle of Wight. To Westminster freestone was brought by land from Reigate and Chaldon in Surrey, ragstone by water from Kent. The only stone common to all three buildings came from Caen in Normandy.[2] Though more

[1] Based on S. Challenger, *Accounts for Works at Marlborough* (Wilts. Archl. Soc. Records Branch, vol. xii, 1956), pp. 10–11.

[2] Though not mentioned in the surviving Dover accounts, Caen stone is still visible in the thirteenth-century portions of the castle.

expensive than the best native freestones (at Winchester 500 Isle of Wight stones suitable for dressings could be had for 17*s.* 6*d.*, while 450 Caen stones cost 23*s.* 6*d.*), it was easily transportable by sea to English ports, and its fine quality ensured its continued use long after England and Normandy were severed politically.

Much of the timber for the king's works was derived from the numerous royal woods in Essex, Hampshire, and elsewhere. But much was purchased, sometimes from London merchants,[1] often at Kingston upon Thames, of whose importance as a market for timber from the Surrey woods there is considerable evidence in these accounts.[2]

Though the information about building technology to be found in these documents is limited, references will be found to the burning and slaking of lime, to the use of timber for templates and centerings, and to the founding and soldering of lead. Terms for some of the specially shaped stones for the fabric of a great Gothic church are given in one of the Westminster accounts, though the precise significance of some of them is uncertain.[3] One of the commonest entries in the accounts is the purchase of withies and hurdles for scaffolding.[4] Hurdles were doubtless used to form the platforms upon which the masons worked, and (as is still the case in Italy) to protect them from the weather. But, as Plate 1 shows, they might also form part of an inclined stairway up which labourers could carry materials in hod or barrow.

[1] Richard Portefer, of London, who sold both timber and lime to the works at Dover, is perhaps the first builder's merchant of whom there is documentary evidence.

[2] It may be significant that in the fourteenth century two of the king's chief carpenters, Hugh Herland and his successor William Toutmond, had property in, and appear to have lived in, Kingston (J. H. Harvey, *English Mediaeval Architects*, 1954, pp. 130, 267).

[3] The commentary on this account written by Willis for Scott's *Gleanings* (1863), pp. 231–8 may still be read with profit.

[4] It is usual to translate *virgae* as 'poles', and the *virgatores* employed at Westminster in 1253 were presumably scaffold-erectors (p. 245). But at Winchester in 1258 *cheverones* (usually translated as 'rafters') as well as *virgae* were bought *ad scaffot*, and in one entry (p. 159) the *virgae* are stated to have been used 'to make hurdles and to tie scaffolding'. Here at least *virgae* would seem therefore to have been withies rather than poles, while the *cheverones* were evidently the standards or poles.

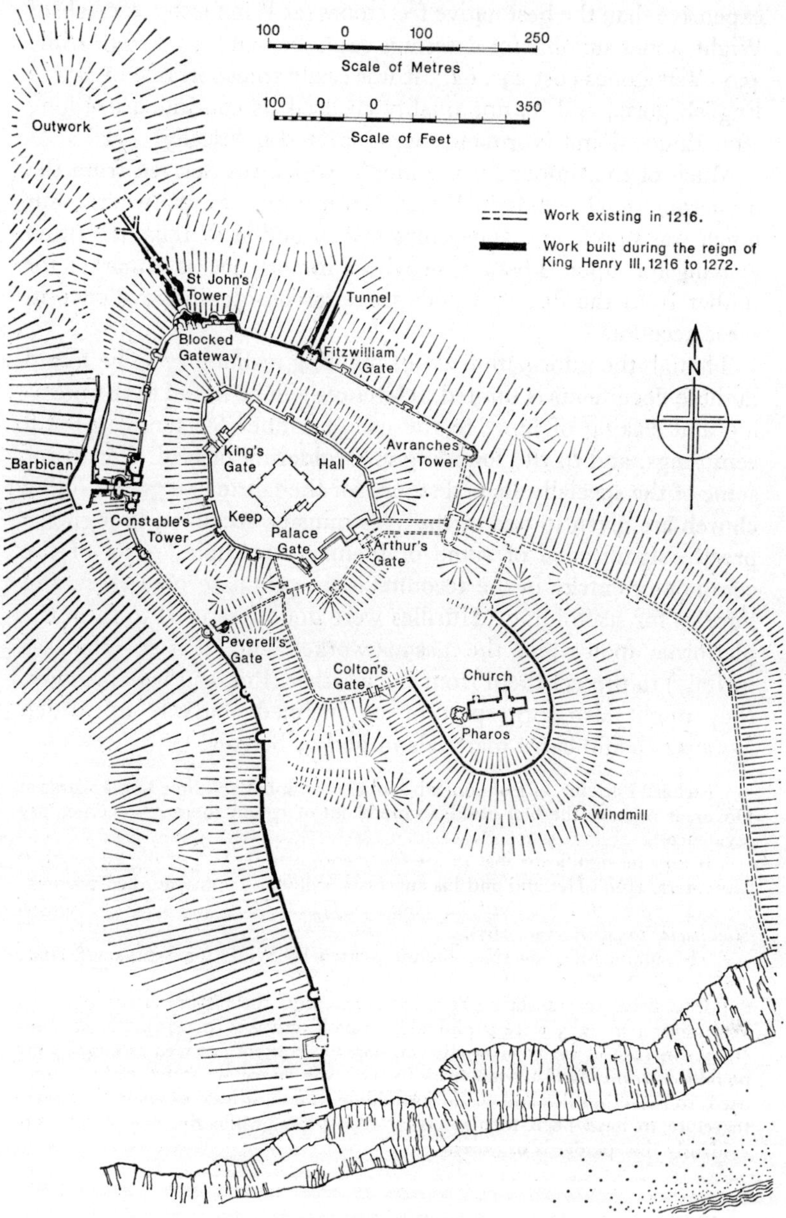

FIG. 1. Dover Castle.

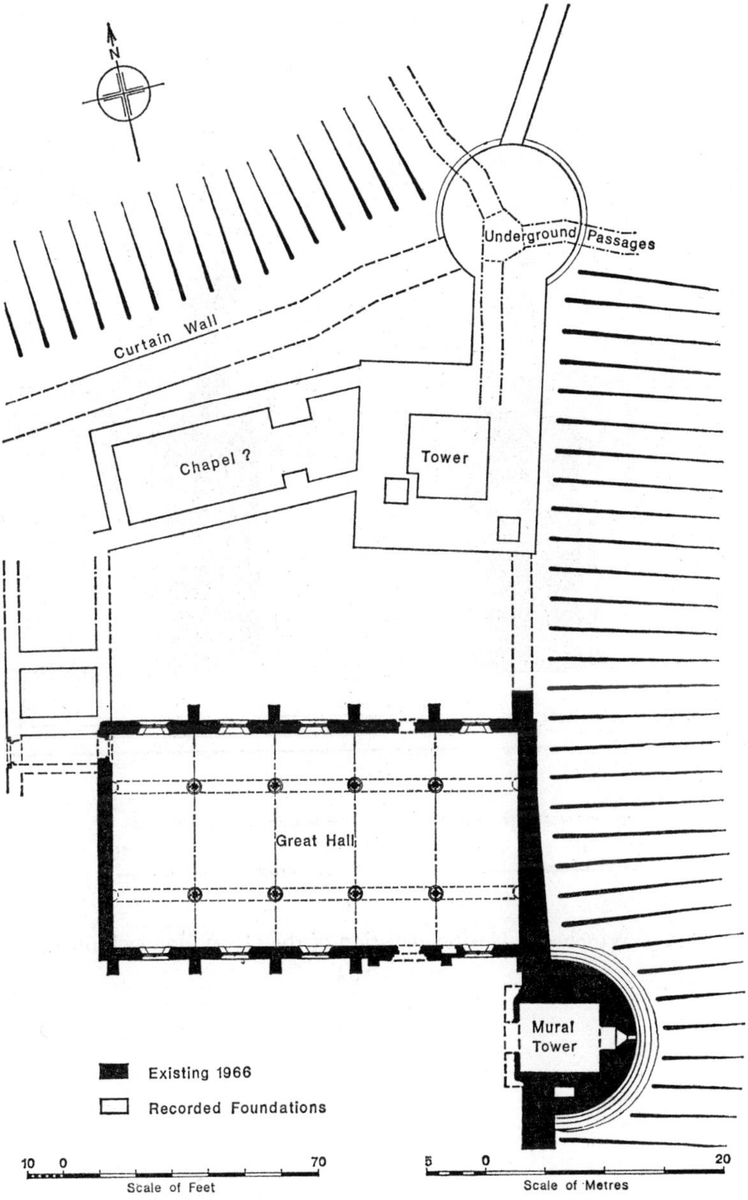

FIG. 2. Winchester Castle: the Great Hall.

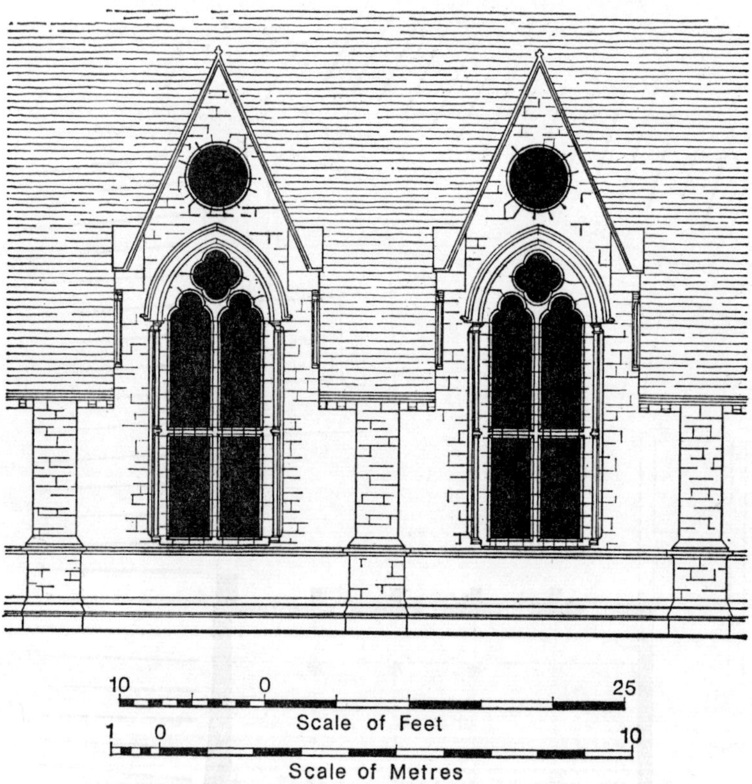

FIG. 3. Winchester Castle: elevation of the Great Hall as built in 1222–34.

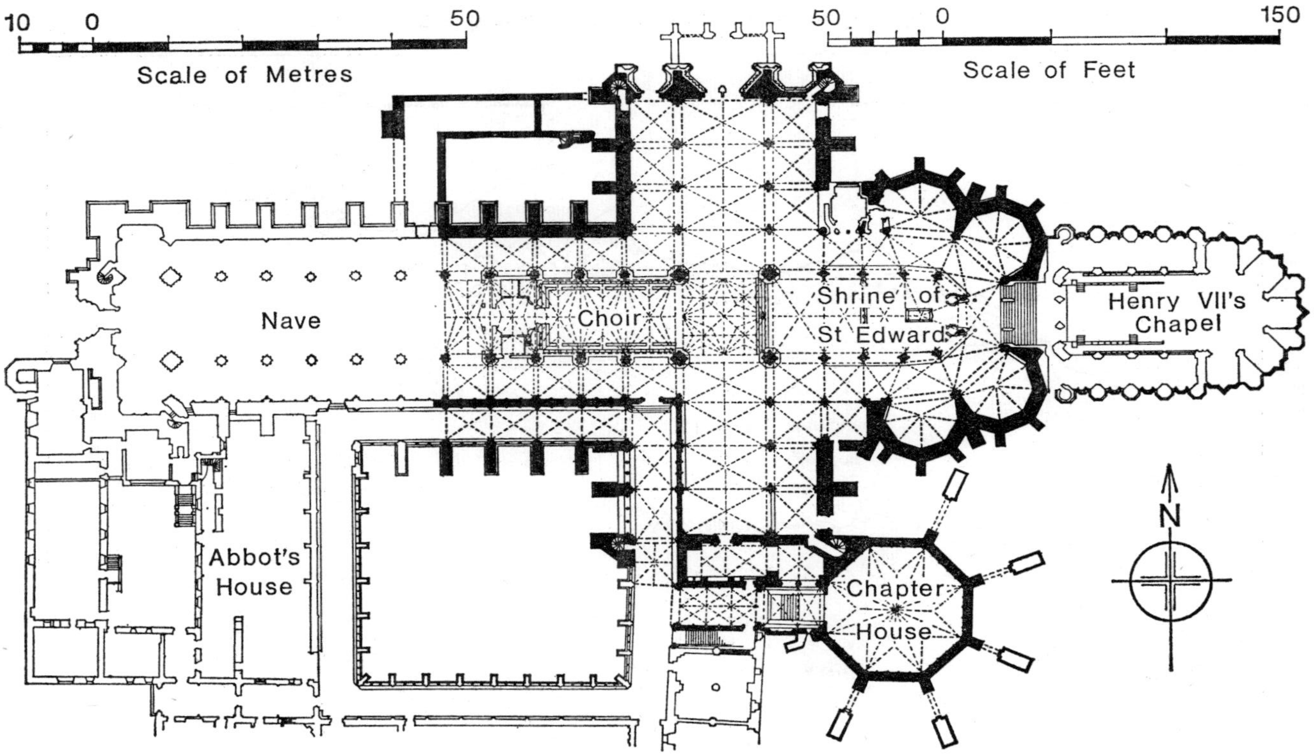

FIG. 4. Westminster Abbey. The portions built by King Henry III are shown in solid black.

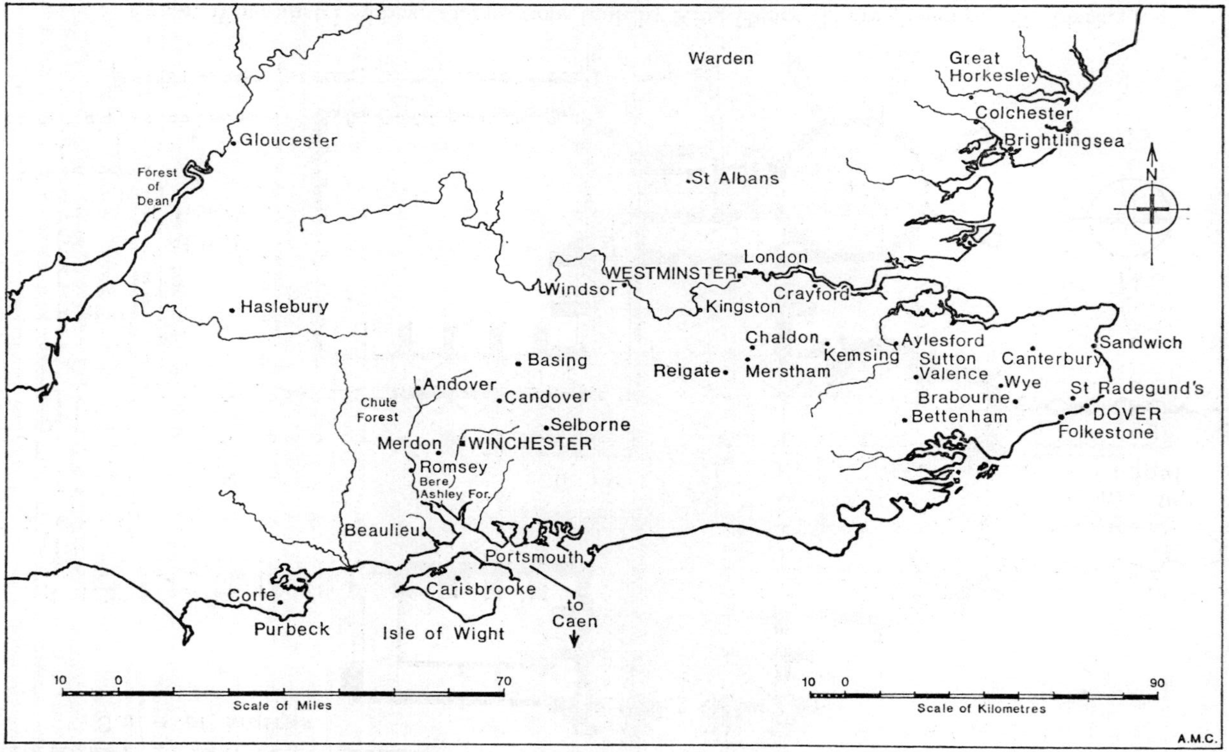

FIG. 5. Map to show places mentioned in the text.

I. DOVER CASTLE

1. Selected writs relating to the works at Dover Castle from 1221 to 1228.

(i) Rex E. Thesaurario & F. & R. Camerariis salutem. Liberate de thesauro nostro Huberto de Burgo Justiciario nostro L marcas ad operacionem castri nostri Dovr'. Teste Huberto de Burgo apud Westmonasterium xxix die Julii, anno etc. v, per eundem (*Rot. Litt. Claus.* i, p. 467).

(ii) Rex E. Thesaurario & F. & R. Camerariis salutem. Liberate de thesauro nostro Willelmo de Essedeford' C li. ad operacionem castri nostri Dovr'.... Teste Huberto de Burgo apud Westmonasterium x die Februarii anno regni nostri vj°. per eundem. (*Rot. Litt. Claus.* i, p. 488.)

(iii) Rex vicecomiti Essex' salutem. Precipimus tibi quod maeremium nostrum quod Constabularius Dovr' prosterni fecit in bailliva tua ad operacionem castri nostri Dovr' per preceptum nostrum cariari facias usque portum extra Colecestr' & custum quod ad hoc posueris per visum & testimonium legalium hominum computabitur tibi ad scaccarium. Teste Huberto de Burgo apud Westmonasterium xj die Junii anno vj° per eundem. (*Rot. Litt. Claus.* i, p. 499.)

(iv) Rex Ricardo de Munfichet salutem. Mandamus vobis quod per visum & testimonium viridariorum & forestariorum nostrorum de bailliva vestra faciatis habere Constabulario Dovr' ad operacionem castri nostri Dovr' tot fusta quot sufficient ad C gistas faciendas tam in bosco de Cestrewald quam aliis boscis baillive vestre ubi melius & competencius videritis expedire. Ita videlicet quod totum maeremium quod de fustis illis fieri poterit cedat in usus nostros & commodum nostrum. Teste Huberto de Burgo apud Westmonasterium xj die Junii, anno vj° per eundem. (*Rot. Litt. Claus.* i, p. 499.)

(v) Rex E. Thesaurario & F. & W. Camerariis salutem. Liberate de thesauro nostro Willelmo de Esseteford' C.li. deferendas usque Dovr' ad operacionem castri nostri de Dovr'. Teste Huberto de Burgo apud Westmonasterium xxiij die Junii, anno regni nostri vj° per eundem & consilium domini Regis. (*Rot. Litt. Claus.* i, p. 500.)

1. Selected writs relating to the works at Dover Castle from 1221 to 1228.

(i) The king greets E. his Treasurer and F. and R. chamberlains of the Exchequer. Deliver from our Treasury to Hubert de Burgh our Justiciar 50 marks towards the work of our castle of Dover.

Attested by Hubert de Burgh at Westminster, 29 July in the 5th year [1221], and issued by authority of the same Hubert.

(ii) The king greets E. his Treasurer and F. and R. chamberlains of the Exchequer. Deliver from our Treasury to William of Ashford £100 towards the work of our castle of Dover.

Attested by Hubert de Burgh at Westminster, 10 February in the 6th year of our reign [1222], and issued by authority of the same Hubert.

(iii) The king greets the sheriff of Essex. We order you to have our timber which the constable of Dover had felled in your bailiwick by our order for the work of our castle of Dover carried to the harbour outside Colchester, and the cost which you shall incur in doing so by view and testimony of law-worthy men shall be credited to you at the Exchequer.

Attested by Hubert de Burgh at Westminster, 11 June in the 6th year [1222], and issued by authority of the same Hubert.

(iv) The king greets Richard de Munfichet. We order you that by view and testimony of our verderers and foresters of your bailiwick you should let the constable of Dover have for the work of our castle of Dover as many tree-trunks as are sufficient to make 100 joists, both in Chesterwell[1] Wood and in the other woods in your bailiwick where you think it can best be arranged, and in such a way that all the timber that can be made from those trunks shall be used for our purposes and for our profit.

Attested by Hubert de Burgh at Westminster, 11 June in the 6th year [1222], and issued by authority of the same Hubert.

(v) The king greets E. his Treasurer and F. and W. chamberlains of the Exchequer. Deliver from our Treasury to William of Ashford £100 to be taken to Dover for the work of our castle of Dover.

Attested by Hubert de Burgh at Westminster, 23 June in the 6th year of our reign [1222] and issued by authority of the same Hubert and the lord king's council.

[1] In Great Horkesley, Essex.

(vi) Rex Constabulario Colecestr' salutem. Precipimus tibi quod habere facias Constabulario Dovr' centum fusta in foresta nostra de Kingeswud' ad maeremium faciendum ad operacionem castri nostri Dovr'. Teste Huberto de Burgo apud Westmonasterium xv Julii anno vj° per eundem. (*Rot. Litt. Claus.* i, p. 504.)

(vii) Rex Constabulario Colecestr' salutem. Precipimus tibi quod exceptis centum fustis que nuper tibi precepimus ut habere faceres Constabulario Dovr' in foresta nostra de Kingeswud'; facias habere eidem Constabulario xx^{ti} fusta in eadem foresta ad maeremium faciendum ad operacionem castri nostri Dovr'. Teste Huberto de Burgo apud Turrim London' xviij die Augusti. per eundem. (*Rot. Litt. Claus.* i, p. 508.)

(viii) Rex vicecomiti Essex' salutem. Precipimus tibi quod maeremium quod prostratum est in foresta nostra de Kingeswud' extra Colecestr' ad operacionem castri nostri Dovr' cariari facias per batellos usque Dovr' & custum quod ad hoc posueris per visum & testimonium legalium hominum computabitur tibi ad scaccarium. Teste Huberto de Burgo apud Westmonasterium xxvij die Januarii anno regni nostri vij°. (*Rot. Litt. Claus.* i, p. 531.)

(ix) Rex E. Thesaurario & F. & W. Camerariis salutem. Liberate de thesauro nostro Roberto de Nereford' & Galfrido de Gurdun C li. ad operacionem castri nostri Dovr'. Teste Huberto de Burgo apud Westmonasterium primo die Februarii anno regni nostri vij°. per eundem. (*Rot. Litt. Claus.* i, p. 532.)

(x) Rex E. Thesaurario & F. & W. Camerariis salutem. Liberate de thesauro nostro Roberto de Nereford' & Galfrido de Gurdun centum libras ad operacionem castri nostri Dovr'. Teste Huberto de Burgo apud Westmonasterium xvj die Maii anno regni nostri vij. per eundem. (*Rot. Litt. Claus.* i, p. 546.)

(xi) Rex Constabulario & sociis suis custodibus operacionis castri Dovr' salutem. Mandamus vobis quod ecclesiam Beate Marie in castro Dovr' sitam reparari faciatis simul cum alia operacione ejusdem castri de denariis nostris ad eandem operacionem assignatis qui sunt in custodia vestra. Teste Huberto de Burgo apud Westmonasterium xiij die Junii anno regni nostri vij. per eundem. (*Rot. Litt. Claus.* i, p. 551.)

(xii) Rex E. Thesaurario & F. & W. Camerariis salutem. Liberate de thesauro nostro Roberto de Nereford' Constabulario castri nostri Dovr'

(vi) The king greets the constable of Colchester. We order you to let the constable of Dover have 100 tree-trunks in our forest of Kingswood[1] in order to make timber for the work of our castle of Dover.

Attested by Hubert de Burgh at Westminster, 15 July in the 6th year [1222] and issued by authority of the same Hubert.

(vii) The king greets the constable of Colchester. We order you that, besides the 100 tree-trunks which we formerly ordered you to let the constable of Dover have in our forest of Kingswood, you are to let the same constable have 20 tree-trunks in the same forest to make timber for the work of our castle of Dover.

Attested by Hubert de Burgh at the Tower of London, 18 August [1222] and issued by authority of the same Hubert.

(viii) The king greets the sheriff of Essex. We order you to have the timber for the work of our castle of Dover which has been felled in our wood of Kingswood outside Colchester carried by boats to Dover, and the cost which you shall incur in doing so by view and testimony of law-worthy men shall be credited to you at the Exchequer.

Attested by Hubert de Burgh at Westminster, 27 January in the 7th year of our reign [1223].

(ix) The king greets E. his Treasurer and F. and W. chamberlains of the Exchequer. Deliver from our Treasury to Robert of Narford and Geoffrey de Gurdun £100 towards the work of our castle of Dover.

Attested by Hubert de Burgh at Westminster, 1 February in the 7th year of our reign [1223] and issued by authority of the same Hubert.

(x) The king greets E. his Treasurer and F. and W. chamberlains of the Exchequer. Deliver from our Treasury to Robert of Narford and Geoffrey de Gurdun £100 towards the work of our castle of Dover.

Attested by Hubert de Burgh at Westminster, 16 May in the 7th year [1223] and issued by authority of the same Hubert.

(xi) The king to the constable and his fellow keepers of the work of the castle of Dover. We direct you to have the church of the Blessed Mary situated within Dover Castle repaired out of the money in your keeping assigned to that work at the same time as the other works of the castle.

Attested by Hubert de Burgh at Westminster, 13 June in the 7th year [1223] and issued by the authority of the same Hubert.

(xii) The king greets E. his Treasurer and F. and W. chamberlains of the Exchequer. Deliver from our Treasury to Robert of Narford, constable

[1] Part of the royal forest of Essex.

& Ricardo de Popleshal' L^{ta} li. ad operacionem ejusdem castri. Teste Huberto de Burgo apud Westmonasterium ix die Sept. anno regni nostri vij per eundem. (*Rot. Litt. Claus.* i, p. 562.)

(xiii) Rex vicecomiti Kanc' salutem. Precipimus tibi quod habere facias Roberto de Nereford' Constabulario nostro Dovr' centum fusta in parco de Sutton' & ea usque Dovr' cariari facias ad operacionem castri nostri Dovr' & custum quod ad hoc posueris computabitur tibi ad scaccarium. Teste Rege apud Bedef' xvij die Julii anno viij. (*Rot. Litt. Claus.* i, p. 636.)

(xiv) Rex Roberto de Lexinton' salutem. Mandamus vobis quod cum qua poteritis festinacione emi faciatis ad opus nostrum centum marcatas plumbi ad operaciones castri nostri Dovr' & duci usque Baltr' & ibidem salvo reponi & cum ibi fuerit coadunatum nobis sine dilacione hoc scire faciatis ut naves illuc mittere possimus ad illud deferendum usque Dovr' & custum quod ad hoc posueritis computabitur vobis ad scaccarium. Teste me ipso apud Bedeford' xij die Augusti anno viij. (*Rot. Litt. Claus.* i, p. 616.)

(xv) Rex vicecomiti Linc' salutem. Precipimus tibi quod mittas usque Bautre & recipias ibidem de Roberto de Lexinton' xxx carratas plumbi ad opus nostrum & ibidem recipias a vicecomite Notingham' quinquaginta marcatas plumbi ad opus nostrum & illas L marcatas una cum predictis xxx carratis plumbi sine dilacione cariari facias usque Dovr' per aquam & custum quod ad hoc posueris computabitur tibi ad scaccarium. Teste Rege apud Westmonasterium x die Nov. anno ix per Justiciarium. (*Rot. Litt. Claus.* ii, p. 6*b*.)

(xvi) Rex vicecomiti Kanc' salutem. Precipimus tibi quod maeremium prosterni & apparari facias in parco de Kemesinges & in parco de Sutton' & in parco de Brayburn' ad palum & alia in castro Dovr' facienda & illud preparari facias & cariari per aquam usque Dovor sicut Willelmus Carpentarius tibi dicet & custum quod ad hoc posueris computabitur tibi ad scaccarium. Teste me ipso apud Winchels' xx die Januarii anno &c ix^{o}. Coram Justiciario. (*Rot. Litt. Claus.* ii, p. 14.)

(xvii) Mandatum est vicecomiti Kanc' quod sit in auxilium emendi buscam in bailliva sua sicut Robertus lator presencium sibi dicet ad denarios domini Regis unde idem lator presencium tibi respondebit ad j rogum faciendum ad operacionem castri Dovr'. Teste Rege apud Rumenel xvij die Januarii. (*Rot. Litt. Claus.* ii, p. 14.)

of our castle of Dover, and Richard of Popes Hall, £50 towards the work of the same castle.

Attested by Hubert de Burgh at Westminster, 9 September in the 7th year of our reign [1223] and issued by authority of the same Hubert.

(xiii) The king greets the sheriff of Kent. We order you to let Robert of Narford, our constable of Dover, have 100 tree-trunks in Sutton Park[1] and have them carried to Dover for the work of our castle of Dover, and the cost which you shall incur will be credited to you at the Exchequer.

Attested by the king at Bedford 17 July in the 8th year [1224].

(xiv) The king greets Robert of Laxton.[2] We direct you as soon as you can to have purchased for our use 100 marks' worth of lead for the works of our castle of Dover and have it taken to Bawtry and kept safe there: and when it has been collected together there you are to let us know without delay so that we can send ships there to carry it from there to Dover: and the cost which you incur will be credited to you at the Exchequer.

Attested by the king at Bedford, 12 August in the 8th year [1224].

(xv) The king greets the sheriff of Lincoln. We order you to send to Bawtry and to receive there from Robert of Laxton 30 chars of lead for our use; and you shall also receive there from the sheriff of Nottingham 50 marks' worth of lead for our use; and you are without delay to have those 50 marks' worth together with the said 30 chars carried by water to Dover, and the cost which you shall incur in doing so shall be credited to you at the Exchequer.

Attested by the king at Westminster 10 November in the 9th year [1224] and issued by authority of the Justiciar.

(xvi) The king greets the sheriff of Kent. We order you to have timber felled and prepared in the parks of Kemsing, Sutton and Brabourne to make palings and other things in Dover Castle, and you are to have it prepared and carried by water to Dover as William the Carpenter shall tell you, and the cost which you shall incur in doing this shall be credited to you at the Exchequer.

Attested by the king at Winchelsea, 20 January in the 9th year [1225], in the presence of the Justiciar.

(xvii) The sheriff of Kent is ordered at the king's expense to assist in the purchase of firewood in his bailiwick in order to make a kiln for the work of Dover Castle as Robert the bearer of these letters shall tell him; and the bearer shall answer to you [the sheriff] for the expenditure.

Attested by the king at Romney, 17 January [1225].

[1] Probably in Sutton Valence.

[2] Then keeper of the honor of Peveril, that is of the royal estates in the Peak, where the lead-mines were situated.

(xviii) Rex Alexandro de Dors' & Henrico de Sancto Albano salutem. Mandamus vobis quod habere faciatis Henrico de Felgeres, Willelmo de Popeshal', Galfrido de Cressy, & Simoni de Grenewey custodibus operacionis castri nostri Dovr' centum li. de exitibus cambii nostri per manus Radulfi Briton' ad eandem operacionem. & computabitur vobis ad scaccarium. Teste domino Rege apud Novum Templum London' xxvj die Februarii anno ix. (*Rot. Litt. Claus.* ii, p. 20.)

(xix) Mandatum est Baronibus de Scaccario quod audiant compotum visorum operacionis castri Dovr' tam de denariis quos receperunt per preceptum domini Regis ad eandem operacionem quam de aliis denariis quos posuerunt in eadem operacione sine precepto domini Regis & in rotulis scaccarii inrotulari faciant. Teste Rege apud Westmonasterium xxix die Aprilis anno nono. (*Rot. Litt. Claus.* ii, p. 34.)

(xx) Rex E. Thesaurario & Camerariis suis salutem. Liberate de thesauro nostro Thurgis' preposito Dovr' centum li. liberandas Ricardo de Nereford' Henrico de Feugeres Jocelino de Oye & Galfrido de Cressy custodibus operacionis castri nostri Dovr' ad eandem operacionem. Teste Rege apud Westmonasterium vij die Augusti anno nono. (*Rot. Litt. Claus.* ii, p. 55.)

(xxi) Rex vicecomitibus London' salutem. Precipimus vobis quod xx carratas plumbi emi facias & liberari dilecto & fideli nostro Thome de Blunvill' constabulario turris London' cariandas usque Dovr' ad operationes nostras in castro Dovr' faciendas & custum tibi computabitur &c. Teste Rege apud Westmonasterium xiij die Maii anno x°. (*Rot. Litt. Claus.* ii, p. 111.)

(xxii) Rex E. Thesaurario & Camerariis suis salutem. Liberate . . . Ricardo de Nereford' & Jocelino de Oye ducentas libras ad operaciones castri nostri Dovr' & xv li. & xviij d. & ob. de eisdem operacionibus de anno preterito de quibus Ricardus & Jocelinus compotum suum reddiderunt. Teste me ipso apud Westmonasterium xxj die Maii anno x°. Coram Justiciario. (*Rot. Litt. Claus.* ii, p. 115.)

(xxiii) Rex vicecomitibus London' salutem. Precipimus vobis quod viginti carratas plumbi que sunt in turri nostra London' quas constabularius noster eiusdem turris vobis liberabit cariari faciatis usque Dovr' & custum quod ad hoc posueritis computabitur vobis ad scaccarium. Teste me ipso apud Westmonasterium v die Julii anno regni nostri x°. (*Rot. Litt. Claus.* ii, p. 126.)

(xviii) The king greets Alexander of Dorset and Henry of St. Albans. We command you to let Henry de Fougères, William of Popes Hall, Geoffrey de Cressy, and Simon of Greenway, keepers of the work of our castle of Dover, have £100 towards the same work out of the issues of our exchange by the hands of Ralph Breton; and it shall be credited to you at the Exchequer.

Attested by the king at the New Temple in London, 26 February in the 9th year [1225].

(xix) The Barons of the Exchequer are ordered to audit the account of the viewers of the work of Dover Castle, both for the money which they received for the same work by order of the king and for other money which they laid out on the same work without the king's order, and to have it enrolled on the rolls of the Exchequer.

Attested by the king at Westminster, 29 April in the 9th year [1225].

(xx) The king greets E. his Treasurer and the chamberlains of the Exchequer. Deliver from our Treasury to Turgis, the reeve of Dover, £100 to be delivered to Richard of Narford, Henry de Fougères, Jocelyn de Oye and Geoffrey de Cressy, keepers of the work of our castle of Dover, towards the cost of the same work.

Attested by the king at Westminster, 7 August in the 9th year [1225].

(xxi) The king greets the sheriffs of London. We order you to cause 20 chars of lead to be bought and delivered to our dear and faithful Thomas de Blundeville, constable of the Tower of London, to be carried to Dover to perform our works in Dover Castle, and the cost will be credited to you at the Exchequer.

Attested by the king at Westminster, 13 May in the 10th year [1226].

(xxii) The king greets his Treasurer and the chamberlains of the Exchequer. Deliver . . . to Richard of Narford and Jocelyn de Oye £200 towards the works of our castle of Dover and £15. 1*s*. 6½*d*. for the works last year for which Richard and Jocelyn have rendered their account.

Attested by the king at Westminster 21 May in the 10th year [1226], in the presence of the Justiciar.

(xxiii) The king greets the sheriffs of London. We order you to have 20 chars of lead which are in our Tower of London, and which our constable of the same Tower will deliver to you, carried to Dover, and the cost which you shall incur in doing this shall be credited to you at the Exchequer.

Attested by the king at Westminster 5 July in the 10th year of our reign [1226].

(xxiv) Rex E. Thesaurario & camerariis suis salutem. Liberate de Thesauro nostro Jocelino de Oye servienti nostro de castro Dovor' C.li. ad operaciones eiusdem castri, Johanni de Stowe & Simoni de Norwic' euntibus . . . ad warnisturam emendam contra passagium nostrum. Et magistro Nicholao magistro Thome Simoni de Norhamt' Roberto de Abbemunt Hugoni de Barentin carpentariis nostris x m. videlicet [cuilibet] eorum duas m. in parte soluscionis liberationum suarum. Et Jordano carpentario nostro iiij m. in parte solucionis liberationis sue. Teste ut supra. (Liberate Roll 11 Henry III, m. 5.)

(xxv) Mandatum est Bertramo de Crioil et Alano Poinant' quod habere faciant constabulario Dovr' xx fusta in bosco archiepiscopi de Betenham ad planchias ad opus pontis turneicii ejusdem castri faciendas, et ea cariari faciant usque ad aquam apud Newenden' carianda inde usque Dovr'. Teste rege apud Windles', xxx die Julii anno etc. xij°. (*Close Rolls 1227–31*, p. 69.)

(xxiv) The king greets E. his Treasurer and chamberlains. Deliver from our Treasury to Jocelyn de Oye our serjeant of Dover castle £100 for the works of the same castle, and to John of Stowe, and Simon of Norwich going . . . to make provision for our passage. And to Master Nicholas, Master Thomas, Simon of Northampton, Robert de Abbemunt, Hugh de Barentin our carpenters 10 marks, namely to [each] of them two marks in part payment of their wages. And to Jordan our carpenter four marks in part payment of his wages.

Attested as above (i.e. by the king at Westminster 13 July) [1227].

(xxv) Bertram de Criel and Alan Poynant are ordered to let the constable of Dover have 20 tree-trunks in the archbishop's wood of Bettenham[1] in order to make planks for the draw-bridge of the same castle, and to have them carried to the river at Newenden, to be carried thence to Dover.

Attested by the king at Windsor, 30 July in the 12th year [1228].

[1] Near Cranbrook, Kent, on the estates of the archbishop of Canterbury, which were then temporarily in the king's hand after the death of Stephen Langton.

2. Particulars of expenditure on Dover Castle from August 1220 to December 1221. (E101/462/8)

Hec est Pacacio facta die Sabbati proxima ante festum Sancti Laurencii per Willelmum de Essedeford & Ricardum de Popeshall' & per visum Galfridi de Gurdune & Gocelini de Oye qui Dicam contra ipsos Willelmum & Ricardum habent.

In xiiij minutis operariis per terminum a festo Sancte Mildrethe virginis usque ad pacacionem supradictam. xvij sol.
Item Rogero carpentario per xx dies v sol. scilicet per diem iij d.
Item Ricardo carpentario per viij dies ij sol. per diem iij d.
Item pro vij circulis ad cuvas operacionis castri relegandas vij d.
Item cuidam cuvario per ij dies vj d. Item cuidam cementario per i diem iij d.
Item Pro furno castri reparando viij d. Item pro remocione xl batellatarum minutorum lapidum a mari usque ad terram xl.d.
Item in lvij tignis de fagina & xxv bordis iiij sol. vj d.
Item pro DCCCC.L. summis harene ductis xij sol. iiij d.
Summa huius particule xlvj sol. ij d.

Die sabbati s. in Die Decollacionis Sancti Johannis Baptiste facta fuit Pacacio Operis per supervisores dictos.

Ad temperandum CC. summas calcis & illas extinguendas v sol. iiij d. in Tassca quodlibet cent. ad temperandum pro xxxij d.
Item ad removendum calcem de Porta Peverelli usque in cameram propinquam ij sol. vj d.
Item Roberto de Witefeld' cementario per x. dies iij sol. iiij d.
Item Willelmo de Colecestre per x dies iij sol. iiij d.
Item Copino cementario per x dies iij sol. iiij d.
Item Roberto cementario per x dies ij sol. xj d.
Item Radulfo Albaspine cementario per iij dies vij d. ob.
Item Ricardo carpentario per vj dies xviij d. pro cintris & templis faciendis
Item in xxx bordis longis ad templa Nove Porte facienda & xxv bordis parvis & C. latarum iiij sol. Item in ij. gatis [ad] aquam hauriendam ij d. ob.
Item in j. lok ad domum custodientem utensilia operacionis ij d.

2. Particulars of expenditure on Dover Castle from August 1220 to December 1221.

This is the payment made on Saturday next before the feast of St. Laurence [8 *August*] *by William of Ashford and Richard of Popes Hall*[1] *by view of Geoffrey de Gurdun and Jocelyn de Oye, who have a tally as a check on the said William and Richard.*

For 14 labourers during the period between the feast of St. Mildred the Virgin [13 July] and the date of the said payment, 17*s.*
And to Roger the carpenter for 20 days, 5*s.*, that is 3*d.* a day
And to Richard the carpenter for 8 days, 2*s.* [that is] 3*d.* a day
And for 7 hoops to bind the tubs for the castle works, 7*d.*
And to a certain cooper for 2 days, 6*d.*
And to a certain mason for 1 day, 3*d.*
And for repairing the castle oven, 8*d.*
And for moving 40 boat-loads of small stones from sea to land, 40*d.*
And for 57 beams of beech and 25 boards, 4*s.* 6*d.*
And for 950 loads of sand brought [to the castle], 12*s.* 4*d.*

Total of this item, 46*s.* 2*d.*

On Saturday, that is on the day of the Beheading of St. John the Baptist [29 *August*] *a payment was made by the said overseers.*

To slake 200 loads of lime and quench them, 5*s.* 4*d.* By task the slaking of each hundred costs 32*d.*
And to remove lime from Peverell's Gate to the adjoining chamber, 2*s.* 6*d.*
And to Robert of Whitfield, mason, for 10 days, 3*s.* 4*d.*
And to William of Colchester for 10 days, 3*s.* 4*d.*
And to Copin, mason, for 10 days, 3*s.* 4*d.*
And to Robert, mason, for 10 days, 2*s.* 11*d.*
And to Ralph Albespine, mason, for 3 days, 7½*d.*
And to Richard, carpenter, for 6 days, 18*d.*, for making centerings and templates
And for 30 long boards to make the templates for the New Gate, and 25 small boards and 100 laths 4*s.*
And for 2 bowls for drawing water, 2½*d.*
And for one lock for the toolshed, 2*d.*

[1] In Coldred parish.

Item in xxxv minutis operariis ad petram portandam & aquam ad Portam novam per iij septimanas xxxiiij sol. Item Guuarino cuvario pro xij circulis & pro j. tina reparanda & cuidam alio cuvario pro xviij circulis & pro alia tina paranda & pro j. cuva religanda xviij d.

Item in MMCCClxij summis Petre & harene portatis ad castrum xxxj sol. vj d.

Item pro x. batellatis minutorum lapidum ductis de Fokestane usque Dovor' vj sol. v d.

Summa huius particule C.sol. viij d.

Die sabbati proxima ante festum Sancti Michahelis anno Regni Regis Henrici iiij^{to} facta fuit pacacio de tribus septimanis.

Item in vij Cimentariis & uno Carpentario per illas iij septimanas & per iij dies. xxij sol.

Item in xlviii minutis Operariis per illum terminum xlviij sol. vj d.

Item in distemperacione CCL summarum calcis vj sol. viij d. C scilicet xxxij d.

Item pro MMMMDC xl. summis harene portatis ad castrum lxi sol. viij d.

Item pro remocione xl. Batellatarum minutorum lapidum a mari usque ad terram iij sol. iiij d.

Item hominibus deferentibus lapides minutos de Folkestane usque Dovor' xv.sol. viij d.

Summa vij li. xvij sol. x d.

Summa harum particularum huc usque xv li. iiij sol. viij d.

Item Willelmo de Grimesbi cissori lapidum & sociis suis pro M pedibus incisis vj li. xiij sol. iiij d. scilicet quodlibet C. incisum per tasscam pro xiij s. iiij d. Item Ricardo Norensi & Radulfo de Popeshall' pro opere Nove Barbekanie lxxi sol. in hoc termino.

Item Radulfo de Herebaldun' vij sol. viij d. pro L. pedibus lapidum incisis & xij d. fuerunt de alia tassca.

Summa totalis de hoc termino usque ad festum Sancti Micahelis xxv li. xvj sol. viij d. per Tailam contra Galfridum de Gurdun' & Gocelinum de Oye.

Die Sabbati proxima ante festum Sanctorum Simonis & Jude facta fuit Pacacio vij dierum.

Item in v. cissoribus lapidum & Cimentariis per xvij dies xxj sol. ix d.

Item in xxiiij minutis Operariis xxvi sol. xi d.

Item in MMM & D & xviii summis harene xlvij sol.

Item in L. summis Calcis temperatis in tassca xvj d.

Summa iiii li. xvii. sol.

And for 35 labourers to carry stone and water to the New Gate for 3 weeks, 34*s*. And to Warin the cooper for 12 hoops and for repairing one cask and to another cooper for 18 hoops and for repairing another cask, and for rebinding one tub, 18*d*.
And for 2,362 loads of stone and sand carried to the castle, 31*s*. 6*d*.
And for 10 boat-loads of small stones brought from Folkestone to Dover, 6*s*. 5*d*.

Total of this item, 100*s*. 8*d*.

On Saturday next before the feast of St. Michael [26 *September*] *in the 4th year of the reign of King Henry a payment was made for 3 weeks.*

And for 7 masons and one carpenter for those 3 weeks and 3 days, 22*s*.
And for 48 labourers for that period, 48*s*. 6*d*.
And for slaking 250 loads of lime, 6*s*. 8*d*., that is for 32*d*. a hundred.
And for 4,640 loads of sand carried to the castle, 61*s*. 8*d*.
And for removing 40 boatloads of small stones from sea to land, 3*s*. 4*d*.
And to men carrying small stones from Folkestone to Dover, 15*s*. 8*d*.

Total, £7. 17*s*. 10*d*.

Total of these items so far, £15. 4*s*. 8*d*.

And to William of Grimsby stone-cutter and his fellows for cutting 1,000 feet, £6. 13*s*. 4*d*., that is each hundred cut by task for 13*s*. 4*d*. And to Richard Norris and Ralph of Popes Hall for the work of the New Barbican, 71*s*. during this period.
And to Ralph of Harbledown, 7*s*. 8*d*. for 50 feet of stone cut, and 12*d*. of this was for another task

Sum total of this period up to the feast of St. Michael [29 September] £25. 16*s*. 8*d*. by tally against Geoffrey de Gurdun and Jocelyn de Oye.

On Saturday next before the feast of Saints Simon and Jude [24 *October*] *a payment was made for 7* [*sic*] *days.*

And for 5 stone-cutters and masons for 17 days, 21*s*. 9*d*.
And for 24 labourers, 26*s*. 11*d*.
And for 3,518 loads of sand, 47*s*.
And for 50 loads of lime slaked by task, 16*d*.

Total, £4. 17*s*.

Item Hugoni de Malinges pro vi. xx[ti]. Planchis ad Pontem Novum faciendum & pro xvj Planchis ad novam Portam faciendam & pro uno flagello & pro xxxii Barris, iiij li.
Item eidem Hugoni pro xiiij Gistis ad Pontem novum. xi.sol.
Item eidem pro CC bordis ad plancandum Turellas. xx sol.
Item pro DCCCC cendulis & l emptis aput Sanwic post festum omnium sanctorum x sol.

Summa harum Particularum. vj li. xii d.

Die Sabbati proxima ante Festum Sancti Nicholai facta fuit pacacio de vj septimanis

Item in xj Cimentariis & Incisoribus per hoc spacium. lv.sol. iij ob.
Item in tribus Carpentariis ad cintros faciendos & alia opera vj.sol. vj d.
Item in materie Cintrorum ad Portam Nouvam. xvij sol. iij ob. scilicet in xiiij trabibus & in xxvij Tingnis & in xiiij Planchis in C. Bordis & in cccc latarum.
Item pro virgis iij ob. Item in uno crible iij ob.
Item in CCC. clavorum grossorum & minutorum. xxiij d.
Item Helie Plumbario & ij hominibus suis per xix dies xij sol. viij d. per diem scilicet viij d.
Item in xxviij minutis operariis xlix sol. vij d. ob.
Item in M.M.DCCC. lxx. summis harene portatis xxxviij sol.
Item in xxij libris staminis & dim. iij sol. ix d.
Item in L. summis Calcis temperatis in tassca. xvj d.
Item in ix batellatis remotis a mari usque ad terram minutorum lapidum ix d.

Summa huius Particule ix li. vij sol. ob.

Item Hugoni de Meaulinges pro xxij gistis longis; quelibet habet in longitudine xxx pedes & aliqua [*sic*] plus ad turrim trabandam de ultra portam nouvam. lxx sol.
Item Willelmo de Grimesbi & sociis suis pro C. pedibus lapidum incisis per antiquam tasscam. xiij sol. iiij d. Item eisdem incissoribus pro DCC. pedibus incisis lapidum. iiij li. iiij sol. Centum scilicet pro xij sol.
Item Radulfo de Herebaldun' pro CC. pedibus lapidum incisis xxiiij sol. scilicet centum pro xij sol.

Summa harum particularum ix li. xi sol. iiij d.

In vigilia Natalis domini facta fuit Pacacio pro operacione Castri Dovor' Anno Regni Regis Henrici vi[to].

Item Hugoni fabro pro utensilibus cimentariorum reparandis xiij d. ob.

And to Hugh of Malling for 6 score planks to make the New Bridge and for 16 planks to make the New Gate and for one whip and for 32 bars, £4.
And to the same Hugh for 14 joists for the New Bridge, 11*s.*
And to the same for 200 boards to plank the towers, 20*s.*
And for 950 shingles bought at Sandwich after the feast of All Saints [1 November], 10*s.*

Total of these items, £6. 12*d.*

On Saturday next before the feast of St. Nicholas [5 *December*] *a payment was made for 6 weeks.*

And for 11 masons and stone-cutters for this period, 55*s.* 1½*d.*
And for three carpenters making centerings and other jobs, 6*s.* 6*d.*
And for wood for the centerings for the New Gate, 17*s.* 1½*d.*, that is for 14 principal beams and 27 beams and 14 planks and 100 boards and 400 laths.
And for withies, 1½*d.* And for one sieve, 1½*d.*
And for 300 nails, large and small, 23*d.*
And to Elias the plumber and his two men for 19 days, 12*s.* 8*d.*, that is 8*d.* a day.
And for 28 labourers, 49*s.* 7½*d.*
And for 2,870 loads of sand carried, 38*s.*
And for 22½ pounds of tin, 3*s.* 9*d.*
And for slaking 50 loads of lime by task, 16*d.*
And for 9 boat-loads of small stones removed from sea to land, 9*d.*

Total of this item, £9. 7*s.* 0½*d.*

And to Hugh of Malling for 22 long joists, each 30 feet long and some longer, to lay in the tower above the New Gate, 70*s.*
And to William of Grimsby and his fellows for cutting 100 feet of stone as part of their old task, 13*s.* 4*d.* And to the same stone-cutters for cutting 700 feet of stone, £4. 4*s.*, that is 100 for 12*s.*
And to Ralph of Harbledown for cutting 200 feet of stone, 24*s.*, that is 100 for 12*s.*

Total of these items, £9. 11*s.* 4*d.*

On Christmas eve in the 6th[1] *year of the reign of King Henry a payment was made for the works of Dover Castle.*

And to Hugh the smith for repairing the masons' tools, 13½*d.*

[1] A clerical error. The date in question fell in the 5th regnal year of Henry III.

Item Eidem pro xix essperdutis ferri operatis ad novam portam. xxviij d. ob. quelibet essperduta operata pro iij ob.
Item cuidam cimentario per ix dies ij sol. ob.
Item Helie plumbario & ij. hominibus suis per v. dies iij sol. iij d.
Item Ricardo Carpentario per xvii dies iiii sol. iii d.
Item Rogero Carpentario per xiiij dies iij sol. vj d.
Item in minutis operariis a festo Sancti Nicholai usque ad hoc Natale supradictum ix sol. ob.
Item pro M. summis harene portatis xiij sol. ij d.

Summa huius particule xxxviij sol. x d.

Summa Totalis a festo Sancti Michahelis usque ad Natale proximo sequens xxxi li. xv sol. ij. ob. per Tailam similiter contra Galfridum de Gurdune & Gocelinum de Oye.

Die Sabbati proxima post festum Sancte Scolastice virginis facta fuit proxima Pacacio post Natale pro operacione.

Item Hugoni fabro pro lxxiij essperdutis operatis & pro pice de verteveles & pro alio ferramento et pro clavis ad novam portam operatis x sol. viij d.
Item pro xlvj li. staminis ad solvendum plumbum & guttar' per castrum vj sol. Item pro vj xx^{ti} & iiij libris plumbi emptis ad domum cooperiendam inter bracinum & domum Turbe xiiii sol. iiii d.

Summa huius particule xxxi sol.

Eadem die facta fuit Pacacio cimentariorum & operariorum
Item Roberto de Wytefelde Cimentario per iij dies xij d.
Item Roberto Pollard Cimentario per vj dies xxi d. scilicet per diem iij d. ob.
Item Ricardo Portefer pro cheverones & bordis & L latis ii sol. v d. ob.
Item in minutis operariis pro castro mundando post magnam nivem & pro muro circa herbarium & pro aliis muris lapsis pro magno gelu xiij sol. v d. ob.
Item Helie plumbario & duobus hominibus suis per vj dies. iiij sol.
Item Ricardo carpentario per xviij dies iiij sol. vj d.
Item Thome de Tanet' Carpentario per iij dies. ix d.
Item ad carcandum xxxij magnas gistas super karrett' aput Sandwic' cum auxilio karetarii v d. ob.
Item Guarino cuvario pro viij circulis ad cuvas & tinas operacionis iiij d.

Summa huius particule xxviij sol. viij d. ob.

Die Sabbati proxima post festum Sancti Mathie Apostoli facta fuit Pacacio operacionis.

Item Helie plumbario pro dim. karetata plumbi & x libris xix sol. iii d.

And to the same for 19 iron bars worked for the New Gate, 28½*d.*, each bar worked for 1½*d.*
And to a certain mason for 9 days, 2*s.* 0½*d.*
And to Elias the plumber and his 2 men for 5 days, 3*s.* 3*d.*
And to Richard the Carpenter for 17 days, 4*s.* 3*d.*
And to Roger the Carpenter for 14 days, 3*s.* 6*d.*
And for labourers from the feast of St. Nicholas [6 December] to this aforesaid Christmas, 9*s.* 0½*d.*
And for 1,000 loads of sand carried, 13*s.* 2*d.*

Total of this item, 38*s.* 10*d.*

Sum total from the feast of St. Michael [29 September] to Christmas next following [25 December], £31. 15*s.* 2½*d.*, by tally similarly against Geoffrey de Gurdun and Jocelyn de Oye.

On Saturday next after the feast of St. Scholastica the Virgin [*13 February*] *the next payment after Christmas was made for the work.*

And to Hugh the smith for working 73 iron bars and for pitch for the hinges and for other iron and for making nails for the New Gate, 10*s.* 8*d.*
And for 46 pounds of tin to solder the leads and gutters about the castle, 6*s.* And for 124 pounds of lead bought to cover the building between the brew-house and the turf house, 14*s.* 4*d.*

Total of this item, 31*s.*

On the same day there was a payment to the masons and labourers
And to Robert of Whitfield, mason, for 3 days, 12*d.*
And to Robert Pollard, mason, for 6 days, 21*d.*, that is 3½*d.* a day.
And to Richard Portefer for rafters and boards and 50 laths, 2*s.* 5½*d.*
And for labourers cleaning up the castle after the great snow and for [removing] the wall round the lawn and the other walls that collapsed on account of the great frost, 13*s.* 5½*d.*
And to Elias the plumber and his two men for 6 days, 4*s.*
And to Richard the carpenter for 18 days, 4*s.* 6*d.*
And to Thomas of Thanet the carpenter for 3 days, 9*d.*
And for loading 32 great joists on a cart at Sandwich with the help of the carter, 5½*d.*
And to Warin the cooper for 8 hoops for tubs and casks for the works, 4*d.*

Total of this item, 28*s.* 8½*d.*

On Saturday next after the feast of St. Matthias the Apostle [*27 February*] *a payment for the works was made.*

And to Elias the plumber for half a char and 10 pounds of lead, 19*s.* 3*d.*

Item in clavis ad domum Turelle inter domum Bracini & domum Turbe vj sol. i d.

Item Copino cimentario per x dies iij sol. iiij d.

Item Roberto Cimentario per x dies xxxv d. Radulfo Albespine cimentario per vj dies xviij d.

Item Ricardo Carpentario per x dies ij sol. vj d.

Item cuidam alii carpentario per ix dies xxvij d.

Item Elie plumbario & ij hominibus suis per v dies iij sol. iiij d.

Item in latis ad domum Turelle inter Bracinum & domum Turbe x d.

Item in xxij minutis operariis pro illa domo & pro aliis minutis operacionibus per castrum xvii sol. ix d.

Summa huius particule lix sol. ix d.

Item Die Sabbati proxima ante festum Sancti Gregorii Hugoni de Maulinges pro lxiiij tingnis de fagina viij sol. j d.

Item Eidem pro xxvj Tingnis de quercu x sol. iiij d. ob.

Item Eidem pro C planchis xvij sol. ad plancandum

Item Eidem pro D bordis minutis de quercu x sol.

Item Eidem pro DC latis de quercu v sol.

Item Eidem pro lviij barris de quercu ad portas per Castrum emendandas vj sol. ij d.

Item Eidem pro CC. Bordis de fagina ij sol.

Item Eidem pro M. latas [*sic*] de fagina v.sol. vj. d.

Summa lxiiij sol. iii ob.

Item in vigilia Sancti Gregorii facta fuit pacacio de ix diebus

Item Roberto de Witefelde cimentario per vij dies xxviij d.

Item Copino cimentario per viij dies ij sol. viij d.

Item Roberto Cimentario per viij dies ij sol. iiij d.

Item Radulfo Albespine cimentario per viij dies xx d.

Item Ricardo Carpentario per x dies ij sol. vj d.

Item cuidam alii carpentario per x dies ij sol. vj d.

Item cuidam alii carpentario per ij dies pro factura de Teliers Balistarum iiij d.

Item operario facienti cleyas per iiij dies ix d.

Item minutis operariis scilicet xxvij per hoc spacium xix sol. ix d. ob.

Item pro ix. gistis & DCCCC lates de quercu emptis in villa Dovor' ad turallam v. sol

Summa huius particule xxxix sol. x d. ob.

And for nails for the building in the tower between the brew-house and the turf house, 6*s*. 1*d*.
And to Copin, mason, for 10 days, 3*s*. 4*d*.
And to Robert, mason, for 10 days, 35*d*. To Ralph Albespine, mason, for 6 days, 18*d*.
And to Richard the carpenter for 10 days, 2*s*. 6*d*.
And to a certain other carpenter for 9 days, 27*d*.
And to Elias the plumber and his two men for 5 days, 3*s*. 4*d*.
And for laths for the building of the tower between the brew-house and the turf house, 10*d*.
And for 22 labourers for that building and for other small jobs about the castle, 17*s*. 9*d*.

Total of this item, 59*s*. 9*d*.

And on Saturday next before the feast of St. Gregory [6 March] to Hugh of Malling for 64 beams of beech, 8*s*. 1*d*.
And to the same for 26 beams of oak, 10*s*. 4½*d*.
And to the same for 100 planks, 17*s*., for planking
And to the same for 500 small oak boards, 10*s*.
And to the same for 600 oak laths, 5*s*.
And to the same for 58 oak bars to mend the gates throughout the castle, 6*s*. 2*d*.
And to the same for 200 beech boards, 2*s*.
And to the same for 1,000 laths of beech, 5*s*. 6*d*.

Total, 64*s*. 1½*d*.

And on the vigil of St. Gregory [*11 March*] *payment was made for 9 days.*
And to Robert of Whitfield, mason, for 7 days, 28*d*.
And to Copin, mason, for 8 days, 2*s*. 8*d*.
And to Robert, mason, for 8 days, 2*s*. 4*d*.
And to Ralph Albespine, mason, for 8 days, 20*d*.
And to Richard, carpenter, for 10 days, 2*s*. 6*d*.
And to a certain other carpenter for 10 days, 2*s*. 6*d*.
And to a certain other carpenter for 2 days for making tillers for crossbows, 4*d*.
And to a labourer making hurdles for 4 days, 9*d*.
And to labourers, that is 27 during this period, 19*s*. 9½*d*.
And for 9 joists and 900 oak laths bought in the town of Dover for the tower, 5*s*.

Total of this item, 39*s*. 10½*d*.

Die Sabbati proxima post annunciacionem Beate Virginis Marie facta fuit pacacio pro Operacione.

Item pro lxi batellatis minutorum lapidum ductis de Folkestane usque Dovor' xl. sol. viij d.

Item pro remocione lxxij batellatarum lapidum a mari usque ad terram vj sol. iiij d.

Item xxix minutis operariis. xv sol. vij d.

Item Ricardo Carpentario per vij dies. xxj.d.

Item Balduino Carpentario per xij dies. iij.sol.

Item M.M. & DCCC summe harene portate. xxxvij sol.

Summa huius particule. C.iiij.sol. iiij d.

Item ad Nundinas apud Wi in clavis xj M. de prig' & minutorum clavorum ix sol. iij. d. Item MMM & dim. clavorum grossorum ad . . . vi sol. vij d.

Item in una pela ad quirandum stabulam karettariorum ij d.

Summa huius Empcionis xvj sol.

In Vigilia Pasce facta fuit Pacacio Operacionis Castri Dovor'.

Item Roberto de Witefeld Cimentario per viij dies. xxxij d.

Item Simoni Cimentario per vj.[1] dies xxviij d.

Item Simoni Cimentario de Dunstapele per unum diem iij d.

Item Copino Cimentario per vij dies. xxviij d.

Roberto Cimentario per vij dies. ij sol. ob.

Item Godman Cimentario per v. dies. x d.

Item Radulfo Albespine cimentario per v dies xii d. ob.

Item xxviij minutis operariis. xvij sol. viij d. ob.

Item in Distemperacione calcis. scilicet cl summarum in Tassca iiij sol.

Item in cccl. clavis grossis emptis in villa Dovor'. xvj d.

Item pro remocione xx batellatarum minutorum lapidum a mari usque terram xx d.

Item in MM & DCCCl summis harene portatis ad castrum xxxvij sol. x d. ob.

Item pro uno crible iij ob.

Item Ricardo Portefer pro vj tingnis. & i scope vij d.

Item in una nova tina & ij bukettis parvis & j. tina reparanda x d.

Item Ricardo Norensi & Radulfo de Popeshal pro curacione de pilers sub novo ponte. v sol.

Item pro xvj batellatis minutorum lapidum ductis de Folkestane usque ad Dovor' x sol. viij d.

Summa huius particule iiij li. xj sol. ij d. ob.

[1] *Sic*, but probably a mistake for vij.

On Saturday next after the Annunciation of the Blessed Virgin Mary [27 March] a payment was made for the work.

And for 61 boat-loads of small stones brought from Folkestone to Dover, 40*s.* 8*d.*
And for removing 72 boat-loads of stones from sea to land, 6*s.* 4*d.*
And to 29 labourers, 15*s.* 7*d.*
And to Richard, carpenter, for 7 days, 21*d.*
And to Baldwin, carpenter, for 12 days, 3*s.*
And for 2,800 loads of sand carried, 37*s.*

Total of this item, 104*s.* 4*d.*

And spent on nails at Wye Fair—11,000 prig-nails and small nails, 9*s.* 3*d.* And for 3,500 large nails for . . ., 6*s.* 7*d.*
And for one shovel to clean the carters' stable, 2*d.*

Total of this purchase, 16*s.*

On the vigil of Easter [10 April] there was a payment for the works of Dover Castle.

And to Robert of Whitfield, mason, for 8 days, 32*d.*
And to Simon, mason, for 6[1] days, 28*d.*
And to Simon the mason of Dunstable for one day, 3*d.*
And to Copin, mason, for 7 days, 28*d.*
To Robert, mason, for 7 days, 2*s.* 0½*d.*
And to Godman, mason, for 5 days, 10*d.*
And to Ralph Albespine, mason, for 5 days, 12½*d.*
And to 28 labourers, 17*s.* 8½*d.*
And for slaking lime, that is 150 loads by task, 4*s.*
And for 350 large nails bought in the town of Dover, 16*d.*
And for removing 20 boat-loads of small stones from sea to land, 20*d.*
And for 2,850 loads of sand brought to the castle, 37*s.* 10½*d.*
And for one sieve, 1½*d.*
And to Richard Portefer for 6 beams and one shovel, 7*d.*
And for one new cask and 2 small buckets and for mending one cask, 10*d.*
And to Richard Norris and Ralph of Popes Hall for putting right the piers underneath the new bridge, 5*s.*
And for 16 boat-loads of small stones brought from Folkestone to Dover, 10*s.* 8*d.*

Total of this item, £4. 11*s.* 2½*d.*

[1] Really 7?

Summa Totalis hucusque per visum Gocelini de Oye usque ad hoc Pasca cum Empcione materiei empte de Hugone de Maulinges facte [*sic*] post Pasca, scilicet viij li. ix sol. vj d. Item xxx li. iiij sol. vj d. per Tailam contra ipsum Gocelinum de hoc termino.

Notandum quod in Vigilia Pasce anno Regni Regis Henrici v^to^ factum fuit quoddam Emptum de Hugone de Meaulinges de materie ad operaciones Castri Dovor' aput Sanwiz, unde hee sunt particule
Item in ij fustes de xxiij pedibus, precium vj sol.
Item pro xlviii cheveruns de quercu de xxj pedibus precium. xxv sol.
Item lxxv cheveruns de fagina ad scatfotandum per operacionem castri vij sol. vj d.
Item CCC bord' ad plancandum lxvj sol.
Item alii bord' scilicet CCC ad plancandum lxv sol.

Summa totalis huius empcionis viij li. ix sol. vj d.

Die Sabbati proxima post clausum Passca anno Regni Regis Henrici v^to^ scilicet in vigilia Sancti Marci Ewangeliste facta fuit Pacacio pro operacione Castri Dovor' per manum Willelmi de Essedeford & Ricardi de Popeshall' & Gocelini de Oye.

Item pro uno batello qui duxit C. & xvj plancas & xviij gistas de Sandwic' usque ad litus Dovor' ij sol.
Item Copino Cimentario per vj dies ij sol.
Roberto Cimentario de Witefeld per vj. dies ij sol.
Item Robin Cimentario per vij dies ij sol. ob.
Item Simoni Cimentario per vij dies ij sol. iiij d.
Item Ricardo Cimentario per iij dies x d. ob.
Item Radulfo Albespine cimentario per vj dies xviij d.
Item Godman Cimentario per vj dies xij d.
Item Stephano Iuveni Cimentario per iiij dies. viij d.
Item pro liiij batellatis lapidum minutorum ductis de Folkestan' xxxvj sol.
Item pro remocione liii batellatarum a mari usque ad terram. iiij sol. vj d.
Item Baldewino Carpentario per xvj dies. iiij sol.
Item in MMDCCCV summis harene portatis xxxvj sol.
Item in xxxviij minutis operariis, aliqui per x dies aliqui minus, xxviij sol. ix d.
Item pro cl summis calcis temperatis iiij sol. in tassca.
Item pro portagio C. summarum calcis iiij sol.

Summa vj li. x sol. viij d.

Sum total so far of expenditure by view of Jocelyn de Oye up to this Easter together with the purchase of timber bought from Hugh of Malling after Easter, that is £8. 9*s*. 6*d*. And there is £30. 4*s*. 6*d*. by a tally against Jocelyn de Oye in this period.

Note that on the vigil of Easter [10 April] in the 5th year of the reign of King Henry a certain purchase of timber for the works of Dover Castle was made from Hugh of Malling at Sandwich, whereof these are the items,

And for 2 timbers 23 feet long, price 6*s*.

And for 48 rafters of oak 21 feet long, price 25*s*.

And 75 poles of beech for scaffolding throughout the works of the castle, 7*s*. 6*d*.

And 300 boards for planking, 66*s*.

And other boards, that is 300 for planking, 65*s*.

Sum total of this purchase, £8. 9*s*. 6*d*.

On Saturday next after the end of Easter [*24 April*] *in the 5th year of the reign of King Henry, that is on the vigil of St. Mark the Evangelist, a payment was made for the works of Dover Castle by the hand of William of Ashford and Richard of Popes Hall and Jocelyn de Oye.*

And for one boat which brought 116 planks and 18 joists from Sandwich to the shore at Dover, 2*s*.

And to Copin, mason, for 6 days, 2*s*.

To Robert the mason of Whitfield for 6 days, 2*s*.

And to Robin, mason, for 7 days, 2*s*. 0½*d*.

And to Simon, mason, for 7 days, 2*s*. 4*d*.

And to Richard, mason, for 3 days, 10½*d*.

And to Ralph Albespine, mason, for 6 days, 18*d*.

And to Godman, mason, for 6 days, 12*d*.

And to Stephen Young, mason, for 4 days, 8*d*.

And for 54 boat-loads of small stones brought from Folkestone, 36*s*.

And for removing 53 boat-loads from the sea to the land, 4*s*. 6*d*.

And to Baldwin, carpenter, for 15 days, 4*s*.

And for 2,805 loads of sand carried, 36*s*.

And for 38 labourers, some for 10 days, some less, 28*s*. 9*d*.

And for 150 loads of lime slaked by task, 4*s*.

And for the portage of 100 loads of lime, 4*s*.

Total, £6. 10*s*. 8*d*.

Die Sabbati proxima post festum Sancti Johannis ante Portam Latinam facta fuit Pacacio pro operacione Castri Dovor'.

Item pro lxxv batellatis minutorum lapidum ductis de Folkestane l sol., quelibet pro viij d.

Item pro remocione earum batellatarum a mari usque ad terram vj sol. iij d.

Item Roberto de Witefeld Cimentario per iiij dies xvj d.

Item Copin Cimentario per iiij dies. xvj d.

Item Simoni Cimentario per vij dies. xxviij d.

Item Robin Cimentario per ix dies. xxxiiij d.

Item Ricardo Cimentario per vij dies. ij sol. ob.

Item Eilmer Cimentario per iij dies. ix d.

Item Albespine Cimentario per iiij dies. xij d.

Item Godman Cimentario per iiij dies. viij d.

Item Stephano Iuveni Cimentario per iiij dies. viij d.

Item Baldelot Carpentario per ix dies ij sol. iij d.

Item in lviij minutis operariis xxxv sol. ij d.

Item pro domo reparanda in qua balistarius est qui servat balistas xvj d.

Item cuidam cooperatori per iiij dies viij d.

Item pro portagio unius batellate de bordis & materie que venit de Sandwic' viij d.

Item pro portagio cuiusdam navati [*sic*] feni in domos castri Dovor', vj d.

Item pro locacione cuiusdam domus in villa Dovor' ubi fenum & materies fuit per tres septimanas x d.

Item pro ij follibus ad fabricam iiij sol.

Item Hugoni fabro pro i securi vj d.

Item pro portagio CC summarum calcis vi sol.

Item pro distemperacione cl xxxiij summarum calcis iiij sol. ix d.

Item in D milibus summarum petre & harene portatis lxvj sol.

Summa ix li. xii sol. vi d. ob.

Item pro vi karettatis plumbi emptis ad festum Sanctorum Philippi & Jacobi de Wiberto de Sandwic' vi li. quelibet karetata pro xxx sol.

Item pro eodem plumbo ducto per aquam de Sandwic' aput Dovor' ii sol.

Item pro portagio eiusdem plumbi a mari usque ad terram viij d.

Item Turgisio preposito pro bosco ad faciendum ii rogos in villa Dovor' li.sol.

On Saturday next after the feast of St. John before the Latin Gate [8 May] a payment was made for the works of Dover Castle.

And for 75 boat-loads of small stones brought from Folkestone, 50*s.*, each for 8*d.*
And for removing those boat-loads from the sea to the land, 6*s.* 3*d.*
And to Robert of Whitfield, mason, for 4 days, 16*d.*
And to Copin, mason, for 4 days, 16*d.*
And to Simon, mason, for 7 days, 28*d.*
And to Robin, mason, for 9 days, 34*d.*
And to Richard, mason, for 7 days, 2*s.* 0½*d.*
And to Eilmer, mason, for 3 days, 9*d.*
And to Albespine, mason, for 4 days, 12*d.*
And to Godman, mason, for 4 days, 8*d.*
And to Stephen Young, mason, for 4 days, 8*d.*
And to Baldelot, carpenter, for 9 days, 2*s.* 3*d.*
And for 58 labourers, 35*s.* 2*d.*
And for repairing the building in which there is the crossbowman who looks after the crossbows, 16*d.*
And to a certain thatcher for 4 days, 8*d.*
And for portage of one boat-load of boards and timber which came from Sandwich, 8*d.*
And for portage of a shipload of hay into the buildings of Dover Castle, 6*d.*
And for hiring a certain building in the town of Dover where the hay and timber was for three weeks, 10*d.*
And for 2 bellows for the forge, 4*s.*
And to Hugh the smith for one axe, 6*d.*
And for the carriage of 200 loads of lime, 6*s.*
And for slaking 183 loads of lime, 4*s.* 9*d.*
And for portage of 5,000 loads of stone and sand, 66*s.*[1]

Total, £9. 12*s.* 6½*d.*

And for 6 chars of lead bought from Wibert of Sandwich on the Feast of Saints Philip and James [1 May], £6, each char for 30*s.*[2]
And for bringing the same lead by water from Sandwich to Dover, 2*s.*
And for portage of the same lead from the sea to the land, 8*d.*
And to Turgis the reeve for wood to make 2 kilns in the town of Dover, 51*s.*

1 Though *D milibus* equals 500,000, it is evident that what the clerk meant must have been 5,000.
2 *Sic.*

Item de Hugone de Meaulinges empt' post Passca xxvi gistas [*sic*] de xxvi pedibus aliqua longior aliqua brevior precium xxiiii sol. iiii d.
Item pro CC longissimis clavis emptis iiii sol.

Summa huius Empcionis plumbi & ligni x li. ii sol. vi d.

Die Sabbati proxima ante festum Sancti Dunstani anno Regni Regis Henrici v^to^ facta fuit pacacio pro operacione Castri Dovor'.

Item pro xxii batellatis minutorum lapidum ductis de Folkestan' usque ad Dovor' xiiii sol. viii d.
Item Hugoni de Rumelli pro C lapidibus incisis xii sol.
Item Roberto de Wytefeld cimentario per unum diem iiii d.
Item Copin cimentario per v dies xx d.
Item Simoni cimentario per v dies xx d.
Item Eilmer cimentario per v dies xv d.
Item Radulfo Albespine per iiii dies xii d.
Item Robin cimentario per v dies xvii d. ob.
Item Ricardo cimentario per i diem iij d. ob.
Item Godman cimentario per v dies x d.
Item Stephano cimentario per v dies x d.
Item Hereberto cimentario per iiii dies xii d.
Item Willelmo cimentario per iiii dies vii d. ob.
Item in xlv minutis operariis xx sol. vi d.
Item pro xxii batellatis lapidum portatis a mari usque ad terram xxii d.
Item pro j batellata materiei portata a mari ad terram viii d.
Item in MMM & viii xx^ti^ & x summis petre & harene portatis xlii sol.
Item pro portagio CC summarum calcis vi sol.
Item pro distemperacione l. summarum calcis xvi d.
Item Dionisio & sociis suis ad temperandum CC summas calcis v sol. iiii d.
Item navi que portavit materiem & bordas de Sandwic' ad Douer' vii sol.
Item hominibus qui carcaverunt navem de materie aput Sandwic' ii sol. ii d.
Item Ricardo Carpentario per iii dies ix d.
Item pro cliiii summis aque portatis iiii sol.

Summa huius vi li. ix sol. ii d. ob.

Pacacio facta in Vigilia Pentecoste[s] *anno Regni Regis Henrici V^to^.*

Item pro clv batellatis lapidum minutorum ductis de Folkestane usque ad Dovor' ciiii sol. iii d. & notandum quod i batellus habuit ix d. de qualibet batellata quia maior aliis erat, omnes vero alii viii d. de qualibet batellata.

And bought from Hugh of Malling after Easter, 26 26-foot joists, some longer, some shorter, 24*s*. 4*d*.
And for 200 very long nails bought, 4*s*.

Total of this purchase of lead and timber, £10. 2*s*. 6*d*.[1]

On Saturday next before the feast of St. Dunstan [*15 May*] *a payment was made for the works of Dover Castle.*

And for 22 boat-loads of small stones brought from Folkestone to Dover, 14*s*. 8*d*.
And to Hugh de Romilly for cutting 100 stones, 12*s*.
And to Robert of Whitfield, mason, for one day, 4*d*.
And to Copin, mason, for 5 days, 20*d*.
And to Simon, mason, for 5 days, 20*d*.
And to Eilmer, mason, for 5 days, 15*d*.
And to Ralph Albespine for 4 days, 12*d*.
And to Robin, mason, for 5 days, 17½*d*.
And to Richard, mason, for one day, 3½*d*.
And to Godman, mason, for 5 days, 10*d*.
And to Stephen, mason, for 5 days, 10*d*.
And to Herbert, mason, for 4 days, 12*d*.
And to William, mason, for 4 days, 7½*d*.
And for 45 labourers, 20*s*. 6*d*.
And for 22 boat-loads of stones carried from sea to land, 22*d*.
And for one boat-load of timber carried from sea to land, 8*d*.
And for portage of 3,170 loads of stone and sand, 42*s*.
And for portage of 200 loads of lime, 6*s*.
And for slaking 50 loads of lime, 16*d*.
And to Denis and his fellows to slake 200 loads of lime, 5*s*. 4*d*.
And to the vessel which brought the timber and boards from Sandwich to Dover, 7*s*.
And to the men who loaded the vessel with timber at Sandwich, 2*s*. 2*d*.
And to Richard, carpenter, for 3 days, 9*d*.
And for portage of 154 loads of water, 4*s*.

Total of this, £6. 9*s*. 2½*d*.

Payment made on the vigil of Whitsun [29 *May*] *in the 5th year of the reign of King Henry.*

And for 155 boat-loads of small stones brought from Folkestone to Dover, 104*s*. 3*d*., and it should be noted that one boat had 9*d*. for every boat-load because it was bigger than the others: all the others had 8*d*. for each boat-load.

[1] *Sic.*

Item pro vi M.CCC. summis harene & petre portatis iiii li. iii sol. x d.
Item pro portagio ccvii summarum calcis a rogo ad operacionem vi sol. ii d.
Item pro portagio cc summarum aque v sol.
Item pro portagio unius batellate de materie a mari ad terram vi d.
Item pro scindendo ad minutas frustras de creie ad duos rogos per nos factos sub rupe scilicet pro clvii summis iiii sol.
Item Roberto de Witefeld Cimentario per iii dies xii d.
Item Her' Cimentario per viii dies ii sol.
Item Copin Cimentario per viii dies ii sol. viii d.
Item Simoni Cimentario per v dies xx d.
Item Eilmer Cimentario per viii dies ii sol. viii d.
Item Robin Cimentario per viii dies ii sol. iiii d.
Item Ricardo Cimentario per viii dies ii sol. iiii d.
Item Hereberto Cimentario per viii dies ii sol.
Item Albespine cimentario per viii dies ii sol.
Item Godman cimentario per viii dies xvi d.
Item Stephano Cimentario per viii dies. xvi d.

Summa Cimentariorum xxi sol. iiii d.

Item ad removendum clv batellatas lapidum a mari ad terram xii sol. xi d.
Item Ricardo carpentario per ix dies ii sol. iii d.
Item Baldelot Carpentario per xvi dies iiii sol.
Item in lxii minutis operariis aliqui per xii dies, aliqui plus, aliqui minus l sol. viii d.
Item in i crible empto ad operacionem castri Dovor' iii ob.
Item in temperacione ccxxv summarum calcis vi sol.
Item duobus hominibus vigilantibus ultra supradictos ii rogos per iii noctes xii d.
Item cuidam plumbario & homini eius per viii dies. iiii sol. scilicet per diem vi d.

Summa huius xv li. vi sol. ob.

Item Radulfo de Popeshall' & Ricardo Norensi pro nova barbakania xxxv sol. viii d.

In Vigilia Sancti Johannis Baptiste facta fuit pacacio pro operacione Castri Dovor'.

Item pro cxlvii batellatis lapidum iiii li. xviii sol. quelibet batallata pro viii d.
Item pro domo Bartolomei Janitoris empta que fuit uxoris sue quando iverunt aput Iherusalem vi sol. viii d.
Item pro arundineto empto aput Sandwic' iiii sol. iiii d.
Item pro cooperture empta scilicet CCCC aput Dovor' de Flandrensibus xx d. ad cooperandum stabulam karettariorum.

And for 6,300 loads of sand and stone carried, £4. 3*s*. 10*d*.
And for portage of 207 loads of lime from the kiln to the work, 6*s*. 2*d*.
And for portage of 200 loads of water, 5*s*.
And for portage of one boat-load of timber from sea to land, 6*d*.
And for breaking chalk up into small pieces for two kilns made by us below the cliff, that is for 157 loads, 4*s*.
And to Robert of Whitfield, mason, for 3 days, 12*d*.
And to Her', mason, for 8 days, 2*s*.
And to Copin, mason, for 8 days, 2*s*. 8*d*.
And to Simon, mason, for 5 days, 20*d*.
And to Eilmer, mason, for 8 days, 2*s*. 8*d*.
And to Robin, mason, for 8 days, 2*s*. 4*d*.
And to Richard, mason, for 8 days, 2*s*. 4*d*.
And to Herbert, mason, for 8 days, 2*s*.
And to Albespine, mason, for 8 days, 2*s*.
And to Godman, mason, for 8 days, 16*d*.
And to Stephen, mason, for 8 days, 16*d*.

Total of masons' wages, 21*s*. 4*d*.

And for removing 155 boat-loads of stones from sea to land, 12*s*. 11*d*.
And to Richard, carpenter, for 9 days, 2*s*. 3*d*.
And to Baldelot, carpenter, for 16 days, 4*s*.
And for 62 labourers, some for 12 days, some more, some less, 50*s*. 8*d*.
And for one sieve bought for the works of Dover Castle, 1½*d*.
And for slaking 225 loads of lime, 6*s*.
And to two men watching over the aforesaid two kilns for 3 nights, 12*d*.
And to a certain plumber and his man for 8 days, 4*s*., that is 6*d*. a day.

Total of this, £15. 6*s*. 0½*d*.

And to Ralph of Popes Hall and Richard Norris for the new barbican, 35*s*. 8*d*.

On the vigil of St. John the Baptist [*23 June*] *a payment was made for the works of Dover Castle.*

And for 167 boat-loads of stones, £4. 18*s*., each boat-load for 8*d*.
And for buying the house of Bartholomew the Janitor which was his wife's, when they went to Jerusalem, 6*s*. 8*d*.
And for reeds bought at Sandwich, 4*s*. 4*d*.
And for thatch bought, that is 4 hundredweight at Dover from Flemings, to cover the carters' stable, 20*d*.

Item Radulfo plumbario pro operacione ii karettarum & x peises plumbi in tassca v sol. viii d.
Item Ricardo Portefer pro CCC summis calcis emptis c.sol. quelibet summa pro iiii d.
Item pro C tignis de fagina vii sol.
Item pro portagio CCC summarum calcis ix sol. quodlibet C. pro iii sol.
Item pro temperacione CCC summarum calcis viii sol. quodlibet C. xxxii d.
Item Roberto de Witefeld Cimentario per iii dies xii d.
Item Copin Cimentario per xiii dies. iiii sol. iiii d.
Item Simoni Cimentario per xv dies v sol.
Item Eilmer Cimentario per xv dies iiii sol. iiii d. ob.
Item Robin Cimentario per xvi dies iiii sol. viii d.
Item Ricardo Cimentario per xv dies iiii sol. iiii d. ob.
Item Waltero Pollard per vi dies xxi d.
Item Henrico filio Roberti Cimentario per xv dies iii sol. ix d.
Item Albespine cimentario per xi dies ii sol. ix d.
Item Godman Cimentario per xi dies xxii d.
Item Stephano Cimentario per xv dies ii sol. vi d.
Item Simoni de Dunstapele Cimentario per iii dies xii d.

Summa Cimentariorum xxxvii sol. iiii d.

Item Ricardo Carpentario per xii dies iii sol.
Item Johanni Carpentario per xiiii dies iii sol. vi d.
Item pro remocione Cxlviii batellatarum lapidum a mari usque ad terram xii sol. iiii d.
Item in una libra staminis & dim. iii d.
Item in laqueis ad novum stabulum karettariorum ii d.
Item pro locacione unius domus per tres septimanas ix d.
Item pro DCCCC M & DCC & xvi summis harene & petrarum vi lib. x sol. x d. ob.
Item in xlvii minutis operariis a Pentecoste usque ad diem Sabbati proximam post Festum Apostolorum Petri & Pauli lxv sol. vi d.
Item pro D & xxxiiii summis aque portatis xiii sol. vi d.
Item pro DCCC arundineti emptis ad domum Gocelini de Oye cooperendam v sol. iiii d. quodlibet C pro viii d.
Item pro iii circulis ad cuvam operacionis ii d.
Item cuidam cooperatori ad cooperendum novum stabulum karetariorum ii sol. in tassca.
Item pro xxv tingnis emptis in villa Dovor' per manum constabularii xx d.
Item Radulfo Plumbario ad cooperendum ii karectatas plumbi & x peises in tassca v sol. & viii d. pro alia turella cooperenda in angulo

Summa huius pacacionis xxvi li. ii sol. iiii d. ob.

And to Ralph, plumber, for working two chars and 10 weighs of lead by task, 5*s.* 8*d.*
And to Richard Portefer for 300 loads of lime bought, 100*s.*, each load for 4*d.*
And for 100 beams of beech, 7*s.*
And for portage of 300 loads of lime, 9*s.*, each 100 for 3*s.*
And for slaking 300 loads of lime, 8*s.*, each 100 for 32*d.*
And to Robert of Whitfield, mason, for 3 days, 12*d.*
And to Copin, mason, for 13 days, 4*s.* 4*d.*
And to Simon, mason, for 15 days, 5*s.*
And to Eilmer, mason, for 15 days, 4*s.* 4½*d.*
And to Robin, mason, for 16 days, 4*s.* 8*d.*
And to Richard, mason, for 15 days, 4*s.* 4½*d.*
And to Walter Pollard for 6 days, 21*d.*
And to Henry son of Robert, mason, for 15 days, 3*s.* 9*d.*
And to Albespine, mason, for 11 days, 2*s.* 9*d.*
And to Godman, mason, for 11 days, 22*d.*
And to Stephen, mason, for 15 days, 2*s.* 6*d.*
And to Simon of Dunstable, mason, for 3 days, 12*d.*

Total of masons' wages, 37*s.* 4*d.*

And to Richard, carpenter, for 12 days, 3*s.*
And to John, mason, for 14 days, 3*s.* 6*d.*
And for removing 148 boat-loads of stones from sea to land, 12*s.* 4*d.*
And for a pound and a half of tin, 3*d.*
And for tie-beams for the new carters' stable, 2*d.*
And for hiring a house for three weeks, 9*d.*
And for 9,716 loads of sand and stones, £6. 10*s.* 10½*d.*
And for 47 labourers from Whitsun to Saturday next after the feast of the Apostles Peter and Paul [3 July], 65*s.* 6*d.*
And for portage of 534 loads of water, 13*s.* 6*d.*
And for 8 hundredweight of reeds bought to thatch Jocelyn de Oye's house, 5*s.* 4*d.*, each hundredweight for 8d.
And for 3 hoops for the tub used for the work, 2*d.*
And to a certain thatcher for covering the new carters' stable, 2*s.* by task-work.
And for 25 beams bought in the town of Dover by the constable, 20*d.*
And to Ralph the plumber for making a roof with 2 chars and 10 weighs of lead by task, 5*s.*; and 8*d.*, for roofing another tower in the corner.

Total of this payment, £26. 2*s.* 4½*d.*

Item Willelmo de Grimesbi & sociis suis pro MM pedibus lapidum incisorum xiii li. iiii sol. cent. scilicet incisum pro xii sol. & notandum quod in CC horum lapidum fuit duplex incisio.

Summa hucusque a Passca predicto usque ad Festum Sancti Johannis proximo sequens per visum & per dicam contra Gocelinum de Oye iiii. xx^ti li. ix li. iii sol.

Die Sabbati proxima ante festum Sancti Laurencii facta fuit pacacio pro operacione castri & maxima fuit illa pacacio quia non habuerunt denarios antequam Dominus Justiciarius illos misit de London' per Galfridum de Gordun' & Simonem de Grenewei & Radulfum Normannum. scilicet centum marcas.

Item Ricardo Portefer & socio suo pro DCCC summis calcis, xiii li. vi sol. viii d. quelibet summa pro iiii d.

Item pro portagio harum DCCC summarum xxiiii sol. cent. pro iii sol.

Item pro temperacione harum DCCC summarum xxi sol. iiii d. C. scilicet pro xxxii d.

Item Hugoni de Meaulinges pro xxv gistis ad pontem novum xxxiii sol. iiii d.

Item pro xv M & DC summis petrarum & harene portatis ad operacionem x lib. vii sol. vii d. ob. scilicet quodlibet C. pro xvi d.

Item pro CC & xxxii batellatis minutorum lapidum ductis de Folkestane usque ad Dovor' vii lib. xiiii sol. viii d.

Item pro remocione harum batellatarum a mari ad terram xix sol. iiii d.

Item pro DCC summis aque portatis ad operacionem & iiii xx^ti xix sol. iiii d. centum scilicet pro xxx d.

Item Hugoni Fabro pro vertevelles porte nove emendand' iiii d.

Item xl minutis operariis per vi septimanas non pacatis lxxix sol. v d.

Item Hugoni de Rumeli per vi dies ii sol.

Item Johanni Longo per vi dies ii sol. Item Willelmo de Grimesbi per vi dies ii sol.

Item Simoni de Dunstapele per ix dies iii sol. ii d. & hii fuerunt cissores lapidum per tot dies quia incisio defuit de tassca

Item Warino cuvario pro iiii circulis iii d.

Item duobus carpentariis per x dies v. sol. cuilibet per diem iii d. pro factura domus Gerardi Balistarii.

Item Ricardo Norensi pro prostracione muri ad nouvam portam xv sol. in tassca.

Item duobus bernardensis pro nova dova perforanda xxvi sol. viii d. in tassca.

Item pro uno crible i d.

Item iii carpentariis pro una domo emendenda in castro xviii d.

Item Ricardo Portefer pro xiiii tingnis ad passus faciendos x d.

Item pro coopertura ad domum Gerardi Balistarii xxviii d.

And to William of Grimsby and his fellows for cutting 2,000 feet of stone, £13. 4*s*., that is a hundred cut for 12*s*., and it should be noted that double cutting was involved in 200 of these stones.

Total so far from Easter aforesaid to the feast of St. John [24 June] next following by view of and by tally against Jocelyn de Oye, £89. 3*s*.

On Saturday next before the feast of St. Laurence [*7 August*] *a payment was made for the work of the castle*, and this was a very large payment because they did not have the cash until the Lord Justiciar sent it from London by Geoffrey de Gordun and Simon of Greenway and Ralph Norman, that is 100 marks [£66. 13*s*. 4*d*.].

And to Richard Portefer and his fellow for 800 loads of lime, £13. 6*s*. 8*d*., each load for 4*d*.
And for portage of these 800 loads, 24*s*., a hundred for 3*s*.
And for slaking these 800 loads, 21*s*. 4*d*., that is a hundred for 32*d*.
And to Hugh of Malling for 25 joists for the new bridge, 33*s*. 4*d*.
And for 15,600 loads of stones and sand carried to the works, £10. 7*s*. 7½*d*., that is a hundred for 16*d*.
And for 232 boat-loads of small stones brought from Folkestone to Dover, £7. 14*s*. 8*d*.
And for removing these boat-loads from sea to land, 19*s*. 4*d*.
And for 780 loads of water carried to the work, 19*s*. 4*d*., that is a hundred for 30*d*.
And to Hugh the smith for mending the hinges of the new gate, 4*d*.
And to 40 labourers unpaid for 6 weeks, 79*s*. 5*d*.
And to Hugh de Romilly for 6 days, 2*s*.
And to John Long for 6 days, 2*s*. And to William of Grimsby for 6 days, 2*s*.
And to Simon of Dunstable for 9 days, 3*s*. 2*d*., and these men were paid as stone-cutters for so many days because the cutting fell short of the task (?).
And to Warin the cooper for 4 hoops, 3*d*.
And to two carpenters for 10 days, 5*s*., each at 3*d*. a day for making the house of Gerard the crossbowman
And to Richard Norris for pulling down the wall by the new gate, 15*s*. by task
And to two barrow-men for cutting the new tunnel, 26*s*. 8*d*. by task
And for one sieve, 1*d*.
And to 3 carpenters for mending one building in the castle, 18*d*.
And to Richard Portefer for 14 beams to make steps, 10*d*.
And for thatch for the house of Gerard the crossbowman, 28*d*.

Item pro xii frustis plumbi emptis apud Sanwic' xiii sol.
Item pro xxv tingnis emptis in villa Dovor' de quodam de Pevenesell' xvi d.

Pacacio Cimentariorum Copin Cimentario per xxiiii dies viii sol.
Item Simoni Cimentario per xxiiii dies viii sol.
Item Eilmer Cimentario per xxiiii dies vii sol.
Item Ricardo Cimentario per xxiiii dies vii sol.
Item Robin Cimentario per xxiiii dies vii sol.
Item Henrico Cimentario per xx dies v sol.
Item Radulfo Albespine per xxi dies v sol. iii d.
Item Godman Cimentario per xxiiii dies iiii sol.
Item Stepphano Cimentario per xxiiii dies iiii sol.
Item Waltero Pollard per xvi dies iiii sol.
Item Simoni Albo London' per ix dies ii sol. vii d. ob.

Summa harum pacacionum individuarum lxi sol. x d. ob.
Summa huius pacacionis xlviii li. iii sol. i d.

Die Sabbati proxima ante Festum Sancti Bartolomei facta fuit Pacacio operacionis castri Dovor' anno Regni Regis Henrici V[to]

Item Ricardo Portefer & Osberto calciatoribus pro ccl summis iiii lib. xl d. quelibet summa pro iiii d.
Item pro portagio earum summarum a rogo ad castrum vii sol. vi d.
Item pro temperacione earum summarum in tassca vi sol. viii d.
Item in vi M. & C. & xxxv summis petrarum & harene iiii lib. i d.
Item pro lxiii batellatis minutorum lapidum ductis de Folkestan' xlvii sol. iii d. & habuit [*sic*] ix d. propter Autumnum.
Item Bernardensis pro remocione lapidum istorum a mari usque ad terram xliiii d.
Item Copin Cimentario per viii dies & dim. ii sol. x d. per diem iiii d.
Item Simoni Cimentario per viii dies & fere j diem ii sol. ix d. per diem iiii d.
Item Simoni Albo Cimentario London' per viii dies & dim. xxx d. per diem iii d. ob.
Eilmer Cimentario per tot dies xxx d.
Item Robin Cimentario similiter per tot dies xxx d. cuilibet per diem iii d. ob.
Item Ricardo Cimentario per ii dies vii d. per diem iii d. ob.
Item Albespine Cimentario per xi dies & dimidium ii sol. x d. quoniam sibi defecerunt de alia superiori pacacione iii dies. & ipse capit per diem iii d.
Item Waltero Pollard per vi dies xxi d. per diem iii d. ob.

And for 12 pieces of lead bought at Sandwich, 13*s.*
And for 25 beams bought in the town of Dover from a man from Pevensey, 16*d.*

Payment to the masons.

to Copin, mason, for 24 days, 8*s.*
to Simon, mason, for 24 days, 8*s.*
to Eilmer, mason, for 24 days, 7*s.*
to Richard, mason, for 24 days, 7*s.*
to Robin, mason, for 24 days, 7*s.*
to Henry, mason, for 20 days, 5*s.*
to Ralph Albespine for 21 days, 5*s.* 3*d.*
to Godman, mason, for 24 days, 4*s.*
to Stephen, mason, for 24 days, 4*s.*
to Walter Pollard for 16 days, 4*s.*
to Simon White of London for 9 days, 2*s.* 7½*d.*

Total of these individual payments, 61*s.* 10½*d.*
Total of this payment, £48. 3*s.* 1*d.*

On Saturday next before the feast of St. Bartholomew [*21 August*] *in the 5th year of the reign of King Henry there was a payment for the works of Dover Castle*

And to Richard Portefer and Osbert, lime-burners, for 250 loads, £4. 40*d.*, each load for 4*d.*
And for portage of those loads from the kiln to the castle, 7*s.* 6*d.*
And for slaking those loads by task, 6*s.* 8*d.*
And for 6,135 loads of stones and sand, £4. 1*d.*
And for 63 boat-loads of small stones brought from Folkestone, 47*s.* 3*d.*, and they had 9*d.* because of the Autumn.[1]
And to the barrow-men[2] for moving those stones from sea to land, 44*d.*
And to Copin, mason, for 8½ days, 2*s.* 10*d.*, at 4*d.* a day.
And to Simon, mason, for 8 days and nearly a day, 2*s.* 9*d.*, at 4*d.* a day.
And to Simon White, mason of London, for 8½ days, 30*d.*, at 3½*d.* a day.
to Eilmer, mason, for the same number of days, 30*d.*
to Robin, mason, similarly for the same number of days, 30*d.*, to each of them 3½*d.* a day.
And to Richard, mason, for 2 days, 7*d.*, at 3½*d.* a day.
And to Albespine, mason, for 11½ days, 2*s.* 10*d.* because he was 3 days short in another payment above, and he receives 3*d.* a day.
And to Walter Pollard for 6 days, 21*d.*, 3½*d.* a day.

1 In other words the harvest.
2 *Bernardensus* is evidently a 'bayarder' or hand-barrow-man.

Item Godman & Stepphano Cimentariis per viii dies & dim. xxxiiii d. per [diem] cuilibet ii d.

Summa horum Cimentariorum xxi sol. iii d. ob.

Item pro carpentacione pontis novi Carpentar' per xvi dies v.sol. iii d.
Item in xxxvi minutis operariis per x dies & dim. xxxviii sol. ix d.

Summa huius Pacacionis per totum xiiii li. xiii sol. ix d. ob.

Item Hugoni de Rumell' pro CCCC pedibus lapidum incisis liiii sol. Ricardo Norensi iii sol. Item Radulfo de Herebaldun' pro CC pedibus lapidum incisis xxiiii sol.
Item Willelmo de Grimesbi & sociis suis pro DCl pedibus incisis lxxvii sol. iiii d.

Summa huius tasche vii li. xviii sol. iiii d.

Die Sabbati proxima ante Nativitatem Beate Marie Virginis facta fuit pacacio anno Regni Regis Henrici V^{to}.

Item Ricardo Portefer & socio suo pro CC summis calcis lxvi sol. viii d.
Item pro viii civeriis rotantibus emptis aput Cantuariam iiii sol.
Item pro xxviii batellatis lapidum minutorum ductis de Folkestan' xxi sol. & notandum quod pro qualibet batellata ix d. propter authumnum & quia multi eorum erant aput Iernemue qui solebant ducere petram.
Item Cimentariis.
Copin per viii dies ii sol. viii d.
Simoni Cimentario per ix dies. iii sol.
Item Simoni Albo per viii dies ii sol. iiii d.
Item Ricardo per viii dies ii sol. iiii d. Pollard per vii dies ii sol. ob. Eilmer per viii dies ii sol. iiii d. Robin per viii dies ii sol. iiii d. Albespine per viii dies ii sol. Godman per viii dies xvi d. Stepphano per viii dies xvi d.

Summa xxi sol. viii d. ob.

Item tribus carpentariis per xi dies & cuidam per i diem viii sol. vi d.
Item pro portagio cc summarum calcis vi sol.
Item pro temperacione earum summarum in tassca v sol. iiii d.
Item Guarino cuvario pro ix circulis v d.
Item in lv minutis operariis per illum terminum xlviii sol. ix d.
Item pro remocione xlvii batellatarum lapidum a mari usque ad terram xlvii d.

And to Godman and Stephen, masons, for 8½ days, 34*d.*, 2*d.* a day to each

Total of these masons, 21*s.* 3½*d.*

And to the carpenter(s) for the carpentry of the new bridge for 16 days, 5*s.* 3*d.*
And for 36 labourers for 10½ days, 38*s.* 9*d.*

Total of this payment in all, £14. 13*s.* 9½*d.*

And to Hugh de Romilly for cutting 400 feet of stone, 54*s.* to Richard Norris, 3*s.* And to Ralph of Harbledown for cutting 200 feet of stone, 24*s.*
And to William of Grimsby and his fellows for cutting 650 feet of stone, 77*s.* 4*d.*

Total of this task-work, £7. 18*s.* 4*d.*

On Saturday next before the Nativity of the Blessed Virgin Mary [*4 September*] *in the 5th year of the reign of King Henry there was a payment.*

And to Richard Portefer and his fellow for 200 loads of lime, 66*s.* 8*d.*
And for 8 wheel-barrows bought at Canterbury, 4*s.*
And for 28 boat-loads of small stones brought from Folkestone, 21*s.* and it should be noted that each boat-load cost 9*d.* because it was Autumn and because many of those who used to bring stone were at Yarmouth.[1]
And to the masons.
to Copin for 8 days, 2*s.* 8*d.*
to Simon, mason, for 9 days, 3*s.*
And to Simon White for 8 days, 2*s.* 4*d.*
And to Richard for 8 days, 2*s.* 4*d.* to Pollard for 7 days, 2*s.* 0½*d.* to Eilmer for 8 days, 2*s.* 4*d.* to Robin for 8 days, 2*s.* 4*d.* to Albespine for 8 days, 2*s.* to Godman for 8 days, 16*d.* to Stephen for 8 days, 16*d.*

Total, 21*s.* 8½*d.*

And to three carpenters for 11 days and to one for 1 day, 8*s.* 6*d.*
And for portage of 200 loads of lime, 6*s.*
And for slaking those loads by task, 5*s.* 4*d.*
And to Warin the cooper for 9 hoops, 5*d.*
And for 55 labourers for the same period, 48*s.* 9*d.*
And for moving 47 boat-loads of stones from sea to land, 47*d.*

[1] No doubt for the herring-fishing.

Item Ricardo Portefer pro xxv. tingnis xx d.
Item cuidam cooperatori & pro coopertura unius domus in castro vi sol.
Item pro vii M. & cl summis petrarum & harene portatis vii marce xiiii d. ob.

Summa xiiii lib. viii sol. vi d.

Item Willelmo de Grimesbi pro DClxx pedibus petrarum incidendis iiii lib.

Die Sabbati scilicet in die Sancti Dionisii facta fuit pacacio.

Ricardo Portefer & socio suo pro CCCC & iiii[or] xx[ti] summis calcis viii lib.
Item pro lxi batellatis minutorum lapidum ductis de Folkestan' liiii sol.
Item pro MMM coopertorii xv sol.
Item pro MCC harundinis vii sol.

Summa harum particularum xi lib. xvi sol.

Hec est Pacacio facta die Sabbati proxima ante festum Luce Euuangeliste.

Item incisoribus lapidum xl sol.
Item xl minutis operariis per vi septimanas iiii lib. xii d.
Item DCMccclxxi summis harene iiii lib. iiii sol. xi d.
Item pro MMM de cailo ad coligendum prope castrum xl sol. pro portagio cccc summarum calcis xii sol.
Item pro distemperacione ccc summarum calcis viii sol.
Item Hugoni de Meaulinges pro materie xiiii sol. iii d.

Summa harum particularum xiiii lib. ii d.

Hec est Pacacio facta die Sabbati scilicet in die Sancti Eadmundi.

Item Ricardo Portefer pro CCCC & xv summis calcis. x marce. v sol., scilicet quelibet summa pro iiii d.
Item pro xxi batellatis minutorum lapidum ductis de Folkestan' usque Dovor' xiiii sol. scilicet quelibet batellata pro viii d.
Item Simoni de Grimesbi incisoribus[1] lapidum pro petra incidenda xx sol.
Cimentariis. Simoni Cimentario per xliiii dies xiiii sol. viii d. per diem iiii d.
Item Copin Cimentario per xxxiiii dies xi sol. iiii d. scilicet per diem iiii d.
Item Simoni Blund Cimentario per xlii dies xii sol. iii d. per diem iii d. ob.
Item Eilmer Cimentario per xli dies xi sol. xi d. ob. per diem iii d. ob.
Item Roberto Potmete Cimentario per xxxiiii dies. ix sol. xi d. per diem. iii d. ob.
Item Waltero Pollard per xl dies xi sol. viii d. per diem iii d. ob.
Item Albaspina Cimentario per xlii dies x sol. vi d. per diem iii d.

[1] *Sic.*

And to Richard Portefer for 25 beams, 20*d.*
And to a certain thatcher for thatching one house in the castle, 6*s.*
And for 7,150 loads of stones and sand carried, £4. 14*s.* 6½*d.*

Total, £14. 8*s.* 6*d.*

And to William of Grimsby for cutting 670 feet of stones, £4.

On Saturday, that is on St. Denis's Day [*9 October*] *there was a payment.*

To Richard Portefer and his fellow for 480 loads of lime, £8.
And for 61 boat-loads of small stones brought from Folkestone, 54*s.*
And for 3,000 of thatch, 15*s.*
And for 1,200 of reed, 7*s.*

Total of these particulars, £11. 16*s.*

This is the payment made on Saturday next before the feast of St. Luke the Evangelist [*16 October*].

And to the stone-cutters, 40*s.*
And to 40 labourers for 6 weeks, £4. 12*d.*
And for 6,371 loads of sand, £4. 4*s.* 11*d.*
And for 30 hundredweight of flints piled near the castle, 40*s.* for portage of 400 loads of lime, 12*s.*
And for slaking 300 loads of lime, 8*s.*
And to Hugh of Malling for timber, 3*d.*

Total of these particulars, £14. 2*d.*

This is the payment made on Saturday, St. Edmund's Day [*20 November*].

And to Richard Portefer for 415 loads of lime, £6. 18*s.* 4*d.*, that is 4*d.* a load.
And for 21 boat-loads of small stones brought from Folkestone to Dover, 14*s.*, each boat-load for 8*d.*
And to Simon of Grimsby, stone-cutter, for cutting stone, 20*s.*
Masons. To Simon, mason, for 44 days, 14*s.* 8*d.*, that is 4*d.* a day.
And to Copin, mason, for 34 days, 11*s.* 4*d.*, that is 4*d.* a day.
And to Simon Blund, mason, for 42 days, 12*s.* 3*d.*, that is 3½*d.* a day.
And to Eilmer, mason, for 41 days, 11*s.* 11½*d.*, that is 3½*d.* a day.
And to Robert Potmete, mason, for 34 days, 9*s.* 11*d.*, that is 3½*d.* a day.
And to Walter Pollard for 40 days, 11*s.* 8*d.*, that is 3½*d.* a day.
And to Albespine, mason, for 42 days, 10*s.* 6*d.*, that is 3*d.* a day.

Item Godman Cimentario per xliiii dies vii sol. iiii d. per diem ii d.
Item Stepphano Cimentario per xlii dies vii sol. per diem ii d.
Item Ricardo Cimentario per xvii dies iiii sol. xi d. per diem iii d. ob.
Item Simoni Spindlere per duos dies viii d. per diem iiii d.
Item pro summagio petre & harene. vii lib. v sol. iii d. scilicet pro xM & DCCC & xiii summis.
Item Radulfo de Popeshall' pro CCCC summis aque x sol. scilicet quodlibet cent. pro ii sol. [*sic*].
Item Cointer pro CCC summis & iiii. xx^{ti} & vi, ix sol. viii d. ob.
Item Stut pro clx summis aque iiii sol.
Item Radulfo de Popeshall pro D iiii xx^{ti} & xv summis portatis de calce a rogo ad castrum xiiii sol. x d. ob.
Item pro distemperacione calcis scilicet pro iiii xx^{ti} & xv summis xv sol. x d. ob.
Item Ricardo Portefer pro materie vi sol. viii d. scilicet pro lxi tingnis ad domum incluse & ad domum putei & item pro C lates.
Item Carpentariis xx sol. vi d.
Item pro remocione C batellatarum minutorum lapidum a mari usque ad terram viii sol. vi d.
Item pro MM prig & cc grossorum clavorum ii sol. vi d.
Item cuidam cooperatori per xvii dies iiii sol. iii d.
Item alii cooperatori per v dies xv d.
Item ad domum incluse & ad domum feni scilicet pro virgis vi d.
Item pro remocione xiiii gistarum a mari usque ad terram iii d.
Item in xxxviii minutis operariis per DCC & vi dies lxxii sol. unde cooperatores habuerunt lx & vi dietas.
Item ad fodiendum viii M & dim. turbarum iii sol. viii d. ob.
Item ad portandum M. & D turbarum xix d.
Item Hugoni de Meaulinges pro xxii gistes & D bordis xxi sol.
Item pro coopertura ad domum iuxta maram & pro virgis xiii d.
Item ad quirendum maram iuxta furnum vi d.
Item ad perpacandum Ricardum Norensem de muro quem fregit xvi d.

Summa harum particularum xxx li. xix sol. x d. ob.

Die Sabbati proxima post festum Sancti Thome Apostoli facta fuit pacacio pro operacione Castri Dovor'.

Item pro xviii M, scilicet pro MMMM & dim. grossorum clavorum & vi M. & dim. aliorum clavorum & vii M. & dim. de prig. xx sol.
Item pro una batella cum materie ducta de Sandwiz xxvi d.
Item incisoribus lapidum scilicet Simoni de Grimesbi & sociis eius pro corbellis incidendis & alia petra xx sol.
Item Ricardo Portefer pro xxviii summis de calce xi sol. viii d. scilicet quelibet summa pro v d. propter hyemem

And to Godman, mason, for 44 days, 7*s.* 4*d.*, that is 2*d.* a day.
And to Stephen, mason, for 42 days, 7*s.*, that is 2*d.* a day.
And to Richard, mason, for 17 days, 4*s.* 11*d.*, that is 3½*d.* a day.
And to Simon Spindlere for 2 days, 8*d.*, that is 4*d.* a day.
And for loads of stone and sand, £7. 5*s.* 3*d.*, that is for 10,813 loads.
And for Ralph of Popes Hall for 400 loads of water, 10*s.*, that is 100 for 2*s.*
And to Cointer for 386 loads, 9*s.* 8½*d.*
And to Stut for 160 loads of water, 4*s.*
And to Ralph of Popes Hall for 595 loads of lime carried from the kiln to the castle, 14*s.* 10½*d.*
And for slaking lime, that is for 95 loads, 15*s.* 10½*d.*
And to Richard Portefer for timber, 6*s.* 8*d.*, that is for 61 beams for the hermit's house and for the well-house and also for 100 laths.
And to carpenters, 20*s.* 6*d.*
And for moving 100 boat-loads of small stones from sea to land, 8*s.* 6*d.*
And for 2,000 prig and 200 large nails, 2*s.* 6*d.*
And to a certain thatcher for 17 days, 4*s.* 3*d.*
And to another thatcher for 5 days, 15*d.*
And for the recluse's house and for the hay-house, that is for withies, 6*d.*
And for moving 14 joists from sea to land, 3*d.*
And for 38 labourers for 706 days, 72*s.*, whereof the thatchers had 66 days
And for digging 8,500 turves, 3*s.* 8½*d.*
And for portage of 1,500 turves, 19*d.*
And to Hugh of Malling for 22 joists and 500 boards, 21*s.*
And for thatch for the house next the pond and for withies, 13*d.*
And for cleaning out the pond by the oven, 6*d.*
And to complete the payment to Richard Norris for the wall which he pulled down, 16*d.*

Total of these particulars, £30. 19*s.* 10½*d.*

On Saturday next after the feast of St. Thomas the Apostle [*25 December*] *a payment was made for the works of Dover Castle.*

And for 18,000 nails, that is for 4,500 large nails and 6,500 other nails and 7,500 prig, 20*s.*
And for one boat with timber brought from Sandwich, 26*d.*
And to stone-cutters, that is to Simon of Grimsby and his mates for cutting corbels and other stone, 20*s.*
And to Richard Portefer for 28 loads of lime, 11*s.* 8*d.*, that is 5*d.* a load because it was winter

Cimentariis. Item Simoni Cimentario per viii dies xxxii d.
Item Roberto Potmete per vii dies ii sol. ob.
Item Albaspine Cimentario per unum diem iii d.
Item pro Tassca. Dionisio & sociis eius ad trahendum terram foras que fuit [ad][1] portam, x sol.
Item Carpentario per xxvii dies vi sol. ix d.
Item pro summagio harene scilicet pro MMMM D iiii^{xx}v summis lx sol. iii d.
Item pro portagio calcis scilicet pro xxviii summis x d.
Item pro distemperacione calcis scilicet pro xxviii summis ix d.
Item Radulfo de Popeshall' pro duobus postibus ii sol.
Item Gocelino de Oye in aiuvacione ad domum suam quam fecit xii sol. & constituit xxv.
Item minutis operariis scilicet xxvi, ix sol.
Item pro D de prig v d.
Item pro CC grossorum clavorum ix d.
Item ad fodendum M. & dim. turbarum. vii d. ob.
Item Ricardo Norensi pro duobus fundamentis quod [*sic*] fecit ad novam portam in tassco iiii sol.
Item Radulfo Albaspine ii sol. de tassco.

Summa harum particularum viii li. ix sol. i d.

Summa hucusque a Festo Sancti Johannis Baptiste usque ad Natale Domini proximo sequens contra Gocelinum de Oye per duas dicas Cliiii lib. viii sol. x d.

Summa recept' huius rotuli CCCxxxi li. ix sol.[2]

Summa summarum CCCxxxi li. viii sol. iii d. ob. & debent vi d.[2]

[1] This word was first written after *foras,* then deleted and not rewritten in its proper place before *portam.*

[2] These two lines are both crossed out in the MS.

Masons. And to Simon, mason, for 8 days, 32*d*.
And to Robert Potmete for 7 days, 2*s*. 0½*d*.
And to Albespine, mason, for one day, 3*d*.
And by task. To Denis and his fellows to draw outside the earth which was in the gateway, 10*s*.
And to the carpenter for 27 days, 6*s*. 9*d*.
And for loads of sand, that is for 4,585 loads, 60*s*. 3*d*.
And for portage of lime, that is for 28 loads, 10*d*.
And for slaking lime, that is for 28 loads, 9*d*.
And to Ralph of Popes Hall for two posts, 2*s*.
And to Jocelyn de Oye to help towards the house which he made, 12*s*., and it cost 25.
And to labourers, that is 26, 9*s*.
And for 500 prig [nails], 5*d*.
And for 200 large nails, 9*d*.
And for digging 1,500 turves, 7½*d*.
And to Richard Norris for two foundations which he made for the new gate by task, 4*s*.
And to Ralph Albespine, 2*s*. for task-work.

Total of these particulars, £8. 9*s*. 1*d*.

Total so far from the feast of St. John the Baptist [24 June] to Christmas next following by two tallies against Jocelyn de Oye, £154. 8*s*. 10*d*.

Total receipts of this roll £331. 9*s*.

Sum total [of expenditure] £331. 8*s*. 3½*d*., and they owe 6*d*.

3. Particulars of expenditure on Dover Castle in 1227. (E101/462/10)

Recepta Ricardi de Neireford' & Goscelini de Oye de scaccario domini Regis Scilicet de Willelmo de Casteles scilicet centum li. xxvi^{to} die [Marcii] anno regni eiusdem regis xi^{mo}. ad operacionem castri Dovor'

Item de eodem scaccario & de eodem Willelmo centum li. die Veneris proxima ante nativitatem Sancti Johannis Baptiste anno eodem

Item de eodem scaccario & de eodem Willelmo centum li. die Iovis proxima ante festum Sancte Margarete anno eodem.

Item de illo scaccario & ipso Willelmo centum & l. li. die Mercurii proxima ante festum Sancti Luce Ewangeliste anno xii^{mo}. regni eiusdem regis secundum rotulos scaccarii.

Expensa inde

Pacacio de operacione castri Dovor' secundo die Maii facta anno supradicto presentibus Johanne Lancelevee tunc temporis subconstabulario domini Willelmi de Abrincis constabulario Dovor' sub Huberto de Burg' custode castri & aliis militibus & servientibus eiusdem presentibus.

Pro CCC & l batellatis petre portatis de Folkestan' Dovor' usque, scilicet ad portum Dovor' xiiii li. xi sol. viii d. quelibet batellata pro x d.

Item pro portagio xxviii maioribus a predicto loco usque ad eundem portum Dovor' xxxii sol. viii d. quelibet pro xiiii d.

Item pro portagio xix batellatis adhuc maioribus xxv sol. iiii d. quelibet batellata pro xvi d.

Pro remocione illius petre a fluctu maris usque ad certam terram ne sabulone postea operiretur antequam per equos possit portari ad castrum xlix sol. vii d. & ob. quelibet batellata pro iii ob.

De sabulone Pro xi mil. Clx summagiis sabulonis portatis ad operacionem castri ix. li. x sol. viii d. de quibus mille CCC summagie quodlibet cent. pro xxii d. & alie summagie quodlibet cent. pro xx d.

3. Particulars of expenditure on Dover Castle in 1227.

The receipts of Richard of Narford and Jocelyn de Oye from the lord king's Exchequer, namely from William of Castles,[1] that is £100 on 26 [March] in the 11th year of the reign of the same king [1227] towards the work of Dover Castle.

And from the same Exchequer and from the said William £100 on Friday next before the nativity of St. John the Baptist the same year [18 June 1227]

And from the same Exchequer and from the said William £100 on Thursday next before the feast of St. Margaret the same year [15 July 1227]

And from that Exchequer and the said William £150 on Wednesday next before the feast of St. Luke the Evangelist in the 12th year of the reign of the same king [13 October 1227] according to the rolls of the Exchequer.[2]

Expenditure

A payment for the work of Dover Castle made on 2 May in the aforesaid year [1227] *in the presence of John Lancelevee, at that time sub-constable of Sir William of Avranches, constable of Dover under Hubert de Burgh, keeper of the castle, and in the presence of other knights and serjeants*[3] *of his.*

For 350 boat-loads of stone brought from Folkestone to Dover, that is to Dover harbour, £14. 11*s.* 8*d.*, each boat-load for 10*d.*

And for carriage of 28 larger ones from the same place to the same Dover harbour, 32*s.* 8*d.*, each for 14*d.*

And for carriage of 19 still larger boat-loads, 25*s.* 4*d.*, each boat-load for 16*d.*

And for removing that stone from the foreshore to dry land lest it should afterwards be covered by sand before it could be carried by horses to the castle, 49*s.* 7½*d.*, each boat-load for 1½*d.*

Sand — For 11,160 loads of sand carried to the works of the castle, £9. 10*s.* 8*d.*, of which 1,300 loads were at the rate of 100 for 22*d.* and the remaining loads at 100 for 20*d.*

1 Probably an under-treasurer of the Exchequer.

2 The rolls in question would be the Issue Rolls.

3 *Servientes* in this context probably means military serjeants belonging to the garrison, but could mean merely 'servants'.

De portagio petre	Pro portagio mille Cx summagiis portatis ad operacionem de petra xvii sol. quodlibet cent. pro xviii d.
De aqua	Pro CCCX summagiis aque portatis ad operacionem & ad fossata viii sol. ix d. quodlibet cent. pro xxx d.
De calce	In centum summis calcis emptis de Ricardo Portefer xl sol. Pro portagio illius calcis a villa Dovor' usque ad operacionem iii sol. Item pro centum summis calcis emptis de Bartholomeo rogario xxxvii sol. vi d. quelibet summa pro iiii d. ob.
De materie	Pro locagio karetarum ad portandum materiem & grossam petram per iiii dies v sol. Pro busca minuta ad passus in fossatis faciendos & glowes ad maunz de pycoys iii sol. Pro xxii gistis curtis ad turellam in fossato extra portam Peverelli xxviii sol. Item in materie ad portam subterraneam versus orientem inchoatam ad cintros iiii sol. iii d.
De liberacionibus servientium	In liberationibus Magistri Ade cementarii. Radulfi de Popeshall magistri fossati. Thome clerici. Hugonis fabri a xxvi[to] die Marcii usque ad tercium diem Maii ad xl dies utraque die computata xl sol. cuilibet per diem iii d. In liberationibus Hogge Pollard servantis operarios per xviii dies tunc primo venientis iiii sol. viii d. Pro roba predicti Radulfi magistri fossati xiii sol. iiii d. In liberationibus Magistri Willelmi carpentarii per tempus supradictum xiii sol. iiii d. per diem iiii d.
De cementariis	Gervasio, Copin, Markere, cementariis per xlii dies ad portam subterraneam xiiii sol. cuilibet per diem iiii d. Pollard', Bigod', Eilmar', Blaunchespine, Waltero de [C]ant' per lxvi dies, xix sol. iiii d. cuilibet per diem iii d. ob. Johanni Scot, Willelmo de Wytefeld, Hugoni Anglico, Henrico de Raculve, Simoni de Wynton', Dawe de Dovor', Petro de Buclaund', Stephano, Batekin' cementariis ad illam eandem operacionem per lxxvi dies xvi sol. vi d. cuilibet per diem iii d. Absaloni & Augustino de Folkestan' per xiiii dies iii sol. vi d.

Portage of Stone	For the portage of 1,110 loads of stone to the work, each 100 for 18*d*.
Water	For 310 loads of water carried to the work and to the ditches, 8*s*. 9*d*., each 100 for 30*d*.
Lime	For 100 loads of lime bought from Richard Portefer, 40*s*. For portage of that lime from the town of Dover to the work, 3*s*. And for 100 loads of lime bought from Bartholomew the lime-burner, 37*s*. 6*d*., each load for 4½*d*.
Timber	For hire of carts to carry timber and large stones for 4 days, 5*s*. For wood to make footways in the ditches and billets for the pick-handles, 3*s*. For 22 short joists for the tower in the ditch outside Peverell's Gate, 28*s*. And for timber for the underground gate begun towards the east, to make centers, 4*s*. 3*d*.
Employees' wages	In the wages of Master Adam the mason, Ralph of Popes Hall, master ditch-digger, Thomas the clerk and Hugh the smith from 26 March to 3 May for 40 days, both days included, to each 3*d*. a day. In the wages of Hogge Pollard supervising the labourers for 18 days, who first arrived then, 4*s*. 8*d*. For a suit of clothes for the said Ralph, master ditch-digger, 13*s*. 4*d*. In the wages of Master William the carpenter for the aforesaid period, 13*s*. 4*d*., at 4*d*. a day.
Masons	To Gervase, Copin, Markere, masons, working for 42 days on the underground gate, 14*s*., to each 4*d*. a day. To Pollard, Bigod, Eilmer, Blaunchespine, Walter of Canterbury, for 66 days, 19*s*. 4*d*., to each 3½*d*. a day. To John Scot, William of Whitfield, Hugh English, Henry of Reculver, Simon of Winchester, Dawe of Dover, Peter of Buckland, Stephen, Batekin, masons engaged on the same work for 76 days, 16*s*. 6*d*., to each 3*d*. a day. To Absalom and Augustine of Folkestone for 14 days, 3*s*. 6*d*.

Carpentariis	In pacacione Einot, Warini, Rogeri de Taned', Ricardi de Tilemanston', Hamonis Chike per xlviii dies xii sol. cuilibet per diem iii d.
Plumbario	Elye plumbario & homini suo per xxviii dies xiiii sol. per diem vi d.
Minutis operariis	In cclxiiii minutis operariis operantibus ad fossata & deservientibus cementariis xx li. iii sol. vi d. alicui per diem ii d. & ob. alicui ii d. alicui iii ob. alicui minus.
De plumbo empto	In tribus karetatis plumbi emptis in villa Dovor' vii li. iiii sol. quelibet karetata pro xlviii sol.
De incisione lapidis	Liberat' Batekino & socio suo pro incisione cccl pedum lapidis de Folkestan' xxxv sol. quodlibet cent. pro x sol.
	Liberat' Gervasio, Johanni longo melioribus incisoribus pro incisione cc. pedum de eadem petra xxiiii sol. cent. pro xii sol.
	Summa lxxiiii li. xiii sol. vii d. ob.

*Pacacio secunda facta in Vigilia Sancti Johannis Baptiste anno regni regis eiusdem xi*mo*. per eosdem superiores pacantes, scilicet a tercia die Maii incohante in presencia superiorum assistencium & per Willelmum de Neireford qui tunc primo pacavit cum aliis.*

De minutis operariis	In pacacione CCCxv minutis operariis ad fossat[a] & cementariis deservientibus lix li. iii sol. x d.
De cementariis	In pacacione Roberti de Wytefeld', Copini, Markere cementariorum pro lxxviii dies xxvi sol. cuilibet per diem iiii d. In pacacione Eilmar', Pollard', Bigod', Walteri, Blanchespin' per centum xxxiiii dies xxxix sol. i d. cuilibet per diem iii d. ob. In pacacione Henrici Anglici, Batekin', Stephani, Willelmi de Wytefeld', Petri de Boclaund', Johannis Scot, Henrici de Raculve, Absalonis, Augustini de Folkestan' & Simonis de Wynton' per centum iiii[xx] & ix dies xlvii sol. iii d. cuilibet per diem iii d.
De plumbario	Elye plumbario & homini suo per turellas operantibus per xxx dies, xv sol.
De carpentariis	Ricardo Corteillier', Eynot, Hamoni Chike, Rogero de Taned', Warino & Karolo carpentariis per centum & xxvi d[i]etas ad pontes emendandos ad unam turellam versus orientem plancandam & gistandam & domos per castrum reparandos xxxii sol. ix d.

Carpenters	In the wages of Einot, Warin, Roger of Thanet, Richard of Tilmanstone, Hamon Chike, for 48 days, 12*s.*, to each 3*d.* a day.
Plumber	To Elias the plumber and his man for 28 days, 14*s.* at 6*d.* a day.
Labourers	To 264 labourers working on the ditches and serving the masons, £20. 3*s.* 6*d.*, some at 2½*d.* a day, some at 2*d.*, some at 1½*d.*, others less.
Lead bought	For three chars of lead bought in the town of Dover, £7. 4*s.*, each char for 48*s.*
Stone-cutting	Paid to Batekin and his fellow for cutting 350 feet of Folkestone stone, 35*s.*, each hundred for 10*s.* Paid to Gervase and John Long, better cutters, for cutting 200 feet of the same stone, 24*s.*, a hundred for 12*s.*

Total £74. 13*s.* 7½*d.*

A second payment made on the Vigil of St. John the Baptist in the 11th year of the reign of the said king [23 June 1227] by the above paymasters, that is starting from 3 May, in the presence of those above mentioned and by William of Narford, who then paid with the others for the first time.

Labourers	In the wages of 315 labourers working on the ditches and serving the masons, £59. 3*s.* 10*d.*
Masons	In the wages of Robert of Whitfield, Copin, Markere, masons, for 78 days, 26*s.*, to each 4*d.* a day. In the wages of Eilmer, Pollard, Bigod, Walter, Blanchespin for 134 days, 39*s.* 1*d.*, each at 3½*d.* a day. In the wages of Henry English, Batekin, Stephen, William of Whitfield, Peter of Buckland, John Scot, Henry of Reculver, Absalom, Augustine of Folkestone and Simon of Winchester for 189 days, 47*s.* 3*d.*, each at 3*d.* a day.
Plumber	To Elias the plumber and his man working on the towers for 30 days. 15*s.*
Carpenters	To Richard Corteillier, Eynot, Hamon Chike, Roger of Thanet, Warin and Charles, carpenters, working for 126 days, mending bridges, planking and joisting a tower on the east side and repairing houses about the castle, 32*s.* 9*d.*

De sabulone — In vi mill. cent. x summagiis harene portatis ad operacionem, centum xi sol. x d. quodlibet cent. pro xxii d. Et notandum quod ideo superius & hic magis habuerunt pro quolibet cent. quia longius illam portaverunt extra murum ad portam subterraneam.

De portagio petre — In portagio v mill. ccclxx summagiis petre illuc portatis iiii li. iii d. ob. quodlibet cent. pro xviii d.

De portagio aque — In portagio mill. cent. xx summagiis aque ad fossata & ad calcem temperatam ibidem liii sol. quodlibet cent. ut superius.

De terra — Pro centum summagiis terre que vocatur arzille emptis de terra cuiusdam paupercule mulieris ad ponendum super turellas inter plancas & sabulonem qui iacet sub plumbo pro putredine materiei iiii d.

De materie — In una veteri nave empta ad plancandum predictam turellam in villa Dovor' xlii sol.

In illa navi custodienda antequam possit dissolvi super ripam per viii noctes xiiii d.

In tingnis & lathis & dim. cent. minutarum columpnarum ad parietem turelle ultra posticum versus Sanctam Margaretam emptis in villa Dovor' xii sol. vi d.

In materie ad passus faciendos in fossatis ad vias hottorum viii d.

In duabus cuvis ad aquam operacionis. In circulis, tinis & bukez emptis & reparatis. ii sol. i d.

De ferro empto — Pro DCCC clavorum grossorum & xi cent. de huseam & C clavis ad plumbi [*sic*] emptis in villa Dovor' ante Pentecost' v sol. vii d. & ob.

In sex esperdutis ferri emptis in villa Dovor' & pice ad verteveles ad portam subterraneam xi d. ob.

In clavis grossis & minutis emptis ad nundinas Sancti Sepulcri anno regni regis Henrici xi^{mo} & pro centum libris stigmatis[1] & aliis minutis necessariis ibidem per clericum, Willelmum carpentarium & Radulfum fabrum. xxi sol. viii d.

In iiii^{or} libris stigmatis[1] emptis in villa Dovor' ante illas nundinas vi d.

[1] *rectius* 'stagminis'.

Sand	For 6,110 loads of sand carried to the work, 111*s.* 10*d.*, each hundred for 22*d.* And it should be noted that above and here they had more for each hundred because they carried it further outside the wall to the underground gate.
Portage of stone	For portage of 5,370 loads of stone carried thither, £4. 3½*d.*, each hundred for 18*d.*
Portage of water	For portage of 1,120 loads of water to the ditches and to slake lime there, 53*s.*, each hundred as above.
Earth	For 100 loads of earth called 'argil'[1] bought from the land of a certain poor woman to place on the towers between the planks and the sand which lies under the lead in order to prevent the timber rotting, 4*d.*
Timber	For an old ship bought in the town of Dover to plank the said tower, 42*s.* For guarding that ship on the shore for 8 nights before it could be broken up, 14*d.* For beams and laths and half a hundred of small posts for the partition wall of the tower above the postern facing towards St. Margaret's, bought in the town of Dover, 12*s.* 6*d.* For timber to make footways in the ditches for the hodmen's paths, 8*d.* For two tubs for water for the works. For buying and repairing hoops, casks and buckets, 2*s.* 1*d.*
Iron purchased	For 800 large nails and 1,100 huseam[2] and 100 lead-nails bought in the town of Dover before Whitsun, 5*s.* 7½*d.* For six iron bars bought in the town of Dover, and for pitch for the hinges of the underground gate, 11½*d.* For nails large and small bought at St. Sepulchre's Fair[3] in the 11th year of the reign of King Henry and for 100 pounds of tin and other small necessaries bought there by the clerk, William the carpenter and Ralph the smith, 21*s.* 8*d.* For 4 pounds of tin bought in the town of Dover before that fair, 6*d.*

[1] Some sort of clay.

[2] 'Hussem', 'hutzeam' or 'houssem' was a variety of nail peculiar to Kent and Sussex (Salzman, *Building in England*, p. 313).

[3] Perhaps at Canterbury, where there was a Benedictine nunnery dedicated to St. Sepulchre.

In locagio karetarum per xi dies trahentium materiem, calcem & petras grossas xiii sol. ix d.

De incisione lapidis — Liberat' Iohanni Longo & socio suo pro incisione D & l pedum lapidis de Folkestan' lvi sol.

Liberat' Bateki[n] & socio eius pro CCC pedibus xxx sol.

De empto calcis — Liberat' Ricardo Portefer pro C summis calcis ab eo emptis in villa Dovor' xxxvii sol. vi d.

Liberat' Bartholomeo rogario pro CCCC summis calcis ab eo emptis vii li. x sol.

De liberationibus servientium — In liberationibus Radulfi magistri fossatorum, clerici, Hugonis fabri, Hogge Pollard a quarta die Maii usque ad diem Sanctorum Johannis & Pauli ad liii dies utraque die computata liii sol.

In liberationibus Huberti custodientis operarios cementariorum & utensilia per xlix dies xii sol. iii d.

In liberationibus Magistri Willelmi carpentarii per liii dies xv sol. viii d. Et notandum quod ipse recepit per hunc terminum per vi dies qualibet die vi d. quoniam cum equo suo in negotio domini regis fuit longe a castro.

Plumbario — Item Elye plumbario pro duabus karetatis & dim. & vi libris plumbi fundendis & cubandis super turellam ubi Gilibertus de Kentewell' manere solebat in tasco v sol. vi d.

De portagio denariorum — Pro portagio centum librarum portatarum a scaccario usque ad Dovor' ante supradictum festum ii sol.

Summa C li. lvii sol. vii d. ob.

Pacacio facta de eadem operacione per superiores camerarios & custodes anno predicto in die Sancte Marie Magdalene.

De materie novi granarii — Liberat' Henrico de Hucham pro cheverons, columpnis gistis ad granarium iuxta granchiam ad bladum castri dulcius observandum per preceptum & assensum domini iusticiarii edificatum viii sol. vi d.

Item Ade Wodemaungere pro iiii^or^ columpnis longis ad illud granarium xiiii d.

Item Ricardo Portefer pro iiii^or^ fustibus longis & viii gistis curtis ad illud idem iiii sol.

For the hire of carts drawing timber, lime, and large stones for 11 days, 13*s.* 9*d.*

Cutting stone

Paid to John Long and his mate for cutting 550 feet of stones from Folkestone, 56*s.*

Paid to Batekin and his fellow for 300 feet, 30*s.*

Lime bought

Paid to Richard Portefer for 100 loads of lime bought from him in the town of Dover, 37*s.* 6*d.*

Paid to Bartholomew the lime-burner for 400 loads of lime bought from him, £7. 10*s.*

Employees' wages

In the wages of Ralph, master of the ditch-diggers, the clerk, Hugh the smith, Hogge Pollard, from 4 May to the day of Saints John and Paul [26 June] for 53 days, both days included, 53*s.*

In the wages of Hubert looking after the masons' labourers and their tools for 49 days, 12*s.* 3*d.*

In the wages of Master William the carpenter for 53 days, 15*s.* 8*d.* And it should be noted that for 6 days during this period he received 6*d.* each day because he and his horse were far from the castle on the king's business.

Plumber

And to Elias the plumber for melting 2½ chars and 6 pounds of lead and laying them on the tower where Gilbert of Kentwell[1] used to stay by task, 5*s.* 6*d.*

Carriage of money

For portage of £100 brought from the Exchequer to Dover before the aforesaid feast, 2*s.*

Total, £102. 17*s.* 7½*d.*

A payment made for the same work by the said chamberlains and keepers on St. Mary Magdalen's Day in the said year [*22 July 1227*].

Timber for the new granary

Paid to Henry of Hitcham for rafters, posts and joists for the granary built next to the barn to keep the corn in the castle sweeter by order and assent of the lord justiciar,[2] 8*s.* 6*d.*

And to Adam Woodmonger for 4 long posts for that granary, 14*d.*

And to Richard Portefer for 4 long timbers and 8 short joists for that same, 4*s.*

[1] Gilbert of Kentwell (in Suffolk) was a knight who had presumably formed part of the garrison in John's reign.

[2] i.e. Hubert de Burgh.

Item pro centum iiii^{xx} & j bordis Hybernie ad illud idem xxi sol. iiii d.

In centum lathis de quercu ad illud idem granarium xii d.

In pacacione vi carpentariorum ad illius granarii carpentacionem xxiiii sol. vi d.

De materie

Item cuidam carpentario per vi dies ad pontes castri emendandos xviii d.

Item in lx bordis Hybernie emptis ad pontes parietes castri vii sol. viii d.

In una grossa trabe veluti standard' empta ad ecclesiam Sancti Martini de Dovor ad portam subterraneam versus orientem & pro j. fuste & pro j trabe parva ibidem empta ix sol.

In maremio ad scaffotandum iuxta aulam novam ii sol.

In j. cuva empta & circulis ibidem viii d.

De ferro

In centum & xii esperdutis ferri emptis in villa Dovor' ad pycoys & ad gunfos & verteveles xv sol. j d.

De Batellatis

Pro CC & viii batellatis petre portatis de Folkestane usque ad ripam Dovor' viii li. j. marca, quelibet pro x d.

Pro remocione eiusdem petre ab aqua usque ad certam terram ne fluctu operiretur xxvi sol. quelibet batellata pro iii ob.

De cementariis

Willelmo Cancellario magistro cementariorum in liberationibus scilicet suis ab ultimo die Maii usque ad diem beate Marie Magdalene ad liii dies utraque die computata per assensum domini regis & eius consilii quando fuerunt apud Dovor' scilicet in crastino Sancti Johannis Baptiste anno eiusdem regni xi^{mo}. xv sol. v d. ob. scilicet per diem iii d. ob.

Roberto de Wytefeld', Copino, Markere per l. dies xvi sol. viii d. cuilibet per diem iiii d.

Eilmer', Pollard', Blanchespin', Rogero Bigod' per lxviii dies xix sol. xi d. cuilibet per diem iii d. ob.

Stephano, Petro de Boclaund', Simoni de Wynton', Willelmo de Wytefeld', Henrico de Raculfe, Absaloni de Riparia per lxxii dies, cuilibet scilicet per diem iii d. xviii sol.

Batekin' cuidam novo incisori ad petram ad murum novum iuxta aulam inscindendam per j diem iii d.

De sabulone

Pro summagiis. v mill. ccc iiii^{xx} de sabulone iiii li. xix sol. ad forum ut supra

And for 181 Irish boards for that same, 21*s*. 4*d*.
For 100 oak laths for that same granary, 12*d*.
For the wages of 6 carpenters for the carpentry-work of that granary, 24*s*. 6*d*.

Timber

And to a certain carpenter for 6 days to mend the bridges of the castle, 18*d*.
And for 60 Irish boards bought for the bridges and partition-walls of the castle, 7*s*. 8*d*.
For one great beam like a standard bought at St. Martin's Church in Dover for the underground gate towards the east, and for 1 piece of timber and for 1 small beam bought there, 9*s*.

For timber to make scaffolding next the new hall, 2*s*.

For 1 tub and hoops bought there, 8*d*.

Iron

For 112 bars of iron bought in the town of Dover for picks and for hooks and eyes,[1] 15*s*. 1*d*.

Boat-loads

For 208 boat-loads of stone carried from Folkestone to the shore at Dover, £8. 13*s*. 4*d*., each for 10*d*.
For moving the same stone from the water to dry land lest it should be covered by the tide, 26*s*., each boat-load for 1½*d*.

Masons

To William Chancellor, master of the masons, that is for his wages from the last day of May to the day of the blessed Mary Magdalen [22 July] for 53 days, both days included, by assent of the lord king and his council when they were at Dover, that is on the morrow of St. John Baptist's day [25 June] in the 11th year of his reign, 15*s*. 5½*d*., that is 3½*d*. a day.
To Robert of Whitfield, Copin, Markere for 50 days, 16*s*. 8*d*., to each 4*d*. a day.
To Eilmer, Pollard, Blanchespine, Roger Bigod for 68 days, 19*s*. 11*d*., to each 3½*d*. a day.
To Stephen, Peter of Buckland, Simon of Winchester, William of Whitfield, Henry of Reculver, Absalom of River, for 72 days, that is to each 3*d*. a day, 18*s*.
To Batekin, a certain new stone-cutter, for cutting stone for the new wall next the hall for 1 day, 3*d*.

Sand

For 5,380 loads of sand, £4. 19*s*., at the same rate as above.

[1] For hinges.

De summagiis petre	Pro iii mill. ccc iiii^{xx} summagiis petre portatis de villa ad operacionem l sol. ix d. ad forum ut supra
De summagiis aque	Pro DClxx summagiis aque illuc portatis xvi sol. ix d. ad forum ut supra
De incisione lapidis	Liberat' Gervasio, Johanni Longo pro incisione cc pedum lapidis de Folkestan' xx sol. Liberat' Johanni Scoto & Batekin' pro incisione cvi pedum de eadem petra. x sol. vii d.
De empcione calcis	Liberat' Bartholomeo rogario pro DCxl summis calcis xii li.
Plumbario	In pacacione Elye plumbario & homini suo per viii dies ad unam turellam & cysternam summe turris operantes iiii sol.
De liberationibus	Magistro Willelmo carpentario pro liberationibus suis a crastino Sanctorum Johannis & Pauli anno regni regis Henrici xi^{mo} usque ad diem Beate Marie Magdalene eodem anno ad xxv dies utraque die computata viii sol. iiii d. In liberationibus Radulfi magistri fossat', Hugonis fabri, clerici, Huberti, Hogge Pollard existentium & custodientium operarios & utensilia per eundem terminum xxxi sol. iii d.
De maremio	Item in maremio ad passus in fossato ad vias hottorum faciendos xxxi d.
De minutis operariis	In pacacione cclxxviii minutis operariis per ipsum terminum xxxii li. x sol.

Pro duabus testis eneis ad duas cysternas sine quibus cysterne non possent bene salvari de pondere xxx librarum, xiii sol. iiii d.

Liberatum Ricardo Norrensi pro j tasca de xviii perticis & quarta parte j pertice ad pedem domini regis in Dovor', & constat pertica illa de xxx pedibus mediis de xlvii pedibus de latitudine ad omnem arduitatem quam illa latitudo posset perferre xxxv li. xvii sol. Et de profundo xxvii pedum.

Summa Cxi li. ix sol. vii d. ob.

Loads of stone	For 3,380 loads of stone carried from the town to the work, 50*s.* 9*d.* at the same rate as above
Loads of water	For 670 loads of water carried thither, 16*s.* 9*d.* at the same rate as above
Cutting stone	Paid to Gervase, John Long for cutting 200 feet of stone from Folkestone, 20*s.* Paid to John Scot and Batekin for cutting 106 feet of the same stone, 10*s.* 7*d.*
Purchase of lime	Paid to Bartholomew the lime-burner for 640 loads of lime, £12.
Plumber	In the wages of Elias the plumber and his man working for 8 days on one tower and on the cistern of the high tower,[1] 4*s.*
Pay	To Master William the carpenter for his wages from the morrow of Saints John and Paul [27 June] in the 11th year of the reign of King Henry to the day of the Blessed Mary Magdalen [22 July] in the same year for 25 days included, 8*s.* 4*d.* In the wages of Ralph the master ditch-digger, Hugh the smith, the clerk, Hubert, Hogge Pollard attending and looking after the labourers and the tools during the same period, 31*s.* 3*d.*
Timber	And for timber to make footways in the ditch for the hodmen's paths, 31*d.*
Labourers	For the wages of 278 labourers for the same period, £32. 10*s.*
	For two brass covers for two cisterns without which the cisterns cannot well be saved, weighing 30 pounds, 13*s.* 4*d.*
	Paid to Richard Norris for one task of 18 perches and a quarter according to the foot of the lord king in Dover,[2] and that perch consists of 30 average feet and 47 feet in breadth at as steep an angle as that breadth involves, £35. 17*s.* And in depth 27 feet.
	Total £111. 9*s.* 7½*d.*

[1] i.e. the twelfth-century keep, whose elaborate system of water-supply is described by E. Macpherson and E. G. J. Amos in *Archaeologia Cantiana* xliv (1931) and *Archaeological Journal* lxxxvi (1929), pp. 253–5.

[2] This statement recalls the tradition that the standard ell was the length of Henry I's own right arm (A. L. Poole, *From Domesday Book to Magna Carta*, 1955, p. 86), but the king's foot mentioned here was probably a standard measure preserved in Dover to enforce the Assize of Measures of 1196.

Pacacio facta per ipsos custodes & per plures superiores assistentes in vigilia Sanctorum Simonis & Jude anno regni regis Henrici xii^{mo}.

De cementariis	In pacacione Roberti, Copini, Markere & Willelmi de Colecestr' cementariorum per centum & xii dies lxx sol. viii d. ut supra Eilmar', Pollard', Roger Bigod', Blanchespine, Batekin' per totum in communi per ccli dies lxxiii sol. ii d. ob. ut supra Stephano, Petro de Boclaund', Willelmo de Wytefeld' & Ricardo carpentario per c. xlii dies xxxv sol. vi d. ad forum ut supra
De sabulone	Pro xij mill. & xxi summagiis sabulonis portatis ad operationes infra castrum & extra xi li. v d. ut supra
De summagiis petre	Pro x mill. iiij^{xx} summagiis petre portatis ad operationes infra & extra castrum vii li. xvi sol. ad forum ut supra
De aqua	Pro mill. cccc & xxxi summagiis aque portatis ad murum iuxta aulam novam & extra castrum xxxv sol. ix d. ut supra.
De maremio	Pro CCC bordis de fagina ad cyntros & duvellis & pro xix fustibus & ij trabibus & vi^{xx} & ij cheverons & centum latis ad cyntros & vias faciendas in fossatis hottoribus & pro DL pessonibus ad passus faciendos in illis fossatis & alibi necessario xxxiiii sol. vi d. ob.
	Pro cuvis & bukez reparatis per ipsum terminum vi d.
	Pro incisione DCCl pedum lapidis de Folkestan' liberat' scilicet Gervasio & sociis eius lxxv sol. quodlibet cent. pro x sol.
De liberationibus	In liberacionibus magistri Willelmi carpentarii a crastino beate Marie Magdalene anno xi^{mo} usque ad diem Omnium Sanctorum anno xii^{mo} utraque die computata ad centum & ii dies xxxiiii sol. per diem iiii d. ut supra. In liberationibus magistri Willelmi cementarii per hunc terminum xxix sol. v d. ob. ut supra.
	In liberationibus Radulfi magistri fossat', clerici, Huberti, Hogge Pollard per hunc terminum vi li. vi sol. ut supra
	In roba Radulfi magistri fossat' xiii sol. iiii d.

A payment made by those keepers and by several others present as abovesaid on the vigil of Saints Simon and Jude in the 12th year of King Henry [*27 October 1227*].

Masons — In the wages of Robert, Copin, Markere and William of Colchester, masons, for 112 days, 70*s.* 8*d.* as above.
To Eilmer, Pollard, Roger Bigod, Blanchespine, Batekin altogether for 251 days, 73*s.* 2½*d.* as above.
To Stephen, Peter of Buckland, William of Whitfield and Richard the carpenter for 142 days, 35*s.* 6*d.* at the same rate as above.

Sand — For 12,021 loads of sand carried to the works within the castle and without, £11. 5*d.* as above.

Loads of stone — For 10,080 loads of stone carried to the works within and without the castle, £7. 16*s.* at the same rate as above.

Water — For 1,431 loads of water carried to the wall by the new hall and outside the castle, 35*s.* 9*d.* as above.

Timber — For 300 boards of beech for centers and staves and for 19 timbers and 2 beams and 122 rafters and 100 laths to make centering and paths in the ditches for the hodmen and for 550 pegs to make steps in those ditches and elsewhere where they were necessary, 34*s.* 6½*d.*

For tubs and buckets repaired during this period, 6*d.*

For cutting 750 feet of Folkestone stone, that is paid to Gervase and his fellows, 75*s.*, at 10*s.* a hundred.

Wages — In the wages of Master William the carpenter from the morrow of the blessed Mary Magdalen in the 11th year [23 July 1227] to All Saints' day in the 12th year [1 November 1227], both days included, for 102 days, 34*s.* at 4*d.* a day as above.
In the wages of Master William the mason during this period, 29*s.* 5½*d.* as above.

In the wages of Ralph the master ditch-digger, the clerk, Hubert, Hogge Pollard during this period, £6. 6*s.*, as above.

For a suit of clothes for Ralph the master ditch-digger, 13*s.* 4*d.*

	In stipendio Hugonis fabri a Natali Domini anno xi^{mo} usque ad Natalem anno xii^{mo} x sol.
	In roba Willelmi carpentarii de hoc anno xiii sol. iiii d.
De minutis operariis	In pacacione centum liii minutis operariis & fuerunt per totum vii millia C.iiii^{xx} operarii lx li. v sol. ix d.
	Et sciendum est quod carius solito locati fuerunt [per] autumpnum & pro caro tempore
De calce	Liberat' Bartholomeo rogario pro DCCC & lx summis calcis xvi li. ii sol. vi d. quelibet summa pro iiij d. ob.
De fabrica	In emendacione pycoys & aliorum utensilium operacionis dum fabrica fuit in faciendo in villa Dovor' v sol. x d. ob.
	Pro locagio karetarum ad petram grossam & materiem portandam iii sol. ix d.
	Pro portagio cl li. de London' usque ad Dovor' ad istam pacacionem faciendam ii sol. viii d.
De materie	Item pro D bordis de Hybernia emptis in villa Dovor' lv sol.
De minutis	In CCCC lathis de quercu emptis in villa Dovor' iiii sol. Pro mille lxx garbis harundinis ad granarium v sol. viii d. Pro virgis & baculis ad coperiendum domum iii d. ob. Pro l summis carbonis emptis in villa Dovor' xxi sol. vi d.
De calce	Item liberat' Bartholomeo rogario pro D summis calcis cum kariagio ix li. vii sol. vi d.
	Pro una fenestra facta in capella Sancte Andree iii sol. vi d.
	Item pro xj mill. sabulonis portandis ad operacionem pro bonitate hyemalis temporis quia magis valet quam in estate x li. x sol.
	Pro portagio quinque mill. summagiorum petre lxxv sol.
	Item pro incisione M. DCCC pedibus lapidis de Folkestan' contra tempus quo operabitur quando dominus rex voluerit viiij li.

Summa Clx li. ix sol. viii d. ob.

For the pay of Hugh the smith from Christmas in the 11th year [1226] to Christmas in the 12th year [1227], 10*s.*

For a suit of clothes for William the carpenter for this year, 13*s.* 4*d.*

Labourers — In the wages of 153 labourers, and there were altogether 7,180 workmen, £60. 5*s.* 9*d.* And it should be known that they were hired at a dearer rate than usual owing to the harvest and because it was a dear time.

Lime — Paid to Bartholomew the lime-burner for 860 loads of lime, £16. 2*s.* 6*d.*, each load for 4½*d.*

Forge — For mending picks and other tools for the work in the town of Dover while the forge was being made, 5*s.* 10½*d.*

For hiring carts to carry large stones and timber, 3*s.* 9*d.*

For the portage of £150 from London to Dover to make this payment, 2*s.* 8*d.*

Timber — And for 500 Irish boards bought in the town of Dover, 55*s.*

Small items —
For 400 oaken laths bought in the town of Dover, 4*s.*
For 1,070 sheaves of reeds for the granary, 5*s.* 8*d.*
For withies and staves to thatch the house, 3½*d.*
For 50 seams of charcoal[1] bought in the town of Dover, 21*s.* 6*d.*

Lime — And paid to Bartholomew the lime-burner for 500 loads of lime with carriage, £9. 7*s.* 6*d.*

For making one window in the chapel of St. Andrew,[2] 3*s.* 6*d.*

And for 11,000 loads of sand carried to the work on account of the goodness of the winter season because it is of better value than in summer,[3] £10. 10*s.*

For portage of 5,000 loads of stone, 75*s.*

And for cutting 1,800 feet of Folkestone stone against the time when work shall be carried out in accordance with the king's wishes, £9.

Total £160 9*s.* 8½*d.*

[1] Alternatively (but less probably) 'coal'.

[2] One of the chapels within the castle.

[3] Salzman's explanation of this entry is that 'the sand was from the sea-shore, and the winter rains washed out a certain amount of the salt which makes sea sand so unsatisfactory for building purposes' (*Building in England*, p. 152).

4. Enrolments of accounts for work at Dover Castle from 1220 to 1229.

(Exchequer, Foreign Account Roll 1 and Pipe Rolls 70, 71, 72, and 73)

Compotus operacionis castri Dovor'

Heres Willelmi de Esseteford' & Willelmus filius & heres Ricardi de Popleshal' reddunt compotum de DCCC & quater xx & iij li. & dim. marca quas patres eorum receperunt de thesauro Regis ad operacionem castri Dovor' de anno v°. vj°. vij°. & viij°. & usque in crastinum Sancti Valentini anno ix°. In thesauro nichil.

Et in operacione castri predicti MCC & quater xx & x li. xiiij sol. & v d. & ob. per breve Regis & per visum predictorum. Et habent de superplus CCCC & vij li. & vij sol. & ix d. & ob. quod totum locatur Huberto de Burgo in magno Rotulo ix in Sudsex' in debito heredis Comitis Arundell'.

(E. 364/1, rot. 1d.)

Compotus operacionis Castri Dovor' a crastino Sancti Valentini anno Regis Henrici tercii ix° usque diem Sancti Pancracii anno x° eiusdem utraque die computata.

Ricardus de Nereford'. Henricus de Feugeriis. Willelmus de Popleshal' & Joscelinus de Oy reddunt compotum de C li. receptis de Henrico de Sancto Albano de Cambio Regis anno eiusdem ix°. Et de DC li. receptis de thesauro Regis anno eodem & anno x. Et de xx li. receptis de Camera Regis per idem tempus. Summa DCC & xx li. In thesauro nichil.

Et in predicta operacione per idem tempus DCC & xxxv li. & xviij d. & ob. Et habent de superplus xv li. & xviij d. & ob.

(E 364/1, rot. 1d.)

Compotus operacionis Castri Dovor' a die Sancti Pancracii anno Regis x° usque in crastinum Sancti Benedicti in Marcio anno xj° eiusdem utraque die computata.

Ricardus de Nereford' & Joscelinus doy reddunt compotum de DCC marcis quas receperunt de thesauro per plures vices infra predictum terminum. In thesauro iij d. & ob.

4. Enrolments of accounts for work at Dover Castle from 1220 to 1229.

Account of the work of Dover Castle

The heir of William of Ashford and William son and heir of Richard of Popes Hall render account of £883. 6*s.* 8*d.* which their fathers received from the king's treasury for the works of Dover Castle in the 5th, 6th, 7th and 8th years [1220–4] and up to the morrow of St. Valentine in the 9th year [15 February 1225]. Paid in cash, nothing.

And in the work of the said castle, £1,290. 14*s.* 5½*d.* by the king's writ and by view of the aforesaid men. And they have spent £407. 7*s.* 9½*d.* more than they have received, which is all allowed to Hubert de Burgh in the Great Roll 9 in Sussex against the debt of the heir of the Earl of Arundel.[1]

Account of the work of Dover Castle from the morrow of St. Valentine in the 9th year of King Henry III [15 February 1225] to St. Pancras' Day in the 10th year [12 May 1226], both days included.

Richard of Narford, Henry de Fougères, William of Popes Hall and Jocelyn de Oye render account of £100 received from Henry of St. Albans from the king's Exchange in his 9th year. And of £600 received from the king's treasury in the same year and in the 10th year. And of £20 received of the king's Chamber during the same period. Total £720. Paid in cash, nothing.

And in the said work during the same period, £735. 1*s.* 6½*d.* And they have spent £15. 1*s.* 6½*d.* more than they have received.[2]

Account of the work of Dover Castle from St. Pancras Day in the 10th year of the king's reign [12 May 1226] to the morrow of St. Benedict in March in the 11th year [22 March 1227], both days included.

Richard of Narford and Jocelyn de Oye render account of 700 marks [£466. 13*s.* 4*d.*] which they received from the treasury at various times within the said period. Paid in cash, 3½*d.*

1 The Earl of Arundel had died in August 1224 and his estates were for the time being at the king's disposal. They were committed to the custody of Hubert de Burgh, who from this feudal windfall was to make good the deficit of £407. 7*s.* 9½*d.* on the Dover account. The sum in question is duly credited to the Arundel account in Pipe Roll 9 Henry III, rot. 11.

2 They were reimbursed by a writ dated 21 May 1226 (above p. 27).

Et in operacione nove turris in fossato iuxta portam Peverelli & empcionibus maremii & plumbi & carriagio sabuli & aque lapidum & calcis empte & plurium aliorum necessariorum ad eandem operacionem & stipendiis custodum dicte operacionis & cementariorum & aliorum operatorum in fossato DC & quater xx & xix marce & xiij sol. & ob. Et quieti sunt.

(E 372/70, rot. 15.)

Compotus Operacionis castri de Dovre a crastino Sancti Benedicti in Martio anno Regis xi^{o} usque ad festum Sancti Martini anno eiusdem xij^{o}.

Ricardus de Nerford' & Willelmus de Nerford' & Jocelinus de Oie reddunt compotum de CCCC & l. li. quas receperunt de thesauro Regis per thesaurarium & camerarios. In thesauro nichil.

Et in operatione eiusdem castri per predictum tempus scilicet in muris. fossatis. portis & boviis. CCCC & xlix li. & x sol. & vij d.

Et debent ix sol. & v d.

(E 372/71, rot. 8.)

Compotus operacionis castri de Dovre a festo Sancti Martini anni xij^{mi} usque ad festum Sancte Agathe anni xiij^{mi}.

Ricardus de Nerford' & Jocelinus de Oie reddunt compotum de CCC & l li. quas receperunt de thesauro Regis per thesaurarium.

In thesauro nichil.

Et in predicta operacione per predictum tempus CCC & xlix [li.] & viij sol. & iij d. Et debent xi sol. & ix d.

Iidem reddunt compotum de eodem debito. In thesauro liberaverunt. Et quieti sunt.

Iidem reddunt compotum de ix sol. & v d. de remanenti compoti sui de anno preterito. In thesauro liberaverunt. Et quieti sunt.

(E 372/72, rot. 10.)

Compotus castri de Dovre a festo Sancte Agathe virginis hoc anno usque ad festum Sancti Dunstani eodem anno.

Jocelinus de Oye reddit compotum de xxv li. & xiiij sol. quos recepit de thesaurario & camerariis. In thesauro nichil.

Et in tribus caretatis blumbi ad capellam cooperiendam & alias domos in castro vj li. & xij sol. Et in operacione predicti castri per predictum tempus & aliis necessariis & minutis expensis. xix li. & xvj d. & ob. Et debet vij d. & ob.

Idem reddit compotum de eodem debito. In thesauro liberavit. Et quietus est.

(E 372/73, rot. 1.)

And in the work of the new tower in the ditch next Peverell's Gate and in purchases of timber and lead and for the carriage of sand and water, stones and lime bought and many other necessaries for the same work, and for the wages of the keepers of the work and the masons and other workmen in the ditch, 699 marks and 13*s.* 0½*d.* [£466. 13*s.* 0½*d.*] And they are quit.

Account of the work of Dover Castle from the morrow of St. Benedict in March in the 11th year of the king's reign [22 March 1227] to the feast of St. Martin in the 12th year [11 November 1227].

Richard of Narford and William of Narford and Jocelyn de Oye render account of £450 which they received from the king's Treasury through the Treasurer and chamberlains. Paid in cash, nothing.

And in the work of the same castle during the said time, that is in walls, ditches, gates and underground passages, £449. 10*s.* 7*d.*

And they owe 9*s.* 5*d.*

Account of the work of Dover Castle from the feast of St. Martin in the 12th year [11 November 1227] to the feast of St. Agatha in the 13th year [5 February 1229].

Richard of Narford and Jocelyn de Oye render account of £350 which they received from the king's Treasury through the Treasurer.

Paid in cash, nothing

And in the said work during the said period, £349. 8*s.* 3*d.*

And they owe 11*s.* 9*d.*

They render account of the same debt. They paid it in cash. And they are quit.

They render account of 9*s.* 5*d.* outstanding from their account of the previous year. They paid it in cash. And they are quit.

Account of Dover Castle from the feast of St. Agatha the Virgin this year [5 February 1229] to the feast of St. Dunstan in the same year [19 May 1229].

Jocelyn de Oye renders account of £25. 14*s.* which he received from the Treasurer and chamberlains. Paid in cash, nothing.

And in three chars of lead to cover the roof of the chapel and other buildings in the castle, £6. 12*s.* And in the work of the said castle during the said period and in other necessaries and small expenses, £19. 1*s.* 4½*d.* And he owes 7½*d.*

He renders account of that debt. He paid it in cash. And he is quit.

Compotus Bertrammi de Kyrioil a predicto festo Sancti Dunstani usque ad festum Sancti Dionisii anno xiiij de eadem operacione.

Idem Bertramus reddit compotum de CC & xxxiij li. & vj sol. & viij d. quos recepit de Thesauro per Thesaurarium & camerarios ad eandem operacionem. In thesauro nichil.

Et in una volta facienda ad exeundum de castro versus campum C li. Et in operacione eiusdem castri & necessariis expensis eiusdem per predictum tempus C & xvij li. & vj sol. & iij d. & ob.

Et debet xvj li. & iiij d. & ob. Sed respondet in Kent.

(E 372/73, rot. 1.)

Account of Bertram de Kyriel[1] *for the same work from the said feast of St. Dunstan* [*19 May 1229*] *to the feast of St. Denis in the 14th year* [*9 October 1229*].

The same Bertram renders account of £233. 6*s.* 8*d.* which he received from the Treasurer and chamberlains for the said work. Paid in cash, nothing.

And in making one vault to go out of the castle towards the field, £100. And in the work of the same castle and in necessary expenses of the same during the said period, £117. 6*s.* 3½*d.*

And he owes £16. 0*s.* 4½*d.* But he answers for it in Kent.

1 Bertram de Kyriel, or Criel, was a Kentish knight who soon afterwards became constable of Dover.

[illegible]

II. WINCHESTER CASTLE

1. Selected writs relating to the works at Winchester Castle in 1222.

(i) Rex E. Thesaurario & F. & R. Camerariis salutem. Liberate de thesauro nostro Magistro Nicholao de Aundely & Magistro Hugoni de Abbemund carpentariis nostris euntibus per preceptum nostrum usque Wintoniam ad domos nostras ibidem reparandas xl sol. ad expensas suas. Teste Huberto de Burgo apud Westmonasterium iiij die Decembris anno vj°. (*Rot. Litt. Claus.* i, p. 483.)

(ii) Rex constabulario de Kerebroc salutem. Precipimus tibi quod permittas mascones nostros venientes in Insulam de Wict' petram ad denarios nostros ibidem fodere secare & inde abducere libere & sine impedimento usque ad castrum nostrum Winton' ad illud reparandum. Teste Huberto de Burgo apud Westmonasterium xij die Aprilis anno regni nostri vj°. (*Rot. Litt. Claus.* i, p. 492.)

(iii) Rex Baillivis suis Suthampt' salutem. Precipimus vobis quod habere faciatis Majori Winton' & Magistro Henrico de Cerne & Alano de Hereford' vj carratas de plumbo ad cooperiendum turrim nostram Winton', & computabitur vobis ad scacarium. Teste Huberto de Burgo apud Westmonasterium xij die Aprilis anno regni nostri vj°. per eundem. (*Rot. Litt. Claus.* i, p. 492.)

(iv) Rex Engelard' de Cygoin' salutem. Mandamus vobis quod non impediatis super cheminagio illos qui venerint pro maeremio in bosco manerii de Candevr' ad operacionem castri nostri Winton' in forestam nostram de Windesor' sed eis liberum cheminagium per forestam nostram habere faciatis promoventes eos & adjuvantes modis quibuscunque poteritis tam in cariagio quam aliis. Teste Huberto de Burgo apud Westmonasterium xxiiij die Aprilis anno vj°. (*Rot. Litt. Claus.* i, p. 493.)

(v) Rex E. Thesaurario & F. & R. Camerariis salutem. Liberate de thesauro nostro Magistro Henrico de Cern' centum libras ponendas in operacione castri nostri Winton' per visum ipsius Magistri Henrici & aliorum quos operacionis illius assignavimus custodes. Teste Huberto de Burgo apud Westmonasterium ij die Maii anno regni nostri vj°. per eundem & dominum Winton'. (*Rot. Litt. Claus.* i, p. 494.)

1. Selected writs relating to the works at Winchester Castle in 1222.

(i) The king greets E. his Treasurer and F. and R. chamberlains of the Exchequer. Deliver from our Treasury to Master Nicholas de Andely and Master Hugh de Abbemunt our carpenters, who are going to Winchester by our order to repair our buildings there, 40*s.* towards their expenses.

Attested by Hubert de Burgh at Westminster, 4 December in the 6th year [1221].

(ii) The king greets the constable of Carisbrooke. We order you to allow our masons who are coming to the Isle of Wight freely and without impediment to dig, cut and take away at our expense stone to our castle of Winchester in order to repair it.

Attested by Hubert de Burgh at Westminster, 12 April in the 6th year of our reign [1222].

(iii) The king greets his bailiffs of Southampton. We direct you to let the Mayor of Winchester and Master Henry of Cerne and Alan of Hereford have 6 chars of lead in order to roof our tower of Winchester,[1] and it shall be credited to you at the Exchequer.

Attested by Hubert de Burgh at Westminster, 12 April in the 6th year of our reign [1222] and issued by his authority.

(iv) The king greets Engelard de Cigogné.[2] We order you not to hinder over tolls those who come to the wood belonging to the manor of Candover in our forest of Windsor for timber for the work of our castle of Winchester, but to let them have free passage through our forest, helping and assisting them in whatever way you can both in carriage and in other things.

Attested by Hubert de Burgh at Westminster, 24 April in the 6th year [1222].

(v) The king greets E. his Treasurer and F. and R. chamberlains of the Exchequer. Deliver from our Treasury to Master Henry of Cerne £100 to be laid out on the work of our castle of Winchester by view of the same Master Henry and the others whom we have assigned as keepers of that work.

Attested by Hubert de Burgh at Westminster, 2 May in the 6th year of our reign [1222] and issued by his authority and that of the Bishop of Winchester.

[1] i.e. the keep of the castle.

[2] Then constable of Windsor.

(vi) Rex E. Thesaurario & F. & R. Camerariis salutem. Liberate de thesauro nostro Magistro Henrico de Cerne centum libras ad operacionem castri nostri Winton'. Teste Huberto de Burgo apud Westmonasterium xxj die Junii anno regni nostri vj^{o} per eundem & dominum Winton'. (*Rot. Litt. Claus.* i, p. 500.)

(vii) Rex Michaeli de Columbariis salutem. Mandamus vobis quod de foresta nostra de Aundevr' faciatis habere per visum & testimonium legalium hominum Magistro Henrico de Cern' maeremium ad operacionem castri nostri Winton' quantum necesse habuerit ad operacionem illam faciendam ita quod visores habeant unam talliam & forestarii contratalliam. Teste Huberto de Burgo apud Westmonasterium xxiiij die Junii anno regni nostri vj^{o} per Episcopum Winton'. (*Rot. Litt. Claus.* i, p. 501.)

(viii) Mandatum est Willelmo Briwer' quod omni occasione postposita faciat habere Magistro Henrico de Cern' & sociis suis custodibus operacionis castri Winton' L fusta in bosco domini Regis de Ber' ad faciendum gistas in castro domini Regis Winton'. Teste Huberto de Burgo apud Glouc' xxix die Julii anno vj^{o} per eundem. (*Rot. Litt. Claus.* i, p. 507.)

(vi) The king greets E. his Treasurer and F. and R. chamberlains of the Exchequer. Deliver from our Treasury to Master Henry of Cerne £100 towards the work of our castle of Winchester.

Attested by Hubert de Burgh at Westminster, 21 June in the 6th year [1222] and issued by his authority and that of the Bishop of Winchester.

(vii) The king greets Michael de Coulommiers.[1] We order you to let Master Henry of Cerne have by view and witness of law-worthy men as much timber from our forest of Andover as he needs for the work of our castle of Winchester, the viewers keeping one tally and the foresters the counter-tally.

Attested by Hubert de Burgh at Westminster, 24 June in the 6th year of our reign [1222], and issued by the authority of the Bishop of Winchester.

(viii) William Briwer is ordered without fail to let Master Henry of Cerne and his fellow keepers of the work of Winchester Castle have 50 tree-trunks in the lord king's wood of Bere[2] in order to make joists in the lord king's castle of Winchester.

Attested by Hubert de Burgh at Gloucester, 29 July in the 6th year [1222] and issued by his authority.

[1] Keeper of the forest of Chute, which adjoined Andover.

[2] This was the forest of Bere Ashley in Hampshire, of which Briwer was the keeper.

2. Fragmentary roll of wages paid at Winchester Castle in 1222.
(C 47/3/8)

[*Liberata cementariis & aliis operariis*] *a die Dominica* . . . *Nativitatem beate* [*Marie*] *usque ad diem Dominicam prox*[*imo sequen*]*tem.*

[Magistro Alb]erto per vi dies, ...
[Magistro] Gerardo per vi dies, ii sol.
[Johanni de A]bendun' per vi dies, ii sol.
[Ranulpho] de Moreva per vi dies, ii sol.
Magistro Henrico per vi dies, ii sol.
Hereberto de Sperkeford' per vi dies, ii sol.
Galfrido de Spersolt' per vi dies, xxii d.
Wimundo fabro per vi dies, xx d.
Johanni de Sancto Albano per vi dies, xx d.
Galfrido de Sancto Albano per vi dies, xx d.
Roberto de Keinesham per vi dies, xx d.
Radulfo Berethorn' per vi dies, xx d.
Ricardo Sired' per vi dies, xx d.
Willelmo de Coldecote per vi dies, xx d.
Gervasio puero per vi dies, xx d.
Alexandro de Bradenestok per vi dies, xx d.
Reginaldo Cornubiensi per vi dies, xx d.
Roberto de Albano per vi dies, xix d.
Ivoni de Sperkeford per vi dies, xix d.
Willelmo Deven' per vi dies, xix d.
Roberto Beawgrant per vi dies, xix d.
Johanni de Bradenestok per vi dies, xix d.
Ricardo Passelewe per vi dies, xix d.
Hugoni de Foleflod' per vi dies, xix d.
Waltero de Ford' per vi dies, xviii d.
Radulfo de Spersolt per vi dies, xviii d.
Galfrido de Sancta Fide per vi dies, xviii d.
Willelmo de Hida per vi dies, xviii d.
Willelmo de Waverleg' per vi dies, [x]vi d.
Simoni de Angr' per vi dies, xvi d.
Giliberto militi per vi dies, xvi d.

2. Fragmentary roll of wages paid at Winchester Castle in 1222.

Paid to masons and other workmen from Sunday . . . the Nativity of the blessed [*Mary*] *. . . to Sunday immediately following* [*either 4–11 or 11–18 September*].

[*Masons*]

[Master Alb]ert for 6 days, ...
[Master] Gerard for 6 days, 2*s.*
John of Abingdon for 6 days, 2*s.*
Ranulf de Moreva for 6 days, 2*s.*
Master Henry for 6 days, 2*s.*
Herbert of Sparkford for 6 days, 2*s.*
Geoffrey of Sparsholt for 6 days, 22*d.*
Wimund the smith for 6 days, 20*d.*
John of St. Albans for 6 days, 20*d.*
Geoffrey of St. Albans for 6 days, 20*d.*
Robert of Keynsham for 6 days, 20*d.*
Ralph Berethorn for 6 days, 20*d.*
Richard Sired for 6 days, 20*d.*
William of Calcott for 6 days, 20*d.*
Gervase the boy for 6 days, 20*d.*
Alexander of Bradenstoke for 6 days, 20*d.*
Reginald of Cornwall for 6 days, 20*d.*
Robert of [St.] Albans for 6 days, 19*d.*
Ivo of Sparkford for 6 days, 19*d.*
William Deven' for 6 days, 19*d.*
Robert Beawgrant for 6 days, 19*d.*
John of Bradenstoke for 6 days, 19*d.*
Richard Passelewe for 6 days, 19*d.*
Hugh of Fullflood for 6 days, 19*d.*
Walter of Ford for 6 days, 18*d.*
Ralph of Sparsholt for 6 days, 18*d.*
Geoffrey of St. Faith for 6 days, 18*d.*
William of Hyde for 6 days, 18*d.*
William of Waverley for 6 days, 16*d.*
Simon of Hanger for 6 days, 16*d.*
Gilbert Knight for 6 days, 16*d.*

Willelmo de Ford' per vi dies, xii d.
Johanni de Ston' per vi dies, xii d.
Willelmo de Sancta Cruce per vi dies, xii d.

Cuchurs

Willelmo Crutall' per v dies, xv d.
Miloni Le Barrir per v dies, xv d.
Nicolao Derbi per v dies, xv d.
Siwardo per v dies, xv d.
Gervasio de Wattevill' per v dies, xv d.
Willelmo Ruffo per v dies, xv d.
Ade de Scam'weia, xix d.

Carpentarii

Waltero de Sancta Maria per v dies, xx d.
Ricardo de Peteresfeld' per v dies, xix d.
Ade Beawsamis per v dies, xii d. ob.
Willelmo de London' per v dies, xvii d. ob.
Simoni de London' per v dies, xvii d. ob.
Henrico Albo per v dies, xv d.
Willelmo de Wiltesir' per v dies, xv d.
Andree filio Walteri per v dies, x d.
Nicolao de Weredham per ii dies, vi d.
Roberto Pilet per v dies, x d.
Martino Excubie per vii noctes & v dies, xi d.
Martino Ruffo per v dies, x d.
Reginaldo Hunne per v dies, x d.
Hugoni de Sropsir' per v dies, x d.
Ricardo Pistori per v dies, x d.
Willelmo Nehek per v dies, x d.
Galfrido filio Albrede per v dies, vii d. ob.
Ricardo de Sancta Cruce per v dies, vii d. ob.
Alano Brun per v dies, vii d. ob.
Willelmo Brun per v dies, vii d. ob.
Herevico de la Bertun' per v dies, vii d. ob.
Ade Dun' per v dies, vii d. ob.
Johanni Scapeto per v dies, vii d. ob.
Ade filio fabri per v dies, vii d. ob.
Willelmo Burel per v dies, vii d. ob.
Reginaldo Puttok per v dies, vii d. ob.
Ade de Lillescliva per v dies, vii d. ob.
Tedbaldo de Billing' per v dies, vii d. ob.

William of Ford for 6 days, 12*d.*
John of Stone for 6 days, 12*d.*
William of St. Cross for 6 days, 12*d.*

Layers

William Critall for 5 days, 15*d.*
Miles le Barrir for 5 days, 15*d.*
Nicholas Derby for 5 days, 15*d.*
Siward for 5 days, 15*d.*
Gervase de Wattevill for 5 days, 15*d.*
William Redhead for 5 days, 15*d.*
Adam of Shambleway, 19*d.*

Carpenters

Walter of St. Mary for 5 days, 20*d.*
Richard of Petersfield for 5 days, 19*d.*
Adam Beawsamis for 5 days, 12½*d.*
William of London for 5 days, 17½*d.*
Simon of London for 5 days, 17½*d.*
Henry White for 5 days, 15*d.*
William of Wiltshire for 5 days, 15*d.*
Andrew son of Walter for 5 days, 10*d.*
Nicholas of Worldham for 2 days, 6*d.*

[*Labourers*]

Robert Pilet for 5 days, 10*d.*
Martin the watchman for 7 nights and 5 days, 11*d.*
Martin Redhead for 5 days, 10*d.*
Reginald Hunne for 5 days, 10*d.*
Hugh of Shropshire for 5 days, 10*d.*
Richard Baker for 5 days, 10*d.*
William Nehek for 5 days, 10*d.*
Geoffrey son of Albreda for 5 days, 7½*d.*
Richard of St. Cross for 5 days, 7½*d.*
Alan Brun for 5 days, 7½*d.*
William Brun for 5 days, 7½*d.*
Hervey of the Barton for 5 days, 7½*d.*
Adam Dun for 5 days, 7½*d.*
John Scapet for 5 days, 7½*d.*
Adam the smith's son for 5 days, 7½*d.*
William Burel for 5 days, 7½*d.*
Reginald Puttok for 5 days, 7½*d.*
Adam de Lillescliva for 5 days, 7½*d.*
Theobald of Billing' for 5 days, 7½*d.*

Willelmo fabro per v dies, vii d. ob.
Waltero Deven' per v dies, vii d. ob.
Petro de Newber' per v dies, vii d. ob.
Nicolao de Shuthwik per v dies, vii d. ob.
Stephano de Prioria per v dies, vii d. ob.
Stephano Duss per v dies, vii d. ob.
Adelardo de Hida per v dies, vii d. ob.
Ade de Lamborn' per v dies, vii d. ob.
Henrico Hune per v dies, vii d. ob.
Willelmo Puke per v dies, vii d. ob.
Simoni de Monte forto per v dies, vii d. ob.
Reginaldo Luveraz per v dies, vii d. ob.
Bertelot filio David per v dies, vii d. ob.
Ricardo Achard' per v dies, vii d. ob.
Henrico de Bristoll' per v dies, vii d. ob.
Johanni Bagge per v dies, viii d. ob.
Roberto de Uverton' per v dies, vii d. ob.
Giliberto de Kent per v dies, vii d. ob.
Thome de Wiltun' per v dies, vii d. ob.
Ricardo Deven' per v dies, vii d. ob.
Radulfo le Criblur per v dies, vii d. ob.
Henrico Modi per v dies, vii d. ob.
Ricardo de Welles per v dies, vii d. ob.
Hugoni Ruffo per v dies, vii d. ob.
Willelmo Mercatori per v dies, vii d. ob.
Petro Sutori per v dies, vii d. ob.
Roberto le Brittun' per v dies, vii d. ob.
Godefrido de Vite per v dies, vii d. ob.
Willelmo de Sumerset' per v dies, vii d. ob.
[Ricardo] de Meredun' per v dies, vii d. ob.
...... de Sumerset per v dies, vii d. ob.
.... per v dies, vii d. ob.
.... per v dies, vii d. ob.

[*Liberata cementariis carpentariis & aliis operariis die Dominica post festum Sancti Luce Ewangeliste*].

Willelmo ...[1]
Reginaldo Puttok ...
Willelmo Burel per v...
Ade de Lillescliva per ...

[1] The heading and the payments to masons and carpenters are missing and the document begins with an imperfect list of labourers.

William the smith for 5 days, 7½*d.*
Walter Deven' for 5 days, 7½*d.*
Peter of Newbury for 5 days, 7½*d.*
Nicholas of Southwick for 5 days, 7½*d.*
Stephen of the priory for 5 days, 7½*d.*
Stephen Duss for 5 days, 7½*d.*
Adelard of Hyde for 5 days, 7½*d.*
Adam of Lambourn for 5 days, 7½*d.*
Henry Hune for 5 days, 7½*d.*
William Puke for 5 days, 7½*d.*
Simon de Montfort for 5 days, 7½*d.*
Reginald Luveraz for 5 days, 7½*d.*
Bertelot son of David for 5 days, 7½*d.*
Richard Achard for 5 days, 7½*d.*
Henry of Bristol for 5 days, 7½*d.*
John Bagge for 5 days, 7½*d.*
Robert of Overton for 5 days, 7½*d.*
Gilbert of Kent for 5 days, 7½*d.*
Thomas of Wilton for 5 days, 7½*d.*
Richard Deven' for 5 days, 7½*d.*
Ralph le Criblur for 5 days, 7½*d.*
Henry Modi for 5 days, 7½*d.*
Richard of Wells for 5 days, 7½*d.*
Hugh Redhead for 5 days, 7½*d.*
William Merchant for 5 days, 7½*d.*
Peter Souter for 5 days, 7½*d.*
Robert the Breton for 5 days, 7½*d.*
Godfrey of the Vine for 5 days, 7½*d.*
William of Somerset for 5 days, 7½*d.*
[Richard] of Merdon for 5 days, 7½*d.*
...... of Somerset for 5 days, 7½*d.*
.... for 5 days, 7½*d.*
.... for 5 days, 7½*d.*

[*Paid to masons, carpenters, and other workmen on Sunday next after the feast of St. Luke the Evangelist* (*23 October*)]

[*Labourers*]

William ...
Reginald Puttok ...
William Burel for 5 [days] ...
Adam de Lillescliva for ...

Tedbaldo de Billing' per v dies ...
Galfrido filio Albrede per v dies ...
Ricardo de Sancta Cruce per v dies, vii [d. ob.]
Alano Brun per v dies, vii d. ob.
Willelmo Brun per v dies, ix d.
Herevico de La Bertun' per v dies, vii d. ob.
Ade Dun per v dies, vii d. ob.
Johanni Scapeto per v dies, vii d. ob.
Ade filio fabri per v dies, vii d. ob.
Willelmo de Farnham per vi dies, ix d.
Stephano de Prioria per vi dies, ix d.
Henrico Hune per vi dies, ix d.
Henrico de Bristoll' per vi dies, ix d.
Willelmo Puke per vi dies, ix d.
Simoni de Monte forto [*sic*] per vi dies, ix d.
Bertelot filio David per vi dies, ix d.
Giliberto de Kent per vi dies, ix d.
Johanni Bagge per vi dies, ix d.
Roberto de Uverton' per vi dies, ix d.
Thome de Wiltun' per vi dies, ix d.
Ricardo le Deven' per vi dies, ix d.
Ade Hune per vi dies, ix d.
Galfrido filio Excubie per vi dies, ix d.
Henrico Modi per vi dies, ix d.
Ricardo de Welles per vi dies, ix d.
Radulfo le Criblur per vi dies, ix d.
Godefrido de Vite per vi dies, ix d.
Samsoni de Hereford' per vi dies, ix d.
Alano de Fremelingham per vi dies, ix d.
Thome Le Norais per vi dies, ix d.
Willelmo Mercatori per vi dies, ix d.
Petro Sutori per vi dies, ix d.
Johanni de Cumptun' per vi dies, ix d.
Reginaldo de Cicestr' per v dies, vii d. ob.
Germano ante opidum per vi dies, ix d.
Ricardo de Merdun' per vi dies, ix d.
Alexandro Calvo per vi dies, ix d.
Martino de Alresford' per vi dies, ix d.
Petro de Bristoll' per vi dies, ix d.
Ade le Waleis per vi dies, ix d.
...... de G]lovernia per vi dies, ix d.
...... martin' per v dies, ix d.
.... per vi dies, ix d.

Theobald of Billing' for 5 days . . .
Geoffrey son of Albreda for 5 days . . . .
Richard of St. Cross for 5 days, 7½*d.*
Alan Brun for 5 days, 7½*d.*
William Brun for 5 days, 9*d.*
Hervey of the Barton for 5 days, 7½*d.*
Adam Dun for 5 days, 7½*d.*
John Scapet for 5 days, 7½*d.*
Adam the smith's son for 5 days, 7½*d.*
William of Farnham for 6 days, 9*d.*
Stephen of the priory for 6 days, 9*d.*
Henry Hune for 6 days, 9*d.*
Henry of Bristol for 6 days, 9*d.*
William Puke for 6 days, 9*d.*
Simon de Montfort for 6 days, 9*d.*
Bertelot son of David for 6 days, 9*d.*
Gilbert of Kent for 6 days, 9*d.*
John Bagge for 6 days, 9*d.*
Robert of Overton for 6 days, 9*d.*
Thomas of Wilton for 6 days, 9*d.*
Richard le Deven' for 6 days, 9*d.*
Adam Hune for 6 days, 9*d.*
Geoffrey son of the watchman for 6 days, 9*d.*
Henry Modi for 6 days, 9*d.*
Richard of Wells for 6 days, 9*d.*
Ralph le Criblur for 6 days, 9*d.*
Godfrey of the Vine for 6 days, 9*d.*
Samson of Hereford for 6 days, 9*d.*
Alan of Framlingham for 6 days, 9*d.*
Thomas le Norais for 6 days, 9*d.*
William Merchant for 6 days, 9*d.*
Peter Souter for 6 days, 9*d.*
John of Compton for 6 days, 9*d.*
Reginald of Chichester for 5 days, 7½*d.*
German *ante opidum* [lit. 'before the town *or* castle'] for 6 days, 9*d.*
Richard of Merdon for 6 days, 9*d.*
Alexander the Bald for 6 days, 9*d.*
Martin of Alresford for 6 days, 9*d.*
Peter of Bristol for 6 days, 9*d.*
Adam the Welshman for 6 days, 9*d.*
. . . . . . of Gloucester for 6 days, 9*d.*
. . . . . . martin for 6 days, 9*d.*
. . . . for 6 days, 9*d.*

.... per vi dies, ix d.
.... per vi dies, ix d.
.... Metter per vi dies, ix d.
..............tori, per vi dies, ix d.
.... de Den', per vi dies, ix d.
Giliberto de Capella per vi dies, ix d.
Roberto de Brummor' per vi dies, ix d.
Matilde per vi dies, vi d.
Agnete [*sic*] per vi dies, vi d.
Lucie per vi dies, vi d.
Ivette per vi dies, vi d.
Orenge per vi dies, vi d.
Grete per vi dies, vi d.
Henrico Nigro per vi dies, ix d.
Waltero de Hereford' per vi dies, ix d.

Caretarii petrarum de Seleborn'

...... de Nortun' ad cariandum l petras, ii sol. vi d.
.... ad cariandum l petras, ii sol. vi d.
Willelmo Bathele ad cariandum centum petras, v sol.
Johanni Patri ad cariandum xxv petras, xv d.
Henrico de Ymesat' ad cariandum l petras, ii sol. vi d.

Caretarii de Insula

Ricardo Lewine per x dies, iiii sol. ii d.
Radulfo Luctatori per viii dies, iii sol. iiii d.
Willelmo le Swon per x dies, iiii sol. ii d.
Willelmo le Scutt per vi dies, ii sol. vi d.
Johanni Belami per ix dies, iii sol. ix d.
Thome filio Johannis per x dies, iiii sol. ii d.
Willelmo Mansel ad secandum centum & l planches in tasca, ix sol.
Henrico de Ymesat pro mille petris de quariria sua de Seleborn', xvii sol. iiii d.

Summa viii li. xviii sol. ii d.

Liberata cementariis carpentariis caretariis & aliis operariis die Dominica proxima post festum Sanctorum Simonis & Jude.

Magistro Alberto per vi dies, xx d.
Magistro Gerardo per vi dies, xx d.
Ranulpho de Moreva per vi dies, xx d.
Hereberto de Sperkeford' per vi dies, xx d.

.... for 6 days, 9*d.*
.... for 6 days, 9*d.*
.... for 6 days, 9*d.*
.... for 6 days, 9*d.*
...... of Dene, for 6 days, 9*d.*
Gilbert of Capell for 6 days, 9*d.*
Robert of Breamore for 6 days, 9*d.*
Matilda for 6 days, 6*d.*
Agnes for 6 days, 6*d.*
Lucy for 6 days, 6*d.*
Ivetta for 6 days, 6*d.*
Orenga for 6 days, 6*d.*
Greta for 6 days, 6*d.*
Henry Black for 6 days, 9*d.*
Walter of Hereford for 6 days, 9*d.*

Carters of stones from Selborne
...... of Norton for carrying 50 stones, 2*s.* 6*d.*
.... for carrying 50 stones, 2*s.* 6*d.*
William Bathele for carrying 100 stones, 5*s.*
John Father for carrying 25 stones, 15*d.*
Henry of Empshot for carrying 50 stones, 2*s.* 6*d.*

Carters of Isle [*of Wight*] *stone*
Richard Lewine for 10 days, 4*s.* 2*d.*
Ralph the wrestler for 8 days, 3*s.* 4*d.*
William le Swon for 10 days, 4*s.* 2*d.*
William le Scutt for 6 days, 2*s.* 6*d.*
John Belami for 9 days, 3*s.* 9*d.*
Thomas son of John for 10 days, 4*s.* 2*d.*
Henry Mansel for cutting 150 planks by task, 9*s.*
Henry of Empshot for 1,000 stones from his quarry at Selborne, 17*s.* 4*d.*

Total £8. 18*s.* 2*d.*

Paid to masons, carpenters, carters and other workmen on Sunday next after the feast of Saints Simon and Jude [*30 October*].

[*Masons*]
Master Albert for 6 days, 20*d.*
Master Gerard for 6 days, 20*d.*
Ranulf de Moreva for 6 days, 20*d.*
Herbert of Sparkford for 6 days, 20*d.*

Magistro Henrico per vi dies, xx d.
Galfrido de Spersolt' per vi dies, xviii d.
Wimundo fabro per vi dies, xvii d.
Galfrido de Sancto Albano per vi dies, xvii d.
Radulfo Berethorn' per vi dies, xvii d.
Roberto de Keinesham per vi dies, xvii d.
Willelmo Deven' per vi dies, xvi d.
Iuoni de Sperkeford' per vi dies, xvi d.
Ricardo Passelewe per vi dies, xvi d.
Hugoni de Foleflod' per vi dies, xvi d.
Johanni de Wintonia per vi dies, xvi d.
Johanni de Bradenstok' per vi dies, xvi d.
Waltero de Ford' per vi dies, xv d.
Radulfo de Spersolt per vi dies, xv d.
Ricardo Wallensi per vi dies, xv d.
Clementi de Sireborn' per vi dies, xv d.
Willelmo de Hida per vi dies, xv d.
Petro de Hida per vi dies, xv d.
Galfrido de Sancta Fide per vi dies, xv d.
Willelmo de Nhutselling' per vi dies, xv d.
Roberto de Kingtun' per vi dies, xv d.
Willelmo de Wauerlegh' per vi dies, xiii d. ob.
Simoni de Angr' per vi dies, xiii d. ob.
Waltero Regi per vi dies, xiii d. ob.
Ade de Sancta Cruce per vi dies, xiii d. ob.
Willelmo de Ford' per vi dies, xi d.
Johanni de Ston' per vi dies, xi d.
Waltero de Sancta Cruce per vi dies, xi d.
Willelmo le Sclatir per v dies, xiii d.
Nicolao Derbi per v dies, xii d. ob.
Waltero de Sancta fide per v dies, xii d. ob.
Willelmo de Farnham per v dies, xv d.
Radulfo de Farnham per v dies, xv d.
Siwardo per v dies, xii d. ob.
Galfrido de Farnham per vi dies, x d. ob.

Carpentarii

Ricardo de Peteresfeld' per v dies, xvi d.
Willelmo de Lond' per v dies, xvi d.
Simoni de Lond' per v dies, xvi d.
Waltero de Lond' per v dies, xvi d.
Gerardo per v dies, xvi d.

Master Henry for 6 days, 20*d.*
Geoffrey of Sparsholt for 6 days, 18*d.*
Wimund the smith for 6 days, 17*d.*
Geoffrey of St. Albans for 6 days, 17*d.*
Ralph Berethorn for 6 days, 17*d.*
Robert of Keynsham for 6 days, 17*d.*
William Deven for 6 days, 16*d.*
Ivo of Sparkford for 6 days, 16*d.*
Richard Passelewe for 6 days, 16*d.*
Hugh of Fullflood for 6 days, 16*d.*
John of Winchester for 6 days, 16*d.*
John of Bradenstoke for 6 days, 16*d.*
Walter of Ford for 6 days, 15*d.*
Ralph of Sparsholt for 6 days, 15*d.*
Richard Welsh for 6 days, 15*d.*
Clement of Sherborne for 6 days, 15*d.*
William of Hyde for 6 days, 15*d.*
Peter of Hyde for 6 days, 15*d.*
Geoffrey of St. Faith for 6 days, 15*d.*
William of Nursling for 6 days, 15*d.*
Robert of Kington for 6 days, 15*d.*
William of Waverley for 6 days, 13½*d.*
Simon of Hanger for 6 days, 13½*d.*
Walter King for 6 days, 13½*d.*
Adam of St. Cross for 6 days, 13½*d.*
William of Ford for 6 days, 11*d.*
John of Stone for 6 days, 11*d.*
Walter of St. Cross for 6 days, 11*d.*
William the slater for 5 days, 13*d.*
Nicholas Derby for 5 days, 12½*d.*
Walter of St. Faith for 5 days, 12½*d.*
William of Farnham for 5 days, 15*d.*
Ralph of Farnham for 5 days, 15*d.*
Siward for 5 days, 12½*d.*
Geoffrey of Farnham for 6 days, 10½*d.*

Carpenters

Richard of Petersfield for 5 days, 16*d.*
William of London for 5 days, 16*d.*
Simon of London for 5 days, 16*d.*
Walter of London for 5 days, 16*d.*
Gerard for 5 days, 16*d.*

Galfrido de Wdestret' per v dies, xvi d.
Ernaldo Le Flemmeng per v dies, xv d.
Ade Beawsamis per v dies, xv d.
Willelmo de Wiltesir' per v dies, xv d.
Danielo de Chushull' per v dies, xv d.
Andree filio Walteri per v dies, x d.
Ricardo Russello per v dies, x d.

Roberto Pilet per v dies, ix d.
Martino Excubie per vii noctes & v dies, ix d.
Martino Ruffo per v dies, vii d. ob.
Reginaldo Hunne per v dies, vii d. ob.
Hugoni de Sropsir' per v dies, vii d. ob.
Ricardo pistori per v dies, vii d. ob.
Willelmo Nhek' per v dies, vii d. ob.
Willelmo Burel per v dies, vi d. ob.
Reginaldo Puttok per v dies, vi d. ob.
Ade de Lillescliva per v dies, vi d. ob.
Tedbaldo de Billing' per v dies, vi d. ob.
Galfrido filio Albr[ede...
Ricardo de Sancta Cr[uce...
Alano Brun ...

[*Liberata cementariis carpentariis caretariis & aliis operariis die Sancti Leonardi*].[1]

Thome filio Johannis ...
R[adulfo Luc]tatori per ...
[Willelmo le] Scutt per ...
Eadmundo de Alresford' per iiii dies
W[illelmo B]athele pro ...
ii sol. vj d.
Galfrido le quareur ...
xv d.
Roberto Lib' pro uno trunco, v d.
Nicholao de Uvntun' pro i trunco, iii d.
Willelmo de Preuet pro i trunco, iii d.
Waltero Puke pro i trunco, iii d.

Summa iiii li. xvi d. ob.

Liberata cementariis & aliis operariis die Dominica proxima post festum Sancti Martini episcopi.

Johanni de Abendun' per v dies, xv d.
Magistro Alberto per v dies, xv d.

[1] Of this section of the document only the last few entries survive, including the total for the week.

Geoffrey of Wood Street for 5 days, 16*d.*
Arnold the Fleming for 5 days, 15*d.*
Adam Beawsamis for 5 days, 15*d.*
William of Wiltshire for 5 days, 15*d.*
Daniel of Chishall for 5 days, 15*d.*
Andrew son of Walter for 5 days, 10*d.*
Richard Russell for 5 days, 10*d.*

[*Labourers*]

Robert Pilet for 6 days, 9*d.*
Martin the watchman for 7 nights and 5 days, 9*d.*
Martin Redhead for 5 days, 7½*d.*
Reginald Hunne for 5 days, 7½*d.*
Hugh of Shropshire for 5 days, 7½*d.*
Richard Baker for 5 days, 7½*d.*
William Nhek for 5 days, 7½*d.*
William Burel for 5 days, 6½*d.*
Reginald Puttok for 5 days, 6½*d.*
Adam de Lillescliva for 5 days, 6½*d.*
Theobald of Billing' for 5 days, 6½*d.*
Geoffrey son of Albreda . . .
Richard of St. Cross . . .
Alan Brun . . .

Paid to masons, carpenters, carters, and other workmen on the day of St. Leonard [*6 November*].

Thomas son of John . . .
Ralph the wrestler for . . .
William le Scutt for . . .
Edmund of Alresford for 4 days
William Bathele for . . . 2*s.* 6*d.*
Geoffrey the quarryman . . . 15*d.*
Robert Lib' for [carrying] one tree-trunk, 5*d.*
Nicholas of Ovington for one tree-trunk, 3*d.*
William of Privet for one tree-trunk, 3*d.*
Walter Puke for one tree-trunk, 3*d.*

Total £4. 1*s.* 4½*d.*

Paid to masons and other workmen on Sunday next after the feast of St. Martin the Bishop [*13 November*].

[*Masons*]

John of Abingdon for 5 days, 15*d.*
Master Albert for 5 days, 15*d.*

Magistro Gerardo per v dies, xv d.
Ranulpho de Moreva per vi dies, xv d.
Hereberto de Sperkeford per vi dies, xv d.
Magistro Henrico per vi dies, xv d.
Galfrido de Spersolt per v dies, xiiii d. ob.
Wimundo fabro per v dies, xv d.
Galfrido de Sancto Albano per vi dies, xii d. ob.
Radulfo Berethorn' per vi dies xii d. ob.
Roberto de Keinesham per vi dies, xii d. ob.
Willelmo Deven' per vi dies, xii d.
Iuoni de Sperkeford' per vi dies, xii d.
Ricardo Passelewe per vi dies, xii d.
Hugoni de Foleflod' per vi dies, xii d.
[Johanni] de Winton' per vi dies, xii d.
[Johanni] de Bradenestok per vi dies, xii d.
Waltero de Ford' per vi dies, x d. ob.
Radulfo de Sparsolt per vi dies, x d. ob.
Ricardo Wallensi per vi dies, x d. ob.
Clementi de Sireborn' per vi dies, x [d.] ob.
Willelmo de Hida per vi dies, x d. ob.
Galfrido de Sancta Fide per vi dies, x d. ob.
Petro de Hida per vi dies, x d. ob.
Willelmo de Nhutselling' per vi dies, x d. ob.
Roberto de Kingtun' per vi dies, x d. ob.
Willelmo de Wauerlegh' per vi dies, . . .
Simoni de Angr' per vi dies, . . .
. . . . . . de Podeham per v[i] dies, . . .
Waltero Regi per vi dies, ix d.
Ade de Sancta Cruce per vi dies, ix d.
Willelmo de Ford per vi dies, vii d. ob.
Johanni de Ston' per vi dies, vii d. ob.
Waltero de Sancta Cruce per vi dies, vii d. ob.

Dawburs

Willelmo de Farnham per v dies, xii d.
Radulfo de Farnham per v dies, xi d.
Willelmo le Sclatir per v dies, xii d.
Nicolao [Der]bi per v dies, xii d.
Waltero de Sancta Fide per v dies, x d.
Siwardo per . . . dies, x d.
[Galfrido] de Farnham per v dies, ix d.

Master Gerard for 5 days, 15*d.*
Ranulph de Moreva for 6 days, 15*d.*
Herbert of Sparkford for 6 days, 15*d.*
Master Henry for 6 days, 15*d.*
Geoffrey of Sparsholt for 5 days, 14½*d.*
Wimund the smith for 5 days, 15*d.*
Geoffrey of St. Albans for 6 days, 12½*d.*
Ralph Berethorn for 6 days, 12½*d.*
Robert of Keynsham for 6 days, 12½*d.*
William Deven' for 6 days, 12*d.*
Ivo of Sparkford for 6 days, 12*d.*
Richard Passelewe for 6 days, 12*d.*
Hugh of Fullflood for 6 days, 12*d.*
[John] of Winchester for 6 days, 12*d.*
[John] of Bradenstoke for 6 days, 12*d.*
Walter of Ford for 6 days, 10½*d.*
Ralph of Sparsholt for 6 days, 10½*d.*
Richard Welsh for 6 days, 10½*d.*
Clement of Sherborne for 6 days, 10½*d.*
William of Hyde for 6 days, 10½*d.*
Geoffrey of St. Faith for 6 days, 10½*d.*
Peter of Hyde for 6 days, 10½*d.*
William of Nursling for 6 days, 10½*d.*
Robert of Kington for 6 days, 10½*d.*
William of Waverley for 6 days, . . .
Simon of Hanger for 6 days, . . .
. . . . . . of Podeham for 6 days, . . .
Walter King for 6 days, 9*d.*
Adam of St. Cross for 6 days, 9*d.*
William of Ford for 6 days, 7½*d.*
John of Stone for 6 days, 7½*d.*
Walter of St. Cross for 6 days, 7½*d.*

Plasterers

William of Farnham for 5 days, 12*d.*
Ralph of Farnham for 5 days, 11*d.*
William the slater for 5 days, 12*d.*
Nicholas Derby for 5 days, 12*d.*
Walter of St. Faith for 5 days, 10*d.*
Siward for . . . days, 10*d.*
Geoffrey of Farnham for 5 days, 9*d.*

[*Carpentarii*]

Ricardo de Peteresfeld' per v dies, xv d.
Willelmo de Lond' per v dies, xv d.
Simoni de Lond' per v dies, xv d.
Waltero de Lond' per v dies, xv d.
Gerardo . . . . per v dies, xv d.
Galfrido de Wdestret per v dies, xv d.
Ernaldo le Flemmeng per v dies, xiiii d.
Danielo de Chushell' per v dies, . . .
Ade Beawsamis per v dies, . . .
Willelmo de Wiltesir' per v [dies,] . . .
Andree filio Walteri per v dies, . . .

Roberto Pilet per v dies, viii d.
Martino Excubie per v noctes, . . .
Martino Ruffo per v dies, . . .
Reginaldo Hunne per v dies, . . .
Hugoni de Sropsir' per v dies, . . .
Ricardo pistori per v dies, vii d. ob.
Willelmo Nhek per iiii dies, vi d.
Willelmo Burel per v dies, vii d.
Reginaldo Puttok per v dies, vi d.
Ade de Lillescliva per vi dies, ix d.
Nicolao de Farnham per v dies, vi d.
Galfrido filio Albrede per v dies, vi d.
Ricardo de Sancta Cruce per v dies, vi d.
Willelmo fabro per v dies, vii d. ob.
Waltero Deven' per v dies, vii d. ob.
Nicolao de Shuthwik per v dies, vi d.
Galfrido filio Excubie per v dies, vi d.
Alano Brun' per v dies, vi d.
Herevico de La Bertun' per v dies, vi d.
Ade Dune per v dies, vi d.
Johanni Scapeto per v dies, vi d.
Ade filio fabri per v dies, vi d.
Roberto de Scam'weia per iii dies, iiii d. ob.
Stephano de Prioria per v dies, vi d.
Henrico Hune per v dies, vi d.
Henrico de Bristoll' per v dies, vi d.
Willelmo Puke per v dies, vi d.

[*Carpenters*]
Richard of Petersfield for 5 days, 15*d.*
William of London for 5 days, 15*d.*
Simon of London for 5 days, 15*d.*
Walter of London for 5 days, 15*d.*
Gerard . . . . for 5 days, 15*d.*
Geoffrey of Wood Street for 5 days, 15*d.*
Arnold the Fleming for 5 days, 14*d.*
Daniel of Chishall for 5 days, . . .
Adam Beawsamis for 5 days, . . .
William of Wiltshire for 5 days, . . .
Andrew son of Walter for 5 days, . . .

[*Labourers*][1]
Robert Pilet for 5 days, 8*d.*
Martin the watchman for 5 nights, . . .
Martin Redhead for 5 days, . . .
Reginald Hunne for 5 days, . . .
Hugh of Shropshire for 5 days, . . .
Richard Baker for 5 days, 7½*d.*
William Nhek for 4 days, 6*d.*
William Burel for 5 days, 7*d.*
Reginald Puttok for 5 days, 6*d.*
Adam de Lillescliva for 6 days, 9*d.*
Nicholas of Farnham for 5 days, 6*d.*
Geoffrey son of Albreda for 5 days, 6*d.*
Richard of St. Cross for 5 days, 6*d.*
William the smith for 5 days, 7½*d.*
Walter Deven' for 5 days, 7½*d.*
Nicholas of Southwick for 5 days, 6*d.*
Geoffrey son of the watchman for 5 days, 6*d.*
Alan Brun for 5 days, 6*d.*
Hervey of the Barton for 5 days, 6*d.*
Adam Dune for 5 days, 6*d.*
John Scapet for 5 days, 6*d.*
Adam son of the smith for 5 days, 6*d.*
Robert of Shambleway for 3 days, 4½*d.*
Stephen of the priory for 5 days, 6*d.*
Henry Hune for 5 days, 6*d.*
Henry of Bristol for 5 days, 6*d.*
William Puke for 5 days, 6*d.*

1 Though there is no sub-heading in the MS., the gap was clearly intended to divide the carpenters from the labourers.

3. Weekly summary of wages paid at Winchester Castle from 6 March 1222 to 24 November, 1224, and particulars of expenditure on materials, transport, etc., in 1222 and part of 1223.

(E 101/491/13)

Expensa facta ad castrum Winton' reparandum per manus Maioris Winton', Magistri Henrici de Cerne & Alani de Hereford' custodum operis castri Winton' anno Regni Regis Henrici sexto ad festum beati Gregorii pape & per manus[1] *Johannis Cobbe, Galfridi de Sancta fide & Rogeri Coleman.*

Liberatum cementariis carpentariis & aliis operariis die Dominica proxima post festum beati Gregorii pape per manus predictorum custodum lxii sol. viii d.

Item liberatum cementariis carpentariis & aliis operariis per visum predictorum die Dominica proxima post festum beati Cutberti de septimana proxima precedenti iiii li. iiii d.

Item liberatum cementariis carpentariis & aliis operariis die Veneris proxima post Annunciacionem beate Virginis scilicet die Crucis adorate per visum predictorum de septimana eadem C & viii sol.

Item liberatum per visum predictorum cementariis carpentariis & aliis operariis die Dominica proxima post festum Sanctorum Tiburcii & Valeriani de septimana proxima precedenti iiii li. xiiii sol. iiii d.

Item liberatum cementariis carpentariis & aliis operariis per visum predictorum die Sancti Georgii martiris de septimana proxima precedenti xi li. iii sol. iii d. ob.

Item liberatum per visum predictorum cementariis carpentariis caretariis & aliis operariis die Dominica proxima post festum Sancti Marci Ewangeliste de septimana proxima precedenti ix li. xvii sol. vi d. ob.

Item liberatum cementariis carpentariis & aliis operariis die Dominica proxima post festum Sancti Johannis ante portam Latinam de septimana proxima precedente [*sic*] x li. ix sol. vii d.

Item liberatum cementariis carpentariis & aliis operariis die Dominica proxima post festum Sanctorum Nerei, Achillei & Pancratii de septimana proxima precedenti xiii li. xviii sol. xi d. ob.

Item liberatum cementariis carpentariis & aliis operariis die Sabbati proxima post festum Sancti Dunstani de septimana proxima precedenti xi li. xv sol. vii d.

[1] Perhaps a slip for *per visum*.

3. Weekly summary of wages paid at Winchester Castle from 6 March 1222 to 24 November 1224, and particulars of expenditure on materials, transport, etc., in 1222 and part of 1223.

Expenses incurred in repairing Winchester Castle by the hands of the Mayor of Winchester, Master Henry of Cerne, and Alan of Hereford, keepers of the work of Winchester Castle in the sixth year of the reign of King Henry at the feast of the blessed Pope Gregory [*6 March 1222*] *and by the hands of*[1] *John Cobbe, Geoffrey of St. Faith, and Roger Coleman.*

Paid to masons, carpenters, and other workmen on Sunday next after the feast of the blessed Pope Gregory [13 March] by the hands of the said keepers £3. 2*s*. 8*d*.

And paid to masons, carpenters, and other workmen by view of the aforesaid on Sunday next after the feast of the blessed Cuthbert [27 March] for the week immediately preceding £4. 0*s*. 4*d*.

And paid to masons, carpenters, and other workmen on Friday next after the Annunciation of the blessed Virgin, that is on Good Friday [1 April] by view of the aforesaid for the week immediately preceding £5. 8*s*. 0*d*.

And paid by view of the aforesaid to masons, carpenters, and other workmen on Sunday next after the feast of Saints Tiburtius and Valerianus [17 April] for the week immediately preceding £4. 14*s*. 4*d*.

And paid to masons, carpenters, and other workmen by view of the aforesaid on St. George's Day [23 April] for the week immediately preceding £11. 3*s*. 3½*d*.

And paid by view of the aforesaid to masons, carpenters, carters, and other workmen on Sunday next after the feast of St. Mark the Evangelist [1 May] for the week immediately preceding £9. 17*s*. 6½*d*.

And paid to masons, carpenters, and other workmen on Sunday next after the feast of St. John before the Latin Gate [8 May] for the week immediately preceding £10. 9*s*. 7*d*.

And paid to masons, carpenters, and other workmen on Sunday next after the feast of Saints Nereus, Achilleus, and Pancras [15 May] for the week immediately preceding £13. 18*s*. 11½*d*.

And paid to masons, carpenters, and other workmen on Saturday next after the feast of St. Dunstan [21 May] for the week immediately preceding £11. 15*s*. 7*d*.

[1] Perhaps a slip for 'by view of'.

ii Rotulus

Item liberatum cementariis carpentariis & aliis operariis die Dominica proxima post festum Sanctorum Marcellini & Petri de septimana proxima precedenti xii li. x sol. iiii d. ob.

Item liberatum cementariis carpentariis & aliis operariis die Dominica proxima post festum Sancti Barnabe apostoli de septimana proxima precedenti per visum predictorum ix li. v sol. ii d. ob.

Item liberatum cementariis carpentariis & aliis operariis die Sanctorum Gervasii & Prothasii de septimana proxima precedenti x li. iii sol. ob.

Item liberatum cementariis carpentariis & aliis operariis per visum predictorum die Dominica proxima post Nativitatem Sancti Johannis Baptiste de septimana proxima precedenti xiiii li. iii d.

Item liberatum cementariis carpentariis & aliis operariis die Dominica proxima post festum apostolorum Petri & Pauli de septimana proxima precedenti ix li. xviii sol.

Item liberatum cementariis carpentariis & aliis operariis die Dominica proxima ante translacionem Sancti Benedicti de septimana proxima precedenti viii li. xvi sol. ix d. ob.

Item liberatum cementariis carpentariis caretariis & aliis operariis die Dominica proxima ante festum beate Margarete Virginis de septimana proxima precedenti vii li. xv sol. x d. ob.

Item liberatum cementariis carpentariis caretariis & aliis operariis die Dominica proxima post festum Sancte Marie Magdalene de septimana proxima precedenti vi li. iiii sol. x d.

Item liberatum cementariis carpentariis caretariis & aliis operariis die Dominica proxima post festum Sancti Jacobi apostoli de septimana proxima precedenti xi li. ix sol. iii d. ob.

Item liberatum cementariis carpentariis & aliis operariis die Dominica proxima post festum beati Petri ad vincula de septimana proxima precedenti vi li. x sol. vi d.

Item liberatum cementariis carpentariis & aliis operariis die Dominica proxima post festum Sancti Laurencii de septimana proxima precedenti per visum predictorum xi li. vi sol. ii d. ob.

Item liberatum cementariis carpentariis & aliis operariis die Dominica proxima post Assumpcionem beate Marie de septimana proxima precedenti vi li. xiii sol. ob.

Item liberatum cementariis carpentariis & aliis operariis die Dominica proxima post festum Sancti Bartholomei apostoli de septimana proxima precedenti xiiii li. xi sol. ii d. ob.

Item liberatum cementariis carpentariis caretariis & aliis operariis die Dominica proxima post decollacionem Sancti Johannis de septimana proxima precedenti iiii li. xviii sol. vi d. ob.

Roll 2

And paid to masons, carpenters, and other workmen on Sunday next after the feast of Saints Marcellinus and Peter [5 June] for the week immediately preceding £12. 10*s*. 4½*d*.

And paid to masons, carpenters, and other workmen on Sunday next after the feast of St. Barnabas the apostle [12 June] by view of the aforesaid £9. 5*s*. 2½*d*.

And paid to masons, carpenters, and other workmen on the day of Saints Gervase and Protasius [Sunday 19 June] for the week immediately preceding £10. 3*s*. 0½*d*.

And paid to masons, carpenters, and other workmen by view of the aforesaid on Sunday next after the Nativity of St. John Baptist [26 June] for the week immediately preceding £14. 0*s*. 3*d*.

And paid to masons, carpenters, and other workmen on Sunday next after the feast of the Apostles Peter and Paul [3 July] for the week immediately preceding £9. 18*s*. 0*d*.

And paid to masons, carpenters, and other workmen on Sunday next before the Translation of St. Benedict [10 July] for the week immediately preceding £8. 16*s*. 9½*d*.

And paid to masons, carpenters, carters, and other workmen on Sunday next before the feast of the Blessed Margaret the Virgin [17 July] for the week immediately preceding £7. 15*s*. 10½*d*.

And paid to masons, carpenters, carters, and other workmen on Sunday next after the feast of St. Mary Magdalen [24 July] for the week immediately preceding £6. 4*s*. 10*d*.

And paid to masons, carpenters, carters, and other workmen on Sunday next after the feast of St. James the Apostle [31 July] for the week immediately preceding £11. 9*s*. 3½*d*.

And paid to masons, carpenters, and other workmen on Sunday next after the feast of the blessed Peter in Chains [7 August] for the week immediately preceding £6. 10*s*. 6*d*.

And paid to masons, carpenters, and other workmen on Sunday next after the feast of St. Laurence [14 August] for the preceding week by view of the aforesaid £11. 6*s*. 2½*d*.

And paid to masons, carpenters, and other workmen on Sunday next after the Assumption of the Blessed Mary [21 August] for the week immediately preceding £6. 13*s*. 0½*d*.

And paid to masons, carpenters, and other workmen on Sunday next after the feast of St. Bartholomew the Apostle [28 August] for the week immediately preceding £14. 11*s*. 2½*d*.

And paid to masons, carpenters, carters, and other workmen on Sunday next after the Decollation of St. John [4 Sept.] £4. 18*s*. 6½*d*.

iii Rotulus[1]

Item liberatum cementariis carpentariis & aliis operariis die Dominica proxima post Nativitatem beate Marie per visum predictorum de septimana proxima precedenti C & xvi sol. i d.

*Item liberatum cementariis carpentariis caretariis & aliis operariis die Dominica proxima post exaltacionem Sancte Crucis de septimana proxima precedenti xiii li. vi sol. ob.

Item liberatum cementariis carpentariis caretariis & aliis operariis die Dominica proxima post festum Sancti Mathei apostoli de septimana proxima precedenti viii li. xvi sol. i d.

Item liberatum cementariis carpentariis caretariis & aliis operariis die Dominica proxima post festum beati Michaelis de septimana proxima precedenti iiii li. xvi sol. ii d.

Item liberatum cementariis carpentariis & aliis operariis die Dominica proxima post festum Sancte Fidis virginis de septimana precedenti viii li. ii sol. xi d. ob.

Item liberatum cementariis carpentariis caretariis & aliis operariis die Dominica proxima ante festum Sancti Luce Ewangeliste de septimana precedenti C & vi sol. viii d. ob.

*Item liberatum cementariis carpentariis & aliis operariis die Dominica proxima post festum Sancti Luce Ewangeliste de septimana precedenti viii li. xviii sol. ii d.

*Item liberatum cementariis carpentariis & aliis operariis die Dominica proxima post festum Sanctorum Simonis & Jude de septimana proxima precedenti viii li. vii sol. iiii d.

*Item liberatum cementariis carpentariis caretariis & aliis operariis die Sancti Leonardi de septimana proxima precedenti iiii li. xvi d. ob.

*Item liberatum cementariis carpentariis & aliis operariis die Dominica proxima post festum Sancti Martini Episcopi de septimana proxima precedenti vi li. iiii sol. iii d. ob.

Item liberatum cementariis carpentariis & aliis operariis die beati Eadmundi Regis de septimana proxima precedenti per visum predictorum C v sol. ii d.

Item liberatum cementariis carpentariis & aliis operariis die Dominica proxima post festum beate Katerine de septimana proxima precedenti lvii sol. xi d. ob.

Item liberatum cementariis carpentariis & aliis operariis die beati Andree apostoli de septimana proxima precedenti per visum predictorum custodum lv sol. x d. ob.

[1] Details of the payments made in weeks marked by an asterisk will be found in No. 2 above.

Roll 3[1]

And paid to masons, carpenters, and other workmen on Sunday next after the Nativity of the Blessed Mary [11 September] by view of the aforesaid for the week immediately preceding £5. 16*s.* 1*d.*

*And paid to masons, carpenters, carters, and other workmen on Sunday next after the Exaltation of the Holy Cross [18 September] for the week immediately preceding £13. 6*s.* 0½*d.*

And paid to masons, carpenters, carters, and other workmen on Sunday next after the feast of St. Matthew the Apostle [25 September] for the week immediately preceding £8. 16*s.* 1*d.*

And paid to masons, carpenters, carters, and other workmen on Sunday next after the feast of the blessed Michael [2 October] for the week immediately preceding £4. 16*s.* 2*d.*

And paid to masons, carpenters, and other workmen on Sunday next after the feast of St. Faith the Virgin [9 October] for the week preceding £8. 2*s.* 11½*d.*

And paid to masons, carpenters, carters and other workmen on Sunday next before the feast of St. Luke the Evangelist [16 October] for the week preceding £5. 6*s.* 8½*d.*

*And paid to masons, carpenters, and other workmen on Sunday next after the feast of St. Luke the Evangelist [23 October] for the week preceding £8. 18*s.* 2*d.*

*And paid to masons, carpenters, and other workmen on Sunday next after the feast of Saints Simon and Jude [30 October] for the week immediately preceding £8. 7*s.* 4*d.*

*And paid to masons, carpenters, carters, and other workmen on St. Leonard's Day [6 November] for the week immediately preceding £4. 1*s.* 4½*d.*

*And paid to masons, carpenters, and other workmen on Sunday next after the feast of St. Martin the Bishop [13 November] for the week immediately preceding £6. 4*s.* 3½*d.*

And paid to masons, carpenters, and other workmen on the day of the blessed Edmund the King [20 November] for the week immediately preceding, by view of the aforesaid £5. 5*s.* 2*d.*

And paid to masons, carpenters, and other workmen on Sunday next after the feast of the blessed Katherine [27 November] for the week immediately preceding £2. 17*s.* 11½*d.*

And paid to masons, carpenters, and other workmen on the day of the blessed Andrew the Apostle [30 November[2]] for the week immediately preceding by view of the aforesaid keepers £2. 15*s.* 10½*d.*

[1] Details of the payments made in weeks marked by an asterisk will be found in No. 2 above.

[2] Presumably a mistake for the following Sunday, that is 4 December.

Item liberatum cementariis carpentariis & aliis operariis die Dominica proxima post Concepcionem beate Virginis de septimana proxima precedenti C & ii sol. xi d. ob.

Item liberatum cementariis carpentariis & aliis operariis die Dominica proxima post festum beate Lucie Virginis de septimana proxima precedenti lxii sol. ob.

Item liberatum cementariis & aliis operariis in vigilia Nativitatis Domini liii sol. ii d. ob.

iiii Rotulus

Item liberatum cementariis & aliis operariis die Sancti Vincencii Martiris de duabus septimanis proximo preteritis C sol. ix d.

Item liberatum cementariis carpentariis & aliis operariis die Dominica proxima post Conversionem Sancti Pauli de septimana proxima precedenti xlvii sol. vi d. ob.

Item liberatum cementariis carpentariis & aliis operariis die beate Agathe virginis de septimana proxima precedenti xv sol. viii d. ob.

Item liberatum cementariis carpentariis & aliis operariis die Dominica proxima post festum beati Mathei [*sic*] apostoli de tribus septimanis proximo preteritis iiii li. xvi sol. x d. ob.

Item liberatum cementariis caretariis & aliis operariis similiter & pro rebus emptis ad castrum reparandum necessariis de duabus septimanis proximo preteritis die Sancti Gregorii pape lxxvii sol. iiii d.

Item liberatum cementariis & aliis operariis die Dominica proxima ante festum Sancti Cutberti de septimana proxima precedenti liii sol. viii d. ob.

Item liberatum cementariis & aliis operariis die Dominica proxima ante festum Sancti Ambrosii Episcopi de duabus septimanis proximo preteritis lv sol. ob.

Item liberatum cementariis carpentariis & aliis operariis die Dominica proxima post festum Sanctorum Tiburcii & Valeriani de duabus septimanis proximo preteritis lxv sol. i d.

Item liberatum cementariis carpentariis & aliis operariis die Jovis proxima ante festum Sancti Georgii de iiii diebus proximo preteritis xlv sol. vi d.

Item liberatum cementariis carpentariis & aliis operariis die Dominica proxima post festum beati Johannis ante portam Latinam de septimana proxima precedenti lvii sol. x d. ob.

Item liberatum cementariis carpentariis & aliis operariis die Dominica proxima ante festum Sancti Dunstani de septimana proxima precedenti C ii sol. ii d.

And paid to masons, carpenters, and other workmen on Sunday next after the Conception of the Blessed Virgin [11 December] for the week immediately preceding £5. 2s. 11½d.
And paid to masons, carpenters, and other workmen on Sunday next after the feast of the blessed Lucy the Virgin [18 December] for the week immediately preceding £3. 2s. 0½d.
And paid to masons and other workmen on Christmas Eve [24 December] £2. 13s. 2½d.

Roll 4

And paid to masons and other workmen on the day of St. Vincent the Martyr [22 January, 1223] for the two weeks last past £5. 0s. 9d.
And paid to masons, carpenters, and other workmen on Sunday next after the Conversion of St. Paul [29 January] for the week immediately preceding £2. 7s. 6½d.
And paid to masons, carpenters, and other workmen on the day of the blessed Agatha the Virgin [5 February] for the week immediately preceding 15s. 8½d.
And paid to masons, carpenters, and other workmen on Sunday next after the feast of the blessed Matthias the Apostle [26 February] for three weeks last past £4. 16s. 10½d.
And paid to masons, carters, and other workmen, and also for the purchase of things needed for the repair of the castle, for two weeks last past on the day of St. Gregory the pope [12 March] £3. 17s. 4d.
And paid to masons and other workmen on Sunday next before the feast of St. Cuthbert [19 March] for the week immediately preceding £2. 13s. 8½d.
And paid to masons and other workmen on Sunday next before the feast of St. Ambrose [2 April] for two weeks last past £2. 15s. 0½d.
And paid to masons, carpenters, and other workmen on Sunday next after the feast of Saints Tiburtius and Valerianus [16 April] for two weeks last past £3. 5s. 1d.
And paid to masons, carpenters, and other workmen on Thursday next before the feast of St. George [20 April] for 4 days last past £2. 5s. 6d.
And paid to masons, carpenters, and other workmen on Sunday next after the feast of the blessed John before the Latin Gate [7 May] for the week immediately preceding £2. 17s. 10½d.
And paid to masons, carpenters, and other workmen on Sunday next before the feast of St. Dunstan [14 May] for the week immediately preceding £5. 2s. 2d.

Item liberatum cementariis carpentariis & aliis operariis die Dominica proxima post festum Sancti Dunstani de septimana proxima precedenti lxx sol. iiii d.

Item liberatum cementariis carpentariis & aliis operariis die Dominica proxima post festum Sancti Augustini Anglorum Apostoli de septimana precedenti vi li. xiii sol. x d. ob.

Item liberatum cementariis carpentariis & aliis operariis die Dominica proxima ante[1] festum Sanctorum Marcelini & Petri de septimana proxima precedenti vii li. xi sol. v d.

Item liberatum cementariis carpentariis & aliis operariis in Vigilia beati Barnabe Apostoli de septimana eadem per visum predictorum custodum operis castri Winton' xi li. vii sol. iii d. ob.

v Rotulus

Item liberatum cementariis carpentariis & aliis operariis & similiter pro rebus emptis ad castrum reparandum necessariis die Dominica proxima post festum beati Johannis Baptiste de septimana proxima precedenti vi li. ix sol. vii d.

Item liberatum cementariis carpentariis & aliis operariis die Dominica proxima post festum apostolorum Petri & Pauli de septimana proxima precedenti C xi sol. v d.

Item liberatum cementariis carpentariis caretariis & pro rebus emptis & aliis operariis die Dominica proxima ante Translacionem Sancti Benedicti de septimana proxima precedenti x li. iii sol. i d.

Item liberatum cementariis carpentariis & aliis operariis & pro rebus emptis ad castrum reparandum die Dominica proxima ante festum beate Margarete Virginis de septimana proxima precedenti ix li. xi sol. vi d. ob.

Item liberatum cementariis carpentariis & aliis operariis similiter & pro rebus emptis ad castrum reparandum necessariis die Dominica proxima post festum beate Marie Magdalene de septimana proxima precedenti vi li. vi sol. v d. ob.

Item liberatum cementariis carpentariis caretariis & aliis operariis & pro rebus emptis per manus predictorum custodum die Dominica proxima ante festum beati Petri ad Vincula de septimana proxima precedenti xi li. xii sol. i d.

Item liberatum cementariis carpentariis caretariis & aliis operariis similiter & pro rebus emptis per manus predictorum custodum die Dominica proxima post festum beati Petri ad Vincula de septimana precedenti viii li. xi sol. x d. ob.

Item liberatum cementariis carpentariis & aliis operariis similiter & pro

[1] Read 'post'.

And paid to masons, carpenters, and other workmen on Sunday next after the feast of St. Dunstan [21 May] for the week next following £3. 10s. 4d.

And paid to masons, carpenters, and other workmen on Sunday next after the feast of St. Augustine the Apostle of the English [28 May] for the preceding week £6. 13s. 10½d.

And paid to masons, carpenters, and other workmen on Sunday next after the feast of Saints Marcellinus and Peter [4 June] for the week immediately preceding £7. 11s. 5d.

And paid to masons, carpenters, and other workmen on the vigil of the blessed Barnabas the Apostle [10 June] for that week by view of the aforesaid keepers of the work of Winchester Castle £11. 7s. 3½d.

Roll 5

And paid to masons, carpenters, and other workmen and also for the purchase of things needed for the repair of the castle, on Sunday next after the feast of the blessed John the Baptist [25 June] for the week immediately preceding £6. 9s. 7d.

And paid to masons, carpenters, and other workmen on Sunday next after the feast of the Apostles Peter and Paul [2 July] for the week immediately preceding £5. 11s. 5d.

And paid to masons, carpenters, carters, and for things bought and for other workmen, on Sunday next before the Translation of St. Benedict [9 July] for the week immediately preceding £10. 3s. 1d.

And paid to masons, carpenters, and other workmen and for things bought to repair the castle on Sunday next before the feast of the blessed Margaret the Virgin [16 July] for the week immediately preceding £9. 11s. 6½d.

And paid to masons, carpenters, and other workmen, and also for the purchase of things needed for the repair of the castle on Sunday next after the feast of the blessed Mary Magdalen [23 July] for the week immediately preceding £6. 6s. 5½d.

And paid to masons, carpenters, carters, and other workmen and for things bought by the hands of the aforesaid keepers on Sunday next before the feast of the blessed Peter in Chains [30 July] for the week immediately preceding £11. 12s. 1d.

And paid to masons, carpenters, carters, and other workmen, and also for things bought by the hands of the aforesaid keepers on Sunday next after the feast of the blessed Peter in Chains [6 August] for the preceding week £8. 11s. 10½d.

And paid to masons, carpenters, and other workmen and also for

rebus emptis ad castrum reparandum necessariis per manus predictorum die Dominica proxima post festum beati Laurencii de septimana precedenti xi li. iii sol. x d. ob.

vi Rotulus

Item liberatum cementariis carpentariis & aliis operariis & pro pluribus rebus emptis ad castrum reparandum necessariis per manus predictorum die Dominica proxima post Assumpcionem beate Virginis de septimana proxima precedenti Summa viii li. viii sol. x d.

Item liberatum cementariis carpentariis caretariis & aliis operariis & pro rebus emptis die Dominica proxima ante Decollacionem Sancti Johannis de septimana precedenti viii li. xi d.

Item liberatum cementariis carpentariis & aliis operariis & pro rebus emptis necessariis ad reparacionem castri per visum predictorum die Dominica proxima post festum beati Egidii de septimana precedenti vii li. x sol. vi d.

Item liberatum cementariis carpentariis caretariis & aliis operariis & pro rebus emptis necessariis ad reparacionem castri die Dominica proxima post Nativitatem beate Virginis de septimana precedenti vii li. xviii sol. iii d. ob.

Item liberatum cementariis carpentariis & aliis operariis & pro rebus emptis necessariis ad reparacionem castri die Dominica proxima post festum beati Mathei apostoli de duabus septimanis proximo preteritis xiii li. iiii sol. ix d.

Item liberatum cementariis carpentariis & aliis operariis & pro rebus emptis necessariis ad reparacionem castri die Dominica proxima ante festum Beati Martini de sex septimanis proximo preteritis cum viii libris liberatis Magistro Stephano cementario pro servicio suo postquam operacio castri incepit Summa xxxi li. viii sol. vi d.

Item liberatum cementariis carpentariis & aliis operariis die Dominica proxima ante festum beati Thome apostoli de sex septimanis proximo preteritis per manus custodum operis vi li. iiii sol.

Item liberatum cementariis carpentariis & aliis operariis in Vigilia Nativitatis Domini de septimana proxima precedenti xvii sol. iiii d.

vii Rotulus

Liberatum cementariis carpentariis & aliis operariis die Dominica proxima post festum beati Barnabe apostoli de septimana proxima precedente [*sic*] C & xvi sol. viii d.

Liberatum cementariis caretariis & aliis operariis die Dominica proxima ante Nativitatem beati Johannis Baptiste de septimane proxima precedente [*sic*] C & xii sol. i d.

things needed for the repair of the castle bought by the hands of the aforesaid on Sunday next after the feast of the blessed Laurence [13 August] for the preceding week £11. 3s. 10½d.

Roll 6

And paid to masons, carpenters, and other workmen and for many things needed for the repair of the castle bought by the hands of the aforesaid, on Sunday next after the Assumption of the blessed Virgin [20 August] for the week immediately preceding Total £8. 8s. 10d.

And paid to masons, carpenters, carters, and other workmen and for things bought, on Sunday next before the Decollation of St. John [27 August] for the preceding week £8. 0s. 11d.

And paid to masons, carpenters, and other workmen and for things needed for the repair of the castle bought by view of the preceding, on Sunday next after the feast of the blessed Giles [3 September] for the week preceding £7. 10s. 6d.

And paid to masons, carpenters, carters, and other workmen and for the purchase of things needed for the repair of the castle on Sunday next after the Nativity of the blessed Virgin [10 September] £7. 18s. 3½d.

And paid to masons, carpenters, and other workmen and for the purchase of things needed for the repair of the castle on Sunday next after the feast of the blessed Matthew the Apostle [24 September] for two weeks last past £13. 4s. 9d.

And paid to masons, carpenters, and other workmen and for things needed for the repair of the castle bought on Sunday next before the feast of the Blessed Martin [5 November] for six weeks last past, together with £8 paid to Master Stephen the mason for his service since work on the castle began Total £31. 8s. 6d.

And paid to masons, carpenters, and other workmen on Sunday next before the feast of the blessed Thomas the Apostle [17 December] for six weeks last past by the hands of the keepers of the work £6. 4s. 0d.

And paid to masons, carpenters, and other workmen on Christmas Eve [24 December] for the week immediately preceding 17s. 4d.

Roll 7

Paid to masons, carpenters, and other workmen on Sunday next after the feast of the blessed Barnabas the Apostle [16 June, 1224] for the week immediately preceding £5. 16s. 8d.

Paid to masons, carters, and other workmen on Sunday next before the Nativity of the blessed John the Baptist [23 June] for the week immediately preceding £5. 12s. 1d.

pro xx chareatis plumbi emptis ad nundinas Sancti Botolphi per manus Maioris Winton' scilicet Elye Westman xxvii li. vi sol.

pro eisdem cariandis per mare apud Suhamton' xxxii sol.

Liberatum cementariis carpentariis & aliis operariis die Dominica proxima post Translacionem & Ordinacionem Sancti Martini Episcopi de duabus septimanis proximo preteritis vii li. iii sol. viii d.

Liberatum cementariis carpentariis & aliis operariis die Dominica proxima ante festum beate Margarete Virginis de septimana precedente [*sic*] C xii sol. x d.

Item liberatum cementariis carpentariis & aliis operariis die Dominica ante festum beate Marie Magdalene de septimana precedente [*sic*] vii li. xviii sol. iii d.

Liberatum cementariis carpentariis & aliis operariis die Dominica proxima post festum beati Jacobi apostoli de septimana precedente [*sic*] lxv sol. vii d. ob.

Liberatum cementariis carpentariis caretariis & aliis operariis die Dominica proxima post festum beati Petri ad Vincula de septimana precedente [*sic*] lxx sol. iii ob.

Liberatum cementariis carpentariis caretariis & aliis operariis die Dominica scilicet die Nativitatis beate Marie de v septimanis proxima [*sic*] preteritis xvi li. vii sol. vii d.

Liberatum cementariis carpentariis & aliis operariis die Dominica proxima post festum Sancti Mathei Apostoli de duabus septimanis proximo precedentibus vii li. vii sol. x d. ob.

Liberatum cementariis & aliis operariis die Dominica scilicet die beati Michaelis de septimana proximo precedente [*sic*] lxxv sol. xi d.

Liberatum cementariis carpentariis & aliis operariis die Dominica proxima post festum beati Michaelis de septimana proxima precedente [*sic*] lxi sol. ii d.

Liberatum carpentariis caretariis & aliis operariis die Dominica proxima ante festum beate Katerine de tribus septimanis preteritis iiii li. xvi sol. xi d. ob.

Summa summarum huius Rotuli DC xxvi li. vi sol. i d.

Expensa in cariagio petrarum de Heselbur' ad columpnas aule infra ballium in castro Winton' anno Regis Henrici sexto ad festum beati Bartholomei apostoli.

Eadem die liberatum Ricardo Sired' ad frangendum & extrahendum C & v petras de quariria de Heselbur' xxiii sol. iiii d.

Eadem die Ade de Wadesyk pro ii caretatis de petris de Heselbur' cariandis ad castrum Winton' xxxii d.

for 20 chars of lead bought at St. Botolph's Fair [Boston] by the hands of the mayor of Winchester, that is Elias Westman £27. 6*s.* 0*d.*

for carrying them by sea to Southampton £1. 12*s.* 0*d.*

Paid to masons, carpenters, and other workmen on Sunday next after the Translation and Ordination of St. Martin the Bishop [7 July] for two weeks last past £7. 3*s.* 8*d.*

Paid to masons, carpenters, and other workmen on Sunday next before the feast of the blessed Margaret the Virgin [14 July] for the preceding week £5. 12*s.* 10*d.*

And paid to masons, carpenters, and other workmen on Sunday next before the feast of the blessed Mary Magdalen [21 July] for the preceding week £7. 18*s.* 3*d.*

Paid to masons, carpenters, and other workmen on Sunday next after the feast of the blessed James the Apostle [28 July] for the preceding week £3. 5*s.* 7½*d.*

Paid to masons, carpenters, carters, and other workmen on Sunday next after the feast of the blessed Peter in Chains [4 August] for the preceding week £3. 10*s.* 1½*d.*

Paid to masons, carpenters, carters, and other workmen on Sunday, that is the Nativity of the blessed Mary [8 September] for 5 weeks last past £16. 7*s.* 7*d.*

Paid to masons, carpenters, and other workmen on Sunday next after the feast of St. Matthew the Apostle [22 September] for the two weeks immediately preceding £7. 7*s.* 10½*d.*

Paid to masons and other workmen on Sunday, that is the day of the blessed Michael [29 September] for the week immediately preceding £3. 15*s.* 11*d.*

Paid to masons, carpenters, and other workmen on Sunday next after the feast of the blessed Michael [6 October] for the week immediately preceding £3. 1*s.* 2*d.*

Paid to carpenters, carters, and other workmen on Sunday next before the feast of the blessed Katherine [24 November] for three weeks past £4. 16*s.* 11½*d.*

Grand total of this roll, £626. 6*s.* 1*d.*

Expenses in the carriage of Haslebury stone for the buttresses of the hall within the bailey of Winchester Castle at the feast of St. Bartholomew the Apostle in the sixth year of the reign of King Henry [*24 August 1222*].

Paid the same day to Richard Sired' to break up and extract 105 stones from Haslebury quarry £1. 3*s.* 4*d.*

On the same day to Adam de Wadesyk for 2 cart-loads of Haslebury stone carried to Winchester Castle 2*s.* 8*d.*

Oseberto de Seld' pro una caretata ii sol.
Waltero piscatori pro una caretata xii d.
Jordano Flur de Melkesham pro ii caretatis bonis v sol.

Liberatum Ricardo Durand' die Dominica proxima post festum beati Dunstani ad cariandum duos Sumirs ad chimeneiam aule infra turrim v sol.
Eadem die Thome filio Johannis pro duabus caretatis cariandis de Heselbur' de petris ad columpnas aule infra Ballium iiii sol.
Eadem die Radulfo Luctatori & sociis suis pro v caretatis de petris de Heselbur' cariandis ad castrum Winton' x sol.
Johanni Le Swon de Twford' pro duabus caretatis iiii sol.
Liberatum die Dominica proxima post festum Sancti Augustini Ricardo Lewine de Twford' & vi sociis suis pro vii caretatis de petris de Heselbur' cariandis ad castrum Winton' xiiii sol.
Ricardo Seger ad cariandum iii petras de Heselbur' ad aulam infra ballium die Dominica proxima post festum Sanctorum Marcellini & Petri ii sol.
In Vigilia Pentecostes scilicet Sancti Barnabe apostoli Ricardo Lewine & v sociis suis pro vi caretatis de petris cariandis de Heselbur' xii sol.
Item liberatum pro eodem cariagio anno Regni Regis Henrici
Item liberatum Ricardo Lewine & iiii sociis suis pro v caretatis de petris Heselbur' cariandis ad castrum Winton' ad magnam aulam die Sancti Johannis Baptiste x sol.
Item liberatum die Dominica proxima post festum beati Petri & Pauli Godefrido palmario pro tribus petris cariandis de Heselbur' per duas vices ii sol. viii d.
Ricardo Harper pro duabus petris cariandis ii sol. iiii d.
Nicolao Gode pro iiii petris cariandis iiii sol. viii d.
Ricardo de Kosham pro ii petris cariandis ii sol. iiii d.

Item liberatum die Dominica proxima post festum beati Grimboldi
Ricardo Leyne & v sociis suis pro vi caretatis cariandis ad castrum Winton' de Heselbur' xii sol.
Item Johanni Wudreman eadem die ad cariandum ii petras xxii d.
Waltero de putta ad cariandum ii petras xxii d.
Jordano de Melkesham ad cariandum i petram xi d.
Nicolao Gode de Kosham ad cariandum ii petras xxii d.
Godefrido de Kosham ad cariandum unam petram & i tabulam xiii d.

To Osbert of Shalden for one cart-load 2*s*. o*d*.
To Walter the fisherman for one cart-load 1*s*. o*d*.
To Jordan Flur of Melksham for two good cart-loads 5*s*. o*d*.

Paid to Richard Durand on Sunday next after the feast of the blessed Dunstan [21 May][1] to carry two somers for the chimney of the hall within the tower 5*s*. o*d*.
On the same day to Thomas son of John for carriage of two cart-loads of Haslebury stone for the buttresses of the hall within the bailey 4*s*. o*d*.
On the same day to Ralph the Wrestler and his mates for carrying 5 cart-loads of Haslebury stone to Winchester Castle 10*s*. o*d*.
To John Le Swon of Twyford for two cart-loads 4*s*. o*d*.
Paid on Sunday next after the feast of St. Augustine [28 May] to Richard Lewine of Twyford and his 6 mates for carrying 7 cart-loads of Haslebury stone to Winchester Castle 14*s*. o*d*.
To Richard Seger to carry 3 pieces of Haslebury stone to the hall within the bailey on Sunday next after the feast of Saints Marcellinus and Peter [4 June] 2*s*. o*d*.
On the vigil of Whitsun, that is on the day of St. Barnabas the Apostle [11 June 1223] to Richard Lewine and his 5 mates for carrying 6 cart-loads of Haslebury stone 12*s*. o*d*.
And paid for the same carriage in the [*7th*] *year of the reign of King Henry*
And paid to Richard Lewine and his 4 mates for carriage of 5 cart-loads of Haslebury stone to Winchester Castle for the great hall on St. John Baptist's Day [24 June] 10*s*. o*d*.
And paid on Sunday next after the feast of the blessed Peter and Paul [2 July]: to Godfrey the palmer for carrying three pieces of Haslebury stone on two occasions 2*s*. 8*d*.
to Richard Harper for carrying two stones 2*s*. 4*d*.
To Nicholas Gode for carrying 4 stones 4*s*. 8*d*.
To Richard of Cosham for carrying 2 stones 2*s*. 4*d*.

And paid on Sunday next after the feast of the blessed Grimbold [*9 July*]*:*
To Richard Leyne and his 5 mates for carrying 6 cart-loads from Haslebury to Winchester Castle 12*s*. o*d*.
And to John Wudreman the same day to carry 2 stones 1*s*. 10*d*.
To Walter of Putte to carry 2 stones 1*s*. 10*d*.
To Jordan of Melksham to carry 1 stone 11*d*.
To Nicholas Gode of Cosham to carry 2 stones 1*s*. 10*d*.
To Godfrey of Cosham to carry one stone and 1 board 1*s*. 1*d*.

[1] Apparently in the same year as subsequent entries which belong to 1223.

Item liberatum die Dominica proxima ante festum beate Margarete Virginis

Thome filio Johannis de Twford' ad cariandum ii petras xxii d.
Johanni Belami ad cariandum ii petras xxii d.
Alexandro de Saldeford' pro ii petris cariandis xxii d.
Godefrido de fonte pro ii petris cariandis xxii d.
Reginaldo de Melkesham pro ii petris cariandis xxii d.
Ade de Melkesham pro una caretata xiiii d.
Godefrido de Hynham pro i caretata xiii d.
Jordano de Melkesham pro i caretata xii d.
Baldewino iuxta boscum pro i caretata xii d.

Item liberatum die beate Margarete Virginis

Balde[w]yno iuxta boscum pro ii petris cariandis de Heselbur' xviii d.
Reginaldo iuxta boscum pro iii petris cariandis xxii d.

Item liberatum quareariis de Heselbur' ad petras extrahendas de quariria sua ad columpnas aule infra Ballium in castro Winton' xvi sol. viii d.

Liberatum die Dominica proxima post festum beate Marie Magdalene

Reginaldo de Melkesham pro tribus petris cariandis xviii d.
Balde[w]yno iuxta Boscum pro una petra carianda xii d.
Jordano de Melkesham pro i petra carianda xi d.
Ade de Binekere ad cariandum unam petram cum ii tabulis xiiii d.
Giliberto de Melkesham pro ii petris cariandis xii d.

Liberatum die Jovis proxima post festum beati Jacobi apostoli

Willelmo Pelling' ad cariandum ii petras de Heselbur' xii d.
Johanni Taleman ad cariandum unam petram vii d.
Nicolao de putta ad cariandum iii petras xviii d.

Liberatum die Dominica proxima ante festum Sancti Laurencii

Giliberto de Melkesham ad cariandam unam petram x d.

Liberatum die beati Mathei apostoli

Reginaldo de Melkesham ad cariandum iii petras xxii d.
Giliberto de Melkesham ad cariandum i petram x d.
Baldewino iuxta boscum ad cariandum ii petras xviii d.

Liberatum die Dominica proxima post Decollacionem Sancti Johannis

Willelmo Pelling' pro tribus caretatis petrarum de Heselbur' iii sol. ix d.
Johanni Taleman pro tribus caretatis iii sol. ix d.

And paid on Sunday next before the feast of the blessed Margaret the Virgin [16 July]:

To Thomas son of John of Twyford to carry 2 stones 1*s.* 10*d.*
To John Belami to carry 2 stones 1*s.* 10*d.*
To Alexander of Shawford for carrying 2 stones 1*s.* 10*d.*
To Godfrey of the well for carrying 2 stones 1*s.* 10*d.*
To Reginald of Melksham for carrying 2 stones 1*s.* 10*d.*
To Adam of Melksham for one cart-load 1*s.* 2*d.*
To Godfrey of Highnam for 1 cart-load 1*s.* 1*d.*
To Jordan of Melksham for 1 cart-load 1*s.* 0*d.*
To Baldwin by the wood for 1 cart-load 1*s.* 0*d.*

And paid on the day of the blessed Margaret the Virgin [20 July]:

To Baldwin by the wood for carrying 2 stones from Haslebury 1*s.* 6*d.*
To Reginald by the wood for carrying 3 stones 1*s.* 10*d.*

And paid to the quarrymen of Haslebury to extract stones from their quarry for the buttresses of the hall within the bailey in Winchester Castle 16*s.* 8*d.*

Paid on Sunday next after the feast of the blessed Mary Magdalen [23 July]:

To Reginald of Melksham for carrying three stones 1*s.* 6*d.*
To Baldwin by the wood for carrying one stone 1*s.* 0*d.*
To Jordan of Melksham for carrying one stone 11*d.*
To Adam of Binegar to carry one stone with 2 boards 1*s.* 2*d.*
To Gilbert of Melksham for carrying 2 stones 1*s.* 0*d.*

Paid on Thursday next after the feast of the blessed James the Apostle [27 July]:

To William Pelling to carry 2 stones from Haslebury 1*s.* 0*d.*
To John Taleman to carry one stone 7*d.*
To Nicholas of Putte to carry 3 stones 1*s.* 6*d.*

Paid on Sunday next before the feast of St. Laurence [6 August]:

To Gilbert of Melksham to carry one stone 10*d.*

Paid on the day of the blessed Matthew the Apostle [21 September]:

To Reginald of Melksham to carry 3 stones 1*s.* 10*d.*
To Gilbert of Melksham to carry 1 stone 10*d.*
To Baldwin by the wood to carry 2 stones 1*s.* 6*d.*

Paid on Sunday next after the Decollation of St. John [3 September]:

To William Pelling for three cart-loads of stone from Haslebury 3*s.* 9*d.*
To John Taleman for three cart-loads 3*s.* 9*d.*

Item Reginaldo de Melkesham ad cariandum iii petras de Heselbur' die Sancti Bartholomei apostoli ad castrum Winton' xviii d.
Eadem die Giliberto de Melkesham ad cariandum i petram vii d.
Baldewyno iuxta boscum ad cariandum ii petras xiiii d.

Summa huius Rotuli ix li. iiii sol. v d.

Expensa in rebus emptis ad reparacionem Castri Winton' necessariis. Liberata per manus Maioris Winton', Magistri Henrici de Cerne & Alani de Hereford' anno Regni Regis Henrici sexto ad festum beati Gregorii pape quando primo inceperunt operacionem Castri predicti, & per manus Rogeri Coleman & Johannis Cobbe.

Liberatum eadem die per manus predictorum scilicet die beati Gregorii pape
Ade de calce pro C sextariis de calce lxxv sol.
pro l bordis xviii d.
pro vi tinis xiiii d.
pro xxv keveruns ad reparandum le astelir viii d.
uni garcioni qui ivit in nuncio apud Seleborn' ii d.
pro una bursa ad imponendum denarios i d.
Willelmo Quareario & Ricardo socio suo pro mille petris tractandis de quariria sua promtis ad cariandum ad castrum Winton' xviii sol. iiii d.
Johanni de Baioco pro sabulo iii sol. vi d.
In duabus civiris ii d.
pro uno trabo ad reparandum cameram infra turrim xiiii d.
pro una serrura vi d.

In die Mercurii proxima sequente pro ii cornicibus ad frangendum murum & iii cuinz iii sol.
eadem die pro una fune viii d.
pro uno doleo viii d.
pro alia fune viii d.
In die Veneris proxima sequente in virgis iii d.
pro plumbo ii d.
Item pro una serrura vi d.
Item Roberto aurifabro pro ii trabis ad dictam cameram reparandam xx d.
pro xx hes de ferro viii sol. iiii d.
pro v frustris de acir ii sol.
pro ii bukettis iii ob.
pro mille clavis laterez xii d.
in virgis i d.

And to Reginald of Melksham on the day of St. Bartholomew the Apostle [24 August] to carry 3 stones from Haslebury to Winchester Castle 1*s.* 6*d.*
On the same day to Gilbert of Melksham to carry 1 stone 7*d.*
To Baldwin by the wood to carry 2 stones 1*s.* 2*d.*

Total of this roll, £9. 4*s.* 5*d.*

Expenditure on the purchase of things needed for the repair of Winchester Castle. Paid by the hands of the Mayor of Winchester, Master Henry of Cerne, and Alan of Hereford on the feast of the blessed Gregory the pope in the sixth year of the reign of King Henry [*12 March 1222*], *and by the hands of Roger Coleman and John Cobbe.*

Paid on the same day by the hands of the aforesaid, that is on the day of the blessed Pope Gregory [*12 March*]
To Adam the lime-man for 100 sesters of lime £3. 15*s.* 0*d.*
for 50 boards 1*s.* 6*d.*
for 6 tubs 1*s.* 2*d.*
for 25 rafters to repair the masons' workshop 8*d.*
to a boy who went with a message to Selborne 2*d.*
for a purse to put pennies in 1*d.*
to William the quarryman and Richard his fellow for drawing a thousand stones from his quarry for carriage to Winchester Castle 18*s.* 4*d.*
to John de Baiuse for sand 3*s.* 6*d.*
for two barrows 2*d.*
for one beam to repair the chamber within the tower 1*s.* 2*d.*
for one lock 6*d.*

On the Wednesday following [*16 March*] for 2 crow-bars to break the wall and 3 wedges 3*s.* 0*d.*
on the same day for a rope 8*d.*
for one cask 8*d.*
for another rope 8*d.*
On the following Friday [*18 March*] for 2 withies 3*d.*
for a lead [vat?] 2*d.*
And for a lock 6*d.*
And to Robert the goldsmith for 2 beams to repair the said chamber 1*s.* 8*d.*
for 20 *hes* of iron 8*s.* 4*d.*
for 5 pieces of steel 2*s.* 0*d.*
for 2 buckets 1½*d.*
for a thousand lath-nails 1*s.* 0*d.*
for withies 1*d.*

Item Willelmo le Specir pro uno ligno ad cameram	xx d.
Ade Dwelie pro mille pedibus de petris de Insula	xl sol.
Summa viii li. iii sol. ob.	
Liberatum per predictos die Sancti Benedicti pro vii saccis de carbone	xiiii d.
Roberto aurifabro pro CCCC caretatis de kaildo	xxvi sol.
In vigilia Annunciacionis beate Marie pro bordis	vi d. ob.
Eadem die iiii^or^ serratoribus	viii d.
pro CC de latis	x d.
pro duabus caretatis de carbone	v sol. iiii d.
pro ii beschis	i d.
pro mille clavis laterez	xiiii d.
pro duabus funibus	ii d. ob.
pro una serrura	i d.
pro ii criblis	iii ob.
pro uno trunco ad fabricam	viii d.
Roberto fabro pro clavis & gunfis	iiii d.
Item pro iiii malleis de ferro	ii sol.
ad cariandum unam caretatam de virgis de bosco Domini Episcopi Winton' ad castrum Winton'	iii d. ob.
Item pro bordis in crastino Floride Pasche	ix sol. iii d. ob.
pro una serrura	ii d.
pro iii caretatis de bosco ad plumbum jactandum	xvi d.
in percameno	i d.
filio Brumman pro clavis plancheriz	ii d. ob.
Item eidem pro D clavis Bordelez	vi d.
pro una civir	i d.
pro uno veteri plumbo	xxviii d.
Willelmo parvo pro una chareata plumbi	xxx sol.
pro eadem carianda ad castrum	iii d. ob.
ad deferendum sabulum ad plumbum iactandum	ii d.
pro v caretatis virgarum cariandis ad castrum de bosco Episcopi	ii sol.
pro vi serruris	iii sol. iiii d.
Item pro virgis	iiii d.
Item pro bordis ad gutturas	viii d.
Item xviii keveruns	viii d.
pro lardo ad solvendum plumbum	i d.
Item pro mille clavis laterez	xiiii d.
Item pro una fune	viii d.

And to William le Specir for one piece of wood for the chamber	1s. 8d.
to Adam Dwelie for a thousand feet of Isle of Wight stone	£2. 0s. 0d.

Total £8. 3s. 0½d.

Paid by the aforesaid on St. Benedict's Day [*21 March*] for 7 sacks of charcoal	1s. 2d.
to Robert the goldsmith for 400 cart-loads of flints	£1. 6s. 0d.
On the vigil of the Annunciation of the blessed Mary [24 March] for boards	6½d.
On the same day to four sawyers	8d.
for 2 hundredweight of laths	10d.
for two cart-loads of charcoal	5s. 4d.
for 2 spades	1d.
for a thousand lath-nails	1s. 2d.
for two ropes	2½d.
for one lock	1d.
for 2 sieves	1½d.
for one trough for the forge	8d.
to Robert the smith for nails and hooks	4d.
And for 4 iron hammers	2s. 0d.
to carry a cart-load of withies from the lord bishop of Winchester's wood to Winchester Castle	3½d.
And for boards on the day after Palm Sunday [28 March]	9s. 3½d.
for one lock	2d.
for 3 cart-loads of wood to cast lead	1s. 4d.
for parchment	1d.
to Brumman's son for plank-nails	2½d.
And to him for 500 board-nails	6d.
for one barrow	1d.
for one old lead[-vat?]	2s. 4d.
to William Small for one char of lead	30s. 0d.
for carrying it to the castle	3½d.
to carry sand to cast lead	2d.
for carriage of 5 cart-loads of withies to the castle from the bishop's wood	2s. 0d.
for 6 locks	3s. 4d.
And for withies	4d.
And for boards for gutters	8d.
And for 18 rafters	8d.
for lard to found lead	1d.
And for a thousand lath-nails	1s. 2d.
And for a rope	8d.

pro ii civiris	ii d.
pro kevildis	iii d.
cuidam nuncio qui ivit pro Girardo le mineur	iiii d.
Item pro C sextariis de calce	lxxv sol.
Johanni de Spena iuxta Niwbur' pro una chareata plumbi	xxx sol.
Ricardo filio Augeri de Bureford' pro una chareata plumbi	xxx sol.

Summa xi li. viii sol. vii d. ob.

Item liberatum die Jovis proxima.

Domino Johanni de Andelia eadem die pro vi^xx quercubus in bosco suo de Kandevr'	vii li.
In carbone	ii sol.
pro xii civires	ix d.
pro una arca	xii d. ob.
pro Bordis	vii d.
pro uno malleo de ferro	xii d.
pro ii serruris	viii d.
Siberno fabro per manus Rogeri Koleman pro ferro	v sol.
Item per manus eiusdem pro duabus summis de ferro apud Andevr'	xxiiii sol.
pro corce ad preparandum les fows ad fabricam Domini Regis	xix d.
Reginaldo palmario & Bernardo socio suo ad cariandum ducentas petras de Seleborn' ad castrum Winton'	xii sol.
Henrico le Quareur pro C petris cariandis	vi sol.
Galfrido le quareur pro C petris cariandis	vi sol.
Henrico de Ymesat' pro ducentis petris cariandis	xii sol.
Willelmo Bathele pro ducentis petris cariandis	xii sol.
Johanni de Okangr' pro ducentis petris cariandis	xii sol.

Summa xi li. xvi sol. vii d. ob.

Liberatum die Dominica proxima ante festum Sancti Marci Ewangeliste pro pluribus rebus captis in septimana proxima precedenti ad castrum Winton' reparandum necessariis.

pro l bordis	v d. ob.
Petro filio Godwini pro xxxi keveruns	xx d.
Willelmo palmario pro xv keveruns	xii d.
pro bosco ad inponendum minerie	xv d.

for 2 barrows	2*d.*
for pegs	3*d.*
to a certain messenger who went for Gerard the miner	4*d.*
And for 100 sesters of lime	£3. 15*s.* 0*d.*
To John of Speen by Newbury for one char of lead	£1. 10*s.* 0*d.*
To Richard son of Auger of Burford for one char of lead	£1. 10*s.* 0*d.*

Total £11. 8*s.* 7½*d.*

And paid on the Thursday following [*31 March*].

To Sir John de Andely on the same day for 120 oaks in his wood at Candover	£7. 0*s.* 0*d.*
For charcoal	2*s.* 0*d.*
for 12 barrows	9*d.*
for a chest	1*s.* 0½*d.*
for boards	7*d.*
for an iron hammer	1*s.* 0*d.*
for 2 locks	8*d.*
to Sibern the smith by the hands of Roger Coleman for iron	5*s.* 0*d.*
And by the hands of the same for two seams of iron at Andover	£1. 4*s.* 0*d.*
for bark to prepare the bellows for the lord king's forge	1*s.* 7*d.*
to Reginald the palmer and Bernard his mate to carry 200 stones from Selborne to Winchester Castle	12*s.* 0*d.*
to Henry the quarryman for carrying 100 stones	6*s.* 0*d.*
to Geoffrey the quarryman for carrying 100 stones	6*s.* 0*d.*
to Henry of Empshot for carrying 200 stones	12*s.* 0*d.*
to William Bathele for carrying 200 stones	12*s.* 0*d.*
to John of Oakhanger for carrying 200 stones	12*s.* 0*d.*

Total £11. 16*s.* 7½*d.*

Paid on Sunday next before the feast of St. Mark the Evangelist [*24 April*] *for various things needed for the repair of Winchester Castle obtained during the week immediately preceding.*

for 50 boards	5½*d.*
to Peter son of Godwin for 31 rafters	1*s.* 8*d.*
to William the palmer for 15 rafters	1*s.* 0*d.*
for wood to put in the mine[1]	1*s.* 3*d.*

[1] This mine may have been a legacy of the siege of 1216, when the castle had been severely damaged.

pro bosco ad illuminandum rogum	xvii sol. i d.
pro carbone	xv d.
pro bordis ad mineriam	iiii d. ob.
in percameno	i d.
ad locandum unum equum ad opus Rogeri Koleman qui ivit ad boscum	vi d.
Gerardo le mineur ad purgandum fundamentum nove turris & ad prosternendum unam partem muris [*sic*]	lx sol.

Summa iiii li. iii sol. viii d.

Item liberatum die Dominica proxima ante Invencionem Sancte Crucis pro rebus captis in septimana proxima precedenti ad castrum reparandum necessariis.

In carbone	xx d.
In bosco ad rogum	vi d.
pro xvi keveruns	x d.
pro una gata & duobus bukettis	iiii d.
In virgis	iii d.
pro xxv bordis	v d.
pro xii bordis ad faciendum civires	iii d.
pro una pelle leporis ad fows	i d.
pro uno criblo	ob.
In cimento	ii d. ob.
In carbone	xx d.
In expensis ad carettas perquirendas apud Basing' & alibi	ii sol. ix d.
Ricardo de Merstedwell' pro xxiii keveruns	x d.
Godwino de Wyttrewa pro xiiii keveruns	xiiii d.
Cuidam nuncio qui ivit apud Weredun' propter fratrem	ix d.
alii nuncio qui ivit apud Sanctam Radegundam propter alium fratrem	ix d.
Item alii qui ivit London' ad Episcopum Winton' ut perquireret cementarios	ii d.
pro x gatis	ix d. ob.

for wood to fire the kiln	17*s*. 1*d*.
for charcoal	1*s*. 3*d*.
for boards for the mine	4½*d*.
for parchment	1*d*.
to hire one horse for the use of Roger Coleman in going to the wood	6*d*.
to Gerard the miner to clear out the foundation of the new tower and to pull down part of the wall	£3. 0*s*. 0*d*.

Total £4. 3*s*. 8*d*.

And paid on Sunday next before the Invention of the Holy Cross [*1 May*] *for things needed to repair the castle obtained during the week immediately preceding.*

for charcoal	1*s*. 8*d*.
for wood for the kiln	6*d*.
for 16 rafters	10*d*.
for one bowl[1] and two buckets	4*d*.
for withies	3*d*.
for 25 boards	5*d*.
for 12 boards to make barrows	3*d*.
for one hare-skin for the bellows	1*d*.
for one sieve	½*d*.
for cement	2½*d*.
for charcoal	1*s*. 8*d*.
for expenses in obtaining carts at Basing and elsewhere	2*s*. 9*d*.
to Richard of Morestead (?) for 23 rafters	10*d*.
to Godwin de Wyttrewe for 14 rafters	1*s*. 2*d*.
to a certain messenger who went to Warden to fetch a brother[2]	9*d*.
to another messenger who went to St. Radegund's to fetch another brother[3]	9*d*.
And to another who went to London to the Bishop of Winchester to obtain masons	2*d*.
for 10 bowls	9½*d*.

[1] Or 'trough'.

[2] Warden was a Cistercian abbey in Bedfordshire. In view of the next entry the 'brother' in question was evidently a Cistercian monk with special knowledge of building whose help was needed at Winchester.

[3] St. Radegund's was a house of Premonstratensian canons near Dover. In 1212 a 'brother Thomas' of St. Radegund's was working for the king at Dover with a squad of carpenters. He appears to have been skilled in mining, for 'brother Thomas's tunnel' is mentioned in the Dover accounts. It may have been his employment at Winchester that led the abbot of Prémontré to write to Hubert de Burgh early in the reign of Henry III authorizing his retention in the king's service provided he did nothing incompatible with his religious calling (*History of the King's Works*, ii, p. 637, n. 11 and references there cited).

pro carbone	xiiii d.
pro una arca ad calcem mensurandam	xii d.
Ade de Calce pro uno rogo faciendo	l sol.
Galfrido de Hida pro duabus columpnis ad fenestras	xviii d.
pro una arca	xv d.
Johanni le verur pro tribus fenestris vitreis ad capellam Sancte Katerine	vi sol.
Morando pro quingentis pedibus petrarum de Insula	xv sol.
Eidem pro ducentis kuinz & esselirs	vii sol.
pro viii tinellis	ii d.
pro vii serruris de Willelmo Muth	vi sol. ii d.
Godefrido de Sancto Jacobo in cuius terra creta ad rogum effoditur	xii d.
Petro de Quidhamtun' pro xlii hes de ferro	xiii sol. vi d.
Magistro Baldewino ad sternendum aulam infra ballium salvo meirimio	lxvi sol. viii d.
Albino le Verur pro iiii fenestris vitreis ad capellam Sancti Thome Martiris	xii sol.
In carbone	xx d.
Galfrido Nigro pro iii sextariis de calce	ii sol. iii d.
Willelmo palmario pro bordis	xxvi sol. vi d.
Waltero de Esford' pro xlv keveruns	xviii d.
Item Petro de Quidhamtun' pro una summa & xvii hes de ferro	xiii sol. vi d.
pro iii bukettis	iiii d.
pro uno doleo	ix d.
In virgis	vii d.
pro funibus ad cameram Domini Regis	i d.

Summa xii li. iii sol. vii d. ob.

Item liberatum die Sabbati proxima post festum Sancti Dunstani pro rebus captis ab Invencione Sancte Crucis ad castrum reparandum necessariis.

Morando pro DC pedibus de petris de Insula de tablamento	xxiiii sol.
pro bosco ad illuminandum rogum	viii d.
In carbone	vii d. ob.
Galfrido Blakeman pro xxviii sextariis de calce	xxv sol.
pro duobus frustris de acir	ii sol. i d.
In stipendiis duorum equorum ad opus constabularii & Rogeri Koleman qui iverunt ad boscum in negociis Domini Regis	x d.

for charcoal 1s. 2d.
for one box to measure lime 1s. 0d.
to Adam the lime-man for making one kiln £2. 10s. 0d.
to Geoffrey of Hyde for two columns for windows 1s. 6d.
for one chest 1s. 3d.
to John the glazier for three glass windows for the Chapel of St. Katherine[1] 6s. 0d.
to Morand for 500 feet of Isle of Wight stone 15s. 0d.
to him for 200 coins and ashlars 7s. 0d.
for 8 small tubs 2d.
for 7 locks from William Muth 6s. 2d.
to Godfrey of St. James, in whose land chalk is dug for the kiln 1s. 0d.
to Peter of Quidhampton for 42 *hes* of iron 13s. 6d.
to Master Baldwin to demolish the hall within the bailey, saving the timber £3. 6s. 8d.
to Albin the glazier for 4 glass windows for the chapel of St. Thomas the Martyr[2] 12s. 0d.
for charcoal 1s. 8d.
to Geoffrey Black for 3 sesters of lime 2s. 3d.
to William the palmer for boards £1. 6s. 6d.
to Walter of Ashford for 45 rafters 1s. 6d.
And to Peter of Quidhampton for one seam and 17 *hes* of iron 13s. 6d.
for 3 buckets 4d.
for one cask 9d.
for withies 7d.
for ropes for the lord king's chamber 1d.

Total £12. 3s. 7½d.

And paid on Saturday next after the feast of St. Dunstan [*21 May*] *for things needed for the repair of the castle obtained since the Invention of the Holy Cross* [*3 May*].

to Morand for 600 feet of Isle of Wight stones for tablements £1. 4s. 0d.
for wood to fire the kiln 8d.
for charcoal 7½d.
to Geoffrey Blackman for 28 sesters of lime £1. 5s. 0d.
for two pieces of steel 2s. 1d.
paid for two horses for the use of the constable and Roger Coleman, who went to the wood on the king's business 10d.

[1] This chapel was in the keep (*History of the King's Works*, ii, p. 862).
[2] For this chapel see *History of the King's Works*, ii, pp. 861–2.

Pagano de Christi monasterio pro septingentis pedibus de tablamento petrarum de Insula	xxviii sol.
Johanni de Andelia pro vi^{xx} & x quercubus in bosco suo de Candevr'	vi libri
Ricardo le Cuvir pro l bordis	xxviii d.
palmario pro l bordis	ii sol. vi d.
In carbone	xxi d.
Item in carbone	xx d.
Capellano ad deferendum brevia pro cementariis	xii d.
Willelmo Bathele pro mille petris tractandis de quariria sua	xviii sol. iiii d.

Summa xi li. viii sol. ix d. ob.

Item liberatum die Dominica proxima ante festum Sancti Barnabe apostoli pro rebus captis a die Sabbati proxima ante festum Sancti Dunstani.

Godwino palmario pro C & lxx bordis	ix sol.
Item eidem pro xxv keveruns	ix d.
Willelmo de Peteresfeld' pro xxiiii keveruns	xi d.
Eidem pro xii keveruns	xi d.
Giliberto de Legha pro vii keveruns	iiii d.
Reginaldo de Blakemer pro vi saccis de carbone	ix d.
pro uno bucello ad tractandam aquam	ix d.
Willelmo le Carbunir pro C bordis de few	xx d.
Morando pro D pedibus de petris de Insula	xx sol.
Pagano de Christi monasterio pro mille & ducentis pedibus de petris de Insula	xlviii sol.
Eidem pro CCCC petris scilicet Cuinz & Esselirs	xiiii sol.
Willelmo Muthe pro tribus serruris & j pendente & duabus clavis	iii sol. iii d.
Henrico le Cuvir pro circulis	iiii d. ob.
Henrico le Quareur ad cariandum C petras de Seleborn'	vi. sol.
Galfrido le Quareur ad cariandum C petras	v sol.
Ricardo & Willelmo socio suo le quareur pro ducentis petris cariandis ad castrum Winton'	x sol.
Henrico de Ymesat' pro ducentis petris cariandis ad castrum Winton'	x sol.
Johanni de Okangr' & sociis suis pro ducentis petris cariandis	x sol.

Summa vii li. viii d. ob.

Item liberatum die Dominica proxima post festum Sancti Barnabe apostoli pro rebus captis in septimana proxima precedenti.

In stipendiis duorum equorum ad videndum boscum	xv d.
Simoni Cornub' pro una fune	vi d. ob.

to Payn of Christchurch for 700 feet of Isle of Wight stones for tablements	£1. 8s. od.
to John de Andely for 130 oaks in his wood at Candover	£6. os. od.
to Richard the cooper for 50 boards	2s. 4d.
to the palmer for 50 boards	2s. 6d.
for charcoal	1s. 9d.
And for charcoal	1s. 8d.
to the chaplain to carry writs for masons[1]	1s. od.
to William Bathele for drawing 1,000 stones out of his quarry	18s. 4d.

Total £11. 8s. 9½d.

And paid on Sunday next before the feast of St. Barnabas the Apostle [*5 June*] *for things obtained since Saturday next before the feast of St. Dunstan* [*14 May*]

to Godwin the palmer for 170 boards	9s. od.
And to him for 25 rafters	9d.
to William of Petersfield for 24 rafters	11d.
to him for 12 rafters	11d.
to Gilbert of Leigh for 7 rafters	4d.
to Reginald of Blackmoor for 6 sacks of charcoal	9d.
for one butt to draw up water	9d.
to William the charcoal-burner for 100 beech boards	1s. 8d.
to Morand for 500 feet of Isle of Wight stones	£1. os. od.
to Payn of Christchurch for 1,200 feet of Isle of Wight stones	£2. 8s. od.
to him for 400 stones, that is coins and ashlars	14s. od.
to William Muthe for 3 locks and 1 padlock and 2 keys	3s. 3d.
to Henry the cooper for hoops	4½d.
to Henry the quarryman to carry 100 stones from Selborne	6s.
to Geoffrey the quarryman to carry 100 stones	5s.
to Richard and his fellow William the quarryman for carrying 200 stones to Winchester Castle	10s.
to Henry of Empshot for carrying 200 stones to Winchester Castle	10s.
to John of Oakhanger and his fellows for carrying 200 stones	10s.

Total £7. os. 8½d.

And paid on Sunday next after the feast of St. Barnabas the Apostle [*12 June*] *for things obtained during the previous week.*

paid for two horses to inspect the wood	1s. 3d.
to Simon the Cornishman for a rope	6½d.

[1] Possibly for their compulsory recruitment by impressment.

Reginaldo de Legha pro xxv keveruns	xi d.
Giliberto de Legha pro l keveruns	xviii d.
Gocelino palmario pro viii keveruns	vi d.
In virgis	v d.
Willelmo palmario pro C & lxxv bordis de fow	v sol. iii d.
Filio Godwini pro xii bordis	xii d.
Carpentariis pro vi^{xx} & x quercubus prosternendis in bosco de Candevr’	ix sol. ii d. ob.
pro eisdem carpentandis ad cariandum salvis Domino Regi omnibus escheitis	xxvii sol. i d.
Servienti nostro ad custodiendum meirimium & boscum ad rogum per xv dies	ii sol. iiii d.
forestario eiusdem bosci	vi d.
pro una fune	iii ob.
In virgis	iiii d.
Waltero de Wald’ pro una arca & una tina	xvi d.
Hawysie pro una tina	iii d.
Ricardo le Cuvir pro v bordis ad hostia	viii d.
Roberto King pro viii gatis & uno buketto & una tina	x d. ob.
pro una mola ad habendum in astelerio	iiii d.
Petro de Peteresfeld’ pro xvi saccis de carbone	xx d.
Willelmo de Brudeport’ pro una fune	vii d.
Unfrido ferrario & Thome de Spen’ pro duabus chareatis plumbi	lx sol.
pro duabus summis de ferro	xix sol.
pro xvi frustris de acir	viii sol.
Willelmo Muthe pro una serrura	iiii d.
Willelmo Bathele pro diversis petris cariandis de Seleborn’	x sol.

Summa vii li. xiiii sol.

Item liberatum die Dominica proxima post festum Sancti Johannis Baptiste de rebus captis a die Dominica proxima post festum Sancti Barnabe.

Thome de Serebroc pro xv keveruns	viii d.
Eidem pro xxiiii keveruns	x d.
pro una scala	iiii d. ob.
Johanni de Bertun’ pro duabus chareatis plumbi	lx sol.
Domine Ymenai pro xii mensuris de caildo	iii sol.
Roberto de Mara pro l bordis ad celandum	xvi d.
Giliberto de Legha pro lxxv bordis	xxi d.
In virgis	iii d.
Radulfo Tocer pro uno trunco ad secandum	vii d.

to Reginald of Leigh for 25 rafters	11*d.*
to Gilbert of Leigh for 50 rafters	1*s.* 6*d.*
to Jocelyn the palmer for 8 rafters	6*d.*
for withies	5*d.*
to William the palmer for 175 boards of beech	5*s.* 3*d.*
to Godwin's son for 12 boards	1*s.* 0*d.*
to the carpenters for felling 130 oaks in Candover wood	9*s.* 2½*d.*
for the carpentry of the same [ready] for carriage, reserving all toppings to the lord king	£1. 7*s.* 1*d.*
to our servant to guard the timber and wood for the kiln for 15 days	2*s.* 4*d.*
to the forester of the same wood	6*d.*
for a rope	1½*d.*
for withies	4*d.*
to Walter of Wield for a chest and a tub	1*s.* 4*d.*
to Hawise for a tub	3*d.*
to Richard the cooper for 5 boards for doors	8*d.*
to Robert King for 8 bowls and a bucket and a tub	10½*d.*
for a whetstone[1] to have in the masons' workshop	4*d.*
to Peter of Petersfield for 16 sacks of charcoal	1*s.* 8*d.*
to William of Bridport for a rope	7*d.*
to Humfrey the iron-worker and Thomas of Speen for two chars of lead	£3. 0*s.* 0*d.*
for two seams of iron	19*s.* 0*d.*
for 16 pieces of steel	8*s.* 0*d.*
to William Muthe for a lock	4*d.*
to William Bathele for carrying divers stones from Selborne	10*s.* 0*d.*

Total £7. 14*s.* 0*d.*

And paid on Sunday next after the feast of St. John the Baptist [*26 June*] *for things obtained since Sunday next after the feast of St. Barnabas* [*12 June*].

to Thomas de Serebroc for 15 rafters	8*d.*
to him for 24 rafters	10*d.*
for a ladder	4½*d.*
to John of Berton for two chars of lead	£3. 0*s.* 0*d.*
to Lady Ymenay for 12 measures of flint	3*s.* 0*d.*
to Robert de la Mare for 50 boards for ceiling	1*s.* 4*d.*
to Gilbert of Leigh for 75 boards	1*s.* 9*d.*
for withies	3*d.*
to Ralph Tocer for a sawing-block	7*d.*

[1] Or 'grindstone'.

Domino Johanni de Andelia pro xx quercubus in bosco suo in Candever ad rogum alium	xx sol.
pro bosco ad illuminandum rogum	xii sol.
In percameno	iii d.
In clavis laterez ad capellam Sancti Joci	xiii d.
Godwino de Yntrewa pro xi bordis ad faciendum fenestras	xiii d. ob.
Willelmo palmario pro vii bordis	xii d.
Giliberto de Legha pro iii bordis	v d.
pro iiii millibus de kevildis	iiii d. ob.
pro xx quercubus sternendis & secandis ad cariandum	iii sol. iiii d.
pro kablis ad tractandum meirimium infra turrim	iiii sol. iiii d.
pro C caretatis de sabulo	iii sol. viii d.
In herba	ii d.
In sepo ad unguenda ingenia ad tractandum meirimium & aquam	iii d.
pro cimento	iii ob.
Ade de Calce ad faciendum secundum rogum	xl sol.
Eidem pro vii sextariis de calce	vi sol. iii d.

Summa viii li. iii sol. ii d.

Item liberatum die Dominica proxima post festum Sanctorum Petri & Pauli pro rebus captis a die Dominica proxima post festum Sancti Johannis Baptiste.

Roberto filio Petri le Carbunir pro xvi saccis de carbone	iii sol.
Waltero de la Bruer pro una summa carbonis	ii sol.
In sepo ad ingenia ungenda	ob.
In virgis	ii d. ob.
Willelmo le Carbunir pro iiii saccis de carbone	v d.
Willelmo palmario pro xxv bordis ad faciendum civeres	iii d.
Willelmo fromundo pro ii mill. clavis laterez	xiii d. ob.
Thome de Serebrok pro xxiiii keveruns	x d.
Eidem pro iii keveruns	i d.

Summa vii sol. xi d. ob.

Liberatum die Dominica proxima ante Translacionem Sancti Benedicti pro rebus emptis a die Dominica proxima post festum beatorum Petri & Pauli.

Roberto filio Ricardi pro vii saccis de carbone	x d. ob.
Ade de Seta pro xvii saccis de carbone	ii sol. iii ob.

to Sir John de Andely for 20 oaks in his wood in Candover for another kiln	£1. 0*s*. 0*d*.
for wood to fire the kiln	12*s*. 0*d*.
for parchment	3*d*.
for lath-nails for the chapel of St. Judoc[1]	1*s*. 1*d*.
to Godwin de Yntrewa for 11 boards to make windows[2]	1*s*. 1½*d*.
to William the palmer for 7 boards	1*s*. 0*d*.
to Gilbert of Leigh for 3 boards	5*d*.
for 4,000 pegs	4½*d*.
for felling 20 oaks and cutting them up for carriage	3*s*. 4*d*.
for cables to haul timber within the tower	4*s*. 4*d*.
for 100 cart-loads of sand	3*s*. 8*d*.
for grass	2*d*.
for tallow to lubricate the engines for drawing timber and water	3*d*.
for cement	1½*d*.
to Adam the lime-man to make a second kiln	£2. 0*s*. 0*d*.
to him for 7 sesters of lime	6*s*. 4*d*.

Total £8. 3*s*. 2*d*.

And paid on Sunday next after the feast of Saints Peter and Paul [*3 July*] *for things obtained since Sunday next after the feast of St. John the Baptist* [*26 June*].

to Robert son of Peter the charcoal-burner for 16 sacks of charcoal	3*s*. 0*d*.
to Walter de la Bruer for one seam of charcoal	2*s*. 0*d*.
for tallow to lubricate the engines	½*d*.
for withies	2½*d*.
to William the charcoal-burner for 4 sacks of charcoal	5*d*.
to William the palmer for 25 boards to make barrows	3*d*.
to William Fromund for 2,000 lath-nails	1*s*. 1½*d*.
to Thomas de Serebroc for 24 rafters	10*d*.
to him for 3 rafters	1*d*.

Total 7*s*. 11½*d*.

Paid on Sunday next before the Translation of St. Benedict [*10 July*] *for things bought since Sunday next after the feast of the blessed Peter and Paul* [*3 July*].

to Robert son of Richard for 7 sacks of charcoal	10½*d*.
to Adam of Sheet for 17 sacks of charcoal	2*s*. 1½*d*.

[1] For this chapel see *History of the King's Works*, ii, p. 862.
[2] i.e. shutters for unglazed windows.

Radulfo de Langris pro xix saccis	xxvii d. ob.
In virgis	iiii d.
Johanni Seman pro iiii saccis de carbone	x d.
Roberto de la mare pro xxi keveruns	ix d.
Godwino de Ymtrewa pro xxv keveruns	vii d.
In virgis	vii d.
Item pro caretata de carbone	ii sol.
pro uno buketto	ii d.
Ricardo de Merstedewell pro xxv keveruns	ix d.
In virgis	iii d.
Siberno fabro pro acir	xv d.
Ade de Calce pro iii sextariis de calce	iii sol.
Waltero scriptori	v marce

Summa iiii li. ii sol. v d. ob.

Liberatum die Dominica proxima ante festum beate Margarete Virginis pro rebus emptis in septimana proxima precedenti.

Roberto de Helda pro xvi saccis de carbone	ii sol.
Alfrich' de Ludeneia pro una summa ferri	ix sol. vi d.
Roberto nigro de Crekkelad' pro una summa ferri	x sol.
Laurencio & Roberto albo de Newbur' pro x frustris de acir	vii sol.
Johanni filio Galfridi de Spena pro una chareata plumbi	xxviii sol.
Item eidem pro una chareata plumbi	xxviii sol.
Johanni de Bertun' pro una chareata plumbi	xxviii sol.
Rogero de Bulindun' pro xxiii fotmellis plumbi	xxvi sol. x d.
Ricardo de Waneting' pro duabus chareatis & xii fotmellis plumbi	lxx sol.
Hoseberto Le Cur de Newbur' pro xi fotmellis	xii sol. x d.
Roberto de Gretham pro xxiii keveruns	ix d.
In virgis	v d.

Summa xi li. iii sol. iiii d.

Liberatum die Dominica proxima post festum Sancti Jacobi apostoli pro rebus emptis a die Dominica proxima ante festum beate Margarete Virginis.

Pagano de Christi monasterio pro mille pedibus de petris de Insula	xl sol.
Ricardo le Quareur de Seleborn' pro mille petris tractandis de quariria sua	xviii sol. iiii d.
Reginaldo Trull' pro xvi saccis de carbone	ii sol.
In percameno	i d.
Pro iii gatis	iii d.

to Ralph of Langrish for 19 sacks	2*s.* 3½*d.*
for withies	4*d.*
to John Seman for 4 sacks of charcoal	10*d.*
to Robert de la Mare for 21 rafters	9*d.*
to Godwin de Ymtrewa for 25 rafters	7*d.*
for withies	7*d.*
And for a cart-load of charcoal	2*s.* 0*d.*
for a bucket	2*d.*
to Richard of Morestead (?) for 25 rafters	9*d.*
for withies	3*d.*
to Sibern the smith for steel	1*s.* 3*d.*
to Adam the lime-man for 3 sesters of lime	3*s.* 0*d.*
to Walter the scribe	£3. 6*s.* 8*d.*

Total £4. 2*s.* 5½*d.*

Paid on Sunday next before the feast of the blessed Margaret the Virgin [*17 July*] *for things bought during the preceding week.*

to Robert de la Held for 16 sacks of charcoal	2*s.* 0*d.*
to Alfric of Lydney for one seam of iron	9*s.* 6*d.*
to Robert Black of Cricklade for one seam of iron	10*s.* 0*d.*
to Laurence and Robert White of Newbury for 10 pieces of steel	7*s.* 0*d.*
to John son of Geoffrey of Speen for one char of lead	£1. 8*s.* 0*d.*
and to him for one char of lead	£1. 8*s.* 0*d.*
to John of Berton for one char of lead	£1. 8*s.* 0*d.*
to Roger of Bullington for 23 fothers of lead	£1. 6*s.* 10*d.*
to Richard of Wantage for two chars and 12 fothers of lead	£3. 10*s.* 0*d.*
to Osbert le Cur of Newbury for 11 fothers	12*s.* 10*d.*
to Robert of Greatham for 23 rafters	9*d.*
for withies	5*d.*

Total £11. 3*s.* 4*d.*

Paid on Sunday next after the feast of St. James the Apostle [*31 July*] *for things bought since Sunday next before the feast of the blessed Margaret the Virgin* [*17 July*].

to Payn of Christchurch for 1,000 feet of Isle of Wight stone	£2. 0*s.* 0*d.*
to Richard the quarryman of Selborne for 1,000 stones to be taken out of his quarry	18*s.* 4*d.*
to Reginald Trull for 16 sacks of charcoal	2*s.* 0*d.*
for parchment	1*d.*
for 3 bowls	3*d.*

Pro xxv keveruns	xii d.
Morando [pro] mille pedibus de petris de Insula	xl sol.
Johanni filio Galfridi de Spena pro duabus chareatis plumbi & vi fotmellis	lxiii sol.
Ricardo de Waneting' pro ii chareatis plumbi	lvi sol.
Johanni de Mundecurt' pro duabus chareatis plumbi	lviii sol.
Reginaldo le Nhotte pro xvi saccis de carbone	ii sol.
Summa xiiii li. viii d.	

In die Jovis proxima post festum beati Petri ad Vincula pro una chareata plumbi de Ricardo de Waneting'	xxix sol.
Radulfo le Carbunir pro carbone	xxii d.
pro CCCC kevildis	iiii d.
pro mille clavis laterez	xiii d.
pro DCCC caretatis de stipula	xxvii d.
ad locandum unum equm ad Bellum Locum	v d.
pro uno equo ad opus Magistri Hugonis eundi ad Boscum	viii d.
pro uno equo ad opus Rogeri Coleman eundi ad boscum	ii d.
pro duabus funibus	ii d.
pro vii mensuris inpletis de kaildo	ii sol.
pro circulis ad ligandum cuvirs	iiii d.
Domine Ymenay pro viii caretatis de kaildo	vi d.
Galfrido filio Michaelis pro xliiii petris de quariria	xiii sol. iiii d.
Phelippo Servienti pro carettis perquirendis	xii d.
Summa liii sol. i d.	

In die Jovis proxima post festum beati Laurencii

Ricardo filio Augeri de Bureford' pro xxii fotmellis plumbi	xxvi sol.
In virgis	i d.
Pagano de Christi monasterio pro mille & ducentis pedibus de petris de Insula	xlviii sol.
In crastino Assumpcionis beate Virginis pro iiii chareatis de glu	x d.
pro sepo & lardo	ii d. ob.
In die Sabbati proxima sequenti Johanni filio Galfridi de Spena pro iii chareatis plumbi & xi fotmellis	vi li. iiii sol. x d.
Ranulpho de Braifeld' pro una chareata virgarum	iiii d. ob.
Waltero le Kene pro una careata virgarum	iii d. ob.
Roberto Pilet ad locandum unum equum per duas vices eundi apud Seleborn'	xii d.
Godwino de Yntrewa pro xxv keveruns	vi d.
In stagno	ob.

for 25 rafters	1*s.* 0*d.*
to Morand for 1,000 feet of Isle of Wight stone	£2. 0*s.* 0*d.*
to John son of Geoffrey of Speen for two chars and 6 fothers of lead	£3. 3*s.* 0*d.*
to Richard of Wantage for 2 chars of lead	£2. 16*s.* 0*d.*
to John de Mundecurt for two chars of lead	£2. 18*s.* 0*d.*
to Reginald le Nhotte for 16 sacks of charcoal	2*s.* 0*d.*

Total, £14. 0*s.* 8*d.*

On Thursday next after the feast of the blessed Peter in Chains [*4 August*]

for one char of lead from Richard of Wantage	£1. 9*s.* 0*d.*
to Ralph the charcoal-burner for charcoal	1*s.* 10*d.*
for 400 pegs	4*d.*
for 1,000 lath-nails	1*s.* 1*d.*
for 800 cart-loads of straw	2*s.* 3*d.*
to hire a horse at Beaulieu	5*d.*
for a horse for the use of Master Hugh when he went to the wood	8*d.*
for a horse for the use of Roger Coleman when he went to the wood	2*d.*
for two ropes	2*d.*
for 7 measures filled with flint	2*s.* 0*d.*
for hoops to bind casks	4*d.*
to Lady Ymenay for 8 cart-loads of flint	6*d.*
to Geoffrey son of Michael for 44 stones from the quarry	13*s.* 4*d.*
to Philip Serjeant for obtaining carts	1*s.* 0*d.*

Total, £2. 13*s.* 1*d.*

On Thursday next after the feast of the blessed Laurence [*11 August*].

to Richard son of Auger of Burford for 22 fothers of lead	£1. 6*s.* 0*d.*
for withies	1*d.*
to Payn of Christchurch for 1,200 feet of Isle of Wight stone	£2. 8*s.* 0*d.*
on the day after the Assumption of the blessed Virgin [16 August] for 4 cart-loads of thatching straw	10*d.*
for tallow and lard	2½*d.*
on the Saturday following [20 August] to John son of Geoffrey of Speen for 3 chars of lead and 11 fothers	£6. 4*s.* 10*d.*
to Ralph of Braishfield for one cart-load of withies	4½*d.*
to Walter le Kene for one cart-load of withies	3½*d.*
to Robert Pilet to hire a horse to go to Selborne on two occasions	1*s.* 0*d.*
to Godwin de Yntrewa for 25 rafters	6*d.*
for tin	½*d.*

pro uno criblo	ob.
Petro de Peteresfeld' pro una summa carbonis	xxii d.
In percameno	iii d.

Summa x li. iiii sol. iii d. ob.

Item in die Sabbati proxima post festum beati Egidii Godwino de Yntrewa pro xxv bordis	xvi d.
Item eidem pro xii keveruns	ix d.
pro lardo & sepo ad plumbum solvendum	iii d.
pro Mille CCCC & l petris de Cadamo	lxvii sol. vi d.
Reginaldo palmario pro una summa carbonis	xx d.
In virgis	iii d.
Item Ricardo de Farlegh' pro duabus caretatis virgarum	viii d.
Item in virgis	iii d.

Summa lxxii sol. viii d.

Item liberatum die Dominica proxima post Exaltacionem Sancte Crucis.

Willelmo palmario pro xx keveruns	xii d.
pro duabus caretatis de glu de Ricardo Alger	vi d.
Ricardo de Torshull' pro una caretata virgarum	iii d.
Willelmo palmario pro xx keveruns	viii d.
pro stagno ad plumbum solvendum	vii d. ob.
ad preparandum bucellum	iii ob.
pro funibus	iii d.
pro lardo & sepo	ii d.
pro CCCC & l petris de Cadmo	xxiii sol. vi d.
Ricardo le Cnave pro una summa carbonis	xx d.
Cuidam cissori misso ad quaririam de Corf	ii sol.
Item pro mille & DCC petris de Kadmo	iiii li. vii sol.

Summa Cxvii sol. ix d.

Liberatum die Mercurii proxima ante festum Sancte Fidis.

Ade de Hetha pro una summa carbonis	ii sol.
pro vii civiris	iiii d. ob.
Willelmo Muthe pro iiii verteveles & ferramento ad almariam capelle Sancti Thome Martiris	ii sol. iii d.
In percameno	iii d.
Reginaldo Fromundo pro xx libris de stagno	ii sol. i d.

for one sieve	½*d.*
to Peter of Petersfield for one seam of charcoal	1*s.* 10*d.*
for parchment	3*d.*

Total £10. 4*s.* 3½*d.*

And on Saturday next after the feast of the blessed Giles [*3 September*]

to Godwin de Yntrewa for 25 boards	1*s.* 4*d.*
And to him for 12 rafters	9*d.*
for lard and tallow to found lead	3*d.*
for 1,450 Caen stones	£3. 7*s.* 6*d.*
to Reginald the palmer for one seam of charcoal	1*s.* 8*d.*
for withies	3*d.*
And to Richard of Farleigh for two cart-loads of withies	8*d.*
And for withies	3*d.*

Total £3. 12*s.* 8*d.*

And paid on Sunday next after the Exaltation of the Holy Cross [*18 September*].

to William the palmer for 20 rafters	1*s.* 0*d.*
for two cart-loads of thatching straw from Richard Alger	6*d.*
to Richard de Torshull for one cart-load of withies	3*d.*
to William the palmer for 20 rafters	8*d.*
for tin to found lead	7½*d.*
to prepare the bushel [measure]	1½*d.*
for ropes	3*d.*
for lard and tallow	2*d.*
for 450 Caen stones	£1. 3*s.* 6*d.*
to Richard le Cnave for one seam of charcoal	1*s.* 8*d.*
to a certain cutter sent to the quarry at Corfe	2*s.* 0*d.*
And for 1,700 Caen stones	£4. 7*s.* 0*d.*

Total £5. 17*s.* 9*d.*

Paid on Wednesday next before the feast of St. Faith [*5 October*].

to Adam of Heath for one seam of charcoal	2*s.* 0*d.*
for 7 barrows	4½*d.*
to William Muthe for 4 hinges and ironwork for the aumbry of the chapel of St. Thomas the Martyr	2*s.* 3*d.*
for parchment	3*d.*
to Reginald Fromund for 20 pounds of tin	2*s.* 1*d.*

In sepo	i d.
Ricardo Kene pro una careata virgarum	iiii d.
ad locandum unum equm ad opus Rogeri Koleman missi ad Hamtun' pro denariis recipiendis	vi d.
Roberto de la Held' pro una summa carbonis	ii sol.
Waltero de la Hecce pro una summa carbonis	ii sol.
Reginaldo palmario pro una summa carbonis	ii sol.
pro una fune	iii d.
pro rubeo plumbo	iii d. ob.
Summa xiiii sol. v d.	

Item liberatum in crastino Sancti Luce Ewangeliste.

Reginaldo Fromundo pro xxi libris de stagno	ii sol. v d.
pro xiii keveruns	vii d.
Eadem die Ricardo le Kuvir pro xv bordis ad cintres	vi d. ob.
In crastino Sanctorum Simonis & Jude pro una summa carbonis	ii sol. i d.
Willelmo de Peteresfeld' pro alia summa carbonis	ii sol. i d.
Radulfo de Peteresfeld' pro xvi saccis de carbone	ii sol. iiii d.
Willelmo de Caldecot' pro ix saccis de carbone	xxii d.
pro ferro apud Romesyam	xx sol.
In stipendiis de fows ad iactandum plumbum de cineribus	iiii d.
Summa xxxi sol. x d. ob.	

Item liberatum die Martis proxima post festum beati Leonardi.

Johanni filio Galfridi de Spena pro una chareata plumbi	xxix sol.
Fromundo pro clavis laterez	iiii d.
Ricardo de Merstedewell' pro l bordis	iii sol. ix d.
pro virgis	v d. ob.
Siberne pro duabus funibus	xxiii d.
Item pro clavis	iii ob.
Summa xxxv sol. vii d.	

Item liberatum die Sancti Andree Apostoli pro rebus captis a festo Beati Martini episcopi ad castrum reparandum.

Ricardo le Cnave pro carbone	ii sol. iiii d.
Godwino de Yntrewa pro vi bordis	ix d.
eidem pro xv bordis	iii sol.

for tallow	1d.
to Richard Kene for one cart-load of withies	4d.
to hire a horse for the use of Roger Coleman when he was sent to Southampton to collect money	6d.
to Robert de la Held for one seam of charcoal	2s. 0d.
to Walter of the Hatch for one seam of charcoal	2s. 0d.
to Reginald the palmer for one seam of charcoal	2s. 0d.
for a rope	3d.
for red lead	3½d.

Total 14s. 5d.

And paid on the morrow of St. Luke the Evangelist [*19 October*].

to Reginald Fromund for 21 pounds of tin	2s. 5d.
for 13 rafters	7d.
on the same day to Richard the cooper for 15 boards for centers	6½d.
On the morrow of Saints Simon and Jude [29 October] for one seam of charcoal	2s. 1d.
to William of Petersfield for another seam of charcoal	2s. 1d.
to Ralph of Petersfield for 16 sacks of charcoal	2s. 4d.
to William of Calcott for 9 sacks of charcoal	1s. 10d.
for iron at Romsey	£1. 0s. 0d.
for the cost of bellows to cast lead from ashes	4d.

Total £1. 11s. 10½d.

And paid on Tuesday next after the feast of the blessed Leonard [*10 November*]

to John son of Geoffrey of Speen for one char of lead	£1. 9s. 0d.
to Fromund for lath-nails	4d.
to Richard of Morestead (?) for 50 boards	3s. 9d.
for withies	5½d.
to Sibern for two ropes	1s. 11d.
And for nails	1½d.

Total £1. 15s. 7d.

And paid on the day of St. Andrew the Apostle [*30 November*] *for things obtained for the repair of the castle since the feast of St. Martin the Bishop* [*11 November*].

to Richard le Cnave for charcoal	2s. 4d.
to Godwin de Yntrewa for 6 boards	9d.
to him for 15 boards	3s. 0d.

Item eidem pro vii bordis xxii d.
Willelmo palmario pro x bordis ii sol. i d.
Item eidem pro v bordis xiiii d.
Item eidem pro ii bordis ad luvarium iiii d.
Giliberto de Legh' pro xii bordis ii sol. iiii d.
pro iiii millibus de kevildis iiii d.
pro clavis laterez iiii d.
pro iiii mensuris de sabulo vi d.

facta computacione contra Paganum de Christi monasterio de denariis sibi accommodatis supra petris de Insula & de lapidibus ab ipso receptis in castro recepit pro ii mill. pedibus de petris de Insula de Tablamento iiii li.
Morando pro D pedibus de petris de Insula xx sol.
Item Pagano pro mille & DCC & lvii kuinz & esselirs lxiii sol. iii d.
Item Morando pro D petris de Insula scilicet kuinz & esselirs xvii sol. vi d.

Summa ix li. xv sol. ix d.

pro xviii chareatis & dim. plumbi emptis ad feriam Sancti Botulfi per manus Maioris Winton' xl marce
pro eisdem ducendis per mare apud Suhamtun' xxxiiii sol. viii d.

Summa summarum huius Rotuli Clxxvi li. ix sol. v d.

Expensa excedit receptam de xv li. xviii [sol.] iii ob.

Endorsed: Rotulus de pluribus rebus emptis in primo anno inceptionis operis ad reparacionem castri necessariis.

And to him for 7 boards 1*s.* 10*d.*
to William the palmer for 10 boards 2*s.* 1*d.*
And to him for 5 boards 1*s.* 2*d.*
And to him for 2 boards for the louver 4*d.*
to Gilbert of Leigh for 12 boards 2*s.* 4*d.*
for 4,000 pegs 4*d.*
for lath-nails 4*d.*
for 4 measures of sand 6*d.*

An account having been drawn up with Payn of Christchurch concerning money lent him on account for Isle of Wight stone and for stone received from him in the castle, he received for 2,000 feet of Isle of Wight stones for tablements £4. 0*s.* 0*d.*
to Morand for 500 feet of Isle of Wight stones £1. 0*s.* 0*d.*
And to Payn for 1,757 coins and ashlars £3. 3*s.* 3*d.*
And to Morand for 500 Isle of Wight stones, that is coins and ashlars 17*s.* 6*d.*
Total £9. 15*s.* 9*d.*

for 18½ chars of lead bought at St. Botolph's Fair [at Boston] by the hand of the Mayor of Winchester £26. 13*s.* 4*d.*
to bring them by sea to Southampton £1. 14*s.* 8*d.*

Grand total of this roll £176. 9*s.* 5*d.*

The expenditure exceeds the receipts by £15. 18*s.* 1½*d.*

Endorsed: a roll of various things needed for the repair of the castle that were bought during the first year after the commencement of the work.

4. Enrolment of account for work at Winchester Castle from 1222 to *circa* 1230.

(Exchequer, Pipe Roll 84, rot. 2^{d})

Compotus Magistri Henrici de Cerne

Magister Henricus de Cerne reddit compotum de quater xx li. ix d. de cablicio foreste de Clarendon' anno vij vendito. Et de CCCC & l li. receptis de episcopo Wintoniensi per diversas particulas sicut recognoscit & sicut continetur in Rotulo de particulis quem liberavit in thesauro. Et de l marcis receptis de Radulfo de Nevill' cancellario. Et de xxx sol. x d. de corticibus & scospellis venditis. Et de lxxvj li. j marca receptis de thesauro. Et de lij li. xv sol. viij d. receptis de Willelmo de Sorewell' tunc vicecomite Sudhantonie. Et de xl li. receptis de prepositis Sudhantonie. Et de xvj li. xiij sol. iiij d. receptis [de] Bartholomeo de Kemeseia tunc vicecomite Sudhantonie. Et de xxx sol. de cablicio de Bere vendito. Et de lx li. receptis de Luca capellano quando fuit clericus de Garderoba Regis. Summa DCCC & xij li. x sol. & vij d. Item CCC & quater xx & x li. receptis de thesauro. Summa summarum M & CC & ij li. x sol. vij d. In thesauro nichil.

Et in operacionibus castri Wintonie de tempore quo idem Henricus fuit custos operacionum eiusdem castri M xx li. xix sol. & j d. per breve Regis & per visum & testimonium Johannis Cobbe & Rogeri Colemann'. Et debet C iiij^{xx} li. xj sol. vj d. Idem reddit compotum de eodem debito. In thesauro nichil. Et in eisdem operacionibus C & lxxvi li. ix sol. j d. per breve Regis & per visum & testimonium Johannis Cole & Walteri Coleman heredis Rogeri Colemann'. Et debet iiij li. ij sol. v d. Sed respondet in Sumerset in Rotulo xlv.

4. Enrolment of account for work at Winchester Castle from 1222 to *circa* 1230.

The account of Master Henry of Cerne

Master Henry of Cerne renders account of £80. 0*s.* 9*d.* for windfallen wood from the forest of Clarendon sold in the seventh year [1222–3]. And of £450 received from the Bishop of Winchester in various sums as he allows and as is contained in the roll of details which he has handed in to the Treasury. And of £33. 6*s.* 8*d.* received from Ralph de Neville the chancellor. And of £1. 10*s.* 10*d.* from the sale of bark and trimmings. And of £76. 13*s.* 4*d.* received from the Treasury. And of £52. 15*s.* 8*d.* received from William of Shorwell, at that time sheriff of Hampshire. And of £40 received from the reeves of Southampton. And of £16. 13*s.* 4*d.* received from Bartholomew of Kempsey, then sheriff of Hampshire. And of £1. 10*s.* from the sale of windfallen wood from the forest of Bere. And of £60 received from Luke the chaplain when he was clerk of the king's Wardrobe. Total £812. 10*s.* 7*d.* And £390 received from the Treasury. Grand total £1,202. 10*s.* 7*d.*

Paid in cash, nothing.

And in the works of Winchester Castle during the period when the same Henry was keeper of the works of the same castle, £1,020. 19*s.* 1*d.* by the king's writ and by view and testimony of John Cobbe and Roger Coleman. And he owes £180. 11*s.* 6*d.* He renders account of the same debt. Paid in cash, nothing. And in the same works, £176. 9*s.* 1*d.* by the king's writ and by view and testimony of John Cole and Walter Coleman, heir of Roger Coleman. And he owes £4. 2*s.* 5*d.* But he answers for it in Somerset in Roll 45.

5. Account of works at Winchester Castle in 1258. (E 101/491/14)

Rotulus de operacionibus factis in castro Winton' anno regni Regis Henrici tercii xlii per visum Ricardi le Bachiere Walteri de Exon' Ricardi de Exon' & Johannis Alure visorum iuratorum in presencia Magistrorum Johannis de Glouernia & Alexandri de Westmonasterio, incipiendo in septimana proxima post festum Sancti Mathie anno predicto.

Turris ultra prisonam tradita fuit Magistro Henrico cementario per predictos magistros Johannem & Alexandrum ad prosternendum & reedificandum ab equalitate aree camere tu[rr]is castri & ad fundamentum faciendum usque ad eandem equalitatem videlicet duo estagia & prisonas pro centum & decem libris unde idem Magister Henricus recepit C solidos die Dominica in festo Sancti Mathie. Item idem Henricus recepit per particulas prout tascam suam expedivit centum & quinque libras. Ita quod plene pacatus est de centum & decem libris.

Summa Cx li.

Septimana proxima post Pasca anno eodem

Cariagium aque	In tribus carettis ad cariendum aquam per totam septimanam, x sol. vj d. pretium carete per diem, vij d.
De calc'	In triginta cistis calci[1] emptis, xx sol. pretium ciste, viij d.
Empciones	In virgis emptis ad faciendum cleyas & ligandum scaffot & huiusmodi, iiij sol. ij d. q. In duodecim cheveronibus alneis emptis ad faciendum scaffot, xij d. In stipendio cuiusdam operarii ad faciendum cleyas de predictis virgis, x d. ob. In gatis emptis ad deferendum mortarium, vij d. In emendacione & reparacione cuvarum ad aquam, xviij d. In una civera empta rotarea, vij d. In quinque civeris virgeis emptis, iiij d. In quadraginta pott' rubei sabulonis, x sol. i d. ob., pretium pott' ij d. q. In quinquaginta pott' albi sabulonis, iij sol. iiij d.

[1] The scribe frequently writes this erroneous form of the genitive in full.

5. Account of works at Winchester Castle in 1258.

Roll of works performed in Winchester Castle in the 42nd year of the reign of King Henry III [1258] by view of Richard le Bachiere, Walter of Exeter, Richard of Exeter, and John Alure, viewers sworn in the presence of Masters John of Gloucester and Alexander of Westminster, beginning in the week next after the feast of St. Matthias [24 February] in the aforesaid year.

The tower over the prison was given to Master Henry the mason by the aforesaid masters John and Alexander to be demolished and rebuilt from the level of the floor of the keep of the castle, and [he undertook] to carry up the foundation to the same level, that is [to build] two stories and the prisons for £110, whereof Master Henry received 100*s.* on Sunday on the feast of St. Matthias [24 February]. And the same Henry received £105 in instalments as he carried out his task, so that he was paid the full £110.

Total £110.

The week following Easter in the said year [31 March–6 April]

Carriage of water — For three carts to carry water throughout the week, 10*s.* 6*d.*, at 7*d.* a day for each cart.

Lime — For the purchase of 30 sesters of lime, 20*s.*, at 8*d.* a sester.[1]

Purchases — For withies bought to make hurdles and tie scaffolding and such-like, 4*s.* $2\frac{1}{4}$*d.* For 12 alder poles bought to make scaffolding, 12*d.* For the pay of a certain workman making hurdles from the said withies, $10\frac{1}{2}$*d.* For hods bought to carry mortar, 7*d.* For mending and repairing casks for water, 18*d.* For the purchase of one wheelbarrow, 7*d.* For 5 hand-barrows bought, 4*d.* For 40 potts[2] of red sand, 10*s.* $1\frac{1}{2}$*d.*, price $2\frac{1}{4}$*d.* a pott. For 50 potts of white sand, 3*s.* 4*d.*

[1] *Cista* is Latin for 'chest', and Salzman accordingly predicates a measure of lime known as a 'chest' (*Building in England*, p. 149). But the 1222 account shows (p. 139) that lime was then being sold in Winchester at 9*d.* a 'sester' (a standard dry measure equivalent to 8 bushels), and it seems more likely that the *cista* for which 8*d.* was being paid in 1258 was in fact the same measure.

[2] This measure of sand appears to have been local to Winchester (Salzman, p. 152). The capacity of a pott is unknown.

Item in stipendiis quater viginti operariorum ad quareram crete ad traendam [*sic*] cretam pro fundamento faciendo per totam septimanam, lx sol.

Summa Cxiij sol. q.

Septimana sequens

Operarii In stipendiis quater viginti operariorum ad quareram ad traendum grossam cretam per quinque dies, l sol., quilibet per diem i d. ob.

Cariagium aque In tribus caretis ad cariendum aquam per totam septimanam, x sol. vj d. pretium carete per diem, vij d.

De calc' In viginti cistis calci emptis, j marca, pretium ciste, viij d.

Rubeus sabulo In viginti & sex pott' rubei sabulonis emptis, iiij sol. x d. ob. pretium pott', ij d. q.

Empciones In quinque caretatis clausture ad includendum calcem petram & attractum super Beumund, xviij d.

In quinquaginta pott' albi sabulonis, iij sol. iiij d., pretium centeni dim. marca

In stipendiis decem carettarum ad cariendum predictam cretam per quinque dies, xxix sol. ij d., quelibet per diem vij d.

Summa Cxij sol. viij d. ob.

Septimana sequens

Operarii In stipendiis quater viginti operariorum ad quareram per tres dies, xl sol., quilibet per diem j d. ob.

Cariagium aque In stipendiis cuiusdam carete ad cariendum aquam per quatuor dies, ij sol. iiij d., videlicet per diem vij d.

De calc' In triginta cistis calci emptis, xx sol. pretium ciste viij d.

Albus sabulo In empcione quinquaginta pott' albi sabulonis, iij sol. vj d. pretium centeni vij sol.

In empcione sexaginta & trium pottorum rubei sabulonis, xij sol. q. pretium pott' ij d. q.

And for the wages of 80 labourers at the chalk quarry drawing chalk to make the foundation throughout the week, 60*s.*

Total, £5. 13*s.* 0¼*d.*

The following week [7–13 April]

Labourers For the wages of 80 labourers at the quarry drawing big [pieces of] chalk for 5 days, 50*s.* each at 1½*d.* a day.

Carriage of water For three carts to carry water throughout the week, 10*s.* 6*d.*, at 7*d.* a cart per day.

Lime For the purchase of 20 sesters of lime, 13*s.* 4*d.*, at 8*d.* a sester.

Red sand For the purchase of 26 potts of red sand, 4*s.* 10½*d.*, at 2¼*d.* a pott.

Purchases For 5 cart-loads of fencing to enclose the lime, stone and [other] materials on Beaumond,[1] 18*d.*

For 50 potts of white sand, 3*s.* 4*d.*, at 6*s.* 8*d.* a 100.

For the wages of 10 carts to carry the aforesaid chalk for 5 days, 29*s.* 2*d.*, each at 7*d.* a day.

Total, £5. 12*s.* 8½*d.*

The following week [14–20 April]

Labourers For the wages of 80 labourers at the quarry for 3 days, 40*s.*, each at 1½*d.* a day.

Carriage of water For the wages of a certain cart carrying water for 4 days, 2*s.* 4*d.* at 7*d.* a day.

Lime For the purchase of 30 sesters of lime, 20*s.*, at 8*d.* a sester.

White sand For the purchase of 50 potts of white sand, 3*s.* 6*d.*, at 7*s.* a 100.

[*Red sand*] For the purchase of 63 potts of red sand, 12*s.* 0¼*d.*, at 2¼*d.* a pott.

[1] An open space between the City Wall and what is now Trafalgar Street. For this information I am indebted to Mr. D. J. Keene.

Empciones In empcione serurarum, guns & vertevellorum & clavorum ad faciendum falcones, xviij d. In cheveronibus emptis ad scaffot' & bordis ad falcones faciendos, xxxij d. In claustura empta ad clausum predictum faciendum, viij d. ob.

In stipendiis duodecim carettarum ad cariandum predictam cretam per quatuor dies, xxviij sol. quelibet per diem vij d.

Summa Cx sol. viij d. ob. & q.

Septimana quarta

Carpentarius In stipendiis Roberti Fassel carpentarii qui fecit quandam domum super Beumund ubi carpentarii & cementarii ponerent utensilia sua, per quatuor dies, xvj d.

Operarii In stipendiis lx operariorum ad quareram per sex dies xlv sol., quilibet per diem i d. ob. In stipendiis unius operarii ibidem per quinque dies, vi d. ob. In stipendiis duorum operariorum ibidem per tres dies, ix d.

Cariagium aque In stipendiis duarum carettar' ad cariendum aquam per totam septimanam, vij sol., quilibet [*sic*] per diem vij d. In stipendiis unius carette ad idem per quinque dies, ij sol. xj d.

De calc' In triginta cistis calci emptis, xx sol. pretium ciste, viij d.

Albus sabulo In l pott' albi sabulonis, iij sol. vj d. pretium centeni, vij sol. Item in viginti & novem pott' eiusdem sabulonis, ij sol. pretium ut supra.

Rubeus sabulo In l pott' rubei sabulonis, ix sol. iiij d. ob. pretium pott', ij d. q.

In empcione duorum [*sic*] cuvarum ad aquam, xvj d.

In stipendiis quatuordecim carettarum ad cariendum predictam cretam per totam septimanam, xlix sol., quelibet per diem vij d.

Summa vij li. ij sol. ix d.

Septimana quinta

Carpentarius In stipendiis unius carpentarii ad faucones & cintros faciendos per totam septimanam, ij sol.

Operarii In stipendiis lxx operariorum ad quareram per totam septimanam, lij sol. vj d., quilibet per diem i d. ob.

In stipendiis unius operarii ad idem per quatuor dies, vj d. quilibet ut supra.

Cariagium aque In stipendiis unius carete ad aquam cariendam per quinque dies, ij sol. xj d., videlicet per diem vij d.

In stipendiis duarum caretarum ad idem & per idem, v sol. x d., per diem vij d.

Purchases For the purchase of locks, hooks and eyes, and nails to make hawks[1], 18*d.* For poles bought for scaffolding and boards to make hawks, 32*d.* For fencing bought to make the aforesaid enclosure, 8½*d.*

For the wages of 12 carts to carry the said chalk for 4 days, 28*s.*, each at 7*d.* a day.

Total £5. 10*s.* 8¾*d.*

The fourth week [21–27 April]

Carpenter For the wages of Robert Fassel, carpenter, who made a building on Beaumond for the carpenters and masons to keep their tools in, for 4 days, 16*d.*

Labourers For the wages of 60 labourers at the quarry for 6 days, 45*s.*, each at 1½*d.* a day. For the wages of one labourer there for 5 days, 6½*d.* For the wages of two labourers there for 3 days, 9*d.*

Carriage of water For the wages of two carts to carry water throughout the week, 7*s.*, each at 7*d.* a day. For the wages of one cart doing the same for 5 days, 2*s.* 11*d.*

Lime For the purchase of 30 sesters of lime, 20*s.*, at 8*d.* a sester.

White sand For 50 potts of white sand, 3*s.* 6*d.*, at 7*s.* a 100. And for 29 potts of the same sand, 2*s.*, price as above.

Red sand For 50 potts of red sand, 9*s.* 4½*d.*, price 2¼*d.* a pott.

For the purchase of two casks for water, 16*d.*

For the wages of 14 carts to carry the aforesaid chalk throughout the week, 49*s.*, each at 7*d.* a day.

Total £7. 2*s.* 9*d.*

The fifth week [28 April–4 May]

Carpenter For the wages of one carpenter making hawks and centering throughout the week, 2*s.*

Labourers For the wages of 70 labourers at the quarry throughout the week, 52*s.* 6*d.*, each at 1½*d.* a day. For the wages of one labourer at the same for 4 days, 6*d.*, at the same rate.

Carriage of water For the wages of one cart carrying water for 5 days, 2*s.* 11*d.*, at 7*d.* a day.

For the wages of two carts doing the same for the same period, 5*s.* 10*d.*, at 7*d.* a day.

[1] i.e. hods.

De calc'	In viginti cistis calci emptis, j marca, pretium ciste viii d. Et pro decem cistis calci, dim. m., pretium ut supra.
Rubeus sabulo	In quadraginta duobus pott' rubei sabulonis vij sol. x d. ob. pretium pott' ij d. q.
Albus sabulo	In viginti quinque pott' albi sabulonis xxj d. pretium centene vij sol.
Empciones	In tresdecim bordis emptis ad falcones faciendos, xv d. ob. In quindecim cheveronibus emptis ad predictam domum faciendam, v d. In virgis emptis ad idem, ob. q. In una civera empta, i d. In ducentis clavis emptis ad cintros faciendos, v d. ob. q. In quatuor civeris emptis, iiij d.
	In stipendiis decem carettarum ad cariendum predictam petram per totam septimanam, xxxv sol. quelibet per diem, vij d.
	Summa vj li. xj sol. ob.

Septimana sexta

Carpentarius	In stipendiis unius carpentarii ad cintros faciendos per duos dies, viij d.
Operarii	In stipendiis lviij operariorum per sex dies, xliij sol. vj d. quilibet per diem i d. ob.
Cariagium aque	In tribus caretis ad cariendum aquam & credam de quarera per totam septimanam, x sol. vj d. videlicet per diem vij d. In duabus caretis ad cariendum cretam predictam per totam septimanam, vij sol. videlicet per diem ut supra.
De calc'	In decem & septem cistis calci emptis, xj sol. iiij d., pretium ciste viij d.
Albus sabulo	In xxv pott' albi sabulonis emptis, xxj d. pretium centeni vij sol.
Rubeus sabulo	In lj pott' rubei sabulonis emptis, ix sol. vj d. ob. pretium pott' ij d. q.
Empciones	In virgis emptis ad scaffot' faciend', xx d. ob. In guns & verteveles ad domum predictam in Beumund, viij d. In duabus gatis emptis ad deferendum morterium, iiij d. ob. In duabus cheveronibus ad scaffot', ij d. Item in xxj cheveronibus ad idem, xj d.
	In stipendiis duodecim carettarum ad cariendum petram, xlij sol. quelibet per diem, vij d.
	Summa vj li. x sol. j d. ob.

Lime For the purchase of 20 sesters of lime, 13*s.* 4*d.*, price 8*d.* a sester. And for 10 sesters of lime, 6*s.* 8*d.*, price as above.

Red sand For 42 potts of red sand 7*s.* 10½*d.*, price 2¼*d.* a pott.

White sand For 25 potts of white sand 21*d.*, at 7*s.* a hundred.

Purchases For 13 boards bought to make hawks, 15½*d.* For 15 rafters bought to make the aforesaid building, 5*d.* For withies bought for the same, ¾*d.* For one barrow bought, 1*d.* For 200 nails bought to make centering, 5¾*d.* For 4 barrows bought, 4*d.*

For the wages of 10 carts carrying the said stone throughout the week, 35*s.*, each at 7*d.* a day.

Total £6. 11*s.* 0½*d.*

The sixth week [5–11 May]

Carpenter For the wages of a carpenter making centering for two days, 8*d.*

Labourers For the wages of 58 labourers for 6 days, 43*s.* 6*d.*, each at 1½*d.* a day.

Carriage of water For 3 carts carrying water and chalk from the quarry throughout the week, 10*s.* 6*d.*, that is 7*d.* a day.

For two carts carrying the said chalk throughout the week, 7*s.*, that is at the same rate.

Lime For the purchase of 17 sesters of lime, 11*s.* 4*d.*, at 8*d.* a sester.

White sand For the purchase of 25 potts of white sand, 21*d.*, at 7*s.* a 100.

Red sand For the purchase of 51 potts of red sand, 9*s.* 6½*d.*, price 2¼*d.* a pott.

Purchases For withies bought to make scaffolding, 20½*d.* For hooks and eyes for the aforesaid building in Beaumond, 8*d.*

For two hods bought to carry mortar, 4½*d.* For two poles for scaffolding, 2*d.* And for 21 poles for the same, 11*d.*

For the wages of 12 carts to carry stone, 42*s.*, each at 7*d.* a day.

Total £6. 10*s.* 1½*d.*

Septimana septima

Carpentarius In stipendiis unius carpentarii ad falcones faciendos & huiusmodi per totam septimanam, ij sol.

Operarius In stipendiis unius copertori ad coperiendum domum predictam in Beimund per tres dies, x d.

Empciones In litera empta ad idem, v sol.

Operarii In stipendiis duorum operariorum ad serviendum predicto copertori per tres dies, ix d.

In stipendiis quinque operariorum ad deferendum terram circa fundamentum & ad predictam terram firmandam, xxij d. ob.

Item in stipendiis xlv operariorum ad quareram per totam septimanam, xxxij sol. ix d. quilibet per diem i d. ob.[1]

De calc' In decem & septem cistis calci emptis, xj sol. iiij d. pretium ciste, vij d.

In stipendiis quatuor carettarum ad cariendum aquam & credam per totam septimanam, xiiij sol., quelibet per diem, vij d.

In quadraginta pott' rubei sabulonis emptis, vij sol. vj d. pretium pott' ij d. q.

In quinquaginta pott' albi sabulonis, iij sol. vj d. pretium centeni vij sol.

In stipendiis octo carettarum ad cariendum petram de quarera, xxviij sol.

Summa Cviij sol. vj d. ob.

Septimana proxima post Pentecost'

Operarii In stipendiis xxxvj operariorum ad quareram de creta per quatuor dies, xviij sol. quilibet per diem i d. ob.

Cariagium aque In stipendiis unius carete ad cariendum aquam & petram de quarera per quatuor dies, ij sol. iiij d. videlicet per diem vij d.

De calc' In quindecim cistis calci emptis, x sol. pretium ciste, viij d. Item in viginti cistis emptis de eodem, j marca.

Albus sabulo In l pottis albi sabulonis emptis, iij sol. vj d. pretium centeni, vij sol. Et in quadraginta pott' rubei sabulonis, vij sol.

[1] This item was inserted later.

The seventh week [12–18 May]

Carpenter For the wages of one carpenter making hawks and suchlike throughout the week, 2*s.*

Workman For the wages of one thatcher thatching the aforesaid building in Beaumond for three days, 10*d.*

Purchases For straw bought for the same, 5*s.*

Labourers For the wages of two labourers to serve the said thatcher for three days, 9*d.*
For the wages of 5 labourers placing earth round the foundation and ramming the said earth, 22½*d.*
And for the wages of 45 labourers at the quarry throughout the week, 32*s.* 9*d.*, each at 1½*d.* a day.

Lime For the purchase of 17 sesters of lime, 11*s.* 4*d.*, at 7*d.* a sester.
For the wages of 4 carts to carry water and chalk throughout the week, 14*s.*, each at 7*d.* a day.
For the purchase of 40 potts of red sand, 7*s.* 6*d.*, price 2¼*d.* a pott.
For the purchase of 50 potts of white sand, 3*s.* 6*d.*, price 7*s.* a 100.
For the wages of 8 carts carrying stone from the quarry, 28*s.*

Total £5. 8*s.* 6½*d.*

The week after Whitsun [19–25 May]

Labourers For the wages of 36 labourers at the chalk-quarry for 4 days, 18*s.*, each at 1½*d.* a day.

Carriage of water For the wages of a cart carrying water and stone from the quarry for 4 days, 2*s.* 4*d.*, that is 7*d.* a day.

Lime For the purchase of 15 sesters of lime, 10*s.*, price 8*d.* a sester. And for the purchase of 20 sesters of the same, 13*s.* 4*d.*

White sand For the purchase of 50 potts of white sand, 3*s.* 6*d.*, at 7*s.* a 100. And for 40 potts of red sand, 7*s.*

Empciones In virgis emptis ad scaffot' faciend', x d. In clavis emptis ad cintros faciendos, vi d. In undecim pottis petr' emptis, xvij d.

In stipendiis sexdecim carettarum ad cariendum petram de quarera per quatuor dies, xxxvij sol. iiij d. quelibet per diem, vij d.

Summa iiij^{or} li. xiiij sol. iij d.

Septimana secunda post Pentecost'

Operarii In stipendiis xxiiij^{or} operariorum ad quareram per totam septimanam, xviij sol. quelibet per diem, vij d.[1]

Cariagium aque In tribus caretis ad cariendum aquam per quatuor dies, vij sol., videlicet per diem, vij d.

De calc' In quindecim cistis calci emptis, x sol., pretium ciste viij d.

Rubeus sabulo In xxxiij pott' rubei sabulonis emptis, vj sol. ij d. q., pretium pott', ij d. q. Et in C pott' albi sabulonis, vij sol.

Empciones In carbone empto ad cineres plumbi fundendos, iiij sol. vj d. ob. In stipendiis cuiusdam plombarii ad predictos cineres fo[n]dendos, xv sol. iv d., videlicet pro xl & vj pedibus plumbi pretium pedis iiij d. In cariagio triginta cuvarum aque ad predictos cineres lavandos, xv d. In stipendiis duorum fabrorum cum follibus suis ad predictos cineres fondendos, iij sol. j d.

In quadraginta cheveronibus ad scaffot' emptis, iij sol. iiij d.

In stipendiis octo caretarum ad cariendum petram de quarera per totam septimanam, xxviij sol. quelibet per diem, vij d.

Summa Ciij sol. viij d. ob. & q.

Usque hic

Septimana tercia post Pentecost'

Operarii In stipendiis viginti operariorum per quinque dies ad quareram, xij sol. vj d., quilibet per diem i d. ob.

Cariagium crete In duabus caretis ad cariendum cretam de quarera per quinque dies, vj sol. x d. videlicet per diem vij d.

De calc' In decem & septem cistis calci emptis, xij sol. pretium ciste viij d. Item in viginti cistis calci emptis j m.

[1] *Sic.* A mistake for *quilibet per diem i d. ob.*

Purchases For withies bought to make scaffolding, 10*d.* For nails bought to make centering, 6*d.* For the purchase of 11 stone potts, 17*d.*

For the wages of 16 carts carrying stone from the quarry for 4 days, 37*s.* 4*d.*, each at 7*d.* a day.

Total £4. 14*s.* 3*d.*

The second week after Whitsun [26 May–1 June]

Labourers For the wages of 24 labourers at the quarry throughout the week, 18*s.*, each at 7*d.* a day [*sic*].[1]

Carriage of water For three carts to carry water for four days, 7*s.*, that is 7*d.* a day.

Lime For the purchase of 15 sesters of lime, 10*s.*, at 8*d.* a sester.

Red sand For the purchase of 33 potts of red sand, 6*s.* 2¼*d.*, price 2¼*d.* a pott. And for 100 potts of white sand, 7*s.*

Purchases For charcoal bought to found lead ash 4*s.* 6½*d.* For the wages of a certain plumber founding the said ash, 15*s.* 4*d.*, that is for 46 feet of lead at 4*d.* a foot. For the carriage of 30 casks of water to wash the said ashes, 15*d.* For the wages of two smiths with their bellows to found the said ashes, 3*s.* 1*d.*

For the purchase of 40 poles for scaffolding, 3*s.* 4*d.*

For the wages of 8 carts to carry stone from the quarry throughout the week, 28*s.*, at 7*d.* a day [each].

Total £5. 3*s.* 8¼*d.*

Up to here.[2]

The third week after Whitsun [2–8 June]

Labourers For the wages of 20 labourers for five days at the quarry, 12*s.* 6*d.*, each at 1½*d.* a day.

Carriage of chalk For two carts to carry chalk from the quarry for five days, 6*s.* 10*d.*, each at 7*d.* a day.

Lime For the purchase of 17[3] sesters of lime, 12*s.*, at 8*d.* a sester. And for the purchase of 20 sesters of lime, 13*s.* 4*d.*

[1] A mistake for 1½*d.* a day.

[2] This (an auditor's note) is written at the bottom of the second membrane of parchment composing the roll.

[3] *Sic.* A mistake for 18.

Rubeus sabulo	In xxj pott' rubei sabulonis, iij sol. xj d. q. pretium pott' ij d. q.
Albus sabulo	In l pott' albi sabulonis emptis, iij sol. iiij d., pretium centeni dim. marca
Empciones	In sex gatis emptis ad deferendum morterium, xij d.
	In stipendiis duarum carettarum ad cariendum aquam per quinque dies, v sol. x d. quelibet per diem vij d.
	Summa lvij sol. ix d. ob.

Septimana quarta post Pentecost'

Operarii	In stipendiis xviij operariorum per quinque dies ad quareram, xj sol. iij d. quilibet per diem i d. ob.
Cariagium crete	In sex caretis ad cariendum cretam de quarera per quinque dies, xvij sol. vj d. videlicet per diem vij d.
De calc'	In decem & septem cistis calci emptis, xij sol. pretium ciste viij d.
Rubeus sabulo	In xxj pott' rubei sabulonis emptis, iij sol. xj d. q. pretium pott' ij d. q.
Albus sabulo	In l. pott' albi sabulonis emptis, iij sol. iiij d. pretium centeni dim. marca.
	In quatuor caretis ad cariendum aquam per quinque dies, xj sol. viij d.
	Summa lix sol. viij d. q.

Septimana quinta post Pentecost'

Operarii	In stipendiis xij^{cim} operariorum per quatuor dies & dim. ad quareram, iiii^{or} sol. ix d., quilibet per diem, i d. ob.
Cariagium aque & crete	In quatuor caretis ad cariendum cretam de quarera & aquam per quatuor dies, ix sol. iiij d. quilibet [*sic*] per diem vij d.
De calc'	In decem & sex cistis calci emptis, x sol. viij d. pretium ciste viij d. Item in viginti cistis de eodem, j marca.
Rubeus sabulo	In viginti duobus pott' rubei sabulonis emptis, iiij sol. vij d. pretium pott' ij d. q.
Albus sabulo	In xxv pott' albi sabulonis emptis, xx d. pretium centeni dim. marca.
	In stipendiis unius operarii ad deferendum terram circa fundamentum turris per quatuor dies & dim., vij d. ob. per diem i d. ob.
	Summa xliiij sol. xj d. ob.

Red sand For 21 potts of red sand, 3*s.* 11¼*d.*, price 2¼*d.* a pott.

White sand For the purchase of 50 potts of white sand, 3*s.* 4*d.*, price 6*s.* 8*d.* a 100.

Purchases For the purchase of six hods to carry mortar, 12*d.*

For the wages of two carts carrying water for five days, 5*s.* 10*d.*, each at 7*d.* a day.

Total £2. 17*s.* 9½*d.*

The fourth week after Whitsun [9–15 June]

Labourers For the wages of 18 labourers for 5 days at the quarry, 11*s.* 3*d.*, each at 1½*d.* a day.

Carriage of chalk For six carts to carry chalk from the quarry for 5 days, 17*s.* 6*d.*, each at 7*d.* a day.

Lime For the purchase of 17[1] sesters of lime, 12*s.*, price 8*d.* a sester.

Red sand For the purchase of 21 potts of red sand, 3*s.* 11¼*d.*, price 2¼*d.*

White sand For the purchase of 50 potts of white sand, 3*s.* 4*d.*, price 6*s.* 8*d.* a 100.

For four carts carrying water for five days, 11*s.* 8*d.*

Total £2. 19*s.* 8¼*d.*

The fifth week after Whitsun [16–22 June].

Labourers For the wages of 12 labourers for 4½ days at the quarry, 4*s.* 9*d.*[2], each at 1½*d.* a day.

Carriage of water & chalk For 4 carts carrying chalk from the quarry and water for 4 days, 9*s.* 4*d.*, each at 7*d.* a day.

Lime For the purchase of 16 sesters of lime, 10*s.* 8*d.*, at 8*d.* a sester. And for 20 sesters of the same, 13*s.* 4*d.*

Red sand For the purchase of 22 potts of red sand, 4*s.* 7*d.* [*sic*], at 2¼*d.* a pott.

White sand For the purchase of 25 potts of white sand, 20*d.*, price 6*s.* 8*d.* a 100.

For the wages of one labourer to lay earth round the foundation of the tower for 4½ days, 7½*d.* at 1½*d.* a day.

Total £2. 4*s.* 11½*d.*

[1] *Sic*, but read 18. [2] *Sic*, but read 6*s.* 9*d.*

Septimana sexta post Pentecost'

Operarii In stipendiis septem operariorum per quatuor dies & dimidium ad quareram, ij sol. xj d. q. quilibet per diem j d. ob.

Cariagium aque & crete In duabus caretis ad cariendum cretam de quarera & aquam per quatuor dies, iiij sol. viij d. quilibet [*sic*] per diem vij d.

De calc' In viginti cistis calci emptis, j marca pretium ciste viij d.

Rubeus sabulo In xxj pott' rubei sabulonis emptis, iiij sol. iiij d. ob. & q. pretium pott' ij d. q.

In xiij pott' albi sabulonis emptis, x d. pretium centeni dim. marca. Item in centum pott' de eodem, vij sol.

In virgis emptis ad ligandum scafot, iiij d. ob.

Summa xxxiij sol. vj d. ob.

Septimana septima post Pentecost'

Operarii In stipendiis quatuor operariorum ad quareram & trium operariorum ad terram portandam circa fundamentum per quatuor dies, iij sol. vj d. quilibet per diem j d. ob.

Cariagium aque & crete In tribus caretis ad cariendum cretam de quarera & aquam per quatuor dies, vij sol. quilibet [*sic*] per diem, vij d.

De calc' In novem cistis calci emptis, vj sol. pretium ciste viij d. Item in triginta cistis de eodem, xx sol.

Rubeus sabulo In decem & quatuor pott' rubei sabulonis emptis, ij sol. vij d. ob. pretium pott' ij d. q.

Albus sabulo In xxv pott' albi sabulonis emptis, xx d. pretium centeni dim. marca.

Empciones In dim. centena bordorum emptis ad cintros faciendos, iij sol. In cheveronibus emptis ad idem, ix d. ob.

Summa xliiij sol. vij d. q.

Septimana octava post Pentecost'

Operarii In stipendiis quatuor operariorum ad quareram & trium operariorum ad terram portandam circa fundamentum per quatuor dies, iii sol. vj d. quilibet per diem j d. ob.

The sixth week after Whitsun [23–29 June]

Labourers For the wages of 7 labourers for 4½ days at the quarry, 2*s.* 11¼*d.*, each at 1½*d.* a day.

Carriage of water & chalk For two carts to carry chalk from the quarry and water for 4 days, 4*s.* 8*d.*, each at 7*d.* a day.

Lime For the purchase of 20 sesters of lime, 13*s.* 4*d.*, price 8*d.* a sester.

Red sand For the purchase of 21 potts of red sand, 4*s.* 4¾*d.*, price 2¼*d.* a pott.

For the purchase of 13 potts of white sand, 10*d.*, price 6*s.* 8*d.* a 100. And for 100 potts of the same, 7*s.*

For withies bought to bind scaffolding, 4½*d.*

Total £1. 13*s.* 6½*d.*

The seventh week after Whitsun [30 June–6 July]

Labourers For the wages of 4 labourers at the quarry and 3 labourers laying earth round the foundation for 4 days, 3*s.* 6*d.*, each at 1½*d.* a day.

Carriage of water & chalk For 3 carts to carry chalk from the quarry and water for 4 days, 7*s.*, each at 7*d.* a day.

Lime For the purchase of 9 sesters of lime, 6*s.*, at 8*d.* a sester. And for 30 sesters of the same, 20*s.*

Red sand For the purchase of 14 potts of red sand, 2*s.* 7½*d.*, price 2¼*d.* a pott.

White sand For the purchase of 25 potts of white sand, 20*d.*, price 6*s.* 8*d.* a 100.

Purchases For the purchase of half a hundred boards to make centering, 3*s.* For the purchase of rafters for the same purpose, 9½*d.*

Total £2. 4*s.* 7¼*d.*

The eighth week after Whitsun [7–13 July]

Labourers For the wages of 4 labourers at the quarry and 3 labourers laying earth round the foundation for 4 days, 3*s.* 6*d.*, each at 1½*d.* a day.

Cariagium aque & crete In tribus caretis ad cariendum cretam de quarera & aquam per quatuor dies, vij sol. videlicet per diem vij d.

De calc' In novem cistis calci emptis, vj sol. pretium ciste viij d. Item in viginti cistis calci emptis, j marca.

In xiij pott' rubei sabulonis emptis, ij sol. v d. q. pretium pott' ij d. q. Et in viginti pott' de eodem, iij sol. ix d.

In xiij pott' albi sabulonis emptis, x d. pretium centeni dim. marca. Et in quinquaginta pott' de eodem, iij sol. vj d.

Summa, xl sol. ij d. q.

Septimana nona post Pentecost'

Operarii In stipendiis quatuor operariorum ad quareram per quatuor dies, ij sol. quilibet per diem j d. ob.

Cariagium petre In una careta ad cariendum petram per idem, ij sol. iij d. videlicet per diem vij d. Et in duabus ad idem, iiij sol. viij d.

De calc' In xv cistis calci emptis, x sol. pretium ciste, viij d. Et in triginta de eodem, xx sol.

Rubeus sabulo In xvj pott' rubei sabulonis emptis, iij sol. j d. q. pretium pott' ij d. q.

Albus sabulo In xxv pott' albi sabulonis emptis, xx d. pretium centeni dim. marca.

Summa, xliij sol. ix d. q.

Septimana in qua fuit festum Sancti Jacobi Apostoli

Operarii In stipendiis quatuor operariorum ad quareram per quatuor dies, ij sol. vj d. quilibet per diem j d. ob.

Cariagium aque & crete In duabus caretis ad cariendum cretam & aquam per quatuor dies, iiij sol. viij d. videlicet per diem, vij d.

De calc' In xv cistis calci emptis, x sol. pretium ciste viij d.

Rubeus sabulo In xvj pott' rubei sabulonis emptis, iij sol. j d. pretium pott' ij d. q. In l de eodem ix sol. iiij d. ob.

Albus sabulo In l pott' albi sabulonis emptis, iij sol. iiij d. pretium centeni dim. marca.

Empciones In duabus gistis emptis ad prisonam, iiij sol. ij d.

Summa, xxxiij sol. j d. ob.

Carriage of water & chalk For three carts carrying chalk from the quarry and water for 4 days, 7*s.*, that is at 7*d.* a day.

Lime For the purchase of 9 sesters of lime, 6*s.*, at 8*d.* a sester. And for the purchase of 20 sesters of lime, 13*s.* 4*d.*

For the purchase of 13 potts of red sand, 2*s.* 5¼*d.*, price 2¼*d.* a pott. And for 20 potts of the same, 3*s.* 9*d.*

For the purchase of 13 potts of white sand, 10*d.*, price 6*s.* 8*d.* a 100. And for 50 potts of the same, 3*s.* 6*d.*

Total, £2. 0*s.* 2¼*d.*

The ninth week after Whitsun [14–20 July]

Labourers For the wages of 4 labourers at the quarry for 4 days, 2*s.*, each at 1½*d.* a day.

Carriage of stone For one cart carrying stone for the same period, 2*s.* 4*d.*, that is at 7*d.* a day. And for two carts for the same, 4*s.* 8*d.*

Lime For the purchase of 15 sesters of lime, 10*s.*, price 8*d.* a sester. And for 30 of the same, 20*s.*

Red sand For the purchase of 16 potts of red sand, 3*s.* 1¼*d.*,[1] price 2¼*d.* a pott.

White sand For the purchase of 25 potts of white sand, 20*d.*, price 6*s.* 8*d.* a 100.

Total, £2. 3*s.* 9¼*d.*

The week containing the feast of Saint James the Apostle [21–27 July]

Labourers For the wages of 4 labourers at the quarry for 4 days, 2*s.* 6*d.*, each at 1½*d.* a day.

Carriage of water and chalk For two carts to carry chalk and water for 4 days, 4*s.* 8*d.*, that is 7*d.* a day.

Lime For the purchase of 15 sesters of lime, 10*s.*, price 8*d.* a sester.

Red sand For the purchase of 16 potts of red sand, 3*s.* 1*d.*,[1] price 2¼*d.* a pott. For 50 of the same, 9*s.* 4½*d.*

White sand For the purchase of 50 potts of white sand, 3*s.* 4*d.*, price 6*s.* 8*d.* a 100.

Purchases For two joists bought for the prison, 4*s.* 2*d.*

Total, £1. 13*s.* 1½*d.*

[1] A mistake. The correct figure is 3*s.*

Septimana sequens

Carpentarius	In stipendiis unius carpentarii per quinque dies ad faciendum necessaria ad prisonam & ad cameras privatas, ij sol.
Operarii	In stipendiis novem operariorum ad quareram per quinque dies, v sol. vij d. ob. quilibet per diem j d. ob.
Cariagium aque & crete	In tribus caretis ad cariendum cretam & aquam per quinque dies, viij sol. ix d. videlicet careta per diem vij d.
De calc'	In xxx cistis calci emptis, xx sol. pretium ciste, viij d.
Rubeus sabulo	In xxx pott' rubei sabulonis emptis, v sol. vij d. ob. pretium pott' ij d. q.
Albus sabulo	In l pott' albi sabulonis emptis, iij sol. iiij d. pretium centeni dim. marca.
Empciones	In bordis & maeremio emptis ad cameras privatas de prisona, iij sol. x d. In virgis emptis ad scaffot, vj d.
	Summa, xlix sol. viij d.

Septimana sequens

Carpentarius	In stipendiis predicti carpentarii per septimanam, ij sol.
Operarii	In stipendiis decem operariorum ad quareram per quinque dies, viij sol. iiij d. quilibet per diem ij d. pro autumpno.
Cariagium aque & crete	In una careta ad quareram per quinque dies, ij sol. xj d. per diem vij d. In duabus caretis ad idem per quatuor dies & dim. v sol. iii d. quelibet per diem vij d.
De calc'	In xxx cistis calci emptis, xx sol. pretium ciste viij d.
Rubeus sabulo	In xxxvj pott' rubei sabulonis emptis, vj sol. ix d. pretium pott', ij d. q.
Albus sabulo	In l pott' albi sabulonis emptis, iij sol. iiij d. pretium centeni dim. marca.
	In vertevellis & guns emptis ad hostia turris, ij sol. vij d.
	Summa, lj sol. ij d.

The following week [28 July–3 August]

Carpenter	For the wages of one carpenter for 5 days making things needed for the prison and for the privy chambers, 2*s.*
Labourers	For the wages of 9 labourers at the quarry for 5 days, 5*s.* 7½*d.*, each at 1½*d.* a day.
Carriage of water and chalk	For 3 carts to carry chalk and water for 5 days, 8*s.* 9*d.*, that is at 7*d.* a cart per day.
Lime	For the purchase of 30 sesters of lime, 20*s.*, price 8*d.* a sester.
Red sand	For the purchase of 30 potts of red sand, 5*s.* 7½*d.*, price 2¼*d.* a pott.
White sand	For the purchase of 50 potts of white sand, 3*s.* 4*d.*, price 6*s.* 8*d.* a 100.
Purchases	For the purchase of boards and timber for the privy chambers of the prison, 3*s.* 10*d.* For the purchase of withies for scaffolding, 6*d.*
	Total, £2. 9*s.* 8*d.*

The following week [4–10 August]

Carpenter	For the wages of the aforesaid carpenter for a week, 2*s.*
Labourers	For the wages of 10 labourers at the quarry for 5 days, 8*s.* 4*d.*, each at 2*d.* a day because it was harvest-time.
Carriage of water & chalk	For one cart at the quarry for 5 days, 2*s.* 11*d.*, at 7*d.* a day. For 2 carts at the same for 4½ days, 5*s.* 3*d.*, each at 7*d.* a day.
Lime	For the purchase of 30 sesters of lime, 20*s.*, price 8*d.* a sester.
Red sand	For the purchase of 36 potts of red sand, 6*s.* 9*d.*, price 2¼*d.* a pott.
White sand	For the purchase of 50 potts of white sand, 3*s.* 4*d.*, price 6*s.* 8*d.* a 100.
	For hooks and eyes bought for the doors of the tower, 2*s.* 7*d.*
	Total, £2. 11*s.* 2*d.*

Septimana Assumpcionis beate Marie

Carpentarius In stipendiis predicti carpentarii per septimanam, ij sol.

Operarii In stipendiis novem operariorum ad quareram per quinque dies, vij sol. vj d. quilibet per diem ii d.

In stipendiis duorum operariorum ibidem per tres dies, xij d. quilibet ut supra.

Cariagium aque & crete In tribus caretis ad cariendum cretam de quarera & aquam per quinque dies, viii sol. ix d. quelibet per diem vij d.

De calc' In xxviij cistis calci emptis, xviij sol. viij d. pretium ciste viij d. Item pro tribus cistis calci, ij sol.

Rubeus sabulo In xxv pott' rubei sabulonis emptis, iiij sol. viij d. q. pretium pott' ij d. q.

In emendatione cuvarum & pro triginta circulis ad idem, xv d. In duobus bukettis emptis ad portandum morterium, ij d. In xxxviij bordis emptis ad cintros faciendos, iij sol. x d.

In duobus centenis albi sabulonis emptis, xiiij sol. pretium centeni, vij sol.

Summa, lxj sol. x d. q.

Septimana sequens

Carpentarii In stipendiis predicti carpentarii per septimanam, ij sol.

In stipendiis unius carpentarii per tres dies, xj d.

In stipendiis duorum secariorum per unum diem ad secandum quoddam lignum, vij d.

Operarii In stipendiis quinque operariorum ad portandum terram ad fundamentum turris per quatuor dies, iij sol. iiij d. quilibet per diem ij d.

Cariagium crete & aque In duabus caretis ad cariendum aquam per quinque dies, v sol. x d. quelibet per diem, vij d.

In sex caretis ad cariendum cretam per quinque dies, xvij sol. vj d. quelibet per diem vij d.

De calc' In xxvj cistis calci emptis, xvij sol. iiij d. pretium ciste viij d.

Rubeus sabulo In xxvij pott' rubei sabulonis, v sol. j d. q. pretium pott' ij d. q.

Albus sabulo In l pott' albi sabulonis emptis, iij sol. vj d. pretium centeni, vij sol.

Empciones In xvii cheverones emptis ad scaffot xij d. In virgis ad idem, vj d. In busca empta ad opus plumarii qui fudit cineres, viij d.

Summa, lviij sol. iij d. q.

The week of the Assumption of the Blessed Mary [11–17 August]

Carpenter For the wages of the aforesaid carpenter for a week, 2*s.*

Labourers For the wages of 9 labourers at the quarry for 5 days, 7*s.* 6*d.*, each at 2*d.* a day.
For the wages of 2 labourers there for 3 days, 12*d.*, each as above.

Carriage of water & chalk For 3 carts to carry chalk from the quarry and water for five days, 8*s.* 9*d.*, each at 7*d.* a day.

Lime For the purchase of 28 sesters of lime, 18*s.* 8*d.*, at 8*d.* a sester. And for 3 sesters of lime, 2*s.*

Red sand For the purchase of 25 potts of red sand, 4*s.* 8¼*d.*, price 2¼*d.* a pott.

For mending casks and for 30 hoops for the same, 15*d.*

For the purchase of 2 buckets to carry mortar, 2*d.* For the purchase of 38 boards to make centering, 3*s.* 10*d.*

For the purchase of 200 [potts] of white sand, 14*s.*, price 7*s.* a hundred.

Total, £3. 1*s.* 10¼*d.*

The week following [18–24 August]

Carpenters For the wages of the aforesaid carpenter for a week, 2*s.*

For the wages of one carpenter for 3 days, 11*d.*

For the wages of two sawyers for one day sawing some wood, 7*d.*

Labourers For the wages of 5 labourers carrying earth to the foundation of the tower for 4 days, 3*s.* 4*d.*, each at 2*d.* a day.

Carriage of chalk & water For two carts to carry water for 5 days, 5*s.* 10*d.*, each at 7*d.* a day.
For 6 carts to carry chalk for 5 days, 17*s.* 6*d.*, each at 7*d.* a day.

Lime For the purchase of 26 sesters of lime, 17*s.* 4*d.*, at 8*d.* a sester.

Red sand For 27 potts of red sand, 5*s.* 1¼*d.*, at 2¼*d.* a pott.

White sand For the purchase of 50 potts of white sand, 3*s.* 6*d.*, price 7*s.* a hundred.

Purchases For the purchase of 17 poles for scaffolding, 12*d.* For withies for the same, 6*d.* For brushwood bought for the plumber who founded the [lead] ashes, 8*d.*

Total, £2. 18*s.* 3¼*d.*

Septimana sequens

Carpentarii	In stipendiis duorum carpentariorum per septimanam, iij sol. viij d.
Operarii	In stipendiis quatuor operariorum per duos dies, xvj d. quilibet per diem ij d.
Cariagium crete & aque	In duabus caretis ad cariendum aquam & cretam per quinque dies, v sol. x d. quelibet per diem vij d.
De calc'	In xx cistis calci emptis, j marca pretium ciste viij d. Item in triginta cistis de eodem, xx sol.
Rubeus sabulo	In xv pott' rubei sabulonis emptis, ij sol. ix d. ob. & q. pretium pott' ij d. q.
Albus sabulo	In xxv pott' albi sabulonis emptis, xxj d. pretium centeni [vij sol.]
Empciones	In virgis emptis ad scaffot, iij d. ob. In duodecim ch[everonibus] emptis ad idem, vij d. In xxj bordis emptis ad hostia facienda & alia necessaria, iij sol. vjd. In clavis emptis ad idem . . . In l grapis factis ferreis ad ligandum turrim, iij sol. iiij d.
	Summa lvij sol. j d. q.

[*Septimana in qua fuit*] *festum Sancti Egidii*

	.... ad prosternendum maeremium in bosco domini electi Wintoniensis ad Turrim ....
	.... ij sol.
	.... per idem, vij sol. iiij d. quilibet per septimanam xxij d.
	.... ij sol.
Operarii	In stipendiis .... dim., xvij d. per diem ij d.
	In stipendiis unius operarii ....
	In tribus equis locatis ad opus .... vj d.
	In quodam allocato ad opus unius .... electi pro maeremio habendo, xx d.
	In expensis unius visorum qui ivit London' ad denarios impetrandos, ij s.
	In una careta ad aquam per sex dies, iij sol. ix d. pretium carete per diem vij d.

The week following [25–31 August]

Carpenters For the wages of two carpenters for a week, 3*s.* 8*d.*

Labourers For the wages of 4 labourers for 2 days, 16*d.*, each at 2*d.* a day.

Carriage of chalk & water For 2 carts to carry water and chalk for 5 days, 5*s.* 10*d.*, each at 7*d.* a day.

Lime For the purchase of 20 sesters of lime, 13*s.* 4*d.*, price 8*d.* a sester. And for 30 sesters of the same, 20*s.*

Red sand For the purchase of 15 potts of red sand, 2*s.* 9¾*d.*, price 2¼*d.* a pott.

White sand For the purchase of 25 potts of white sand, 21*d.*, price [7*s.*] a 100.

Purchases For withies bought for scaffolding, 3½*d.* For 12 poles bought for the same, 7*d.* For 21 boards bought to make doors and other requisites, 3*s.* 6*d.* For nails bought for the same purpose . . . For making 50 iron clamps to bind the tower, 3*s.* 4*d.*

Total £2. 17*s.* 1¼*d.*

The week containing the Feast of Saint Giles [1–7 September]

.... to fell timber for the tower in the wood belonging to the bishop elect of Winchester[1] .... 2*s.*

.... for the same 7*s.* 4*d.* each at 22*d.* a week.

.... 2*s.*

Labourers For the wages of .... ½, 17*d.*, at 2*d.* a day.

For the wages of one labourer......................

For 3 horses hired for the use .... 6*d.*

For a certain man allowed for one............ of the bishop elect to obtain timber, 20*d.*

For the expenses of one of the viewers who went to London to obtain money, 2*s.*

For one cart fetching water for 6 days, 3*s.* 9*d.*, price of the cart per day, 7*d.*

[1] Aymer de Valence, half-brother of the king, who had been elected Bishop of Winchester in 1250, but was not consecrated until 1260.

De calc' In sex cistis calci emptis, iiij sol. pretium ciste, viij d.

Rubeus sabulo In xv pottis rubei sabulonis, ij sol. ix d. ob. & q. pretium pott' ij d. q.

Albus sabulo In xxv pott' albi sabulonis emptis, xxj d. pretium centeni vij sol.

In mangnis veteribus muris de domo que quondam fuit Ismayne Aurebur per [preceptum?] magistrorum Johannis & Alexandri, iiij marce & dim. In duabus carettatis busce emptis ad opus plumbarii, xj d. ob. In uno quarteron' bordorum empto ad cintros faciendos, xv d. In l grapes emptis ad turrim ligandam, iii sol. iiij d. In clavis emptis ad cintros faciendos, xix d. In octo circulis ad ligandum quandam cuvam, iiij d. In plumbo empto de Johanne Edgar, xlvj sol. videlicet una charrea.[1]

Summa, viij li. 1 d. ob. q.

Memorandum quod convencionatum fuit coram magistris J. cementario et Alexandro carpentario in nundinis Sancti Egidii die Jovis proxima ante exaltacionem Sancte Crucis visoribus tunc ibidem presentibus quod magister Johannes Withe saceret[2] ad custum suum proprium alias viginti quercus quas dominus electus dedit domino Regi in parco de Merdune & quadrabit. Et secabit plankas & pl[a]ncabit ad idem custum. Et convencionatum fuit cum eodem Johanne pro omnibus predictis faciendis per decem marcas. Quas idem Johannes de vicecomite & visoribus recepit per particulas per talliam inde inter eos factam.

Summa, x marce

Septimana in qua fuit festum Nativitatis beate Marie anno eodem

Memorandum de hostio tesauri In stipendiis unius cementarii ad reparandum quoddam hostium in turri quod multum indigebat reparacioni per septimanam, ij sol. In stipendiis duorum cementariorum ad idem & per idem, iij sol. quilibet per septimanam, xviii d.

In stipendiis unius cementarii ad idem & per idem, xvij d. In stipendiis duorum cementariorum ad idem per duos dies, xvj d.

[1] The last two words appear to have been added later.
[2] For *secaret*.

Lime For the purchase of 6 sesters of lime, 4*s*., price 8*d*. a sester.

Red sand For 15 potts of red sand, 2*s*. 9¾*d*., price 2¼*d*. a pott.

White sand For the purchase of 25 potts of white sand, 21*d*., price 7*s*. a 100.

For the great old walls of the house that used to belong to Ismayne Aurebur, purchased by [order] of Masters John and Alexander for £3. For 2 cart-loads of brushwood bought for the use of the plumber, 11½*d*. For a quarter of boards bought to make centering, 15*d*. For 50 clamps bought to bind the tower, 3*s*. 4*d*. For nails bought to make centering, 19*d*. For 8 hoops to bind a certain cask, 4*d*. For lead bought from John Edgar, 46*s*., that is one char.

Total, £8. 0*s*. 1¾*d*.

Memorandum that at St. Giles' Fair on Thursday before the Exaltation of the Holy Cross [12 September] it was agreed before Masters John the mason and Alexander the carpenter, and in the presence of the viewers, that Master John Withe[1] should at his own expense saw and square the other 20 oaks which the lord bishop elect gave to the lord king in his park of Merdon.[2] And he will cut the planks and plank [the floor?] at his own cost, And it was agreed with the said John that he should do all this for £6. 13*s*. 4*d*., which the said John received from the sheriff and viewers by instalments in accordance with a tally made between them.

Total, £6. 13*s*. 4*d*.

The week in the same year containing the feast of the blessed Mary [8–14 September]

Note concerning the Treasury doorway For the wages of a mason repairing a certain doorway in the tower which much needed repair, for one week, 2*s*. For the wages of two masons doing the same for the same period, 3*s*., each at 18*d*. a week.

For the wages of a mason doing the same for the same period, 17*d*. For the wages of two masons doing the same for two days, 16*d*.

[1] The name is difficult to read. [2] In the parish of Hursley.

In stipendiis unius operarii per totam septimanam in castro ad serviendum eisdem cementariis, ix d.

In tribus caretis ad cariendum aquam & cretam per septimanam, x sol. vj d. In xxx cistis calci emptis, xx sol. In xl pott' rubei sabulonis, vij sol. vj d. In C pott' albi sabulonis, vij sol.

In duabus carettatis busce emptis ad plumer', xx d. In sepo cera & pice emptis ad idem, v d. ob. In duabus caretatis busce emptis ad fundendum plumbum ad ligaturas Turris, xiiij d. In virgis emptis ad scaffot, viij d. ob.

Summa, lvij sol. vj d.

Septimana sequens

In stipendiis trium operariorum ad prosternendum predictum murum emptum & dividendum petram a sabulone, ij sol. iij d. In stipendiis unius operarii ad idem per quatuor dies, vj d. In stipendiis unius carete ad cariendum eandem petram ad castrum per septimanam, iij sol. vj d. per diem, vij d.

In una careta ad cariendum cretam de quarera & aquam per totam septimanam, iij sol. ix d. per diem, vij d.

In novem cistis calci emptis, vj sol. pretium ciste, viij d.

In uno quarteron' bordorum empto ad cintros faciendos, ix d. Item in bordis emptis ad idem, xv d.

In clavis emptis ad cintros faciendos, j d. In quadam civer' & uno crebro emptis, ij d.

In maeremio cariato de placia ante castrum ubi carpentatum fuit usque turrim, vij d. In tribus caretatis busce emptis ad plumer', xvij d. ob. In quadam parva cabla empta ad maeremium traendum, ij sol. vj d. In virgis emptis ad scaffot, iij d. ob. In cepo empto ad plumer', i d. In duodecim libris stangminis ad idem, xviij d.

Summa, xxiiij sol. viij d.

For the wages of a labourer to serve the said masons in the castle for a whole week, 9*d.*

For three carts to carry water and chalk during the week, 10*s.* 6*d.* For the purchase of 30 sesters of lime, 20*s.* For 40 potts of red sand, 7*s.* 6*d.* For 100 potts of white sand, 7*s.*

For two cart-loads of brushwood bought for the plumbery, 20*d.* For tallow, wax, and pitch bought for the same, 5½*d.* For two cart-loads of brushwood bought to found lead for the clamps of the tower,[1] 14*d.* For withies bought for scaffolding, 8½*d.*

Total, £2. 17*s.* 6*d.*

The week following [15–21 September]

For the wages of three labourers pulling down the wall that was purchased and separating the stone from the sand, 2*s.* 3*d.* For the wages of one labourer doing the same for 4 days, 6*d.* For the wages of one cart to carry the same stone to the castle for a week, 3*s.* 6*d.*, at 7*d.* a day.

For one cart to carry chalk from the quarry and water throughout the week, 3*s.* 9*d.* [*sic*], at 7*d.* a day.

For the purchase of 9 sesters of lime, 6*s.*, price 8*d.* a sester.

For one quarter of boards bought to make centering, 9*d.* And for boards bought for the same purpose, 15*d.*

For nails bought to make centering, 1*d.* For the purchase of a barrow and a sieve, 2*d.*

For the carriage of timber to the tower from the place before the castle where the carpenters worked, 7*d.* For 3 cart-loads of firewood bought for the plumbery, 17½*d.* For the purchase of a certain small cable to draw timber, 2*s.* 6*d.* For withies bought for scaffolding, 3½*d.* For tallow bought for the plumbery, 1*d.* For 12 pounds of tin for the same, 18*d.*

Total, 24*s.* 8*d.*

[The remainder of the roll is missing. Sewn up with it is a fragment of another roll of which the text is printed below. The total of £233. 14*s.* 2½*d.*, given at the end of this fragment, corresponds to the total claimed by the sheriff of Hampshire in 1258–9 for works carried out under a writ of June 1256 (*Calendar of Liberate Rolls 1251–60*, pp. 307–8: Pipe Roll E 372/103, rot. 1). The works recorded in the roll printed above

[1] The tower was evidently being secured by iron ties and bands run in lead.

De gradu de camera Rosamunde usque capellam prope lectum

In stipendiis sex carpentariorum ad faciendum quendam gradum lingneum subtus gradum petrinum per unam septimanam, xij sol. quilibet per septimanam, ij sol.

In stipendiis duodecim talliatorum talliantium petram ad predictum gradum per quindecim dies, xl sol. quilibet per septimanam xx d.

In stipendiis decem operariorum ad frangendum murum ubi hostia de novo facta sunt & ad separandum mortarium de petra & ad ministrandum cementariis per idem, xx sol. quilibet per diem ij d.

In stipendiis sex cucheriorum ad idem & per idem, xxiiij sol. quilibet per septimanam ij sol.

In decem cistis calci emptis ad idem, dim. marca.

In albo & rubeo sabulone empto ad idem, iij sol.

In stipendiis cuiusdam carpentarii ad faciendum quoddam hostium de novo ibidem. Bordis & vertevellis & huiusmodi emptis ad idem, dim. marca.

Summa, Cxij sol. ix d.

In fenestris & hostiis de novo in turri emendatis & aliis emendandis que indigebant emendacione videlicet gutteriis emendendis & muris rimandis & emendandis, xlj sol. j d. ob.

Summa, xlj sol. j d. ob.

Summa probata CCxxxiij li. xiiij sol. ij d. ob.

may have been among those ordered by a writ of November 1256 (*Cal. Liberate Rolls 1251–60*, p. 343), for which the sheriff also accounted in November 1258–9 (Pipe Roll as cited), but the particulars do not correspond, and it appears more likely that they were authorized by some other writ whose text has not survived.]

Concerning the stair from Rosamund's Chamber to the chapel next the [king's] bed

For the wages of 6 carpenters making a certain wooden stair below the stone stair, for one week, 12*s*., each at 2*s*. a week.

For the wages of 12 stone-cutters cutting stone for the said stair for a fortnight, 40*s*., each at 20*d*. a week.

For the wages of 10 labourers breaking through the wall where the doorways are newly made and separating the mortar from the stone and serving the masons, for the same period, 20*s*., each at 2*d*. a day.

For the wages of six layers doing the same for the same period, 24*s*., each at 2*s*. a week.

For the purchase of 10 sesters of lime for the same, 6*s*. 8*d*.

For the purchase of white and red sand bought for the same, 3*s*.

For the wages of a certain carpenter making a new door there: for boards and eyes and such-like bought for the same, 6*s*. 8*d*.

Total, £5. 12*s*. 9*d*.

For newly repairing windows and doors in the tower and other things that needed repair, namely repairing gutters and examining and repairing walls, 41*s*. 1½*d*.

Total, 41*s*. 1½*d*.

Total checked £233. 14*s*. 2½*d*.

III. WESTMINSTER

1. Selected writs relating to royal works at Westminster, 1249–1269

(i) Rex Thesaurario & Camerariis suis salutem. Liberate de Thesauro nostro custodibus operationum nostrarum Westmonasterii quater xx & decem libras & novem solidos ad perficiendum pacacionem que debetur operariis predictarum operacionum usque ad diem Sabbati proximam post festum beate Fidis Virginis. Liberate etiam de eodem Thesauro nostro eisdem custodibus octo libras & tres solidos quos posuerunt per preceptum nostrum in quatuor carratis plumbi emptis & missis usque Windes'.

Teste Rege apud Westmonasterium ix die Octobris.

(Liberate Roll 33 Henry III, m. 2.)

(ii) Rex injungit Magistro Johanni de Sancto Omero, quod garderobam camere regis apud Westmonasterium perpingi faciat, sicut pictura illius garderobe inchoatur; et quod faciat unum lectrinum ponendum in novo capitulo Westmonasterii ad similitudinem illius quod est in capitulo Sancti Albani, vel decentius et pulcrius, si fieri poterit; et ad hoc faciendum, colores et maeremium et necessarias liberaciones usque ad adventum regis Lond' ei inveniri faciet. Et custum ad hoc appositum, cum rex illud sciverit, reddi faciet. Et mandatum est abbati Westmonasteriensi, Edwardo filio Odonis et Philippo Luvel quod liberaciones et alia necessaria ut supra inveniri faciant.

Teste rege apud Wind' xxiii. die Septembris.

(*Close Rolls 1247–51*, p. 203.)

(iii) Rex Thesaurario & Camerariis suis salutem. Liberate de Thesauro nostro custodibus operacionum Ecclesie Westm' tria milia DCC quater viginti & novem libras xvj solidos x denarios & obolum quos posuerunt per preceptum nostrum in eisdem operationibus factis a termino Pasche anno etc. xxxj° usque ad Pentecost' anno etc. xxxiij°.

Teste Rege apud Westmonasterium xxv die Aprilis anno etc. xxxiij°.

(Liberate Roll 33 Henry III, m. 2.)

(iv) Mandatum est Edwardo de Westmonasterio quod faciat habere Magistro Johanni de Sancto Odomero denarios ad operaciones regis quas rex ei injunxit faciendas, et ad expensas suas; et cum rex sciverit quantum ei liberaverit, breve suum de Liberate eidem Edwardo inde habere faciet.

Teste rege apud Clarend' viij. die Decembris.

(*Close Rolls 1247–51*, p. 245.)

(v) Mandatum est thesaurario et camerariis quod pacari faciant operariis regis Westmonasterii stipendia sua usque ad Natale Domini anno etc.

1. Selected writs relating to royal works at Westminster, 1249–1269

(i) The king greets his Treasurer and chamberlains [of the Exchequer]. Deliver from our Treasury to the keepers of our works of Westminster £90. 9*s.* to complete the payment owing to the workmen employed on the said works up to the Saturday next after the feast of the blessed Faith the Virgin [9 October]. Deliver also from our same Treasury to the same keepers £8. 3*s.* which they laid out by our order on buying four chars of lead and sending them to Windsor.

Attested by the king at Westminster, 9 October [1249].

(ii) The king commands Master John of St. Omer to cause the wardrobe of the king's chamber at Westminster to be painted throughout as the painting of that wardrobe was begun; and to make a lectern to be placed in the new chapter-house at Westminster similar to the one in the chapter-house at St. Albans, and if possible even more handsome and beautiful; and for this purpose the king will arrange for the provision of colours and timber and for the necessary expenditure until the king returns to London. And when the king knows how much this has cost, he will have him reimbursed. And the abbot of Westminster, Edward son of Odo and Philip Lovel are directed to provide for the payments and other necessaries as above.

Attested by the king at Windsor, 23 September [1249].

(iii) The king to his Treasurer and chamberlains [of the Exchequer]. Deliver from our Treasury to the keepers of the works of the church of Westminster £3,789. 16*s.* 10½*d.* which they have laid out by our order on performing those works between Easter in the 31st year of our reign [1247] and Whitsun in the 33rd year [1249].

Attested by the king at Westminster, 25 April in the 33rd year [1249].

(iv) Edward of Westminster is directed to let Master John of St. Omer have money for the king's works which the king has ordered him to carry out, and for his expenses; and when the king knows how much he has paid him, he will let the said Master Edward have his writ of *Liberate* for that amount.

Attested by the king at Clarendon, 8 December [1249].

(v) The Treasurer and chamberlains [of the Exchequer] are ordered to have the wages of the king's workmen at Westminster paid up to

xxxiiij[to]. Et cum rex sciverit summam, breve suum de Liberate eis inde habere faciet.

Teste rege apud Clarend' xiij. die Decembris.

(*Close Rolls 1247–51*, pp. 245–6.)

(vi) Rex Thesaurario & camerariis suis salutem. Liberate de thesauro nostro dilecto clerico nostro Edwardo de Westmonasterio cccc xxxj li. x sol. v d. & ob. ad perficiendum inde pacaciones operariis nostris de Westmonasterio a die sancte Fidis Virginis usque ad vigiliam Natalis Domini, anno regni nostri xxxiiij.

Teste ut supra.

(Liberate Roll 34 Henry III, m. 11.)

(vii) Mandatum est vicecomiti Kancie quod omnes illos de balliva sua, qui petram grisiam habent ad vendendum, distringat ad petram illam cariandam usque Westmonasterium ad operaciones nostras ibidem inde faciendas. Et rex de precio venditoribus illius petre ibidem satisfieri faciet. Teste rege apud Westmonasterium v. die Februarii.

(*Close Rolls 1247–51*, p. 262.)

(viii) Mandatum est W. de Haverhull' et Edwardo de Westmonasterio quod mutuo aut alio modo, prout melius poterunt, perquirant ccc. marcas, et eas liberent custodibus operacionum ecclesie Westmonasterii ad fabricam ejusdem ecclesie, ita quod pro defectu pecunie fabrica illa non remaneat. Teste rege apud Clarend' xxiiij. die Julii.

(*Close Rolls 1247–51*, p. 307.)

(ix) Rex thesaurario et camerariis suis salutem. Mandamus vobis quod operariis operacionum nostrarum Westm' pacari faciatis stipendia de sex septimanis proximo preteritis. Teste rege apud Wintoniam xiij. die Novembris.

(*Close Rolls 1247–51*, p. 375.)

(x) Mandatum est Edwardo de Westmonasterio quod de denariis quos vicecomes Norff' mittit usque Westmonasterium ei liberandos solvi faciat stipendia operariorum ecclesie Westmonasterii, provisuri [*sic*] quod sexcenti vel octingenti in adventu regis operentur ibidem. Teste rege apud Norwicum xix. die Marcii.

(*Close Rolls 1247–51*, p. 423.)

(xi) Quia rex vellet quod operaciones ecclesie Westmonasterii multum expedirentur, mandatum est Henrico, magistro predictarum operacionum, quod totum opus marmoreum quod fieri poterit sine periculo in hac hyeme levari faciat. Teste rege apud Walingford' xxx. die Octobris.

(*Close Rolls 1251–3*, p. 174.)

(xii) Mandatum est Edwardo de Westmonasterio quod, statim visis litteris istis, magnam novam campanam pendere faciat, ita quod pulsari possit in vigilia Beati Edwardi, nec a London' recedat antequam id fieri

Christmas in the 34th year [1249]. And when the king knows the total, he will let them have his writ of *Liberate*.

Attested by the king at Clarendon, 13 December [1249].

(vi) The king greets his Treasurer and chamberlains. Deliver from our Treasury to our beloved clerk Edward of Westminster £431. 10*s*. 5½*d*. to complete the payment of our workmen of Westminster from St. Faith's day [6 October] to Christmas Eve [24 December] in the 34th year of our reign.

Attested as above [At Westminster 21 January, 1250].

(vii) The sheriff of Kent is directed to compel all those in his bailiwick[1] who have ragstone to sell to carry that stone to Westminster in order to perform our works there with it. And the king will arrange for the sellers of that stone to be satisfied for the cost there.

Attested by the king at Westminster, 5 February [1250].

(viii) William of Haverhill[2] and Edward of Westminster are directed to obtain, by loan or by any other means, as best they can, £200, and to pay them to the keepers of the works of the church of Westminster for the building of the said church, so that that building is not held up for lack of money.

Attested by the king at Clarendon, 24 July [1250].

(ix) The king greets his Treasurer and chamberlains of the Exchequer. We direct you to pay the wages of the workmen engaged on our works at Westminster for the six weeks last past.

Attested by the king at Winchester, 13 November [1250].

(x) Edward of Westminster is directed to pay the wages of the workmen engaged on the church at Westminster from the money which the sheriff of Norfolk is sending to Westminster, taking care that 600 or 800 men are working there when the king arrives.

Attested by the king at Norwich, 19 March [1251].

(xi) Because the king wishes that the works of the church of Westminster should be greatly speeded up, Henry, the master of the said works, is directed to have all the marble work raised this winter that can be done without danger.

Attested by the king at Wallingford, 30 October [1252].

(xii) Edward of Westminster is ordered, immediately he has seen these letters, to have the great new bell hung, so that it can be rung on the eve of the blessed Edward [4 January], and he is not to leave London until

[1] i.e. the county of Kent.

[2] Then the king's Treasurer.

fecerit. Maeremium eciam querat ad cumulum novi operis regis ecclesie Westmonasterii et ad stalla monachorum in eadem ecclesia facienda. Et, quamcito poterit, operari faciat circa factoram [*sic*] stallorum illorum. Teste rege apud Clarendon' xxv. die Novembris. Per regem.

(*Close Rolls 1251–3*, p. 280.)

(xiii) Mandatum est Philippo Lovel Thesaurario et Edwardo de Westmonasterio quod per denarios de Thesauro Regis vel aliunde de debitis Regis faciant revocare operarios ecclesie Westmonasterii qui decesserunt ut intimatum fuit Regi ita quod opus predictum sub debita maturitate procedat, quia oportet quod consecretur ad ultimum in festo Translationis Sancti Edwardi quod erit in quindena Sancti Michaelis.

(Patent Roll 39 Henry III, Part 1, m. 3.)

(xiv) Quia cementarii et alii operarii apud Westmonasterium pro defectu denariorum recedere volunt, ut rex audivit, mandatum est Philippo Luvel, thesaurario regis, quod scrutatis diligenter debitis que regi debentur ubi melius expedire viderit, vel de comitatibus Sussex' et Suth', vel de itineribus justiciariorum ibidem vel alibi, cum omni celeritate perquirat denarios ad operacionem illam usque ad cccc. libras, ita quod pro defectu denariorum operacio illa non impediatur. Et rex de denariis quos ad hoc liberaverit faciet ei habere breve de Liberate. Teste rege apud Wodest' xiij. die Februarii.

(*Close Rolls 1254–6* p. 274.)

(xv) Rex Thesaurario & camerariis suis salutem. Liberate de Thesauro nostro quinque milia marcarum ad operaciones nostras Westm' ita quod pecunia illa liberetur citra festum Natalis Domini. Teste Rege apud Geudef' xx die Junii.

(Liberate Roll 40 Henry III, m. 7.)

(xvi) Mandatum est eidem quod magistris Ricardo de Eltham, Willelmo de Wauz, cementariis, Odoni carpentario, Eduuardo vitreario, Henrico fabro, Waltero clerico operacionum regis Westmonasterii et Gilberto carpentario Wind' et Agneti uxori magistri Johannis le Macun et Argentine uxori magistri Alexandri carpentarii regis faciat habere robas suas contra instans festum Pentecostes de dono regis sicut eas prius habere consueverunt. Teste rege apud Westmonasterium iiij. die Maii.

(*Close Rolls 1256–9*, pp. 218–19.)

(xvii) Quia caminus camere Regis apud Westmonasterium debilis est, mandatum est Johanni de Crachale Thesaurario Regis quod statim post

he has had this done. He is also to seek timber to make the roof of the king's new work at the church of Westminster, and for the monks' stalls in the said church. And, as soon as he can, he is to put the work of those stalls in hand.

Attested by the king at Clarendon, 25 November [1252]. Issued by the king's authority.

(xiii) Philip Lovel, Treasurer, and Edward of Westminster are ordered, with money from the King's treasury or elsewhere from money owed to the King to recall the workmen of the church of Westminster who, as the king is informed, have left, so that the aforesaid work may proceed at its due speed. For it is necessary that it should be consecrated at the latest on the feast of the Translation of St. Edward [13 October] which will fall on the 15th day after Michaelmas.

[Undated, but enrolled between two patents dated 7 November 1254.]

(xiv) Because the masons and other workmen at Westminster want, so the king has heard, to leave for lack of money, Philip Lovel, the king's Treasurer, is ordered carefully to examine the debts owing to the king, and from whatever source he thinks best, whether from the counties of Sussex and Hampshire, or from the sessions of the justices there or elsewhere, with all speed to obtain money for that work up to the sum of £400, so that that work shall not be hindered for lack of money. And for the money which he pays out for this purpose the king will let him have a writ of *Liberate*.

Attested by the king at Woodstock, 13 February [1256].

(xv) The king greets his Treasurer and chamberlains [of the Exchequer]. Deliver from our Treasury £3,333. 6*s*. 8*d*. for our works at Westminster, so that this money be delivered before Christmas.

Attested by the king at Guildford, 20 June [1256].

(xvi) He[1] is also directed to let Masters Richard of Eltham, William de Wauz, masons, Master Odo the carpenter, Master Edward the glazier, Master Henry the smith, Walter the clerk of the king's works at Westminster, and Gilbert the carpenter at Windsor, and Agnes the wife of Master John the Mason, and Argentine the wife of Master Alexander the king's carpenter, have their suits of clothes against the coming feast of Whitsun by the king's gift as they have previously been accustomed to have them.

Attested by the king at Westminster, 4 May [1258].

(xvii) Since the chimney of the king's chamber at Westminster is weak, John of Crakehall, the king's treasurer, is ordered to see that the

[1] Peter des Rivaux, keeper of the Wardrobe.

parleamentum Regis quod erit post instans Pascha predictum caminum prosterni & unum bonum caminum & fortem ibidem construi faciat. Et Rex cum sciverit custum quod ad hoc posuerit ei inde breve de liberate Rex fieri faciet. Teste ut supra. Vacat.

(Liberate Roll 43 Henry III, m. 5.)

(xviii) Quia rex injunxit magistro Johanni de Glouc', cementario suo, quod caminum camere regis apud Westmonasterium, qui minatur ruinam, reparari, et conductum aque que sub terra ducitur ad lavatorium regis et ad alia loca Westmonasterii emendari faciat, et quod inter coquinas regis et Tamisiam quendam conductum fieri faciat quo sordes coquinarum illarum defluere possint usque in Tamisiam, quia fetor aque sordide que per aulas nostras deportatur corrumpit homines conversantes in eisdem; et quod defectus aliarum domorum regis Westmonasterii reparari faciat reparacione qua necessario indigent; mandatum est Johanni de Crakhal', thesaurario, quod ad hec omnia facienda Martino de Chaunflur, clerico recepte, et eidem Johanni denarios habere faciat. Et, cum rex sciverit quantum ei liberaverint, breve de Liberate inde sibi habere faciet. Teste rege apud Westmonasterium xxx. die Aprilis.

(*Close Rolls 1256–9*, p. 380.)

(xix) Henricus dei gratia Rex Anglie Dominus Hibernie Dux Normannie Aquitannie & Comes Andegavie Magistro Johanni de Gloucestr' cementario suo & custodibus operacionum Westm' saiutem. Precipimus vobis quod quinque ymagines regum excisas in franca petra & quandam petram ad supponendum pedibus unius ymaginis beate Marie faciatis habere custodibus operacionum ecclesie sancti Martini London' ad easdem operaciones de dono nostro.

Teste meipso apud Westmonasterium xij° die Maii anno regni nostri xliij°.

(Westminster Abbey Muniments 15999(c).)

(xx) Mandatum est Edwardo de Westmonasterio, suppriori et sacriste Westmonasterii quod veterem fabricam ecclesie Westmonasterii prosterni faciant usque ad vestiarium quod est juxta sedem regis et eandem ecclesiam de pecunia ad operaciones ecclesie illius assignata relevari faciant prout alia fabrica ibidem incepta requirit. Reparari eciam faciant altaria in alis dicte nove fabrice et ipsa prout opus fuerit includi ita quod monachi ejusdem domus divina ibidem possint celebrare. Teste rege apud Wodestok' iij. die Junii.

(*Close Rolls 1256–9*, p. 390.)

aforesaid chimney is pulled down immediately after the king's parliament which will be after this Easter [13 April] and that a good and strong one is built there. And when the king knows the cost that has been laid out for this he will cause a writ of *liberate* to be made out for him [John] on that account.

Attested as above [by the king at Westminster 7 April, 1259]. Cancelled.[1]

(xviii) Since the king has directed Master John of Gloucester, his mason, to cause the chimney of the king's chamber at Westminster, which threatens to fall, to be repaired, and to have the conduit of water which runs underground to the king's lavatory and to other places in Westminster, repaired, and to cause a certain conduit to be made between the king's kitchens and the Thames, through which the waste from those kitchens can flow away into the Thames, because the stench of the dirty water which is carried through our halls infects men frequenting them; and to have such other repairs as are needed carried out to the king's other buildings at Westminster, John of Crakehall, the Treasurer, is ordered to make money to carry out all these tasks available to Martin de Chanflur, clerk of the Receipt, and to the same John. And when the king knows how much has been paid to him, he will let him [the Treasurer] have a writ of *Liberate* for that sum.

Attested by the king at Westminster, 30 April [1259].

(xix) Henry, by the grace of God, King of England, Lord of Ireland, Duke of Normandy and Aquitaine and Count of Anjou sends greetings to Master John of Gloucester his mason and the keepers of the works at Westminster. We order you to supply to the keepers of the works of the church of St. Martin at London for those works by our gift five statues of kings cut in freestone and a certain stone to support the feet of a statue of the blessed Mary.

Witnessed by me at Westminster 12 May in the 43rd year of our reign [1259].

(xx) Edward of Westminster, the sub-prior and the sacrist of Westminster are ordered to have the old fabric of the church of Westminster pulled down as far as the vestry which is by the king's seat, and to have the same church rebuilt out of the money assigned for the works of that church in such manner as the new[2] fabric begun there requires. They are also to have the altars in the aisles of the said new fabric repaired, and to have them enclosed as necessary, so that the monks of that house can celebrate divine service there.

Attested by the king at Woodstock, 3 June [1259].

[1] Presumably in favour of the following writ.

[2] Literally 'the other'.

(xxi) Henricus dei gratia Rex Anglie Dominus Hibernie Aquitannie & Comes Andegavie Magistro Johanni de Glouc' cementario suo salutem. Mandamus vobis quod statim visis litteris istis scire nobis faciatis distincte & aperte utrum custus plumbi empti et custus reparacionis domorum nostrarum Westmonasterii computetur infra summam xxviij M.C. xxvij li. xv s. x d. ob. quam nobis transmisistis vel non. Et hoc non omittatis.

Teste meipso apud Merton' vi die Octobris anno regni nostri xliij.

(Westminster Abbey Muniments 15999(d).)

xxii) Rex dilecto clerico suo Waltero de Merton' salutem. Cum nuper ante recessum nostrum ab Anglia ordinaremus quod denarii provenientes de exitu sigilli nostri Anglie, salva racionabili et moderata sustentacione clericorum cancellarie nostre quos exhibere debemus, custodibus operacionum nostrorum Westmonasterii liberarentur ad operaciones predictas inde faciendas, vos a tempore quo recessimus ab Anglia denarios predictos recepistis nec ad operaciones predictas prefatis custodibus inde quicquam liberastis, ut audivimus, super quo non mediocriter movemur. Quocirca vobis mandamus quod denarios predictos a tempore predicto receptos, salva sustentacione predicta, una cum illis quos ab eodem sigillo recipietis usque adventum nostrum in Angliam prefatis custodibus ad predictas operaciones nostras inde faciendas liberetis; et quantum prefatis custodibus liberaveritis nobis significetis. Teste rege apud Sanctum Adomarum xx. die Februarii anno etc. xliiij.

(*Close Rolls 1259–61*, p. 241.)

(xxiii) Henricus dei gratia Rex Anglie Dominus Hibernie Dux Aquitannie Edwardo de Westmonasterio & Roberto de Beverlaco custodibus operacionum suarum Westmonasterii salutem. Mandamus vobis quod de quarera quam emitis ad operaciones predictas faciatis habere dilectis nobis in Christo fratribus Predicatoribus London' duo milia libere petre ad studia sua perficienda de dono nostro & petram illam venire facias London'.

Teste me ipso apud Turrim Londonie xiij die Februarii anno regni nostri xlv^to^.

(Westminster Abbey Muniments, 16000(b).)

(xxiv) Rex dilectis sibi Ricardo de Bamfeld' & Bartholomeo de Castello custodibus cambiorum suorum Lond' & Cantuar' salutem. Quia ad perfectionem operacionum nostrarum Westm' denariis ad presens quamplurimum indigemus vobis mandamus quod omnes denarios quos de exitibus cambiorum predictorum recepturi estis a tempore confectionis presencium Thesaurario & camerariis nostris ad Scaccarium nostrum modis omnibus persolvatis per manus eorum dilecto clerico nostro Ade Stratton' & sociis suis custodibus operacionum predictarum ulterius liberandos ad easdem operaciones inde faciendas.

(xxi) Henry, by the grace of God, King of England, Lord of Ireland, Duke of Normandy and Aquitaine and Count of Anjou sends greetings to Master John of Gloucester his mason. We command that as soon as you have seen these letters you shall inform us clearly and openly whether the purchase of lead and the cost of the repair of our buildings at Westminster are accounted within the sum of £28,127. 15*s.* 10½*d.* which you have sent us, or not. And you are to do this without fail.

Witnessed by myself at Merton, 6 October in the 43rd year of our reign [1259].

(xxii) The king greets his beloved clerk Walter of Merton. Before our departure from England we lately directed that the money deriving from the issues of our seal of England should, allowing for the reasonable and moderate maintenance of the clerks of our Chancery whom we are bound to support, be paid to the keepers of our works at Westminster in order to perform the said works. You have received the said money since the time when we left England, but, as we have heard, have not paid any of it to the said keepers for the said works, as a result of which we are in no small measure displeased. Wherefore we order you to pay to the said keepers, to carry on our said works, the said money that has been received since the said time, reserving the said maintenance, together with what you shall have received from the said seal up to the time of our arrival in England, and you are to inform us how much you have paid to the said keepers.

Attested by the king at St. Omer, 20 February in the 44th year [1260].

(xxiii) Henry, by the grace of God, King of England, Lord of Ireland and Duke of Aquitaine sends greetings to Edward of Westminster and Robert of Beverley, keepers of his works at Westminster. We command you that from the quarry which you are buying for the aforesaid work you should supply to our beloved in Christ the Friars Preachers of London 2,000 freestones by our gift to complete their buildings for study and you should arrange for the stone to be brought to London.

Witnessed by myself at the Tower of London, 13 February in the 45th year of our reign [1261].

(xxiv) The king greets his beloved Richard de Bamfeld and Bartholomew de Castello, wardens of the mints of London and Canterbury. Since we are at present greatly in need of money to complete our works of Westminster, we order you to pay to our Treasurer and chamberlains at our Exchequer all the money which you shall receive from the issues of the aforesaid mints from the date of the present [letters]. They will pass it on to our beloved clerk Adam Stratton and his fellows,

Et hoc pro aliquo mandato nostro vobis directo seu dirigendo nullatenus omittatis. Teste Rege apud Westmonasterium xviij die Januarii.

(Patent Roll 53 Henry III, m. 23.)

(xxv) Rex omnibus etc. salutem. Sciatis quod dilecta nobis Alesia de Lascy liberavit per preceptum nostrum custodibus operacionum nostrarum Westm' per undecim annos videlicet de annis regni nostri xliij xliiij xlv xlvj xlvij° xlviij° xlix° l° lj° lij° liij° tria milia & septingentas & quinquaginta & quatuor libras, quatuordecim solidos & octo denarios de fine suo trescentarum[*sic*] sexaginta duarum librarum trium solidorum & octo denariorum annuorum quem nobiscum fecit pro habenda custodia terrarum & heredis Edmundi de Lascy defuncti qui de nobis tenuit in capite usque ad legitimam etatem heredis eiusdem Edmundi & quinquaginta libras Henrico de Lascy heredi predicti Edmundi infra etatem existenti ad sustentacionem suam de dono nostro. Et centum & sex libras Nicholao de Leukenor' quondam custodi garderobe nostre die Mercurii in vigilia apostolorum Simonis & Jude anno regni nostri lj°. Et centum & decem marcas priori de parco de Helawe de decem marcis annuis quas idem prior percipit de molendinis de Castreford' de qua quidem peccunia eadem Alesia habet litteras nostras patentes & tallias de scaccario operacionum nostrarum Westm & breve nostrum de Allocate de predictis centum & decem marcis quas etiam dei [*sic*] litteras nostras patentes simul cum istis litteris nostris patentibus eadem Alesia tenetur restituere ad Scaccarium nostrum factis sibi prius allocacione & quietancia de peccunia supradicta.

In cuius etc.

Teste ut supra.

(Patent Roll 54 Henry III, m. 28.)

keepers of the aforesaid works, therewith to carry out the work. And you are not to omit to do this on account of any other mandate of ours that has been or will be directed to you.

Attested by the king at Westminster, 18 January [1269].

(xxv) The king greets all to whom the present letters shall come. Know that our beloved Alice de Lacy has delivered by our order to the keepers of our works of Westminster during eleven years, to wit from 43 to 53 Henry III [October 1258 to October 1269] £3,754. 14*s.* 8*d.* of her fine of £362. 3*s.* 8*d.* a year which she made with us to have the wardship of the lands and heir of the late Edmund de Lacy, who held from us in chief, until Edmund's heir came of age, and £50 to Henry de Lacy, heir of the same Edmund, being under age, for his maintenance of our gift, and £106 to Nicholas of Lewknor, sometime keeper of our Wardrobe, on Wednesday, the vigil of the feast of the Apostles Simon and Jude in the fifty-first year of our reign [27 October 1267][1] and 110 marks to the prior of Healaugh Park of the ten marks a year which he received from the mills of Castleford. For all this money the same Alice has our letters patent and tallies of the Exchequer of our works of Westminster and our writ of *allocate* for the aforesaid 110 marks, and the said letters patent together with these letters patent, the same Alice is bound to surrender at our Exchequer once she has received allowance and quittance of the above mentioned sum.

In witness of which etc.

Attested as above [i.e. by the king at Westminster, 6 November 1269].

[1] In 1267, 27 October fell on a Thursday, so either the scribe has mistaken the weekday, or the payment was made in 1266 when October 27 did fall on a Wednesday. As the feast itself would fall within the next regnal year, it might be a natural mistake to forget that the vigil of the feast fell within the preceding regnal year.

2. Receipts of the Keepers of the works at Westminster from 1249 to 1253 and advances made to workmen in 1249–52 (E 101/466/29)

Recepta denariorum post Natale ad fabricam ecclesie beati Petri Westmonasteriensis anno regni Regis Henrici tercii xxxiij°. quarto anno incepti operis.

Die martis in vigilia beati Mathie Apostoli anno regni regis Henrici xxxiij° de Scacario. C li.

Die Sabbati post Clausum Pasche anno regni regis Henrici xxxiij° de Scacario CC li.

Item. Die martis que vocatur Hokeday anno regni regis Henrici xxxiij de Scacario C libri

Item. Die Sabbati in vigilia Pentecost' de Scacario. CCC et xxxiij li. vj sol. viij d.

Memorandum quod magister Henricus tenetur respondere de lx sol. et viij d. de pacacione facta in Pentecost'.[1]

Summa Recepte denariorum a festo Epiphanie usque Pentecost' anno regni Regis xxxiij° vij c. & xxxiij li. vi sol. viij d.

Item. *Recepta denariorum per dominum Philippum Lovel & fratrem Philippum subpriorem Westmonasteriensem cum domino Eadwardo clerico & magistro Henrico cementario.*

Die martis proxima post translacionem beati Benedicti anno regni Regis Henrici [xxxiij] de Thesauro CCC & xxxiij li. vj sol. viij d. de quibus facta fuit Pacacio a crastino Sancte Trinitatis usque Sabbatum post festum apostolorum Petri & Pauli per v. Ebdomadas precedentes.

Item. Die Sabbati in vigilia decollacionis beati Johannis Baptiste. L. marce de domino W. Tesaurario mutuo recepte anno regni regis Henrici xxxiij°. de quibus perpacata est franca petra a festo apostolorum Petri & Pauli usque Sabbatum in vigilia decollacionis beati Johannis per viij ebdomadas.[2]

[1] This entry has been written later over an erasure.
[2] The whole of this entry has been cancelled.

2. Receipts of the Keepers of the works at Westminster from 1249 to 1253 and advances made to workmen in 1249–52

The receipts of moneys after Christmas for the fabric of the church of the blessed Peter at Westminster in the 33rd year of the reign of King Henry and the fourth year since the beginning of the work [*1249*].

On Tuesday on the eve of the feast of the blessed Matthias the apostle [23 February] in the 33rd year of the reign of King Henry from the Exchequer, £100.

On Saturday after the first Sunday after Easter [17 April] in the 33rd year of the reign of King Henry from the Exchequer, £200.

Also. On Tuesday which is called Hokeday [20 April] in the 33rd year of the reign of King Henry from the Exchequer, £100.

Also. On Saturday on Whitsun Eve [22 May] from the Exchequer, £333. 6*s*. 8*d*. (Note that Master Henry is bound to answer for 60*s*. and 8*d*. of the payment made at Whitsun.)

Total receipts of moneys from the feast of Epiphany [6 January] to Whitsun [23 May] in the 33rd year of the reign of King Henry, £733. 6*s*. 8*d*.

Also. *The receipts of moneys by Sir Philip Lovel and Brother Philip the sub-prior of Westminster together with Sir Edward the clerk and Master Henry the mason.*

On Tuesday following the feast of the Translation of the blessed Benedict [13 July] in the 33rd year of the reign of King Henry from the Treasury, £333. 6*s*. 8*d*. from which a payment was made for the period from the morrow of the Holy Trinity [31 May] to Saturday after the feast of the Apostles Peter and Paul [3rd July] for five weeks.

Also. On Saturday on the eve of the feast of the beheading of the blessed John the Baptist [28 August] £33. 6*s*. 8*d*. received on loan from Sir W[illiam] the Treasurer in the 33rd year of the reign of King Henry from which full payment was made for freestone for eight weeks from the feast of the Apostles Peter and Paul [29 June] to Saturday on the eve of the feast of the Beheading of the blessed John the Baptist [28 August].

Item. Die Iovis in crastino Nativitatis beate Marie de Tallagio London' C marce anno regni regis Henrici xxxiij° de quibus fit Pacacio a Die Sabbati proxima post festum apostolorum Petri & Pauli usque sabbatum in vigilia beati Jacobi per iij ebdomadas.

Item. Die dominica proxima post festum Sancti Michaelis de Tesauro CCCC li. anno regni regis Henrici xxxiij° de quibus facta fuit Pacacio a Die sabbati in vigilia beati Jacobi usque Sabbatum post festum Sancti Michaelis per x ebdomadas & solute fuerunt Thesaurario L marce.

Item. Die Sabbati ante translacionem beati Eadwardi de Tesauro iiij^{xx} & x li. ix sol. Item. eodem die pro iiij^{or} careiis plumbi liberatis apud Wind' per preceptum Regis viij li. iij sol.

Item. Die Martis in festo beati Thome apostoli de tesauro .CCC.li. anno regni regis Henrici xxxiiij de quibus fit pacacio Stipendiorum operariorum Westmonasterii a Die sabbati proxima post festum beate Fidis virginis usque diem Veneris in vigilia Natalis per xj^{cim} ebdomadas.

Item. Die Sabbati post Purificacionem ad perpacacionem empcionum ante Natale faciendam de Thesauro C xxxj li. x sol. v d. ob.

Summa recepte tempore domini Philippi & prioris. MCCCXXX li. ij sol. v d. ob.[1]

Summa totalis Recepte Anni quarti. M.M.lxiij li. ix sol. d. ob.

Recepta denariorum Post Natale ad fabricam Ecclesie beati Petri Westmonasteriensis & ad alias operaciones eiusdem loci anno regni Regis Henrici tercii xxxiiij^{to} Quinto anno operis incipiente.

prima pacacio Die Veneris ante Cathedram beati Petri anno regni regis Henrici xxxiiij^{to}. Lxvj li. xiij sol. iiij d.

Die Martis sequenti in festo cathedre beati Petri xxxiij li. vj sol. viij d. de quibus facta fuit Pacacio per iij ebdomadas ij & dies post Natale scilicet a crastino Epiphanie usque Sabbatum ante Purificacionem quinto anno operis incepti.

[1] This entry was added later.

Also. On Thursday on the morrow of the Nativity of the blessed Mary [9 September] from the tallage of London £66. 13*s*. 4*d*. in the 33rd year of the reign of King Henry from which payment was made for three weeks from the Saturday after the feast of the Apostles Peter and Paul [3 July] to the Saturday on the eve of the feast of the blessed James [24 July].

Also. On Sunday following the feast of St. Michael [3 October] in the 33rd year of the reign of King Henry, £400 from the Treasury from which payment was made for ten weeks from Saturday on the eve of the feast of the blessed James [24 July] to the Saturday after the feast of St. Michael [2 October] and £33. 6*s*. 8*d*. were repaid to the Treasurer.

Also. On Saturday before the feast of the Translation of the blessed Edward [9 October] from the Treasury, £90. 9*s*. Also on the same day received for four chars of lead delivered to Windsor by the king's order, £8. 3*s*.

Also. On Tuesday on the feast of the blessed Thomas the Apostle [21 December] in the 34th year of the reign of King Henry, £300 from the Treasury from which payment of the workmen's wages was made for eleven weeks from the Saturday following the feast of the blessed Faith the Virgin [9 October] to Friday on Christmas Eve [24 December].

Also. On Saturday following the feast of the Purification [6 February 1250] from the Treasury to make a full payment of purchases made before Christmas, £131. 10*s*. $5\frac{1}{2}$*d*.

Total receipts in the time of Sir Philip and the prior, £1,330. 2*s*. $5\frac{1}{2}$*d*.

Sum total of receipts in the fourth year of the work, £2,063. 9*s*. $1\frac{1}{2}$*d*.

The Receipt of moneys for the fabric of the church of the blessed Peter at Westminster and for other works at the same place after Christmas in the 34th year of the reign of King Henry at the beginning of the fifth year of the work [*1250*].

first
nent

On Friday before the feast of the blessed Peter *in Cathedra* [18 February] in the 34th year of the reign of King Henry, £66. 13*s*. 4*d*.

On Tuesday following, the feast of the blessed Peter *in Cathedra* [22 February], £33. 6*s*. 8*d*. from which a payment was made for three weeks and two days after Christmas, namely from the morrow of Epiphany [7 January] to Saturday before the feast of the Purification [29 January] in the fifth year since the work began.

Item. Die Mercurii ante festum beati Gregorii anno regno regis Henrici xxxiiij^to de Tesauro. lxvj li. xiij sol. iiij d. de quibus pacate sunt pro franca petra, Grisa petra & calce, xxxiiij li. xix sol. ix d. que allocate sunt in pacacione facta a purificacione usque festum beati Gregorii per vj ebdomadas.

secunda pacacio

Item. die Mercurii post Palmas anno regni regis Henrici xxxiiij^o C & xxx li.

Item. Die Iovis post Hockeday de Scacario ad predictam receptionem perficiendam[1] xxxiiij sol. v d. ob.

tercia pacacio

Item. Die Sabbati ante festum beati Alfegi de Scacario CCC li. & xxxij sol. ij d. ob. per breve domini Regis patens anno regni Regis Henrici xxxiiij^to de quibus facta fuit Pacacio per quindenam ante Pascham & per quindenam post Pascham.

Item. De Ramis Arborum & aliis escaetis in bosco de Cray. vj li. xiij sol. iiij d. extra Recepta per breve patens.

Die veneris ante Pentecost' anno regni regis Henrici xxxiiij^to. cclxvj li. xiij sol. iiij d. de quibus fit pacacio per iiij^or ebdomadas.

Item. Die martis ante festum beati Barnabe Apostoli anno regni regis Henrici xxxiiij^to de Scacario. x li. ad meremium apud Crey & apud Ki[n]geston' emendum.

Item. Die Jovis in festo commemoracionis beati Pauli de Scacario C li. a^o xxxiiij^to. de quibus fit pacacio licenciatis per vj ebdomadas.

Item. Die mercurii in vigilia translacionis beati Thome martiris de Tesauro. ccxxxiij li. vj sol. viij d. de quibus fit Pacacio per predictas vj ebdomadas anno regni regis Henrici xxxiiij^to.

Item. Die Sabbati proxima ante festum beati Jacobi de Tesshauro C & j li. de quibus facta fuit perpacacio france petre per ix^vem ebdomadas de iiij^xx li. & xv li. ij sol. ix d.

Item. Die veneris proxima ante Assumpcionem beate Marie per manus Thesaurarii & domini Eadwardi C li. de quibus perp[ac]ata sunt arreragia a crastino Sancte Trinitatis usque sabbatum post festum Apostolorum Petri & Pauli per vj ebdomadas.

Item. Die Lune ante Nativitatem beate Marie de domino Eadwardo clerico L marce anno regni regis Henrici xxxiiij^to de quibus fiunt Prestita operariis.

[1] *ad predictam receptionem perficiendam* has been added in a smaller hand.

Also. On Wednesday before the feast of the blessed Gregory [9 March] in the 34th year of the reign of King Henry from the Treasury £66. 13*s.* 4*d.* from which there was paid for freestone, ragstone, and lime, £34. 19*s.* 9*d.* which are allowed for in the payment made for six weeks from the feast of the Purification to the feast of the blessed Gregory [2 February to 12 March].

ıd
nent

Also. On Wednesday after Palm Sunday [23 March] in the 34th year of the reign of King Henry, £130.

Also. On Thursday after Hokeday [14 April] from the Exchequer to complete the aforesaid receipt, 34*s.* 5½*d.*

Also. On Saturday before the feast of the blessed Alphege [16 April] from the Exchequer, £301. 12*s.* 2½*d.* by a writ patent of the Lord King in the 34th year of the reign of King Henry [October 1249 to October 1250], from which payment was made for a fortnight before Easter and a fortnight after Easter.

l
nent

Also. From the sale of branches of trees and other loppings in the wood of Cray, besides the receipt by writ patent, £6. 13*s.* 4*d.*

On Friday before Whitsun in the 34th year of the reign of King Henry [13 May 1250], £266. 13*s.* 4*d.*, from which payment was made for four weeks.

Also. On Tuesday before the feast of the blessed Barnabas in the 34th year of the reign of King Henry [7 June 1250], £10 from the Exchequer to buy timber at Cray and at Kingston.

Also. On Thursday on the feast of the Commemoration of the blessed Paul [30 June] from the Exchequer £100 in the 34th year, from which payment was made to those leaving during a period of six weeks.

Also. On Wednesday on the eve of the feast of the Translation of the blessed Thomas the martyr [6 July] from the Treasury, £233. 6*s.* 8*d.*, from which payment was made for the aforesaid six weeks in the 34th year of the reign of King Henry.

Also. On Saturday before the feast of the blessed James [23 July] from the Treasury, £101, from which was made a full payment for freestone for nine weeks of £95. 2*s.* 9*d.*

Also. On Friday before the feast of the Assumption of the blessed Mary [12 August] by the hands of the Treasurer and Sir Edward, £100, from which the arrears were completely paid from the morrow of Holy Trinity [23 May] to Saturday following the feast of the Apostles Peter and Paul [2 July] for six weeks.

Also. On Monday before the feast of the Nativity of the blessed Mary in the 34th year of the reign of King Henry [5 September 1250] from Sir Edward the clerk £33. 6*s.* 8*d.*, from which advances were made to workmen.

Ad pacacionem xiij^{cim} ebdomadarum

Item. Die Sabbati post Nativitatem beate Marie de Tesaurario L marce anno regni regis Henrici xxxiiij^{to}. de quibus fit Pacacio france petre per quindenam. de r[es]iduo fit.

Item. die Veneris proxima post festum sancti Michaelis de priore de Hurl' xx li.

Item. Ebdomada prima post festum Sancti Michaelis per vices de Scacario .vj^{c}.li. anno regni regis Henrici xxxiiij^{to} de quibus fit Pacacio xiij^{cim} Ebdomadarum.

ad pacacionem xij^{cim} ebdomadarum

Die dominica post festum beati Martini de Tesauro cc li. xiiij sol. v d. ob. anno regni regis Henrici xxxv^{to} de quibus fit Pacacio de stipendiis per vj ebdomadas a die Sabbati post festum Sancti Michaelis usque festum beati Martini.

Item. Ante Natale & post Natale de Tesauro cc lxij li. xviij sol. ij d. de quibus fit pacacio usque Natale per xij Ebdomadas.

Item. eodem tempore de Thesauro ad quandam crucem magnam emendam xxxiij li. vj sol. viij d.

Summa Totalis Recepte quinto anno incepti operis. MMvj^{c} li. xxv sol. xj d. ob. Anno Regni Regis Henrici xxxv^{to}.

Recepta denariorum post Natale ad fabricam Ecclesie beati Petri Westmonasteriensis & ad alias operaciones eiusdem Loci anno regni Regis Henrici tercii xxxv^{to}. Anno Sexto operis incipiente.

per ij vices pacata post viij ebdomadas

Item. Die mercurii post festum beati Gregorii de Tessauro C lxxiij li. ix sol. v d. ob.
Die veneris in vigilia Annunciacionis beate Marie de Tessauro C.li. anno regni regis Henrici xxxv^{to}

Item.[1] Die veneris ante Palmas xx li. de Turri que prius acomodate fuerunt apud Westmonasterium prout continetur in Rotulo anno regni regis Henrici xxxv^{to} ad pacaciones post Cineres faciendas.

Item. Die martis post Palmas. vj li. x s. v d. ob. ad ducentas libras & iiij^{xx} libras perficiendas post Nathale receptas.

Item.[2] eodem die per breve continens CC li. Recepte sunt lxxiij li. x s. vj.d. ob.

Item. Infra Pascham de Thesauro xxxix li. anno regni regis Henrici xxxv^{to}.

[1] The first ten words of this entry have been struck out; the last five have been added later, perhaps to explain the deletion.

[2] The first eight words of this entry have been struck out.

the ...ment ...f 13 ...eeks

Also. On Saturday after the feast of the Nativity of the blessed Mary in the 34th year of the reign of King Henry [10 September 1250] from the Treasurer £33. 6*s.* 8*d.* from which payment for freestone was made for a fortnight. It was made from the residue.

Also. On Friday following the feast of St. Michael [30 September] from the prior of Hurley, £20.

Also. The first week after Michaelmas [1–8 October] in the 34th year of the reign of King Henry in instalments from the Exchequer, £600, from which payment was made for thirteen weeks.

the ...ment ...f 12 ...eeks

On Sunday after the feast of the blessed Martin in the 35th year of the reign of King Henry [13 November 1250] from the Treasury, £200. 14*s.* 5½*d.*, from which payment was made for six weeks from Saturday after the feast of St. Michael [1 October] to the feast of the blessed Martin [11 November].

Also. Before and after Christmas from the Treasury, £262. 18*s.* 2*d.*, from which payment was made for twelve weeks to Christmas.

Also. In the same period from the Treasury to buy a certain great cross, £33. 6*s.* 8*d.*

Sum total of receipts during the fifth year of the work, £2,601. 5*s.* 11½*d.* in the 35th year of the reign of King Henry.

The Receipt of moneys after Christmas for the fabric of the Church of the blessed Peter at Westminster and for other works at the same place in the 35th year of the reign of King Henry III at the beginning of the sixth year of the work [*1251*].

...aid two ...tal- ...ents ...er 8 ...eeks

On Wednesday after the feast of the blessed Gregory [15 March] from the Treasury, £173. 9*s.* 5½*d.*

Also. On Friday on the eve of the feast of the Annunciation of the blessed Mary [24 March] in the 35th year of the reign of King Henry, £100 from the Treasury.

Also. On Friday before Palm Sunday [7 April], £20 from the Tower[1] which had previously been borrowed at Westminster as is contained in the Roll in the 35th year of the reign of King Henry: to make payments after Ash Wednesday [1 March].

Also. On Tuesday after Palm Sunday [11 April], £6. 10*s.* 5½*d.* to complete £280 received since Christmas.

Also. On the same day by a writ containing £200[1] there was received £73. 10*s.* 6½*d.*

Also. Within the time of Easter in the 35th year of the reign of King Henry, £39 from the Treasury.

[1] The sum of £220 covered by the deletions noted opposite is not included in the total given below.

Item. Die martis in vigilia crucis C & vij li. xj sol.

Item. Die mercurii ante festum beati Dunstani de Tesauro ccc li. anno regni regis Henrici xxxv^{to} de quibus arreragia ante pascham pacata sunt & Omnia per iiij^{or} ebdomadas post Pascham pacata sunt xlv li. vj sol. x d. ob.

Item. Die martis ante festum beati Johanni Baptiste anno regni regis [Henrici] xxxv^{to} de Scacario x marce ad meremium emendum ad stalla ad opus domini Eadwardi.

Item. Die Sabbati in festo beate Marie Magdalene de Scacario CCC li. de quibus fit pacacio stipendiorum & quarumdam empcionum per viij ebdomadas precedentes; & ex alia parte ad feretrum l^{a} marce.

Item. Die lune ante festum beati Mathei apostoli anno regni regis Henrici xxxv^{to}. de changia CC li. xx marce ad perpacacionem empcionum predictarum viij^{to} Ebdomadarum ante Pentecost' & post Pentecost' faciendam.

Item. Die Sabbati in crastino beate Fidis virginis de Scacario vj^{c} lxvj li. xiij sol. iiij d.

Item. ad opus Johannis le Senter & Petri pictoris xx li.

Item. Die Iovis in crastino beate Lucie virginis & die Veneris sequenti de Scacario lviij li. xvj s. v d. de quibus licentiati ante Natale fuerunt pacati.

Item. Ebdomada post Epiphaniam de Scacario C s. ad prestitum faciendum pro petra de Came.

Item. die mercurii in vigilia Conversionis beati Pauli de Scacario viij li. ad perpacacionem petre de Came.

Item. Die Lune post festum cathedre beati Petri anno regni regis Henrici xxxvj^{to} de scacario V^{c} li. de quibus fit perpacacio per xj^{cim} ebdomadas ante Natale & per vii^{tem} ebdomadas post Natale.

Summa totalis Anni Sexti Operis incepti MMvj^{c}xj li. xvij sol. x d. ob. anno regni regis Henrici xxxvj^{to}.

Recepta denariorum post Natale ad diversas Operaciones Westmon' anno regni regis Henrici xxxvj^{to}.

Dominica post quindenam Pasche de Scacario CCCC li. ad pacacionem faciendam a die Sabbati post festum cathedre beati Petri usque predictam dominicam per v. ebdomadas ante Pascham & per vj dies post Pascham anno regni regis

Also. On Tuesday on the eve of the Cross [2 May], £107. 11*s.*

Also. On Wednesday before the feast of the blessed Dunstan [17 May], £300 in the 35th year of the reign of King Henry, from which were paid both the arrears before Easter and everything for four weeks after Easter [amounting to] £45. 6*s.* 10½*d.*

Also. On Tuesday before the feast of the blessed John the Baptist [20 June] in the 35th year of the reign of King Henry from the Exchequer £6. 13*s.* 4*d.* for Sir Edward's use to buy timber for the stalls.

Also. On Saturday on the feast of the blessed Mary Magdalen [22 July] from the Exchequer, £300, from which were made payment for wages of workmen and certain purchases for the 8 preceding weeks; and from elsewhere for the shrine, £33 6*s.* 8*d.*

Also. On Monday before the feast of the blessed Matthew the Apostle in the 35th year of the reign of King Henry [18 September 1251] from the Mint £213. 6*s.* 8*d.* to make full payment of the purchases made in the aforesaid eight weeks before and after Whitsun.

Also. On Saturday on the morrow of the feast of the blessed Faith the Virgin [7 October] from the Exchequer, £666. 13*s.* 4*d.*

Also. For John le Senter and Peter the painter, £20.

Also. On Thursday on the morrow of the feast of the blessed Lucy the Virgin [14 December] and the following Friday [15 December] from the Exchequer, £58. 16*s.* 5*d.*, from which those leaving before Christmas were paid.

Also. During the week after Epiphany [Monday 8 to Saturday 13 January 1252] from the Exchequer 100*s.* to make an advance for Caen stone.

Also. On Wednesday on the eve of the Conversion of the blessed Paul [24 January 1252] from the Exchequer £8 for the final payment for Caen stone.

Also. On Monday after the feast of the blessed Peter *in Cathedra* in the 36th year of the reign of King Henry [26 February] from the Exchequer, £500, from which were made the final payments for 11 weeks before Christmas and for 7 weeks after Christmas.

Sum total of the sixth year of the work, £2,611. 17*s.* 10½*d.* in the 36th year of the reign of King Henry.

The Receipt of moneys after Christmas for divers works at Westminster in the 36th year of the reign of King Henry [*1252*].

On the Sunday after the fortnight of Easter [7 April] from the Exchequer, £400 to make payment from Saturday after the feast of the blessed Peter *in Cathedra* [24 February] to the said

Henrici xxxvj^{to}. Item ad opus Magistri le Senter de Scacario xx li.

Item. Die martis in festo beati Barnabe apostoli de Scacario xv li. ad francam Petram de Came anno regni regis Henrici xxxvj^{to}. Omnia predicta Recepta alocata sunt in prima pacacione vij anni operis.

Item. Die veneris ante festum beati Johannis Baptiste magistro Alexandro ad meremium emendum apud Ki[n]gestun x li. de Scacario.

Item. Die veneris in vigilia beati Petri apostoli de Scacario CC li. anno regni regis Henrici xxxvj^{to}.

Item. Die Lune sequenti in crastino comemoracionis beati Pauli de Scacario xiij marce pro fretis duarum Navatarum marmoris pacandis. *cancelled* quia alocate sunt infra C li. infrascriptas.

Item. Die Sabbati in vigilia Translacionis beati Thome martiris de Tetharo [*sic*] C li. anno regni regis Henrici xxxvj^{to}.

Item. Die veneris proxima ante festum beati Kenelmi martiris de Scacario magistro Alexandro ad meremium apud Kingeston x li.

Item. Die Sabbati post festum beati Jacobi de Scacario CCCC li. anno regni regis Henrici xxxvj^{to}. de quibus CC li. fuerunt ad perpacionem predictam & CC li. ad pacacionem a festo Sancte Trinitatis usque festum Sancti Michaelis.

Item. Die Lune post festum assumpcionis beate Marie per dominum Eadwardum lxxv marce de quibus liberate fuerunt magistro Henrico xl marce ad taschas perpacandas. Et magistro Johanni le Senter ad metallum purgandum & ad alia xxxv marce.

Item. xlvj sol. viij d. pro ix^{m} & vij^{c} stagminis de Cornubia ad Westmonasterium. Die martis ante translacionem beati Eadwardi de Scacario ix^{c} li. de quibus fit pacacio Empcionum a festo Sancte Trinitatis usque Sabbatum in vigilia Sancti Michaelis per xviij ebdomadas & Pacacio stipendiorum a festo apostolorum Petri & Pauli usque Sabbatum in vigilia Sancti Michaelis per xiij^{cim} ebdomadas & residuum reservatum fuit ad pacacionem sequentem.

Die Sabbati ante festum beati Martini anno regni regis Henrici

Sunday for five weeks before Easter and for six days after Easter in the 36th year of the reign of King Henry.

Also for Master le Senter from the Exchequer, £20.

Also. On Tuesday on the feast of the blessed Barnabas the Apostle [11 June] from the Exchequer £15 for Caen freestone in the 36th year of the reign of King Henry.

All the aforesaid receipts are allocated to the first payment of the seventh year of the work.

Also. On Friday before the feast of the blessed John the Baptist [21 June] to Master Alexander to buy timber at Kingston, £10 from the Exchequer.

Also. On Friday on the eve of the feast of the blessed Peter the Apostle [28 June] in the 36th year of the reign of King Henry, from the Exchequer, £200.

Also. On the following Monday, the morrow of the Commemoration of the blessed Paul [1 July], from the Exchequer, £8. 13*s.* 4*d.* to pay for freight of two shiploads of marble, *cancelled* because they are included in the £100 below.

Also. On Saturday on the vigil of the feast of the Translation of the blessed Thomas the Martyr [6 July] in the 36th year of the reign of King Henry, from the Treasury, £100.

Also. On Friday before the feast of the blessed Kenelm the Martyr [12 July] from the Exchequer for Master Alexander to buy timber at Kingston, £10.

Also. On Saturday after the feast of the blessed James [27 July] in the 36th year of the reign of King Henry, from the Exchequer £400, of which £200 were to make the said payment in full and £200 were to pay for the period from the feast of Holy Trinity [26 May] to the feast of St. Michael [29 September].

Also. On Monday after the feast of the Assumption of the blessed Mary [19 August] by Sir Edward £50, of which £26. 13*s.* 4*d.* were delivered to Master Henry to make final payments for task-works. And Master John le Senter had £23 6*s.* 8*d.* to refine metal and for other things.

Also. 46*s.* 8*d.* for carriage of 97 hundredweight of tin from Cornwall to Westminster. On Tuesday before the feast of the Translation of the blessed Edward [8 October] from the Exchequer, £900 from which payments were made for purchases from the feast of Holy Trinity [26 May] to Saturday on the vigil of the feast of St. Michael [28 September] for 18 weeks and the rest was kept for the next payment.

On Saturday before the feast of the blessed Martin [9 November] in the 37th year of the reign of King Henry, from the Exchequer

xxxvij^mo de Scacario CC cum remanenti prioris Pacacionis ad pacacionem faciendam a festo Sancti Michaelis usque Sabbatum ante festum Sancti Martini per v ebdomadas.

Item. ad opus Johannis le Senter x.li. Item Die Martis ante festum beati Nicholai ad opus eiusdem Johannis le Sentor ad perpacacionem Campane xvij li. xix sol. ij d.

Item. Ebdomada iij^a post Purificacionem Die Sabbati ante Septuagesimam de Tesauro C li. anno regni regis Henrici xxxvij^o de quibus fit pacacio stipendiorum a Die Sabbati ante festum beati Martini usque Sabbatum in festo beati Andree per iij ebdomadas & pro franca petra usque vigiliam Natalis per vj ebdomadas.

Item. Die Sabbati in festo cathedre beati Petri xx li. ad tascham introitus capituli.

Item. Die Mercurii post festum beati Mathie pro vitro acquietando. iiij li. xv sol. iij d. anno regni regis Henrici xxxvij^o.

Item. Die Jovis post festum beati Mathie de tesauro cc li. anno regni regis Henrici xxxvij^o.

Item. Die Lune post festum beati Gregorii Lx li. ad pacacionem Empcionum a festo beati Martini usque purificacionem faciendam. Item de Garderoba domini Regis de prestito C s. liberatis [*sic*] magistro Henrico licentiatio cum iij mansipulis.

Summa Recepte sexti & vij. anni. MMvij^c xxv li. xiij d.

Item. anno viij^vo Operis de Thesauro L iij sol. iiij d. ad quandam Navatam de petra de Came in festo Annunciacionis beate Marie anno regni regis Henrici xxxvij^o.

Item. Die Jovis in crastino beati Johannis ante portam latinam de Tesauro vj^c.li. anno regni regis Henrici xxxvij^o de quibus fit Pacacio a festo Purificacionis usque in vigiliam Pasche per xj. ebdomadas.

[£]200 together with the remainder of the previous payment to make payments for five weeks from the feast of St. Michael [29 September] to the Saturday before the feast of St. Martin [9 November].

Also. for John le Senter, £10. Also on Tuesday before the feast of the blessed Nicholas [3 December] for the same John le Senter in full payment for the bell, £17. 19*s.* 2*d.*

Also. On the Saturday before Septuagesima, three weeks after the Purification [22 February][1] in the 37th year of the reign of King Henry [1253] from the Treasury £100, from which payment was made for wages for three weeks from Saturday before the feast of the blessed Martin [9 November] to Saturday on the feast of the blessed Andrew [30 November] and for freestone for six weeks until Christmas Eve [24 December].

Also. On Saturday on the feast of the blessed Peter *in Cathedra* [22 February] £20 towards the task-work of the entrance to the chapter-house.

Also. On Wednesday after the feast of the blessed Matthias [26 February] in the 37th year of the reign of King Henry to pay off the glass, £4. 15*s.* 3*d.*

Also. On Thursday after the feast of the blessed Matthias [27 February] in the 37th year of the reign of King Henry from the Treasury, £200.

Also. On Monday after the feast of the blessed Gregory [17 March] £60 to pay for purchases made between the feast of the blessed Martin [11 November 1252] and the Purification [2 February 1253]. Also from the lord king's Wardrobe an advance of 100*s.* delivered to Master Henry leaving with three servants.

Total Receipts for the sixth and seventh years, £2,725. 1*s.* 1*d.*

Also. In the eighth year of the work from the Treasury 53*s.* 4*d.* for a certain shipload of Caen stone on the feast of the Annunciation of the blessed Mary in the 37th year of the reign of King Henry [25 March 1253].

Also. On Thursday on the morrow of the feast of the blessed John before the Latin Gate [8 May][2] in the 37th year of the reign of King Henry from the Treasury £600, from which payment was made for eleven weeks from the feast of the Purification [2 February] to the eve of Easter [19 April].

[1] The Saturday before Septuagesima fell on 15 Feb., only 2 weeks after the Purification [2 Feb.]. The following Saturday was the Saturday before Sexagesima, and it is probable that the clerk confused the two Sundays.

[2] The feast of St. John before the Latin Gate [6 May] fell on a Tuesday in 1253.

Die Sabbati ante festum beati Augustini de Scacario xij li. ad duas Navatas france petre de Came adquietandas.

Item. Die Iovis post festum Sancte Trinitatis de Scacario xx li. ad meremium emendum.

Item. Die Veneris sequenti de Scacario xxx li. de quibus pro freto marmoris pacato C & ix s. viij d.

Summa recepte huius pacacionis vj^{c}lxiiij li. xiij sol. iiij d.[1]

Die Martis proxima post festum apostolorum Petri & Pauli de Thesauro C li.

Item. Die Veneris sequenti .xxxvij li. xviij sol. iij d. de quibus pacata sunt stipendia operariorum per iij ebdomadas post Pascham.

Item. Die Veneris post Translacionem beati Thome martiris de Scacario xlvj li. xvij d.

Item. Die Martis ante festum beate Margarete & Die mercurii ante festum beate Margarete. Cxlvj li. xiij sol. iij d. de quibus pacata sunt stipendia operariorum.

Item. Recepta ante festum beati Bartholomei de prestito mercatorum. CCC xxxiii li. vj sol. viij d.

Item. de Scacario xx li. ad stipendia licenciatorum pacanda. Item C s. ad opus aurifab'.

Item. Die Mercurii post Nativitatem beate Marie de remanenti. xl^{ta} marce de Tallagio de Havering' xxxiij sol. iiij d.

Item. dominica in festo Sancte Crucis per dominum Edwardum. xxvj sol. viij d. que liberate [*sic*] fuerunt Roberto de Turri ad quandam quareriam discoperiendam.

Item. Die Lune in crastino beati Mathei de vicecomite Norhamton'. lxvj li. xiij sol. iiij d. de quibus liberate sunt Roberto de Turri ad quarriam discoperiendam viij li.

Die Martis post festum beati Luce Ewangeliste de Scacario. CC li. de quibus pacate fuerunt quedam empciones.

Item. Die Veneris in vigilia Omnium Sanctorum CC li. ad pacandum stipendia Anno regni regis Henrici xxxviij^{vo}.

Item. Die Mercurii in crastino beati Martini ad pacandum stipendia licenciatorum Lxvj li. xiij sol. iiij d.

Item. Die Sabbati in vigilia beati Andree ad stipendia xviij fabrorum per xij^{cim} ebdomadas xviij li. xix sol. ij d. ob.

[1] This entry has been interlineated.

On Saturday before the feast of the blessed Augustine [24 May] from the Exchequer, £12 to pay off two shiploads of Caen freestone.

Also. On Thursday after the feast of Holy Trinity [19 June] from the Exchequer, £20 to buy timber.

Also. On the following Friday [20 June] from the Exchequer, £30 from which a payment of £5. 9*s.* 8*d.* was made for freight of marble.

(Total of the receipts of this payment, £664. 13*s.* 4*d.*)

On Tuesday following the feast of the Apostles Peter and Paul [1 July] from the Treasury, £100.

Also. On the following Friday [4 July] £37. 18*s.* 3*d.* from which payment was made for workmen's wages for three weeks after Easter.

Also. On Friday after the feast of the Translation of the blessed Thomas the Martyr [11 July] from the Exchequer, £46. 1*s.* 5*d.*

Also. On Tuesday before the feast of the blessed Margaret and on Wednesday before the same feast [15 and 16 July], £146. 13*s.* 3*d.* from which the wages of workmen were paid.

Also. Received before the feast of St. Bartholomew [24 August] from merchants' loans, £333. 6*s.* 8*d.*

Also from the Exchequer £20 to pay the wages of those leaving. Also 100*s.* for the goldsmith[s].

Also. On Wednesday after the feast of the Nativity of the blessed Mary [10 September] from the remainder of 40 marks from the tallage of Havering, 33*s.* 4*d.*

Also. On Sunday on the feast of Holy Cross [14 September] through Sir Edward, 26*s.* 8*d.* which were delivered to Robert of the Tower to open up a certain quarry.

Also. On Monday on the morrow of the feast of the blessed Matthew [22 September] from the sheriff of Northamptonshire, £66. 13*s.* 4*d.* from which £8 were delivered to Robert of the Tower to open up a quarry.

On Tuesday after the feast of the blessed Luke the Evangelist [21 October] from the Exchequer, £200 from which payment was made for certain purchases.

Also. On Friday on the eve of All Saints [31 October] in the 38th year of the reign of King Henry, £200 to pay the wages.

Also. On Wednesday on the morrow of the feast of the blessed Martin [12 November] to pay the wages of those leaving, £66. 13*s.* 4*d.*

Also. On Saturday on the eve of the feast of the blessed Andrew [29 November] for the wages of 18 smiths for 12 weeks, £18. 19*s.* 2½*d.*

Item. Die Jovis ante festum beati Nicholai de Scacario Cxxxiij li. vj sol. viij d.

Summa MM.xlij li. v sol. vj d. ob.

Summa totalis recepte v. annorum. X^{m} vij^{c}.li. Liiij s. x d.

Summa recepte per breve domini Regis patens a pascha usque ad vincula beati Petri M xij li. xij sol. ij d. ob. infra quas computati sunt. xxxij sol. ij d. & ob. recepti ante pascham. Item summa recepte medio tempore. C $iiij^{xx}$ li. & vj li. xiij sol. iiij d.

Prestita post Natale anno Regni Regis Henrici tercii xxxiij° & quarto anno incepti operis.[1]

Die Mercurii in festo beati Mathie Willelmo clerico ad Robam de prestito xiij sol. iiij d.

Eodem die super tascham capital' in claustro de prestito ix li.

Item eidem lx sol. de tascha xij li. (plena solucio).[2]

Die dominica in octabis clausi Pasche Willelmo plumbario super tascham de xiij marcis pro conductu lx sol.

Magistro bene pro Ogivis cissis ad tascham de prestito xv sol.

Die Martis sequenti que vocatur Hokeday magistro Odoni carpentario de prestito xl sol.

Die Mercurii post Hokeday Henrico de Ponte super ferrum de prestito x li. Item xii li. x sol. pac'

Item Die Veneris post Hocheday Willelmo plumbario super tascham de prestito xx sol. Item. iiij li. xiij sol. iiij d. pac'.

Die Sabbati in vigilia beati Marci magistro Alexandro ad metallum ponderandum & cariandum xxx sol.

Die Sabbati in vigilia beati Marci quariariis de prestito xl sol.

Item Die Lune in crastino Pentecost' pro Pavimento camere Regis de prestito lx sol.

eodem die Johanni de Meleton' super tascham claustri de Prestito. x sol.

eodem die magistro Ricardo Paris super marmore C sol.

eodem die magistro Alexandro ad Nemus de prestito iiij li.

Item magistro Albrico super tascham in claustro de xxx li. xl sol.

Item die Mercurii ante festum beati Kenelmi magistro Alexandro ad pilos emendos de prestito xl sol.

[1] All the entries under this heading have been struck through.

[2] These two words have been added in the margin.

Also. On Thursday before the feast of the blessed Nicholas [4 December] from the Exchequer, £133. 6s. 8d.

Total £2,042. 5s. 6½d.

Sum total of the receipts of five years £10,702. 14s. 10d.

Total of the receipts by the lord king's writ patent from Easter to the feast of the blessed Peter in Chains [20 April to 1 August], £1,012. 12s. 2½d. within which are accounted 32s. 2½d. received before Easter. And total of the receipts meanwhile, £186. 13s. 4d.

Advances after Christmas in the 33rd year of the reign of King Henry and the fourth year of the work [1249].

On Wednesday on the feast of the blessed Matthias [24 February] to William the clerk for a suit of clothes by way of advance, 13s. 4d.

On the same day for the task-work of the capitals in the cloister, by way of advance, £9.

And to the same [mason] 60s. towards a task-work costing £12 (full payment).

On the second Sunday after Easter [18 April] to William the plumber towards a task-work of £8. 13s. 4d. for the conduit, 60s.

To Master Bene for cutting vaulting-ribs at task by way of advance, 15s.

On the following Tuesday [20 April] which is called Hokeday to Master Odo the carpenter by way of advance, 40s.

On Wednesday after Hokeday [21 April] to Henry of Bridge for iron by way of advance, £10. Also £12. 10s. paid.

Also on Friday after Hokeday [23 April] to William the plumber towards task-work by way of advance, 20s. Also £4. 13s. 4d. paid.

On Saturday on the eve of the feast of the blessed Mark [24 April] to Master Alexander for the weighing and carriage of metal, 30s.

On Saturday on the eve of the feast of the blessed Mark [24 April] to quarrymen by way of advance, 40s.

Also on Monday on the morrow of Whitsun [24 May] for the pavement of the King's chamber by way of advance, 60s.

On the same day to John of Milton towards the task-work of the cloister by way of advance, 10s.

On the same day to Master Richard Paris for marble, 100s.

On the same day to Master Alexander towards the cost of a wood, by way of advance, £4.

Also to Master Aubrey towards task-work in the cloister worth £30, 40s.

Also on Wednesday before the feast of the blessed Kenelm [14 July] to Master Alexander to buy piles by way of advance, 40s.

Item eodem die fossatoribus de Flete xxx sol.
Item die Veneris in vigilia beati Kenelmi magistro Albrico super tascham xiij li.
Item die Sabbati in festo sancti Kenelmi pro pavimento camere Regis xl sol.
Item eodem die magistro Johanni Sentori x marce.
Item magistro Alexandro eodem die ad pilos Berefridi xl sol.
Item eodem die Johanni Norman & socio suo super tascham de prestito xx sol.
Item Rogero de Reygate super francam petram de prestito iiij li.
Item Calfonario de prestito xx li. die martis post festum Sancti Michaelis.

Memorandum quod magister Johannes le Senter recepit de prestito v^{c} libras metalli de quibus liberavit Domino Roberto de Sotindon'. C & dimidium per dominum Eadwardum & sic dictus Johannes tenetur respondere de CCC & dimidiam.

Prestita quinti anni

Godefrido de Suerk' per vices ad marmor de prestito. vij li. xv sol. de quibus alocate sunt iiij li. super quandam Navatam marmoris per breve.
Item Die Jovis ante Pentecost' anno regni regis Henrici xxxiiij^{to} Domino Willelmo tessaurario pro bordis adquietandis. xx sol. Item domino Eadwardo ad idem x sol.
Item in vigilia Pentecost' magistro Alexandro ad meremium per duas vices xvj li xiij sol. iiij d. de priori pacacione.
Item eodem die quariariis ad francam petram per duas vices xvj. li.

Item Die Veneris in crastino commemoracionis beati Pauli quarriariis	xxvij li.	de C. li. tunc receptis
Item eodem Die magistro Alexandro ad meremium	x li.	
Item eodem Die magistro Odoni ad scafota	c sol.	

Item memorandum quod Godefridus tenetur respondere de C solidis receptis die Translacionis beati Thome martiris. Item die sabbati ante Assumpcionem beate Marie de x solidis de prestito Nautis liberatis cum iiij li. & iiij sol. illius Navis tunc non appreciate que omnia allocata sunt in magno Rotulo Pacacionum.
Item die lune ante festum beati Mathei apostoli anno regni regis Henrici xxxv^{to} de prestito domino Eadwardo c sol. de ducentis libris receptis de cambia.

Also on the same day to the ditchers of the Fleet, 30*s*.
Also on Friday on the vigil of the feast of the blessed Kenelm [16 July] to Master Aubrey towards task-work, £13.
Also on Saturday on the feast of the blessed Kenelm [17 July] for the pavement of the king's chamber, 40*s*.
Also on the same day to Master John Senter, £6. 13*s*. 4*d*.
Also to Master Alexander on the same day for the piles of the Belfry, 40*s*.
Also on the same day to John Norman and his fellow for task-work by way of advance, 20*s*.
Also to Roger of Reigate for freestone by way of advance, £4.
and to the lime-burner by way of advance,
£20 on Tuesday after the feast of St. Michael [5 October]

Note that Master John le Senter received by way of advance five hundredweight of metal, of which he delivered to Sir Robert of Shottenden one and a half hundredweight through Sir Edward and so the said John is bound to answer for three and a half hundredweight.

Advances in the fifth year [*1250*]

To Godfrey of Southwark on various occasions for marble by way of advance, £7. 15*s*. of which £4 are allocated by writ towards the cost of a certain shipload of marble.
Also on Thursday before Whitsun [12 May] in the 34th year of the reign of King Henry to Sir William the Treasurer to pay for boards, 20*s*. Also to Sir Edward for the same, 10*s*.
Also on Whitsun Eve [14 May] to Master Alexander for timber on two occasions, £16. 13*s*. 4*d*. from a previous payment.
Also on the same day to quarrymen for freestone on two occasions, £16.
Also on Friday on the morrow of the commemoration of the blessed Paul [1 July] to quarrymen £27 }
Also on the same day to Master Alexander for timber £10 } of £100 then received
Also on the same day to Master Odo for scaffolding £5 }
Also note that Godfrey is bound to answer for £5 received on the day of the Translation of the blessed Thomas the martyr [7 July].
Also on Saturday before the feast of the Assumption of the blessed Mary [13 August] 10*s*. advanced to sailors together with £4. 4*s*. for that ship which was not then valued, which are all allocated in the great Roll of Payments.
Also on Monday before the feast of the blessed Matthew the Apostle [19 September] in the 35th year of the reign of King Henry by way of advance to Sir Edward £5 of the £200 received from the Mint.

Item Memorandum. Die lune proxima post festum Assumpcionis beate Marie anno regni regis Henrici xxxvj^{to} pro vectura IX^{m}vij^{C} stagminis de Cornubia ad Westmonasterium per mare iij marce & dim.

Item Johanni le Senter eodem die xx marce. Item eidem ad carbonem & buscham emendam x li.

Item Magistro Henrico ad opus tasch' xl marce.

Memorandum quod die lune post festum Sancti Nicholai Gilot recepit C metali de prestito. Magistro Johanne plegio.

Memorandum quod die Martis in crastino beati Mathie apostoli dictus Gilot solvit C libras metalli.

Also to be noted. On Monday following the feast of the Assumption of the blessed Mary in the 36th year of the reign of King Henry [19 August 1252] for transporting 97 hundredweight of tin from Cornwall to Westminster by sea, £2. 6*s*. 8*d*.

Also to John le Senter on the same day, £13. 6*s*. 8*d*. Also to the same to buy charcoal and firewood, £10.

Also to Master Henry for task-work, £26. 13*s*. 4*d*.

Note that on Monday after the feast of St. Nicholas [9 December 1252] Gilot received a hundredweight of metal in advance. Master John stood surety.

Note that on Tuesday on the morrow of the feast of the blessed Matthias the Apostle [25 February 1253] the said Gilot melted a hundred pounds of metal.

3. Payments for works at Westminster Abbey from 2 February to 19 April, 1253
(E 101/467/4)

[torn off]

xxxiiij li. xix sol. vj d.

Summa totalis istius partis cvj li. v sol. ix d.

Asseditores

	d. Willelmus Bledelauwe	xxvj. sol. viij d.
Ebdomada viij^{a} die Lune deest	Alfredus Westm' per vij ebdomadas	xiiij sol. x d.
	Rogerus Luton'	
	Henricus de Risberwe	
	Willelmus Donestapele	xxiij sol. ij d.
	Willelmus de Reding	
Ebdomada iij^{a} die Lune venerunt	Willelmus Tothule	
	Reginaldus Mepham	xix sol. ij d.
Eadem ebdomada die Martis	Johannes Wolecumb	xviij sol. x d.
Ebdomada iiij^{a} die Martis in crastino beati Mathie		
Ebdomada viij^{a} continente festum Annunciationis signati per d. desunt per taschiam		
Ebdomada xj^{a} rediit	d.Willelmus Sevenok'	x sol. ij d.
	d.Petrus Merssam	
	d.Eadmundus Herlauwe	viij sol. iiij d.
	d.Henricus Kersauleton	
Ebdomada xj^{a} rediit de tasch'	d.Hugo Blak'	x sol. ij d.
	d.Ricardus Canterbir'	
	d.Simon Lincol'	viij sol. iiij d.
	d.Johannes redehede	
	d.Johannes Denniton'	
Ebdomada vij^{a} die Lune deest	d.Willelmus Paumer per iij ebdomadas	vj sol. ij d.
	d.Reginaldus Abbendon	viij sol. iiijd.

3. Payments for works at Westminster Abbey from 2 February to 19 April, 1253

[torn off]

£34. 19*s.* 6*d.*

Sum total of this portion, £106. 5*s.* 9*d.*

Layers

	d. William Bledlow	26*s.* 8*d.*
He left on Monday in the 8th week	Alfred Westminster for 7 weeks	14*s.* 10*d.*
	Roger Luton	
They came on Monday in the 3rd week	Henry of Risborough	
	William Dunstable	23*s.* 2*d.* (each)
	William of Reading	
	William Tothill	
	Reginald Meopham	19*s.* 2*d.*
On Tuesday in the same week	John Wolecumb	18*s.* 10*d.*
On Tuesday, the morrow of the blessed Matthias [25 February] in the 4th week[1]		
Those marked d. were absent on task-work in the 8th week containing the feast of the Annunciation [25 March]		
He returned in the 11th week	d. William Sevenoaks	10*s.* 2*d.*
	d. Peter Merstham	
	d. Edmund Harlow	8*s.* 4*d.* (each)
	d. Henry Carshalton	
He returned from task-work in the 11th week	d. Hugh Black	10*s.* 2*d.*
	d. Richard Canterbury	
	d. Simon Lincoln	
	d. John Redhead	8*s.* 4*d.* (each)
	d. John Denton	
He left on Monday in the 7th week	d. William Palmer for 3 weeks	6*s.* 2*d.*
	d. Reginald Abingdon	8*s.* 4*d.*

[1] No name follows in the MS.

Ebdomada v^a die Lune ante Cyneres venerunt	Sansun Meleton per vij ebdomadas, xiiij sol. x d.
	d. Adam de Sancto Leodegaro per iij ebdomadas, vj sol. vj d.
Ebdomada $viij^a$ die Lune venit	Walterus de Sorne per iiij ebdomadas, viij sol. iiij d.
Ebdomada x^a die Lune venit	Willelmus Atebore per quindenam, iiij sol.

Summa xvj li. ij sol. ij d.

Empciones a purificacione usque in vigiliam Pasche per xj ebdomadas

pro tascha introitus capituli	xxv li.
In tascha iij formarum ecclesie	xj li.
Item eidem pro tascha capelle domini Regis	ix li. vj sol. viij d.
Item Gileberto Normanno pro tascha muri iuxta berefridum	C sol.
Item Willelmo Yxewerth' pro ij ymaginibus	liij sol. iiij d.
Philippo Hildeley pro xiij capetrellis	xiij sol.
Item Bernardo & Reginaldo cum sociis pro MMV^C & iiij pedibus de asseler' cissis ad tascham	lxx sol. iij d. ob.
Henrico Cheraulton' cum sociis pro V^M & V^C crete ad pend'	xviij sol. iiij d.
Item pro $iiij^{xx}xvj$ pedibus & dim. de bosol' & $Mviij^Cxj$ pedibus de grossis columpnis & C & $iiij^{xx}$ & iiij pedibus de gracilibus columpnis cissis ad tascham	xij li. xvij sol. iij d. & ob.
[Ade Dobin' pro vj passibus ad introitum capituli	vij sol.][1]
Hugoni Waleford pro altari ad capellam curie	vij sol.
Item pro discariacione marmoris cum navata france petre de Came	vij sol.
Henrico fabro pro vigiliis	xl sol.
Item Ricardo fabro pro vigiliis	xvj sol.
Item pro ij navatis france petre de Came	x li. iiij sol. viij d.
Item pro V^MCCCC & quartron france petre	xvj li. v sol. vj d.
Item Rogero Reygate pro MM ix^C & iij quartron petre	ix li. xiij sol. iiij d. ob.

[1] Deleted.

They came on Monday before Ash Wednesday [3 March]	Samson Milton for 7 weeks	14*s.* 10*d.*
	Adam of St. Leger for 3 weeks	6*s.* 6*d.*
He came on Monday in the 8th week	Walter of Shorne for 4 weeks	8*s.* 4*d*
He came on Monday in the 10th week	William Atebore for a fortnight	4*s.* 0*d.*

Total, £16. 2*s.* 2*d.*

Purchases from the Purification [*2 February*] *to the eve of Easter* [*19 April*] *for 11 weeks.*

For the task-work of the entrance to the chapter-house	£25.
For the task-work of 3 [sets of] tracery for the church	£11.
And to the same for the task-work of the lord king's chapel	£9. 6*s.* 8*d.*
And to Gilbert Norman for the task-work of the wall next to the belfry	100*s.*
And to William Ixworth for 2 statues	53*s.* 4*d.*
To Philip Hillsley for 13 capitals	13*s.*
And to Bernard and Reginald with their fellows for 2,504 feet of ashlar cut at task	70*s.* 3½*d.*
To Henry Carshalton with his fellows for 55 hundredweight of chalk for vaults	18*s.* 4*d.*
And for 96½ feet of *bosol'* and 1,811 feet of thick columns and 184 feet of thin columns cut at task	£12. 17*s.* 3½*d.*
[To Adam Dobin for 6 steps at the entrance to the chapter-house	7*s.*][1]
To Hugh Waleford for the altar for the chapel of the court	7*s.*
And for unloading marble together with a shipload of Caen freestone	7*s.*
To Henry the smith for night-work	40*s.*
To Richard the smith for night-work	16*s.*
And for 2 shiploads of Caen freestone	£10. 4*s.* 8*d.*
And for 54¼ hundredweight of freestone	£16. 5*s.* 6*d.*
And to Roger Reigate for 29¾ hundredweight of stone	£9. 13*s.* 4½*d.*

[1] Entry deleted.

Item pro xiiij^{cim} navatis grise petre	iiij li. vij sol. iij d.
Item Ricardo calfonario pro MMMC calcis	vij li. xv sol.
Item Agneti pro MCCC calcis	lxv sol.
Athel' de Ey pro CCCC & xlix careret' sabulonis	iij sol.
Willelmo porcario pro Mlviij caret' sabulonis cariandis	xxj sol. ij d.
Ade merenario pro CCC tignis & MM & CCC[1] bordis	xvli. ij sol. iiij d.
Ledulfo pro M bordis	C sol.
Hugoni merenario pro CCC bordis	xv sol. vj d.
Willelmo Breis pro vj^{C} bordis	vj sol. viij d.
Roberto Otis pro xvj tabulis de sape	xl sol. viij d.
Johanni Stoil pro CC & quartron de salceto ad scafota	xiij sol. vj d.
Benedicto & Matheo pro vectura meremii	xiiij sol. j d.
Ricardo de Estchepe pro virgis & craticulis	lx sol. viij d.
Ricardo Ogul' pro virgis & craticulis	iiij li. ij sol. viij d.
pro CCC & iij quartron busche	xiij sol. iij d. ob.
Item pro bochetis & utensilibus emend'	vij sol. viij d.
Henrico de Ponte pro clavis & alio ferramento	ix li.v sol. v d.
Ricardo de Celer' pro V^{M}IX^{C} & iiij cha[r]ges ferri cum vectura	xiij li. xij sol. & viij d.
Item Josep pro clutis ad carram	xij d.
Ricardo de Crokeley pro CC & V^{xx} ulnis de canevas	lxxix sol. viij d. ob.
Waltero Box pro viij summis vitri & oleo	iiij li. xiij sol. ix d.
Item Laurencio vitriario pro viij summis vitri	lx sol.
Eadwardo vitriario pro ceruris & emendacione utensilium	v sol. j d.
Matilde de Bekeles [pro] Lj duodenis auri	xxiiij sol. xj d.
Waltero Adrian pro colore ad aulam Regis	l sol. iij d.
Warino pictori pro ij ymaginibus pingendis cum colore	xj sol.
Johanni Sige pro iiij caretatis tegularum fractis [*sic*]	xx d.
Hamoni pro literio	xix d.
Fratri de Templo [pro] viij^{C} & quartron tignorum de salseto	iiij li. ij sol. vj d.

[1] Number uncertain.

And for 14 shiploads of ragstone	£4. 7s. 3d.
And to Richard the lime-burner for 31 hundredweight of lime	£7. 15s. 0d.
And to Agnes for 13 hundredweight of lime	65s.
To Athel' of Eye for 449 cart-loads of sand	3s.
To William the swine-herd for carting 1,058 cart-loads of sand	21s. 2d.
To Adam the timber-merchant for 300 beams and 2,300 boards	£15. 2s. 4d.
To Ledulf for 1,000 boards	100s.
To Hugh the timber-merchant for 300 boards	15s. 6d.
To William Breis for 600 boards	6s. 8d.
To Robert Otis for 16 planks of softwood	40s. 8d.
To John Stoil for 2¼ hundredweight of osiers for scaffolding	13s. 6d.
To Benedict and Matthew for conveyance of timber	14s. 1d.
To Richard of Eastcheap for withies and hurdles	60s. 8d.
To Richard Ogul for withies and hurdles	£4. 2s. 8d.
For 3¾ hundredweight of firewood	13s. 3½d.
And for repairing(?) buckets and utensils	7s. 8d.
To Henry of Bridge for nails and other ironwork	£9. 5s. 5d.
To Richard of the cellar for 59 hundredweight and 4 loads of iron with transport	£13. 12s. 8d.
And to Joseph for clouts for a cart	12d.
To Richard of Crokeley for 340[1] ells of canvas	79s. 8½d.
To Walter Box for 8 seams of glass and for oil	£4. 13s. 9d.
And to Lawrence the glazier for 8 seams of glass	60s.
To Edward the glazier for locks and for repairing utensils	5s. 1d.
To Matilda of Bexley for 51 dozen of gold	24s. 11d.
To Walter Adrian for colour for the king's hall	50s. 3d.
To Warin the painter for painting 2 images with colour	11s.
To John Sige for 4 cart-loads of broken tiles	20d.
To Hamon for straw	19d.
To a Brother of the Temple for 8¼ hundredweight of willow logs	£4. 2s. 6d.

[1] As '200 and 5 score' would be a strange way of writing '300' it is assumed that C here means the 'long hundred' of 120, making the figure 340.

Item Roberto de Turri pro meremio	iiij sol. iij d.
Roberto de Beverley pro iiij[or] clavibus	xxxij sol.

Summa CC li. lxxij sol. v d. ob.
CC li. lxxvj sol. viij d. ob.

Memorandum de liij sol. iiij d. pro franca petra de Came in festo . . . ionis beate Marie

Hec est pacacio facta die Veneris de V[C] li. die Jovis precedenti in crastino beati Johannis ante portam Latinam receptis.

pro xxiij chareis plumbi	l li.
pro tascha introitus capituli	xxv li.
pro tascha formarum	xj li.
pro tascha capelle	ix li.
pro tascha muri	c sol.
remanent de j sacco iij sol. ij d. ob.	
De ij[do] sacco	
Willelmo Yxelewerth pro duabus ymaginibus	liij sol. iiij d.
Philippo Hildeley pro tascha	xiij sol.
Bernardo & sociis pro asselers	lxx sol. iiij d. ob.
pro cretis cissis ad tascham	xviij sol. iiij d.
pro marmore cisso ad tascham	xij li. xvij sol. iij d. ob.
In stipendiis alborum cissorum	lxviij li. ix sol. ix d.
Item ad stipendia marmorariorum de eodem sacco	x li. xvij sol. ij d.
Item eisdem marmorariis de tercio [sacco]	xxiiij li. iij sol. iiij d.
In stipendiis cubitorum	xvj li. ij sol. ij d.
In stipendiis carpentariorum cum Johanne & W. turnur cum operariis	xlvij li. xiij sol. v d.
pictori circa aulam	cx sol. d.
Item Petro Pictori	lxiiij sol.
Item ad stipendia polisorum de eodem sacco	lx sol. &
Item de iiij[to] saco ad stipendia pollisorum	vj li. xij d.
Item in stipendiis fabrorum	xvj li. iij. sol. iiij d.
Item vitriariis	xvj li. xvj sol. xj d.
Item plumbatoribus	x li. xij sol. ix d. ob.
Item in stipendiis custodum, clericorum cum bigis diurnis	vij li. vij sol. xj d.
Item pro craticulis	iiij li. ij sol. viij d.
Item de iiij[to] sacco ad stipendia minutorum operariorum	xxxix li. viij sol. d ob.
Item de quinto sacco ad stipendia eorundem	xxj li. x sol. x d.
Item fabris pro vigiliis	lvj sol.

And to Robert of the Tower for timber	4*s*. 3*d*.
To Robert of Beverley for 4 keystones	32*s*.

Total £203. 12*s*. 5½*d*.
£203. 16*s*. 8½*d*.

Note of 53*s*. 4*d*. for Caen freestone paid on the feast of the Purification of the blessed Mary [2 February].

This is the payment made on Friday of £500 received on the preceding Thursday, the morrow of the blessed John before the Latin Gate.[1]

For 23 chars of lead	£50
For the task-work of the entrance to the chapter-house	£25
For the task-work of window-tracery	£11
For the task-work of the chapel	£9
For the task-work of the wall	100*s*.
there remains from the 1st sack, 3*s*. 2½*d*.	
From the 2nd sack	
To William Ixworth for two images	53*s*. 4*d*.
To Philip Hillsley for task-work	13*s*.
To Bernard and his fellows for ashlar	70*s*. 4½*d*.
For chalk cut at task	18*s*. 4*d*.
For marble cut at task	£12. 17*s*. 3½*d*.
In wages of white cutters	£68. 9*s*. 9*d*.
And for the wages of marblers from the same sack	£10. 17*s*. 2*d*.
And to the same marblers from the third [sack]	£24. 3*s*. 4*d*.
In wages of layers	£16. 2*s*. 2*d*.
In wages of carpenters with John and W. the turner, with labourers	£47. 13*s*. 5*d*.
To a painter [working] upon the hall	110*s*. 1*d*.
And to Peter the Painter	64*s*.
And for the wages of polishers from the same sack	60*s*. &
And from the 4th sack for the wages of polishers	£6 1*s*.
And for smiths' wages	£16 3*s*. 4*d*.
And to glaziers	£16 16*s*. 11*d*.
And to plumbers	£10 12*s*. 9½*d*.
And for the wages of keepers and clerks, with daily carts	£7 7*s*. 11*d*.
And for hurdles	£4 2*s*. 8*d*.
And from the 4th sack for the wages of labourers	£39. 8*s*. 1½*d*.
And from the 5th sack for the wages of the same	£21. 10*s*. 10*d*.
And to the smiths for night-work	56*s*.

[1] In 1253 the feast of St. John before the Latin Gate (6 May) fell on a Tuesday, so the morrow would have been a Wednesday, not a Thursday.

pro franca petra	xxv li. xviij sol. x d. ob.
Item pro franca petra de Came	x li. iiij sol. viij d.
Item Magistro Johanni apud Sanctum Albanum	iiij sol. iiij d.
Item pro grisa petra	iiij li. vij sol. iij d.
Item pro calce	xj li.
Item pro virgis	lx sol. viij d.
pro clavibus cissis ad tascham	xxxij sol.
pro sabulone	iij sol.
Item eidem pro cera	vj sol. viij d.
pro cariagio sabulonis	xxj sol. ij d.
pro fretto marmoris	iiij li. ix sol. viij d.
Ludulfo pro bordis	c sol.
pro altari & discariacione petre de Came	xiiij sol.
Fratri de Templo pro meremio	iiij li. ij sol. vj d.
Item de quinto sacco pro meremio Ade	lxiiij sol. d. ob.
Item eidem Ade pro meremio de vj^to^ sacco	xj li. xviij sol. ij d. ob.
Item Hugoni cum aliis merenariis pro meremio bordis & tabulis de sape cum vectura	iiij li. x sol. v d.
Henrico de ponte pro clavis ferri & alio ferramento	ix li. viij sol. v d.
pro iij navatis marmoris	xx li.
pro boketis cum buscha	xx sol. xj d. ob.
pro ferro Glovernie	xiij li. xij sol. viij d.
pro canevas	lxxix sol. viij d. ob.
pro custura canevas	vj sol. viij d.
Waltero Box pro vitro & oleo	iiij li. xiij sol. ix d.
Item Laurencio pro vitro	lxv sol. j d.
Item pro tegulis literio & meremio	vij sol. vj d.
Item pro pullitione	xiiij sol. xj d.
Item pro auge	ij sol.
Item Jacobo Junctori pro tabulis iungendis	lxiiij sol. ij d.
pro arreragiis Rogeri Wonbe	xvj d.
pro cariagio ferri	iij sol. iiij d.
Item pro iiij diebus	xij d.
Matilde de Boxele pro auro	xxiiij sol. xj d.
Item in expensis . . .	v sol.
Item pro diversis agendis	vj sol. iij d.

For freestone	£25. 18*s*. 10½*d*.
And for Caen freestone	£10. 4*s*. 8*d*.
And to Master John at St. Albans	4*s*. 4*d*.
And for ragstone	£4. 7*s*. 3*d*.
And for lime	£11
And for withies	60*s*. 8*d*.
For keystones cut at task	32*s*.
For sand	3*s*.
And to the same for wax	6*s*. 8*d*.
For carriage of sand	21*s*. 2*d*.
For freight of marble	£4. 9*s*. 8*d*.
To Ludulf for boards	100*s*.
For an altar and for unloading Caen stone	14*s*.
To a Brother of the Temple for timber	£4. 2*s*. 6*d*.
And to Adam from the fifth sack for timber	64*s*. 1½*d*.
And to the same Adam for timber, from the 6th sack	£11. 18*s*. 2½*d*.
And to Hugh with other timber-merchants for timber, boards, and planks of softwood with transport	£4. 10*s*. 5*d*.
To Henry of Bridge for iron nails and other ironwork	£9. 8*s*. 5*d*.
For 3 shiploads of marble	£20
For buckets with firewood	20*s*. 11½*d*.
For Gloucester iron	£13. 12*s*. 8*d*.
For canvas	79*s*. 8½*d*.
For stitching canvas	6*s*. 8*d*.
To Walter Box for glass and oil	£4. 13*s*. 9*d*.
And to Lawrence for glass	65*s*. 1*d*.
And for tiles, straw, and timber	7*s*. 6*d*.
And for polishing	14*s*. 11*d*.
And for a trough	2*s*.
And to James the joiner for joining planks[1]	64*s*. 2*d*.
To Roger Wonbe for arrears	16*d*.
For carriage of iron	3*s*. 4*d*.
And for 4 days	12*d*.
To Matilda of Boxley for gold	24*s*. 11*d*.
And in expenses . . .	5*s*.
And for doing various things	6*s*. 3*d*.

[1] It is possible that *tabulis* should here be translated as 'tables' rather than as 'planks'.

Et restat in sacco xj li. (*deleted*)

Item de eodem sacco pro pictura xxix sol. ix d.

& restant in sacco ix li. x sol. iij d.

Item pro ij navatis petre de Came xij li. die Sabbati ante festum beati Augustini de Scaccario recepte

Item die Veneris in crastino accessionis [*sic*] de remanenti duorum saccorum quariariis de prestito xix li. xi sol. pro $vj^{M}vj^{C}$ petre.

Item die Lune xx li. pro meremio.

Item die Veneris sequenti quariariis de prestito pro $vj^{M}vj^{C}$ & dim. petre xx li.

Item pro freto marmoris iiij li. x sol. d. ob.

Item pro freto marmoris cix sol. x d. ob.

Item tribus operariis licentiatis per ix ebdomadas xxx sol. de remanenti vj sacci.

And there remains in the sack £11 (*deleted*)
And from the same sack for painting 29*s*. 9*d*.
and there remains in the sack £9. 10*s*. 3*d*.
And for 2 ship-loads of Caen stone £12 received from the Exchequer on Saturday before the feast of the blessed Augustine [24 May].
And on Friday, the morrow of the Ascension [30 May] from the remainder of two sacks to the quarrymen by way of advance for 66 hundredweight of stone £19 11*s*.
And on Monday [2 June] for timber £20.
Anc on the following Friday [6 June] to the quarrymen by way of advance for 66½ hundredweight of stone £20.
And for freight of marble £4. 10*s*. 1½*d*.
And for freight of marble 109*s*. 10½*d*.
And to three departing labourers for 9 weeks, 30*s*. from the remainder of the 6th sack

4. Account of works at Westminster Abbey and Palace from 1 February to 19 April, 1253 (E 101/466/30)

Compotus diversarum Operacionum Ecclesie, Capituli, Berefridi & Curie Westmonasterii, Anno regni regis Henrici xxxvij^{o} Operis incepti viij^{vo}.

Hec est Pacacio facta a die Sabbati in vigilia Purificacionis beate Marie usque Sabbatum in vigilia Pasche per undecim Ebdomadas continentes iiij^{or} festa quorum primum est Cementariorum secundum domini Regis & sic de singulis ita quod festum Paraceve est domini Regis anno regni regis Henrici xxxvij^{o}.

In stipendiis lxxiiij alborum cissorum, xlv marmorariorum, xxiiij cubitorum, iiij carpentariorum. xiij pollisorum, xx fabrorum, xv vitriariorum cum clericis & custodibus c.iiij^{xx}. xij li. & viij sol.

In stipendiis magistri Johannis cum carpentario & serviente apud Sanctum Albanum circa lectron. lxxiiij sol.

In stipendiis C. & xxxj minutorum Operariorum cum ix bigis diurnis. lxiiij li. xij sol. vij d. & ob.

Empciones

In ij ymaginibus ad taschiam cissis	liiij sol. iiij d.
In chapittellis, clavibus, asselers cum creta ad taschiam cissis	c xv sol. iiij d.
In taschia introitus Capituli	xxv li.
In taschia formarum Ecclesie	xj li.
In iij Navatis marmoris	xxxiiij li. ix sol. viij d.
In ij Navatis france Petre de Came	xxiiij li. xviij sol.
In xxiiij^{M} france Petre de Reygate	lxxij li.
In M.M. Calcis ad ecclesiam & capitulum	C sol.
In meremio salceti & alneti ad scafota cum portagio & vectura	iiij li. vij sol.
In virgis & craticulis ad scafota	vij li. iij sol. iiij d.
In boketis & emendacione utensilium	vij sol. viij d.
In V^{M}.IX^{C}. ferri tenacis de Glovernia cum clavis ferri & alio ferramento	xx li.
In CC.V^{xx} ulnis de canavasio ad fenestras capituli	iiij li. vj sol. iiij d. ob.
In xvj summis vitri colorati & albi	vij li. xviij sol. ix d.
In meremio ad lectronem apud Sanctum Albanum	iiij sol. iiij d.

Summa totalis. Ecclesie & Capituli. CCCC. iiij^{xx}.v.li. xviij sol. v.d.

4. Account of works at Westminster Abbey and Palace from 1 February to 19 April, 1253

The account of divers works of the church, the chapter-house, belfry, and the Court of Westminster in the 37th year of the reign of King Henry, and the eighth year since the work began [1253].

This is the payment made from Saturday on the vigil of the Purification of the blessed Mary [1 February] to Saturday, Easter Eve [19 April] for eleven weeks containing four feasts of which the first is the masons', the second the lord king's and so on, so that Good Friday [18 April] is the lord king's in the 37th year of the reign of King Henry.

For wages of 74 white cutters, 45 marblers, 24 layers, 4 carpenters, 13 polishers, 20 smiths, 15 glaziers, with clerks and keepers, £192. 8*s.*

For wages of Master John with a carpenter and a servant at St. Albans working on the lectern, 74*s.*

For wages of 131 labourers with nine carts daily, £64. 12*s.* 7½*d.*

Purchases

For cutting two images by task, 53*s.* 4*d.*

For capitals, bosses, ashlars, with chalk cut by task, 115*s.* 4*d.*

For the task-work of the entrance of the chapter-house, £25.

For the task-work of tracery for the Church, £11.

For 3 shiploads of marble, £34. 9*s.* 8*d.*

For 2 shiploads of Caen freestone, £24. 18*s.*

For 240 hundredweight of Reigate freestone, £72.

For 20 hundredweight of chalk for the church and the chapter-house, 100*s.*

For willow and alder timber for scaffolding with portage and carriage, £4. 7*s.*

For withies and hurdles for scaffolding, £7. 3*s.* 4*d.*

For buckets and mending of utensils, 7*s.* 8*d.*

For 59 hundredweight of tough Gloucester iron with iron nails and other ironwork, £20.

For 340[1] ells of canvas for the windows of the chapter house, £4. 6*s.* 4½*d.*

For 16 seams of coloured and white glass, £7. 18*s.* 9*d.*

For timber for the lectern at St. Albans, 4*s.* 4*d.*

Sum total of the Church and chapter-house, £485. 18*s.* 5*d.*

[1] This is assuming that C. here means the 'long hundred' of 120.

Opus Berefridi

In Stipendiis xxvj carpentariorum, ix^{vem} plumbatorum	xxxviij li. xiij sol. ix d.
In stipendiis minutorum operariorum cum carpentariis	x li. xv sol.
In taschia muri iuxta Berefridum operandi	C sol.

Empciones

In xvij Navatis Grise Petre	c ij sol. ij d.
In MM. cccc calcis	vj li.
In M.V^{c} caretatis sabulorum ad taschiam fodendis & cariandis	xxiiij sol. ij d.
In grosso meremio Bordis & lateis	xxxvj li. iiij sol. x d.
In V^{c} & dim. Busche	xxj sol.
In xxiij chareis Plumbi	L li.
In clavis ferri ad plumbandum Berefridum	Lviij sol.
In tegulis ad murum & domum iuxta Berefridum	vij sol.
In cordis ad campanas	vj sol. iij d.

Summa Berefridi. c & lvij li. xij sol. ij d.

Opus Curie

In Stipendiis Magistri Petri de Hispania Pictoris	lxiiij sol.
In stipendiis x. Pictorum in magna aula ultra mensam pingentium	c & x sol. j d.

Empciones

In Quinquaginta una duoden[is] auri ad picturam	xxiiij sol. xj d.
In aliis diversis coloribus ad predictam Picturam	xxix sol. ix d.
In taschia capelle infra Gardinum Curie	ix li.
In quodam altari eiusdem capelle	xiiij sol.

Summa totalis Curie xxj li. ij sol. & ix d.

Summa totalis Ecclesie Capituli Berefridi & Curie vj^{c}.lxiiij li. xiij sol. iiij d.

The work of the Belfry

For wages of 26 carpenters, 9 plumbers, £38. 13*s*. 9*d*.
For wages of labourers with the carpenters, £10. 15*s*.
For the task-work of making the wall next to the Belfry, 100*s*.

Purchases

For 17 shiploads of ragstone, 102*s*. 2*d*.
For 24 hundredweight of lime, £6.
For digging and carrying 1,500 cart-loads of sand by task, 24*s*. 2*d*.
For heavy timber, boards, and laths, £36. 4*s*. 10*d*.
For five and a half hundredweight of firewood, 21*s*.
For 23 chars of lead, £50.
For iron nails for leading the Belfry, 58*s*.
For tiles for the wall and building next the Belfry, 7*s*.
For cords for the bells, 6*s*. 3*d*.

Total of the Belfry, £157. 12*s*. 2*d*.

The work of the Court

For the wages of Master Peter of Spain the painter, 64*s*.
For the wages of 10 painters painting in the great hall above the table, 110*s*. 1*d*.

Purchases

For 51 dozen of gold for the painting, 24*s*. 11*d*.
For various other colours for the said painting, 29*s*. 9*d*.
For the task-work of the chapel within the garden of the Court, £9.
For a certain altar for the same chapel, 14*s*.

Sum total of the Court, £21. 2*s*. 9*d*.

Sum total of the church, the chapter-house, the belfry, and the Court, £664. 13*s*. 4*d*.

5. Memoranda concerning payments for works at Westminster Abbey from 28 April to 17 May, 1253

(E 101/683/1)[1]

Hugoni Cant'	ij sol.
Ricardo Kerwente	
Waltero Tabbur'	
Willelmo Tothul'	
Willelmo Somersete	
Willelmo Ketinge	
Willelmo Borhache	ij sol. iij d. ob.
Willelmo Kitebrig'	
Willelmo Gudbure	
Johanni avelove	
Johanni Greton'	
Simoni scafatur	
Nicholao de Forde	xxij d. ob.
Thome Noreis	
Ricardo Batrichesey	
Rogero Wygorn'	
Galfrido Werne	xv d.
Gileberto Kitebrige	
Simoni Torvey	
Waltero Marchant	
Radulfo Hendon'	
Willelmo Benflete	
Johanni Botefant'	
Johanni de Sancto Albano	
Waltero Kenenford'	
Simoni Oxn'	
Johanni de ponte Walteri	
Roberto Hokeley	
Johanni Sauyar	
Nicholao Polen	
Willelmo Wodestok	xv d.
Waltero Bacon	

[1] Five names have been added later opposite the following wage-brackets: W. Porcarius (2*s*. $3\frac{1}{2}$ *d.*), R. Lichf', A. Miting', S. Clericus and W. Covel' (15 *d.*)

5. Memoranda concerning payments for works at Westminster Abbey from 28 April to 17 May, 1253[1]

[*Labourers*]

Hugh Cant'	
Richard Caerwent	2*s*.
Walter Tabor (?)	
William Tothill	
William Somerset	
William Keating	
William Borhache	2*s*. 3½*d*.
William Kitebrig'	
William Goldbury	
John Havelove	
John Gretton	
Simon the scaffolder	
Nicholas of Forde	22½*d*.
Thomas Noreis	
Richard Battersea	
Roger of Worcester	
Geoffrey Werne	
Gilbert Kitebrige	15*d*.
Simon Turvey	
Walter Marchant	
Ralph Hendon	
William Benfleet	
John Botefant	
John of St. Albans	
Walter Kenenford	
Simon Oxney (?)	
John of Bridgwater	
Robert Hockley	
John Sawyer	
Nicholas Polen	
William Woodstock	15*d*.
Walter Bacon	

[1] Five names have been added later opposite the following wage-brackets: W. the swineherd (2*s*. 3½*d*.). R. Lichfield, A. Miting, S. Clerk and W. Cowley (15*d*).

Reginaldo Salomon'	
Ricardo Martin	
Thome Bradwell'	
Johanni Cleygate	
Willelmo Bradewey	
Roberto Taddeham	
Johanni Greneford'	
Ernaldo Ferley	
Johanni Lond'	xv d.
Roberto Ledrede	xij d. ob.
Morel'	x d.

Summa totalis xxiiij li. xvj sol. xj d.

Summa totalis operariorum xxvij li. x sol. ob.

Hec est Pacacio facta die Martis post festum Apostolorum Petri & Pauli pro stipendiis & taschiis a die Lune in crastino clausi Pasche usque Sabbatum proximum ante festum Sancti Dunstani ultimo celebratum per iij ebdomadas continentes iij festa quorum primum est domini Regis, ij cementariorum, tercium domini Regis, anno regni regis H. xxxvij.

Pro stipendiis l albis [*sic*] ciss', xviij marmorariorum, xxx cubitorum, xxix carpentariorum, xiiij pollisorum, xix fabrorum, xiiij vitriariorum, iiij^{xx} taschiatorum cum custodibus & clericis iiij^{xx} li. lxxviij sol. x d. ob.

In stipendiis CC operariorum per iij ebdomadas predictas xvj li. xiiij d.

Item ad stipendia . . . . . . xxxvij li. x . . . sol. iij d. die Veneris ante festum Translacionis beati Thome martiris

ad pacacionem stipendiorum predictorum operariorum ix li. xvij sol. iij d.

Item mercator' de Came pro franca petra cxvij sol.

Item quariariis de Reygate de prestito super francam petram xxij li.

Item xv li. ix sol. . . .

Item per manum magistri Alexandri pro iij caretatis carbonis lignei	iiij sol. viij d.
Item pro caretata carbonis	xxij d.
Item . . . . . pro minori	xiij d.
Calfonar' de prestito	xl sol.
. . . . de Came	lx sol.
In [perpacacionem] Ricardo de Elteham pro	xvij d.

Operarii cum carpentariis

Johanni Sike
Ricardo Robine
Willelmo Pecok'

Reginald Solomon	
Richard Martin	
Thomas Bradwell	
John Claygate	
William Bradway	
Robert Taddeham	
John Greenford	
Arnold Farley	
John London	15*d.*
Robert Leatherhead	12½*d.*
Morel	10*d.*

Total, £24. 16*s.* 11*d.*

Total for labourers, £27. 10*s.* 0½*d.*

This is the payment made on Tuesday after the feast of the Apostles Peter and Paul [1 July] for wages and task-works from Monday on the day after the end of Easter [28 April] to Saturday before the feast of St. Dunstan [17 May] for 3 weeks containing 3 feasts, of which the first is the lord king's, the second the masons', the third the lord king's, in the 37th year of the reign of King Henry [1253].

For the wages of 50 white cutters, 18 marblers, 30 layers, 29 carpenters, 14 polishers, 19 smiths, 14 glaziers, 80 task-workers, with keepers and clerks, £83. 18*s.* 10½*d.*

For the wages of 200 labourers for the said three weeks, £16. 1*s.* 2*d.*

And . . . . £37. 1..*s.* 3*d.* on Friday before the feast of the Translation of the blessed Thomas the Martyr. [4 July] . . . .

To pay the wages of the said labourers, £9. 17*s.* 3*d.*

And to a merchant of Caen for freestone, £5. 17*s.* 0*d.*

And to the Reigate quarrymen in advance for freestone, £22. Also £15. 9*s* . . .

And by the hand of Master Alexander [the carpenter] for 3 cart-loads of charcoal	4*s.* 8*d.*
And for a cart-load of charcoal	1*s.* 10*d.*
And . . . . for a smaller one	13*d.*
To the lime-burner in advance	£2. 0*s.* 0*d.*
. . . . . . of Caen (?)	£3. 0*s.* 0*d.*
To complete the payment to Richard of Eltham for	1*s.* 5*d.*

Labourers with the carpenters

John Sike
Richard Robine
William Pecok

Thome Sotton' Eadmundo Brasin Roberto Aldeham Waltero Sertesey Johanni Neck'[1] Waltero Noris Rogero Testard Roberto Brone Johanni Chilhuth' Stephano Gardin' Henrico caret' Roberto Standon' Simoni Coco Willelmo gardin'	iij sol. d. ob.
	liij sol. d. ob.

Virgatores

Roberto de Turri	v sol. iiij d.
Richero de Cruce Hamoni	iij sol. ix d.

Clerici

Galfrido clerico	vij sol.
Willelmo clerico Johanni clerico	vij sol.

Bige diurne

Johanni Bouton' bigam Willelmo porcher bigam	v sol.

Hec sunt prestita per tres vices facta Quariariis ante & post Pentecost' de xix li. xj sol. in pacacione ante Pentecost' alocatis
Item de xx li. post Pentecost' in pacacione alocatis
Item die Veneris ante Translacionem beati Thome Martiris de xxij li.

Rogero Reigate per iij vices	xiij li.
Algar Brige per iij vices	xiiij li.
Ricardo Crouden'	xj li.
Radulfo de Lamhuthe	viij li. x sol.
Willelmo Brige	viij li. xj sol.
Willelmo Karre	viij li. x sol.

[1] Deleted: *pro peregrinacione ix sol. ix d. ob.* has been added opposite this name.

Thomas Sutton Edmund Brasin Robert Aldham Walter Chertsey John Neck[1] Walter Norris Roger Testard Robert Brone John Chilhuth Stephen Gardiner Henry the carter Robert Standon Simon Cook William Gardiner	3*s*. 1½*d*.
	£2. 13*s*. 1½*d*.

Erectors of scaffolding

Robert of the Tower	5*s*. 4*d*.
Richer of the Cross Hamo	3*s*. 9*d*.

Clerks

Geoffrey the clerk	7*s*. 0*d*.
William the clerk John the clerk	7*s*. 0*d*.

Daily carts

John Bouton's cart William Porcher's cart	5*s*. 0*d*.

These are advances made on three occasions to the quarrymen before and after Whitsun: £19. 11*s*. 0*d*. allocated before Whitsun; £20 allocated after Whitsun; and on Friday before the Translation of the blessed Thomas the Martyr [4 July] £22

to Roger Reigate on three occasions	£13. 0*s*. 0*d*.
to Algar Bridge on three occasions	£14. 0*s*. 0*d*.
to Richard Croydon	£11. 0*s*. 0*d*.
to Ralph of Lambeth	£8. 10*s*. 0*d*.
to William Bridge	£8. 11*s*. 0*d*.
to William Karre	£8. 10*s*. 0*d*.

[1] Deleted: '9*s*. 9½*d*. on account of his pilgrimage' has been added opposite this name

Item die Veneris post Translacionem beati Thome de scaccario, vj li.
xvij sol. (?) de quibus Algaro ad perpacacionem per
ix ebdomadas xv li. ix sol. vj d.
pro cariagio petre xv sol.

Item Rogero Reygate ad perpacacionem ix ebdomadarum pro petra viij li. x sol. vij d. ob.

.... xvij d.

xxv li. ......

Item ad perpacacionem .... per x ebdomadas
Ricardo Crouden .... vj d.
Radulfo de Lamhuth ....
Willelmo de Brige .... lj sol...
Willelmo de C .... lxxj sol. vj d.

Summa prestitorum quariariis liij li. xij d.

And on Friday after the Translation of the blessed Thomas [11 July] from the Exchequer, £6. 17*s*. (?), from which there was paid to Algar in full payment for 9 weeks £15. 9*s*. 6*d*.

For carriage of stone 15*s*.

And to Roger Reigate in full payment of stone for 9 weeks, £8. 10*s*. 7½*d*.

. . . . 1*s*. 5*d*.

£25. . . . .

And in full payment . . . . for 10 weeks to

Richard Croydon . . . . 6*d*.

Ralph of Lambeth . . . .

To William of Bridge. . . . . £2. 11*s*. . . .

To William of C[. . . . . .] . . . . £3. 11*s*. 6*d*.

Total advances to quarrymen £53. 1*s*. 0*d*.

6. Payments for works at Westminster Abbey from 28 April to 6 December, 1253

(E 101/467/1)

Ebdomada Prima post Pascham. Continente festum apostolorum Philippi & Jacobi per diem Jovis quod est domini Regis & festum Invencionis Sancte Crucis per diem Sabbati quod est cementariorum.

In stipendiis xxxix alborum cissorum, xiiii marmorariorum, xx cubitorum, xxxii carpentariorum cum Johanne apud Sanctum Albanum, iii pictorum, xiii pollisorum, xix^{cim} fabrorum, xiiii vitriariorum cum iiii^{or} plumbatoribus xiiij li. xij sol.

In stipendiis cl minutorum operariorum cum custodibus clericis & duabus bigis diurnis. vj li. & xvj sol.

Summa stipendiorum xxj li. viij sol.

Empciones

Henrico fabro

Bernardo de Sancta Osida pro v^{c}iiij^{xx} & viii pedibus de asselers cissis ad taschiam xiiij sol. viij d.

Item Henrico de Chersaulton' pro vj^{c} & dim. crete ad pend' cissis ad taschiam xxvj d.

Item Nicholao Scot & sociis suis pro portagio petre vj sol. vij d.

Item pro MMMvj^{c} france petre x li. xvj sol.

Rogero de Reygate pro M france petre lxv sol., pro ij navatis grise petre. xiij sol. iij d.

Item pro v^{c} calcis xxv sol.

Ade merenario pro meremio bordis & latis xxxiij sol. x d.

Item Jacobo junctori pro tabulis ad cameras domini Regis & Regine & pro panellis ad lectum domini Regis lxiiij sol. ij d.

Item Ricardo de Estchepe pro virgis & craticulis iiij sol. vj d.

Item Ricardo Ogul pro craticulis v sol.

Ricardo cuvario pro bochetis iij sol. vj d.

Waltero Box pro cordis viij sol. vj d.

Henrico de Ponte pro grese ad martella acuenda iiij sol.

Item eidem Henrico pro clavis ferri xiij sol.

Ricardo de Celer' pro MMCCCC ferri tenacis de Glovernia iiij li. xvj sol.

Item pro cariagio dicti ferri iij sol. iiij d.

Item Michaeli Tony pro xxiij chareis plumbi l li.

Item Pain pro cyneribus plumbi fundendis xl s.

6. Payments for works at Westminster Abbey from 28 April to 6 December, 1253

The first week after Easter. Containing the feast of the Apostles Philip and James [1 May] on Thursday which is the lord king's and the feast of the Invention of the Holy Cross [3 May] on Saturday which is the masons'.

For wages of 39 white cutters, 14 marblers, 20 layers, 32 carpenters together with John at St. Albans, 3 painters, 13 polishers, 19 smiths, 14 glaziers, and 4 plumbers, £14. 12*s*.

For wages of 150 labourers, with keepers, clerks, and [the charges of] two carts daily, £6. 16*s*.

Total wages, £21. 8*s*.

Purchases

To Henry the smith.

To Bernard of St. Osyth for cutting 588 feet of ashlars by task, 14*s*. 8*d*.

And to Henry of Carshalton for cutting six hundredweight and a half of chalk for the vaults by task, 2*s*. 2*d*.

And to Nicholas Scot and his fellows for portage of stone, 6*s*. 7*d*.

And for 36 hundredweight of freestone, £10. 16*s*.

To Roger of Reigate for 10 hundredweight of freestone, 65*s*., for two shiploads of ragstone, 13*s*. 3*d*.

And for five hundredweight of lime, 25*s*.

To Adam the timber merchant for timber, boards, and laths, 33*s*. 10*d*.

And to James the joiner for tables for the chambers of the lord king and the queen and for panels for the lord king's bed, 64*s*. 2*d*.

And to Richard of Eastcheap for withies and hurdles, 4*s*. 6*d*.

And to Richard Ogul for hurdles, 5*s*.

To Richard the cooper for buckets, 3*s*. 6*d*.

To Walter Box for cords, 8*s*. 6*d*.

To Henry of Bridge for a whetstone to sharpen mauls, 4*s*.

And to the aforesaid Henry for iron nails, 13*s*.

To Richard of the cellar for 24 hundredweight of tough Gloucester iron, £4. 16*s*.

And for carriage of the same iron, 3*s*. 4*d*.

And to Michael Tony for 23 chars of lead, £50.

And to Pain for smelting lead ashes, 40*s*.

Item Johanni Sige pro xiij M. & dim. tegularum cum portagio & cavillis xxviij sol. xj d.

Summa empcionum xxvij li. xij s. iiij d.

Summa totalis ebdomade xlix li. iiij d.

Ebdomada secunda post Pascham continente festum Beati Johannis ante Portam Latinam per diem Martis quod est domini Regis.

In stipendiis xxxix alborum cissorum, xv marmorariorum, xxvj cubitorum, xxxij carpentariorum cum Johanne et socio suo apud Sanctum Albanum, duobus[1] pictorum cum serviente, xiij^cim^ pollisorum, xix fabrorum, xiiij^cim^ vitriariorum cum iiij^or^ plumbatoribus xv li. x s. d.

In stipendiis clxxvj operariorum cum custodibus clericis cum ij bigis diurnis, ix li. xvij sol. ij d.

Summa stipendiorum xxv li. vij sol. iij d.

Empciones

Magistro Albrico pro arreragiis formarum & ....

lxvj sol., pro liij pedibus de parpen' pretium pedis iiij d., lix pedibus de folsur' cum fil' pretium pedis iij d. ob., CC & xxj pedibus & dim. pretium pedis iij d., l assisis pretium assise v d., xlij chamberand', xxij pedibus maignanz, ccxliij pedibus cerches, ix pedibus de bosseus & vij passibus cissis ad taschiam vij li. xiij sol. j d.

Item pro ix capitellis, lxviij pedibus de escus, MV^c^iiij^xx^xj pedibus de cerches liiij sol. & iiij d.

Item pro MMV^c^ dim. quart. pendent' crete viij sol. vij d.

Item pro MMCC & iij quart. france petre vj li. xvj sol. vj d.

Rogero de Reygate pro viij^c^ quart. france petre liij sol. vij d. ob.

Ricardo Calfonario pro ccc calcis xv s.

Agnes pro CC dim. calcis xij sol. vj d.

Item Ricardo de Estchep pro ij duodenis craticularum cum virgis ix sol. vij d.

Ricardo Oggol pro v duodenis craticularum cum virgis xij sol. vj d.

Henrico de Ponte pro clavis ferri & gressiis xix sol. viij d.

Benedicto pro vectura portagio & pesagio xxiij charrearum plumbi ix sol. iiij d.

Richero pro literia xviij d.

Summa totalis empcionum xxvij li. xij sol. x d. ob.

Summa totalis ebdomade liij li. & d. ob.

Ebdomada tertia sine festo.

In stipendiis xxxix alborum cissorum, xv marmorariorum, xxvj cubitorum,

[1] *Sic.*

And to John Sige for 13,500 tiles together with portage and tile-pins, 28*s.* 11*d.*

Total purchases, £27. 12*s.* 4*d.*

Sum total of the week, £49. 0*s.* 4*d.*

The second week after Easter containing the feast of the blessed John before the Latin Gate [6 May] on Tuesday which is the lord king's.

For wages of 39 white cutters, 15 marblers, 26 layers, 32 carpenters together with John and his fellow at St. Albans, two painters with a servant, 13 polishers, 19 smiths, 14 glaziers, and four plumbers, £15. 10*s.* 1*d.*

For wages of 176 labourers, with keepers, clerks, and [the charges of] two carts daily, £9. 17*s.* 2*d.*

Total wages, £25. 7*s.* 3*d.*

Purchases. To Master Aubrey for the arrears owed for tracery and ......, 66*s.*, for 53 feet of parpent stone at 4*d.* a foot, 59 feet of voussoirs with fillets at 3½*d.* a foot, 221½ feet at 3*d.* a foot, 50 *assises* at 5*d.* each, 42 jambs, 22 feet of mullions, 243 feet of *cerches*,[1] 9 feet of *bosseus*, and seven steps cut by task, £7. 13*s.* 1*d.*

And for 9 capitals, 68 feet of skew-stones, 1,591 feet of *cerches*,[1] 54*s.* 4*d.*

And for 25¾ hundredweight of chalk for the vaults, 8*s.* 7*d.*

And for 22 hundredweight and three quarters of freestone, £6. 16*s.* 6*d.*

To Roger of Reigate for eight hundredweight and a quarter of freestone, 53*s.* 7½*d.*

To Richard the lime-burner for three hundredweight of lime, 15*s.*

To Agnes for two hundredweight and a half of lime, 12*s.* 6*d.*

And to Richard of Eastcheap for two dozen hurdles together with withies, 9*s.* 7*d.*

To Richard Oggol for five dozen hurdles together with withies, 12*s.* 6*d.*

To Henry of Bridge for iron nails and whetstones, 19*s.* 8*d.*

To Benedict for carriage, portage, and pesage of 23 chars of lead, 9*s.* 4*d.*

To Richer for straw, 1*s.* 6*d.*

Sum total of the purchases, £27. 12*s.* 10½*d.*

Sum total of the week, £53. 0*s.* 1½*d.*

The third week [*after Easter*], without a feast day.

For wages of 39 white cutters, 15 marblers, 26 layers, 32 carpenters

[1] These appear to have been stones cut so as to form a segment of a circle (cf. Salzman, p. 109).

xxxij carpentariorum cum Johanne & sociis suis apud Sanctum Albanum, Petri pictoris, xv^cim pollisorum, xvij fabrorum, xiiij vitriariorum cum vj plumbatoribus xvii li. xj s.

Item in stipendiis CC minutorum operariorum cum custodibus clericis & duabus bigis diurnis xiij li. iij sol. x d.

Summa stipendiorum. xxx li. xiiij sol. x d.

Empciones ix cissoribus pro xxxvj assisis & dim. cissis ad taschiam. Item pro lxvj pedibus de parpens. Item pro xiiij pedibus & dim. de folsuris cum filo. Item pro xxix pedibus & dim. de rotundis folsuris. Item pro c.xvj pedibus de chamerand'. Item pro xij pedibus de formellis. Item pro xxxiiij pedibus de boseus. Item pro xj pedibus de chapement bowe. Item pro iiij^xx & x & dim. pedibus de scutis. Item pro c. & iiij^xx pedibus de tablemento. Item xxvij cissoribus pro MCC & j pedibus de asslers vj li. xij sol. vij d. ob.

Item in cxlvj pedibus & dim. de grossis colunis marmoris. In cxli pedibus & dim. de gracilibus colunis marmoris, ix pedibus de bos', vj pedibus & dim. de tablemento & vj basis & vj chapitris & xvj pedibus & dim. & dim. quartron de grossis rotundis. ix li. xvij sol. viij d. ob.

Summa taschiarum xvi li. x sol. iiij d.

pro MMviij^c france petre viij li. viij sol.
Rogero de Reygate pro vj^c petre xxxix sol.
Ricardo Calfonario pro cc calcis x sol.
Agneti pro cccc & iij quartron calcis. xxiij sol. ix d.
Item pro cccc & xl caretatis sabulonis fodendis & cariendis viij sol. x d.
Item Ricardo Estchepe pro iiij duodenis craticularum xij s. vj d.
Ricardo Ogul pro vj duodenis craticularum cum virgis xv sol.
Henrico de Ponte pro xj garbis asseri clavis ferri cum dimidia duodena cenevectoriorum xxv sol. vj d.
Item in C tegulis cavatis ad capellam Regis xviij d.

Summa empcionum xxxj li. xiiij sol. v d.

Summa totalis ebdomade lxij li. ix sol. iij d.

Ebdomada quarta sine festo

In stipendiis xli alborum cissorum, xvj marmorariorum, xxxj cubitorum, xxxij carpentariorum cum Johanne & sociis apud Sanctum Albanum, Petri pictoris, xv pollisorum, xvij fabrorum, xiij vitriariorum cum vj plumbatoribus xviij li. iiij sol.

Item in stipendiis ccxiij operariorum cum custodibus clericis & ij bigis diurnis xiiij li. d.

Summa totalis stipendiorum xxxij li. iiij sol. j d.

together with John and his fellows at St. Albans, Peter the painter, 15 polishers, 17 smiths, 14 glaziers, and six plumbers, £17. 11*s.*

And for wages of 200 labourers and keepers, clerks, and [the charges of] two carts daily, £13. 3*s.* 10*d.*

Total wages, £30. 14*s.* 10*d.*

Purchases. To nine cutters for cutting 36½ *assises* at task. And for 66 feet of parpent stone. And for 14½ feet of voussoirs with fillets. And for 29½ feet of rounded voussoirs. And for 116 feet of jambs. And for 12 feet of tracery. And for 34 feet of *boseus*. And for 11 feet of *chapement bowe*. And for 90½ feet of skew-stones. And for 180 feet of *tablement.*[1] And for 27 cutters for [cutting] 1,201 feet of ashlars, £6. 12*s.* 7½*d.*

And for [cutting] 146½ feet of thick marble columns. For [cutting] 141½ feet of thin marble columns, 9 feet of *boseus*, 6½ feet of *tablement*, and 6 bases, and 6 capitals, and 16⅝ feet of great round stones, £9. 17*s.* 8½*d.*

Total task-work, £16. 10*s.* 4*d.*

For 28 hundredweight of freestone, £8. 8*s.*

To Roger of Reigate for six hundredweight of stone, 39*s.*

To Richard the lime-burner for two hundredweight of lime, 10*s.*

To Agnes for four hundredweight and three quarters of lime, 23*s.* 9*d.*

And for digging and carrying 440 cart-loads of sand, 8*s.* 10*d.*

And to Richard Eastcheap for 4 dozen hurdles, 12*s.* 6*d.*

To Richard Ogul for 6 dozen hurdles with withies, 15*s.*

To Henry of Bridge for 11 sheaves of steel, iron nails, and half a dozen barrows, 25*s.* 6*d.*

And for 100 curved tiles for the king's chapel, 1*s.* 6*d.*

Total purchases, £31. 14*s.* 5*d.*

Sum total of the week, £62. 9*s.* 3*d.*

The fourth week [*after Easter*] without a feast day.

For wages of 41 white cutters, 16 marblers, 31 layers, 32 carpenters together with John and his fellows at St. Albans, Peter the painter, 15 polishers, 17 smiths, 13 glaziers, and 6 plumbers, £18. 4*s.*

And for wages of 213 labourers and keepers, clerks, and [the charges of] two carts daily, £14. 0*s.* 1*d.*

Sum total of wages, £32. 4*s.* 1*d.*

Empciones Pro xl assisis pretium assise v d. Item pro viij pedibus scenhon pretium pedis ij d.

Item pro l pedibus & dim. de formellis pretium pedis ij d. Pro xlj buscellis pretium buscelli iij d. Pro clxxiiij pedibus & dim. Chamerand' pretium pedis ij d. ob. Pro lviij pedibus & dim. de parpen pretium pedis iiij d., pro viij pedibus de folsuris rotundis pretium pedis iij d. Item pro xij pedibus de rotundis folsuris cum filet pretium pedis iij d. ob., pro lxvj pedibus de Scenh' pretium pedis [d.] iij quad. iiij li. xviij sol. x d.

Item pro ij navatis petre de Came xij li. Pacate.

Item pro MMMC & iij quartron france petre ix li. x sol. vj d.

Item Rogero de Reygate pro vj^{c} & dim. petre xlij sol. iij d., pro ij navatis grise petre xiij s. iij d.

Item Ricardo Calfonario pro cccc & dim. calcis xxij sol. vj d.

Agneti pro cc & quartron calcis xj sol. iij d.

Item Ricardo Estchepe pro virgis iiij sol. iiij d.

Item Ricardo Ogul pro craticulis xv sol.

Ricardo Cuvario pro utensilibus emendandis xviij d.

Henrico de Ponte pro clavis ferri xvj sol. x d. ob.

Summa empcionum xx li. xvj sol. iij d. ob.

Summa totalis ebdomade liij li. iiij d. ob.

Ebdomada quinta continente festum Assencionis quod cementariorum.

In stipendiis xlj alborum cissorum, xvj marmorariorum, xxxj cubitorum, xxxij carpentariorum cum Johanne & sociis apud Sanctum Albanum, Petro [*sic*] Pictoris, xv pollisorum, xvij fabrorum, xiij vitriariorum cum vj plumbatoribus xviij li. & x sol.

In stipendiis CC & xiij operariorum cum custodibus & clericis & ij bigis diurnis xij li. xix d.

Summa stipendiorum xxx li. xj sol. vij d.

Empciones pro xxj essicis, vj pedibus & dim. parpen, lxxiij pedibus de folsuris cum filo, viij pedibus de rotundis folsuris, xxxviij bosseus & xlv pedibus de chamerand', cxxxiij pedibus de formellis, cxviij lothenges, xvij pedibus de esscument', MMMix^{c}xxxvj pedibus de asselers, ix li. iiij sol. ij d.

Item Ade de Aldewyche cum sociis pro V^{M}V^{c} pendentis crete cissis ad taschiam xiiij sol. viij d.

Item pro MMM france petre ix li.

Rogero de Reygate pro viij^{c} petre lij sol.

Item Ricardo Calfonario pro V^{c} & iij quart. calcis xxviij sol. ix d.

Agneti Calfonarie pro CC & dim. calcis xij sol. vj d.

Item Ricardo de Estchepe pro virgis & baculis v sol. vij d.

Purchases. For 40 *assises* at 5*d*. each. And for 8 feet of splayed stones at 2*d*. a foot. And for 50½ feet of tracery at 2*d*. a foot. For 41 *buscell'* at 3*d*. each. For 174½ feet of jambs at 2½*d*. a foot. For 58½ feet of parpent stone at 4*d*. a foot, for 8 feet of rounded voussoirs at 3*d*. a foot. And for 12 feet of rounded voussoirs with fillets at 3½*d*. a foot, for 66 feet of splayed stone at 1¾*d*. a foot, £4. 18*s*. 10*d*.

And for two shiploads of Caen stone, £12 paid.

And for 31 hundredweight and three quarters of freestone, £9. 10*s*. 6*d*.

And to Roger of Reigate for six hundredweight and a half of stone, 42*s*. 3*d*., for two shiploads of ragstone, 13*s*. 3*d*.

And to Richard the lime-burner for 4 hundredweight and a half of lime, 22*s*. 6*d*.

To Agnes for two hundredweight and a quarter of lime, 11*s*. 3*d*.

And to Richard Eastcheap for withies, 4*s*. 4*d*.

And to Richard Ogul for hurdles, 15*s*.

To Richard the cooper for repairing utensils, 1*s*. 6*d*.

To Henry of Bridge for iron nails, 16*s*. 10½*d*.

Total purchases, £20. 16*s*. 3½*d*.

Sum total of the week, £53. 0*s*. 4½*d*.

The fifth week [*after Easter*] containing the feast of the Ascension [29 May] which was the masons'.

For wages of 41 white cutters, 16 marblers, 31 layers, 32 carpenters together with John and his fellows at St. Albans, Peter the painter, 15 polishers, 17 smiths, 13 glaziers, and 6 plumbers, £18. 10*s*.

For wages of 213 labourers with keepers and clerks, and [the charges of] two carts daily, £12. 1*s*. 7*d*.

Total wages, £30. 11*s*. 7*d*.

Purchases. For 21 *assises*, 6½ feet of parpent stone, 73 feet of voussoirs with fillets, 8 feet of rounded voussoirs, 38 *bosseus*, 45 feet of jambs, 133 feet of tracery, 118 lozenge-shaped stones, 17 feet of skew-stones, 3,936 feet of ashlar, £9. 4*s*. 2*d*.

And to Adam of Aldwych and his fellows for cutting 55 hundredweight of chalk for the vaults by task, 14*s*. 8*d*.

And for 30 hundredweight of freestone, £9.

To Roger of Reigate for 8 hundredweight of stone, 52*s*.

And to Richard the lime-burner for 5 hundredweight and three quarters of lime, 28*s*. 9*d*.

To Agnes the lime-burner for two hundredweight and a half of lime, 12*s*. 6*d*.

And to Richard of Eastcheap for withies and staves, 5*s*. 7*d*.

Ricardo Ogul pro v duodenis craticularum xij sol. vj d.
Henrico de Ponte pro clavis ferri & cera cum pice xiiij sol.
pro ceruris curie xx d.
Laurentio vitriario pro ij summis vitri colorati, iiij summis albi vitri & viij pisis vitri albi, lij sol.
Richer de Cruce [pro] xxx fescellis literi ad fabricas iij sol. iiij d.

Summa totalis empcionum xxviij li. xiiij d.

Summa totalis ebdomade lviij li. xij sol. & ix d.

Ebdomada sexta sine festo

In stipendiis xlj alborum cissorum, xvj marmorariorum, xxxv cubitorum, xxxiij carpentariorum, Petro [*sic*] pictoris, xv pollisorum, xviij fabrorum, xiij vitriariorum cum vj plumbatoribus xix li. & xix d.
In stipendiis CC & xiij minutorum operariorum cum custodibus & clericis & ij bigis diurnis xiiij li. & j d.

Summa totalis stipendiorum xxxiij li. & xx den.

Empciones xlj cissoribus pro diversis taschiis france petre ad taschiam cisse iiij li. xvj sol. vj d.
Item Rogero de Turri pro iiij orbilouns xxxiiij sol.
Item pro ij clavibus & viij capitrellis cum MMclxvj pedibus de asselers ad taschiam iiij li. ij sol. vij d. ob.
Item pro taschia xxxiij marmorariorum per iij ebdomadas ad taschiam circa marmor xj li. xvij d.
Item debentur Agneti Calfonarie xl sol.
Item pro MMMMV^{c} pend' crete cissis ad taschiam xij sol.
Item pro MMMMvj^{c} france petre xiij li. xvj sol.
Item Rogero de Reygate pro ix^{c} & dim. france petre lxj sol. ix d.
Item pro ij navatis grise petre xiij sol. iij d.
Ricardo Calfonario pro vij^{c} calcis xxxv sol.
Agneti Calfonarie pro cc calcis x sol.
Item Willelmo porcario pro vj^{c} & lx caretatis sabulonis xiij sol. ij d. ob.
Ricardo de Estchepe pro ij duodenis craticularum vj sol.
Ricardo Ogul' pro vij duodenis craticularum cum virgis xvij sol. vj d.
Ade merinario pro bordis & lateis xv sol. vij d.
Jacobo Junur pro panellis ad lectum domini Regis iungendis & pro tabulis ad scacarium & aliis tabulis de sape lxvj sol. vj d.
Henrico Nec' pro xj^{c} buschie xix sol.
Willelmo Jacobo pro CC & quartron buschie v sol. vij d. ob.
Ricardo Coper pro bokettis ij sol.
Benedicto merenario pro vectura meremii v sol.

To Richard Ogul for 5 dozen hurdles, 12*s.* 6*d.*

To Henry of Bridge for iron nails and wax and pitch, 14*s.*, for locks for the courtyard, 1*s.* 8*d.*

To Lawrence the glazier for two seams of coloured glass, four seams of white glass and 8 weys of white glass, 52*s.*

To Richer of the Cross for 30 bundles of straw for the workshops, 3*s.* 4*d.*

Sum total of purchases, £28. 1*s.* 2*d.*

Sum total of the week, £58. 12*s.* 9*d.*

The sixth week [*after Easter*] without a feast day.

For wages of 41 white cutters, 16 marblers, 35 layers, 33 carpenters, Peter the painter, 15 polishers, 18 smiths, 13 glaziers, and 6 plumbers, £19. 1*s.* 7*d.*

For wages of 213 labourers and keepers and clerks and [the charges of] two carts daily, £14. 0*s.* 1*d.*

Sum total of wages, £33. 1*s.* 9*d.*

Purchases. To 41 cutters for divers task-works cutting freestone, £4. 16*s.* 6*d.*

And to Roger of the Tower for four *orbilons*, 34*s.*

And for [cutting] 2 keystones and 8 capitals together with 2,166 feet of ashlar by task, £4. 2*s.* 7½*d.*

And for the task-work of 33 marblers working for 3 weeks on the marble, £11. 1*s.* 5*d.*

And 40*s.* are owed to Agnes the lime-burner.

And for cutting 45 hundredweight of chalk for the vault by task, 12*s.*

And for 46 hundredweight of freestone, £13. 16*s.*

And to Roger of Reigate for 9 hundredweight and a half of freestone, 61*s.* 9*d.*

And for two shiploads of ragstone, 13*s.* 3*d.*

To Richard the lime-burner for 7 hundredweight of lime, 35*s.*

To Agnes for two hundredweight of lime, 10*s.*

And to William the swine-herd for 660 cart-loads of sand, 13*s.* 2½*d.*

To Richard of Eastcheap for 2 dozen hurdles, 6*s.*

To Richard Ogul for 7 dozen hurdles with withies, 17*s.* 6*d.*

To Adam the timber-merchant for boards and laths, 15*s.* 7*d.*

To James the joiner for joining panels for the king's bed, and for chess-boards and other softwood boards, 66*s.* 6*d.*

To Henry Nec' for 11 hundredweight of firewood, 19*s.*

To William James for two hundredweight and a quarter of firewood, 5*s.* 7½*d.*

To Richard the cooper for buckets, 2*s.*

To Benedict the timber-merchant for carriage of timber, 5*s.*

Henrico de Ponte pro quartron de gatis iij sol. v d.
Item eidem pro xxij garbis asseri cum clavis ferri xliiij sol. v d.
Henrico fabro pro incude & coreo ad folles coperiendos x sol. ij d.
Johanni Sige pro MM tegulis cum cavillis iiij sol. iij d.

Summa empcionum lij li. x sol. ij d. ob.

Summa totalis ebdomade iiij^{xx} & v li. xj sol. x d. ob.

Summa totalis debiti a Pascha usque vigiliam Pentecost' per vj ebdomadas CCClxj li. xiiij sol. viij d. ob.[1]

Ebdomada prima post Pentecost' sine festo

In stipendiis xlii alborum cissorum, xviij marmorariorum, xxviij cubitorum, xxxiij carpentariorum, Petri pictoris, xv pollisorum, xvij fabrorum, xiiij vitriariorum, iiij plumbatorum cum j serviente xix li. xiiij sol. x d.

In stipendiis cc & xx minutorum operariorum cum custodibus clericis & duabus bigis diurnis xiiij li. viij sol. vij d.

Summa stipendiorum xxxiiij li. iij sol. v d.

Empciones Pro ar[r]eagiis marmorariorum xv li. xvj sol. vij d.
In MMCC & dim. france petre vij li. xij d.
Rogero de Reygate pro V^{c} & dim. france petre xxxv sol. ix d.
Item Ricardo Calfonario pro V^{c} & iij quart. calcis xxviij sol. ix d.
Agnes pro ccc calcis xv sol.
Item Ricardo de Estchep' vj sol. & ij d.
Ricardo Oggol pro craticulis x sol.
Ricardo cuvario pro bokettis & emendacione utensilium iij sol. & vj d.
Henrico de Ponte pro clavis ferri ix sol. d. ob.
Nicholao Scot pro portagio france petre infra Pentecost' xiij d.

Summa empcionum xxviij li. vj sol. xj d. ob.

Summa totalis ebdomade lxij li. x sol. iiij d. ob.

Ebdomada secunda continente festum Johannis Baptiste per diem Martis quod est domini Regis.

In stipendiis liij alborum cissorum, xlix marmorariorum, xxviij cubitorum, xxxiij carpentariorum, Petri pictoris, xv pollisorum, xvij fabrorum, xiiij vitriariorum, iiij plumbatorum cum serviente, xx li. xv d. ob.

[1] This third total is written on a slip of parchment sewn on to the roll.

To Henry of Bridge for a quarter of *gat'*,[1] 3*s*. 5*d*.
And to the same for 22 sheaves of steel and for iron nails, 44*s*. 5*d*.
To Henry the smith for an anvil and for leather to cover bellows, 10*s*. 2*d*.
To John Sige for two thousand tiles with tile-pins, 4*s*. 3*d*.

Total purchases, £52. 10*s*. 2½*d*.

Sum total of the week, £85. 11*s*. 10½*d*.

Sum total due from Easter to Whitsun Eve for 6 weeks, £361. 14*s*. 8½*d*.

The first week after Whitsun without a feast day.
For wages of 42 white cutters, 18 marblers, 28 layers, 33 carpenters, Peter the painter, 15 polishers, 17 smiths, 14 glaziers, 4 plumbers with one servant, £19. 14*s*. 10*d*.
For wages of 220 labourers and keepers, clerks, and [the charges of] two carts daily, £14. 8*s*. 7*d*.

Total wages, £34. 3*s*. 5*d*.

Purchases. For arrears owed to marblers, £15. 16*s*. 7*d*.
For 23 hundredweight and a half of freestone, £7. 1*s*.
To Roger of Reigate for 5 hundredweight and a half of freestone, 35*s*. 9*d*.
And to Richard the lime-burner for 5 hundredweight and three quarters of lime, 28*s*. 9*d*.
To Agnes for 3 hundredweight of lime, 15*s*.
And to Richard of Eastcheap, 6*s*. 2*d*.
To Richard Oggol for hurdles, 10*s*.
To Richard the cooper for buckets and repairing utensils, 3*s*. 6*d*.
To Henry of Bridge for iron nails, 9*s*. 1½*d*.
To Nicholas Scot for portage of freestone at Whitsun, 1*s*. 1*d*.

Total purchases, £28. 6*s*. 11½*d*.

Sum total of the week, £62. 10*s*. 4½*d*.

The second week after Whitsun containing the feast of John the Baptist [24 June] on Tuesday which is the lord king's.
For wages of 53 white cutters, 49 marblers, 28 layers, 33 carpenters, Peter the painter, 15 polishers, 17 smiths, 14 glaziers, 4 plumbers with a servant, £20. 1*s*. 3½*d*.

[1] As Henry of Bridge was a regular purveyor of nails, *gat'* may have been the sort of nails called 'gaddes'.

Item in stipendiis cc & xx minutorum operariorum cum custodibus & clericis & ij bigis diurnis xij li. viij d.

Summa totalis stipendiorum xxxij li. xxiij d. & ob.

Empciones Pro vij^{c}lvj lothenges, lviij assisis, xx pedibus & dim. de parpen, iiij^{xx}iiij pedibus & dim. de folsur' cum filo, xxxix pedibus de formellis, cclxviij pedibus de serches, c & vij pedibus de scutis, iiij^{xx}v folsur' chanferite. Item pro V^{m}lX^{c}iiij^{xx} asselers cissis ad taschiam xvj li. xj sol. ij d.

Pro MMMvij^{c} pendentis crete cissis ad taschiam ix sol. xj d.

Pro navata france petre de Came vij li.

Item pro MMvj^{c} & iij quartron france petre viij li. vj d.

Rogero Reygate pro vj^{c} & dim. petre xlij sol. iij d.

Ricardo Calfonario pro V^{c} calcis xxv sol.

Agneti Calfonarie pro CC dim. calcis xij sol. vj d.

Contra mulierem de Ey' pro sabulone vj sol.

Alano de Ey' pro sabulone vj sol. viij d.

Ricardo Ogul pro virgis x sol.

Henrico de Ponte pro clavis ferri xvj sol. iiij d. ob.

Pekin pro ceruris xxiij d.

Summa empcionum xxxviij li. iij s. vj d. ob.

Summa totalis ebdomade lxx li. v sol. x d.

Ebdomada tercia sine festo

In stipendiis lvj alborum cissorum, xlix marmorariorum, xxviij cubitorum, xxiij carpentariorum, j pictoris, Ade dealbatoris cum serviente, xv pollisorum, xvij fabrorum, xiiij vitriariorum, iiij plumbatorum cum serviente, xix li. iij sol.

Item in stipendiis cc & xx minutorum cum custodibus & clericis & ij bigis diurnis xij li. viij sol.

Summa stipendiorum xxxj li. xj sol.

Empciones pro stipendiis plumbatorum per vj ebdomadas lxxj sol.

In MM & iij quartron france petre vj li. iiij sol. vj d.

Rogero Reygate pro vj^{c} petre xxxix sol.

pro MMMM & ix^{c} crete ad pendentia xxix sol. iiij d. ob.

pro ij navatis grise petre xij sol. vj d.

Ricardo Calfonario pro CCCC & dim. calcis xxij sol. vj d.

Agneti Calfonarie pro ccc & dim. calcis xvij sol. vj d.

Ricardo Estchepe pro virgis & craticulis vij sol.

Ricardo Ogul pro craticulis & virgis xiiij sol. vj d.

Carbonario pro carbone vij sol. iiij d.

And for wages of 220 labourers and keepers, clerks, and [the charges of] two carts daily, £12. 0*s*. 8*d*.

Sum total of wages, £32. 1*s*. 11½*d*.

Purchases. For 756 lozenge-shaped stones, 58 *assises*, 20½ feet of parpent stone, 84½ feet of voussoirs with fillets, 39 feet of tracery, 268 feet of *serches*, 107 feet of skew-stones, 85 chamfered voussoirs. And for cutting 5,980 ashlars by task, £16. 11*s*. 2*d*.

For cutting 37 hundredweight of chalk for the vaults by task, 9*s*. 11*d*.

For a shipload of Caen freestone, £7.

And for 26 hundredweight and three quarters of freestone, £8. 0*s*. 6*d*.

To Roger Reigate for 6 hundredweight and a half of stone, 42*s*. 3*d*.

To Richard the lime-burner for 5 hundredweight of lime, 25*s*.

To Agnes the lime-burner for 2 hundredweight and a half of lime, 12*s*. 6*d*.

To a woman of Eye for sand, 6*s*.

To Alan of Eye for sand, 6*s*. 8*d*.

To Richard Ogul for withies, 10*s*.

To Henry of Bridge for iron nails, 16*s*. 4½*d*.

To Pekin for locks, 1*s*. 11*d*.

Total purchases, £38. 3*s*. 6½*d*.

Sum total of the week, £70. 5*s*. 10*d*.

The third week [*after Whitsun*] without a feast day.

For wages of 56 white cutters, 49 marblers, 28 layers, 23 carpenters, one painter, Adam the plasterer and a servant, 15 polishers, 17 smiths, 14 glaziers, and 4 plumbers with a servant, £19. 3*s*.

And for wages of 220 labourers with keepers, clerks, and [the charges of] two carts daily, £12. 8*s*.

Total wages, £31. 11*s*.

Purchases. For wages of plumbers for 6 weeks, 71*s*.

For 20 hundredweight and three quarters of freestone, £6. 4*s*. 6*d*.

To Roger Reigate for 6 hundredweight of stone, 39*s*.

For 49 hundredweight of chalk for the vaults, 29*s*. 4½*d*.

For 2 shiploads of ragstone, 12*s*. 6*d*.

To Richard the lime-burner for 4 hundredweight and a half of lime, 22*s*. 6*d*.

To Agnes the lime-burner for 3 hundredweight and a half of lime, 17*s*. 6*d*.

To Richard Eastcheap for withies and hurdles, 7*s*.

To Richard Ogul for hurdles and withies, 14*s*. 6*d*.

To a charcoal burner for charcoal, 7*s*. 4*d*.

Henrico de Ponte pro clavis ferri vj sol. iiij d.
Laurentio vitriario pro ij summis vitri colorati & j summa albi xxx sol.
Rogero Borser pro vij summis vitri colorati lxxvij sol.
Richero de Cruce pro ij petris ad marmor polisandum vj sol.
Magistro Odoni pro literio ad loges ij sol. viij d.

Summa empcionum xxiij li. vij sol. ij d. ob

Summa totalis ebdomade liiij li. xviij sol. ij d. ob.

Ebdomada quarta continente festum Beati Thome Martiris per diem lune quod est cementariorum.

In stipendiis lx alborum cissorum, xlix marmorariorum, xiiij cubitorum, xxj carpentariorum, Johannis cum carpentario & serviente apud Sanctum Albanum, Petri pictoris, xv pollisorum, xvij fabrorum, xiij vitriariorum, iiij plumbatorum cum vij servientibus xxj li. v sol. iij d. ob.

In stipendiis cc & xv minutorum operariorum cum custodibus, clericis & ij bigis diurnis, xi li. xvij sol. x d. ob.

Summa stipendiorum xxxiij li. iij sol. ij d.

Empciones pro diversis modis france petre ad taschiam cisse viij li. xj sol. x d.

Item pro diversis modis marmoris ad taschiam cissi xxiiij sol. vij d.
Item pro MMvij^{c} & iij quartron france petre viij li. vj sol. vj d.
Item Rogero Reygate pro M. C & iij quartron france petre lxxvj sol. iiij d. ob.
Ricardo Calfonario pro V^{c} & dim. calcis xxvij sol. vj d.
Item Agneti Cafonarie pro C calcis v sol.
Ricardo Estchepe pro virgis iij sol.
Ricardo Ogul pro ij duodenis craticul' & virgis vij sol.
Hamoni virgatori pro carbon' xx d.
Item Henrico de Ponte pro C ferri xv sol. j d.
Item eidem pro clavis ferri x sol.

Summa empcionum xxv li. ix sol. ob.

Summa totalis ebdomade lviij li. xij sol. ij d. ob.

Ebdomada Quinta sine festo

In stipendiis lx alborum cissorum, xlix marmorariorum, xiiij cubitorum, xvj carpentariorum, Johannis cum carpentario & serviente apud Sanctum Albanum, Petri pictoris, xv pollisorum, xvij fabrorum, vj vitriariorum, iiij plumbatorum cum vij servientibus, xxj li. v sol. iij d. ob.

In stipendiis cc & xv minutorum operariorum cum custodibus clericis ij bigis diurnis, xiij li. xix sol. vj d. ob.

Summa stipendiorum xxxv li. iiij sol. x d.

To Henry of Bridge for iron nails, 6*s.* 4*d.*
To Lawrence the glazier for 2 seams of coloured glass and 1 seam of white glass, 30*s.*
To Roger Borser for 7 seams of coloured glass, 77*s.*
To Richer of the Cross for 2 stones to polish marble, 6*s.*
To Master Odo for straw for the lodges, 2*s.* 8*d.*

Total purchases, £23. 7*s.* 2½*d.*

Sum total of the week, £54. 18*s.* 2½*d.*

The fourth week [*after Whitsun*] containing the feast of the blessed Thomas the Martyr [7 July] on Monday which is the masons'.
For wages of 60 white cutters, 49 marblers, 14 layers, 21 carpenters, John with a carpenter and a servant at St. Albans, Peter the painter, 15 polishers, 17 smiths, 13 glaziers, 4 plumbers with 7 servants, £21. 5*s.* 3½*d.*
For wages of 215 labourers with keepers, clerks, and [the charges of] two carts daily, £11. 17*s.* 10½*d.*

Total wages, £33. 3*s.* 2*d.*

Purchases. For cutting different kinds of freestone by task. £8. 11*s.* 10*d.*
And for cutting different kinds of marble by task, 24*s.* 7*d.*
And for 27 hundredweight and 3 quarters of freestone, £8. 6*s.* 6*d.*
And to Roger Reigate for 11 hundredweight and 3 quarters of freestone, 76*s.* 4½*d.*
To Richard the lime-burner for 5 hundredweight and a half of lime, 27*s.* 6*d.*
And to Agnes the lime-burner for 1 hundredweight of lime, 5*s.*
To Richard Eastcheap for withies, 3*s.*
To Richard Ogul for 2 dozen hurdles and withies, 7*s.*
To Hamon the scaffolder for charcoal, 1*s.* 8*d.*
And to Henry of Bridge for 1 hundredweight of iron, 15*s.* 1*d.*
And to the same for iron nails, 10*s.*

Total purchases, £25. 9*s.* 0½*d.*

Sum total of the week, £58. 12*s.* 2½*d.*

The fifth week [*after Whitsun*] without a feast day.
For wages of 60 white cutters, 49 marblers, 14 layers, 16 carpenters, John with a carpenter and a servant at St. Albans, Peter the painter, 15 polishers, 17 smiths, 6 glaziers, 4 plumbers, 7 servants, £21. 5*s.* 3½*d.*
For wages of 215 labourers with keepers, clerks, and [the charges of] two carts daily, £13. 19*s.* 6½*d.*

Total wages, £35. 4*s.* 10*d.*

Empciones Johanni Benet pro iij capitrellis iij sol.
Item pro MMMMV^c & xxviij pedibus de asselers cissis ad taschiam cxiij sol. ij d. ob.
Item pro MMMCCCC & iij quartron france petre x li. viij sol. vj d.
Rogero Reygate pro vij^c & iij quartron petre l sol. iiij d. ob.
Ricardo Calfonario pro V^c & dim. calcis xxvij sol. vj d.
Agneti pro dim. C calcis ij sol. vj d.
Ricardo de Estchepe pro virgis & craticulis v sol. x d.
Ricardo Ogul pro v duodenis craticularum xij sol. vj d.
Ade merenario pro V^m lateis l sol.
Item Rogero de Berking pro ij caretatis carbonis iiij sol. iiij d.
David clerico pro v caretatis carbonis x sol.
Item Henrico de Ponte pro clavis ferri ad plumbum xij sol. ix d.
Item eidem pro cera & pice ad cymentum xv d.
Johanni Sige pro $xvij^M$ tegularum cum cariagio xxxix sol. iiij d.

Summa empcionum xxxvj li. xv sol. d.

Summa totalis ebdomade lxij li.

Ebdomada sexta continente festum Magdalene per diem Martis quod est domini Regis & festum beati Jacobi per diem Veneris quod est Cementariorum.

In stipendiis lxvj alborum cissorum, xlix marmorariorum, xiiij cubitorum, xvj carpentariorum, Johannis cum carpentario & serviente apud Sanctum Albanum, Petri pictoris, xv pollisorum, xvij fabrorum, vj vitriariorum, iiij plumbatorum cum vij servientibus xxij li.
In stipendiis C & xl minutorum operariorum cum j biga diurna, custodibus clericis, vij li. ix sol.

Summa stipendiorum xxix li. ix sol.

Empciones In diversis modis france petre ad taschiam cisse cxix sol. iij d. ob.
Item in diversis modis marmoris ad taschiam cissi, xxij sol. ix d.
In MM & C france petre vj li. vj sol.
Item Rogero Reygate pro CCC & dim. petre xxij sol. ix d.
Agneti pro C. calcis v sol.
Ricardo Calfonario pro $iiij^c$ xx sol.
Radulfo Bleur pro iij caretatis carbonis vj sol. vj d.
Ricardo cupario pro utensilibus emendandis xiij d.
Ricardo de Celario pro V^M $iiij^c$.iiij. charg' ferri de Glovernia x li. xvj sol.
Item pro cariagio dicti ferri vj sol. iiij d.
Henrico de Ponte pro clavis ad ecclesiam & berefridum x sol. x d. ob.

Summa empcionum xxviij li. vj sol. d.

Summa totalis ebdomade lvij li. xv sol. j d.

Purchases. To John Benet for 3 capitals, 3*s*.
And for cutting 4,528 feet of ashlars by task, 113*s*. 2½*d*.
And for 34 hundredweight and 3 quarters of freestone, £10. 8*s*. 6*d*.
To Roger Reigate for 7 hundredweight and 3 quarters of stone, 50*s*. 4½*d*.
To Richard the lime-burner for 5 hundredweight and a half of lime, 27*s*. 6*d*.
To Agnes for half a hundredweight of lime, 2*s*. 6*d*.
To Richard of Eastcheap for withies and hurdles, 5*s*. 10*d*.
To Richard Ogul for 5 dozen hurdles, 12*s*. 6*d*.
To Adam the timber-merchant for 5 thousand laths, 50*s*.
And to Roger of Barking for 2 cart-loads of charcoal, 4*s*. 4*d*.
To David the clerk for 5 cart-loads of charcoal, 10*s*.
And to Henry of Bridge for iron nails for lead, 12*s*. 9*d*.
And to the same for wax and pitch for cement, 1*s*. 3*d*.
To John Sige for 17,000 tiles with carriage, 39*s*. 4*d*.

Total purchases, £26. 15*s*. 1*d*.

Sum total of the week, £62.

The sixth week [*after Whitsun*] containing the feast of Mary Magdalen [22 July] on Tuesday which is the lord king's and the feast of the blessed James [25 July] on Friday which is the masons'.
For wages of 66 white cutters, 49 marblers, 14 layers, 16 carpenters, John with a carpenter and a servant at St. Albans, Peter the painter, 15 polishers, 17 smiths, 6 glaziers, 4 plumbers with 7 servants, £22.
For wages of 140 labourers with [the charges of] 1 cart daily, keepers, and clerks, £7. 9*s*.

Total wages, £29. 9*s*.

Purchases. For cutting different kinds of freestone by task, 119*s*. 3½*d*.
And for cutting different kinds of marble by task, 22*s*. 9*d*.
For 21 hundredweight of freestone, £6. 6*s*.
And to Roger Reigate for 3 hundredweight and a half of stone, 22*s*. 9*d*.
To Agnes for 1 hundredweight of lime, 5*s*.
To Richard the lime-burner for 4 hundredweight [of lime], 20*s*.
To Ralph Bleur for 3 cart-loads of charcoal, 6*s*. 6*d*.
To Richard the cooper for repairing utensils, 1*s*. 1*d*.
To Richard of the cellar for 54 hundredweight and 4 loads of Gloucester iron, £10. 16*s*.
And for carriage of the same iron, 6*s*. 4*d*.
To Henry of Bridge for nails for the church and the belfry, 10*s*. 10½*d*.

Total purchases, £28. 6*s*. 1*d*.

Sum total of the week, £57. 15*s*. 1*d*.

Ebdomada septima continente festum beati Petri ad Vincula per diem Veneris quod est domini Regis.

In stipendiis lxviij alborum cissorum xlix marmorariorum, xiiij cubitorum, xvj carpentariorum, Johannis apud Sanctum Albanum circa lectron cum carpentario & serviente, Petri pictori[s], xv pollisorum, xvj fabrorum, vj vitriariorum, iiij plumbatorum cum vij servientibus, cum custodibus & clericis, xviij li. xj sol. v d.

In stipendiis vj^{xx} & xiij operariorum cum biga vij li. ij d. ob.

Summa stipendiorum xxv li. xj sol. vij d. ob.

*Empciones** In iij navatis marmoris xxvij li. iij sol. vij d.

In MM.IX^{c} & iij quartron france petre viij li. xviij sol. vj d.

Rogero Reygate pro viij^{c} petre, lij sol.

Ricardo Calfonario pro CCCC & dim. calcis xxij sol. vj d.

Agneti pro C & dim. calcis vij sol. vj d.

Ricardo Estchepe pro virgis vj sol. viij d.

Roberto Cofere pro ceruris ix d.

Henrico de Ponte pro clavis ferri ad nundinas Westmon' xxxiiij sol. xj d.

Summa empcionum xlij li. v sol. vj d.

Summa totalis ebdomade lxvij li. xvij sol. d. ob.

Ebdomada octava sine festo

In stipendiis lxxviij alborum cissorum, xlix marmorariorum, xiiij^{cim} cubitorum, xvj carpentariorum cum Johanne apud Sanctum Albanum cum serviente, Petri Pictoris, xv pollisorum, xvj fabrorum, vj vitriariorum, iiij plumbatorum cum vij servientibus & cum custodibus & clericis, xix li. xix sol. vij d.

In stipendiis vj^{xx}.xv operariorum cum biga diurna viij li. x sol. ix d.

Summa totalis stipendiorum xxviij li. x sol. iiij d.

Empciones Pro diversis modis france petre ad taschiam cisse viij li. xiiij sol. iiij d.

Item pro taschia introitus capituli l sol.

Item pro diversis modis marmoris ad taschiam cissi xl sol. ij d.

Item pro navata petre de Came xiij li. vj sol.

Item pro MMCCC & j quartron france petre vj li. x sol. vj d.

Rogero Reygate pro vj^{c} & iij quartron petre xliij sol. x d. ob.

Ricardo Calfonario pro CCCC & quartron calcis xxj sol. iij d.

Ledulfo pro M bordis C sol.

Waltero Box pro xij^{cim} chareis plumbi cum portagio vectura & pesagio xxvj li. xij sol.

* *Marginal note:* Memorandum de xij li. ij sol. & xj d. debitis pro marmore.

The seventh week [*after Whitsun*] containing the feast of the blessed Peter in Chains [1 August] on Friday which is the lord king's.

For wages of 68 white cutters, 49 marblers, 14 layers, 16 carpenters, John at St. Albans working on the lectern with a carpenter and a servant, Peter the painter, 15 polishers, 16 smiths, 6 glaziers, 4 plumbers with 7 servants, together with keepers and clerks, £18. 11*s*. 5*d*.

For wages of 133 labourers with [the charges of] a cart, £7. 0*s*. 2½*d*.

Total wages, £25. 11*s*. 7½*d*.

*Purchases**

For 3 shiploads of marble, £27. 3*s*. 7*d*.

For 29 hundredweight and 3 quarters of freestone, £8. 18*s*. 6*d*.

To Roger Reigate for 8 hundredweight of stone, 52*s*.

To Richard the lime-burner for 4 hundredweight and a half of lime, 22*s*. 6*d*.

To Agnes for 1 hundredweight and a half of lime, 7*s*. 6*d*.

To Richard Eastcheap for withies, 6*s*. 8*d*.

To Robert Cofere for locks, 9*d*.

To Henry of Bridge for iron nails at the fair at Westminster, 34*s*. 11*d*.

Total purchases, £42. 5*s*. 6*d*.

Sum total of the week, £67. 17*s*. 1½*d*.

The eighth week [*after Whitsun*] without a feast day.

For wages of 78 white cutters, 49 marblers, 14 layers, 16 carpenters and John at St. Albans with a servant, Peter the painter, 15 polishers, 16 smiths, 6 glaziers, 4 plumbers with 7 servants, together with keepers and clerks, £19. 19*s*. 7*d*.

For wages of 135 labourers with [the charges of] a cart daily, £8. 10*s*. 9*d*.

Sum total of wages, £28. 10*s*. 4*d*.

Purchases. For cutting different kinds of freestone by task. £8. 14*s*. 4*d*.

And for task-work on the entrance of the chapter-house, 50*s*.

And for cutting different kinds of marble by task, 40*s*. 2*d*.

And for a shipload of Caen stone, £13. 6*s*.

And for 23 hundredweight and 1 quarter of freestone, £6. 10*s*. 6*d*.

To Roger Reigate for 6 hundredweight and 3 quarters of stone, 43*s*. 10½*d*.

To Richard the lime-burner for 4 hundredweight and a quarter of lime, 21*s*. 3*d*.

To Ledulf for a thousand boards, 100*s*.

To Walter Box for 12 chars of lead, with portage, carriage, and weighing, £26. 12*s*.

* *Marginal note:* Memorandum concerning £12 2*s*. 11*d*. owed for marble.

Henrico de Ponte pro assero, clavis, cera & pice xlix sol. ij d. pro MMMM cavillarum vj d.

Summa emcionum lxx li. xij sol. ij d. ob.

Summa totalis ebdomade iiij^{xx}xix li. ij sol. vj d. ob.

Ebdomada Prima post Pacacionem stipendiorum per viij^{to} ebdomadas continente festum Assumpcionis Beate Marie per diem Veneris quod est cementariorum.

In stipendiis lxviij alborum cissorum, xlix marmorariorum, xiiij^{cim} cubitorum, xvj carpentariorum cum J. apud Sanctum Albanum cum serviente, Petri pictoris, Ade dealbatoris cum serviente, xv pollisorum, xvj^{cim} fabrorum, duo vitriariorum, cum clericis & virgatoribus xviij li. xij sol. vj d.

In stipendiis vj^{xx}xviij minutorum operariorum cum biga diurna, viij li. xviij sol.

Summa stipendiorum xxvij li. x sol. vj d.

Empciones pro MCC & iij quartron france petre lxxvj sol. vj d.
Item Rogero Reygate pro vj^{c} & dim. petre xlij sol. iij d.
Ricardo Calfonario pro CCCC & dim. calcis xxij sol. vj d.
Willelmo porcario pro M caretatis sabulonis fodendis & cariandis ad taschiam xxj sol. vij d.
Ricardo Eschepe pro craticulis iij sol. vij d.
Willelmo Jacob' pro quartron buschie ix d.
pro ij caretatis carbonis iij sol. ij d.
Henrico de Ponte pro clavis ferri vij sol. vij d. ob.

Summa empcionum viij li. xviij sol.

Summa ebdomade xxxvj li. viij sol. v d. ob.

Ebdomada secunda sine festo

In stipendiis lxviij alborum cissorum, xlix marmorariorum, xiiij cubitorum, xvj carpentariorum cum Johanne apud Sanctum Albanum cum serviente, Petro pictore, Ada dealbatore cum serviente, xv pollisorum, xvj fabrorum, ij vitriariorum cum clericis & virgatoribus xviij li. xij sol. & vj d.

In stipendiis vj^{xx}xviij minutorum operariorum cum biga diurna viij li. vij sol. viij d.

Summa totalis stipendiorum xxvij li. iij sol. viij d.

Empciones In diversis taschiis france petre & marmoris xiij li. xj sol. ix d. ob.
In Mix^{c} & dim. france petre cxvij sol.
In V^{c} france petre de Reygate xxxij sol. vj d.
Ricardo Calfonario pro V^{c} calcis, xxv sol.
Agneti pro C & dim. calcis vij sol. vj d.
Ricardo de Estchepe pro craticulis xxvij d.

To Henry of Bridge for steel, nails, wax, and pitch, 49*s*. 2*d*.
For 4,000 tile-pins, 6*d*.

Total purchases, £70. 12*s*. 2½*d*.

Sum total of the week, £99. 2*s*. 6½*d*.

The first week after the payment of wages for 8 weeks, containing the feast of the Assumption of the Blessed Virgin Mary [15 August] on Friday which is the masons'.
For wages of 68 white cutters, 49 marblers, 14 layers, 16 carpenters with John at St. Albans with a servant, Peter the painter, Adam the plasterer with a servant, 15 polishers, 16 smiths, 2 glaziers, with clerks and scaffold-erectors, £18. 12*s*. 6*d*.
For wages of 138 labourers with [the charges of] a cart daily, £8. 18*s*.

Total wages, £27. 10*s*. 6*d*.

Purchases. For 12 hundredweight and 3 quarters of freestone, 76*s*. 6*d*.
And to Roger Reigate for 6 hundredweight and a half of stone, 42*s*. 3*d*.
To Richard the lime-burner for 4 hundredweight and a half of lime, 22*s*. 6*d*.
To William the swine-herd for digging and carrying a thousand cart-loads of sand by task, 21*s*. 7*d*.
To Richard of Eastcheap for hurdles, 3*s*. 7*d*.
To William James for a quarter of firewood, 9*d*.
For 2 cart-loads of charcoal, 3*s*. 2*d*.
To Henry of Bridge for iron nails, 7*s*. 7½*d*.

Total purchases, £8. 18*s*.

Total of the week, £36. 8*s*. 5½*d*.

The second week, without a feast day.
For wages of 68 white cutters, 49 marblers, 14 layers, 16 carpenters, and John at St. Albans with a servant, Peter the painter, Adam the plasterer with a servant, 15 polishers, 16 smiths, 2 glaziers, with clerks and scaffold-erectors, £18. 12*s*. 6*d*.
For wages of 138 labourers with [the charges of] a cart daily, £8. 7*s*. 8*d*.

Sum total of wages, £27. 3*s*. 8*d*.

Purchases. For divers task-works in freestone and marble, £13. 11*s*. 9½*d*.
For 19 hundredweight and a half of freestone, 117*s*.
For 5 hundredweight of Reigate freestone, 32*s*. 6*d*.
To Richard the lime-burner for 5 hundredweight of lime, 25*s*.
To Agnes for a hundredweight and a half of lime, 7*s*. 6*d*.
To Richard of Eastcheap for hurdles, 2*s*. 3*d*.

Ricardo Oggel pro craticulis iij sol.
Nicolao Duket pro navata carbonis xv sol.
Henrico de Ponte pro clavis ferri xx sol. iiij d. ob.

Summa empcionum xxiiij li. xiiij sol. v d.

Summa totalis ebdomade lj li. xviij sol. j d.

Ebdomada tercia continente festum decollacionis Sancti Johannis Baptiste per diem Veneris quod est Domini Regis

In stipendiis xlix alborum cissorum, xxxj marmorariorum, xiij cubitorum, xiij carpentariorum, magistri Johannis cum serviente, magistri Petri, j dealbatoris cum serviente, xv pollisorum, xviij fabrorum, ij vitriariorum, xiij li. xv sol. viij d. ob.

Item in stipendiis iiij^{xx} & xj minutorum operariorum cum custodibus & clericis & j biga diurna, c & vj sol. viij d. ob.

Summa totalis stipendiorum xix li. ij sol. & v d.

Empciones In MV^{c} & dim. france petre iiij li. xiij sol.
Rogero de Reygate pro ij^{c} & dim. france petre xvj sol. vj d.
Ricardo Calfonario pro iiij^{c} & dim. calcis xxij sol. vj d.

Summa empcionum vj li. xij sol.

Summa ebdomade xxv li. xiiij sol. v d.

Ebdomada quarta sine festo

In stipendiis xlix alborum cissorum, xxxj marmorariorum, xiij cubitorum, xiij carpentariorum, magistri Johannis cum serviente apud Sanctum Albanum, Petri pictoris, Ade dealbatoris cum serviente, xv pollisorum, xviij fabrorum, ij vitriariorum, custodum cum clericis, xv li. vj sol. ij d.

In stipendiis iiij^{xx}xj minutorum operariorum cum biga diurna c & xv sol. ix d.

Summa stipendiorum xxj li. xxiij d.

Empciones In diversis modis france petre ad taschiam cisse vj li. xv d. ob.
In diversis modis marmoris ad taschiam cissi lxv sol. ix d. ob.
Item pro ix^{c} & iij quartron france petre lviij sol. vj d.
Item Rogero de Reygate pro V^{c} & quartron xxxiiij sol. d. ob.
Ricardo Calfonario pro CC & dim. calcis xij sol. vj d.
Ricardo Estchepe pro craticulis iij sol. iij d.
Henrico de Ponte pro clavis ferri ad ecclesiam & berefridum xiiij sol. iiij d.

Summa taschiarum ix li. vij sol. ob.

Summa empcionum vj li. ij sol. viij d.

Summa ebdomade xxxvj li. xj sol. vij d. ob.

To Richard Oggel for hurdles, 3*s.*
To Nicholas Duket for a shipload of coal, 15*s.*
To Henry of Bridge for iron nails, 20*s.* 4½*d.*

Total purchases, £24. 14*s.* 5*d.*
Sum total of the week, £51. 18*s.* 1*d.*

The third week, containing the feast of the Beheading of St. John the Baptist [29 August] on Friday which is the lord king's.
For wages of 49 white cutters, 31 marblers, 13 layers, 13 carpenters, Master John with a servant, Master Peter, 1 plasterer with a servant, 15 polishers, 18 smiths, 2 glaziers, £13. 15*s.* 8½*d.*
For wages of 91 labourers, with keepers and clerks, and [the charges of] a cart daily, 106*s.* 8½*d.*

Sum total of wages, £19. 2*s.* 5*d.*

Purchases. For 15 hundredweight and a half of freestone, £4. 13*s.*
To Roger of Reigate for 2 hundredweight and a half of freestone, 16*s.* 6*d.*
To Richard the lime-burner for 4 hundredweight and a half of lime, 22*s.* 6*d.*

Total purchases, £6. 12.
Total of the week, £25. 14*s.* 5*d.*

The fourth week, without a feast day.
For wages of 49 white cutters, 31 marblers, 13 layers, 13 carpenters, Master John with a servant at St. Albans, Peter the painter, Adam the plasterer with a servant, 15 polishers, 18 smiths, 2 glaziers, keepers, and clerks, £15. 6*s.* 2*d.*
For wages of 91 labourers with [the charges of] a cart daily, 115*s.* 9*d.*

Total wages, £21. 1*s.* 11*d.*

Purchases. For different kinds of freestone cut by task, £6. 1*s.* 3½*d.*
For different kinds of marble cut by task, 65*s.* 9½*d.*
And for 9 hundredweight and 3 quarters of freestone, 58*s.* 6*d.*
And to Roger of Reigate for 5 hundredweight and a quarter [of stone], 34*s.* 1½*d.*
To Richard the lime-burner for 2 hundredweight and a half of lime, 12*s.* 6*d.*
To Richard Eastcheap for hurdles, 3*s.* 3*d.*
To Henry of Bridge for iron nails for the church and the belfry, 14*s.* 4*d.*

Total task-work, £9. 7*s.* 0½*d.*
Total purchases, £6. 2*s.* 8*d.*
Total of the week, £36. 11*s.* 7½*d.*

Ebdomada quinta continente festum Nativitatis beate Marie per diem Lune quod est cementariorum.

In stipendiis xlix alborum cissorum, xv marmorariorum, xiij cubitorum, xiij carpentariorum, magistri Johannis cum serviente, Petri pictoris, Ade dealbatoris cum serviente, xv pollisorum, xviij fabrorum, ij vitriariorum cum custodibus & clericis, xv li.

In stipendiis iiij^{xx}xj minutorum operariorum cum biga diurna iiij li. xiij sol. ix d.

Summa stipendiorum xix li. xiij sol. ix d.

Empciones pro vij^{c} & dim. france petre xlv sol.
Rogero Reygate pro c & iij quartron petre xj sol. iiij d. ob.
Willelmo de Came pro V^{c} esselers xj sol. xj d.
Ricardo Calfonario pro iiij^{c} calcis xx sol.
Ricardo Estchepe pro virgis ij sol. viij d. ob.
Hamoni pro ij caretatis carbonis v sol. xj d.
Henrico de Ponte pro clavis ferri ad ecclesiam & berefridum ix sol. viij d.

Summa empcionum v li. [*blank*] vij d.

Summa ebdomade xxv li. iiij d.

Ebdomada sexta sine festo

In stipendiis lvj alborum cissorum, xv marmorariorum, xxiij cubitorum, xiij carpentariorum, Johannis apud Sanctum Albanum cum serviente, Petri pictoris, Ade dealbatoris cum serviente, xv pollisorum, xviij fabrorum, ij vitriariorum cum custodibus & clericis xvij li.

In stipendiis cviij minutorum operariorum cum biga diurna, vj li. xvij sol.

Summa stipendiorum xxiij li. xvij sol.

Empciones In diversis modis france petre ad taschiam cisse vj li. v sol. x d.
In diversis modis marmoris ad taschiam cissi iiij li. vij sol. x d. ob.
pro fretto navatis marmoris lxvj sol. viij d.
Item in Mvj^{c} france petre iiij li. xvj sol.
Rogero Reygate pro CCC france petre xix sol. vj d.
Item Ricardo pro CCCC & dim. calcis xxij sol. vj d.
Item Ade merenario pro bordis & lateis, xxiij sol. vj d.
Ricardo Estchepe pro virgis vij sol. ij d.
Ricardo Cuver pro bokettis iij sol. ij d.
Item pro v caretatis carbonis xij sol. viij d.
Item Johanni de Gisors pro xxviij chareis & xv li. plumbi cum portagio [&] pesagio lxiij li. x sol. vj d.
Item pro vectura & portagio apud Westmonasterium vij sol. ij d.
Henrico de Ponte pro clavis ecclesie & berefridi xix sol. ix d. ob.

The fifth week containing the feast of the Nativity of the Blessed Virgin Mary [8 September] on Monday which is the masons'.

For wages of 49 white cutters, 15 marblers, 13 layers, 13 carpenters, Master John with a servant, Peter the painter, Adam the plasterer with a servant, 15 polishers, 18 smiths, 2 glaziers with keepers and clerks, £15.

For wages of 91 labourers and [the charges of] a cart daily, £4. 13*s*. 9*d*.

Total wages, £19. 13*s*. 9*d*.

Purchases. For 7 hundredweight and a half of freestone, 45*s*.

To Roger Reigate for 1 hundredweight and 3 quarters of stone, 11*s*. 4½*d*.

To William of Caen for 5 hundredweight of ashlar, 11*s*. 11*d*.

To Richard the lime-burner for 4 hundredweight of lime, 20*s*.

To Richard Eastcheap for withies, 2*s*. 8½*d*.

To Hamon for 2 cart-loads of charcoal, 5*s*. 11*d*.

To Henry of Bridge for iron nails for the church and the belfry, 9*s*. 8*d*.

Total purchases, £5. [6]*s*. 7*d*.

Total of the week, £25. 0*s*. 4*d*.

The sixth week, without a feast day.

For wages of 56 white cutters, 15 marblers, 23 layers, 13 carpenters, John at St. Albans with a servant, Peter the painter, Adam the plasterer with a servant, 15 polishers, 18 smiths, 2 glaziers, with keepers and clerks, £17.

For wages of 108 labourers with [the charges of] a cart daily, £6. 17*s*.

Total wages, £23. 17*s*.

Purchases. For different kinds of freestone cut by task, £6. 5*s*. 10*d*.

For different kinds of marble cut by task, £4. 7*s*. 10½*d*.

For freight of a shipload of marble, 66*s*. 8*d*.

And for 16 hundredweight of freestone, £4. 16*s*.

To Roger Reigate for 3 hundredweight of freestone, 19*s*. 6*d*.

And to Richard for 4 hundredweight and a half of lime, 22*s*. 6*d*.

And to Adam the timber-merchant for boards and laths, 23*s*. 6*d*.

To Richard Eastcheap for withies, 7*s*. 2*d*.

To Richard Cooper for buckets, 3*s*. 2*d*.

And for 5 cart-loads of charcoal, 12*s*. 8*d*.

And to John of Gisors for 28 chars and 15 lbs. of lead with portage [and] weighing, £63. 10*s*. 6*d*.

And for carriage and portage [of the lead] at Westminster, 7*s*. 2*d*.

To Henry of Bridge for nails for the church and the belfry, 19*s*. 9½*d*.

Willelmo de Aqua pro tasso straminis viij sol.
pro portagio buschie ij sol. vj d. pacati

Summa empcionum sine freto marmoris iiij^{xx} li. & v li. iij sol. viij d.

Summa totalis ebdomade CIX li. viij d.

Ebdomada septima sine festo

In stipendiis lviij alborum cissorum, xiiij marmorariorum, xxvj cubitorum, xiij carpentariorum, Johannis apud Sanctum Albanum cum serviente, Petri pictoris, Ade dealbatoris cum serviente, xv pollisorum, xviij fabrorum, iij vitriariorum cum custodibus & clericis, xvij li. vij sol.

In stipendiis vj^{xx} minutorum operariorum cum biga diurna vij li. xij sol. d.

Summa stipendiorum xxiiij li. xix sol. d.

Empciones pro MVIII^{c} & quartron france petre C & ix sol. vj d.
Item Rogero de Reygate pro vij^{c} & dim. france petre xlv sol. vj d.
pro ij navatis marmoris
Item Ricardo Calfonario pro CCCC & iij quartron calcis xxiij sol. ix d.
Item Ricardo Ogul pro craticulis & virgis xx sol.
Ricardo cuvier' pro utensilibus ij sol.
Henrico de Ponte pro clavis ecclesie & berefridi cum cera & pice xij sol. ij d. ob.

Summa empcionum x li. xij sol. xj d.

Summa ebdomade xxxv li. xij sol. ob.

Ebdomada octava continente festum Beati Michaelis per diem Lune quod est domini Regis.

In stipendiis lx alborum cissorum, xiiij marmorariorum, xxxj cubitorum, xiiij carpentariorum, Johannis apud Sanctum Albanum, Petri Pictoris, Ade dealbatoris cum serviente, xv pollisorum, xviij fabrorum, iij vitriariorum cum custodibus & clericis xv li. xv sol. ix d. ob.

In stipendiis VII^{xx}xv minutorum operariorum cum ij bigis diurnis viij li. iiij sol. ix d. ob.

Summa totalis stipendiorum xxiiij li. vij d.

Empciones In diversis modis france petre ad taschiam cisse xj li. xvij d. ob.
Item in diversis modis marmoris ad taschiam cissi lxxv sol. iiij d.
Item pro MCCC & dim. france petre lxxix sol. vj d.
Rogero de Reygate pro CCC & dim. xxij sol. ix d.
Item Ricardo Calfonario pro IX^{c} & quartron calcis xxxj sol. & iij d.

To William of Water for a rick of straw, 8*s*.
For portage of firewood, 2*s*. 6*d*. paid.[1]

Total purchases without the freight of marble, £85. 3*s*. 8*d*.

Sum total of the week, £109. 0*s*. 8*d*.

The seventh week, without a feast day.
For wages of 58 white cutters, 14 marblers, 26 layers, 13 carpenters, John at St. Albans with a servant, Peter the painter, Adam the plasterer with a servant, 15 polishers, 18 smiths, 3 glaziers with keepers and clerks, £17. 7*s*.
For wages of 120 labourers with [the charges of] a cart daily, £7. 12*s*. 1*d*.

Total wages, £24. 19*s*. 1*d*.

Purchases. For 18 hundredweight and a quarter of freestone, 109*s*. 6*d*.
And to Roger of Reigate for 7 hundredweight and a half of freestone, 45*s*. 6*d*.
For 2 shiploads of marble[2]
And to Richard the lime-burner for 4 hundredweight and 3 quarters of lime, 23*s*. 9*d*.
And to Richard Ogul for hurdles and withies, 20*s*.
To Richard the cooper for utensils, 2*s*.
To Henry of Bridge for nails for the church and the belfry together with wax and pitch, 12*s*. 2½*d*.

Total purchases, £10. 12*s*. 11½*d*.

Total of the week, £35. 12*s*. 0½*d*.

The eighth week containing the feast of the blessed Michael [29 September] on Monday which is the lord king's.
For wages of 60 white cutters, 14 marblers, 31 layers, 14 carpenters, John at St. Albans, Peter the painter, Adam the plasterer with a servant, 15 polishers, 18 smiths, 3 glaziers, with keepers and clerks, £15. 15*s*. 9½*d*.
For wages of 155 labourers and [the charges of] 2 carts daily, £8. 4*s*. 9½*d*.

Sum total of wages, £24. 0*s*. 7*d*.

Purchases. For different kinds of freestone cut by task, £11. 1*s*. 5½*d*.
For different kinds of marble cut by task, 75*s*. 4*d*.
And for 13 hundredweight and a half of freestone, 79*s*. 6*d*.
To Roger of Reigate for 3 hundredweight and a half [of stone], 22*s*. 9*d*.
And to Richard the lime-burner for 9 hundredweight and a quarter of lime, 31*s*. 3*d*.

[1] Added in the margin, and not included in the total. [2] Cost not stated.

Agneti Calfonarie pro C & dim. calcis vij sol. vj d.
Item Ricardo de Estchepe pro virgis v sol. viij d.
Item Henrico de Ponte pro clavis ferri xviij sol. j d.
Summa empcionum xxiij li. xvj sol. vj d.
Summa ebdomade xlvij li. xvij sol. d. ob.

Ebdomada Nona sine festo

In stipendiis xlij alborum cissorum, xiiij marmorariorum, xxxj cubitorum, xiiij carpentariorum, Johannis cum serviente apud Sanctum Albanum, Petri Pictoris, Ada dealbatoris cum serviente, xv pollisorum, xviij fabrorum, iij vitriariorum cum custodibus & clericis xviij li. iij sol. x d.

In stipendiis vij^{xx} & xv minutorum operariorum cum vj bigis diurnis x li. v sol. ix d.

Summa stipendiorum xxviij li. ix sol. vij d.

Empciones In diversis modis france petre ad taschiam cisse vj li. iiij sol. viij d.

Item pro MC & quartron france petre lxxiij sol. d. ob.
Rogero de Reygate CC & quartron petre xiiij sol. vij d. ob.
Item pro navata france petre de Came
Item pro marmore apud Corve xviij li. xix sol. ob.
Item pro navata grise petre v sol. ix d.
Item magistro Willelmo de Waz pro prestito xv sol. vj d.
Item Ricardo Calfonario pro viij^{c} calcis xxx sol.
Item Agneti Calfonarie pro CC calcis x sol.
Item Willelmo porcario pro Mvj^{c} & dim. c sabulonis xxxv sol. viij d.
Item Mauricio de Aqua pro meremio iiij li. xiij sol. iiij d.
Ricardo Estchepe pro virgis iij sol. d.
Ricardo Ogul pro V duodenis craticularum xij sol. vj d.
Item Pekin pro emendatione de ceruris xx d.
Henrico de Ponte pro clavis iiij sol. vj d. ob.
Summa empcionum xlj li. v sol. vj d.
Summa totalis ebdomade lxix li. xv sol. d.

Ebdomada decima continente festum Translacionis beati Eadwardi per diem lune quod cementariorum, et festum beati Luce Evangeliste per diem Sabbati quod est domini Regis.

To Agnes the lime-burner for 1 hundredweight and a half of lime, 7*s.* 6*d.*
And to Richard of Eastcheap for withies, 5*s.* 8*d.*
And to Henry of Bridge for iron nails, 18*s.* 1*d.*

Total purchases, £23. 16*s.* 6*d.*

Total of the week, £47. 17*s.* 1½*d.*

The ninth week, without a feast day.
For wages of 42 white cutters, 14 marblers, 31 layers, 14 carpenters, John with a servant at St. Albans, Peter the painter, Adam the plasterer with a servant, 15 polishers, 18 smiths, 3 glaziers, with keepers and clerks, £18. 3*s.* 10*d.*
For wages of 155 labourers with [the charges of] 6 carts daily, £10. 5*s.* 9*d.*

Total wages, £28. 9*s.* 7*d.*

Purchases. For different kinds of freestone cut by task, £6. 4*s.* 8*d.*
And for 11 hundredweight and a quarter of freestone, 73*s.* 1½*d.*
To Roger of Reigate for 2 hundredweight and a quarter of stone, 14*s.* 7½*d.*
And for a shipload of Caen freestone,[1]
And for marble at Corfe, £18. 19*s.* 0½*d.*
And for a shipload of ragstone, 5*s.* 9*d.*
And to Master William de Waz an advance of 15*s.* 6*d.*
And to Richard the lime-burner for 8 hundredweight of lime, 30*s.*
And to Agnes the lime-burner for 2 hundredweight of lime, 10*s.*
And to William the swine-herd for 16 hundredweight and a half of sand, 35*s.* 8*d.*
And to Maurice of Water for timber, £4. 13*s.* 4*d.*
To Richard Eastcheap for withies, 3*s.* 1*d.*
To Richard Ogul for 5 dozen hurdles, 12*s.* 6*d.*
And to Pekin for mending locks, 1*s.* 8*d.*
To Henry of Bridge for nails, 4*s.* 6½*d.*

Total purchases, £41. 5*s.* 6*d.*

Sum total of the week, £69. 15*s.* 1*d.*

The tenth week, containing the feast of the Translation of the blessed Edward [13 October] on Monday which is the masons', and the feast of the blessed Luke the Evangelist [18 October] on Saturday which is the lord king's.

[1] Cost not stated.

In stipendiis lviij alborum cissorum, xvj marmorariorum, xxxiij cubitorum, xv carpentariorum, Johanne cum serviente apud Sanctum Albanum, Petri pictoris, Ade dealbatoris cum serviente, xvj pollisorum, xviij fabrorum, iij vitriariorum, j plumbatoris cum custodibus & clericis xvj li. v sol.

In stipendiis vij^xx & xvjjj[1] minutorum operariorum cum vj bigis diurnis vij li.

Summa stipendiorum xxiij li. v sol.

Empciones Magistro Albrico pro taschia form' vj li. x d.
In diversis modis france petre cisse ad taschiam lxxj sol. iij d.
Item in diversis modis marmoris ad taschiam cissi iiij li. xiij sol. d.
Item pro MCC & quartron france petre lxxix sol. vij d. ob.
Rogero de Reygate pro ccc petre xix sol. vj d.
Item pro petra de quareria Regis pro C & quartron viij sol. ix d.
Ricardo Calfonario pro vj^c & dim. calcis xxij sol. vj d.
Agneti Calfonarie pro CCC calcis xv sol.
Ricardo Estchepe pro virgis v sol. vij d.
Ricardo Ogul pro duodena & dim. craticularum iij sol. ix d.
Ricardo Cuvario pro dim. duodena boketis xxv d.
pro v caretatis carbonis xiij sol. viij d.
Item Willelmo plumbario pro taschia berefridi x li.
Rogero plumbario pro taschia berefridi C & xiij sol. iiij d.
Henrico de Ponte pro clavis ad ecclesiam & berefridum xij sol. ij d.

Summa empcionum xxxiij li. x d. ob.

Summa ebdomade lxij li. xv sol. x d. ob.

Ebdomada undecima sine festo

In stipendiis lviij alborum cissorum, xv marmorariorum, xxxiiij cubitorum, xiiij carpentariorum cum Johanne & serviente apud Sanctum Albanum, Petri pictoris, dealbatoris cum serviente, xv pollisorum, xviij fabrorum, ij vitriariorum, j plumbarii cum serviente, cum virgatoribus & clericis xix li. iiij d.

Item in stipendiis vij^xx & xvij operariorum cum vj bigis diurnis x li. viij sol. iiij d.

Summa stipendiorum xxix li. viij sol. viij d.

Empciones In diversis modis france petre ad taschiam cisse lxxiij sol. v d. ob.
Item pro viij^c iij quartron france petre lvj sol. iiij d. ob.
de quareria domini Regis iij quartron v sol. iij d.
Rogero Reygate pro CC petre xiij sol.
Ricardo Calfonari pro V^c & quartron calcis xxvj sol. iij d.
Agnes Calfonarie pro CCC calcis xv sol.

[1] The figure intended is not quite clear. The clerk appears to have written xvj and then to have added two more digits.

For wages of 58 white cutters, 16 marblers, 33 layers, 15 carpenters, John with a servant at St. Albans, Peter the painter, Adam the plasterer with a servant, 16 polishers, 18 smiths, 3 glaziers, 1 plumber, with keepers and clerks, £16. 5*s*.
For wages of 158 [?] labourers with [the charges of] 6 carts daily, £7.
Total wages, £23. 5*s*.

Purchases. To Master Aubrey for the task-work of tracery, £6. 0*s*. 10*d*.[1]
For different kinds of freestone cut by task, 71*s*. 3*d*.
And for different kinds of marble cut by task, £4. 13*s*. 1*d*.
And for 12 hundredweight and a quarter of freestone, 79*s*. 7½*d*.
To Roger of Reigate for 3 hundredweight of stone, 19*s*. 6*d*.
And for 1 hundredweight and a quarter of stone from the king's quarry, 8*s*. 9*d*.
To Richard the lime-burner for 6 hundredweight and a half of lime, 22*s*. 6*d*.
To Agnes the lime-burner for 3 hundredweight of lime, 15*s*.
To Richard Eastcheap for withies, 5*s*. 7*d*.
To Richard Ogul for a dozen and a half of hurdles, 3*s*. 9*d*.
To Richard the cooper for half a dozen buckets, 2*s*. 1*d*.
For 5 cart-loads of charcoal, 13*s*. 8*d*.
And to William the plumber for the task-work of the belfry, £10.
To Roger the plumber for the task-work of the belfry, 113*s*. 4*d*.
To Henry of Bridge for nails for the church and the belfry, 12*s*. 2*d*.
Total purchases, £33. 0*s*. 10½*d*.
Total of the week, £62. 15*s*. 10½*d*.

The eleventh week, without a feast day.
For wages of 58 white cutters, 15 marblers, 34 layers, 14 carpenters, with John and a servant at St. Albans, Peter the painter, the plasterer with a servant, 15 polishers, 18 smiths, 2 glaziers, 1 plumber with a servant, and scaffold-erectors and clerks, £19. 0*s*. 4*d*.
And for wages of 157 labourers with [the charges of] 6 carts daily, £10. 8*s*. 4*d*.
Total wages, £29. 8*s*. 8*d*.

Purchases. For different kinds of freestone cut by task, 73*s*. 5½*d*.
And for 8 hundredweight and 3 quarters of freestone, 56*s*. 4½*d*.
Stone from the lord king's quarry, 3 quarters, 5*s*. 3*d*.
To Roger Reigate for 2 hundredweight of stone, 13*s*.
To Richard the lime-burner for 5 hundredweight and a quarter of lime, 26*s*. 3*d*.
To Agnes the lime-burner for 3 hundredweight of lime, 15*s*.

[1] Added later and not included in the total.

Ricardo Estchepe pro virgis vj sol. x d.
Henrico de Ponte pro clavis ecclesie & berefridi xx sol. d. ob.

Summa empcionum x li. x sol. iij d. ob.

Summa totalis ebdomade xxxix li. xix sol.

Ebdomada duodecima continente festum Apostolorum Simonis & Jude quod est domini Regis, Anno Regni Regis Henrici xxxviiij^vo^ incipiente & festum Omnium Sanctorum per diem Sabbati quod est cementariorum.

In stipendiis lviij alborum cissorum, xv marmorariorum, xxxiiij cubitorum, xiiij carpentariorum cum Johanne & serviente suo apud Sanctum Albanum, Petri pictoris, dealbatoris cum serviente, xv pollisorum, xviij fabrorum, ij vitriariorum, plumbatoris cum serviente, iiij virgatorum, cum clericis, xviij li. x sol.

In stipendiis vij^xx^ operariorum cum vj bigis diurnis ix li. viij sol.

Summa stipendiorum xxvij li. xviij sol.

Empciones In diversis modis france petre ad taschiam cisse cum creta ad pendentia iiij li. xvj sol. iiij d.
In diversis modis marmoris ad taschiam cissi lxix sol. ob.
Item de quareria domini Regis C & quartron france petre viij sol. ix d.
Item Rogero Reygate pro CC & quartron petre xiiii sol. vij d. ob.
Item pro vij^c^ france petre xlv sol. vj d.
Item Ricardo Calfonario pro CCCC calcis xx sol.
Agneti Calfonarie pro dim. C calcis ij sol. vj d.
Ricardo Estchepe pro craticulis vij sol. viij d.
Ricardo Ogul pro vjj duodenis craticularum xvij sol. vj d.
pro vectura meremii x sol.
Hamoni pro carbone iij sol. iiij d.
Henrico de Ponte pro clavis ferri iiij sol. iiij d.

Summa empcionum xiiij li. ix sol. vij d.

Summa ebdomade xlij li. vij sol. vij d.

Ebdomada Prima post Festum Omnium Sanctorum sine festo grossa stipendia alborum cissorum solent decrescere.

In stipendiis lviij alborum cissorum, xj marmorariorum, xj cubitorum, xiiij carpentariorum, Johannis apud Sanctum Albanum cum serviente, Petri pictoris, Ade dealbatoris cum serviente, xvj pollisorum, xviij fabrorum, duorum vitriariorum, cum clericis & custodibus, xviij li.

In stipendiis vij^xx^ minutorum operariorum cum iij bigis diurnis vij li. xij sol

Summa stipendiorum xxv li. xij sol.

To Richard Eastcheap for withies, 6*s.* 10*d.*
To Henry of Bridge for nails for the church and the belfry, 20*s.* 1½*d.*
Total purchases, £10. 10*s.* 3½*d.*
Sum total of the week, £39. 19*s.*

The twelfth week, containing the feast of the Apostles Simon and Jude [28 October] which is the lord king's, at the beginning of the 38th year of the reign of King Henry, and the feast of All Saints [1 November] on Saturday which is the masons'.
For wages of 58 white cutters, 15 marblers, 34 layers, 14 carpenters, and John and his servant at St. Albans, Peter the painter, the plasterer with a servant, 15 polishers, 18 smiths, 2 glaziers, a plumber with a servant, 4 scaffold-erectors, and clerks, £18. 10*s.*
For wages of 140 labourers with [the charges of] 6 carts daily, £9. 8*s.*
Total wages, £27. 18*s.*

Purchases. For different kinds of freestone cut by task together with chalk for the vaults, £4. 16*s.* 4*d.*
For different kinds of marble cut by task, 69*s.* 0½*d.*
And from the lord king's quarry 1 hundredweight and a quarter of freestone, 8*s.* 9*d.*
And to Roger Reigate for 2 hundredweight and a quarter of stone, 14*s.* 7½*d.*
And for 7 hundredweight of freestone, 45*s.* 6*d.*
And to Richard the lime-burner for 4 hundredweight of lime, 20*s.*
To Agnes the lime-burner for half a hundredweight of lime, 2*s.* 6*d.*
To Richard Eastcheap for hurdles 7*s.* 8*d.*
To Richard Ogul for 7 dozen hurdles, 17*s.* 6*d.*
For carriage of timber, 10*s.*
To Hamon for charcoal, 3*s.* 4*d.*
To Henry of Bridge for iron nails, 4*s.* 4*d.*
Total purchases, £14. 9*s.* 7*d.*
Total of the week, £42. 7*s.* 7*d.*

The first week after the feast of All Saints [1 November], without a feast day. [In this week] the high wages of the white cutters are usually reduced.
For wages of 58 white cutters, 11 marblers, 11 layers, 14 carpenters, John at St. Albans with a servant, Peter the painter, Adam the plasterer with a servant, 16 polishers, 18 smiths, 2 glaziers, with clerks and keepers, £18.
For wages of 140 labourers with [the charges of] 3 carts daily, £7. 12*s.*
Total wages, £25. 12*s.*

Empciones In diversis modis france petre & marmoris ad taschiam cissi iiij li. xiiij sol. iij d.

Item in CCC & dim. de quareria domini Regis xxiiij sol. vj d.

Item Rogero de Reygate pro CCCC & dimid. france petre xxix sol. iij d.

Item pro MCCC petre iiij li. iiij sol. vj d.

Item Ricardo Calfonario pro C & dim. calcis vij sol. vj d.

Ricardo Estchepe pro virgis ix sol. vj d.

Ricardo Ogul pro iiij duodenis craticularum x sol.

Henrico de Ponte pro cepo & uncto ij sol. iiij d.

Summa empcionum xiij li. xxij d.

Summa ebdomade xxxviij li. xiij sol. x d.

Ebdomada secunda continente festum beati Martini per diem Martis quod est domini Regis.

In stipendiis xxxiiij alborum cissorum, vij marmorariorum, v asseditorum, ix carpentariorum, Johannis cum serviente apud Sanctum Albanum, Petri pictoris, xiij fabrorum, ij vitriariorum, iij virgatorum cum iij clericis, viij li. iij sol. iiij d. ob.

Item in stipendiis xxx minutorum operariorum cum duabus bigis diurnis xxxv sol.

Summa stipendiorum ix li. xviij sol. iiij d. ob.

Empciones Rogero plumbario pro charea plumbi ultra porticum ecclesie ad taschiam operati xj sol. x d.

Item pro IX^{c} & dim. france petre lxj sol. ix d.

pro dim. C petre domini Regis iij sol. vj d.

Rogero Reygate pro CCCC & quartron petre xxvij sol. vij d. ob.

Ricardo Estchepe pro virgis iiij sol.

Henrico de Ponte pro oleo & ve[r]nis ij sol. iij d. ob.

Hamoni pro carbone iiij sol.

Summa empcionum C & xv sol.

Summa ebdomade xv li. xiij sol. iiij d. ob.

Ebdomada tertia continente festum beati Eadmundi per diem Jovis quod est cementariorum.

In stipendiis xxxv alborum cissorum, vij marmorariorum, v cubitorum, ix^{vem} carpentariorum, Johannis de Sancto Albano cum serviente, magistri Petri pictoris, xiij fabrorum, ij vitriariorum cum custodibus & clericis, ix li. xviij sol. ob.

In stipendiis xxxv operariorum cum duabus bigis diurnis xl sol.

Summa stipendiorum xj li. xviij sol. ob.

Purchases. For different kinds of freestone and marble cut by task, £4. 14*s*. 3*d*.
And for 3 hundredweight and a half [of stone] from the lord king's quarry, 24*s*. 6*d*.
And to Roger of Reigate for 4 hundredweight and a half of freestone, 29*s*. 3*d*.
And for 13 hundredweight of stone, £4. 4*s*. 6*d*.
And to Richard the lime-burner for 1 hundredweight and a half of lime, 7*s*. 6*d*.
To Richard Eastcheap for withies, 9*s*. 6*d*.
To Richard Ogul for 4 dozen hurdles, 10*s*.
To Henry of Bridge for tallow and grease, 2*s*. 4*d*.

Total purchases, £13. 1*s*. 10*d*.

Total of the week, £38. 13*s*. 10*d*.

The second week [after the feast of All Saints] containing the feast of the blessed Martin [11 November] on Tuesday which is the lord king's.
For wages of 34 white cutters, 7 marblers, 5 layers, 9 carpenters, John with a servant at St. Albans, Peter the painter, 13 smiths, 2 glaziers, 3 scaffold-erectors, and 3 clerks, £8. 3*s*. 4½*d*.
For wages of 30 labourers with [the charges of] 2 carts daily, 35*s*.

Total of wages, £9. 18*s*. 4½*d*.

Purchases. To Roger the plumber for working on a char of lead above the church porch by task, 11*s*. 10*d*.
And for 9 hundredweight and a half of freestone, 61*s*. 9*d*.
For half a hundredweight of the lord king's stone, 3*s*. 6*d*.
To Roger Reigate for 4 hundredweight and a quarter of stone, 27*s*. 7½*d*.
To Richard Eastcheap for withies, 4*s*.
To Henry of Bridge for oil and varnish, 2*s*. 3½*d*.
To Hamon for charcoal, 4*s*.

Total purchases, 115*s*.

Total of the week, £15. 13*s*. 4½*d*.

The third week [after the feast of All Saints] containing the feast of the blessed Edmund [20 November] on Thursday which is the masons'.
For wages of 35 white cutters, 7 marblers, 5 layers, 9 carpenters, John of St. Albans with a servant, Master Peter the painter, 13 smiths, 2 glaziers, with keepers and clerks, £9. 18*s*. 0½*d*.
For wages of 35 labourers with [the charges of] 2 carts daily, 40*s*.

Total wages, £11. 18*s*. 0½*d*.

Empciones xxvj taschiatoribus pro diverso modo france petre ad taschiam cisse cij sol. v d.

Item vj marmorariis pro diverso modo marmoris ad taschiam cissi xxxj sol. x d.

Item de quareria Regis pro dim. C petre iij sol. vj d.

Rogero Reygate pro CCC petre xix sol. vj d.

Item pro vj^c & iij quartron petre xliij sol. x d. ob.

Item Ricardo Ogul pro ij duodenis craticularum v sol.

Henrico de Ponte pro cera pice & carbone marino v sol. j d.

Summa empcionum x li. xj sol. ij d. ob.

Summa totalis ebdomade xxij li. ix sol. iij d.

Ebdomada quarta continente festum Sancte Katerine per diem Martis quod est domini Regis.

In stipendiis xxxv alborum cissorum, vij marmorariorum, iiij cubitorum, ix^vem carpentariorum, Johannis apud Sanctum Albanum cum serviente, Magistri Petri Pictoris, xiij fabrorum, ij vitriariorum, ij plumbatorum cum servientibus cum clericis & iij custodibus, viij li. xj sol.

In stipendiis xxxvij operariorum cum ij bigis diurnis, xlj sol. x d. ob.

Summa totalis stipendiorum x li. xij sol. x d. ob.

Empciones In MCC crete ad taschiam cisse ij sol. vj d.

Item de quareria Regis pro quartron xxj d.

Rogero de Reygate pro CCCC & quartron petre xxvij sol. vij d. ob.

Item pro MC & quartron petre lxxiij sol. d. ob.

Ricardo Estchepe pro virgis iij sol. x d.

Item Henrico de Ponte pro assero & clavis ferri ad berefridum vj sol. vij d. ob.

Summa empcionum CXV sol. v d. ob.

Summa totalis ebdomade xvj li. viij sol. iiij d.

Ebdomada quinta continente festum beati Nicholai per diem sabbati quod est cementariorum.

In stipendiis xxxv alborum cissorum, vij marmorariorum, iiij cubitorum, ix carpentariorum, Johannis apud Sanctum Albanum cum serviente, magistri Petri, xiij fabrorum, ij vitriariorum, ij plumbatorum cum servientibus, custodibus & clericis, viij li. xviij sol.

In stipendiis xxxvij minutorum operariorum cum ij bigis xlj sol. x d. ob.

Summa stipendiorum x li. xix sol. x d. ob.

Empciones De quareria domini Regis pro iij quartron france petre iiij sol. x d. ob.

Rogero de Reygate pro CCC & dim. france petre xxij sol. ix d.

Item pro ix^c & quartron france petre lx sol. d. ob.

Item Henrico de Ponte pro carbone marino x sol.

Purchases. To 26 task-workers cutting different kinds of freestone by task, 102*s*. 5*d*.

And to 6 marblers for cutting different kinds of marble by task, 31*s*. 10*d*.

And for half a hundredweight of stone from the king's quarry, 3*s*. 6*d*.

To Roger Reigate for 3 hundredweight of stone, 19*s*. 6*d*.

And for 6 hundredweight and 3 quarters of stone, 43*s*. 10½*d*.

And to Richard Ogul for 2 dozen hurdles, 5*s*.

To Henry of Bridge for wax, pitch, and sea-coal, 5*s*. 1*d*.

Total purchases, £10. 11*s*. 2½*d*.

Sum total of the week, £22. 9*s*. 3*d*.

The fourth week [after All Saints] containing the feast of St. Katherine [25 November] on Tuesday which is the lord king's.

For wages of 35 white cutters, 7 marblers, 4 layers, 9 carpenters, John at St. Albans with a servant, Master Peter the painter, 13 smiths, 2 glaziers, 2 plumbers with servants, with clerks and 3 keepers, £8. 11*s*.

For wages of 37 labourers with [the charges of] 2 carts daily, 41*s*. 10½*d*.

Sum total of wages, £10. 12*s*. 10½*d*.

Purchases. For cutting 12 hundredweight of chalk by task, 2*s*. 6*d*.

And from the king's quarry a quarter [of stone] 1*s*. 9*d*.

To Roger of Reigate for 4 hundredweight and a quarter of stone, 27*s*. 7½*d*.

And for 11 hundredweight and a quarter of stone, 73*s*. 1½*d*.

To Richard Eastcheap for withies, 3*s*. 10*d*.

And to Henry of Bridge for steel and for iron nails for the belfry, 6*s*. 7½*d*.

Total purchases, 115*s*. 5½*d*.

Sum total of the week, £16. 8*s*. 4*d*.

The fifth week [after All Saints] containing the feast of the blessed Nicholas [6 December] on Saturday which is the masons'.

For wages of 35 white cutters, 7 marblers, 4 layers, 9 carpenters, John at St. Albans with a servant, Master Peter, 13 smiths, 2 glaziers, 2 plumbers with servants, keepers, and clerks, £8. 18*s*.

For wages of 37 labourers with [the charges of] 2 carts, 41*s*. 10½*d*.

Total wages, £10. 19*s*. 10½*d*.

Purchases. From the lord king's quarry 3 quarters of freestone, 4*s*. 10½*d*.

To Roger of Reigate for 3 hundredweight and a half of freestone, 22*s*. 9*d*.

And for 9 hundredweight and a quarter of freestone, 60*s*. 1½*d*.

And to Henry of Bridge for sea-coal, 10*s*.

Endorsements

1. Memorandum quod die Jovis ante festum Decollacionis beati Johannis de Magistro Johanne le Senter xxxiij[c] ferri. Item dictus Johannes le Senter recepit eodem die de ballivis domini Regis MMMMCC metalli. Item restant in deposito CC & fere dim. cupri.
2. Memorandum quod Ebdomada iiij[ta] Die Martis in crastino beati Thome Martiris Magister Albricus cum iij sociis incepit taschiam iij formarum.
3. Memorandum quod die Lune in crastino beati Bartholomei inceperunt operarii in quarreria domini Regis.
4. Hec est liberacio vitri facta magistro Henrico die Lune post ad vincula beati Petri anno regni regis Henrici xxxvij[o] videlicet ij summe vitri colorati precium summe xij sol. & ij. Summe vitri albi precium summe vj sol. Summa denariorum xxxvj sol. de quibus tenetur respondere. In taschia fenestrarum sic taxata pro pede operato vitris colorati viij d. pro pede operato vitri albi iiij d.
   Item die Martis in crastino Nativitatis beate Marie eidem Henrico vj Pise vitri colorati precium iiij sol. Item eidem ij summe vitri albi xij sol. dim. summa vitri colorati precium vj sol.

Endorsements

1. Note that on Thursday [28 August] before the feast of the Beheading of St. John the Baptist 33 hundredweight of iron [was received] from Master John le Senter. And the aforesaid John le Senter received on the same day 42 hundredweight of metal from the king's bailiffs. And there remains in store nearly 2 and a half hundredweight of copper.

2. Note that in the fourth week [after Whitsun] on Tuesday [8 July] on the morrow of the feast of the blessed Thomas the Martyr, Master Aubrey with 3 fellows began the task-work of 3 pieces of tracery.

3. Note that on Monday [25 August] on the morrow of the feast of the blessed Bartholomew the labourers began in the lord king's quarry.

4. This is the glass that was delivered to Master Henry on Monday [4 August] after the feast of the blessed Peter in Chains, in the 37th year of the reign of King Henry [1253] namely, two seams of coloured glass at 12*s*. a seam, and two seams of white glass at 6*s*. a seam. Total 36*s*., for which he is bound to answer. For the task-work of the windows priced thus, 8*d*. for working a foot of coloured glass, and 4*d*. for working a foot of white glass.

   And on Tuesday [9 September], the morrow of the feast of the Nativity of the blessed Virgin Mary, 6 weys of coloured glass costing 4*s*. [were delivered] to the aforesaid Henry. And two seams of white glass [costing] 12*s*. and half a seam of coloured glass costing 6*s*.

7. Payments for works at Westminster Palace from 5 May to 11 October, 1259

(E 101/467/3)

Custus positus in camino camere Domini Regis apud Westmonasterium reparando, conducto aque que sub terra ad lavatorium ducitur emendando, defectubus domorum domini Regis apud Westmonasterium reparandis, et quodam conducto faciendo inter coquinas & Tamisiam propter fetorem aque sordide que per aulam Regis deportatur & corrumpit homines in aula conversantes secundum quod continetur in brevi regis Thesaurario & camerariis scaccarii inde directo per Martinum de Campo Florum & magistrum Johannem cementarium.

1. Prima pacacio facta per predictos Martinum & Johannem die Lune proxima post Invencionem Sancte Crucis usque in festo Sanctorum Nerei & Archillei.

Unde eadem ebdomada in cent. & uno quarter' france petre empte de Radulfo de Lamh' vjj sol. vj d. liberati eidem Radulfo precium centene vj sol.

Item in uno quarter' france petre empte de Ricardo de Croyden' vj sol. liberati Ricardo de Cycestr'.

Item in dim. centum & uno quarter' france petre empte de Randulfo de Waltham iiij^or^ sol. vj d. liberati Ricardo de Cycestr'.

Et in una navata grise petre empte de Ricardo le Corner vj sol. per talliam Et in una navata grise petre empte de Roberto filio Alicie v sol.	lib' Ricardo de Cycestr'

Cementarii circa caminum prima ebdomada, videlicet	Robertus de Beverleye & capit iij sol. Johannes de Burgel' ij sol. ij d. Henricus de Waltham ij sol. ij d. Willelmus de Hampton' ij sol. ij d.	lib' Ricardo de Cycestr'

Johanni Pollard pro busca prosternenda & carianda ad calcem faciendam xx sol. lib' Waltero clerico

7. Payments for works at Westminster Palace from 5 May to 11 October, 1259

The costs laid out by Martin de Chanflur and Master John the mason in repairing the chimney of the lord king's chamber at Westminster, in mending the conduit which goes underground to the lavatory,[1] in repairing the defects of the lord king's houses at Westminster and in making a certain conduit between the kitchens and the Thames because of the stench of dirty water which is conveyed away through the king's hall and infects men frequenting the hall, as is contained in the king's writ directed in respect of this to the Treasurer and chamberlains of the Exchequer.

1. The first payment made by the aforesaid Martin and John on Monday following the feast of the Invention of the Holy Cross [5 May] to the feast of Saints Nereus and Achilleus [12 May].

Wherefore in the same week for one hundredweight and a quarter of freestone bought from Ralph of Lambeth, 7*s.* 6*d.* paid to the same Ralph at 6*s.* a hundredweight.

And for a quarter[2] of freestone bought from Richard of Croydon, 6*s.* paid to Richard of Chichester.

And for three quarters of a hundredweight of freestone bought from Ranulf of Waltham, 4*s.* 6*d.* paid to Richard of Chichester.

And for a shipload of ragstone bought from Richard le Corner, 6*s.* by tally And for a shipload of ragstone bought from Robert son of Alice, 5*s.*	paid to Richard of Chichester

Masons working on the chimney the first week, namely:

Robert of Beverley taking 3*s.* John de Burgel', 2*s.* 2*d.* Henry of Waltham, 2*s.* 2*d.* William of Hampton, 2*s.* 2*d.*	paid to Richard of Chichester

To John Pollard for cutting and carrying firewood to make lime, 20*s.* paid to Walter the clerk.

[1] The word is here used in its original meaning of a washing place.

[2] *Sic.* But comparison with the corresponding entry in E 101/467/2 suggests that 'a quarter' is here an error for 'a hundredweight'.

In duabus novis seruris emptis & duabus veteribus seruris emendandis ad hostia domorum domini regis ij sol. vj d. liberati Waltero fabro.

Summa stipendiorum huius pacacionis ix sol. vj d.

Summa totalis huius pacacionis lxv sol.

2. Pacacio facta a die Lune in festo Sanctorum Nerei & Archillei anno &c. usque dominicam in vigilia Sancti Augustini per quindecim dies continentes festum Assencionis domini quod domini regis fuit.

Cementarii circa caminum	Reginaldo Sturmin iiij^{or} sol. Johannes le Burgenun iiij^{or} sol. Philippus de Hyndel' iiij^{or} sol. Henrico de Waltham iiij^{or} sol. et Willelmus de Hampton iiij^{or} sol.	pro quindena proximo preterita. Summa xx sol.

Cementarii ad lotorium. Willelmus de Bradele iiij^{or} sol. Thomas de Kenefeg iiij sol. Et Rogerus de Oxon' cubitarius per idem tempus iiij sol. Summa xij sol.[1]

Carpentarii, videlicet	Willelmus de Waldis Johannes de Padinthon' Henricus de Knythebrugg'	quorum quilibet capit per septimanam xxvj d. Summa per quindenam xij sol.
Minuti operarii:	Ricardus de Lycefelt Simon Russel Roger de la Cherring' Robertus de Oxon'	xxvij d. ob. Summa ix sol. ij d.

Summa secunde pacacionis stipendiorum liij sol. ij d.

Empciones de predicta quindena, videlicet Algar' de Brig' pro Ciij quarter' france petre de Chalved' x sol. vj d. Willelmo de Brug' pro j. quarter' france petre de eadem quarrura xviij d. Radulfo de Lamh' pro C dim. france petre de eadem ix sol. Radulfo de Wautham pro C france petre de eadem vj sol. Item pro j quarter' xviij d. Petro de Mercheham pro C france petre vj sol.

Summa xxxiiij sol. vj d.[2]

Summa totalis vj li. xviij sol. iiij^{or} d.[2]

[1] Substituted for 'per unicam septimanam xxij d. Summa totalis ix sol. x d.'.
[2] Underlined for deletion.

For the purchase of two new locks and the repair of two old locks for the doors of the lord king's houses, 2*s.* 6*d.* paid to Walter the smith.

Total wages of this payment, 9*s.* 6*d.*

Sum total of this payment, 65*s.*

2. The payment made from Monday on the feast of Saints Nereus and Achilleus [12 May] in the same year to Sunday on the vigil of the feast of St. Augustine [25 May] for fifteen days containing the feast of the Ascension of the Lord [22 May] which was the lord king's.

Masons working on the chimney:

Reginald Sturmin, 4*s.* John le Burgenun, 4*s.* Philip of Hillsley,[1] 4*s.* Henry of Waltham, 4*s.* and William of Hampton, 4*s.*	for the fortnight last past. Total, 20*s.*

Masons at the lavatory: William of Bradley, 4*s.* Thomas of Kenfig, 4*s.* And Roger of Oxford, layer, for the same period, 4*s.* Total 12*s.*

Carpenters, namely:	William de Waldis[2] John of Paddington Henry of Knightsbridge	each of them takes per week 2*s.* 2*d.* Total for the fortnight, 12*s.*
Labourers:	Richard of Lichfield Simon Russel Roger of Charing Robert of Oxford	at 2*s.* 3½*d.* Total, 9*s.* 2*d.*

Total of the second payment of wages, 53*s.* 2*d.*

Purchases for the said fortnight, namely to Algar of Bridge for one hundredweight and three quarters of Chaldon freestone, 10*s.* 6*d.* To William of Bridge for one quarter of freestone from the same quarry, 18*d.* To Ralph of Lambeth for one hundredweight and a half of freestone from the same quarry, 9*s.* To Ralph of Waltham for one hundredweight of freestone from the same quarry, 6*s.* And for a quarter [of freestone], 18*d.* To Peter of Merstham for one hundredweight of freestone, 6*s.*

Total, 34*s.* 6*d.*

Sum total, £6. 18*s.* 4*d.*

[1] Or 'Ilsley' (Berks.). [2] Perhaps William 'of the Wolds'.

Memorandum xxxvj sol. ij d. qui deficiunt in rotulo sed adduntur v sol. vj d. & ita remanent xxx sol. viij d. ad locandum inde demantur viij sol. vj d. & remanent ad loquand' xxij. ij d.

3. Pacacio facta de operacionibus curie domini regis apud Westmonasterium videlicet de camino lavatorio & coquina a die Lune in festo Sancti Augustini usque in vigilia Pentecost' scilicet per unam hebdomadam sine festo.

Albi cissores contra [*sic*] *caminum* vj sol. vj d.	Reginaldus Sturmi	
	Johannes Burg'	
	Philippus de Hyldesl'	xxvj d.
	Henricus de Wautham	
	Willelmus de Hampton'	
Cubitores	Johannes le Harpur	
	Ricardus de Kerewr'	xxvj d.
	Radulfus de Walet'	
	Willelmus de Bledelawe	
	Robertus de Beverle	iij sol.
die Martis venit. deest die Jovis	Willelmus de Tham'	xij d.
	Summa xxiij sol. vj d.[1]	
Albi cyssores circa lavatorium vj sol. vj d.	Willelmus de Bradel'	xxvj d.
	Thomas de Kenefeg'	
Cubitores ebdomada j venit	Radulfus de Oxonia	iiij sol.
ebdomada iij venit	Robertus Pik'	xxvj d.
	Summa x sol. vj d.[2]	
Fabri circa caminum ebdomada iij	Magister Henricus faber	iiij sol.
	Willelmus de Offinton'	xviij d.
	Ricardus faber	iij sol.
	Summa viij sol. vj d.	
Carpentarii circa operacionem coquine		
ebdomada ij venit iiij sol. iiij d.	Willelmus de Wauzs	
	Johannes de Padinton'	xxvj d.
	Henricus de Knythebr'	
ebdomada iij venit	Nicholaus de Eye	xxvj d.
	Summa viij sol. viij d.[3]	

[1] Substituted for 45s. 2d. [2] Substituted for 19s. 6d.
[3] Substituted for 15s. 2d.

Note of 36*s*. 2*d*. which is missing on the roll, but 5*s*. 6*d*. are added and thus 30*s*. 8*d*. remain to be allowed, from which 8*s*. 6*d*. are subtracted and 22*s*. 2*d*. remain to be allowed.

3. The payment made for the works of the lord king's court at Westminster namely on the chimney, lavatory, and kitchen from Monday on the feast of St. Augustine [26 May] to the vigil of Whitsun [31 May] that is for one week without a feast day.

White cutters on the chimney: 6*s*. 6*d*.	Reginald Sturmi John Burg' Philip of Hillsley Henry of Waltham William of Hampton	2*s*. 2*d*.
Layers:	John the Harper Richard of Carwardine Ralph of Walden William of Bledlow	2*s*. 2*d*.
	Robert of Beverley, 3*s*.	
Came on Tuesday, left on Thursday	William of Thame, 12*d*.	
	Total, 23*s*. 6*d*.[1]	
White cutters on the lavatory:		
6*s*. 6*d*.	William of Bradley Thomas of Kenfig	2*s*. 2*d*.
Layers:		
He came week 1	Ralph of Oxford, 4*s*.	
He came week 3	Robert Pike, 2*s*. 2*d*.	
	Total, 10*s*. 6*d*.[1]	

Smiths working on the fire-place in week 3:

	Master Henry the smith,	4*s*.
	William of Uffington,	18*d*.
	Richard the smith,	3*s*.
	Total, 8*s*. 6*d*.	

Carpenters on the work in the kitchen:

He came week 2 4*s*. 4*d*.	William de Wauzs John of Paddington Henry of Knightsbridge	2*s*. 2*d*.
He came week 3	Nicholas of Eye	2*s*. 2*d*.
	Total, 8*s*. 8*d*.[1]	

[1] See notes 1–3 opposite.

Minuti operarii circa caminum ebdomada iij	Simon le scaffot'	xviij d.
	Willelmus Mylers Johannes le porter	xv d.
deest die Veneris	Johannes Neck	x d.
eadem die Mercurii venit	Martinus	
	Summa v sol. viij d.	
Portitores france petre ad caminum per ij dies	Willelmus de Pret'well Johannes curaunt Fukel Reginaldus fuell' Johannes Gyng'	v d.
	Summa xxv d.	
Minuti operarii circa lavatorium per quindenam	Ricardus de Lichefeud Symon Russell Rogerus de Cherrinke	ij sol. iij d. ob.
	Summa vj sol. x d. ob.	
Minuti operarii circa officium coquine		
ebdomada iij venit	Edmundus de Bracino Johannes Mityng' Elyas le breveter	xv d.
	Summa iij sol. ix d.	
Minuti operarii in fabrica		
ebdomada iij venit	Welbilowed Alexander faber Robertus Jobbe	xv d.
eadem die Veneris venit	Adam de Awelthon'	x d.
	Summa iiij sol. vij d.	
Operarii circa fossatum in curia Regis ebdomada ante Pentecost'	Galfridus Wrenn' Duraunt de Eye Hugo de Berking' Thomas de Eye Willelmus de Fecham	xv d.
	Summa vj sol. iij d.	

Summa stipendiorum tercie pacacionis iiij li. xiiij sol. ij d.

Labourers on the fire-place in week 3:

	Simon the scaffolder,	18*d*.
	William Mylers	15*d*.
	John the porter	
He left on Friday	John Neck	10*d*.
He came in the same week on Wednesday	Martin	10*d*.
	Total, 5*s*. 8*d*.	

Porters of freestone to the chimney for two days:

William of Prittlewell	5*d*.
John Curaunt	
Fukel	
Reginald Fuell'	
John Gyng'	
Total, 2*s*. 1*d*.	

Labourers on the lavatory for a fortnight:

Richard of Lichfield	2*s*. 3½*d*.
Simon Russel	
Roger of Charing	
Total, 6*s*. 10½*d*.	

Labourers on the kitchen:

He came week 3	Edmund of the malt-house	15*d*.
	John Miting	
	Elias the Breveter	
	Total, 3*s*. 9*d*.	

Labourers in the smithy:

He came week 3	Welbilowed	15*d*.
	Alexander the smith	
	Robert Jobbe	
He came the same week on Friday	Adam of Alton	10*d*.
	Total, 4*s*. 7*d*.	

Labourers on the trench in the king's court, the week before Whitsun:

Geoffrey Wrenn	15*d*.
Durand of Eye	
Hugh of Barking	
Thomas of Eye	
William of Feckenham	
Total, 6*s*. 3*d*.	

Total wages of the third payment, £4. 14*s*. 2*d*.

Empciones ad operaciones curie a die Lune proxima post assencionem domini usque in vigilia Pentecost' cum quibusdam emptis de ebdomada precedenti

Franca petra ad caminum

Algaro de Brig' pro Ciij quarter' france petre de Chalved' x sol. vj d.
Radulfo de Lamh' pro CC iij quarter' de eadem quarura xvj sol. vj d.
Ricardo de Croind' pro dim. C de eadem quarura iij sol.

Summa pro franca petra xxx sol.

Franca petra ad lavatorium

Radulfo de Wauttham pro C france petre vj sol.
Willelmo de Brug' pro dim. C france petre iij sol.
Petro de Mucham pro dim. C france petre iij sol.

Summa xij sol.

Empciones diverse ad operaciones curie

Agneti Caffour' pro CCC dim. calcis ad opus camini, lavatorii & coquine xvij sol. vj d. per iij tallias
Henrico de Ponte pro vj gatis & iij luch' xiij d.
Et pro portagiis france petre talliate ad caminum xxj d.
Et Ricardo de Eschip pro ij duodecim craticularum & vj fasciculis virgarum cum portagiis & vectura v sol. iij d.
Ricardo le cuvir pro iij bukettis ix d.

Summa xxvj sol. iiij d.

Roberto le engles & sociis suis pro pollicione lavatorii curie Domini Regis iiij sol.
Henrico de ponte pro ij millibus minitorum [*sic*] clavorum ferri xv d. & pro C dim. ferri tenacis ad opus camini xxv sol.
Et pro iij quarter' carbonis marini cum portagio & vecturis iij sol. vj d.

Summa xxxiij sol. x d.

Item pro portagio iij navatarum grise petre ad tascham de aqua usque ad gardinum xxj d.
Et pro plumbo assidendo in coquina domini Regis cum ij dietis vj sol. iiij d.

Summa viij sol. j d.

Ricardo de celar' pro xxxvj chareis sablonis ad tascham cariendis xj d.
Item Radulfo de Ponte pro xxxvj chareis ad tascham cariandis xj d.

Summa xxij d.

The purchases for the works of the court from Monday following the Ascension of the Lord [26 May] to the vigil of Whitsun [31 May] together with certain things bought the previous week.

Freestone for the chimney:

To Algar of Bridge for one hundredweight and three quarters of Chaldon freestone, 10*s*. 6*d*.

To Ralph of Lambeth for two hundredweight and three quarters of stone from the same quarry, 16*s*. 6*d*.

To Richard of Croydon for half a hundredweight of stone from the same quarry, 3*s*.

Total for freestone, 30*s*.

Freestone for the lavatory:

To Ralph of Waltham for one hundredweight of freestone, 6*s*.

To William of Bridge for half a hundredweight of freestone, 3*s*.

To Peter of Merstham for half a hundredweight of freestone, 3*s*.

Total, 12*s*.

Divers purchases for the works of the court:

To Agnes the lime-burner for three hundredweight and a half of lime for the chimney, lavatory, and kitchen, 17*s*. 6*d*. by three tallies.

To Henry of Bridge for six bowls and three spades, 1*s*. 1*d*.

And for portage of freestone hewn for the chimney, 1*s*. 9*d*.

And to Richard of Eastcheap for two dozen hurdles and six bundles of withies with portage and transport, 5*s*. 3*d*.

To Richard the cooper for three buckets, 9*d*.

Total, 26*s*. 4*d*.

To Robert the English and his fellows for polishing the lavatory of the lord king's court, 4*s*.

To Henry of Bridge for two thousand small iron nails, 1*s*. 3*d*. and for one and a half hundredweight of tough iron for the chimney, 25*s*.

And for three quarters of sea-coal with portage and transport, 3*s*. 6*d*.

Total, 33*s*. 10*d*.

And for portage of three shiploads of ragstone at task from the water to the garden, 1*s*. 9*d*.

And for fixing lead in the lord king's kitchen with two days' work, 6*s*. 4*d*.

Total, 8*s*. 1*d*.

To Richard of the cellar for carrying 36 cart-loads of sand at task, 11*d*.

And to Ralph of Bridge for carrying 36 cart-loads at task, 11*d*.

Total, 1*s*. 10*d*.

4. Pacacio de operacionibus curie a die Jovis infra ebdomadam Pentecost' anno regni Henrici xliij° usque dominicam proximam ante Nativitatem beati Johannis baptiste

Cementarii		
desunt secunda scilicet die Lune in crastino Sancte Trinitatis	Magister Ricardus de Eltham	ij sol. iij d.
	Magister Willelmus de Wauzs	iij sol.
	Walterus de Monden'	xiij d.
	Robertus Pik' Thomas Kenefeg'	vj sol. j d.
deest secunda	Walterus de Waleden'	xiij d.
	Ricardus de Kerwordin Radulfus de Waled'	v sol. j d.
desunt secunda die Martis	Ade filius Warini Johannes de Maldun'	xvij d.
ebdomada secunda venit. deest iij die	Robertus de Beverle	ij sol. vj d.
deest ij die Jovis	Gilebertus Norman	ix d.
deest iij die	Reginaldus Sturmi	xxij d.
	Johannes Burg' Philippus de Hyldel' Johannes le Harper Willelmus de Hampton' Henricus de Wautham	iiij sol.
ebdomada tercia venit	Rogerus de Cicestre	ij sol. ij d.
	Summa lvij sol. x d.	
Cubitores	Willelmus de Bledelewe	v sol. j d.
deest tercia die	Radulfus Oxon'	ij sol. xj d.
ebdomada secunda venit. deest iij die	Henricus de Risebur'	xxij d. Item xiij d.
deest tercia	Willelmus de Bradele	ij sol. xj d.
ebdomada tercia venit	Barethor' Westmon' Willelmus de Asse	ij sol. ij d.
	Summa xviij sol. ij d.	

Carpentarii circa coquinam & gutteram ebdomada secunda

	Willelmus de Waus Henricus de Kintebur'	iiij sol.

4. The payment for the works of the court from Thursday within the week of Pentecost [5 June] in the 43rd year of the reign of King Henry [1259] to the Sunday before the feast of the Nativity of the blessed John the Baptist [22 June].

Masons		
They left the second week, namely on Monday the morrow of Holy Trinity [9 June]	Master Richard of Eltham Master William de Wauzs Walter of Munden	2*s*. 3*d*. 3*s*. 13*d*.
	Robert Pike Thomas Kenfig	6*s*. 1*d*.
He left the second week	Walter of Walden	1*s*. 1*d*.
	Richard of Carwardine Ralph of Walden	5*s*. 1*d*
They left on Tuesday in the second week	Adam son of Warin John of Maldon	1*s*. 5*d*.
He came week 2, left week 3 on [*blank*] day	Robert of Beverley	2*s*. 6*d*.
He went the second week on Thursday	Gilbert Norman	9*d*.
He left week 3 on [*blank*] day	Reginald Sturmi	22*d*.
	John Burg' Philip of Hillsley John the Harper William of Hampton Henry of Waltham	4*s*.
He came week 3.	Roger of Chichester	2*s*. 2*d*.
	Total, 57*s*. 10*d*.	
Layers	William of Bledlow	5*s*. 11*d*.
He left the third week on [*blank*] day	Ralph of Oxford	2*s*. 11*d*.
He came week 2, left week 3 on [*blank*] day	Henry of Risborough	1*s*. 10*d*. Also 13*d*.
He left the third [week]	William of Bradley	2*s*. 11*d*.
He came the third week.	Bartholomew of Westminster William of Ash	2*s*. 2*d*.
	Total, 18*s*. 2*d*.	

Carpenters working on the kitchen and gutter the second week.

William de Waus Henry of Knightsbridge	4*s*.

ebdomada tercia venit die Jovis	Hudin Rogerus	xiij d.
	Summa x sol. ij d.	
ebdomada secunda venit de tribus dietis	Walterus clericus Willelmus clericus	iij sol. vj d.
	Summa iiij sol. iij d.	
	Ricardus faber	vij sol.
deest secunda	Ricardus frater eius	xxij d.
	Summa viij sol. x d.	

Minuti Operarii

deest secunda	Symon scaffot'	ix d.
desunt tercia	Walterus filius Elye Martinus Willelmus Milers	xx d.
deest de iij dietis in ebdomada Pent'	Robertus de Oxon' Rogerus de Chering'	ij sol. iij d. ob. Item vij d. ob.
deest ij	Johannes le portur	vij d. ob.
	Galfridus Wrenn' Duraunt de Eye Hugo de Berking' Thomas de Eye Willelmus de Fecham	ij sol. xi d.
ebdomada ij venerunt	Welbilove Robertus Chubbe Stephanus le Gardiner Johannes Malekin Symon Russell	ij sol. iij d. ob.
ebdomada ij venerunt J stan'	Willelmus de Cofley Johannes Miting Willelmus de Hendon' Robertus de Eye Walterus de Bracino Johannes Cocus Ricardus de Hampslhap' Hugo de Notingeham Johannes Havelove Willelmus de Guldebur' Johannes de Essex Thomas de Thothull	xv d.

He came the third week on Thursday	Odo Roger	13*d*.
	Total, 10*s*. 2*d*.	
He came the second week. For three days	Walter the clerk William the clerk	3*s*. 6*d*.
	Total, 4*s*. 3*d*.	
	Richard the smith	7*s*.
He left the second week	Richard his brother	1*s*. 10*d*.
	Total, 8*s*. 10*d*.	

Labourers

He left the second week	Simon the scaffolder	9*d*.
They left the third week	Walter son of Elias Martin William Milers	1*s*. 8*d*.
He was absent three days in Whitsun week	Robert of Oxford Roger of Charing	2*s*. 3½*d*. Also 7½*d*.
He left in the second week	John the porter	7½*d*.
	Geoffrey Wrenn Durand of Eye Hugh of Barking Thomas of Eye William of Feckenham	2*s*. 11*d*.
They came the second week	Welbilove Robert Chubbe Stephen the gardener John Malekin Simon Russell	2*s*. 3½*d*.
They came the second week	William of Cowley John Miting William of Hendon Robert of Eye Walter of the malt-house John the cook Richard of Hanslope Hugh of Nottingham John Havelove	1*s*. 3*d*.
J. Stan'	William of Goldbury John of Essex Thomas of Tothill	

desunt eadem die Martis	Willelmus de Enefeuld Elyas le Brevetor	ij d. ob.

Summa liij sol. ob.

circa mundacionem necessariorum curie domini regis	Magister Warinus cum tribus hominibus suis per iij dies. Item per ij dies cum uno homine iiij sol. v d.

Summa stipendiorum quarte pacacionis viij li. xviij sol. v d. ob.

Ebdomada Pentecost' operabantur in curia Domini Regis circa caminum & coquinam per diem Jovis, Veneris & Sabbati ebdomada secunda fuit festum Sancti Barnabe per diem Mercurii quod fuit domini regis ebdomada tercia sine festo

Memorandum de xl sol. liberatis Magistro Alexandro ad maeremium emendum ad opus curie die Sabbati proxima ante Nativitatem Sancti Johannis baptiste, unde pro xviij magnis peciis quercus ad cameram forinecam in curia regis xix sol. iij d. ob. Et pro xiij minoribus peciis quercus ad eandem viij sol. viij d. ob. Et pro vectura predicti maeremii de Kingeston' usque Westmonasterium ij sol.

Summa xxx sol.

Empciones diverse ad operaciones curie a die Jovis infra ebdomadam Pentecost' usque ad dominicam proximam ante Nativitatem Sancti Johannis Baptiste.

Algaro de Brug' pro CC dim. france petre ad diversas operaciones curie, camini, cisterne & coquine	xv sol.
Radulfo de Lamh' pro C dim. france petre ad idem	ix sol.
Willelmo de Brug' pro C dim. france petre ad idem	ix sol.

Summa france petre xxxiij sol.

Ricardo le fort pro navata grise petre ad idem	vj sol.
Matheo de ponte pro navata grisse petre ad idem	vj sol. vj d.
Et Agneti Calfonarie pro CCC calcis ad opus cisterne & gutterie post Pentecost' sumpte	xv sol.
Radulfo de Ponte pro j quarter' sablonis ad tascham cariati ad predictas operaciones	vij d. ob.
Item eidem pro dim. C. xiij caretatis sablonis ad opus curie ebdomada iij.	xix d.

Summa xxix sol. viij d. ob.

They left the same week on Tuesday	William of Enfield Elias the Breveter	2½*d.*
	Total, 54*s.* 0½*d.*	

Cleaning out the necessary offices in the lord king's court.

Master Warin with his three men for three days. Also for two days with one man, 4*s.* 5*d.*

Total wages of the fourth payment, £8. 18*s.* 5½*d.*

During Whitsun week work was done in the lord king's court on the chimney and the kitchen on Thursday, Friday, and Saturday. In the second week there was the feast of St. Barnabas on the Wednesday [11 June] which was the lord king's. There was no feast day in the third week.

Note about 40*s.* delivered to Master Alexander to buy timber for the court on Saturday before the feast of the Nativity of St. John the Baptist [21 June]. Whereof for 18 great pieces of oak for the latrine in the king's court, 19*s.* 3½*d.* And for 13 small pieces of oak for the same, 8*s.* 8½*d.* And for transporting the aforesaid timber from Kingston to Westminster, 2*s.*

Total, 30*s.*

Various purchases for the works of the court from Thursday in Whitsun week [5 June] to the Sunday before the Nativity of St. John the Baptist [22 June].

To Algar of Bridge for two hundredweight and a half of freestone for divers works of the court, chimney, cistern, and kitchen, 15*s.*

To Ralph of Lambeth for one hundredweight and a half of freestone for the same, 9*s.*

To William of Bridge for one hundredweight and a half of freestone for the same, 9*s.*

Total of freestone, 33*s.*

To Richard le Fort for a shipload of ragstone for the same, 6*s.*

To Matthew of Bridge for a shipload of ragstone for the same, 6*s.* 6*d.*

And to Agnes the lime-burner for three hundredweight of lime for the cistern and the gutter taken after Whitsun, 15*s.*

To Ralph of Bridge for a quarter of sand carried by task to the aforesaid works, 7½*d.*

And to the same for 73 cart-loads of sand for the court in the third week, 19*d.*

Total, 29*s.* 8½*d.*

Henrico de ponte pro j. mille clavorum ad lathas ix d.
Et pro xv li. picis ad cisternam curie ix sol. iiij d. ob.
Et pro iiij^or li. picis v libris cere ad idem iiij sol. viij d. ob.
Et pro ij millibus clavorum ferri & VC grossiorum ad opus coquine iij sol. vj d.

Summa xviij sol. iiij d.

Willelmo le Clus' pro ferramento ad opus curie, scilicet coquine xxvj d.
Eidem pro martellis fabricandis ante Pentecost' & post iij sol. v d. ob. per ij tall'
Et pro diversis coloribus ad caminum & latera parie[tum] ex utraque parte camini depingenda xj sol. vij d.
Et pro dim. quarter' carbonis lignei ad cysternam cimentandam vij d.
Et pro iij clavibus cum emendacione quarundam serure in curia regis viij d.

Summa xviij sol. v d.

Item Willelmo de Tothull super tascha de magna gutteria xx sol.
Et Willelmo de Midhurst & socio suo pro portagio france petre in curia xv d.

Summa xxj sol. iij d.

Et pro morterio de calce & sablone facto empto de Domino Hugone & [*sic*] Sancto Albano monacho iij sol.
Item Willelmo de Gardino carpentario per iij dies vj d.

Summa iij sol. vj d.

Summa totalis empcionum vj li. iiij sol. ij d. ob.

5. Pacacio facta de operacionibus curie a die Lune in vigilia Nativitatis Sancti Johannis Baptiste anno regni regis Henrici xliij° usque dominicam in festo apostolorum Petri & Pauli per j ebdomadam scilicet continentem festum Nativitatis Sancti Johannis Baptiste per diem Martis quod fuit cementariorum.

[*Carpentarii*]	Willelmus de Waud'	
	Henricus de Knthebur'	
	Odin	
	Rogerus de Westmonasterio	ij sol. ij d.
	Symon Bukethot	
	Rogerus Cornswos	
	Summa xiij sol.	
	Walterus clericus	xxj d.
Plumbariis de iij ebdomadis	Willelmus Plummer	viij sol. vj d.
	Johannes serviens eius	iiij sol. iij d.

To Henry of Bridge for a thousand nails for laths, 9*d.*
And for 15 pounds of pitch for the cistern of the court, 9*s.* 4½*d.*
And for four pounds of pitch and five pounds of wax for the same, 4*s.* 8½*d.*
And for two thousand iron nails and five hundred larger nails for the kitchen, 3*s.* 6*d.*
Total, 18*s.* 4*d.*
To William le Clus' for ironwork for the court, namely for the kitchen, 2*s.* 2*d.*
And to the same for making mauls before and after Whitsun, 3*s.* 5½*d.* by 2 tallies.
And for divers colours to paint the chimney and the walls on each side of the chimney, 11*s.* 7*d.*
And for half a quarter of charcoal to cement the cistern, 7*d.*
And for three keys and mending certain locks in the king's court, 8*d.*
Total, 18*s.* 5*d.*
And to William of Tothill for the task-work of the great gutter, 20*s.*
And to William of Midhurst and his fellow for portage of freestone in the court, 1*s.* 3*d.*
Total, 21*s.* 3*d.*
And for mortar made of lime and sand bought from Dom Hugh of St. Albans, monk, 3*s.*
And to William of the Garden, carpenter, for three days, 6*d.*
Total, 3*s.* 6*d.*
Sum total of purchases, £6. 4*s.* 2½*d.*

5. The payment made for the works of the court from Monday on the eve of the Nativity of St. John the Baptist in the 43rd year of the reign of King Henry [23 June 1259] to Sunday on the feast of the Apostles Peter and Paul [29 June] namely for one week, containing the feast of the Nativity of St. John the Baptist [24 June] on Tuesday which was the masons'.

[*Carpenters*]	William de Waud'	
	Henry of Knightsbridge	
	Odo	
	Roger of Westminster	2*s.* 2*d.*
	Simon Bukethot	
	Roger Cornswos	
	Total, 13*s.*	
	Walter the clerk	21*d.*
Plumbers for 3 weeks	William Plummer	8*s.* 6*d.*
	John his servant	4*s.* 3*d.*

ebdomada iij[a] die Mercurii venit	Simon	xij d.
eadem die Iovis	Johannes Govayr	vj d.
ebdomada j[a] post Pentecost' die sabbati venit. deest iij die Veneris	Ricardus	iiij[or] sol. vj d.
ebdomada ij[a] venit. deest iij die Veneris	Johannes de Radigg'	iiij sol.
ebdomada j[a] venit post Pentecost' die Sabbati. deest iij die Veneris	Deudone	iij sol. vj d.
ebdomada iij[a] venit. deest eadem die Veneris	Garcio	x d.

Summa xxviij sol. x d.

Operarii cum Carpentariis	Walterus Norr' Willelmus de Syreburne Stephanus le Gardiner Johannes Portir Duraunt de Eye	xij d. ob.
circa gutteram	Rogerus de Chering' Galfridus Wrenn' Hugo de Berking' Willelmus de Fecham Thomas de Eye Philippus de Turb' Adam Didewerth' Robertus de Oxon' Hugo de Notingeham Johannes de Chelhuth' Johannes de Essex	xiv d. ob.

	He came week 3 on Wednesday	Simon	12*d.*
	The same week on Thursday	John Govayr	6*d.*
[*Painters*]	He came the first week after Pentecost on Saturday. He left week 3 on Friday	Richard	4*s.* 6*d.*
	He came week 2, left week 3 on Friday	John of Reading	4*s.*
	He came the first week after Whitsun, left week three on Friday	Deudone	3*s.* 6*d.*
	He came week 3, and left the same week on Friday	a boy	10*d.*

Total, 28*s.* 10*d.*

Labourers with the Carpenters	Walter Norris William of Sherborne Stephen the Gardener John Porter Durand of Eye	12½*d.*
on the gutter	Roger of Charing Geoffrey Wrenn Hugh of Barking William of Feckenham Thomas of Eye Philip of Turvey Adam Dedworth Robert of Oxford Hugh of Nottingham John of Chelsea John of Essex	14½*d.*

eadem die Mercurii venerunt	Johannes Miting Walterus de Bracin Johannes Havelove Thomas de Thothull' Rogerus de Knarebur'	x d.
eadem die Jovis	Willelmus fayrwyf Nicholaus de Eboraco Hugo le paumer Philippus filius Willelmi Egidius de Essex	vij d. ob.

Summa xxiij sol.

Summa stipendiorum quinte pacacionis cum tasch' Cv sol.

Empciones ad opus curie

videlicet pro navata grise petre ad gutteram	v sol. vj d.
Elye de Melton' pro navata crete ad idem	ij sol. iiij d.
Hamon le Greger [*sic*] pro navata crete ad idem	ij sol. vij d.
Ricardo de Denitun' pro navata crete ad idem	ij sol. ij d.
Thome le long' pro navata crete ad idem	ij sol. vij d.
Item Ricardo de Deniton' pro navata crete ad idem	ij sol. ij d.
Henrico de Ponte pro iiij millibus clavorum ferri iij sol. vj d. precium M. x d. ob.	
Johanni Gyng' & sociis suis pro portagio	iiij sol ij d.
Ricardo Calfonario pro iij quart' calcis	iij sol. ix d.
Agneti Calfonarie pro iij C calcis	xv sol.
Willelmo de Gardin pro C calcis	v sol.
Radulfo de Ponte pro sablone cariando ad thascham	xviij d.
Waltero de Camera pro biga sua per iij dietas	xij d.
pro emendacione utensilium	xiij d. ob.
Item Henrico pro navata grise petre ad gutteram	v sol.
Aufrido de Strode pro navata eiusdem	vj sol.
Roberto Syrloc pro navata eiusdem	vj sol. ad idem
Ricardo le fort pro navata grise petre	vj sol.

Willelmo de Tothull' ad pacacionem [tasche] sue in curia ad gutteram xxxv sol. under pro pertica de xx^{ti} pedibus cepit xl d. & prius habuit xx sol. & fuerunt xvj perticate & dim.

Item Henrico de Ponte pro dim. mill. de grossis clavis xx d. & pro iiij^{or} mill. & dim. clavorum ad cindulas xlv d. & pro iiij mill. minorum clavorum ij sol. vj d.

Summa Cxviij sol. iij d. ob.

6. Pacacio facta de Operacionibus curie a die Martis proxima post festum Apostolorum Petri & Pauli anno regni regis Henrici xliij^{o} usque dominicam in vigilia beate Thome martiris, videlicet per v dies.

They came the same week on Wednesday	John Miting Walter of the malt-house John Havelove Thomas of Tothill Roger of Knaresborough	10*d.*
They came the same week on Thursday	William fayrwyf Nicholas of York Hugh le paumer Philip son of William Giles of Essex.	7½*d.*

Total, 23*s.*

Total wages of the fifth payment with task-work, 105*s.*

The purchases for the court

Namely for a shipload of ragstone for the gutter, 5*s.* 6*d.*
To Elias of Milton for a shipload of chalk for the same, 2*s.* 4*d.*
To Hamon le Greger for a shipload of chalk for the same, 2*s.* 7*d.*
To Richard of Denton for a shipload of chalk for the same, 2*s.* 2*d.*
To Thomas le long for a shipload of chalk for the same, 2*s.* 7*d.*
Also to Richard of Denton for a shipload of chalk for the same, 2*s.* 2*d.*
To Henry of Bridge for 4,000 iron nails, 3*s.* 6*d.* at 10½*d.* a thousand.
To John Gyng' and his fellows for portage, 4*s.* 2*d.*
To Richard the lime-burner for three quarters of lime, 3*s.* 9*d.*
To Agnes the lime-burner for 3 hundredweight of lime, 15*s.*
To William of the Garden for a hundredweight of lime, 5*s.*
To Ralph of Bridge for carrying sand by task, 1*s.* 6*d.*
To Walter of the Chamber for his cart for three days, 12*d.*
For mending utensils, 13½*d.*
Also to Henry for a shipload of ragstone for the gutter, 5*s.*
To Alfred of Strood for a shipload of the same, 6*s.*
To Robert Syrloc for a shipload of the same, 6*s.* for the same
To Richard le fort for a shipload of ragstone, 6*s.*
To William of Tothill to complete the payment for his task on the gutter in the court, 35*s.*, whereby for a perch of 20 feet he took 40*d.* and he previously had 20*s.* and there were 16½ perches.
And to Henry of Bridge for 500 large nails, 20*d.* and 4,500 nails for shingles, 45*d.* and for 4,000 smaller nails, 2*s.* 6*d.*

Total, 118*s.* 3½*d.*

6. The payment made for the works of the court from Tuesday following the feast of the Apostles Peter and Paul in the 43rd year of the reign of King Henry [1 July 1259] to Sunday on the eve of the blessed Thomas the martyr [6 July], that is for five days.

Carpentarii	Willelmus de Wauzs	
	Henricus de Knyth'brig'	
W. carpentarius recepit	Rogerus Westmon'	xxij d.
	Simon Buketot	
	Rogerus Cornwus	
	Summa ix sol. ij d.	
	Walterus clericus	xxj d.
Operarii	Stephanus Gardiner	
	Galfridus Werenne	
	Thomas de Eye	
	Rogerus de Chering'	xij d. ob.
	Johannes Malekin	
	Adam de Sidewrth'[1]	
	Robertus de Sidwod'	
	Summa ix sol. ob.	

Empciones	Matheo de Ponte pro navata grise petre	vj sol. vj d.
	Roberto Syrloc pro navata grise petre	vj sol.
	Philippo de Brig' pro navata grise petre	v sol. vj d.
W. carpentarius recepit	Ricardo Calfonario pro cent. & quarter. calcis	vj sol. iij d.

Summa totalis pacacionis huius septimane xlii sol. vd. ob.

Summa stipendiorum sexte pacacionis xviij sol. ij d. ob.

7. Pacacio facta a die Lune in festo Translacionis beati Thome Martiris anno regni regis xliij° usque dominicam in festo Sancte Margarete.

Cementarii	Ricardus de Colecestre	iiij^{or} sol.
deest secunda	Guydo de Brun'	xxij d.
	Gervasius de Westmonasterio	iiij sol.
	Henricus Wyting'	
	Summa xiij sol. x d.	
Carpentarii	Willelmus de Waud'	iiij sol. iiij d.
	Henricus de Knithebrig	
	Rogerus de Westmonasterio	
	Symon de Norhaunt'	iiij sol.
	Rogerus Corwous	
	Summa xx sol. viij d.	

[1] *Sic.* But elsewhere his name is 'Didworth'.

Carpenters	William de Wauzs	22*d*.
W. the carpenter received it	Henry of Knightsbridge	
	Roger Westminster	
	Simon Buketot	
	Roger Cornwus	
	Total, 9*s*. 2*d*.	
	Walter the clerk, 1*s*. 9*d*.	
Labourers	Stephen Gardiner	12½*d*.
	Geoffrey Werenne	
	Thomas of Eye	
	Roger of Charing	
	John Malekin	
	Adam of Dedworth	
	Robert de Sidwod	
	Total, 9*s*. 0½*d*.	

Purchases

To Matthew of Bridge for a shipload of ragstone, 6*s*. 6*d*.

To Robert Syrloc for a shipload of ragstone, 6*s*.

To Philip of Bridge for a shipload of ragstone, 5*s*. 6*d*.

W. the carpenter received it — To Richard the lime-burner for a hundredweight and a quarter of lime, 6*s*. 3*d*.

Sum total of this week's payment, 42*s*. 5½*d*.

Total wages of the sixth payment, 18*s*. 2½*d*.

7. The payment made from Monday on the feast of the Translation of the blessed Thomas the martyr in the 43rd year of the reign of King Henry [7 July 1259] to the Sunday on the feast of St. Margaret [20 July]

Masons	Richard of Colchester	4*s*.
He left the second [week]	Guy of Bourne	22*d*.
	Gervase of Westminster	4*s*.
	Henry Wyting	
	Total, 13*s*. 10*d*.	
Carpenters	William de Waud'	4*s*. 4*d*.
	Henry of Knightsbridge	
	Roger of Westminster	4*s*.
	Simon of Northampton	
	Roger Corwous	
	Total, 20*s*. 8*d*.	

	Walterus clericus	
	Summa iij sol. vj d.	
Operarii	Stephanus Gardenir Rogerus de Chering' Galfridus Wrenn' Willelmus de Guldebur'	ij sol. iij d. ob.
	Thomas clericus Nicholaus de Sancto Sepulcro Thomas de Eye	v d.
	Robertus Sidwod	ij sol. iij d. ob.
	Walterus de Malthws Walterus ate Stile	v d.
	Item vij operarii per diem beati Pauli	xvij d. ob.
	Item Gerardo	xij d.
	Item Ricardo de Selar' cum biga	iij sol. viij d.
	Summa xix sol. viij d.	

Summa stipendiorum septime pacacionis lxixj [*sic*] sol. ij d.

Empciones per xv dies precedentes

liberatum Magistro W. de Wald'	scilicet Radulfo de Wautham pro CCC dim. france petre	xxj sol.
	Item Radulfo de Lamh' pro C[1] quarter. france petre	vij sol. vj d.
	Item Philippo de Ponte pro navata grise petre	v sol. vj d.

Item Roberto Syrloc pro navata grise [petre] ad fundamentum camere forinsece	vj sol.
Item Agneti Calfonarie pro C j. quarter. calcis	vj sol. iij d.
Item Willelmo de Gardino pro j quarter. calcis ad opus curie	xv d.
Item Radulfo de Ponte pro areragiis cariagii sablonis	xvj d.
Item Willelmo de Thothull super tascha de fundamento camere fodendo & faciendo	x sol.
Item Willelmo de Clus' pro batell' martellorum & ij paribus wectrium	xvij d.
Item in j serura & j clavi ad opus curie	vj d.
Item Willelmo Bledelawe [cum] j operario per j. diem circa cisternam	vj d. ob.
Item Roberto de Oxeneford per iij dies in septimana in Pentecost' circa coquinam	vij d. ob.
Item ij operariis circa cameram Regine mundandam	v d.
Item ij carpentariis per j diem in curia operantibus	vj d.

Summa lxij sol. x d.

Summa totalis vj li. vj sol.

[1] There has been a confused deletion after 'C', but the clerk's intention seems to have been 'C quart'.

Walter the clerk

Total, 3*s*. 6*d*.

Labourers	Stephen Gardener Roger of Charing Geoffrey Wrenn William of Goldbury	2*s*. $4\frac{1}{2}$*d*.
	Thomas the clerk Nicholas of St. Sepulchre Thomas of Eye	5*d*.
	Robert Sidwod	2*s*. $3\frac{1}{2}$*d*.
	Walter of the malt-house Walter atte Stile	5*d*.

And to seven labourers for the day of the blessed Paul [30 June], $17\frac{1}{2}$*d*.
And to Gerard, 12*d*.
And to Richard of the cellar with his cart, 3*s*. 8*d*.

Total, 19*s*. 8*d*.

Total wages of the seventh payment, 63*s*. 2*d*.[1]

Purchases for the preceding fifteen days

Paid to Master W. of Walden	Namely to Ralph of Waltham for three hundredweight and a half of freestone, 21*s*. And to Ralph of Lambeth for one hundredweight and a quarter of freestone, 7*s*. 6*d*. And to Philip of Bridge for a shipload of ragstone, 5*s*. 6*d*.

And to Robert Syrloc for a shipload of ragstone for the foundation of the latrine, 6*s*.
And to Agnes the lime-burner for a hundredweight and a quarter of lime, 6*s*. 3*d*.
And to William of the garden for a quarter of lime for the court, 15*d*.
And to Ralph of Bridge for the arrears of the carriage of sand, 16*d*.
And to William of Tothill towards the task-work for the digging and making of the foundation of the latrine, 10*s*.
And to William de Clus' for battering [masons'] mauls and for two sets of crowbars, 1*s*. 5*d*.
And for a lock and key for the court, 6*d*.
And to William Bledlow, [with] a labourer, for a day on the cistern, $6\frac{1}{2}$*d*.
And to Robert of Oxford for three days in Whitsun week on the kitchen $7\frac{1}{2}$*d*.
And to two labourers cleansing the queen's [outer] chamber,[2] 5*d*.
And to two carpenters working for one day in the court, 6*d*.

Total, 62*s*. 10*d*.

Sum total, £6. 6*s*.

[1] From the sum total given below this seems to be the figure intended, but the wages actually amount to only 57*s*. 8*d*.

[2] i.e. latrine.

8. Pacacio facta de operibus curie domini regis apud Westmonasterium a die Lune in crastino beate Margarete virginis anno [regni] regis Henrici xliij^{o} usque dominicam proximam post festum beati Petri ad Vincula per quindecim scilicet dies continentes tria festa quorum primum est domini regis, secundum cementariorum, tercium domini regis.

Robertus Pik	Guydo de Brun'	iiij^{or} d. pro festo
deest ij^{a} die Mercurii	Ricardus de Colecestr'	ij sol. vj d. Item iiij^{or} d.
	Gervasius Westmon' Henricus Wyting'	iij sol. viij d. Item iiij d.
	Ricardus de Eynesham	xxij d.
	Summa xiij sol.	
	Willelmus de Wald' Henricus de Knythebrig' Rogerus de Westmonasterio Simon de Norht' Rogerus Cornwos	iij sol. viij d. Item iiij d.
	Reginaldus de Estwik Thomas de Wyndesor	iij sol. viij d.
ebdomada ij^{a} venit	Ricardus le Cuver	xxij d.
eadem die Mercurii post prandium venit	Gilbertus de Guldeford	xiiij d.
	Walterus clericus	iij sol. vj d.
	Summa xxxiij sol. x d.	
W. carpentarius	Stephanus le Gardiner Rogerus de Cherring' Robertus Sidwod	xxij d. ob.
deest ij^{a} Magister Alexander	Willelmus de Guldebur'	x d.
ebdomada ij^{a} venit	Willelmus de Feckam'	xij d. ob.
ebdomada ij^{a} venit	Radulfus de Ponte cum biga	xx d.
W. carpentarius		
	Summa ix sol. ij d.	

Et Willelmo de Thotull' ad perpacacionem tasche sue de fundamento camere forinsece — x sol.

Eidem super tascha de guttera circa lavacrum curie facienda — vij sol. vj d.

8. The payment made for the works of the court of the lord king at Westminster from Monday on the morrow of the feast of the blessed Margaret the Virgin in the 43rd year of the reign of King Henry [21 July 1249] to Sunday following the feast of the blessed Peter in Chains [3 August] namely for a fortnight, containing three feast days of which the first is the lord king's, the second the masons', and the third is the lord king's.

Robert Pik,	Guy of Bourne	4*d.* for a feast day
He left on Wednesday in the 2nd week	Richard of Colchester	2*s.* 6*d.* Also 4*d.*
	Gervase [of] Westminster Henry Wyting	3*s.* 8*d.* Also 4*d.*
	Richard of Eynsham	22*d.*
	Total, 13*s.*	
	William de Wald' Henry of Knightsbridge Roger of Westminster Simon of Northampton Roger Cornwos	3*s.* 8*d.* Also 4*d.*
	Reginald of Eastwick Thomas of Windsor	3*s.* 8*d.*
He came week 2	Richard the cooper	22*d.*
He came the same week on Wednesday after lunch	Gilbert of Guildford	14*d.*
	Walter the clerk	3*s.* 6*d.*
	Total, 33*s.* 10*d.*	
W. the carpenter	Stephen the Gardener Roger of Charing Robert Sidwod	1*s.* 10½*d.*
He left week 2. Master Alexander	William of Goldbury	10*d.*
He came week 2	William of Feckenham	12½*d.*
He came week 2. W. the carpenter	Ralph of Bridge with a cart	20*d.*
	Total, 9*s.* 2*d.*	

And to William of Tothill to complete the payment for his task-work on the foundation of the latrine, 10*s.*

To the same towards the task-work of making a gutter around the lavatory of the court, 7*s.* 6*d.*

Et pro j cent. magnorum bordorum emptorum ad gutteram magne aule	xiiij sol. viij d.
Et Ricardo de Croiden' pro j cent. france petre ad cayum faciendum	vj sol.
Et Willelmo de Brig' pro j cent. & j quarter' ad idem	vij sol. vj d.
Et Randulfo de Regat' pro j quarter' ad idem	xviij d.
Et Radulfo de Lamh' pro j quarter' ad idem	xviij d.
Et Ricardo Calfonario pro j cent. calcis empti ad idem	v sol.
Et Agneti Calfonarie pro ij cent. ad idem	x sol.
Et pro ij mill. clavorum ferri ad lathas & dim. cent. de dornail' ad opus curie	iij sol. vj d.
Et pictoribus de areragiis unius diete	xij d.
Et Willelmo de Clus' fabro pro emendacione martellorum cementariorum	vj d.

Summa stipendiorum octave pacacionis lxxv sol. Summa lxviij sol. viij d. Summa totalis vj li. ij sol. viij d.

Et remansit in sacco xxvij sol. j d.

9. Pacacio facta de operacionibus curie domini Regis apud Westmonasterium a die Lune proxima post festum beati Petri advincula anno regni regis Henrici xliij° usque dominicam in festo Sancti Laurencii, scilicet per ebdomadam sine festo.

Willelmus de Wald' Henricus de Knithebur' Rogerus de Westmonasterio Simon Norhanton' Rogerus Cornwos Reginaldus de Estwyk' Gilebertus de Guldeford Ricardus le cuuir	xxvj d.
Robertus de Audebur'	xviij d.
Walterus clericus	xxj d.
Summa xx sol. vij d.	
Stephanus Gardenir Hugo de Berkink' Thomas de Eye	xv d.
Robertus de Oxonia Johannes portir Johannes de Oxonia	vij d. ob.

And for a hundred great boards bought for the gutter of the great hall, 14*s*. 8*d*.

And to Richard of Croydon for one hundredweight of freestone to make a quay, 6*s*.

And to William of Bridge for a hundredweight and a quarter for the same, 7*s*. 6*d*.

And to Ranulf of Reigate for one quarter [of freestone] for the same, 1*s*. 6*d*.

And to Ralph of Lambeth for one quarter for the same, 1*s*. 6*d*.

And to Richard the lime-burner for one hundredweight of lime bought for the same, 5*s*.

And to Agnes the lime-burner for two hundredweight for the same, 10*s*.

And for two thousand iron nails for laths and half a hundred doornails for the court, 3*s*. 6*d*.

And to the painters for arrears for a day's work, 12*d*.

And to William de Clus' the smith for mending the masons' mauls, 6*d*.

Total wages of the eighth payment, 75*s*. Total, 68*s*. 8*d*.

Sum total, £6. 2*s*. 8*d*. and there remained in the sack 27*s*. 1*d*.

9. The payment made for the works of the lord king's court at Westminster from Monday following the feast of the blessed Peter in Chains [4 August 1259] in the 43rd year of the reign of King Henry to Sunday on the feast of St. Laurence [10 August] that is for a week without a feast day.

William de Wald' Henry of Knightsbridge Roger of Westminster Simon Northampton Roger Cornwos Reginald of Eastwick Gilbert of Guildford Richard the cooper	2*s*. 2*d*.
Robert of Albury	1*s*. 6*d*.
Walter the clerk	1*s*. 9*d*.
Total, 20*s*. 7*d*.	
Stephen Gardener Hugh of Barking Thomas of Eye	15*d*.
Robert of Oxford John Porter John of Oxford	7½*d*.

Geraud' de Bisel' pro camera forinseca purganda	vj d.

Summa vj sol. j.d. ob.

Summa stipendiorum none pacacionis xxvj sol. viij d. ob.

Summa totalis huius pacacionis xxvj sol. viij d. ob.

10. Pacacio facta de operacionibus curie a die dominica in festo beati Laurencii anno regis Henrici xliij° usque dominicam in festo beati Bartholomei per xv dies continentes festum asumpcionis beati Marie quod est cementariorum.

Willelmus de Waus	
Henricus de Knitebreg'	
Rogerus de Westmonasterio	
Simon Norht'	
Rogerus Cornwos	iiij sol. iiij d.
Reginaldus de Estwyk'	
Gilebertus de Guldefort	
Ricardus le Cuver	
Thomas de Windleshore	
Robertus de Audebur'	iij sol.

Summa xlij sol.

Walterus clericus	iij sol. vj d.
Stephanus le Gardener	ij sol. iij d. ob.
Thomas de Eye	xv d.
Rogerus de Cherrink'	ij sol. iij d. ob.
Robertus de Oxonia	vij d. ob.
Hugo de Berkink'	xvij d. ob.
Johannes le portor	vij d. ob.
Johannes de Oxonia	

Summa xij sol. viij d.

Summa stipendiorum decime pacacionis lxvj sol. vij d. ob.

Willelmo de Thothull' ad perpacacionem thasche de guttera in curia Regis vij sol. vj d. Et pro j quarter' calcis de Angnete Calfonaria xv d. Et pro CC lattarum xvj d. Et pro j pelve ad capella[m] xvj d. Et pro C bordorum magnorum emptorum apud Kingeston' xij sol. vj d. Et pro CC dim. de clavis ad plang' & MMM de clavis ad scindulas & pro MM de clavis ad lathas viij sol. vj d. Et Willelmo de Thothull' pro cariagio sablonis ad opus curie iiij sol. v d. ob. Et pro ij seruris ad ostium thesauri xij d.

Summa xxxvij sol. x d. ob.

Summa totalis huius ultime pacacionis iiij li. xij sol. vj d. ob.

Gerard of Bisley for cleansing the latrine, 6*d.*

Total, 6*s.* 1½*d.*

Total wages of the ninth payment, 26*s.* 8½*d.*

Sum total of this payment, 26*s.* 8½*d.*

10. The payment made for the works of the court from Sunday on the feast of blessed Laurence in the 43rd year of the reign of King Henry [10 August 1259] to Sunday on the feast of blessed Bartholomew [24 August] for fifteen days containing the feast of the Assumption of the blessed Mary [15 August] which was the masons'.

William de Waus Henry of Knightsbridge Roger of Westminster Simon Northampton Roger Cornwos Reginald of Eastwick Gilbert of Guildford Richard the cooper Thomas of Windsor	4*s.* 4*d.*
Robert of Albury	3*s.*
Total, 42*s.*	
Walter the clerk	3*s.* 6*d.*
Stephen the Gardener	2*s.* 3½*d.*
Thomas of Eye	1*s.* 3*d.*
Roger of Charing	2*s.* 3½*d.*
Robert of Oxford	7½*d.*
Hugh of Barking	1*s.* 5½*d.*
John the porter John of Oxford	7½*d.*
Total, 12*s.* 8*d.*	

Total wages of the tenth payment, 66*s.* 7½*d*[1]

To William of Tothill in full payment for the task-work of the gutter in the king's court, 7*s.* 6*d.* And for one quarter of lime from Agnes the lime-burner, 1*s.* 3*d.* And for 200 laths, 1*s.* 4*d.* And for one basin for the chapel, 1*s.* 4*d.* And for 100 great boards bought at Kingston, 12*s.* 6*d.* And for two and a half hundred of nails for planks and 3,000 nails for shingles and 2,000 nails for laths, 8*s.* 6*d.* And to William of Tothill for carriage of sand for the court, 4*s.* 5½*d.* And for two locks for the treasury door, 12*d.*

Total, 37*s.* 10½*d.*

Sum total of this last payment, £4. 12*s.* 6½*d.*

[1] The true total is 54*s.* 8*d.*, which was actually used to arrive at the sum total given below.

11. Pacacio facta die Lune in crastino Sancti Bartholomei anno regis Henrici xliij° usque dominicam post festum decollacionis beati Johannis Baptiste per j ebdomadam continentem predictum festum quod fuit domini Regis

Willelmus de Waus Henricus de Knithebur' Rogerus de Westmonasterio Simon de Norht' Rogerus Cornwos Reginaldus de Estwyk' Gilebertus de Gudefort Ricardus le Cuver Thomas de Windleshor' Robertus de Audebur'	xxij d.
Summa xviij sol. iiij d.	
Walterus clericus	xxj d.
Stephanus le gardener Rogerus de Chering'	xij d. ob.
Summa iij sol. x d.	
Summa totalis xxij sol. ij d.	
Summa stipendiorum xj^e pacacionis xxij sol. ij d.	

12. Hec est pacacio facta a die Lune proxima post festum decollacionis beati Johannis Baptiste anno regni regis Henrici xliij° usque in die Sabbati ante festum translacionis beati Edwardi Regis per vj ebdomadas, continencia [*sic*] ij festa, scilicet festum Nativitatis beate Marie per diem Lune quod est cubitorum & carpentariorum & festum beati Michaelis per diem Lune quod est Domini Regis.

	Willelmus de Waus Henricus de Cyntebr' Rogerus Cornwos Reginaldus de Estwyk' Ricardus le Cuver	xij sol. viij d.
	Robertus de Audebur'	viij sol. ix d.
Desunt vj	Rogerus de Westmonasterio Thomas de Windleshor'	x sol. vj. d.
Deest j die Jovis	Gilebertus de Gudefort	xiij d.

11. The payment made from Monday on the morrow of the feast of St. Bartholomew [25 August] in the 43rd year of the reign of King Henry to Sunday after the feast of the beheading of the blessed John the Baptist [31 August] for one week containing the aforesaid feast day which was the lord king's.

William de Waus Henry of Knightsbridge Roger of Westminster Simon of Northampton Roger Cornwos Reginald of Eastwick Gilbert of Guildford Richard the cooper Thomas of Windsor Robert of Albury	1*s.* 10*d.*
Total, 18*s.* 4*d.*	
Walter the clerk,	1*s.* 9*d.*
Stephen the Gardener Roger of Charing	12½*d.*
Total, 3*s.* 10*d.*	

Sum total, 22*s.* 2*d.*

Total wages of the eleventh payment, 22*s.* 2*d.*

12. This is the payment made from Monday following the feast of the beheading of the blessed John the Baptist [1 September] in the 43rd year of the reign of King Henry to Saturday before the feast of the Translation of the blessed Edward the king [11 October] for six weeks containing two feasts, namely the feast of the Nativity of the blessed Mary [8 September] on Monday which is the layers' and carpenters,' and the feast of the blessed Michael [29 September] on Monday which is the lord king's.

	William de Waus Henry of Knightsbridge Roger Cornwos Reginald of Eastwick Richard the cooper	12*s.* 8*d.*
	Robert of Albury	8*s.* 9*d.*
They left week 6	Roger of Westminster Thomas of Windsor	10*s.* 6*d.*
He left week 1 on Thursday	Gilbert of Guildford	1*s.* 1*d.*

	Walterus clericus	vij sol.
	Simon de Norhanton'[1]	xij sol. viij d.[1]
	Summa C sol. xiiij d.	
Ebdomada iij venit. deest v	Deudone	iiij sol. iiij d.
Ebdomada iiij venit. deest v	Ricardus pictor	iij sol.
	Summa vij sol. iiij d.	
Ebdomada ij venit. deest iij die Mercurii	Radulfus de Oxonia	ij sol. ij d.
	Robertus Busch'	x sol. ij d.
	Ricardus de Reherfeld	viij sol.
Ebdomada iij venit. deest eadem die Mercurii	Galfridus de Piro	viij d. ob.
Ebdomada iij die Martis	Hugo de Mertune	vij sol. viij d.
Ebdomada iij venit die Veneris deest iiij die Martis	Robertus le Blund	xvij d.
Ebdomada iij venit die Veneris	Ricardus de Kinesham	vj sol. vj d. ob.
	Roger Wombe	iij sol. viij d.
	Summa xl sol. iiij d.	
Ebdomada prima venit	Stephanus le Gardenir Rogerus de la Cherrink'	vij sol. j d.
Ebdomada ij venit	Walterus de Nyweport Girardus Bisel' Gillot de Perham	v sol. x d.
desunt vj	Ricardus de Lichefeld Adam Miting Simon Rossel	Item eidem v d.[1] iiij sol. vij d.
Ebdomada iij venit die Veneris	Johannes de Enesham	iij sol. x d. ob.
	Fukes	xij d. ob.
	Johannes Stronge[1]	ij sol iij d. ob.[1]

[1] Added later.

	Walter the clerk	7*s.*
	Simon of Northampton	12*s.* 8*d.*
	Total, 100*s.* 14*d.*[1]	
He came week 3, left week 5	Deudone	4*s.* 4*d.*
He came week 4, left week 5	Richard the painter	3*s.*
	Total, 7*s.* 4*d.*	
He came week 2, and went week 3 on Wednesday	Ralph of Oxford	2*s.* 2*d.*
	Robert Busch'	10*s.* 2*d.*
	Richard of Rotherfield[2]	8*s.*
He came week 3, left the same week on Wednesday	Geoffrey de Piro	8½*d.*
He came week 3 on Tuesday	Hugh of Merton	7*s.* 8*d.*
He came week 3 on Friday left week 4 on Tuesday	Robert le Blund	1*s.* 5*d.*
He came week 3 on Friday	Richard of Eynsham	6*s.* 6½*d.*
	Roger Wombe	3*s.* 8*d.*
	Total, 40*s.* 4*d.*	
They came week 1	Stephen the Gardener Roger of Charing	7*s.* 1*d.*
They came week 2	Walter of Newport Gerard of Bisley Gillot of Parham	5*s.* 10*d.*
They left week 6	Richard of Lichfield Adam Miting Simon Russell	Also to him 5*d.* 4*s.* 7*d.*
He came week 3 on Friday	John of Eynsham	3*s.* 10½*d.*
	Fukes	12½*d.*
	John Stronge	2*s.* 3½*d.*

[1] This was the correct total before Simon of Northampton's 12*s.* 8*d.* was added.

[2] In E 101/467/2 he appears as Ricardus 'de Bureford', i.e. of Burford.

Henricus de Bedeminist'[1] xij d. ob.
Biga diurna per iiij dies ii sol.
Summa lij sol. iiij d.[2]
Summa stipendiorum xij^{e} pacacionis xiiij li. xviij sol. iij d. ob.
Summa summarum stipendiorum l li. xviij sol. vj d.

[*Empciones a die Lune proxima post festum decollacionis beati Johannis Baptiste usque in die Sabbati ante festum translacionis beati Edwardi regis per vj ebdomadas*][3]

Ebdomada prima sine festo

Ebdomada secunda continens festum Nativitatis beate Marie Virginis quod est cementariorum in empcionibus grise petre eadem ebdomada & clavorum ferri

Willelmo Prudfot pro j navata v sol. ix d.
Edmundo filio Radulfi pro j navata grise petre v sol. ix d.
Henrico Mereweder pro j navata grise petre v sol. ix d.
Roberto de Hakeford' pro eadem v sol. ix d.
Ricardo Makefair pro eadem iiij sol. vj d.
Henrico de Ponte pro vij^{M} clavorum ad sindulas x sol. vj d. precium cuiuslibet M. xviij d.
Et pro MM clavorum ad lattas de quercu ij sol.
Summa empcionis secunde ebdomade xl sol.

Ebdomada tercia sine festo in empcionibus grise petre & clavorum ferri eadem ebdomada

Willelmo Prudfot pro j navata grise petre v sol. ix d.
Edmundo filio Roberti [*sic*] pro eadem v sol. ix d.
Ricardo filio Josselini pro eadem iiij sol. vj d.
Henrico de Ponte pro vj^{M}, viij sol., precium cuiuslibet M, xvj d. & pro [C]C grosse [*sic*] clavorum ad plang' iij sol. ij d., precium C, xix d. & eidem Henrico pro MMMM grosse clavorum, scilicet dorenail vj sol. viij d., precium cuiuslibet M, xx d. Et pro MM clavorum ad latas de quercu ij sol. Et pro MM clavorum ad latas de foul' xxij d. Et pro CC tingelnal' vj d.
Hugoni maerenario pro xviij tingnis de quercu & xvj punsuns de eadem viij sol. vj d. ob. Et pro iiij perticis & dim. muri facti ad thascham iij sol. vj d.
Et pro CC rossis ad murum cooperiendum xviij d.
& pro litera ad dictum murum vj d.
Summa empcionum tercie ebdomade lj sol. vij d. ob.[4]

Ebdomada quarta sine festo
Ricardo Curtais pro C. caretarum & dim. sablonis iij sol.

[1] Added later.
[2] This is the correct total before the insertion of the later entries.
[3] There is no heading in the MS.
[4] Reading uncertain. The correct total of *lij sol. ij d. ob.* may be intended.

Henry of Bedminster 12½*d.*
A cart daily for four days 2*s.*

Total 52*s.* 4*d.*

Total wages of the twelfth payment, £14. 18*s.* 3½*d.*

Sum total of wages, £50. 18*s.* 6*d.*

[*Purchases from Monday following the feast of the beheading of the blessed John the Baptist* [*1 September*] *to Saturday before the feast of the Translation of the blessed Edward the king* [*11 October*] *for six weeks.*]

The first week with no feast day.

The second week containing the feast of the Nativity of the blessed Mary the Virgin [8 September] which is the masons', in purchases of ragstone the same week and iron nails.

To William Prudfot for one shipload, 5*s.* 9*d.*

To Edmund son of Ralph for one shipload of ragstone, 5*s.* 9*d.*

To Henry Mereweder for one shipload of ragstone, 5*s.* 9*d.*

To Robert of Hackford for the same, 5*s.* 9*d.*

To Richard Makefair for the same, 4*s.* 6*d.*

To Henry of Bridge for 7,000 nails for shingles, 10*s.* 6*d.*, price of each thousand 1*s.* 6*d.*

And for two thousand nails for oak laths, 2*s.*

Total purchases of the second week, 40*s.*

The third week without a feast in purchases of ragstone and iron nails the same week.

To William Prudfot for a shipload of ragstone, 5*s.* 9*d.*

To Edmund son of R[alph] for the same, 5*s.* 9*d.*

To Richard son of Jocelin for the same, 4*s.* 6*d.*

To Henry of Bridge for 6,000 [nails], 8*s.* price of each thousand 16*d.*, and for 200 large nails for planks, 3*s.* 2*d.*, price of a hundred 19*d.* and to the same Henry for 4,000 large nails namely doornails, 6*s.* 8*d.*, price of a thousand 20*d.* And for 2,000 nails for oak laths, 2*s.* And for 2,000 nails for beech laths, 1*s.* 10*d.* And for 200 tingelnail, 6*d.*

To Hugh the timber-merchant for 18 oak timbers and 16 puncheons of the same timber, 8*s.* 6½*d.*

And for making four and a half perches of a wall by task-work, 3*s.* 6*d.*

And for two hundredweight of reeds to cover the wall, 1*s.* 6*d.*

And for straw for the said wall, 6*d.*

Total of purchases for the third week, 51*s.* 7½*d.*[1]

The fourth week with no feast day.

To Richard Curtais for 150 cart-loads of sand, 3*s.*

[1] See note 4 opposite.

Ricardo de celario pro C caretarum sablonis ij sol.
Willelmo de Braye pro M latarum de quercu ad herberchar' viij sol. viij d.
Et pro V charr' plumbi fundendi[s] & assidendi[s] in gutter' aule Domini Regis xxv sol.
Et pro portagio predicti rossis ad aquam & vectura per aquam de Wyhyfeld usque Westmonasterium vj d.
Et pro iiij M. et C dim. tingol' ad cooperiendum herberch' xiij sol. viij d. per ij tallias

Summa empcionis quarte ebdomade lij sol. x d.

Ebdomada quinta sine festo
Henrico de Ponte pro MM scingularum & MM clavorum ad latas iiij sol. viij d.
Et pro CC dim. calcis xij sol. vj d.
Et ij clavibus & emendacione ij serurarum v d.
Et pro MMMM clavorum ad tegulas vj d. Item j d. ob.
Item Ricardo cuteis pro V quarter' sabelonis cariandis cum biga iij sol. ij d.
Item Waltero de la chaumbre pro C caretarum sabelonis pro ij dietis ij sol. viij d.
Item pro ij seruris xv d. ob.
Item Henrico de Ponte pro M & VC calvis [*sic*] ferri ad sendulas ij sol. iij d.
Willelmo de Sempeveld pro VC de tingles xviij d.

Summa xxix sol. j d.[1]

Summa summarum viij li. xiij sol. vij d. ob.

Item magistro Willelmo pictori & tribus servientibus suis pingentibus caminum & parietes ex utraque parte camini in thalamo Domini Regis per iiij ebdomadas xxxvj sol. vj d.
Et pro diversis coloribus ad dictum caminum depingendum vij sol. vj d.

Summa stipendiorum & colorum circa caminum xliiij sol.

Item quindecim minutis operariis & ij bigis diurnis per quindenam circa herbarium Domini Regis operantibus xxij sol. xj d.
Item memorandum de C solidis prestitis ad pacacionem faciendam de operacionibus per iij ebdomodas ante predictum tempus
Ricardo Curteys pro iij dietis cum biga xij d.
Item eidem vij d.
Item iij plumbariis pro j ebdomada & pro iij dietis antea vj sol. iij d.
Item Radulfo Cordewanir iiij d. d. ob.
Item iij carpentariis & ij operariis per ij dietas xij d.

Summa viij li. xvj sol. j d. ob.

[1] Several erasures and deletions and one incorrect total (superseded by the one printed but not deleted in the MS.) have here been omitted. The last two items in the account for the 5th week were added later, and comparison with E 101/467/2 (p. 375) shows that they in fact represent the expenditure in the 6th and last week.

To Richard of the cellar for 100 cart-loads of sand, 2*s*.
To William of Bray for 1,000 oak laths for the *herberchar'*,[1] 8*s*. 8*d*.
And for melting and laying five chars of lead on the gutter of the lord king's hall, 25*s*.
And for portage of the said reeds to the water and transport by water from Wyhyfeld to Westminster, 6*d*.
And for 4,150 tiles to roof the *herberchar'*,[1] 13*s*. 8*d*. by two tallies.

Total purchases of the fourth week, 52*s*. 10*d*.

The fifth week with no feast day.
To Henry of Bridge for 2,000 shingles and 2,000 nails for laths, 4*s*. 8*d*.
And for two hundredweight and a half of lime, 12*s*. 6*d*.
And for two keys and repairing two locks, 5*d*.
And for 4,000 pegs for tiles, 6*d*. Also 1½*d*.
Also to Richard Cu[r]teis for carrying five quarters of sand with a cart, 3*s*. 2*d*.
And to Walter of the Chamber for 100 cart-loads of sand for two days, 2*s*. 8*d*.
For two locks, 1*s*. 3½*d*.
And to Henry of Bridge for 1,500 iron nails for shingles, 2*s*. 3*d*.
To William of Smithfield for 500 tiles, 1*s*. 6*d*.

Total, 29*s*. 1*d*.

Sum total, £8. 13*s*. 7½*d*.

And to Master William the painter and his three servants painting the chimney and the walls on each side of the chimney in the chamber of the lord king for four weeks, 36*s*. 6*d*.
And for divers colours to paint the said chimney, 7*s*. 6*d*.

Total wages and colours for the chimney, 44*s*.

And to fifteen labourers and two carts daily working for fifteen days on the lord king's lawn, 22*s*. 11*d*.
And note that 100*s*. were advanced to pay for the works for three weeks before the aforesaid time.
To Richard Curteys for three days' work with his cart, 12*d*.
And to the same, 7*d*.
And to three plumbers for one week and three days at an earlier period, 6*s*. 3*d*.
And to Ralph Cordwainer, 4½*d*.
And to three carpenters and two labourers for two days' work, 12*d*.

Total, £8. 16*s*. 1½*d*.

[1] The precise significance of *herberchar'* is doubtful. The word *herlebecheria* occurs at Clarendon, where it is thought to have meant a scullery (*History of the King's Works*, ii, p. 912).

Memorandum quod Martinus de Campo Florum solvit magistro Alexandro carpentario lxxiij sol. vij d. ob. ad pacacionem curie Domini Regis die Martis proxima post festum apostolorum Petri & Pauli.

Item magistro Alexandro xx sol. ad maeremium emendum.

De xi liberatis

Memorandum quod Martinus de Campo Florum solvit Matheo de Ponte de Elesfort et sociis suis pro j navata grise petre vj sol. vj d. die Sabbati post festum apostolorum Petri & Pauli. Item idem cepit de eisdem ix libris xlij sol. ad pacacionem curie domini Regis.

Memorandum de xl sol. liberatis magistro Alexandro ad maeremium emendum ad opus curie Domini Regis die Sabbati proxima ante Nativitatem beati Johannis Baptiste

unde pro xviij grossis peciis de quercu ad cameram forinsecam in curia Domini Regis construendam xix sol. iij d. ob.

Et pro xiij minoribus peciis de quercu ad eandem viij sol. viij d. ob.

Pro cariagio eiusdem maeremii usque monesterium ij sol.

Summa xxx sol. & ita remanent x sol. penes magistrum Alexandrum.

Item memorandum de C solidis sumptis de scaccario & liberatis magistro Alexandro ad maeremium emendum apud Kingeston' in vigilia apostolorum Petri & Pauli

Item de x sol. residuis de priori empcione

Summa Cx sol.

unde in decem M cindularum de quercu ad cooperturam predicte camere lxx sol. precium mill. vij sol.

Et in xlj peciis de quercu ad ea[n]dem cameram xxj sol. x d.

Et in xlix bordis minutis de quercu xiij d.

Et pro iij grossis postibus de quercu vij sol. vj d.

Pro cariagio predicti maeremii ij sol.

Summa Cij sol. v d. & ita remanent penes magistrum Alexandrum vij sol. vij d. in toto.

Memorandum de xxix peciis grossis & minutis de quercu emptis apud Kingeston' die Sabbati proxima post festum apostolorum Petre & Pauli pro xij sol. ix d.

Et cariag' eiusdem maeremii per aquam ij sol.

Summa xiiij^or sol. ix d.

ad quod magister Alexander habuit vij sol. vij d. de denariis ei prius liberatis ad maeremium emendum & ita debentur ei adhuc vij sol. ij d. quos ei solvit Martinus de Campo Florum.

Note that Martin de Chanflur paid Master Alexander the carpenter 73*s*. 7½*d*. to pay for the court of the lord king on Tuesday after the feast of the Apostles Peter and Paul [1 July].
And to Master Alexander 20*s*. to buy timber.

Concerning [£?]11 paid.
Note that Martin de Chanflur paid Matthew of Bridge of Aylesford and his fellows for one shipload of ragstone 6*s*. 6*d*. on Saturday after the feast of the Apostles Peter and Paul [5 July]. Also from those £9 he took 42*s*. to make payment for the court of the lord king.

Note of 40*s*. delivered to Master Alexander to buy timber for the lord king's court on Saturday before the feast of the Nativity of the blessed John the Baptist [21 June].
whereof for 18 large pieces of oak to build the latrine in the lord king's court, 19*s*. 3½*d*.
And for 13 smaller pieces of oak for the same, 8*s*. 8½*d*.
For the carriage of the same timber to the monastery, 2*s*.
Total, 30*s*. and thus there remains 10*s*. in the possession of Master Alexander.
Also note of 100*s*. taken from the Exchequer and delivered to Master Alexander to buy timber at Kingston on the eve of the feast of the Apostles Peter and Paul [28 June].
Also of 10*s*. remaining from the previous purchase
Total, 110*s*.
whereof for 10,000 oak shingles to roof the aforesaid chamber, 70*s*. at 10*s*. a thousand: and in 41 pieces of oak for the same chamber, 21*s*. 10*d*.
And for 49 small oak boards, 13*d*.
And for three large oak posts, 7*s*. 6*d*.
For carriage of the aforesaid timber 2*s*.
Total, 102*s*. 5*d*. and thus there remains in the possession of Master Alexander, 7*s*. 7*d*. in all.

Note about 29 pieces of oak, large and small, bought at Kingston the Saturday following the feast of the Apostles Peter and Paul [5 July] for 12*s*. 9*d*.
And carriage of the same timber by water, 2*s*.
Total, 14*s*. 9*d*.
for which Master Alexander had 7*s*. 7*d*. of moneys previously delivered to him to buy timber and thus there are still owed to him 7*s*. 2*d*. which Martin de Chanflur paid to him.

Memorandum quod de xx sol. argenti liberatis magistro Alexandro apposuit idem die Sabbati proxima post Translacionem beati Thome Martiris apud Kingeston' in xxix peciis de quercu viij sol. xj d.
Et in VC latharum emptis ibidem iij sol.
Et in cariagio eiusdem maeremii per aquam ij sol.
Summa xiij sol. xj d. et ita restant vj sol. j d.

Memorandum quod Martinus de Campo florum & magister Johannes cementarius receperunt ad scaccarium C sol. ad operaciones eis iniunctas perficiendas.
Idem recepit adhuc ad easdem viij marcas. Idem recepit adhuc ad easdem viij li. viij sol. Item xl sol. per manus domini E. clerici & postea fuerunt ei persoluti. Item xl sol. Item xx li. iiij^{or} sol. vj d. Item C sol. Item Cx sol. vj d.

Memorandum quod Martinus de Campo florum liberavit magistro Alexandro carpentario viij^{o} marcas quas receperat ad scaccarium ad pacandum pro operibus de Westmonasterio. Item eidem xl sol. ad maeremium emendum die Sabbati proxima ante Nativitatem Sancti Johannis Baptiste.
Item C sol. liberat' eidem ad meeremium emendum.

Note that of 20*s.* in silver delivered to Master Alexander, he laid out on Saturday following the feast of the Translation of the blessed Thomas the Martyr [12 July] at Kingston on 29 pieces of oak, 8*s.* 11*d.*
And on 500 laths bought there, 3*s.*
And in carriage of the same timber by water, 2*s.*
Total 13*s.* 11*d.*, and thus remains 6*s.* 1*d.*

Note that Martin de Chanflur and Master John the mason received at the Exchequer 100*s.* to complete the works enjoined on them.
He further received for the same, £5. 6*s.* 8*d.*
He further received for the same, £8. 8*s.*
Also 40*s.* by the hands of Sir E. the clerk and afterwards they were paid to him in full.
Also 40*s.* Also £20. 4*s.* 6*d.* Also 100*s.* Also 110*s.* 6*d.*

Note that Martin de Chanflur delivered to Master Alexander the carpenter £5. 6*s.* 8*d.* which he had received at the Exchequer to make payment for the Westminster works. Also to the same 40*s.* to buy timber on Saturday before the feast of the Nativity of St. John the Baptist [21 June]
Also 100*s.* delivered to him to buy timber.

8. Payments for works at Westminster Palace from 27 October to 21 December, 1259
(E 101/622/19)

14. Pacacio facta a die lune in vigilia Apostolorum Symonis & Jude anno regis Henrici xliiij^{o} incipiente usque in die sabbati proxima post festum Sancti Martini. videlicet per iij. ebdomadas continentes tria festa. primum fuit cementariorum. secundum Domini Regis. tercium cementariorum.

Carpentarii circa cooperacionem coquine Regis & Domorum Vicinarum.

	Willelmus de Waus	
	Roger Cornwous	vj ij d.
	Henricus de Knitth'	
Ebdomada ij^{a}	Robertus de Aldebury	iiij sol. iij d.
	Gilebertus carpentarius	
	Johannes Greneford	iiij sol. iiij d.
	Johannes de Padinton'	
	Summa xxxv sol. ix d.	

Cementarii circa quamdam fenestram in domo Justiciariorum Judeorum.

	Johannes de Oxon'	vj sol. ij d.
Ebdomada ij	Ricardus de Sicestr'	
	Johannes Eltham	xxvj d.
desunt iij^{a}	Reginaldus Sturmin	
	Walterus clericus	v sol. iij d.
	Summa xvij sol. xj d.	

Fabri circa caminum sustinendum in camera Domini regis.

Magister H. faber	xij sol.
Symon	vj sol. ij d.
Willelmus de Offinton'	iiij sol. iij d.
Thorold	iiij sol. ix d.
Summa xxvij s. ij d.	

Operarii

	Stephanus de Gardin	iij sol. j d. ob.
	Rogerus de Cherringe	
deest ij^{a}	Johannes Curaunt	x d.
	Summa vij sol. j d.	

8. Payments for works at Westminster Palace from 27 October to 21 December, 1259

14. The payment made from Monday on the eve of the Apostles Simon and Jude [27 October] at the beginning of the 44th year of King Henry [1259] to Saturday next after the feast of Saint Martin [15 November], that is to say for 3 weeks including three feasts. The first was the masons', the second the lord king's, the third the masons'.

Carpenters [working] upon the roofing of the king's kitchen and the adjacent buildings

	William de Waus Roger Cornwous Henry of Knightsbridge	6*s*. 2*d*.
2nd week	Robert of Albury	4*s*. 3*d*.
	Gilbert the carpenter John Greenford John of Paddington	4*s*. 4*d*.
	Total, 35*s*. 9*d*.	

Masons [working] upon a certain window in the building of the Justices of the Jews

	John of Oxford	6*s*. 2*d*.
Week 2 Left in the third	Richard of Chichester John Eltham Reginald Sturmin	26*d*.
	Walter the clerk	5*s*. 3*d*.
	Total, 17*s*. 11*d*.	

Smiths [working] upon supporting a chimney in the lord king's chamber

Master H[enry] the smith	12*s*.
Simon	6*s*. 2*d*.
William of Uffington	4*s*. 3*d*.
Thorold	4*s*. 9*d*.
Total, 27*s*. 2*d*.	

Labourers

	Stephen of the Garden Roger of Charing	3*s*. 1½*d*.
Left in the second	John Corant	10*d*.
	Total, 7*s*. 1*d*.	

Empciones

pro ij. mill. minuti [*sic*] clavorum ad lathas & pro j. mill. maiorum iij sol. vj.d.

Item pro iiij^{or} mill. & dim. clavorum ad lathas & pro M.M. gross[i]oribus. & pro CCC dim. clavorum ad cendulas cum vectura per aquam ix sol. ob.

Et pro C calcis v sol.

Item pro quadam serura cum clave & emendacione serure xviij d.

Summa empcionum xix s. ob.

Summa totalis C.vj.s. xj d. ob.

15. Pacacio de Operacionibus Curie regis Westmonasterii facta a die Lune proxima post festum beati Martini anno regis Henrici xliiij^{to} usque dominicam in festo Sancti Andree apostoli proximo sequenti, per xv scilicet dies continentes festum beati Edmundi regis & martiris quod fuit domini regis & festum beate Caterine virginis quod fuit carpentariorum & cementariorum de C xviij sol. iij d. ob. receptis de thesauro vigilia beate Lucie virginis & ipso die beate Lucie pacatis per manus Ade clerici & magistri Alexandri carpentarii.

Cementarii

videlicet cementariis operantibus circa fenestram & bancos in domo Judeorum & circa gistas ultra cameram senescallorum sublevandas. videlicet Johanni de Oxonia per xv dies iiij^{or} sol. Et Ricardo de Colecestr' per j ebdomadam circa idem ij sol. Et Bartholomeo Westm' per eamdem ebdomadam ij sol. Et Waltero clerico per xv dies iij sol. vj d.

Summa xj s. vj d.

Carpentarii

videlicet Willelmo de Waud' Rogero Cornwus Henrico de Knyth'brug' Gilberto carpentario Johanni de Greneford Johanni de Padinton' operantibus circa coquinam regis scindulandam & gistas predictas sublevandas per predictam quindenam xxiiij sol. cuilibet illorum scilicet iiij sol. Et Roberto de Aldebir' circa idem per idem tempus ij sol. ix d.

Summa xxvj sol. ix d.

Fabri

videlicet magistro H. fabro circa ferramentum ad sustentandum & efforciandum tuellum camini camere regis per predictam quindenam viij^{to} sol. Et Simoni fabro per idem tempus iiij^{or} sol. Et Willelmo de Offinton' per idem tempus ij sol. ix d. Et Thoraudo per idem tempus

Purchases

For 2,000 small nails for laths and for 1,000 larger ones, 3*s*. 6*d*.

Item for 4,500 nails for laths and for 2,000 bigger ones and for 350 nails for shingling, with conveyance by water, 9*s*. 0½*d*.

And for 1 hundredweight of lime, 5*s*.

Item for a certain lock with a key and for repair of a lock, 18*d*.

Total of purchases, 19*s*. 0½*d*.

Sum total, £5. 6*s*. 11½*d*.

15. The payment for works at the king's court of Westminster made from Monday next after the feast of the blessed Martin [17 November] in the 44th year of King Henry [1259] to Sunday on the feast of Saint Andrew the apostle next following [30 November], that is to say for 15 days including the feast of the blessed Edmund King & Martyr [20 November], which was the lord king's and the feast of the blessed Catherine the Virgin [25 November], which was the carpenters' and masons'—of £5. 18*s*. 3½*d*. received from the Treasury on the eve of the blessed Lucy the Virgin [12 December] and paid on the same day of the blessed Lucy [13 December] by the hands of Adam the clerk and Master Alexander the carpenter.

Masons

That is to say masons working upon a window and benches in the building [of the Justices] of the Jews and upon raising joists above the stewards' chamber, that is to say to John of Oxford for 15 days, 4*s*. And to Richard of Colchester for 1 week upon the same, 2*s*. And to Bartholomew of Westminster for the same week, 2*s*. And to Walter the clerk for 15 days, 3*s*. 6*d*.

Total, 11*s*. 6*d*.

Carpenters

That is to say to William de Waud', Roger Cornwus, Henry of Knightsbridge, Gilbert the carpenter, John of Greenford, John of Paddington, working upon shingling the king's kitchen and raising the aforesaid joists during the aforesaid fortnight, 24*s*., to each of them that is to say, 4*s*. And to Robert of Albury [working] upon the same for the same time, 2*s*. 9*d*.

Total, 26*s*. 9*d*.

Smiths

That is to say to Master H[enry] the smith [working] upon ironwork to support and strengthen the flue of the chimney of the king's chamber for the aforesaid fortnight, 8*s*. And to Simon the smith for the same time, 4*s*. And to William of Uffington for the same time, 2*s*. 9*d*. And

iij sol. j d. Et omnibus predictis fabris pro vigiliis suis de nocte per j. mensam ad predictum ferramentum festinandum vj sol. viij d.

Summa xxiiij^or sol. vj d.

Operarii

Et operariis deservientibus cementariis & carpentariis videlicet Stephano de Gardino per predictos xv dies ij sol. j d. Et Rogero de Cherring' per idem tempus ij sol. j d.

Et tribus operariis juvantibus fabros & scaffot' circa caminum predictum per j ebdomadam iij sol. j d. ob. cuilibet illorum scilicet xij d. ob.

Et duobus operariis videlicet Waltero Norr' Willelmo de Scyreburn' qui scyaverunt ligna per j. ebdomadam & iiij^or dies iij sol. ix d.

Summa xj sol. ob.

Tasche plumbariorum

Willelmo de Strande & Johanni Govair' pro viij^to char' plumbi ad tascham fundendis iactandis & cubandis ultra cameram senescallorum xl sol. precium char' v sol.

Et magistro Odoni pro carecta sua per j diem eunte ad plumbum & buscam vj d.

Et Willelmo de Clus' super tascha de ferramento ad fenestram in domo Judeorum cum emendacione quorumdam aliorum in curia regis iiij^or sol.

Summa xliiij sol. vj d.

Summa totalis huius pacacionis c xviij sol. iij d. ob.

16. Pacacio facta a die Lune in crastino Sancti Andree apostoli anno regis Henrici xliiij^o usque dominicam in crastino Sancte Lucie virginis per xv dies continentes festum beati Nicholai per diem sabbati quod fuit domini regis & festum concepcionis beate virginis per diem Lune quod fuit carpentariorum de C xv sol. receptis de Thesauro, que pacacio fiebat per visum Magistri Alexandri carpentarii & Ade clerici de recepta.

Carpentarii

videlicet Willelmo de Waud' Rogero Westm' Rogero Cornwus Gilberto carpentario Henrico de Knyth' Johanni de Padinton' per predictos xv dies operantibus circa sedes Justiciariorum de Banco & emendacionem pontis regis & cooperturam coquine xxiiij^or sol. videlicet cuilibet illorum iiij^or sol. Et Roberto de Aldebir' peridem tempus ij s. ix d. Et Johanni de Greneford per j. ebdomadam xxij d.

Summa xxviij sol. vij d.

to Thorold for the same time, 3*s*. 1*d*. And to all the aforesaid smiths for their night work for one month to hasten the said ironwork, 6*s*. 8*d*.
Total, 24*s*. 6*d*.

Labourers

And to labourers assisting the masons and carpenters, that is to say to Stephen of the Garden for the aforesaid 15 days, 2*s*. 1*d*. And to Roger of Charing for the same time, 2*s*. 1*d*.

And to three labourers helping the smiths and scaffolders on the aforesaid chimney for 1 week, 3*s*. 1½*d*. To each of them that is to say, 12½*d*.

And to two labourers, that is to say to Walter Norris [and] William of Sherborne, who were sawing wood for 1 week and 4 days, 3*s*. 9*d*.
Total, 11*s*. 0½*d*.

Plumbers' task-works

To William of Strand and John Govair for founding, casting, and laying 8 chars of lead at task above the stewards' chamber, 40*s*. price per char, 5*s*.

And to Master Odo for going with his cart for one day for lead and firewood, 6*d*.

And to William de Clus' upon task-work for ironwork for a window in the building [of the Justices] of the Jews with repair of certain others in the king's court, 4*s*.
Total, 44*s*. 6*d*.
Sum total of this payment, £5. 18*s*. 3½*d*.

16. The payment made from Monday on the morrow of Saint Andrew the apostle [1 December] in the 44th year of King Henry [1259] to Sunday on the morrow of Saint Lucy the Virgin [14 December] for 15 days including the feast of the blessed Nicholas [6 December] on Saturday, which was the lord king's and the feast of the Conception of the Blessed Virgin [8 December] on Monday which was the carpenters'—of £5. 15*s*. received from the Treasury, which payment was made by the view of Master Alexander the carpenter and of Adam, clerk of the Receipt.

Carpenters

That is to say to William de Waud', Roger of Westminster, Roger Cornwus, Gilbert the carpenter, Henry of Knightsbridge, John of Paddington, working for the aforesaid 15 days upon the seats of the Justices of the Bench and repair of the king's bridge and roofing of the kitchen, 24*s*., that is to say to each of them, 4*s*. And to Robert of Albury for the same time, 2*s*. 9*d*. And to John of Greenford for 1 week, 22*d*.
Total, 28*s*. 7*d*.

Cementarii

Johanni de Oxon' circa gistas ultra cameram senescallorum elevandas per predictum tempus iiij^or sol. Et Waltero clerico per idem tempus. iij sol. vj d. Et cuidam plumbario per j. dietam iiij d.

Summa vij sol. x d.

Fabri

Magistro Henrico fabro qui operabatur circa ferramentum camini per j. ebdomadam iiij^or s. Et Simoni fabro xxvj d. Et Willelmo de Offinton' xviij d. Et Thoraud' xx^ti d.

Summa ix sol. iiij d.

Minuti operarii

videlicet Stephano de Gardino per predictum quindenam xxv d.

Et Rogero de Cherring' per idem tempus xxv d.

Et duobus Scyhurs scilicet Waltero Norr' & Willelmo de Scyreburn' qui secaverunt ligna ad emendacionem pontis regis per iij. dies xv d. videlicet utrique illorum vij d. ob.

Summa v sol. v d.

Cariagium

videlicet Matheo carectario per iij ebdomadas & ij dies eunti cum carecta sua ad sablonem & argillum per iij. ebdomadas[1] vj sol. Et Ricardo de Celar' cum carecta sua per quindenam eunti ad idem iij sol. iiij d.

Et Waltero de Camera cum biga per ebdomadam & iiij^or dies ij sol. vj d.

Et magistro Odoni pro carecta sua ad buscam trahendam per j diem, vj d.

Summa xij sol. iiij^or d.

Plumbarii

videlicet Johanni Govair' & Willelmo de Strand pro viij^to char' plumbi ad tascham fundendis iactandis & cubandis ultra cameram senescallorum xl sol. precium char' v sol.

Fabri ad tascham

Et Willelmo de Clus' ad perpacacionem ferramenti de fenestra Judaismi iiij^or sol. ij d.

Eidem pro ferramento ad ostia sedis Justiciariorum de Banco xiiij d.

Summa xlv sol. iiij^or d.

Empciones

videlicet pro C. Busce empto ad plumbum fundendum	iiij^or sol.
Et pro j. quarter. calcis empto London'	xv d.
Et pro iiij^or fasciculis virgarum ad scaffot' camini	x d.

Summa vj sol. j d.

Summa totalis predicte pacacionis C.xiiij^or sol. xj d.

[1] *Sic.*

Masons

To John of Oxford raising joists above the stewards' chamber for the aforesaid time, 4*s*. And to Walter the clerk for the same time, 3*s*. 6*d*. And to a certain plumber for one day, 4*d*.

Total, 7*s*. 10*d*.

Smiths

To Master Henry the smith who was working upon the ironwork of the chimney for one week, 4*s*. And to Simon the smith, 26*d*. And to William of Uffington, 18*d*. And to Thorold, 20*d*.

Total, 9*s*. 4*d*.

Labourers

That is to say to Stephen of the Garden for the aforesaid fortnight, 25*d*.

And to Roger of Charing for the same time, 25*d*.

And to two sawyers, that is to say to Walter Norris and to William of Sherborne who sawed wood for the repair of the king's bridge for 3 days, 15*d*., that is 7½*d*. to each of them.

Total, 5*s*. 5*d*.

Carriage

That is to say to Matthew the carter for 3 weeks and 2 days going with his cart for sand and clay for 3 weeks, 6*s*.

And to Richard of the Cellar going with his cart for a fortnight for the same, 3*s*. 4*d*.

And to Walter of the Chamber with a cart for a week and 4 days, 2*s*. 6*d*.

And to Master Odo for his cart carrying firewood for one day, 6*d*.

Total, 12*s*. 4*d*.

Plumbers

That is to say to John Govair and to William of Strand for founding, casting, and laying 8 chars of lead at task above the stewards' chamber, 40*s*. price per char, 5*s*.

Smiths at task

And to William de Clus' in full payment for the ironwork of the window of the Jewry, 4*s*. 2*d*.

To the same for ironwork for the doors of the seat of the Justices of the Bench, 14*d*.

Total, 45*s*. 4*d*.

Purchases

That is to say for a hundredweight of firewood bought to found lead, 4*s*.

And for 1 quarter of lime bought at London, 15*d*.

And for 4 bundles of withies for the scaffolding of the chimney, 10*d*.

Total, 6*s*. 1*d*.

Sum total of the aforesaid payment, £5. 14*s*. 11*d*.

Et ita deest j d. qui in computando defuit ad finem pacacionis
Et adhuc debetur operariis de j. ebdomada ante Natale domini que amuntat C sol.

17. Pacacio facta de operacionibus curie domini regis a die dominica in crastino sancte Lucie virginis anno regis Henrici. xliiij° usque dominicam in festo beati Thome apostoli per j. ebdomadam.

Carpentarii	Willelmus de Waudis	
	Rogerus Westm'	
	Rogerus Cornwus	
	Gilbertus carpentarius	xxvj d.
	Henricus de Knyth'brig'	
	Johannes de Greneford	
	Johannes de Padinton'	
	Robertus de Aldebir'	xviij d.
Cementarii	Johannes de Oxon'	xxvj d.
	Walterus clericus	xxj d.
Operarii	Stephanus de Gardino	
	Rogerus de Cherring'	xv d.
	Walterus Norr'	
	Willelmus de Scyreburn'	

Et Johanni Govayr' & Willelmo de Strande pro. xij. char' & dim. plumbi fundendis & cubandis super cameram senescallorum ad tascham lxij sol. vj d.
Et Henrico de Ponte pro scyng'naill', bordnayll'. & clavis ad planchias x sol. vj d. per duas tallias.

Summa totalis iiij^or^ li. xvij sol. xj d.

Endorsed: Operaciones Westmonasterii.

And there is thus 1*d.* short which was missing in the reckoning at the end of the account.

And there is still owed to the workmen for one week before Christmas [25 December] [a sum] which amounts to 100*s.*

17. The payment made for the works at the court of the lord king from Sunday on the morrow of Saint Lucy the Virgin in the 44th year of King Henry [14 December 1259] until Sunday on the feast of the blessed Thomas the apostle [21 December] for 1 week.

Carpenters	William de Waudis Roger of Westminster Roger Cornwus Gilbert the carpenter Henry of Knightsbridge John of Greenford John of Paddington	26*d.*
	Robert of Albury	18*d.*
Masons	John of Oxford	26*d.*
	Walter the clerk	21*d.*
Labourers	Stephen of the Garden Roger of Charing Walter Norris William of Sherborne	15*d.*

And to John Govayr and to William of Strand for founding and laying 12½ chars of lead above the stewards' chamber at task, 62*s.* 6*d.*

And to Henry of Bridge for shingle-nails, board-nails, and nails for planks, 10*s.* 6*d.* by two tallies.

Sum total, £4. 17*s.* 11*d.*

Endorsed: Works of Westminster.

9. Account of works at Westminster Palace from 3 May to 25 December, 1259
(E 101/467/2)

Recepta ad operaciones curie regis Westmonasteriensis faciendas, videlicet a festo Invencionis Sancte Crucis anno regni Henrici tercii xl° tercio usque festum Sancti Michaelis sequens, lxxix li. xvij d. Item ad predictas operaciones post festum Sancti Michaelis, xlvii li. xxi d. ob.

Summa totalis recepte C xxvj li. iii sol. ij d. ob.

Rotulus de expensis factis circa operaciones curie domini regis apud Westmonasterium a die Lune post Inventionem Sancte Crucis anno regni Henrici filii Johannis Regis Anglie xl°tercio usque Natale domini proximum sequens, videlicet circa caminum camere domini regis prosternendum & reficiendum & tuellum eiusdem camini extra cum ferro ligandum et efforciandum. Et lotorium curie reparandum. Et unam gutteram magnam de coquina regis usque in Thamisiam de novo faciendam. Et unam cisternam novam in curia regis. Et quamdam cameram forincecam communem in curia regis super Thamisiam de novo construendam. Et magnam cameram senescallorum regis cum plumbo de novo cooperiendam. Et coquinas regis scindulandas, una cum emendacione domorum curie regis per diversa loca.

Prima pacacio

Pacacio prima de predictis operibus curie regis facta fuit de predicto die Lune post Invencionem Sancte Crucis usque Dominicam in Vigilia Sanctorum Nerey & Achillei per unam scilicet ebdomadam continentem festum Sancti Johannis ante portam Latina mquod fuit cementariorum & carpentariorum.

Cementarii. videlicet Roberto de Beverlaco tallianti circa caminum regis per eamdem ebdomadam iij sol. Et Johanni Burg'lun per eandem xxvi d. Et Henrico de Wautham per eandem xxvj d. Et Willelmo de Hampton' per eamdem xxvi d.

Summa cementariorum ix sol. vi d.

Franca petra. Et pro v quarter' petre de Chalveden' emptis de Radulfo de Lamh' ad opus camini predicti, vij sol. vi d. Et pro C france petre

9. Account of works at Westminster Palace from 3 May to 25 December, 1259

Receipts for carrying on the works at the king's court at Westminster, that is from the feast of the Invention of the Holy Cross [3 May] in the 43rd year of the reign of Henry III [1259] up to the feast of St. Michael following [29 September], £79. 1*s*. 5*d*. Item towards the said works after the feast of St. Michael, £47. 1*s*. 9½*d*.

Sum total of receipts, £126. 3*s*. 2½*d*.

Roll of expenditure on the works of the court of the lord king at Westminster from Monday after the Invention of the Holy Cross [5 May] in the 43rd year of the reign of Henry son of John, King of England [1259], up to Christmas following, that is pulling down and rebuilding the chimney of the chamber of the lord king and tying and strengthening the shaft of the chimney outside with iron. And repairing the lavatory[1] of the court. And making anew one great gutter from the king's kitchen to the Thames. And [making] one new cistern in the king's court. And constructing anew a certain common latrine in the king's court over the Thames. And covering anew with lead the great chamber of the king's stewards. And shingling the king's kitchens, together with mending the buildings of the king's court in various places.

First Payment

The first payment for the aforesaid works of the king's court was made from the said Monday after the Invention of the Holy Cross [5 May] up to the Sunday on the eve of Saints Nereus and Achilleus [11 May] for one week containing the feast of St. John before the Latin Gate [6 May] which was the masons' and carpenters'.

Masons, namely Robert of Beverley cutting [stone] in connection with the king's chimney during the said week, 3*s*. And to John Burg'lun during the same [week] 2*s*. 2*d*. And to Henry of Waltham during the same, 2*s*. 2*d*. And to William of Hampton during the same, 2*s*. 2*d*.

Masons' total, 9*s*. 6*d*.

Freestone. And for 5 quarters of Chaldon stone bought from Ralph of Lambeth for use in the said chimney, 7*s*. 6*d*. And for 1 hundredweight

[1] The word is here used in its original meaning of a 'washing-place'.

ad idem empto de Ricardo de Croiden', vj sol. Et pro iij quarter' france petre ad idem emptis de Randulfo de Wautham, iiij^or sol. vi d.
Summa france petre xviij sol.

Grisa petra. Et pro j navata grise petre ad opus guttere predicte empta de Ricardo le Cornur, vj sol. Et pro j navata grise petre ad idem empta de Roberto filio Alicie, v sol. Et pro navata grise petre ad idem empta de Ricardo filio Jocelini, iiij^or sol.
Summa grise petre, xv sol.

Ad calcem. Et ad prosternendum & cariandum vetera robora in foresta Wyndes' usque aquam unde fiet calx ad operaciones, xx sol. Et in duabus seruris novis ad ostia curie, & duabus seruris reparandis, ij sol. vj d.
Summa, xxij sol. vj d.
Summa totalis prime pacacionis lxv sol.

Secunda pacacio

Pacacio secunda de predictis operibus facta fuit a die Lune in festo Sanctorum Nerey & Achillei anno regni Henrici xliij° usque dominicam in vigilia Sancti Augustini per xv scilicet dies continentes festum Assencionis Domini quod fuit domini regis.

Cementarii. videlicet Johanni Burg'lun tallianti circa caminum per predictam quindenam cum quatuor sociis suis, videlicet Reginaldo Sturmy, Henrico de Wautham, Willelmo de Hampthon', Philippo de Hildesl', xx sol, cuilibet illorum scilicet iiij^or sol. Et Willelmo de Bradele cum duobus sociis suis talliantibus circa lotorium curie regis per eamdem quindenam, videlicet Thome de Kenefeg' & Radulfo de Oxonia, xij sol., cuilibet illorum trium, iiij^or sol.
Summa stipendiorum cementariorum, xxxij sol.

Carpentarii. Carpentariis circa reparacionem cumuli coquine regis adusti, videlicet Willelmo de Waudis cum duobus sociis suis, scilicet Johanni de Padinton', Henrico de Knythebrig' per predictos xv dies, xii sol., cuilibet illorum trium iiij^or sol.
Summa stipendiorum carpentariorum, xij sol.

Operarii. Et operariis deservientibus cementariis & carpentariis, videlicet Ricardo de Lichefeud per quindenam, ij sol. iij d. ob.
Et Simoni Russell' per idem tempus, ij sol. iij d. ob.
Et Rogero de Cherring' per idem tempus, ij sol. iij d. ob.
Et Roberto de Oxonia per idem tempus, ij sol. iij d. ob.
Summa stipendiorum operariorum, ix sol. ij d.

Franca petra. Et pro CCiij quarter' france petre ad opus camini & lotorii emptis de Algaro de Brugg', xvj sol. vi d.
Et pro j quarter' france petre ad idem empto de Willelmo de Brug', xviii d. Et pro C dim. france petre ad idem emptis de Radulfo de

of freestone for the same bought from Richard of Croydon, 6*s*. And for 3 quarters of freestone for the same bought from Ranulf of Waltham, 4*s*. 6*d*.

Freestone, total 18*s*.

Ragstone. And for 1 shipload of ragstone for use in the said gutter bought from Richard le Corner, 6*s*. And for 1 shipload of ragstone for the same bought from Robert son of Alice, 5*s*. And for a shipload of ragstone for the same bought from Richard son of Jocelin, 4*s*.

Ragstone, total 15*s*.

For lime. And to fell and carry to the water the old oaks in Windsor Forest with which lime will be made for the works, 20*s*. And in two new locks for the doors of the court, and repairing two locks, 2*s*. 6*d*.

Total, 22*s*. 6*d*.

Sum total of the first payment, 65*s*.

Second Payment

The second payment for the aforesaid works was made from Monday on the feast of Saints Nereus and Achilleus [12 May] in the 43rd year of the reign of Henry to the Sunday on the eve of St. Augustine [25 May] for 15 days containing the feast of the Lord's Ascension [22 May] which was the lord king's.

Masons, namely John Burg'lun cutting [stone] for the chimney for the aforesaid fortnight with his four fellows, namely Reginald Sturmy, Henry of Waltham, William of Hampton, Philip of Hillsley 20*s*., that is to each of them 4*s*. And to William of Bradley with his two fellows cutting [stone] for the lavatory of the king's court for the same fortnight, namely to Thomas of Kenfig and Ralph of Oxford, 12*s*., to each of the three, 4*s*.

Total masons' wages, 32*s*.

Carpenters. To carpenters repairing the scorched roof of the king's kitchen, namely William de Waudis with his two fellows, that is John of Paddington and Henry of Knightsbridge, for the aforesaid 15 days, 12*s*., to each of the three, 4*s*.

Total carpenters' wages, 12*s*.

Labourers. And to labourers serving the masons and carpenters, namely to Richard of Lichfield for a fortnight, 2*s*. 3½*d*. And to Simon Russell for the same time, 2*s*. 3½*d*. And to Roger of Charing for the same time, 2*s*. 3½*d*. And to Robert of Oxford for the same time, 2*s*. 3½*d*.

Total labourers' wages, 9*s*. 2*d*.

Freestone. And for 2 hundredweight and three quarters of freestone for the chimney and lavatory bought of Algar of Bridge, 16*s*. 6*d*. And for 1 quarter of freestone for the same bought of William of Bridge,

Lamh', ix sol. Et pro C j quarter' france petre ad idem empts de Randulfo de Wautham, vij sol. vi d. Et pro C france petre ad idem empto de Petro de Merstham, vj sol.

Summa france petre, xl. sol. vj d.

Summa totalis secunde pacacionis, iiij^{or} li. xiij sol. viij d.

Tercia pacacio

Pacacio tercia facta fuit a die Lune in festo Sancti Augustini anno regni Henrici xliij^{o} usque vigiliam Pentecost' per unam ebdomadam sine festo.

Cementarii. Albis cissoribus & cubitoribus circa caminum regis, videlicet Reginaldo Sturmy, Johanni Burg'lun, Philippo de Hyldesl', Henrico de Wautham, Willelmo de Hampthon', Johanni le Harpur, Ricardo de Keruurth', Radulfo de Waleden', Willelmo de Bledelawe, xix sol. vj d., cuilibet predictorum ix, xxvj d. Et Roberto de Beverlaco per eamdem ebdomadam iij sol. Et Willelmo de Tham' per duos dies xij d. Cementariis ad lotorium, videlicet Willelmo de Bradele, Thome de Kenefeg', Radulfo de Oxon', Roberto Pik' per eamdem ebdomadam, viij sol. viij d., cuilibet scilicet predictorum quatuor, xxvi d.

Summa stipendiorum cementariorum xxxij sol. ij d.

Fabri. Et magistro Henrico de Lewes circa ferramentum quod supportavit mantellum camini camere regis antequam prosterneretur per predictam ebdomadam iiij^{or} sol. Et Willelmo de Offinton' circa idem per idem tempus xviij d. Et Ricardo fabro circa idem per eamdem ebdomadam iij sol.

Summa stipendiorum fabrorum viij sol. vj d.

Carpentarii. Et quatuor carpentariis circa cumulum coquine regis adustum reparandum per eamdem ebdomadam, videlicet Willelmo de Waudis, Johanni de Padinton', Nicholao de Eye, Henrico de Knythebrig' viij sol. viij d., cuilibet illorum quatuor scilicet xxvi d.

Summa carpentariorum viij sol viij d.

Operarii. Et minutis operariis videlicet Simoni le Scaffoter per illam ebdomadam viij d. Et Willelmo Millers xv d. Et Johanni Porter xv d. Et Johanni Neck' per quatuor dies x d. Et Martino per idem tempus x d. Et quinque operariis videlicet Willelmo de Prit'well, Johanni Corant, Fulconi, Reginaldo Fuhell', Johanni Gyng' per duos dies ferentibus francam petram talliatam de astelar' usque in cameram regis ad opus predicti camini xxv d. cuilibet illorum quinque scilicet v d. Et tribus operariis qui fuerunt cum fabris per ebdomadam predictam, iij sol. ix d. cuilibet illorum xv d. Et Ade de Auhlton' per quatuor dies x d. Et operariis cum cementariis

1*s*. 6*d*. And for a hundredweight and a half of freestone for the same bought of Ralph of Lambeth, 9*s*. And for 1 hundredweight and a quarter of freestone for the same bought of Ranulf of Waltham, 7*s*. 6*d*. And for 1 hundredweight of freestone for the same bought of Peter of Merstham, 6*s*.

Total of freestone, £2. 0*s*. 6*d*.

Sum total of the second payment, £4. 13*s*. 8*d*.

Third Payment

The third payment was made from Monday on the feast of St. Augustine [26 May] in the 43rd year of the reign of Henry to the eve of Whitsun [31 May] for one week without a feast.

Masons. To white cutters and layers working on the king's chimney, namely Reginald Sturmy, John Burg'lun, Philip of Hillsley, Henry of Waltham, William of Hampton, John the Harper, Richard of Carwardine, Ralph of Walden, William of Bledlow, 19*s*. 6*d*., to each of the aforesaid nine, 2*s*. 2*d*. And to Robert of Beverley for the same week, 3*s*. And to William of Thame for two days, 1*s*. To the masons at the lavatory, namely William of Bradley, Thomas of Kenfig, Ralph of Oxford, Robert Pike, for the same week, 8*s*. 8*d*., that is to each of the said four, 2*s*. 2*d*.

Total masons' wages, £1. 12*s*. 2*d*.

Smiths. And to Master Henry of Lewes working during the said week on the ironwork which supported the mantel of the chimney of the king's chamber before it was pulled down, 4*s*. And to William of Uffington about the same for the same time, 1*s*. 6*d*. And to Richard the smith about the same for the same week, 3*s*.

Total smiths' wages, 8*s*. 6*d*.

Carpenters. And to four carpenters repairing the scorched roof of the king's kitchen during the same week, namely William de Waudis, John of Paddington, Nicholas of Eye, Henry of Knightsbridge, 8*s*. 8*d*., that is to each of those four, 2*s*. 2*d*.

Total carpenters' [wages], 8*s*. 8*d*.

Labourers. And to labourers, namely to Simon the Scaffolder for that week, 8*d*. And to William Millers, 1*s*. 3*d*. And to John Porter, 1*s*. 3*d*. And to John Neck for four days, 10*d*. And to Martin for the same time, 10*d*. And to five labourers, namely William of Prittlewell, John Corant, Fulk, Reginald Fuhell, John Gyng' for two days carrying cut freestone from the lodge to the king's chamber for the said chimney, 2*s*. 1*d*., that is to each of those five, 5*d*. And to three labourers who were with the smiths during the said week, 3*s*. 9*d*., to each of them, 1*s*. 3*d*. And to Adam of Alton for four days, 10*d*. And to labourers with the masons repairing the offices of the king's kitchen,

reparantibus officinas coquine regis, videlicet Edmundo de Bracino per illam ebdomadam xv d. Et Johanni Mityng' per idem tempus xv d. Et Elye le Breuetur per idem tempus xv d. Et operariis qui foderunt fundamentum ad gutteram magnam, videlicet Galfrido Wrenn', Durando de Eye, Hugoni de Berking', Thome de Eye, Willelmo de Feck'ham, vj sol. iij d. cuilibet predictorum quinque xv d. Et operariis deservientibus cementariis circa lotorium, videlicet Ricardo de Lichefeud, Simoni Russell', Rogero de Cherring' per xv dies vi sol. x d. ob., cuilibet illorum trium per primam ebdomadam xij d. ob. propter festum interveniens. Et per secundam ebdomadam xv d.

Summa operariorum xxix sol. ij d. ob.

Tasche. Et Roberto Anglico & sociis suis pro lotorio curie regis ad tascham polliendo iiij^{or} sol. Et pro portagio france petre talliate de astelar' usque in cameram regis ad opus camini xxi d. Et pro portagio trium navatarum grise petre de aqua usque ad manus operancium gutteram coquine, xxi d. Et pro plumbo in coquina regis assidendo & officinis quibusdam coquine regis reficiendis ad tascham vi sol. iiij^{or} d.

Summa tascharum xiii sol. x d.

Franca petra. Et pro CCiij quarter' france petre ad caminum regis emptis de Algaro de Brig' xvi sol. vi d. Et pro CC iij quarter' france petre ad idem emptis de Radulfo de Lamh' xvi sol. vi d. Et pro dim. cent. france petre ad idem empto de Ricardo de Croyden' iij sol. Et pro C france petre ad lotorium curie regis empto de Randulfo de Wautham vj sol. Et pro dim. cento france petre ad idem empto de Willelmo de Brug' iij sol. Et pro dim. cent. france petre ad idem empto de Petro de Mertsham iij sol.

Summa france petre xlviij sol.

Plumbum. Et pro quatuor chareis plumbi emptis ad Nundinas beati Botulfi per manus Ricardi Box' London' ad gutteras magne aule regis & coopperturam domorum curie regis per loca emendandas viij li. viij sol. *Ferramentum.* Et pro C et dim. ferri tenacis emptis London' ad opus camini predicti xxv sol. Et pro iij quarter' carbonis marini ad fabricandum ferramentum ad opus predicti camini, cum portagio & vectura per aquam iij sol. vj d. Et pro MM clavorum ferri ad scindulas emptis London' de Henrico de Ponte xvi d.

Summa ix li. xvij sol. x d.

Calx. Et pro CCC dim. calcis ad opus predictorum camini & lotorii emptis de Agnete Calfonaria London' xvij sol. vj d.

namely to Edmund of the malt-house for that week, 1*s.* 3*d.* And to John Mityng for the same time, 1*s.* 3*d.* And to Elias the Brevetur for the same time, 1*s.* 3*d.* And to the labourers who dug the foundation for the great gutter, namely Geoffrey Wrenn, Durand of Eye, Hugh of Barking, Thomas of Eye, William of Feckenham, 6*s.* 3*d.*, to each of the aforesaid five, 1*s.* 3*d.* And to the labourers serving the masons at the lavatory, namely Richard of Lichfield, Simon Russell, Roger of Charing for 15 days, 6*s.* 10½*d.*, to each of those three, 12½*d.* for the first week on account of the feast falling within it. And for the second week, 1*s.* 3*d.*

Total labourers' [wages], £1. 9*s.* 2½*d.*

Task-work. And to Robert English and his fellows for polishing the lavatory of the king's court by task, 4*s.* And for the portage of cut freestone from the lodge to the king's chamber for the chimney, 1*s.* 9*d.* And for the portage of three shiploads of ragstone from the water to the hands of those working on the kitchen gutter, 1*s.* 9*d.* And for laying lead in the king's kitchen and for remaking certain offices of the king's kitchen at task, 6*s.* 4*d.*

Total of task-work, 13*s.* 10*d.*

Freestone. And for 2 hundredweight and 3 quarters of freestone for the king's chimney bought from Algar of Bridge, 16*s.* 6*d.* And for 2 hundredweight and 3 quarters of freestone for the same bought from Ralph of Lambeth, 16*s.* 6*d.* And for half a hundredweight of freestone for the same bought of Richard of Croydon, 3*s.* And for 1 hundredweight of freestone for the lavatory of the king's court bought from Ranulf of Waltham, 6*s.* And for half a hundredweight of freestone for the same bought of William of Bridge, 3*s.* And for half a hundredweight of freestone for the same bought of Peter of Merstham, 3*s.*

Total of freestone, £2. 8*s.* 0*d.*

Lead. And for four chars of lead bought at St. Botolph's Fair [at Boston] by the hands of Richard Box of London to repair the gutters of the great hall and the roofing of the buildings of the king's court in various places, £8. 8*s.* *Ironwork.* And for a hundredweight and a half of tough iron bought in London for the aforesaid chimney, £1. 5*s.* And for 3 quarters of sea-coal to work the iron for the said chimney, together with portage and carriage by water, 3*s.* 6*d.* And for 2,000 iron nails for shingles bought in London from Henry of [London] Bridge, 1*s.* 4*d.*

Total, £9. 17*s.* 10*d.*

Lime. And for 3 hundredweight and a half of lime for the said chimney and lavatory bought from Agnes the lime-burner of London, 17*s.* 6*d.*

Sabulon'. Et Ricardo de Celar' pro xxxvj chareis sablonis fodendis & cariandis ad tascham xi d. Et Radulfo de Ponte pro fossur' & cariagio totidem charearum sablonis ad tascham xj d.

Virge. Craticule. Et relicte Ricardi de Estchepe pro ij duodenis craticularum & vi fasciculis virgarum ad scaffot' faciend' ad caminum regis predictum v sol. iij d. Et Henrico de Ponte pro vi gat' & iij lusch' xiij d. Et Ricardo le Cuver pro iij bukettis ix d.

Summa xxvj sol. v d.

Summa totalis tercie pacacionis xviii li. iiii^or^ sol. vii d. ob.

Quarta pacacio

Pacacio quarta fiebat de die Iovis infra ebdomadam Pentecost' anno regni xliij^o^ usque dominicam proximam ante Nativitatem Sancti Johannis Baptiste per quindenam scilicet & tres dies continentes festum beati Barnabe apostoli per diem Martis quod fuit domini regis.

Cementarii. videlicet Ricardo de Eltham cementario per iij dies in ebdomada Pentecost' circa caminum regis ij sol. iij d. Et Willelmo de Waudis per predictos tres dies circa idem iij sol. Et Waltero de Munden' per idem tempus xiij d. Et Roberto Pik' circa opus camini per quindenam & tres dies v sol. j d. Et Thome de Kenefeg' circa idem per idem tempus v sol. j d. Et Radulfo de Waleden per idem tempus circa idem v sol. i d. Et Ricardo de Keruurth' per idem tempus circa idem v sol. i d. Et Ade filio Warini per iiij^or^ dies circa idem xvij d. Et Johanni de Maldon' per idem tempus xvij d. Et Gilberto Norman per iiij^or^ dies circa idem xviij d. Et Waltero de Waleden' per tres dies circa idem xiij d. Et Johanni Burg'lun, Philippo de Hildesl', Johanni Le Harpur, Willelmo de Hampton', Henrico de Wautham per xv dies circa idem xx sol. cuilibet illorum quinque scilicet iiij^or^ sol. Et Roberto de Beverlaco per j ebdomadam circa idem ij sol vj d. Et Reginaldo Sturmy per eamdem ebdomadam xxij d. Et Rogero de Cicestr' per j ebdomadam integram sine festo xxvj d.

Cubitores & assessores. videlicet Willelmo de Bledelawe per quindenam & tres dies circa opus camini v sol. j d. Et Radulfo de Oxon' per ebdomadam in qua cecidit festum & tres dies ii sol. xj d. Et Henrico de Riseber' per idem tempus ij sol. xi d. Et Willelmo de Bradele per idem tempus ij sol. xi d. Et Bartholomeo Westmon' per j ebdomadam integram xxvj d. Et Willelmo de Assch' per eamdem ebdomadam xxvi d.

Summa stipendiorum cementariorum lxxvi sol. ix d.

Sand. And to Richard of the Cellar for 36 cart-loads of sand dug and carried by task, 11*d*. And to Ralph of Bridge for digging and carrying as many cart-loads of sand by task, 11*d*.

Withies, Hurdles. And to Richard of Eastcheap's widow for 2 dozen hurdles and 6 bundles of withies for making scaffolds for the said king's chimney, 5*s*. 3*d*. And to Henry of Bridge for 6 bowls and 3 spades, 13*d*. And to Richard le Cuver for 3 buckets, 9*d*.

Total, £1. 6*s*. 5*d*.

Sum total of the third payment, £18. 4*s*. 7½*d*.

Fourth Payment

The fourth payment was made from Thursday in Whitsun week [5 June] in the 43rd year of the reign [of Henry] to Sunday next before the Nativity of St. John the Baptist [22 June], that is for a fortnight and three days, containing on Tuesday[1] the feast of the blessed Barnabas the apostle [11 June] ,which was the king's.

Masons: namely to Richard of Eltham mason for 3 days in Whitsun week on the king's chimney, 2*s*. 3*d*. And to William de Waudis for the said three days on the same, 3*s*. And to Walter of Munden for the same time, 1*s*. 1*d*. And to Robert Pike on the work of the chimney for a fortnight and three days, 5*s*. 1*d*. And to Thomas of Kenfig on the same for the same time, 5*s*. 1*d*. And to Ralph of Walden for the same time on the same, 5*s*. 1*d*. And to Richard of Carwardine for the same time on the same, 5*s*. 1*d*. And to Adam son of Warin for 4 days on the same, 1*s*. 5*d*. And to John of Maldon for the same time, 1*s*. 5*d*. And to Gilbert Norman for 4 days on the same, 1*s*. 6*d*. And to Walter of Walden for three days on the same, 1*s*. 1½*d*. And to John Burg'lun, Philip of Hillsley, John the Harper, William of Hampton, Henry of Waltham for 15 days on the same, 20*s*., that is to each of those five, 4*s*. And to Robert of Beverley for 1 week on the same, 2*s*. 6*d*. And to Reginald Sturmy for the same week, 1*s*. 10*d*. And to Roger of Chichester for 1 whole week without the feast, 2*s*. 2*d*.

Layers and Setters: namely to William of Bledlow for a fortnight and three days on the work of the said chimney, 5*s*. 1*d*. And to Ralph of Oxford for the week in which the feast fell and three days, 2*s*. 11*d*. And to Henry of Risborough for the same time, 2*s*. 11*d*. And to William of Bradley for the same time, 2*s*. 11*d*. And to Bartholomew of Westminster for 1 whole week, 2*s*. 2*d*. And to William of Ash for the same week, 2*s*. 2*d*.

Total masons' wages, £3. 16*s*. 9*d*.

[1] A mistake for Wednesday.

Carpentarii. videlicet Willelmo de Waudis per xv dies circa coquinam regis adustam & gutteram cooperiendam cum planch' iiij^or sol. Et Henrico de Knyth'brig' per idem tempus circa idem iiii^or sol. Et Odoni carpentario per tres dies circa idem xiij d. Et Rogero Cornwus per idem tempus xiij d.

Summa carpentariorum x sol. ij d.

Fabri. Et Ricardo fabro circa ferramentum ad caminum regis per quindenam & tres dies vij sol. Et Ricardo fabro juniori per unam ebdomadam xxij d.

Summa viij sol. x d.

Tasche. videlicet Willelmo de Thotull' super tascha de guttera magna coquine facienda xx sol. Et Willelmo de Midhurst & sociis suis pro portagio france petre talliate ad caminum regis xv d. Et Willelmo de Clus' pro fabricacione & emendacione martellorum cementariorum de tempore precedente iij sol. v d. ob. Et Willelmo de Gardino per tres dies festos intendenti ad recipiendum materialia necessaria operacionibus predictis vj d.

Summa xxv sol. ij d. ob.

Operarii. Et operariis deservientibus predictis cementariis & carpentariis per predictum tempus, videlicet Simoni Le Scaffotur per tres dies infra ebdomadam Pentecost' circa scaffot' ad caminum regis ix d. Et Waltero filio Elie, Martino, Willelmo Millers per j ebdomadam & tres dies juvantibus ad caminum predictum v sol., cuilibet illorum trium scilicet xx d. Et Rogero de Cherring', Galfrido Wrenn', Durando de Eye, Hugoni de Berking', Thome de Eye, & Willelmo de Feck'ham qui fecerunt fundamentum guttere magne predicte per predictum tempus xvij sol. vj d., cuilibet predictorum sex ij sol. xj d. Et Roberto de Oxon',[1] Willelmo Welbilove, Roberto Chubbe, Stephano de Gardino, Johanni Malekin, Simoni Russell' deservientibus cementariis & carpentariis per predictam quindenam xiij sol. ix d. cuilibet scilicet illorum quinque [*sic*] ij sol. iij d. ob. Et Willelmo de Coffle, Johanni Mityng', Willelmo de Hendon', Roberto de Eye, Waltero de Bracino, Johanni Coco, Ricardo de Hampslap', Hugoni de Notyngham', Johanni Havelove, Willelmo de Guldebur', Johanni de Essex, Thome de Thotull', per j ebdomadam cariantibus rebbussam ad equandum aream gardini iuxta cisternam xv sol., cuilibet illorum xij scilicet xv d. Et Willelmo de Enefeud, Elie Le Brevetur per duos dies v d. utrique illorum scilicet ij d. ob. per diem. Et Johanni Porter per iij dies vij d. ob. Et magistro Warino London' cum tribus hominibus suis ad mundandum cameras forinsecas regine & senescallorum in curia regis per quatuor dies iiij sol. v d.

Summa stipendiorum operariorum lvij sol. v.d. ob.

[1] This name was added later.

Carpenters. Namely to William de Waudis for 15 days on the king's scarched kitchen and covering the gutter with planks, 4*s.* And to Henry of Knightsbridge for the same time on the same, 4*s.* And to Odo the carpenter for three days on the same, 1*s.* 1*d.* And to Roger Cornwus for the same time, 1*s.* 1*d.*

Total carpenters' [wages], 10*s.* 2*d.*

Smiths. And to Richard the smith working on the ironwork for the king's chimney for a fortnight and three days, 7*s.* And to Richard the smith the younger for one week, 1*s.* 10*d.*

Total, 8*s.* 10*d.*

Task-works. Namely to William of Tothill on the task of making the great gutter of the king's kitchen, £1. And to William of Midhurst and his fellows for portage of the cut freestone to the king's chimney, 1*s.* 3*d.* And to William de Clus' for making and mending the masons' mauls during the said time, 3*s.* 5½*d.* And to William of the garden attending for three feast days to receive the materials needed for the said works, 6*d.*

Total, £1. 5*s.* 2½*d.*

Labourers. And to labourers serving the said masons and carpenters for the said time, namely to Simon the Scaffolder for three days within Whitsun week on the scaffold for the king's chimney, 9*d.* And to Walter son of Elias, Martin, William Millers for 1 week and three days helping at the said chimney, 5*s.*, that is to each of those three, 1*s.* 8*d.* And to Roger of Charing, Geoffrey Wrenn, Durand of Eye, Hugh of Barking, Thomas of Eye, and William of Feckenham who made the foundation of the said great gutter during the said time, 17*s.* 6*d.*, to each of the aforesaid six, 2*s.* 11*d.* And to Robert of Oxford,[1] William Welbilove, Robert Chubbe, Stephen of the garden, John Malekin, Simon Russell serving the masons and carpenters during the said week, 13*s.* 9*d.*, that is to each of those five [*sic*], 2*s.* 3½*d.* And to William of Cowley, John Mityng, William of Hendon, Robert of Eye, Walter of the malt-house, John Cook, Richard of Hanslope, Hugh of Nottingham, John Havelove, William of Goldbury, John of Essex, Thomas of Tothill, for 1 week carrying rubbish to level the surface of the garden by the cistern, 15*s.*, that is to each of those 12, 1*s.* 3*d.* And to William of Enfield, Elias the Breveter for two days, 5*d.*, that is to each of them 2½*d.* a day. And to John Porter for 3 days, 7½*d.* And to Master Warin of London with his three men to clean out the queen's and the stewards' latrines in the king's court for four days, 4*s.* 5*d.*

Total labourers' wages, £2. 17*s.* 5½*d.*

[1] This name was added later.

Franca petra. Et pro CC dim. france petre ad caminum, cisternam & lotorium emptis de Algaro de Brug' xv sol. Et pro C dim. france petre ad idem emptis de Radulfo de Lamh' ix sol. Et pro C dim. france petre ad idem emptis de Willelmo de Brug' ix sol.

Summa france petre xxxiij sol.

Grisa petra. Et pro navata grise petre ad opus magne guttere empta de Ricardo le Fort vj sol. Et pro navata grise petre ad idem empta de Matheo de Ponte vj sol. vj d.

Summa grise petre xij sol. vj d.

Calx, Sablon'. Et Agneti Calfonarie pro CCC calcis ad opus guttere predicte & cisterne xv sol. Et Radulfo de Ponte pro xxv chareis sablonis cariatis ad tascham vij d. ob. Eidem pro lxxiij chareis sablonis cariatis per tascham xix d. Et pro morterio de calce & sablone empto de domino Hugone de Sancto Albano monacho iij sol.

Summa xx sol. ij d. ob.

Ferramentum. Et Willelmo de Clus' pro quodam ferramento ad quamdam fenestram in coquina regis xxvi d. Et pro tribus clavibus novis emptis cum emendacione quarumdam serurarum in curia regis viij d. Et Henrico de Ponte London' pro MMM clavorum ad lathas & v^c^ grossorum clavorum ad opus coquine regis iiij^or^ sol. iij d. Et pro xix libris picis & v libris cere emptis ad opus cisterne regis xiiij^or^ sol. j d. Et pro dim. cent. carbonis lignei ad cisternam cimentandam vij d.

Summa xxi sol. ix d.

Maeremium. Et pro xviij grossis peciis quercus emptis apud Kyngeston' ad opus camere forinsece constructe in curia regis xix sol. iij d. ob. Et pro xiij minoribus peciis quercus ad idem tunc emptis ibidem viij sol. viij d. ob. Eg pro cariagio predicti maeremii de Kyng' usque Westmonasterium ij sol.

Summa maeremii xxx sol.

Summa totalis quarte pacacionis xiiij^or^ li. xv sol. x d. ob.

Quinta pacacio

Pacacio quinta fiebat de die Lune in vigilia Nativitatis Sancti Johannis Baptiste anno regni Henrici predicti xliij^o^ usque dominicam in festo apostolorum Petri & Pauli per j ebdomadam scilicet continentem predictum festum beati Johannis quod fuit carpentariorum.

Carpentarii. Et Willelmo de Waudis, Henrico de Knythebrug', Odoni, Rogero de Westmonasterio, Simoni de Norht', Rogero Cornws carpentariis incipientibus operari circa constructuram camere forincece in curia regis per illam ebdomadam xiij sol., cuilibet predictorum sex xxvi d.

Summa carpentariorum xiij sol.

Freestone. And for two hundredweight and a half of freestone for the chimney, cistern, and lavatory bought of Algar of Bridge, 15*s*. And for a hundredweight and a half of freestone for the same bought of Ralph of Lambeth, 9*s*. And for a hundredweight and a half of freestone for the same bought of William of Bridge, 9*s*.

Total of freestone, £1. 13*s*. 0*d*.

Ragstone. And for a shipload of ragstone for the great gutter bought of Richard le Fort, 6*s*. And for a shipload of ragstone for the same bought of Matthew of Bridge, 6*s*. 6*d*.

Total of ragstone, 12*s*. 6*d*.

Lime, Sand. And to Agnes the lime-burner for three hundredweight of lime for the said gutter and cistern, 15*s*. And to Ralph of Bridge for 25 loads of sand carried by task, 7½*d*. To the same for 73 loads of sand carried by task, 19*d*. And for mortar of lime and sand bought of dom. Hugh of St. Albans the monk, 3*s*.

Total, £1. 0*s*. 2½*d*.

Ironwork. And to William de Clus' for certain ironwork for a certain window in the king's kitchen, 2*s*. 2*d*. And for three new keys bought together with mending certain locks in the king's court, 8*d*. And to Henry of London Bridge for 3,000 lath-nails and 500 large nails for the king's kitchen, 4*s*. 3*d*. And for 19 pounds of pitch and 5 pounds of wax bought for the king's cistern, 14*s*. 1*d*. And for half a hundredweight of charcoal to cement the cistern, 7*d*.

Total, £1. 1*s*. 9*d*.

Timber. And for 18 large pieces of oak bought at Kingston for the latrine built in the king's court, 19*s*. 3½*d*. And for 13 smaller pieces of oak for the same bought then at the same place, 8*s*. 8½*d*. And for carriage of the said timber from Kingston to Westminster, 2*s*.

Total of timber, £1. 10*s*. 0*d*.

Sum total of the fourth payment, £14. 15*s*. 10½*d*.

Fifth Payment

The fifth payment was made from Monday on the eve of the Nativity of Saint John the Baptist [23 June] in the 43rd year of the reign of Henry aforesaid to Sunday on the feast of the Apostles Peter and Paul [29 June] that is for one week, containing the said feast of the Blessed John which was the carpenters'.

Carpenters. And to William de Waudis, Henry of Knightsbridge, Odo, Roger of Westminster, Simon of Northampton, Roger Cornwus, carpenters beginning to work on the building of the latrine in the king's court for that week, 13*s*., to each of the said six, 2*s*. 2*d*.

Total carpenters' [wages], 13*s*. 0*d*.

Plummers. Et Willelmo de Strande per tres ebdomadas circa conductum lotorii & cisterne reparandum viij sol. vj d. Et Johanni Govayr per j diem vj d. Et Johanni homini suo per tres ebdomadas iiij^{or} sol. iij d. Et Simoni le plummer per iiij^{or} dies xij d.

Summa xiiij^{or} sol. iij d.

Pictores. Et Ricardo pictori circa parietem ex utraque parte camini regis depingendum per ix dies iiij^{or} sol. vj d. Et Johanni de Rading' per viij dies circa idem iiij^{or} sol. Et Deudon' per xv dies circa idem iij sol. vj d. Et cuidam garcioni preparanti colores predictorum pictorum per j ebdomadam x d. Et in coloribus diversis emptis ad idem xi sol vij d.

Summa xxiiij^{or} sol. v d.

Operarii. Et quinque operariis deservientibus carpentariis per predictam ebdomadam videlicet Waltero Norr', Willelmo de Scyreburn', Stephano de Gardino, Johanni Porter, Durando de Eye, v sol. ij d. ob. cuilibet illorum scilicet xij d. ob. Et xi operariis circa fundamentum magne guttere fodendum, videlicet Rogero de Cherring', Galfrido Wrenn', Hugoni de Berkyng', Willelmo de Feckham, Thome de Eye, Philippo de Turfeye, Ade de Diddewrth', Roberto de Oxon', Hugoni de Notyngham, Johanni de Chelchuth', Johanni de Essex per predictam ebdomadam xi sol. v d. ob. cuilibet illorum scilicet xij d. ob. Et Johanni Miting', Waltero de Bracino, Johanni Havelove, Thome de Thotull', Rogero de Knarebur' per quatuor dies circa idem & aream gardini adequandam cum rebbusa iiij^{or} sol. ij d. cuilibet scilicet illorum quinque x d. Et Willelmo Fayrwif, Nicholao de Eboraco, Hugoni le Paumer, Philippo filio Willelmi, Egidio de Essex per tres dies circa idem iij sol. j d. ob. cuilibet predictorum quinque vij d. ob.

Summa operariorum xxiij sol. xj d. ob.

Tasch'. videlicet Willelmo de Thotull' ad perpacacionem tasch' de magna gutera, que continebat xvi perticas & dim., unde cepit pro pertica de xx^{ti} pedibus iij sol. iiij^{or} d. xxxv sol. Et Johanni Ging' & sociis suis pro portagio france petre & velute ad tascham iiij^{or} sol. ij d. Et Radulfo de Ponte pro cariagio dim. cent. char' sablonis ad tasch' xviij d.

Summa xl sol. viij d.

Grisa petra. Et pro j navata grise petre ad gutteram & cayam desub camera forinceca predicta faciendas empta de Elia de Meleton' vj sol. vj d. Et pro navata grise petre ad idem empta de Henrico Eldegrom' v sol. Et Alvredo de Strode pro navata grise petre ad idem

Plumbers. And to William of Strand for three weeks repairing the conduit of the lavatory and the cistern, 8*s.* 6*d.* And to John Govayr for 1 day, 6*d.* And to John his man for three weeks, 4*s.* 3*d.* And to Simon the plumber for 4 days, 12*d.*

Total, 14*s.* 3*d.*

Painters. And to Richard the painter painting the wall on either side of the king's chimney for 9 days, 4*s.* 6*d.* And to John of Reading for 8 days on the same, 4*s.* And to Deudon' for 15 days on the same, 3*s.* 6*d.* And to a certain boy preparing colours for the aforesaid painters for one week, 10*d.* And for various colours bought for the same, 11*s.* 7*d.*

Total, 24*s.* 5*d.*

Labourers. And to five labourers serving the carpenters during the aforesaid week, namely Walter Norris, William of Sherborne, Stephen of the garden, John Porter, Durand of Eye, 5*s.* 2½*d.*, that is, to each of them, 12½*d.* And to 11 labourers digging the foundation of the great gutter, that is to Roger of Charing, Geoffrey Wrenn, Hugh of Barking, William of Feckenham, Thomas of Eye, Philip of Turvey, Adam of Dedworth, Robert of Oxford, Hugh of Nottingham, John of Chelsea, John of Essex for the said week, 11*s.* 5½*d.*, that is, to each of them, 12½*d.* And to John Miting, Walter of the malthouse, John Havelove, Thomas of Tothill, Roger of Knaresborough for four days about the same and levelling the surface of the garden with rubbish, 4*s.* 2*d.*, that is, to each of those five 10*d.* And to William Fayrwif, Nicholas of York, Hugh le Paumer, Philip son of William, Giles of Essex for three days about the same, 3*s.* 1½*d.*, to each of the aforesaid five, 7½*d.*

Total labourers' [wages], 23*s.* 11½*d.*

Task-work. That is, to William of Tothill to complete the payment for the task of the great gutter, which contained 16½ perches, for which he received 3*s.* 4*d.* per perch of 20 feet, 35*s.* And to John Ging' and his mates for the portage of freestone and *petra veluta*[1] by task, 4*s.* 2*d.* And to Ralph of Bridge for carriage of half a hundred cart-loads of sand by task, 18*d.*

Total, 40*s.* 8*d.*

Ragstone. And for one shipload of ragstone bought from Elias of Milton to make the gutter and the quay beneath the aforesaid latrine, 6*s.* 6*d.* And for a shipload of ragstone for the same bought from Henry Eldegrom, 5*s.* And to Alfred of Strood for a shipload of ragstone for the same, 6*s.* And for a shipload of ragstone for the

1 Some sort of 'coarse' or 'rough' stone: probably ragstone.

vj sol. Et pro navata grise petre ad idem empta de Roberto Scyrlok' vj sol. Et pro navata grise petre ad idem empta de Ricardo Forti vi sol.
Summa grise petre xxix sol. vi d.

Creta. Et pro navata crete ad idem empta de Elya de Meleton' ii sol. iiij^or d. Et pro navata crete ad idem empta de Hamone le Cogger ii sol. vii d. Et pro navata crete ad idem empta de Thoma Longo ij sol. vij d. Et pro ij navatis crete emptis de Ricardo de Denynton' iiii^or sol. iiij^or d.
Summa albe crete xj sol. x d.

Calx. Et pro C. iij quarter' calcis ad opus guttere & caii predicti emptis de Ricardo calfonario London' viij sol. ix d. Et pro CCC calcis emptis ad idem de Agnete calfonaria xv sol.
Summa calcis xxiij sol. ix d.

Ferramentum. Et Henrico de Ponte London' pro vij mill. clavorum ad lathas ab ipso emptis vj sol. Eidem pro v^c grossorum clavorum xx d. Item eidem pro iiij^or mill. & dim. clavorum ad cindulas iij sol. x d. Et Ricardo le Cuver pro emendacione utensilium xiii d.
Summa xij sol. vj d.

Maeremium. videlicet in xli peciis quercus emptis apud Kyngeston' ad opus camere forinsece curie regis xxi sol x d. Et pro xlix parvis bordis ad idem emptis ibidem xiij d. Et pro tribus grossis postibus de quercu ad idem emptis ibidem vij sol. vi d. Et pro cariagio predicti maeremii per aquam usque Westmonasterium ij sol. Et pro x mill. cindularum emptis ad opus predicte camere & coquinas regis cooperiendas lxx sol. precium millenarii vij sol. Et pro cariagio predictarum scindularum per aquam per vices de Kyng' usque Westmonasterium vi sol. j d.
Summa C viii sol. vj d.
Summa totalis quinte pacacionis xv li. ij sol. iiij^or d. ob.

Sexta pacacio

Pacacio sexta fiebat de die Lune in crastino Apostolorum Petri & Pauli anno regni Henrici predicti xliij^o usque dominicam in vigilia translacionis beati Thome Martiris per j ebdomadam integram videlicet sine festo interveniente.

Carpentarii. videlicet v carpentariis operantibus circa carpentariam predicte camere forinsece in curia regis, Willelmo de Waudis, Henrico de Knyth'brig', Rogero Westm', Simoni de Norht', Rogero Cornwus per predictam ebdomadam x sol. x d. cuilibet scilicet illorum xxvi d.
Summa carpentariorum x sol. x d.

same bought from Robert Scyrlok, 6*s*. And for a shipload of ragstone for the same bought of Richard le Fort, 6*s*.

Total of ragstone, 29*s*. 6*d*.

Chalk. And for a shipload of chalk for the same bought from Elias of Milton, 2*s*. 4*d*. And for a shipload of chalk for the same bought from Hamon le Cogger, 2*s*. 7*d*. And for a shipload of chalk for the same bought from Thomas Long, 2*s*. 7*d*. And for 2 shiploads of chalk for the same bought from Richard of Denton, 4*s*. 4*d*.

Total of white chalk, 11*s*. 10*d*.

Lime. And for 1¾ hundredweight of lime for the gutter and the aforesaid quay bought from Richard the lime-burner of London, 8*s*. 9*d*. And for 3 hundredweight of lime bought for the same from Agnes the lime-burner, 15*s*.

Total of lime, 23*s*. 9*d*.

Ironwork. And to Henry of London Bridge for 7,000 lath-nails bought from him, 6*s*. To the same for 500 large nails, 20*d*. And to the same for 4,500 nails for shingles, 3*s*. 10*d*. And to Richard the cooper for mending utensils, 13*d*.

Total, 12*s*. 6*d*.

Timber. That is for 41 pieces of oak timber bought at Kingston for the latrine of the king's court, 21*s*. 10*d*. And for 49 small boards bought there for the same, 13*d*. And for three large oak posts bought there for the same, 7*s*. 6*d*. And for carriage of the aforesaid timber by water to Westminster, 2*s*. And for 10,000 shingles bought to cover the aforesaid chamber and kitchens, 70*s*., price 7*s*. a thousand. And for carriage of the aforesaid shingles by water from Kingston to Westminster at various times, 6*s*. 1*d*.

Total, 108*s*. 6*d*.

Sum total of the fifth payment, £15. 2*s*. 4½*d*.

Sixth Payment

The sixth payment was made from Monday on the morrow of the feast of the Apostles Peter and Paul [30 June] in the 43rd year of the reign of Henry aforesaid to Sunday on the eve of the Translation of the blessed Thomas the Martyr [6 July] for one whole week, that is, without any intervening feast.

Carpenters. That is to 5 carpenters working on the carpentry of the aforesaid latrine in the king's court, William de Waudis, Henry of Knightsbridge, Roger of Westminster, Simon of Northampton, Roger Cornwus, 10*s*. 10*d*. for the aforesaid week, that is, to each of them 26*d*.

Total carpenters' [wages], 10*s*. 10*d*.

Operarii. Et operariis deservientibus predictis carpentariis per idem tempus, videlicet Stephano de Gardino, Rogero de Cherring' xxv d. utrique illorum scilicet xij d. ob. Et quinque operariis cariantibus rebbusam ad equandum aream gardini circa cisternam, videlicet Galfrido Wrenn', Thome de Eye, Johanni Malekyn, Ade de Diddeuurth', Roberto de Sidwod' per quinque dies v sol. ij d. ob., cuilibet illorum scilicet xij d. ob.

Summa operariorum vij sol. iij d. ob.

Grisa petra. Et pro navata grise petre ad predictam gutteram & cayum faciend' empta de Matheo de Ponte vj sol. vj d. Et pro navata grise petre ad idem empta de Roberto Scyrlok' vi sol. Et pro navata grise petre ad idem empta de Philippo de Ponte v sol. vj d.

Summa grise petre xviij sol.

Calx. Et pro C j quarter' calcis emptis de Ricardo calfonario London' ad opus guttere & caii desub camera forinseca predicta vi sol. iij d.

[*Maeremium.*] Et pro xxix peciis de quercu ad opus eiusdem camere emptis apud Kyng' xij sol. ix d. Et pro cariagio eiusdem maeremii per aquam apud Westmonasterium de Kyng' ij sol.

Summa calcis & maeremii xxi sol.

Summa totalis sexte pacacionis lvij sol. j d. ob.

Septima pacacio

Pacacio septima fiebat a die Lune in festo Translacionis beati Thome Martiris anno regni Henrici predicti xliij° usque dominicam in festo beate Margarete Virginis per xv scilicet dies continentes predictum festum beati Thome quod fuit domini regis.

Cementarii. Tribus cementariis talliantibus ad cayum predictum per eamdem quindenam, videlicet Ricardo de Colecestr', Gervasio de Westmonasterio, Henrico Wyting' xij sol., cuilibet illorum scilicet iiij^or^ sol. Et Guydoni de Brun' per primam ebdomadam xxij d.

Summa cementariorum xijj sol. x.d.

Carpentarii. Et quinque carpentariis videlicet Willelmo de Waudis, Henrico de Knythebrug', Rogero de Westmonasterio, Simoni de Norht', Rogero Cornwus operantibus circa carpentariam predicte camere forinsece & coquinam regis scindulandam xx sol. cuilibet scilicet predictorum quinque iiij^or^ sol.

Summa carpentariorum xx sol.

Operarii. Et quinque operariis deservientibus predictis cementariis & carpentariis, videlicet Stephano de Gardino, Rogero de Cherring',

Labourers. And to the workmen serving the aforesaid carpenters for the same period, namely Stephen of the garden and Roger of Charing, 25*d*., that is to each of them 12½*d*. And to five labourers carrying rubbish to level the surface of the garden round the cistern, namely Geoffrey Wrenn, Thomas of Eye, John Malekyn, Adam of Dedworth, Robert de Sidwod for five days, 5*s*. 2½*d*., that is to each of them, 12½*d*.

Total labourers' [wages], 7*s*. 3½*d*.

Ragstone. And for a shipload of ragstone to make the aforesaid gutter and quay bought from Matthew of Bridge, 6*s*. 6*d*. And for a shipload of ragstone for the same bought from Robert Scyrlok, 6*s*. And for a shipload of ragstone for the same bought from Philip of Bridge, 5*s*. 6*d*.

Total of ragstone, 18*s*.

Lime. And for one hundredweight and one quarter of lime bought from Richard the lime-burner of London for the gutter and quay beneath the aforesaid latrine, 6*s*. 3*d*.

[*Timber*.] And for 29 pieces of oak for the said chamber bought at Kingston, 12*s*. 9*d*. And for the carriage of the said timber by water from Kingston to Westminster, 2*s*.

Total of lime and timber, 21*s*.

Sum total of the sixth payment, 57*s*. 1½*d*.

Seventh Payment

The seventh payment was made from Monday in the feast of the Translation of the blessed Thomas the Martyr [7 July] in the 43rd year of the reign of Henry aforesaid to Sunday on the feast of the blessed Margaret the Virgin [20 July], that is for 15 days, containing the aforesaid feast of the blessed Thomas which was the king's.

Masons. To three masons cutting for the aforesaid quay for the same fortnight, namely Richard of Colchester, Gervase of Westminster, Henry Wyting, 12*s*., that is to each of them 4*s*. And to Guy of Bourne for the first week, 22*d*.

Total masons' [wages], 13*s*. 10*d*.

Carpenters. And to five carpenters, namely William de Waudis, Henry of Knightsbridge, Roger of Westminster, Simon of Northampton, Roger Cornwus working on the carpentry of the aforesaid latrine and shingling the king's kitchen, 20*s*., that is to each of the aforesaid five, 4*s*.

Total carpenters' [wages], 20*s*.

Labourers. And to five labourers serving the aforesaid masons and carpenters, namely Stephen of the garden, Roger of Charing,

Galfrido Wrenn', Willelmo de Guldebur', Roberto de Sidwode per predictam quindenam xi sol. v d. ob. cuilibet illorum xxvij d. ob. Et quinque operariis videlicet Nicholao de Sancto Sepulcro, Thome de Eye, Thome clerico, Waltero de Bracino, Waltero ad Scaleram, operantibus per ij dies, xxv d., cuilibet illorum quinque scilicet v d. Et Gerardo de Bisele ad emundandum cameram forinsecam regine xij d. Et septem operariis qui discarcaverunt naviculatam maeremii ad opus predicte camere forinsece communis & detulerunt illud ad manus carpentariorum xvii d. ob.

Summa operariorum xvj sol.

Tasche. Et Willelmo de Thotull' super tascha de cayo sub camera forinseca assidendo x sol. Et Willelmo de Bledelawe cum j operario per j diem in curia regis circa cisternam assidendam vi d. ob. Et pro areragiis duorum carpentariorum per j diem operancium in coquina regis vi d. Et pro areragiis j operarii per iii dies circa opus camini in ebdomada Pentecost' vij d. ob. Et pro purgacione camere forinsece regine per j vicem duobus operariis v d. Et Willelmo de Clus' pro fabricacione martellorum cementariorum xvij d. Et Ricardo de Celar' pro cariagio sablonis per xv dies iij sol. viii d.

Summa tascharum xvij sol. ij d.

Franca petra. Et pro iiij^{or} cent. iij quarter' france petre ad opus caii predicti emptis de Radulfo de Lamh' xxviij sol. vi d.

Summa xxviij sol. vj d.

Grisa petra. Et pro navata grise petre ad opus guttere & caii predicte empta de Philippo de Ponte v sol. vj d. Et pro navata grise petre ad idem empta de Roberto Scyrlok' vj sol.

Calx. Et Agneti Calfonarie London' pro C j quarter' calcis emptis ad opus predicti cayi vj sol. iij d. Et Ricardo Calfonario London' pro j quarter' calcis empto ad idem xv d. Et Radulfo de Ponte pro cariagio sablonis ad tascham xvj d. Et pro j serura empta ad opus curie regis vi d.

Summa grise petre etc. xx sol. x d.

Maeremium. Et pro xxix peciis quercus ad opus predicte camere forinsece emptis apud Kyng' viij sol. xj d. Et pro v^{c} latharum ad idem emptis ibidem iij sol. Et pro cariagio predicti maeremii per aquam de Kyngeston' usque Westmonasterium ij sol.

Summa maeremii xiij sol. xi d.

Summa totalis septime pacacionis vj li. x sol. iij d.

Octava pacacio

Pacacio octava fiebat de die Lune in crastino beate Margarete Virginis anno regni Henrici predicti xliij^{o} usque dominicam proximam post

Geoffrey Wrenn, William of Goldbury, Robert de Sidwode for the aforesaid fortnight, 11*s.* 5½*d.*, to each of them, 27½*d.* And to five labourers, namely Nicholas of St. Sepulchre, Thomas of Eye, Thomas the clerk, Walter of the malt-house, Walter at stile, working for 2 days, 25*d.*, that is to each of those five, 5*d.* And to Gerard of Bisley to clean out the queen's latrine, 12*d.* And to seven labourers who unloaded a small boat-load of timber for the aforesaid common latrine and brought it to the hands of the carpenters, 17½*d.*

Total labourers' [wages], 16*s.*

Task-work. And to William of Tothill for the task of laying the quay beneath the latrine, 10*s.* And to William of Bledlow with one labourer in the king's court setting the cistern in place, 6½*d.* And for the arrears of two carpenters working for 1 day in the king's kitchen, 6*d.* And for the arrears of 1 labourer working on the chimney for 3 days in Whitsun week, 7½*d.* And for cleansing the queen's latrine on one occasion, to two labourers, 5*d.* And to William de Clus' for forging masons' mauls, 17*d.* And to Richard of the cellar for the carriage of sand for 15 days, 3*s.* 8*d.*

Total task-work, 17*s.* 2*d.*

Freestone. And for 4 hundredweight and three quarters of freestone for the aforesaid quay bought from Ralph of Lambeth, 28*s.* 6*d.*

Total, 28*s.* 6*d.*

Ragstone. And for a shipload of ragstone for the aforesaid gutter and quay bought from Philip of Bridge, 5*s.* 6*d.* And for a shipload of ragstone for the same bought from Robert Scyrlock, 6*s.*

Lime. And to Agnes the lime-burner of London for 1 hundredweight and 1 quarter of lime bought for the aforesaid quay, 6*s.* 3*d.* And to Richard the lime-burner of London for 1 quarter of lime bought for the same, 15*d.* And to Ralph of Bridge for carriage of sand by task, 16*d.* And for one lock bought for the king's court, 6*d.*

Total ragstone &c., 20*s.* 10*d.*

Timber. And for 29 pieces of oak for the aforesaid latrine bought at Kingston, 8*s.* 11*d.* And for 500 laths for the same bought there, 3*s.* And for carriage of the aforesaid timber by water from Kingston to Westminster, 2*s.*

Total timber, 13*s.* 11*d.*

Sum total of the seventh payment, £6. 10*s.* 3*d.*

Eighth Payment

The eighth payment was made from Monday on the morrow of the blessed Margaret the Virgin [21 July] in the 43rd year of the reign of the aforesaid Henry to Sunday next after the feast of the blessed

festum beati Petri ad Vincula per xv scilicet dies continentes festum beate Marie Magdalene per diem Martis quod fuit cementariorum & carpentariorum & festum beati Jacobi per diem Veneris quod fuit domini regis & predictum festum beati Petri per diem Veneris similiter quod fuit cementariorum & carpentariorum.

Cementarii. videlicet Ricardo de Colecestr' per ix dies tallianti ad cayum predictum ij sol. x d. Et Guydoni de Brun' per j diem circa idem iiij^{or} d. Et Ricardo de Eynesham per j diem operanti in curia regis per loca ad emendandum quedam xxij d. Et Gervasio de Westm' per predictam quindenam tallianti ad predictum cayum iiij^{or} sol. Et Henrico Wyting' per idem tempus circa idem iiij^{or} sol.

Summa cementariorum xiij sol.

Carpentarii. Et quinque carpentariis videlicet Willelmo de Waudis, Henrico de Knythebrig', Rogero Westm', Simoni de Norht', Rogero Cornws operantibus circa cameram forinsecam & coquinas regis scindulandas xx sol. cuilibet scilicet predictorum quinque iiij^{or} sol. Et Reginaldo de Estwik', Thome de Wyndesor' circa idem per idem tempus vij sol. iiij^{or} d. utrique illorum scilicet iij sol. viij d. Et Ricardo le Cuver per j ebdomadam circa idem xxij d. Et Gilberto de Guldeford circa idem per iiij^{or} dies xiiij^{or} d.

Summa carpentariorum xxx sol. iiij d.

Operarii. Et operariis deservientibus predictis cementariis & carpentariis per predictam quindenam videlicet Stephano de Gardino, Rogero de Cherring', Roberto de Sydwod' v sol. vij d. ob. cuilibet scilicet predictorum trium xxij d. ob. Et Willelmo de Guldebur' per iiij^{or} dies x d. Et Willelmo de Feck'ham per j ebdomadam xij d. ob.

Summa operariorum vij sol. vj d.

Tasch'. videlicet Willelmo de Thotull' ad perpacacionem tasche de cayo assidendo cum franca petra x sol. Item eidem Willelmo super tasch' de guttera circa lotorium in curia regis facienda vij sol. vj d. Et duobus pictoribus pro areragiis j diete circa parietes circa caminum regis depingendos xij d. Et Willelmo de Clus' pro fabricacione & emendacione martellorum cementariorum vj d. Et Radulfo de Ponte cum biga sua carianti sablonem per quinque dies xx d.

Summa tascharum xx sol. viij d.

Franca petra. videlicet pro C france petre ad opus caii predicti empto de Ricardo de Croiden' vi sol. Et pro C j quarter' france petre ad idem emptis de Willelmo de Brug' vij sol. vj d. Et pro j quart' france petre

Peter in Chains [3 August], that is for 15 days containing the feast of the blessed Mary Magdalen on Tuesday [22 July] which was the masons' and carpenters', and the feast of the blessed James on Friday [25 July] which was the king's, and the said feast of the blessed Peter likewise on Friday [1 August] which was the masons' and carpenters'.

Masons. That is to Richard of Colchester for 9 days cutting [stone] for the aforesaid quay, 2*s*. 10*d*. And to Guy of Bourne for 1 day on the same, 4*d*. And to Richard of Eynsham working in the king's court for 1 day mending things in various places, 22*d*. And to Gervase of Westminster cutting [stone] for the aforesaid quay during the said fortnight, 4*s*. And to Henry Wyting about the same during the same time, 4*s*.

Total masons' [wages], 13*s*.

Carpenters. And to five carpenters, namely William de Waudis, Henry of Knightsbridge, Roger of Westminster, Simon of Northampton, Roger Cornws, working on the latrine and shingling the king's kitchens, 20*s*., that is to each of the said five, 4*s*. And to Reginald of Eastwick, Thomas of Windsor about the same for the same time, 7*s*. 4*d*., that is to each of them, 3*s*. 8*d*. And to Richard the cooper for one week about the same, 22*d*. And to Gilbert of Guildford about the same for 4 days, 14*d*.

Total carpenters' [wages], 30*s*. 4*d*.

Labourers. And to labourers serving the aforesaid masons and carpenters for the said fortnight, namely Stephen of the garden, Roger of Charing, Robert de Sydwod, 5*s*. 7½*d*., that is to each of the aforesaid three, 22½*d*. And to William of Goldbury for 4 days, 10*d*. And to William of Feckenham for 1 week, 12½*d*.

Total labourers' [wages], 7*s*. 6*d*.

Task-work. That is to William of Tothill to complete payment for the task of laying the quay with freestone, 10*s*. And to the said William for the task of making a gutter round the lavatory in the king's court, 7*s*. 6*d*. And to two painters for one day's arrears for painting the walls about the king's chimney, 12*d*. And to William de Clus' for forging and mending masons' mauls, 6*d*. And to Ralph of Bridge carrying sand with his cart for five days, 20*d*.

Total task-work, 20*s*. 8*d*.

Freestone. That is for one hundredweight of freestone for the aforesaid quay bought from Richard of Croydon, 6*s*. And for a hundredweight and a quarter of freestone for the same bought from William of Bridge, 7*s*. 6*d*. And for 1 quarter of freestone for the same bought

ad idem empto de Randulfo de Regat' xviii d. Et pro j quarter' france petre ad idem empto de Radulfo de Lamh' xviij d.

Summa xvi sol. vj d.

Calx. Et pro C calcis ad opus predicti caii empto de Ricardo Calfonario v sol. Et pro CC calcis ad idem emptis de Agnete Calfonar' x sol.

Summa calcis xv sol.

Bord'. Et pro C magnorum bordorum Estric' ad gutter' magne aule regis emendand' & renovand' xiiij sol. viij d.

Ferramentum. Et pro MM clavorum ad lathas & dim. cent. dor'nayll' emptis de Henrico de ponte London' iij sol. vj d.

Summa xviij sol. ij d.

Summa totalis viij^{ve} pacacionis vj li. xiiij^{or} denarii.

Nona pacacio

Pacacio nona fiebat de die Lune proxima post festum beati Petri ad vincula anno regni Henrici predicti xliij^{o} usque dominicam in festo beati Laurencii martiris per unam ebdomadam sine festo.

Carpentarii. Et viij carpentariis videlicet Willelmo de Waudis, Henrico de Knythebrig', Rogero Westm', Simoni de Norht', Rogero Cornwus, Reginaldo de Estwik', Gilberto de Guldeford, Ricardo le Cuver operantibus circa cameram forincecam communem in curia regis & coquinas regis scindulandas per predictam ebdomadam xvij sol. iiij^{or} d. cuilibet scilicet predictorum viij^{to} xxvi d. Et Roberto de Aldebir' per idem tempus circa idem xviij d.

Summa carpentariorum xviij sol. x d.

Operarii. Et tribus operariis videlicet Stephano de Gardino, Hugoni de Berking', Thome de Eye deservientibus carpentariis per eamdem ebdomadam iij sol. ix d. cuilibet scilicet illorum xv d. Et tribus operariis videlicet Roberto de Oxon', Johanni Porter & Johanni de Oxon' per tres dies amoventibus terram de cayo predicto xxij d. ob. cuilibet scilicet illorum trium vij d. ob. Et Gerardo de Bis' pro emundacione camere forinsece domine regine per j vicem vi d.

Summa operariorum vi sol. j d. ob.

Summa totalis ix^{e} pacacionis xxiiij^{or} sol. xi d. ob.

Decima pacacio

Pacacio decima fiebat a die Lune in crastino beati Laurencii martiris anno regni Henrici predicti xliij^{o} usque dominicam in festo Sancti

from Ranulf of Reigate, 18*d.* And for 1 quarter of freestone for the same bought from Ralph of Lambeth, 18*d.*

Total, 16*s.* 6*d.*

Lime. And for one hundredweight of lime for the aforesaid quay bought from Richard the lime-burner, 5*s.* And for two hundredweight of lime for the same bought from Agnes the lime-burner, 10*s.*

Total of lime, 15*s.*

Boards. And for 100 great Eastland boards to repair and renew the gutters of the king's great hall, 14*s.* 8*d.*

Ironwork. And for 2,000 lath-nails and half a hundred door-nails bought from Henry of London Bridge, 3*s.* 6*d.*

Total, 18*s.* 2*d.*

Sum total of the eighth payment, £6. 1*s.* 2*d.*

Ninth Payment

The ninth payment was made from Monday next after the feast of the blessed Peter in Chains [4 August] in the 43rd year of the reign of the aforesaid Henry to the Sunday on the feast of the blessed Laurence the Martyr [10 August], for one week without a feast.

Carpenters. And to 8 carpenters, namely William de Waudis, Henry of Knightsbridge, Roger of Westminster, Simon of Northampton, Roger Cornwus, Reginald of Eastwick, Gilbert of Guildford, Richard the cooper, working on the common latrine in the king's court and shingling the king's kitchens during the said week, 17*s.* 4*d.*, that is to each of the aforesaid eight, 26*d.* And to Robert of Albury working for the same time on the same, 18*d.*

Total of carpenters' [wages], 18*s.* 10*d.*

Labourers. And to three labourers, namely Stephen of the garden, Hugh of Barking, Thomas of Eye, serving the carpenters during the same week, 3*s.* 9*d.*, that is to each of them, 15*d.* And to three labourers, that is Robert of Oxford, John Porter, and John of Oxford for three days moving earth from the aforesaid quay, 22½*d.*, that is to each of these three, 7½*d.* And to Gerard of Bisley for cleaning out the latrine of our lady the queen on one occasion, 6*d.*

Total of labourers' [wages], 6*s.* 1½*d.*

Sum total of the ninth payment, 24*s.* 11½*d.*

Tenth Payment

The tenth payment was made from Monday on the morrow of the blessed Laurence the Martyr [11 August] in the 43rd year of the reign of Henry aforesaid to Sunday on the feast of St. Bartholomew

Bartholomei apostoli per xv scilicet dies continentes festum Assumpcionis beate Marie per diem Veneris quod fuit carpentariorum.

Carpentarii. videlicet ix carpentariis, Willelmo de Waudis, Henrico de Knyth'brig', Rogero de Westmonasterio, Simoni de Norht', Rogero Cornwus, Reginaldo Estwyk', Gilberto de Guldeford, Ricardo le Cuver, Thome de Wyndes' operantibus circa construccionem camere forinsece & coquinas regis scindulandas per predictam quindenam xxxix sol., cuilibet illorum scilicet iiij^or^ sol. iiij^or^ d. Et Roberto de Aldebir' circa idem per predictum tempus iij sol.

Summa carpentariorum xlij sol.

Operarii. Et duobus operariis deservientibus carpentariis per predictam quindenam, videlicet Stephano de Gardino & Rogero de Cherring' iiij^or^ sol. vij d. utrique illorum scilicet xxvij d. ob. Et Hugoni de Berking' per j ebdomadam & j diem circa fundamentum camere forinsece curie regis preparandum xvij d. ob. Et Thome de Eye per j ebdomadam circa idem xv d. Et Roberto de Oxon', Johanni Porter & Johanni de Oxon' circa idem per tres dies xxij d. ob. cuilibet scilicet illorum trium vij d. ob.

Summa operariorum ix sol. ij d.

Tasche. Et Willelmo de Thotull' ad perpacacionem tasche de guttera circa lotorium in curia regis vij sol. vi d. Item eidem Willelmo pro cariagio sablonis ad opus predicte guttere iiij^or^ sol. v d. ob.

Summa xi sol. xi d. ob.

Calx. Et pro j quarter' calcis ad opus guttere circa lotorium empto de Agnete Calfonar' London' xv d.

Maeremium. Et pro C magnorum bordorum ad opus camere forinsece predicte empto apud Kyng' xij sol. vi d. Et pro CC latharum de quercu ad idem emptis ibidem xvi d. Et pro CC dim. clavorum ferri ad planch' & MMM clavorum ad scindulas & MM clavorum ad lathas ad opus predicte camere & coquine regis viij sol. vi d. Et pro duabus seruris novis emptis ad ostium thesauri xij d. Et pro j pelve stagnea ad deferendum cereum quemdam in capella Sancti Stephani per preceptum domini regis xvi d.

Summa xxv sol. xi d.

Summa totalis x^e^ pacacionis iiij^or^ li. ix sol. ob.

Undecima pacacio

Pacacio undecima fiebat a die Lune in crastino beati apostoli Bartholomei anno regni Henrici predicti xliij^o^ usque dominicam in vigilia beati Egidii per j scilicet ebdomodam continentem festum decollacionis Sancti Johannis Baptiste per diem Veneris quod fuit domini regis.

the Apostle [24 August], that is for 15 days containing the feast of the Assumption of the blessed Mary on Friday [15 August] which was the carpenters'.

Carpenters, namely to 9 carpenters, William de Waudis, Henry of Knightsbridge, Roger of Westminster, Simon of Northampton, Roger Cornwus, Reginald Eastwick, Gilbert of Guildford, Richard the cooper, Thomas of Windsor, working on the construction of the latrine and the shingling of the king's kitchens during the said fortnight, 39*s*., that is to each of them 4*s*. 4*d*. And to Robert of Albury on the same for the same time, 3*s*.

Total carpenters' [wages], 42*s*.

Labourers. And to two labourers serving the carpenters during the said fortnight, namely Stephen of the garden and Roger of Charing, 4*s*. 7*d*., that is to each of them 27½*d*. And to Hugh of Barking preparing the foundation of the latrine of the king's court for one week & one day, 17½*d*. And to Thomas of Eye on the same for one week, 15*d*. And to Robert of Oxford, John Porter, and John of Oxford on the same for three days, 22½*d*., that is 7½*d*. to each of those three.

Total labourers' [wages], 9*s*. 2*d*.

Task-work. And to William of Tothill to complete the task of the gutter round the lavatory in the king's court, 7*s*. 6*d*. And to the said William for the carriage of sand for the said gutter, 4*s*. 5½*d*.

Total, 11*s*. 11½*d*.

Lime. And for 1 quarter of lime for the gutter round the lavatory bought from Agnes the lime-burner of London, 15*d*.

Timber. And for 100 great boards for the said latrine bought at Kingston, 12*s*. 6*d*. And for 200 oak laths for the same bought at the same place, 16*d*. And for two and a half hundred of iron nails for planks and 3,000 nails for shingles and 2,000 nails for laths for the said latrine and king's kitchen, 8*s*. 6*d*. And for two new locks bought for the door of the treasury, 12*d*. And for one tin basin to carry a certain wax-light in St. Stephen's Chapel by the lord king's order, 16*d*.

Total, 25*s*. 11*d*.

Sum total of the tenth payment, £4. 9*s*. 0½*d*.

Eleventh Payment

The eleventh payment was made from Monday on the morrow of the blessed Apostle Bartholomew [25 August] in the 43rd year of the reign of the aforesaid Henry to Sunday on the eve of the blessed Giles [31 August], that is for one week containing the feast of the beheading of St. John the Baptist on Friday [29 August], which was the lord king's.

Carpentarii. Novem carpentariis videlicet Willelmo de Waudis, Henrico de Knythebrig', Rogero de Westmonasterio, Symoni de Norht', Rogero Cornwus, Reginaldo de Estwik', Gilberto de Gudeford, Ricardo le Cuver, Thome de Wyndesor' per predictam ebdomadam operantibus circa cameram forinsecam predictam & coquinas regis scindulandas xvi sol. vj d. cuilibet scilicet predictorum xxij d. Et Roberto de Aldebir' circa idem per eamdem ebdomadam xv d.

Summa carpentariorum xvij sol. ix d.

Operarii. Et duobus operariis videlicet Stephano de Gardino, Rogero de Cherring' deservientibus predictis carpentariis per predictam ebdomadam xxv d. utrique illorum scilicet xij d ob.

Summa operariorum xxv d.

Summa totalis xi^{e} pacacionis xix sol. x d.

Duodecima pacacio

Pacacio duodecima fiebat a die Lune in festo Sancti Egidii anno regni Henrici predicti xliij^{o} usque dominicam in vigilia Translacionis beati Edwardi regis per sex ebdomadas continentes festum Nativitatis beate Marie per diem Lune quod fuit carpentariorum & festum beati Michaelis per diem Lune similiter quod fuit domini regis.

Cubitores. videlicet Roberto Busch' cubitori per v ebdomadas operanti circa gutteram exeuntem de camera forinseca regine usque Thamisiam x sol. ij d. Et Radulfo de Oxon' per j ebdomadam integram circa idem xxvi d. Et Ricardo de Bureford per iiij^{or} ebdomadas circa idem viij sol. Et Galfrido de Piro per ij dies circa idem viij d. ob. Et Hugoni de Merthon' per iiij^{or} ebdomadas circa idem vij sol. viij d. Et Roberto le Blund per iiij^{or} dies circa idem xvij d. Et Ricardo de Eynesham per iij ebdomadas circa idem vi sol. vi d. ob. Et Rogero de Essex' per xv dies circa idem iij sol. viij d.

Summa cubitorum xl sol. iiij^{or} d.

Carpentarii. Et sex carpentariis videlicet Simoni de Norht', Willelmo de Waudis, Henrico de Knythebrug', Rogero Cornwus, Reginaldo de Estwik', Ricardo le Cuver' per sex ebdomadas operantibus circa cameram forincecam predictam & coquinas regis scindulandas lxxvi sol. cuilibet scilicet predictorum sex xij sol. viij d. Et Roberto de Aldebir' per idem tempus viij sol. ix d. Et Rogero de Westmonasterio & Thome de Wyndesor' per quinque ebdomadas circa idem xxi sol. utrique illorum scilicet x sol. vi d. Et Gilberto de Guldeford per iij dies circa idem xiij d.

Summa carpentariorum C vi sol. x d.

Carpenters. To nine carpenters, namely William de Waudis, Henry of Knightsbridge, Roger of Westminster, Simon of Northampton, Roger Cornwus, Reginald of Eastwick, Gilbert of Guildford, Richard the cooper, Thomas of Windsor working for the said week on the said latrine and shingling the king's kitchens, 16*s*. 6*d*., that is to each of the aforesaid, 22*d*. And to Robert of Albury on the same for the same week, 15*d*.

Total carpenters' [wages], 17*s*. 9*d*.

Labourers. And to two labourers, that is Stephen of the garden, Roger of Charing serving the said carpenters during the said week, 25*d*., that is to each of them 12½*d*.

Total labourers' [wages], 25*d*.

Sum total of the 11th payment, 19*s*. 10*d*.

Twelfth Payment

The twelfth payment was made from Monday on the feast of St. Giles [1 September] in the 43rd year of the reign of the aforesaid Henry to Sunday on the eve of the Translation of the blessed King Edward [12 October] for six weeks containing the feast of the Nativity of the blessed Mary on Monday [8 September] which was the carpenters' and the feast of the blessed Michael, also on Monday [29 September] which was the lord king's.

Layers, namely Robert Busch layer working for 5 weeks on the gutter going from the queen's latrine to the Thames, 10*s*. 2*d*. And to Ralph of Oxford for one whole week on the same, 26*d*. And to Richard of Burford for 4 weeks on the same, 8*s*. And to Geoffrey de Piro for 2 days on the same, 8½*d*. And to Hugh of Merton for 4 weeks on the same, 7*s*. 8*d*. And to Robert le Blund for 4 days on the same, 17*d*. And to Richard of Eynsham for 3 weeks on the same 6*s*. 6½*d*. And to Roger of Essex for 15 days on the same, 3*s*. 8*d*.

Total layers' [wages], 40*s*. 4*d*.

Carpenters. And to six carpenters, namely Simon of Northampton, William de Waudis, Henry of Knightsbridge, Roger Cornwus, Reginald of Eastwick, Richard the cooper for six weeks working on the aforesaid latrine and shingling the king's kitchens, 76*s*., that is to each of the aforesaid six, 12*s*. 8*d*. And to Robert of Albury for the same time, 8*s*. 9*d*. And to Roger of Westminster and Thomas of Windsor for five weeks on the same, 21*s*., that is to each of them 10*s*. 6*d*. And to Gilbert of Guildford for 3 days on the same, 13*d*.

Total carpenters' [wages], 106s. 10*d*.

Pictoribus. Et Magistro Willelmo pictori cum hominibus suis circa Jesse in mantello camini regis depingendum & circa picturam parietum ipsius camere regis innovandam & abluendam xliij sol. x d. Et in coloribus diversis emptis ad idem vij sol. vi d.

Plummer'. Et tribus plumbariis per j ebdomadam & iii dies circa gutteram aule regis reparandam & foramina supra cameram senescallorum consolidanda vi sol. iij d.

Summa lvij sol. vij d.

Operarii. Et duobus operariis deservientibus carpentariis per predictum tempus videlicet Stephano de Gardino, Rogero de Cherring' xiiij^or^ sol. ij d. utrique illorum scilicet per sex ebdomadas predictas vij sol. j d. Et tribus operariis videlicet Waltero de Neuport', Gerardo de Bisel', Willelmo de Perham per quinque ebdomadas deservientibus predictis cubitoribus xvij sol. vj d. cuilibet predictorum trium scilicet v sol. x d. Et Ricardo de Lichefeud per quatuor ebdomadas & ij dies circa idem v sol. Et Ade Miting' Et Simoni Russell' per tres ebdomadas circa idem ix sol. ij d. utrique illorum scilicet iiij^or^ sol. vij d. Et Johanni de Eynesham per tres ebdomadas & duos dies circa idem iij sol. x d. ob. Et Fulconi per j ebdomadam cum festo xij d. ob.

Summa operariorum l sol. ix d.

Tasche. Et pro iiij^or^ perticis cuiusdam muri terrei constructi ad claudendum inter predictam cameram forinsecam & clausum capellanorum regis iij sol. vj d.

Plummer'. Et Johanni Govayr' & socio suo pro v chareis plumbi fundendis & ponendis in guter' magne aule regis xxv sol.

Et tribus carpentariis pro areragiis j diete xij d. Et Radulfo le veriur per ij dies iiij^or^ d. ob.

Sabulon'. Et Ricardo Curteys pro CC dim. charearum sablonis cariatarum ad tascham iij sol. vi d. Et pro carecta sua locata per quinque dietas xxvij d. Et Ricardo de Celario pro cariagio C sablonis ad tascham ij sol. Eidem pro carecta sua cum duobus equis ad dietam per quatuor dies ij sol. Et Waltero de camera pro cariagio C sablonis ad tascham ij sol. Eidem pro carecta sua per duas dietas viij d. Et xv operariis cum duabus bigis diurnis per xv dies circa herbarium domini regis reparandum & turbandum xxij sol. xi d.

Summa lxv sol. ij d. ob.

Grisa petra. Ebdomada prima pro navata grise petre ad predictam gutteram empta de Willelmo Prudfot' v sol. ix d. Et pro navata grise petre ad idem empta de Edmundo filio Radulfi v sol. ix d. Et pro navata grise petre ad idem empta de Henrico Muriweder v sol.

Painters. And to Master William the painter with his men painting a [Tree of] Jesse on the mantel of the king's chimney and renewing and cleaning the painting on the walls of the king's chamber itself, 43*s.* 10*d.* And for various colours bought for the same, 7*s.* 6*d.*

Plumbers. And to three plumbers for one week and 3 days repairing the gutter of the king's hall and soldering holes over the stewards' chamber, 6*s.* 3*d.*

Total, 57*s.* 7*d.*

Labourers. And to two labourers serving the carpenters during the said time, namely Stephen of the garden, Roger of Charing, 14*s.* 2*d.*, that is to each of them for the said six weeks, 7*s.* 1*d.* And to three labourers, namely Walter of Newport, Gerard of Bisley, William of Parham serving the said layers for five weeks, 17*s.* 6*d.*, that is to each of the said three, 5*s.* 10*d.* And to Richard of Lichfield for four weeks and 2 days on the same, 5*s.* And to Adam Miting and Simon Russell for three weeks on the same, 9*s.* 2*d.*, that is to each of them, 4*s.* 7*d.* And to John of Eynsham for three weeks and two days on the same, 3*s.* 10½*d.* And to Fulk for one week containing a feast, 12½*d.*

Total labourers' [wages], 50*s.* 9*d.*

Task-work. And for 4 perches of a certain earthen wall built to form an enclosure between the aforesaid latrine and the close of the king's chaplains, 3*s.* 6*d.*

Plumbers. And to John Govayr' and his mate for founding 5 chars of lead and fixing them in the gutter of the king's great hall, 25*s.*

And to three carpenters for arrears of one day's work, 12*d.* And to Ralph le Veriur for 2 days 4½*d.*

Sand. And to Richard Curteys for carriage of 250 cart-loads of sand by task, 3*s.* 6*d.* And for the hire of his cart for 5 days, 27*d.* And to Richard of the cellar for the carriage of one hundred [cart-loads] of sand by task, 2*s.* To him for his cart with two horses by the day for 4 days, 2*s.* And to Walter of the chamber for the carriage of one hundred [cart-loads] of sand by task, 2*s.* To him for his cart for two days, 8*d.* And to 15 labourers with two carts daily for 15 days making good and turfing the king's lawn, 22*s.* 11*d.*

Total, 65*s.* 2½*d.*

Ragstone. In the first week for a shipload of ragstone for the aforesaid gutter bought from William Prudfot, 5*s.* 9*d.* And for a shipload of ragstone for the same bought from Edmund son of Ralph, 5*s.* 9*d.* And for a shipload of ragstone for the same bought from Henry Muriweder, 5*s.* 9*d.* And for a shipload of ragstone for the same

ix d. Et pro navata grise petre ad idem empta de Roberto de Hakeford v sol. ix d. Et pro navata grise petre ad idem empta de Ricardo Makevayr iiij^or^ sol. vi d.

Summa xxvij sol. vi d.

Ferramentum. Et Henrico de Ponte pro vij mill. clavorum ferri ad cindulas ad cooperturam predicte camere forinsece regis & ad coquinas scindulandas x solid. vj d. Eidem pro MM clavorum ad lathas ad idem ij sol.

Summa xij sol vj d.

Grisa petra. Item ebdomada secunda pro navata grise petre empta de Willelmo Prudfot' ad predictam gutteram v sol. ix d. Et pro navata grise petre empta de Edmundo filio Radulfi v sol. ix d. Et pro navata grise petre ad idem empta de Ricardo filio Jocelini iiij^or^ sol. vj d.

[*Creta.*] Et pro ij navatis albe crete ad idem emptis de Johanne Eldegrom' ij sol. vi d.

Summa xviij sol. vi d.

Maeremium. Et pro xviij cheveronibus & xvi punsuns quercus ad opus predicte camere forincece viij sol. vi d. ob. Et pro CC ross' ad crestandum murum terreum ante cameram forinsecam predictam emptis apud Wytheflet' cum vectura per aquam usque Westmonasterium ij sol. Et pro littera ad ipsum murum faciendum vj d.

Summa xi sol. ob.

Ferramentum. Et pro vi mill. tyng'naill' ad opus predicte camere & coquinarum regis viij sol. precium mill. sexdecim denarii. Et pro CC grossorum claviorum ad planch' iij sol. ij d. Et pro iiij^or^ mill. de rofnaill' ad idem vi sol. viij d. Et pro MM clavorum ad lathas de quercu ij sol. Et pro MM clavorum ad lathas de fohu xxij d. Et pro CC ting'naill' vj d.

Summa xxij sol. ij d.

Item ebdomada quarta pro j mill. latharum quercus empto de Willelmo de Braye viij sol. viij d. Et pro iiij^or^ mill. planarum tegularum & C & dim. tegularum cavarum ad cooperturam domorum curie regis xiij sol. viij d.

Item ebdomada quinta pro CC dim. calcis ad gutteram camere forinsece emptis London' xij sol. vi d. Et pro MM tyng'naill' & MM clavorum ad lathas emptis de Henrico de Ponte London' iiij^or^ sol. viij d.

Et pro iiij^or^ mill. cavillarum ad tegulas vij d. ob. Et pro duabus clavibus novis emptis cum emendacione quarumdam serurarum curie regis xx d. ob.

Item ebdomada sexta pro v^c^ tegularum emptis de Willelmo de Smethefeud xviij d. Et Henrico de Ponte London' pro M v^c^ clavorum ad cindulas ij sol. iij d.

Summa xlv sol. vij d.

Summa totalis xij^e^ pacacionis xxij li. xviij sol.

bought from Robert of Hackford, 5*s*. 9*d*. And for a shipload of ragstone for the same bought from Richard Makevayr, 4*s*. 6*d*.

Total, 27*s*. 6*d*.

Ironwork. And to Henry of [London] Bridge for 7,000 iron nails for shingles to cover the king's said latrine and to shingle the kitchens, 10*s*. 6*d*. To him for 2,000 nails for laths for the same, 2*s*.

Total, 12*s*. 6*d*.

Ragstone. And in the second week for a shipload of ragstone bought from William Prudfot for the said gutter, 5*s*. 9*d*. And for a shipload of ragstone bought from Edmund son of Ralph, 5*s*. 9*d*. And for ragstone for the same bought from Richard son of Jocelin, 4*s*. 6*d*.

[*Chalk*.] And for 2 shiploads of white chalk for the same bought from John Eldegrom, 2*s*. 6*d*.

Total, 18*s*. 6*d*.

Timber. And for 18 rafters and 16 oak puncheons for the said latrine 8*s*. 6½*d*. And for two hundredweight of reeds to make a cresting for the earthen wall in front of the said latrine bought at Wytheflet with transport by water to Westminster, 2*s*. And for straw to make the said wall, 6*d*.

Total, 11*s*. 0½*d*.

Ironwork. And for 6,000 tyngnaill for the said latrine and king's kitchens, 8*s*., price 16*d*. a thousand. And for 200 large nails for planks, 3*s*. 2*d*. And for 4,000 rofnaill for the same, 6*s*. 8*d*. And for 2,000 nails for oaken laths, 2*s*. And for 2,000 nails for beech laths, 22*d*. And for 200 tingnaill, 6*d*.

Total, 22*s*. 2*d*.

And in the fourth week for 1,000 oak laths bought of William of Bray, 8*s*. 8*d*. And for 4,000 flat tiles and a hundred and a half of curved tiles to cover the buildings of the king's court, 13*s*. 8*d*. And in the fifth week for 2 hundredweight and a half of lime for the gutter of the latrine bought in London, 12*s*. 6*d*. And for 2,000 tyngnaill and 2,000 nails for laths bought from Henry of London Bridge, 4*s*. 8*d*.

And for 4,000 pegs for tiles, 7½*d*. And for two new keys bought together with the mending of certain locks in the king's court, 20½*d*.

And in the sixth week for 500 tiles bought from William of Smithfield, 18*d*. And to Henry of London Bridge for 1,500 nails for shingles, 2*s*. 3*d*.

Total, 45*s*. 7*d*.

Sum total of the 12th payment, £22. 18*s*.

Terciadecima pacacio

Pacacio terciadecima fiebat a die Lune in festo translacionis beati Edwardi regis anno regni Henrici predicti xliij° usque dominicam proximam ante festum apostolorum Simonis & Jude per xv scilicet dies continentes predictum festum beati Edwardi quod fuit carpentariorum & festum beati Luce Ewangeliste per diem sabbati quod fuit domini regis.

Carpentarii. Tribus carpentariis videlicet Willelmo de Waudis, Rogero Cornwus, Henrico de Knythebrug' circa coquinas regis cooperiendas per predictam quindenam xij sol. cuilibet scilicet predictorum trium iiij^{or} sol. Et Roberto de Aldebir' per idem tempus ij sol. ix d.

Summa carpentariorum xiiij^{or} sol. ix d.

Plummer'. Et Johanni le plumm[er]e per duos dies operanti circa defectus plummer' ultra cameram senescallorum emendandos viij d. ob.

Operarii. Et duobus operariis deservientibus predictis carpentariis & plummario per predictum tempus videlicet Stephano de Gardino, Rogero de Cherring' iiij^{or} sol. ij d. utrique illorum scilicet xxv d. per quindenam.

Summa iiij^{or} sol. x d. ob.

Ferramentum. Et pro MM grossorum clavorum ad lathas & j mill. minorum clavorum ad idem emptis de Henrico de ponte London' iiij^{or} sol. Et pro vj mill. clavorum ad cindulas ad opus coquinarum regis emptis de eodem vj sol.

Summa x sol.

Summa totalis xiij^{e} pacacionis xxix sol. vij d. ob.

Quartadecima pacacio

Pacacio quartadecima fiebat a die Lune in vigilia apostolorum Simonis & Jude anno regni Henrici predicti xliij° usque dominicam proximam post festum beati Martini per tres ebdomadas continentes predictum festum predictorum apostolorum per diem Martis quod fuit cementariorum & carpentariorum & festum Omnium Sanctorum per diem Sabbati quod fuit domini regis & festum beati Martini per diem Martis similiter quod fuit cementariorum & carpentariorum.

Cementarii. Cementario operanti circa fenestram in domo Judeorum videlicet Johanni de Oxon' per tres ebdomadas vi sol. ij d. Et tribus cementariis videlicet Ricardo de Cicestr', Johanni de Eltham, Reginaldo Sturmy per j ebdomadam talliantibus ad eamdem fenestram vj sol. vj d. cuilibet illorum trium scilicet xxvi d.

Summa cementariorum xij sol. viij d.

Thirteenth Payment

The thirteenth payment was made from Monday on the feast of the Translation of the blessed King Edward [13 October] in the 43rd year of the reign of the said Henry to Sunday next before the feast of the Apostles Simon and Jude [26 October], that is for 15 days containing the said feast of the blessed Edward which was the carpenters' and the feast of the blessed Luke the Evangelist on Saturday [18 October], which was the lord king's.

Carpenters. To three carpenters, namely William de Waudis, Roger Cornwus, Henry of Knightsbridge, working on covering the king's kitchens during the said fortnight, 12*s.*, that is to each of the said three, 4*s.* And to Robert of Albury for the same time, 2*s.* 9*d.*

Total carpenters' [wages], 14*s.* 9*d.*

Plumbers. And to John the plumber working for two days to mend the defects of the lead-work above the stewards' chamber, 8½*d.*

Labourers. And to two labourers serving the said carpenters and plumbers during the said time, namely Stephen of the garden, Roger of Charing, 4*s.* 2*d.*, that is to each of them 25*d.* for the fortnight.

Total, 4*s.* 10½*d.*

Ironwork. And for 2,000 large nails for laths and 1,000 small nails for the same bought from Henry of London Bridge, 4*s.* And for 6,000 nails for shingles for the king's kitchens, bought from the same, 6*s.*

Total, 10*s.*

Sum total of the 13th payment, £1. 9*s.* 7½*d.*

Fourteenth Payment

The fourteenth payment was made from Monday on the eve of the Apostles Simon and Jude [27 October] in the 43rd year of the reign of the said Henry to Sunday next after the feast of the blessed Martin [16 November] for three weeks containing the said feast of the said apostles on Tuesday [28 October], which was the masons', and the feast of All Saints on Saturday [1 November], which was the lord king's, and the feast of the blessed Martin on Tuesday [11 November], which was likewise the masons' and carpenters'.

Masons. To a mason working on the window in the Jews' house,[1] namely to John of Oxford for three weeks, 6*s.* 2*d.* And to three masons, namely Richard of Chichester, John of Eltham, Reginald Sturmy for one week cutting stone for the same window, 6*s.* 6*d.*, that is to each of those three, 26*d.*

Total masons' [wages], 12*s.* 8*d.*

[1] That is, the building occupied by the Justices of the Jews.

Carpentarii. Et tribus carpentariis videlicet Willelmo de Waudis, Henrico de Knythebr', Rogero Cornwus per tres ebdomadas operantibus circa coquinas regis scindulandas xviij sol. vj d. cuilibet illorum trium scilicet vi sol. ij d. Et Roberto de Aldebir' per idem tempus iiij^or^ sol. iij d. Et Gilberto carpentario, Johanni de Greneford, Johanni de Padinton' per xv dies circa idem xiij sol. cuilibet scilicet illorum trium iiij^or^ sol. iiij d.

Summa carpentariorum xxxv sol. ix d.

Fabri. Et fabris circa ferramentum faciendum quod sustentat tuellum extra cameram regis contra impetus ventorum, videlicet magistro Henrico de Lewes per predictas tres ebdomadas circa predictum ferramentum fabricandum xij sol. Et Simoni fabro per idem tempus vi sol. ij d. Et Willelmo de Offinton' per idem tempus circa idem iiij^or^ sol. iij d. Et Thoraud' per idem tempus circa idem iiij^or^ sol. ix d.

Summa xxvij sol. ij d.

Operarii. Et duobus operariis, videlicet Stephano de Gardino & Rogero de Cherring' deservientibus predictis cementariis & carpentariis per predictas tres ebdomadas vj sol. iij d., utrique illorum scilicet iij sol. j d. ob. Et Johanni Churant per quatuor dies x d.

Summa operariorum vij sol. j d.

Ferramentum. Et pro MM minutorum clavorum ad lathas & j mill. maiorum clavorum ad idem iij sol. vj d. Item pro iiij^or^ mill. & v^c^ clavorum ad lathas v sol. Et pro MM grossorum clavorum & CCC dim. clavorum ad scindulas ix sol. ob. Et pro quadam serura nova cum clave ad ostium quoddam in curia regis xviij d.

Summa xix sol. ob.

Summa totalis xiiij^me^ pacacionis Cj sol. viij d. ob.

Quintadecima pacacio

Pacacio quintadecima fiebat a die Lune proxima post festum Sancti Martini anno regni Henrici predicti xliiij^o^ usque dominicam in festo Sancti Andree apostoli per xv dies continentes festum beati Edmundi regis & martiris per diem Jovis quod fuit domini regis & festum beate Caterine virginis per diem Martis quod fuit cementariorum & carpentariorum.

Cementarii. videlicet Johanni de Oxon' operanti circa fenestram & bancos in domo Judeorum & circa gistas sublevandas ex una parte in camera senescallorum per predictam quindenam iiij^or^ sol. Et Ricardo de Colecestr' per j ebdomadam circa idem ij sol. Et Bartholomeo de Westmonasterio per j ebdomadam circa idem ij sol.

Summa cementariorum viij sol.

Carpenters. And to three carpenters, namely William de Waudis, Henry of Knightsbridge, Roger Cornwus working for three weeks on the shingling of the king's kitchens, 18*s*. 6*d*., that is to each of those three, 6*s*. 2*d*. And to Robert of Albury for the same time, 4*s*. 3*d*. And to Gilbert the carpenter, John of Greenford, John of Paddington working for 15 days on the same, 13*s*., that is to each of these three, 4*s*. 4*d*.

Total carpenters' [wages], 35*s*. 9*d*.

Smiths. And to smiths making the ironwork which supports the flue of the chimney outside the king's chamber against the pressure of the wind, namely to Master Henry of Lewes making the said ironwork during the said three weeks, 12*s*. And to Simon the smith for the same time, 6*s*. 2*d*. And to William of Uffington for the same time on the same, 4*s*. 3*d*. And to Thorold for the same time on the same, 4*s*. 9*d*.

Total, 27*s*. 2*d*.

Labourers. And to two workmen, namely Stephen of the garden and Hugh of Charing serving the said masons and carpenters during the said three weeks, 6*s*. 3*d*., that is to each of them, 3*s*. 1½*d*. And to John Churant for four days, 10*d*.

Total labourers' [wages], 7*s*. 1*d*.

Ironwork. And for 2,000 small nails for laths and 1,000 larger nails for the same, 3*s*. 6*d*. And for 4,500 nails for laths, 5*s*. And for 2,000 large nails and 350 nails for shingles, 9*s*. 0½*d*. And for a certain new lock with a key for a certain door in the king's court, 18*d*.

Total, 19*s*. 0½*d*.

Sum total of the 14th payment, £5. 1*s*. 8½*d*.

Fifteenth Payment

The fifteenth payment was made from Monday next after the feast of St. Martin [17 November] in the 44th year of the reign of the said Henry to Sunday on the feast of St. Andrew the Apostle [30 November] for 15 days, containing the feast of the blessed Edmund the King and Martyr on Thursday [20 November], which was the lord king's and the feast of the blessed Catherine the Virgin on Tuesday [25 November], which was the masons' and carpenters'.

Masons, namely to John of Oxford working on the window and benches in the house [of the Justices] of the Jews and on raising the joists on one side in the stewards' chamber, 4*s*. And to Richard of Colchester for one week on the same, 2*s*. And to Bartholomew of Westminster for one week on the same, 2*s*.

Total masons' [wages], 8*s*.

Carpentarii. Et sex carpentariis videlicet Willelmo de Waudis, Rogero Cornwus, Henrico de Knithebrug', Gilberto carpentario, Johanni de Greneford, Johanni de Padinton' per predictam quindenam circa coquinas regis & sedem Justiciariorum de Banco emendandam xxiiij^{or} sol. cuilibet predictorum sex iiij^{or} sol. Et Roberto de Aldebir' per idem tempus ij sol. ix d.

Summa carpentariorum xxvi sol. ix d.

Fabri. Et magistro Henrico de Lewes circa ferramentum ad caminum fabricandum per predictam quindenam viij sol. Et Simoni fabro per idem tempus iiij^{or} sol. Et Willelmo de Offinton' per idem tempus ij sol. ix d. Et Thoraudo per idem tempus iij sol. j d. Et predictis fabris pro vigiliis suis de nocte per j mensem circa predictum ferramentum festinandum vi sol viij d.

Summa fabrorum xxiiij^{or} sol. vj d.

Operarii. Et operariis deservientibus predictis cementariis & carpentariis per predictum tempus, videlicet Stephano de Gardino per idem tempus xxv d. Et Rogero de Cherring' per idem tempus xxv d. Et tribus operariis videlicet Waltero de Sancto Albano, Willelmo Millers & Johanni de Stan' juvantibus & facientibus scaffot' ad predictum ferramentum ponendum per j ebdomadam iij sol. j d. ob. cuilibet illorum scilicet xij d. ob. Et duobus scyhur' videlicet Willelmo de Scyreburn', Waltero Norr' per j ebdomadam & iiij^{or} dies iij sol. ix d.

Summa xj sol. ob.

Tasche plummer'. Et Johanni Govair' & Willelmo de Strande pro viij^{to} chareis plumbi fundendis & cubandis supra cameram senescallorum per tascham xl sol. capiendo pro charea v sol. Et Willelmo de Clus' super tascham de ferramento ad fenestram domus Judeorum faciendo cum quibusdam aliis emendandis iiij^{or} sol. Et pro carecta magistri Odonis per j dietam ad buscam & plumbum carianda vj d.

Summa xliiij^{or} sol. vj d.

Summa totalis xv^{e} pacacionis C xiiij^{or} sol. ix d. ob.

Sextadecima pacacio

Pacacio sextadecima fiebat a die Lune in crastino Sancti Andree apostoli anno regni Henrici predicti xliiij^{o} usque dominicam in crastino Sancte Lucie Virginis per xv scilicet dies continentes festum beati Nicholai per diem Sabbati quod fuit domini regis & festum Concepcionis beate Marie per diem Lune quod fuit carpentariorum.

Carpentarii. Sex carpentariis operantibus circa sedem Justiciariorum de Banco & coquinas regis scindulandas, videlicet Willelmo de Waudis,

Carpenters. And to six carpenters, namely William de Waudis, Roger Cornwus, Henry of Knightsbridge, Gilbert the carpenter, John of Greenford, John of Paddington for the said fortnight working on the king's kitchens and repairing the seat of the Justices of the Bench, 24*s.*, to each of the said six, 4*s.* And to Robert of Albury for the same time, 2*s.* 9*d.*

Total carpenters' [wages], 26*s.* 9*d.*

Smiths. And to Master Henry of Lewes forging ironwork for the chimney during the said fortnight, 8*s.* And to Simon the smith for the same time, 4*s.* And to William of Uffington for the same time, 2*s.* 9*d.* And to Thorold for the same time, 3*s.* 1*d.* And to the said smiths for their labours by night for one month in order to hasten the said ironwork, 6*s.* 8*d.*

Total smiths' [wages], 24*s.* 6*d.*

Labourers. And to labourers serving the said masons and carpenters during the said time, namely Stephen of the garden for the same time, 25*d.* And to Roger of Charing for the same time, 25*d.* And to three labourers, namely Walter of St. Albans, William Millers, and John of Stanway (?) helping and making the scaffold to fix the said ironwork for one week, 3*s.* 1½*d.*, that is to each of them 12½*d.* And to two sawyers, namely William of Sherborne, Walter Norris for one week and 4 days, 3*s.* 9*d.*

Total, 11*s.* 0½*d.*

Plumbers' task-work. And to John Govair' and William of Strand for founding and laying 8 chars of lead above the stewards' chamber by task, 40*s.*, taking 5*s.* a char. And to William de Clus' for the task of making ironwork for the window of the house [of the Justices] of the Jews, together with mending certain other things, 4*s.* And for Master Odo's cart for one day to carry firewood and lead, 6*d.*

Total, 44*s.* 6*d.*

Sum total of the 15th payment, £5. 14*s.* 9½*d.*

Sixteenth Payment

The sixteenth payment was made from Monday on the morrow of St. Andrew the Apostle [1 December] in the 44th year of the reign of the said Henry to Sunday on the morrow of St. Lucy the Virgin [14 December] for 15 days, containing the feast of the blessed Nicholas on Saturday [6 December] which was the lord king's and the feast of the Conception of the blessed Mary on Monday [8 December] which was the carpenters'.

Carpenters. To six carpenters working on the seat of the Justices of the Bench and shingling the king's kitchens, namely William de Waudis,

Rogero de Westmonasterio, Rogero Cornwus, Gilberto carpentario, Henrico de Knith'brig', et Johanni de Padinton' per predictam quindenam xxiiij^or sol. cuilibet illorum sex scilicet iiij^or sol. Et Johanni de Greneford per j ebdomadam xxij d. Et Roberto de Aldebir' per xv dies ij sol. ix d.

Summa carpentariorum xxviij sol. vij d.

Cementarii. Et Johanni de Oxon' per predictam quindenam circa predictas gistas sublevandas iiij^or sol. Et Johanni le plummer per j diem iiij^or d.

Summa iiij^or sol. iiij^or d.

Fabri. Et Magistro Henrico de Lewes per primam ebdomadam circa predictum ferramentum fabricandum iiij^or sol. Et Simoni fabro xxvi d. Et Thoraudo xx d. Et Willelmo de Offinton' xviij d. per eamdem ebdomadam.

Summa fabrorum ix sol. iiij d.

Operarii. Et duobus operariis videlicet Stephano de Gardino & Rogero de Cherring' deservientibus predictis carpentariis per predictos xv dies iiij^or sol. ij d. utrique illorum scilicet xxv d. Et duobus scihurs videlicet Waltero Norr' & Willelmo de Scyreburn' per iij dies xv d. utrique illorum vij d. ob.

Summa operariorum v sol. v d.

Plummer'. Et Johanni Govair' & Willelmo de Strande pro viij^to chareis plumbi fundendis & cubandis supra cameram senescallorum per tasch' capiendo pro charea quinque solidos xl sol.

Ferramentum. Et Willelmo de Clus' ad perpacacionem tasche de ferramento ad fenestram domus Judeorum iiij^or sol. ij d. Eidem Willelmo pro ferramento ad sedem Justiciariorum de Banco faciendo xiiij^or d.

Summa xlv sol. iiij^or d.

Cariagium sablonis & argilli. Et Matheo de Eye cum biga sua eunti ad sablonem & argillum ponenda sub plumbo ultra cameram senescallorum per iij ebdomadas vj sol. Et Ricardo de Celar' cum biga sua cum duobus equis per xv dies iij sol. iiij^or d. Et Waltero de Camera cum biga sua eunte ad idem per j ebdomadam & ij dies ij sol. vj d. Et magistro Odoni pro carecta sua locata per j diem vj d.

Summa xij sol. iiij^or d.

Calx. Et pro j quarter' calcis empto London' ad massonandum circa gistas predictas xv d. Et pro iiij^or fasciculis virgarum ad scaffot' x d. Et pro C busce empto de Willelmo Jacob ad plumbum fundendum iiij^or sol.

Summa vi sol. j d.

Summa tocius xvj^e pacacionis C xi sol. v d.

Roger of Westminster, Roger Cornwus, Gilbert the carpenter, Henry of Knightsbridge, and John of Paddington for the said fortnight, 24*s*., that is to each of those six, 4*s*. And to John of Greenford for one week, 22*d*. And to Robert of Albury for 15 days, 2*s*. 9*d*.

Total carpenters' [wages], 28*s*. 7*d*.

Masons. And to John of Oxford for raising the said joists during the said fortnight, 4*s*. And to John the plumber for one day, 4*d*.

Total, 4*s*. 4*d*.

Smiths. And to Master Henry of Lewes for the first week forging the said ironwork, 4*s*. And to Simon the smith, 26*d*. And to Thorold, 20*d*. And to William of Uffington, 18*d*. for the same week.

Total smiths' [wages], 9*s*. 4*d*.

Labourers. And to two labourers, namely Stephen of the garden and Roger of Charing serving the said carpenters for the said 15 days, 4*s*. 2*d*., that is to each of them, 25*d*. And to two sawyers, namely Walter Norris and William of Sherborne for 3 days, 15*d*., to each of them, 7½*d*.

Total labourers' [wages], 5*s*. 5*d*.

Plumbers. And to John Govair' and William of Strand for founding and laying 8 chars of lead on the stewards' chamber by task, taking 5*s*. a char, 40*s*.

Ironwork. And to William de Clus' to complete the payment for the task of the ironwork for the window of the Jews' house, 4*s*. 2*d*. To the same William for making ironwork for the seat of the Justices of the Bench, 14*d*.

Total, 45*s*. 4*d*.

Carriage of Sand and Clay. And to Matthew of Eye going with his cart to fetch sand and clay to place beneath the lead above the stewards' chamber for 3 weeks, 6*s*. And to Richard of the cellar with his cart with two horses for 15 days, 3*s*. 4*d*. And to Walter of the chamber with his cart going to do the same for one week and 2 days, 2*s*. 6*d*. And to Master Odo for his cart hired for one day, 6*d*.

Total, 12*s*. 4*d*.

Lime. And for 1 quarter of lime bought in London in order to make good the masonry round the said joists, 15*d*. And for 4 bundles of withies for scaffolding, 10*d*. And for a hundredweight of firewood bought from William James in order to found lead, 4*s*.

Total, 6*s*. 1*d*.

Sum total of the 16th payment, £5. 11*s*. 5*d*.

Septimadecima pacacio

Pacacio septimadecima fiebat a die dominica in crastino Sancte Lucie Virginis anno regni Henrici xliiij° usque dominicam in festo beati Thome Apostoli per j ebdomadam scilicet sine festo.

Carpentarii. Septem carpentariis videlicet Willelmo de Waudis, Rogero de Westmonasterio, Rogero Cornwus, Gilberto carpentario, Henrico de Knyth'brug', Johanni de Greneford, Johanni de Padinton' per predictam ebdomadam circa pontem regis emendandum & sedem Justiciariorum de Banco perficiendam xv sol. ij d., cuilibet predictorum sex [*sic*] xxvi d. Et Roberto de Aldebur' per eamdem ebdomadam xviij d.

Summa carpentariorum xvi sol. viij d.

Cementarii. Et Johanni de Oxon' per predictam ebdomadam circa gistas sublevandas & rabata ultra extremitatem pannorum plumbi iuxta parietes cum plastra reparanda xxvi d. Et Willelmo de Bledelawe pro areragiis unius diete circa fenestram assidendam in domo Judeorum iiij^or^ d. ob.

Summa cementariorum ij sol. vj.d. ob.

Plummer'. Et Johanni Govayr' & Willelmo de Strande pro xij chareis & dim. plumbi per tascham fundendi & cubandi ultra magnam cameram senescallorum regis lxij sol. vj d.

Summa lxij sol. vj d.

Operarii. Et duobus operariis videlicet Stephano de Gardino & Rogero de Cherring' deservientibus carpentariis & cementariis per predictam ebdomadam ij sol. vj d. utrique illorum scilicet xv d. Et duobus scyhurs videlicet Waltero Norr' & Willelmo de Scyreburn' per eamdem ebdomadam xxx d. utrique illorum xv d. Et cuidam operario pro areragiis ij dietarum cum cementariis in domo Judeorum v d. Et Rogero de Cherring' pro tribus diebus inter festum beati Thome apostoli & diem Natalis Domini circa lotoria curie regis reparanda vij d. ob.

Summa operariorum vi sol. ob.

Ferramentum. Et pro duobus mill. de scyng'naill' emptis de Henrico de Ponte ad opus domorum curie regis ij sol. vi d. Et pro iiij^or^ mill. scyng'naill' & CC bordnaill' & CC clavorum ad planch' ad idem viij sol. Et pro CCC ferri emptis London' cum portagio & vectura per aquam ad ferramentum ad opus camini regis l sol. precium cent. xvi sol. vi d. Et pro x quarter' carbonis marini ad predictum ferramentum fabricandum x sol.

Summa lxx sol. vj d.

Seventeenth Payment

The seventeenth payment was made from Sunday on the morrow of St. Lucy the Virgin [14 December] in the 44th year of Henry's reign to Sunday on the feast of the blessed Thomas the Apostle [21 December], that is for one week without a feast.

Carpenters. To seven carpenters, namely William de Waudis, Roger of Westminster, Roger Cornwus, Gilbert the carpenter, Henry of Knightsbridge, John of Greenford, John of Paddington working during the said week repairing the king's landing-bridge and completing the seat of the Justices of the Bench, 15*s.* 2*d.*, to each of the said 6 [*sic*], 26*d.* And to Robert of Albury for the same week, 18*d.*

Total carpenters' [wages], 16*s.* 8*d.*

Masons. And to John of Oxford during the said week raising the joists and repairing the rebates above the end of the webs of lead next the walls with plaster, 26*d.* And to William of Bledlow for arrears of one day setting the window in the Jews' house, 4½*d.*

Total masons' [wages], 2*s.* 6½*d.*

Plumbers. And to John Govayr and William of Strand for founding and laying 12½ chars of lead above the great chamber of the king's stewards, 62*s.* 6*d.*

Total, 62*s.* 6*d.*

Labourers. And to two labourers, namely Stephen of the garden and Roger of Charing serving the carpenters and masons during the said week, 2*s.* 6*d.*, that is to each of them, 15*d.* And to two sawyers, namely Walter Norris and William of Sherborne for the same week, 30*d.*, to each of them, 15*d.* And to a certain labourer for arrears of 2 days working with the masons in the Jews' house[1] 5*d.* And to Roger of Charing for three days between the feast of the blessed Thomas the Apostle [21 December] and Christmas Day [25 December] repairing the lavatory of the king's court, 7½*d.*

Total labourers' [wages], 6*s.* 0½*d.*

Ironwork. And for 2,000 scyngnaill bought from Henry of London Bridge for the buildings of the king's court, 2*s.* 6*d.* And for 4,000 scyngnaill and 200 bordnaill and 200 nails for planks for the same, 8*s.* And for 3 hundredweight of iron bought in London with portage and transport by water for the ironwork of the king's chimney, 50*s.*, price 16*s.* 6*d.* a hundred. And for 10 quarters of sea-coal to forge the said ironwork, 10*s.*

Total, 70*s.* 6*d.*

[1] See note on p. 377.

Summa totalis xvij[e] pacacionis vij li. xviij sol. iij d.

Summa summarum omnium expensarum circa minutas operaciones curie regis Westmonasterii in stipendiis operariorum & omnibus empcionibus factis a die Lune proxima post Invencionem Sancte Crucis anno regni Henrici filii regis Johannis regis Anglie xliij[o] usque Natale proximum sequens Cxxvj li. xvij sol. viij d. ob.

Inde debet dominus rex xiiii[or] sol. vj d. qui adhuc solvendi sunt pro ferramento ad caminum regis.

Endorsed: Compotus de minutis operacionibus factis apud Westmonasterium per Martinum de Campo Florum & Johannem Cementarium.

Sum total of the 17th payment, £7. 18*s*. 3*d*.

Grand total of all expenditure on the minor works at the king's court at Westminster, in workmen's wages and all purchases, from Monday next after the Invention of the Holy Cross [4 May] in the 43rd year of the reign of Henry son of King John, King of England, to Christmas next following, £126. 17*s*. 8½*d*.

Thereof the lord king owes 14*s*. 6*d*. which have still to be paid for ironwork for the king's chimney.

Endorsed: Account of minor works carried out at Westminster by Martin de Chanflur and John the Mason.

10. Payments for works at Westminster Abbey and Palace from 26 July to 17 October, 1265
(E 101/683/3)

Pac[acio] .... die Sa[bbati .... an]no xlix. De arreragiis stipendiorum .... ebdomadas .... usque diem Sabbati proximam ante festum Sancti Mathei .... ebdomade in s .... iiij rotulos per dictum tempus

	Magister Robertus de Beverl'	lvj sol.
	Magister Alexander Carpentarius Magister Johannes de Sopele	xxj sol.
	Johannes de Eltham	xiiij sol.
	Radulfus filius Ade Galfridus de Horton	viij sol. viij d.
ve j. de vj. re viij die Martis	Willelmus de Tam'	viij sol. iij d.
ve j. de iiii	Willelmus de Lichefeld	iii sol. vj d.
	Willelmus de Denynton' Reginaldus Stormyn Bartholomeus de Westmonasterio	viij sol. ... d.
	Adam de Saperton' Walterus de Munden' Johannes Burgillun Radulfus Chaunterel Wellelmus de Fermesham Ricardus de Colecestr' Thomas Mantel Robertus de Wyke Matheus de Rems	viij sol. ij d.
ve j. de vj. re vij.	Willelmus de Dereby	vij sol. j d.
ve j. de vj. die L. re eadem die Martis	Johannes Somer	vij sol. x d. ob.
	Robertus Caperun Henricus de Cernes	vj sol.
ve ij.	Radulfus de Bello Henricus de Lond'	v sol. j d.
ve j. de ij	Robertus de Rofa	xiij d.

10. Payments for works at Westminster Abbey and Palace from 26 July to 17 October, 1265

Payment [for the Church and Court made on] Saturday [19 September] in the 49th year [1265] for arrears of wages [for 8] weeks [from 26 July] to Saturday next before the feast of St. Matthew [19 September] . . . . weeks in . . . . 4 rolls for the said time.

[*White cutters*]	Master Robert of Beverley	56*s.*
	Master Alexander the Carpenter Master John of Sopley	21*s.*
	John of Eltham	14*s.*
	Ralph son of Adam Geoffrey of Horton	8*s.* 8*d.*
a.1, d.6, r.8 (Tu.)[1]	William of Thame	8*s.* 3*d.*
a.1, d.4	William of Lichfield	3*s.* 6*d.*
	William of Denton Reginald Sturmin Bartholomew of Westminster	8*s.* ..*d.*
	Adam of Sapperton Walter of Munden John Burgillun Ralph Chaunterel William de Frensham Richard of Colchester Thomas Mantel Robert of Wyke Matthew of Rheims	8*s.* 2*d.*
a.1, d.6, r.7	William of Derby	7*s.* 1*d.*
a.1, d.6 (Mon.), r.6 (Tu.)	John Somer	7*s.* 10½*d.*
	Robert Caperun Henry of Sheen	6*s.*
a.2	Ralph of Battle Henry of London	5*s.* 1*d.*
a.1, d.2	Robert of Rochester	13*d.*

[1] These marginal notes indicate the weeks in which individual workmen came on or off the payroll. a = arrived, d = departed, r = returned.

ve v	Nicholaus de Ardern'	iii.sol.
ve vj	Ricardus de Watham	iii sol. j d.
	Summa xiiij li. ix sol.	
	Petrus de Certesh' Radulfus de Lincoln'	viij sol. ij d.
	Summa xvj sol. iiij d.	
	Willelmus de Bledel'	viij sol. x d.
	Willelmus de Wycumb' Willelmus de Reding' Ricardus de Cantuaria	viij sol. ij d.
ve iij. de iiij die Veneris re vij	Willelmus de Tothull'	xix d. ob.
ve iij die Jov. de iiij. die Veneris	Radulfus Briselanc'	xv d.
ve vij	Hugo de Wycumb'	ij sol.
	Summa xxxviij sol. ij d. ob.	
	Godefridus le Iunur	xij sol.
ve j. de iij	Magister Willelmus de Feldsted'	iij sol.
	Gilebertus carpentarius	xj sol. iij d.
	Godefridus Turnur Willelmus de Wald' Simon de Norhampt' Abraham filius Alani Robertus de Theye Johannes de Greneford' Simon de Stelbrug'	viij sol. ij d.
ve j. de v. re vj	Robertus Sampson	v sol.
ve v.	Gilbertus de Watham	iiij sol.
ve j. de iij	Johannes de Feldsted'	xxvj d.
ve j. de v. re vij die L. de eadem die Ven.	Robertus de Eye	v sol. ix d.
ve iiij	Willelmus attefrithe	v sol. j d.
	Summa cv sol. v d.	
	Magister Walterus de Durh'	xiij sol. d. ob.
	Ricardus le Blunt	xj sol. iij d.
	Dewdon' de Westmonasterio Thomas de Giseburn'	vij sol. vj d.
ve iij de v.	Philippus de Brok	ij sol.
ve v.	Stet' de Paris	iiij sol. vij d.
ve viij die Mercurii	Willelmus de Sancto Albano	xij d.

Summa xlvi sol. xj d. ob.

a.5	Nicholas of Arden	3*s.*
a.6	Richard of Waltham	3*s.* 1*d.*
	Total, £14. 9*s.* 0*d.*	
[*Marblers*]	Peter of Chertsey, Ralph of Lincoln	8*s.* 2*d.*
[*Layers*]	William of Bledlow	8*s.* 10*d.*
	William of Wycombe, William of Reading, Richard of Canterbury	8*s.* 2*d.*
a.3, d.4 (Fri.)	William of Tothill	19½*d.*
a.3 (Th.), d.4 (Fri.) r.7	Ralph Briselance	15*d.*
a.7	Hugh of Wycombe	2*s.*
	Total, 38*s.* 2½*d.*	
[*Carpenters*]	Godfrey the joiner	12*s.*
a.1, d.3	Master William of Felsted	3*s.*
	Gilbert the Carpenter	11*s.* 3*d.*
	Godfrey Turner, William de Wald', Simon of Northampton, Abraham son of Alan, Robert of Tey, John of Greenford, Simon of Stalbridge	8*s.* 2*d.*
a.1, d.5, r.6	Robert Sampson	5*s.*
a.5	Gilbert of Waltham	4*s.*
a.1, d.3	John of Felsted	26*d.*
a.1, d.5, r.7 (Mon.), d.7 (Fri.)	Robert of Eye	5*s.* 9*d.*
a.4	William atte Frithe	5*s.* 1*d.*
	Total, 105*s.* 5*d.*	
[*Painters*]	Master Walter of Durham	13*s.* 1½*d.*
	Richard le Blunt	11*s.* 3*d.*
	Dewdon of Westminster, Thomas of Gisburn	7*s.* 6*d.*
a.3, d.5	Philip of Brook	2*s.*
a.5	Stet' of Paris	4*s.* 7*d.*
a.8 (Wed.)	William of St. Albans	12*d.*
	Total, 46*s.* 11½*d.*	

ve vij	Magister Henricus faber	v sol. iij d.
	Ricardus faber	xij sol.
	Willelmus de Sar'	viij sol. ij d.
	Willecok faber	ij sol.
	Summa xxvij sol. v d.	
	Magister Willelmus Plumbarius	xiiij sol.
	Alexander de Waleden'	v sol. vij d. ob.
	Summa xix sol. vij d. ob.	
	Eadwardus vitriarius	xj sol. iij d.
	Willelmus Suwerk	viij sol. ij d.
	Summa xix sol. v d.	
	Robertus Pollisur	v sol. viij d.
	Johannes de Wygorn'	v sol.
	Summa x sol. viij d.	
	Walterus Norr' } Johannes Bissop }	v sol.
	Summa x sol.	
	Magister Robertus Pistor	vj sol. x d.
ve ij	Ricardus Curteys	vij sol.
	Summa xiij sol. x d.	
	Walterus de Sancto Albano	v sol. iiij d.
	Gilebertus de Wymbeld', Willelmus de Bosco, Ricardus Bluet, Petrus de Gardino, Willelmus de Lichefeld', Willelmus de Wanleswrth', Galfridus de Bracino, Aluredus de Langedich, Robertus de Oxon', Johannes . . . ., Adam de Wynton', Stephanus de Geldeford, Willelmus de Ware, Heyne de fonte, Wylch' de Heye, Simon de Berking', Johannes Porter, Stephanus Gardin', Rogerus de Westmonasterio }	iiii sol. iij d. ob.

[*Smiths*] a.7	Master Henry the smith	5*s*. 3*d*.
	Richard the smith	12*s*.
	William of Salisbury	8*s*. 2*d*.
	Willecok the smith	2*s*.
	Total, 27*s*. 5*d*.	
[*Plumbers*]	Master William the plumber	14*s*.
	Alexander of Walden	5*s*. 7½*d*.
	Total, 19*s*. 7½*d*.	
[*Glaziers*]	Edward the glazier	11*s*. 3*d*.
	William Southwark	8*s*. 2*d*.
	Total, 19*s*. 5*d*.	
[*Polishers*]	Robert the polisher	5*s*. 8*d*.
	John of Worcester	5*s*.
	Total, 10*s*. 8*d*.	
[*Sawyers*]	Walter Norris }	
	John Bishop }	5*s*.
	Total, 10*s*.	
[ ][1]	Master Robert Baker	6*s*. 10*d*.
a.2	Richard Curtieys	7*s*.
	Total, 13*s*. 10*d*.	
[*Labourers*]	Walter of St. Albans	5*s*. 4*d*.
	Gilbert of Wimbledon }	
	William of the Wood }	
	Richard Bluet }	
	Peter of the garden }	
	William of Lichfield }	
	William of Wandsworth }	
	Geoffrey of the malt-house }	
	Alfred of Longditch }	
	Robert of Oxford }	
	John . . . . }	
	Adam of Winchester }	
	Stephen of Guildford }	
	William of Ware }	
	Heyne of (the ?) Well }	
	Wylch' of Eye }	
	Simon of Barking }	4*s*. 3½*d*.
	John Porter }	
	Stephen Gardiner }	
	Roger of Westminster }	

[1] Trade uncertain.

	Willelmus Barbator
	Rogerus de Welinton'
	Radulfus de Taverham
	Hugo de Hurle
	Galfridus de Oxon'
	Petrus de Cadamo
	Willelmus de Bruges
	Walterus de Norhampt'
	Ricardus Justic'
	Hugo de Berking'
ve j. de v	Ricardus Womb'
ve j. de iij	Thomas pistor
ve iij de iiij die Ven. rev. vij	Rogerus de Sancto Albano
ve iij. die	Walterus [C?]roft
Jov	Johannes de Cleygate
Veneris	....
	Summa ....
	Summa totalis stipendiorum huius rotuli xxxvj li. xv sol.

Ebdomada prima [continens festum beati Petri ad Vincula per die]m Sabbati [quod est cementariorum].

Ebdomada secunda sine [festo].

Ebdomada tercia continens festum [beati Laurencii] per diem [Lune] quod est domini Regis. Et festum Assumpcionis beate Marie per diem Sabbati quod est cementariorum.

Ebdomada iiij sine festo.

Ebdomada v continens festum Sancti Bartholomei per diem Lune quod est domini Regis. Et festum Decollacionis Sancti Johannis Baptiste per diem Sabbati quod est cementariorum.

Ebdomada vj sine festo.

Ebdomada vij continens festum Nativitatis beate Marie per diem Martis quod est domini Regis.

Ebdomada viij continens festum Sancte Crucis per diem Lune quod est cementariorum.

Pacacio Ecclesie & Curie facta die Sabbati in vigilia Sancti Luce Evangeliste anno xlix de arreragiis stipendiorum iiij ebdomadarum in isto rotulo collectarum per viij ebdomadas. iiij rotuli continentes a festo beati Petri ad vincula usque diem Sabbati post festum Exaltacionis Sancte Crucis anno predicto. quarum alie iiij ebdomade per dictos iiij rotulos de medietate stipendiorum proportionaliter fuerunt pacate. Et de perpacacione empcionum per predictas viij ebdomadas per visum Magistrorum Roberti de Beverl', magistri Alexandri Carpentarii Willelmi de Berking' tunc sacriste Westmon' & aliorum custodum operis.

	William Barber
	Roger of Wellington
	Ralph of Taverham
	Hugh of Hurley
	Geoffrey of Oxford
	Peter of Caen
	William of Bride
	Walter of Northampton
	Richard Justice
	Hugh of Barking
a.1, d.5	Richard Womb'
a.1, d.3	Thomas Baker
a.3, d.4 (Fri.), r.7	Roger of St. Albans
a.3 (Th.) . . . . (Fri.)	Walter [C]roft
	John of Claygate
	Total, ...
	Sum total of wages on this roll, £36. 15*s*.

The first week [containing the feast of St. Peter in Chains on] Saturday [1 August] [which is the masons'].

The second week without [a feast].

The third week containing the feast of [St. Laurence] on [Monday 10 August] which is the lord king's, and the feast of the Assumption of the blessed Mary on Saturday [15 August] which is the masons'.

Week 4 without a feast.

Week 5 containing the feast of St. Bartholomew on Monday [24 August] which is the lord king's, and the feast of the Beheading of St. John the Baptist on Saturday [29 August] which is the masons'.

Week 6 without a feast.

Week 7 containing the feast of the Nativity of the blessed Mary on Tuesday [8 September] which is the lord king's.

Week 8 containing the feast of the Holy Cross on Monday [14 September] which is the masons'.

Payment for the Church and Court made on Saturday, the vigil of St. Luke the Evangelist [17 October] in the 49th year [1265] for the arrears of wages for 4 of the 8 weeks included in this roll. 4 rolls containing from the feast of the blessed Peter in Chains [1 August] to Saturday after the feast of the Exaltation of the Holy Cross [19 September] in the aforesaid year. The other 4 weeks have been paid proportionately by the said 4 rolls in respect of half the wages. And for the full payment of purchases made throughout the aforesaid 8 weeks by view of Masters Robert of Beverley, Alexander the Carpenter, and William of Barking, then sacrist of Westminster, and of the other keepers of the works.

Opus Curie [*sic*]

In stipendiis xxij alborum cissorum, ij marmorariorum, vij cubitorum, xv carpentariorum, iiij fabrorum, ij vitriariorum xxiiij li. xv sol. ix d. ob.

In stipendiis ij pollitorum, ij seratorum, xxxvij minutorum operariorum cum ij bigis diurnis viij li. xiij sol. ob.

Roberto de Bekel' pro vj^{c}xl pedibus de assel' cissis ad tascham vj sol. x d.

Radulfo de Corf in perpacacione j navate marmoris lvj sol.

Rogero de Reygate & sociis suis pro V^{m}CCC quarter' viii pond. france petre xvj li.

Ricardo Justic' pro portagio france petre & plumbi per dies feriales vij sol.

Pro iij navatis grise petre xxviij sol. viij d

Ricardo Calfonario pro Mvj^{c}iij quarter' calcis iiij li. iij sol. ix d.

Roberto de Pollingefeld in perpacacione lij peciarum maeremii de quercu liij sol. v d.

Johanni de lestrand in parte solucionis tasche Ecclesie xxvj sol. viij d.

Johanni de Newdegat' & sociis suis pro viij peciis, xij tignis de quercu viij sol. vij d.

Ricardo Crockere pro xxiiij planchiis, vij conevector' vij sol. x d.

Willelmo Alex' pro vj^{c} lat' de fago xiiij d.

Petro Ventre & socio suo in parte solucionis xxxviij peciarum de quercu xxij sol.

Willelmo Cristemess' pro cariagio diversi maeremii & custod' apud Kingeston' x sol. vj d.

Ricardo Atteleg' pro MMC bordis de fago & j M. busce xlij sol.

Alicie de Estchep' pro vij duodenis cratium & virgarum ad scafota xvij sol. vj d. ob.

Rogero de Dorking' pro pluribus passagiis diversi maeremii de Kingeston' x sol. vj d.

Roberto le Cuver pro vj bokettis & emendacione utensilium xxvij d.

Galfrido de Sancto Albano pro Ciiij^{xx}x peciis ferri, xiiij picis, x libris cepi, vj libris uncti, j garba asseri & iij ligonibus cum diversis clavis ferri vj li. xvj sol.

Nicholao atteberwe pro lxj peciis ferri vij sol. vj d.

Johanni Tegulatori pro C tegulis cavatis xvj d.

Summa lxxvj li. iiij sol. x d. ob.

Work on the Church[1]

In the wages of 22 white cutters, 2 marblers, 7 layers, 15 carpenters, 4 smiths, 2 glaziers, £24. 15*s.* 9½*d.*

In the wages of 2 polishers, 2 sawyers, 37 labourers, with 2 carts daily, £8. 13*s.* 0½*d.*

To Robert of Beckley for 640 feet of ashlar cut at task, 6*s.* 10*d.*

To Ralph of Corfe in full payment for 1 shipload of marble, 56*s.*

To Roger of Reigate and his fellows for 53 hundredweight, one quarter and 8 pounds of freestone, £16.

To Richard Justice for carriage of freestone and lead on holidays, 7*s.*

For 3 shiploads of ragstone, 28*s.* 8*d.*

To Richard the lime-burner for 16 hundredweight and 3 quarters of lime, £4. 3*s.* 9*d.*

To Robert de Pollingefeld in full payment for 52 pieces of oak timber, 53*s.* 5*d.*

To John of the Strand in part-payment for task-work for the Church, 26*s.* 8*d.*

To John of Newdigate and his fellows for 8 pieces and 12 beams of oak, 8*s.* 7*d.*

To Richard Crocker for 24 planks and 7 barrows, 7*s.* 10*d.*

To William Alexander for 600 laths of beech, 14*d.*

To Peter Ventre and his fellow in part-payment for 38 pieces of oak, 22*s.*

To William Christmas for carriage of divers timber and guarding at Kingston, 10*s.* 6*d.*

To Richard Attlee for 2,100 beech boards and 10 hundredweight of firewood, 42*s.*

To Alice of Eastcheap for 7 dozen hurdles and withies for scaffolding, 17*s.* 6½*d.*

To Roger of Dorking for conveying sundry timber [by water] from Kingston on several occasions, 10*s.* 6*d.*

To Robert the cooper for 6 buckets and the repair of utensils, 27*d.*

To Geoffrey of St. Albans for 190 pieces of iron, 14 .... of pitch, 10 pounds of tallow, 6 pounds of grease, 1 sheaf of steel, and 3 mattocks with sundry iron nails, £6. 16*s.*

To Nicholas Attenborough for 61 pieces of iron, 7*s.* 6*d.*

To John Tiler for 100 curved tiles, 16*d.*

Total, £76. 4*s.* 10½*d.*

[1] *Curie* in the MS. is here an obvious slip for *Ecclesie.*

Opus Curie

In stipendiis vij pictorum, ij plumbariorum	lxvj sol. vij d.
In perpacacione magistri Petri pro vij plastrariis cum opere ad tascham	iiij li. vj sol. vij d. ob.
Willelmo Heremit' in perpacacionem tasche recepte dealbande	xiij sol. iiij d.
Magistro Waltero de Durham in perpacacione tasche ymagin' capelle Sancti Stephani	xx sol.
Roberto de Plumsted' & sociis pro pluribus servariis Curie mundandis	xxj sol. viij d.
Matheo fabro pro diversis curie factis ad tascham	xxxij d.
Philippo de Douegat' pro portagio & vectura vij charrearum plumbi et CCCC ferri	iiij sol. iij d.
Johanni de Brugge pro M dim^{c} quarter' france petre	lxiiij sol. vj d.
David' Calfonario pro viij^{c} calcis	xl sol.
Pro iiij navatis grise petre	xxv sol. viij d.
Willelmo Jacob pro xxxviij tignis de alneto cum C busce de quercu	v sol. vij d.
Radulfo de Hamsted' pro ij duodenis cratium	iiij sol.
Waltero de Douegat' pro j quarter' stagni	iij sol. vj d.
Willelmo Pag' pro xxx libris albi plumbi, x libris rubei plumbi, iij libris de vermilun, dimidia libra de azur', ij libris de verniz, ij libris de virid', ij libris de orpiment & ocre & de arreragiis iiij summarum vitri & j quarter' de sinople	xxj sol. x d. ob.
Reginaldo le Chaundeler pro iiij galon' olei, dimidia libra & j uncia azur', j quarter' de sinople, ij duodenis stagni colorati	xv sol. ij d.
Johanni de Aven' pro ij libris iij unciis azur'	xxxij sol. j d.
Dewdon' pro ovis ad colores	ij d. ob.
Roberto de Oxon' pro X^{M} cavillarum ad tegulas	xv d. ob.
Blosme pro cariagio j mill' tegularum	iij d.

Summa xxi li., ix sol. iij d.

Summa totalis dictarum pacacionum Ecclesie & Curie iiij^{xx}xvij li. xiiij sol. d. ob.

Work on the Court

In the wages of 7 painters and 2 plumbers, 66*s.* 7*d.*

In full payment of Master Peter for 7 plasterers with work at task, £4. 6*s.* 7½*d.*

To William Hermit in full payment for the task of whitewashing the Receipt of the Exchequer, 13*s.* 4*d.*

To Master Walter of Durham in full payment of the task of [painting] images in St. Stephen's Chapel, 20*s.*

To Robert of Plumstead and his fellows for clearing out several fish-ponds in the Court, 21*s.* 8*d.*

To Matthew the smith for several works for the Court done at task, 32*d.*

To Philip of Dowgate for portage and conveyance of 7 chars of lead and 4 hundredweight of iron, 4*s.* 3*d.*

To John of Bridge for 10 hundredweight and 3 quarters of free-stone, 64*s.* 6*d.*

To David the lime-burner for 8 hundredweight of lime, 40*s.*

For 4 shiploads of ragstone, 25*s.* 8*d.*

To William James for 38 pieces of alder and a hundredweight of oak for firewood, 5*s.* 7*d.*

To Ralph of Hampstead for 2 dozen hurdles, 4*s.*

To Walter of Dowgate for 1 quarter of tin, 3*s.* 6*d.*

To William Page for 30 pounds of white lead, 10 pounds of red lead, 3 pounds of vermilion, half a pound of azure, 2 pounds of varnish, 2 pounds of green, 2 pounds of orpiment and ochre, and for arrears of 4 seams of glass and 1 quarter of sinople, 21*s.* 10½*d.*

To Reginald the chandler for 4 gallons of oil, half a pound and 1 ounce of azure, 1 quarter of sinople, 2 dozen ,[1] 15*s.* 2*d.*

To John of Avon for 2 pounds, 3 ounces of azure, 32*s.* 1*d.*

To Dewdon for eggs for colours, 2½*d.*

To Robert of Oxford for 10,000 tile-pins, 15½*d.*

To Blosme for carriage of 1,000 tiles, 3*d.*

Total, £21. 9*s.* 3*d.*

Sum total of the aforesaid payments for the Church and Court, £97. 14*s.* 1½*d.*

[1] The correct translation of *stagni colorati* is not clear. Literally translated the words mean 'tin' and 'coloured'.

11. Three undated memoranda concerning payments for works at Westminster (E 101/683/2, 4, and 5)

ebdomada iiij[a] venit	Willelmus Gardin'	x sol. ij d. ob.
ebdomada v[a] die Mercurii, die Veneris sequenti deest ebdomada xj[a] rediit	Philippus Dilewe	ij sol. iij d. ob.
	Johannes Stanewey	viij sol. xj d. ob.
Operarii cum fabris ebdomada xiij[a] desunt	Walterus de Degemerfelde Adam Auleton' . . . . Flore	xiij sol. vj d. ob.
ebdomada vj[a] die Lune venit	Philippus Walensis	vij sol. x d.
xij[a] deest	Walterus Stan . . . . . de	
	Jos' Westm' Henricus Brasin	vij sol. xj d.
in crastino Animarum desunt	Willelmus Tothule Walterus Wendeleswerth Odin Sutor' Willelmus Windles'	vij sol. xj d.
ebdomada ix[a] deest	Laurencius de Hendon'	iij sol. iiij d.
Servienti dealbatorum		. . . sol. vj d. ob.
Operarii cum Carpentariis	Johannes Sige	xij sol. vj d. ob.
ebdomada vij[a] deest ebdomada ix[a] rediit	Johannes Chilhuthe	xj sol. iij d.
In Gardinis	Stephanus Gardin'	xiij sol. vj d. ob.
ebdomada viij[a] die Martis in crastino Sancti Michaelis venerunt		
	Ricardus Roine Henricus de Chering'	v sol. v d.
Biga diurna	Robertus Buriton'	xxj sol. viij d.
ebdomada viij[a] die Martis venit	Magister Odo bigam	viij sol. viij d.

11. Three undated memoranda concerning payments for works at Westminster[1]

came in the 4th week	William Gardiner	10*s.* 2½*d.*
came in the 5th week on Wednesday, departed on the following Friday, returned in the 11th week	Philip of Dilwyn	2*s.* 3½*d.*
	John Stanway	8*s.* 11½*d.*
Labourers with the smiths		
departed in the 13th week	Walter of Dogmersfield Adam Alton . . . . Floore	13*s.* 6½*d.*
came on Monday in the 6th week	Philip Welsh	7*s.* 10*d.*
departed in the 12th week	Walter Stan . . . de	. . .
	Jos' Westminster Henry Brasin	7*s.* 11*d.*
departed on the morrow of All Souls [3 November]	William Tothill Walter Wandsworth Odo the souter William Windsor	7*s.* 11*d.*
departed in the 9th week	Lawrence of Hendon	3*s.* 4*d.*
[*Labourers*] *serving the plasterers*		.. *s.* 6½*d.*
Labourers with the carpenters		
	John Sige	12*s.* 6½*d.*
departed in the 7th week, returned in the 9th	John Chilhuthe	11*s.* 3*d.*
In the garden	Stephen the gardener	13*s.* 6½*d.*
came on Tuesday on the morrow of Michaelmas [30 September][2]	Richard Roine Henry of Charing	5*s.* 5*d.*
Daily Carts		21*s.* 8*d.*
came on Tuesday in the 8th week	Master Odo, cart	8*s.* 8*d.*

[1] Westminster is not referred to in any of these three documents, but the first shares several names with E 101/683/1 (No. 5) of 1253, the second is in the same hand as E 101/467/4 (No. 3, also of 1253), and the third may reasonably be presumed to be a product of the Westminster works.

[2] 30 September fell on a Tuesday in 1236, 1242, 1253, 1259, 1264, and 1281. As several of the workmen named also occur in No. 5 of 1253, 1253 is the most likely date.

ebdomada ix^a die Lune	Nicholaus caretarius	
	Willelmus Porcher	vij sol.
ebdomada xiij^a deest	Willelmus	
ebdomada x^a die Martis	Nicholaus	

(E 101/683/2)

Memorandum de taschiis & Expensis

Radulfus le Hare Ricardus Donestapele
Simon le Noreis per xj^cim ebdomadas ceperunt pro taschiis

Adam Merton per
Petrus de Roff' per

Alii minus bene peragentes taschiam
Matheus de Rem per xj^cim ebdomadas
Ricardus Norman per iiij^or ebdomadas & iij dies
Henricus de Rems per iiij ebdomadas & iij dies
R. de Came per x^cem dies operabiles ut dicitur

Memorandum quod tempore taschiarum tantum contentato(?) recepturi per dietas

Radulfus le Hare per xj^cim ebdomadas	xxij sol. ij d.
Ricardus Donestapele per xj^cim ebdomadas	xxij sol. ij d.
A. Noreis per idem	xxij sol. ij d.
Petrus de Roff' per idem	xxij sol. ij d.
Adam Merton per septem ebdomadas	xiiij sol. ij d.
Ricardus Chivening' per novem dies operabiles	iij sol. ij d.
Item Matheus de Rems per xj^cim ebdomadas	xxij sol. ij d.
Ricardus Norman, Henricus de Rems } per iiij ebdomadas & tres dies	xviij sol.
Ricardus de Came per quindenam ut dicitur	iiij sol.

Summa dietarum vij li. x sol. ij d.
& pro taschiis receperunt x li. xviij d.
& sic restant de lucro lxviij sol. viij d.

(E 101/683/4)

xiij cementarii licenciati & debentur eis pro prima septimana	xxxv sol.
Et pro ij^a septimana debentur eisdem	xxvij sol. iij d.
xxviij cubatores & debentur eis pro prima septimana	lxij sol. vj d.
Et pro ij^a septimana debentur eisdem	xxxviij sol. iiij d.
vj^xx minuti operarii & debentur eis pro prima septimana	vij li. x sol. ix d.
Item C & xviij operarii in secunda septimana & debentur eis pro eadem	iiij li. xviij sol. x d.

Summa xx li. xij sol. viij d.

In stipendiis fabrorum pro ij septimanis	xxxvij sol. vj d.
In stipendiis carpentariorum pro ij septimanis	x sol. iiij d.

came on Monday in the 9th week	Nicholas the carter William Porcher	7*s*.
departed in the 13th week	William	
came on Tuesday in the 10th week	Nicholas	

Note concerning task-works and expenditure

Ralph le Hare Richard Dunstable
Simon Norris received for 11 weeks on task-works

Adam Merton for
Peter of Rochester for

Others failing to complete tasks
Matthew of Rheims for 11 weeks
Richard Norman for 4 weeks and 3 days
Henry of Rheims for 4 weeks and 3 days
Richard of Caen for 10 working days as it is said

Note that [if only the] time spent on task-work were paid for, they would receive at day-rates:

Ralph le Hare for 11 weeks	22*s*. 2*d*.
Richard Dunstable for 11 weeks	22*s*. 2*d*.
A. (?) Norris for the same	22*s*. 2*d*.
Peter of Rochester for the same	22*s*. 2*d*.
Adam Merton for seven weeks	14*s*. 2*d*.
Richard Chevening for nine working days	3*s*. 2*d*.
And Matthew of Rheims for 11 weeks	22*s*. 2*d*.
Richard Norman, Henry of Rheims for 4 weeks and three days	18*s*.
Richard of Caen for a fortnight as it is said	4*s*.

Total of day-wages, £7. 10*s*. 2*d*.
And they received for task-work £10. 1*s*. 6*d*.
And so there remains a gain of £3. 8*s*. 8*d*.

13 masons leaving, and there is owed to them for the first week	35*s*.
And owed to the same for the 2nd week	27*s*. 3*d*.
28 layers, and there is owed to them for the first week	62*s*. 6*d*.
And owed to the same for the 2nd week	38*s*. 4*d*.
120 labourers, and there is owed to them for the first week	£7. 10*s*. 9*d*.
And 118 labourers in the second week, and there is owed to them for the same	£4. 18*s*. 10*d*.

Total, £20. 12*s*. 8*d*.

In the wages of the smiths for 2 weeks	37*s*. 6*d*.
In the wages of the carpenters for 2 weeks	10*s*. 4*d*.

tegulatoribus pro ij septimanis	xviij sol. ix d.
plumbariis pro ij[a] septimana	v sol. vj d. ob.
pictoribus pro ij septimanis	lix sol. vj d. ob.
carectariis pro ij septimanis	ix sol.
Summa vij li. viij d.	
Item & de empcionibus in ij[a] septimana	xvij li. xiij sol.
Summa totalis xlv li. vj sol. iiij d.	

De presenti septimana nichil tactum est

Summa cementariorum licenciatorum xxvj septimana	v sol. vj d.
cubatores	lxij sol.
operarii	cij sol. xj d.
Summa viij li. x sol. v d.	
Cubatores licenciati xxvij septimana	lvij sol. xj d.
operarii	lxvij sol. iij d. ob.
Summa vj li. v sol. ij d. ob.	

Summa totalis xiiij li. xv sol. vij d. ob.

Et est summa pacata xij li. ij sol. j d. Item vij d. pro alia pacacione.

(E 101/683/5)

To the tilers for 2 weeks	18*s*. 9*d*.
To the plumbers for the 2nd week	5*s*. 6½*d*.
To the painters for 2 weeks	59*s*. 6½*d*.
To the carters for 2 weeks	9*s*.
Total, £7. 0*s*. 8*d*.	
And for purchases in the 2nd week	£17. 13*s*. 0*d*.
Sum total, £45. 6*s*. 4*d*.	
For the present week nothing mentioned	
Total of masons leaving in the 26th week	5*s*. 6*d*.
Layers	62*s*. 0*d*.
Labourers	102*s*. 11*d*.
Total, £8. 10*s*. 5*d*.	
Layers leaving in the 27th week	57*s*. 11*d*.
Labourers	67*s*. 3½*d*.
Total, £6. 5*s*. 2½*d*.	

Sum total, £14. 15*s*. 7½*d*.

And the sum paid was £12. 2*s*. 1*d*. And 7*d*. for another payment.

12. Payments for works at Westminster in August and September, 1270
(C 47/3/43, m. 12)

Pacacio cementariorum & .... *usque ad festum Assumpcionis beate Marie*

Magister Robertus de		
Galfridus clericus		
Johannes de . . . ltham		
Ricardus de Dunmawe		
Radulfus de Wymburne		
Willelmus Curtoys		
Ricardus de Walmesford'		
Matheus de Rem		
Johannes Somer	ix . .	
Alexander de Tothull'	vj sol.	
Henricus de Cernes		
Gervasius de Westmonasterio		
Walterus de Suwell'		
Henricus Taillard'		
Thomas de Bernewell'		
Wyot de Broune		
Nicolaus de Maldon'		
Lucas de la Charring'		
Henricus de Stokwell'		
Gillot de Cadamo		
Johannes de Sipenham		
Willelmus Jolivet		
Thomas de Leuesham		
Robertus de Christi Ecclesia		
Ricardus de Cestre		
Willelmus le Blunt		
Ricardus de Appel . . .		
Johannes de R		
Ricardus de He . . .		
Willelmus de Glascu		
Robertus de Wyke		
Johannes de Weting'	}	j sol.
Radulfus Chanterel	}	
Radulfus de Donmawe		xxvj d.
Thomas de Cantuar'		iiij sol. iiij d.

Summa xvj li. viij sol. ij d.

12. Payments for works at Westminster in August and September, 1270

Payment of masons and . . . . until the feast of the Assumption of the blessed Mary

Master Robert of [Beverley]	
Geoffrey the clerk	
John of [E]ltham	
Richard of Dunmow	
Ralph of Wimborne	
William Curtoys	
Richard of Wansford	
Matthew of Rheims	
John Somer	9 . .
Alexander of Tothill	6*s.*
Henry of Sheen	
Gervase of Westminster	
Walter of Southwell	
Henry Taillard	
Thomas of Barnwell	
Wyot of Bourne	
Nicholas of Maldon	
Luke of la Charing	
Henry of Stockwell	
Gillot of Caen	
John of Cippenham	
William Jolivet	
Thomas of Lewisham	
Robert of Christchurch	
Richard of Chester	
William le Blunt	
Richard of Apple . . .	
John of R	
Richard of He	
William of Glasgow	
Robert of Wyke	
John of Weting' } Ralph Chanterel }	1*s.*
Ralph of Dunmow	26*d.*
Thomas of Canterbury	4*s.* 4*d.*
Total, £16. 8*s.* 2*d.*	

Radulfus de Corf ix sol.

Petrus de Certesh'
Thomas Cok
Adam Dobin
Henricus Golde
Alanus de Corf
Willelmus Bataille
Walterus Doket
} viij sol. ij ......

Summa lxvij s. iiij d.

Willelmus de Bledel' ix sol.
Willelmus de Wycumb' viij sol.
Hugo de Wycumb'
Willelmus de Tothull
Willelmus ....
Alvredus ....
Henricus ....
Henricus ....[1]

On the dorse

..... Johannis per diem Veneris [quod] est domini Regis

..... Nativitatis beate Marie per diem Lune quod est cementariorum

..... Sabbati in vigilia Sancte Crucis anno liiii° de stipendiis & emptionibus ... prox. post festum Assu[mptionis beate Marie] predictum per iiij ebdomadas continentes ij festa quorum [primum est domini] Regis & secundum cementariorum.

...... fratris Ranulphi & aliorum custodum operis

...... cissorum, viij marmorariorum, viij cubitorum, xiij carpentariorum, iiij fabrorum cum j plumbario ad tascham xvj ...
xxxvij li. viij sol. j d.

..... ij pollitorum, ij seratorum, xliiij minutorum operariorum, cum j biga diurna. ix li. xvij sol. x d.

.... [im]agine ecclesie facta ad tascham. xiij sol. iiij d.

...... xx pedibus de assel' cissis ad tascham, xxxiij sol. v d.

.... emendacione utensilium x sol. ij d.
.... xxiij d.

.... de Lamheth' & [sociis] suis pro M.M.M. D. france petre, x li. x sol.

... calfonario & sociis suis pro M. ix^{c} calcis, iiij li. xv sol.

.... & sociis pro M.M. & cent. latarum de quercu, xiij sol. iiij d.

.... & sociis suis pro xiiij peciis de quercu, viij sol. xj d.

[1] The remainder of the document is almost totally illegible, but among the few names that can be distinguished are those of 'Magister Henricus', 'Magister Walterus', and 'Magister Thomas'.

Ralph of Corfe[1] 9*s.*
Peter of Chertsey
Thomas Cok
Adam Dobin
Henry Golde } 8*s.* . . .
Alan of Corfe
William Bataille
Walter Doket

Total, £3. 7*s.* 4*d.*

William of Bledlow[2] 9*s.*
William of Wycombe 8*s.*
Hugh of Wycombe
William of Tothill
William . . . .
Alfred . . . .
Henry . . . .
Henry . . . . . .

. . . . . Decollation of St. John on Friday, [which] is the lord king's [29 August]

. . . . . . birth of the blessed Mary on Monday, which is the masons' [8 September]

. . . . . . Saturday on the eve of St. Cross in the 54th year [13 September 1270] for wages and purchases . . . . next after the said feast of the Assumption of the blessed Mary for 4 weeks containing 2 feasts, of which the first is the lord king's and the second the masons'.

. . . . of brother Ranulf and the other keepers of the work

. . . . cutters, 8 marblers, 8 layers, 13 carpenters, 4 smiths, with 1 plumber at taskwork 16 . . . . . .

£37. 8*s.* 1*d.*

. . . . . . 2 polishers, 2 sawyers, 44 labourers, with 1 cart daily, £9. 17*s.* 10*d.*

. . . . image of the church done by task, 13*s.* 4*d.*

. . . . . . 20 feet of ashlars cut by task, 33*s.* 5*d.*

. . . . repair of tools, 10*s.* 2*d.*

. . . . 23*d.*

. . . . of Lambeth and his [fellows] for 35 hundredweight freestone, £10. 10*s.*

. . . . lime-burner and his fellows for 19 hundredweight of lime, £4. 15*s.*

. . . . and his fellows for 2,100 oaken laths, 13*s.* 4*d.*

. . . . and his fellows for 14 pieces of oak, 8*s.* 11*d.*

[1] These are the 8 marblers mentioned later in the roll.

[2] These are presumably the 8 layers mentioned later in the roll.

. . . . . orreys & sociis suis in parte solucionis C.ij peciarum de quercu, l tignis de eodem, lxxix sol. viij d.

. . . . . Newheth' pro cariagio dicti meremii per terram & aquam usque ad Westmonasterium, xxix sol.

. . . . & sociis suis pro lxij tignis de quercu, xxxix sol. v d.

. . . . . born' & sociis suis pro iiij^{xx} x planch' de querc', xxxvij sol. iii d.

. . . . . pro vectura cuiusdam partis dicti meremii, vj d.

. . . . pro iij duodenis iiij cratibus, j duodena viij fescilis virgorum, xj sol. viij d.

. . . . pro emendacione utensilium, xxiij d. ob.

. . . . pro mill. cavillarum ad tegulas curie, j d. ob.

. . . . Albo pro diversis clavis ferri, xviij sol. x d. ob.

. . . . pro vectura ij charrearum plumbi, iij d. ob.

. . . . petram, vij d. ob.[1]

[1] After this only a few disjointed words are legible.

.... [N]orreys and his fellows in part payment for 102 pieces of oak, 50 beams of the same timber, 79*s.* 8*d.*

.... Newhythe for carriage of the said timber by land and water to Westminster, 29*s.*

.... and his fellows for 62 beams of oak, 39*s.* 5*d.*

.... born and his fellows for 90 oak planks, 37*s.* 3*d.*

...... for carrying a certain part of the said timber, 6*d.*

...... for 40 hurdles, 20 bundles of withies, 11*s.* 8*d.*

.... for mending tools, 23½*d.*

.... for 1,000 pegs for the tiles in the [king's] court, 1½*d.*

.... White for various iron nails, 18*s.* 10½*d.*

.... for carriage of 2 chars of lead, 3½*d.*

.... stone, 7½*d.*

13. Summary of expenditure on works at Westminster in 1258 (25 June–3 August) and in 1263–4 (E 101/505/33)

Summa stipendiorum tascharum cum diversis empcionibus Ecclesie Westm' per vj ebdomadas a die Martis in crastino Nativitatis Sancti Johannis Baptiste anno xlij usque diem Sabbati post festum beati Petri advincula ccviij li. xiij sol. vij d. ob. per unum Rotulum.

Summa stipendiorum tascharum cum diversis empcionibus ecclesie Westm' per xij ebdomadas a die Lune proxima ante festum beati Petri advincula anno xlvij usque diem Sabbati post festum Sancti Luce Ewangeliste cccxxxv li. ix sol. ob. per unum Rotulum.

Summa stipendiorum ecclesie per v ebdomadas a die Lune in vigilia Sancti Edmundi regis anno xlviij incipiente usque diem Sabbati in crastino Sancti Thome apostoli liiij li. xij sol. ix d. ob. per j Rotulum.

Summa stipendiorum ecclesie per vij ebdomadas a die Lune in crastino Sanctorum Fabiani & Sebastiani anno xlviij usque diem Sabbati proximam post Cineres xxvij li. xv sol. vj d. per unum Rotulum.

Summa predictorum iiij Rotulorum Ecclesie per xxx ebdomadas DCxxvj li. x sol. xj d. ob.

Summa stipendiorum tascharum cum diversis empcionibus Curie Westm' per xij ebdomadas a die Lune proxima ante festum beati Petri advincula anno xlvij usque diem Sabbati post festum Sancti Luce Ewangeliste cciiij^{xx}ix li. xiiij sol. iij d. per unum Rotulum.

Summa stipendiorum Curie per unam ebdomadam a die Lune proxima ante festum Sancti Thome Apostoli anno xlviij usque diem Sabbati in crastino dicti festi xiiij li. ij sol. x d. ob. per j Rotulum.

Summa predictorum duorum Rotulorum Curie per xiij ebdomadas CCCiij li. xvj sol. j d. ob.

Summa totalis stipendiorum tascharum cum diversis empcionibus Ecclesie & Curie Westm' per xliij ebdomadas in sex Rotulis predictis ix^{c}xxxij li. viij sol. j d.

13. Summary of expenditure on works at Westminster in 1258 (25 June–3 August) and in 1263–4

Total of wages and tasks with various purchases for the Church of Westminster for 6 weeks from Tuesday on the morrow of the Nativity of St. John the Baptist [25 June] in the 42nd year [1258] until Saturday after the feast of the blessed Peter in Chains [3 August], £208. 13*s*. 7½*d*. by one roll.

Total of wages and tasks with various purchases for the Church of Westminster for 12 weeks from Monday next before the feast of the blessed Peter in Chains [30 July] in the 47th year [1263] until Saturday after the feast of St. Luke the Evangelist [20 October], £335. 9*s*. 0½*d*. by one roll.

Total of wages for the Church for 5 weeks from Monday on the eve of St. Edmund the King [19 November] at the beginning of the 48th year [1263] until Saturday, the morrow of St. Thomas the Apostle [22 December], £54. 12*s*. 9½*d*. by one roll.

Total of wages for the Church for 7 weeks from Monday, the morrow of Saints Fabian and Sebastian [21 January] in the 48th year [1264] until Saturday after Ash Wednesday [8 March], £27. 15*s*. 6*d*. by one roll.

Total of the aforesaid 4 rolls for the Church for 30 weeks, £626. 10*s*. 11½*d*.

Total of wages and tasks with various purchases for the Court at Westminster for 12 weeks from Monday next before the feast of the blessed Peter in Chains [30 July] in the 47th year [1263] until Saturday after the feast of St. Luke the Evangelist [20 October], £289. 14*s*. 3*d*. by one roll.

Total of the wages for the Court for one week from Monday next before the feast of St. Thomas the Apostle [17 December] in the 48th year [1263] until Saturday on the morrow of the said feast [22 December], £14. 2*s*. 10½*d*. by one roll.

Total of the aforesaid two rolls for the Court for 13 weeks, £303. 16*s*. 1½*d*.

Sum total of wages and tasks with several purchases for the Church and Court of Westminster for 43 weeks in the six aforesaid rolls, £932. 8*s*. 1*d*.

14. Memorandum of the total expenditure on works at Westminster up to Michaelmas 1261
(Westminster Abbey Muniments, 16000(*e*))

Summa custus operacionum Westm' ab Inceptione earundem usque in die dominica proxima post festum beati Michaelis anno regni Regis Henrici xlv^{to}. Et cc lx li. restant solvende pro stipendiis alborum cissorum et minutorum operariorum. Et pro franca petra & calce & aliis empcionibus que non compotantur in hac summa

xxix mill. ccc xlv li. xix sol. viij^{to} d.

14. Memorandum of the total expenditure on works at Westminster up to Michaelmas 1261

The total costs of the works at Westminster from their commencement until the Sunday following the feast of the blessed Michael in the 45th year of the reign of King Henry [1 October 1261]. And £260 remains to be paid for the wages of white cutters and labourers and for freestone and lime and other purchases which are not counted in this total:

£29,345. 19*s*. 8*d*.

15. Enrolments of the accounts of the Keepers of the works at Westminster from 1264 to 1272
(Exchequer, Pipe Rolls 110, 112, 113, 114, 115, 116)

Compotus operacionum ecclesie Westm' & domorum Regis ibidem a crastino Epi[p]hanie anno xlviij usque ad Natale domini anno lj° per magistros Robertum de Beverle. Alexandrum carpentarium. Johannem de Spalding' custodes operacionum predictarum & per visum Ade de Stratton' clerici per breve Regis.

Iidem reddunt compotum de CCCCxxxvj li. viij sol. vij d. receptis de Thesauro Regis per manus fratris Henrici Prioris Sancte Radegundis Thesaurarii & camerariorum anno xlix. Et de iiij^xx li. receptis de eodem thesauro per manus magistri Thome de Wymundeham thesaurarii & camerariorum. Et de xxxiij li. dim. marca receptis de garderoba Regis per manus Radulfi de Sandwico custodis eiusdem garderobe anno xlviij. Et de Mxxviij li. xij sol. vj d. de exitu sigilli Regis per manum Johannis Le Fauconer per totum predictum tempus. Et de Clxvj li. xiij sol. iiij d. de exitu cambiorum London' & Cantuar' per manum Willelmi filii Ricardi custodis eorundem. Et de xl li. de exitu eiusdem cambii per manum Bartholomei de Castello. Et de xiij li. j marca receptis de Johanne Adryen & Luca de Batencurt ballivis London'. Et de DCCC lxxvij li. xiiij sol. receptis de Alesia de Lacy de fine pro habenda custodia terrarum Edmundi de Lacy quondam viri sui. Et de lxiij li. dim. marca receptis de Hawisia de London' de fine pro habenda custodia terrarum que fuerunt Patricii de Chawurces. Et de xl li. receptis de civibus London' de auxilio ad reparacionem domorum Regis apud Westmonasterium. Et de xx li. receptis de abbate de Seleby de fine pro habenda carta. Et de C li. receptis de Hugone de Windes' pro Gileberto comite Gloucestrie de fine mille librarum. Et de xlviij li. receptis de Ami[ci]a comitissa Devon' de firma de Melkesham. Et de xx li. receptis de Johanne de Havering' de fine pro habenda custodia ballie que fuit Ricardi de Hareden' in foresta de Savernak'. Et de x marcis receptis de magistro Willelmo de Sancto Albano de fine pro terra.

Summa MMDCCCClxxiiij li. viij sol. v d. In thesauro nichil

15. Enrolments of the accounts of the Keepers of the works at Westminster from 1264 to 1272

Account of the works at the church of Westminster and the king's buildings there, from the morrow of the Epiphany in the 48th year (of Henry III) [7 January 1264] until Christmas in the 51st year [25 December 1266], by Masters Robert of Beverley, Alexander the carpenter, [and] John of Spalding, keepers of the aforesaid works, and by the view of Adam of Stratton, clerk, by the king's writ.

The same render account of £436. 8*s*. 7*d*. received from the king's Treasury in the 49th year by the hands of brother Henry, Prior of St. Radegund's, Treasurer, and the chamberlains. And of £80 received from the same Treasury by the hands of Master Thomas of Wymondham, Treasurer, and the chamberlains. And of £33. 6*s*. 8*d*. received from the king's Wardrobe by the hands of Ralph of Sandwich, keeper of the same Wardrobe in the 48th year. And of £1,028. 12*s*. 6*d*. from the issue of the king's seal, by the hand of John Le Fauconer throughout all the aforesaid time. And of £166. 13*s*. 4*d*. from the issue of the mints of London and Canterbury by the hand of William fitzRichard, warden of the same. And of £40 from the revenue of the same exchange by the hand of Bartholomew de Castello. And of £13. 13*s*. 4*d*. received from John Adryen and Luke de Batencourt, bailiffs of London. And of £877. 14*s*. received from Alice de Lacy from a fine for having wardship of the lands of Edmund de Lacy, formerly her husband. And of £63. 6*s*. 8*d*. received from Hawise of London from a fine for having wardship of the lands which belonged to Patrick of Chaworth. And of £40 received from the citizens of London, from an aid for the repair of the king's buildings at Westminster. And of £20 received from the abbot of Selby from a fine for having a charter. And of £100 received from Hugh of Windsor on behalf of Gilbert, Earl of Gloucester, from a fine of £1,000. And of £48 received from Amice, Countess of Devon, from the farm of Melksham. And of £20 received from John of Havering from a fine for having custody of the bailiwick in the forest of Savernake that was Richard of Harding's. And of £6. 13*s*. 4*d*. received from Master William of St. Albans from a fine for having land.

Total, £2,974. 8*s*. 5*d*. Paid in cash, nothing.

Et in marmore libera petra tam de Cadamo quam de Reygate. grisia petra. creta. plastre. calce. windagio & cariagio predictorum ad operaciones predicte ecclesie per totum predictum tempus CCCCiiij^{xx}vij li. xvj sol. x d. Item xxiij sol. Et pro grosso maeremio & maeremio ad columpnas faciendas ad stalla monachorum. maeremio prosternendo in diversis locis. bordis. tignis. lathis. cleiis. virgis. busca & quibusdam parvis utensilibus ad easdem operaciones per idem tempus cum cariagio premissorum CCviij li. ix sol. j d. Et in plumbo. ferro. acero. carbone ad ferramenta facienda tegula ad domos operariorum cooperiendas. cordis. vitro. cera. pice & aliis necessariis ad fenestras vitreas & ad cementum & cariagio omnium premissorum Ciiij^{xx}xviij li. xxiij d. ob. Et in stipendiis quorumdam cementariorum & carpentariorum. minutorum operariorum & operacionibus traditis ad tascam cementariis & carpentariis & expensis quorumdam missorum ad diversa loca pro negocio dictarum operacionum MCiiij^{xx}x li. vj sol. ij d. ob. per predictum tempus quorum omnium particulas liberaverunt in thesauro.

Summa MMiiij^{xx}v li. xvij sol. j d.

Et in libera & grisea petra. creta. calce. plastre ad camina cum cariagio predictorum. coloribus & aliis necessariis ad picturas camere Regis maeremio. bordis. plumbo. ferro. acero. clavis & aliis necessariis ad operaciones domorum Regis per predictum tempus Diiij^{xx}viij li. iij sol. v d. Et in stipendiis quorumdam cementariorum carpentariorum. pictorum. plumbariorum. vitreariorum. minutorum operariorum & operacionibus traditis ad tascam & expensis quorumdam missorum ad diversa loca pro negocio earundem operacionum. Dviij li. viij sol. iij d. ob.

Summa Miiij^{xx}xvj li. xj sol. viij d.

Summa omnium precedencium misarum MMMCiiij^{xx}ij li. viij sol. ix d. ob.

Et habent de superplus CCviij li. iiij d. ob. quod totum debetur diversis hominibus quorum nomina continentur in quodam rotulo quem predicti liberaverunt in thesauro sub sigillis eorum quod superplusagium allocatur custodibus operacionum in rotulo lvj in compoto suo de eisdem operacionibus in rotulo compotorum. quia magister Robertus cementarius & Adam de Stratton' recognoverunt coram Baronibus quod satisfecerunt predictis hominibus de predictis debitis quorum nomina liberaverunt in thesauro.

(E 372/110, rot. 13^{d}.)

And in marble, freestone both from Caen and from Reigate, ragstone, chalk, plaster, limestone, windage and carriage, of the aforesaid to the works at the aforesaid church throughout all the said time, £487. 16*s.* 10*d.* Item 23*s.* And for heavy timber and timber for making columns for the monks' stalls, for felling timber in several places, for boards, beams, laths, hurdles, withies, firewood, and for certain small necessaries for the same works throughout the same time, with carriage of the same, £208. 9*s.* 1*d.* And in lead, iron, steel, [and] charcoal for making ironwork, tiles for covering the workmen's buildings, ropes, glass, wax, pitch, and other things necessary for glass windows and for cement, and in carriage of all the things abovementioned £198. 1*s.* 11½*d.* And in the wages of certain masons, carpenters, and labourers, and in works put out at task to masons and carpenters, and in the expenses of certain messengers sent to various places on business connected with the said works, £1,190. 6*s.* 2½*d.* for the aforesaid time, the particulars of all of which they have delivered into the Treasury.

Total, £2,085. 17*s.* 1*d.*

And in free- and ragstone, chalk, lime, [and] plaster for chimneys with carriage of the aforesaid; in colours and other things necessary for painting the king's chamber; in timber, boards, lead, iron, steel, nails, and other things necessary for the works of the king's buildings throughout the aforesaid time, £588. 3*s.* 5*d.* And in the wages of certain masons, carpenters, painters, plumbers, glaziers, [and] labourers, and in works put out at task, and in the expenses of certain messengers sent to several places on business connected with the same works, £508. 8*s.* 3½*d.*

Total, £1,096. 11*s.* 8*d.*

Total of all the preceding expenditure, £3,182. 8*s.* 9½*d.*

And they have a balance in their favour of £208. 0*s.* 4½*d.*, all of which is owed to several men, whose names are contained in a certain roll, which the aforesaid [accountants] have delivered into the Treasury under their seals. This balance is allowed to the keepers of the works in roll 56 in their account for the same works in the Roll of Accounts,[1] because Master Robert the mason and Adam of Stratton acknowledged before the Barons [of the Exchequer] that they have satisfied the aforesaid men, whose names they have delivered in the Treasury, for the aforesaid debts.

[1] This was the section of the Pipe Roll devoted to the enrolment of special accounts.

Compotus operacionum ecclesie Westm' & domorum Regis ibidem a festo Natalis Domini anno lj^{o} usque ad festum Sancti Michaelis anno lij per magistrum Robertum de Beverlaco cementarium & fratrem Ranulphum conversum abbacie Cumbermere positum loco Alexandri carpentarii & Johannem de Spalding' per breve regis directum Ade de Stratton' clerico custodi operacionum earundem per visum & testimonium eiusdem Ade.

Iidem reddunt compotum de Cxl li. receptis de thesauro Regis per manum Thome de Wimundeham Thesaurarii Regis & camerariorum per predictum tempus. Et de CCCCxxxv li. j marca receptis de exitibus sigilli Regis per manum Johannis le Faucaner. Et de Dlxvj li. j marca receptis de Alesia Comitissa Lincolnie de fine pro habenda custodia terre & heredis Edmundi de Lacy. Et de xiij li. receptis de Isabella Comitissa Albem' de firma de Stratton'. Et de x li. receptis de Hawisia de Lond' pro habenda custodia terre & heredis Patricii de Chawurc'. Et de xxiiij li. receptis de Amicia Comitissa Devon' de firma de Melkesham. Et de ij marcis receptis de Alicia que fuit uxor Willelmi de Sancto Albano pro terra eiusdem Willelmi. Et de viij li. dim. marca receptis de Johanne Adrian & Luca de Batencurt custodibus civitatis Lond'. Et de xx li. receptis de magistro Ricardo de Stanes de exitibus episcopatus London' de prestito. Et de l marcis receptis de Ada de Stratton' de prestito quas l marcas Rex assignavit ei de debito Saer' filii Henrici sicut recepit. Et de l marcis receptis de Roberto de Northon' vicecomite Norffolk' & Suffolk' per manum Simonis Passelewe. Et de dim. marca de Thoma de Mimmes de fine pro terra. Et de xx sol. de Galfrido de la Forde de fine pro eodem. Et de dim. marca de Henrico Horn de fine pro eodem. Et de x marcis de Radulfo Rasur de fine pro eodem. Et de C sol. de Radulfo le Kayer de fine pro eodem. Et de dim. marca de Radulfo le Men de fine pro eodem. Et de xx sol. de Waltero de Otteford de fine pro eodem. Et de j marca de Nicholao le carpenter de Suthwerk' de fine pro eodem. Et de xx sol. de Andrea le Moun' de fine pro eodem. Et de xx sol. de Thoma Rokke plumbario de fine pro eodem. Et de dim. marca de Galfrido de Colet' de fine pro eodem sicut continetur in quodam rotulo de particulis quem predictus Adam liberavit in thesauro.

Summa MCCCiij li. vj sol. viij d. In thesauro nichil.

Account of the works at the church of Westminster, and the king's buildings there, from the feast of Christmas in the 51st year [*25 December 1266*] *until the feast of St. Michael in the 52nd year* [*29 September 1267*], *by Master Robert of Beverley, mason, and brother Ranulf, lay-brother of the abbey of Combermere, put in the place of Alexander the carpenter, and John of Spalding by the king's writ directed to Adam of Stratton, clerk, keeper of the same works, by the view and witness of the said Adam.*

The same render account of £140 received from the king's Treasury by the hand of Thomas of Wymondham, the king's Treasurer, and the chamberlains during the aforesaid time. And of £435. 13*s*. 4*d*. received from the issues of the king's seal by the hand of John Le Faucaner. And of £566. 13*s*. 4*d*. received from Alice, Countess of Lincoln, from a fine for having wardship of the land and the heir of Edmund de Lacy. And of £13 received from Isabella, Countess of Aumale, from the farm of Stratton. And of £10 received from Hawise of London for having wardship of the land and the heir of Patrick of Chaworth. And of £24 received from Amice, Countess of Devon, from the farm of Melksham. And of £1. 6*s*. 8*d*. received from Alice, who was the wife of William of St. Albans, for the land of the same William. And of £8. 6*s*. 8*d*. received from John Adrian and Luke de Batencourt, keepers of the city of London. And of £20 received from Master Richard of Staines from the revenues of the bishopric of London by way of imprest. And of £33. 6*s*. 8*d*. received from Adam of Stratton by way of imprest, which sum the king assigned to him from the debt of Saer fitzHenry just as he received it. And of £33. 6*s*. 8*d*. received from Robert of Norton, sheriff of Norfolk and Suffolk, by the hand of Simon Passelewe. And of 6*s*. 8*d*. received from Thomas of Mimms from a fine for land. And of 20*s*. from Geoffrey de la Forde from a fine for the same. And of 6*s*. 8*d*. from Henry Horn from a fine for the same. And of £6. 13*s*. 4*d*. from Ralph Rasur from a fine for the same. And of 100*s*. from Ralph le Kayer from a fine for the same. And of 6*s*. 8*d*. from Ralph le Men from a fine for the same. And of 20*s*. from Walter of Otford from a fine for the same. And of 13*s*. 4*d*. from Nicholas the carpenter of Southwark from a fine for the same. And of 20*s*. from Andrew le Moun' from a fine for the same. And of 20*s*. from Thomas Rokke, plumber, from a fine for the same. And of 6*s*. 8*d*. from Geoffrey de Colet' from a fine for the same, as is contained in a certain roll of particulars, which the aforesaid Adam delivered into the Treasury.

Total, £1,303. 6*s*. 8*d*. Paid in cash, nothing.

Et in libera petra tam de Cadamo quam de Reigat'. grisea petra. creta. plastr'. calce. windagio. bukettis & cariagio omnium predictorum ad operaciones predictas sicut continetur in rotulo de particulis quem predicti liberaverunt in thesauro CCiiij^{xx}iij li. xiiij sol. x d. ob. Et in grosso maeremio bordis tignis tam de quercu quam de alneto. cleiis. latis. virgis. uncto. visco & quibusdam parvis utensilibus ad easdem operaciones cum cariagio predictorum lxxvij li. ix sol. iiij d. sicut continetur ibidem. Et in plumbo. ferro. acero. carbone. busca ad ferramenta facienda. seruris. cordis. vitro. cera. pice. & aliis necessariis ad fenestras vitreas tam apud Havering' quam apud Westmonasterium & ad cementum faciendum cum cariagio eorundem Clx li. v sol. ix d. sicut continetur ibidem. Et in tegulis. cavillis. litera. arundine, emptis ad cooperiendum muros operacionum predictarum & diversas domos Regis cum cariagio predictorum sicut continetur ibidem xj li. ix sol. ix d. ob. Et in stipendiis quorumdam cementariorum pavatorum ante pheretrum Sancti Edwardi. carpentariorum. pictorum. plumbariorum. vitreariorum. minutorum operariorum & operationibus [traditis] cementariis. carpentariis. pictoribus ad tascham & expensis quorumdam missorum ad diversa loca pro negociis dictarum operacionum per predictum tempus sicut continetur ibidem DCxiiij li. x sol. j d. ob.

Et in duobus leuncellis. duobus turellis. duabus platis. tribus cuppis de cupro faciendis. deaurandis ad sedem Regis in magna aula Westmonasterii & quinque clavibus cupreiis ad lavatorium in parva aula cum quinque ymaginibus stagneis ad idem lavatorium. & uno tuello de cupro ad quandam cisternam iuxta cameram Regis sicut continetur ibidem xxxiiij li. xix d. Et pro auro in folio & aliis necessariis ad picturas circa lectum Regis in camera Regis ibidem. liij li. v sol. ij d. ob.

Summa misarum MCCxxxiiij li. xvj sol. viij d. Et debent lxviij li. x sol. Iidem reddunt compotum de eodem debito. In thesauro nichil. Et in garderoba Regis Nicholao de Leukenor' tunc custodi eiusdem garderobe lxvi li. xiij sol. iiij d. per breve Regis. Et Magistro Waltero pictori Regis pro dampnis & gravaminibus que sustinuit in servicio Regis tempore turbacionis habite in regno xl sol. per breve Regis. Et habent de superplus xl d. qui allocantur eis in rotulo sequenti in compoto suo de eisdem operacionibus.

(E 372/112, rot. 1^{d}.)

Compotus operacionum ecclesie Westm' & domorum Regis ibidem a festo Sancti Michaelis anno lij^{o} usque ad natale domini anno liiij^{o} per Magistrum Robertum de Beverlaco cementarium & fratrem Ranulphum

And in freestone, both from Caen and from Reigate, ragstone, chalk, plaster, lime, windage, buckets, and in carriage of all the aforesaid to the aforesaid works, as is contained in a roll of particulars which the aforesaid have delivered in the Treasury, £283. 14*s.* 10½*d.* And in heavy timber, boards, beams of both oak and alder, hurdles, laths, withies, grease, and glue, and in certain small necessaries for the same works, with carriage of the aforesaid, £77. 9*s.* 4*d.*, as is contained there. And in lead, iron, steel, charcoal, [and] firewood for making ironwork; locks, ropes, glass, wax, pitch and other things necessary for glass windows, both at Havering and at Westminster, and for making cement, with carriage of the same, £160. 5*s.* 9*d.* as is contained there. And in tiles, tile-pins, litter, [and] reeds, bought for covering the walls of the aforesaid works and several of the king's buildings, with carriage of the aforesaid as is contained there, £11. 9*s.* 9½*d.* And in the wages of certain masons, paviors [working] in front of the shrine of St. Edward, carpenters, painters, plumbers, glaziers, labourers, and in works put out at task to masons, carpenters, [and] painters, and in the expenses of certain messengers sent to various places on business connected with the said works throughout the aforesaid time, as is contained there, £614. 10*s.* 1½*d.*

And in fashioning and gilding two small lions, two turrets, two plates [and] three cups of copper for the king's throne in the great hall of Westminster and in five copper taps for the lavatory in the small hall with five tin images for the same lavatory; and in one spout of copper for a certain cistern next the king's chamber as is contained there, £34. 19*d.* And for gold leaf, and other things necessary for paintings around the king's bed in the king's chamber there, £53. 5*s.* 2½*d.*

Total expenditure, £1,234. 16*s.* 8*d.* And they owe £68. 10*s.* The same render account of the same debt. Paid in cash, nothing. And [they paid] into the king's Wardrobe to Nicholas of Lewknor, the keeper of the same Wardrobe, £66. 13*s.* 4*d.* by the king's writ. And [they paid] to Master Walter, the king's painter, for damages and injuries which he received in the king's service at the time of the disturbance in the kingdom, 40*s.* by the king's writ. And they have a balance in their favour of 40*d.* which is allowed to them in the following roll in their account of the same works.

Account of the works at the church of Westminster, and the king's buildings there, from the feast of St. Michael in the 52nd year [29 *September* 1267] *until Christmas in the 54th year* [25 *December* 1269], *by Master Robert of Beverley, mason, and brother Ranulf, lay-brother of the abbey of*

conversum abbacie de Cumbermere & per visum & testimonium Ade de Stratton' clerici & custodis earundem operacionum.

Iidem reddunt compotum de Miiij^{xx}xvij li. ix sol. ij d. receptis de thesauro Regis per manum Thome de Wymundeham Thesaurarii Regis & camerariorum per predictum tempus. Et de DCxj li. j marca de exitibus sigilli Regis per manum Johannis le Fauconer per idem tempus. Et de CCCCiiij^{xx} li. x sol. iiij d. receptis de Alesia Comitissa Lincoln' de fine pro habenda custodia terre & heredis Edmundi de Lacy. Et de xx marcis receptis de abbate de Abbodesbir' pro habenda confirmacione. Et de xx marcis receptis de Priore de Spalding' pro eodem. Et de l li. receptis de Hawisia que fuit uxor Patricii de Chawurc' de fine pro habenda custodia terrarum & heredum dicti Patricii. Et de l marcis receptis de Priore & conventu Sancti Benedicti de Hulmo de fine. Et de lx li. receptis de Philippo Marmiun de arreragiis firme sue de Thamewurth' & Wiginton'. Et de xx marcis receptis de Priore & conventu Sancte Trinitatis Lond' pro habenda custodia eiusdem prioratus de tempore vacacionis. Et de xx marcis receptis de Burgensibus de Rotomag' pro habenda carta. Et de v marcis receptis de abbate de Nuttel' pro habenda confirmacione. Et de x marcis receptis de Magistro Johanne de Chisull' de fine pro habenda custodia terre & heredis Johannis de Bernival. Et de x marcis receptis de Priore Karl' pro habenda confirmacione. Et de xviij li. xj sol. ix d. receptis de oblacionibus provenientibus de altari Sancti Edwardi per manus Ade de Wicumb monachi & sacriste eiusdem loci. Et de x sol. receptis de Rogero le Gardiner apud Westmonasterium de exitibus gardini Regis ibidem.

Summa MMCCCCxxij li. xv d. In thesauro nichil.

Et in libera petra tam de Cadamo quam de Reygat'. grisia petra. creta. plastr'. calce. windagio & cariagio omnium predictorum ad easdem operaciones sicut continetur in Rotulo de particulis quem predicti liberaverunt in Thesauro DCCxlvj li. xv sol. iij d. ob. Et in grosso maeremio. bordis tignis tam de quercu quam de alneto. cleiis lathis virgis uncto visco & quibusdam parvis utensilibus ad easdem operaciones cum cariagio predictorum sicut continetur in eisdem particulis iiij^{xx}xij li. v sol. xj d. ob. Et in plumbo ferro acero carbone busca ad ferramenta facienda. seruris. cordis. vitro. cera. pice. & aliis necessariis ad fenestras vitreas & ad cementum faciendum. & canabo ad claudendas fenestras eiusdem ecclesie; cum cariagio eorundem sicut continetur in Rotulo de eisdem particulis; Cliij li. xv sol. x d. ob. Et in tegulis cavillis. litera. arundine stipula emptis ad cooperiendum

Combermere, and by the view and witness of Adam of Stratton, clerk and keeper of the same works.

The same render account of £1,097. 9*s*. 2*d*. received from the king's Treasury by the hand of Thomas of Wymondham, the king's Treasurer, and the chamberlains during the said time. And of £611. 13*s*. 4*d*. from the issues of the king's seal by the hand of John le Fauconer during the same time. And of £480. 10*s*. 4*d*. received from Alice, Countess of Lincoln, from a fine for having wardship of the land and heir of Edmund de Lacy. And of £13. 6*s*. 8*d*. received from the abbot of Abbotsbury for having confirmation [of a charter]. And of £13. 6*s*. 8*d*. received from the prior of Spalding for the same. And of £50 received from Hawise, who was the wife of Patrick of Chaworth, from a fine for having wardship of the lands and heirs of the said Patrick. And of £33. 6*s*. 8*d*. received from the prior and convent of St. Benet Holme from a fine. And of £60 received from Philip Marmiun of the arrears of his farm of Tamworth and Wigginton. And of £13. 6*s*. 8*d*. received from the prior and convent of the Holy Trinity of London, for having custody of the same priory during a vacancy. And of £13. 6*s*. 8*d*. received from the citizens of Rouen for having a charter. And of £3. 6*s*. 8*d*. received from the abbot of Notley for having confirmation. And of £6. 13*s*. 4*d*. received from Master John of Chishall from a fine for having wardship of the land and heir of John de Bernival. And of £6. 13*s*. 4*d*. received from the prior of Carlisle for having confirmation. And £18. 11*s*. 9*d*. received from the offerings coming from the altar of St. Edward by the hands of Adam of Wycombe, monk and sacrist of the same place. And of 10*s*. received from Roger the gardener at Westminster from the revenues of the king's garden there.

Total, £2,422. 15*d*. Paid in cash, nothing.

And in freestone both from Caen and from Reigate, ragstone, chalk, plaster, lime, windage, and carriage of all the aforesaid to the same works, as is contained in a roll of particulars which the aforesaid have delivered into the Treasury, £746. 15*s*. 3½*d*. And in heavy timber, boards, beams of both oak and alder, hurdles, laths, withies, grease, glue, and in certain small necessaries for the same works, with carriage of the aforesaid as is contained in the same particulars, £92. 5*s*. 11½*d*. And in lead, iron, steel, charcoal, and firewood for making ironwork; in locks, ropes, glass, wax, pitch, and other things necessary for glass windows and for making cement, and canvas for closing the windows of the same church, with carriage of the same, as is contained in the roll of the same particulars, £153. 15*s*. 10½*d*. And in tiles, tile-pins, litter, reeds, [and] straw bought for covering

turrim eiusdem ecclesie inceptam & muros operacionum predictarum; & ad diversas domos Regis cum cariagio eorundem, sicut continetur in Rotulo de eisdem particulis viij li. xj sol. j d. ob. Et in quadam imagine stagnea facienda ad cisternam Regis inter cameram Regis & cameram Regine & quadam imagine crucifixi empta & posita in parva capella iuxta lectum Regis. & stipendiis iiij^{or} aurifabrorum operancium circa novum feretrum beati Edwardi sicut continetur in Rotulo de eisdem particulis vj li. xij sol. viij d. Et in auro in folio. aimallis. diversis coloribus & aliis necessariis ad picturas voltarum ecclesie supradicte & magne camere Regis sicut continetur ibidem lxviij li. xviij sol. ix d. ob. Et in stipendiis quorumdam cementariorum pavatorum ante feretrum beati Edwardi. carpentariorum. pictorum. plumbariorum. vitriariorum. minutorum operariorum. & diversis operacionibus positis & factis ad tascham & expensis quorumdam nunciorum missorum ad diversa loca pro negociis dictarum operacionum per predictum tempus sicut continetur in Rotulo de eisdem particulis. MCCCxliiij li. xix sol. v d.

Summa misarum MMCCCCxxj li. xix sol. iij ob. Et debent ij sol. iij ob.

Iidem reddunt compotum de eodem debito. In thesauro nichil. Et in superplus quod habent in rotulo precedenti in compoto suo de eisdem operacionibus xl d. Et habent de superplus xv d.

(E 372/113, rot. 1^{d}.)

Compotus operacionum ecclesie Westm' & domorum Regis ibidem a Natali domini hoc anno per magistrum Robertum de Beverlaco cementarium & fratrem Ranulphum conversum abbacie de Cumbermare & per visum & testimonium Ade de Stratton' clerici & custodis earundem operacionum usque ad festum purificacionis beate virginis anno l^{mo} quinto.

Iidem reddunt compotum de CCCCiiij^{xx}vij li. ij sol. iij d. ob. receptis de thesauro Regis per manum Thome de Wimundeham & magistri Johannis de Chishull' & camerariorum per predictum tempus videlicet lix li. x sol. x d. de tempore Thome & CCCCxxvij li. xj sol. v d. ob. de tempore magistri Johannis. Et de CCCCxj li. xiij sol. iiij d. receptis de exitibus sigilli regis per manum Johannis le Fauconer per idem tempus. Et de CCClv li. x sol. iiij d. receptis de Alesia comitissa Lincolnie de fine pro habenda custodia. Et de l marcis receptis de abbate de Seleby de fine conventus pro habenda custodia abbacie de Seleby cum ipsam vacare contigerit. Et de l marcis receptis de Hawisia de London' de fine pro habenda custodia terrarum & heredum Patricii de Chawurc'. Et de xl li. receptis de Philippo Marmiun de firma de Thamewurth'. Et de iij sol. x d. receptis de

the tower of the same church, which has been begun, and the walls of the aforesaid works; and for several of the king's buildings, with carriage of the same, as is contained in the roll of the same particulars, £8. 11*s*. 1½*d*. And in making a certain tin figure for the king's cistern [which is] between the king's chamber and the queen's chamber; and a certain image of the Crucified bought and placed in the small chapel next to the king's bed. And in the wages of 4 goldsmiths working on the new shrine of the blessed Edward as is contained in a roll of the same particulars, £6. 12*s*. 8*d*. And in gold leaf, enamels, various colours, and other things necessary for painting the vaults of the aforesaid church and the king's great chamber, as is contained there, £68. 18*s*. 9½*d*. And in the wages of certain masons, paviors [working] in front of the shrine of the blessed Edward, carpenters, painters, plumbers, glaziers, labourers, and in several works put out and done at task, and in the expenses of certain messengers sent to various places on business connected with the said works during the aforesaid time, as is contained in the roll of the same particulars, £1,344. 19*s*. 5*d*.

Total expenditure, £2,421. 19*s*. 1½*d*. And they owe 2*s*. 1½*d*.

The same render account of the same debt. Paid in cash, nothing. And in the balance which they have in the preceding roll in their account of the same works, 40*d*. And they have a balance of 15*d*.

Account of the works at the church of Westminster and the king's buildings there, from Christmas this year [25 December 1269], by Master Robert of Beverley, mason, and brother Ranulf, lay-brother of the abbey of Combermere, and by the view and witness of Adam of Stratton, clerk and keeper of the same works, until the feast of the Purification of the Blessed Virgin in the 55th year [2 February 1271].

The same render account of £487. 2*s*. 3½*d*. received from the king's Treasury by the hand of Thomas of Wymondham and Master John of Chishall and the chamberlains during the aforesaid time, that is to say: £59. 10*s*. 10*d*. for the time of Thomas and £427. 11*s*. 5½*d*. for the time of Master John. And of £411. 13*s*. 4*d*. received from the issues of the king's seal, by the hand of John Le Fauconer during the same time. And of £355. 10*s*. 4*d*. received from Alice, Countess of Lincoln, from a fine for having wardship. And of £33. 6*s*. 8*d*. received from the abbot of Selby from a fine from the convent for having custody of the abbey of Selby, when it next happens to be vacant. And of £33. 6*s*. 8*d*. received from Hawise of London from a fine for having wardship of the lands and heirs of Patrick of Chaworth. And of £40 received from Philip Marmiun from the farm

Johanne de Sutton' sacrista Westmonasteriensi de oblacionibus altaris beati Edwardi.

Summa MCCClxj li. iij sol. j d. ob. In thesauro nichil.

Et in marmore. libera petra tam de Cadamo quam de Reigate grisea petra plastro creta cariagio omnium predictorum windagiis & diversis utensilibus ad easdem operaciones per predictum tempus sicut continetur in rotulo de particulis quem predicti liberaverunt in thesauro CCCClix li. xij sol. ix d. Et in grosso maeremio bordis tignis tam de quercu quam de alneto latis cleiis virgis uncto visco & quibusdam parvis utensilibus ad easdem operaciones cum cariagio predictorum sicut continetur in rotulo de eisdem particulis; liij li. xv sol. xj d. ob. Et in plumbo ferro acero carbone busca ad ferramenta facienda, serruris cordis vitro cera pice & aliis necessariis ad fenestras vitreas & ad cementum faciendum. canabo ad fenestras predicte ecclesie claudendas cum cariagio omnium predictorum sicut continetur ibidem; Cxl li. xiiij sol. Et in tegulis cavillis litera stipula ad cooperiendum muros eiusdem ecclesie sicut continetur ibidem iiij li. xj sol. iiij d. ob. Et in auro in folio & admallis diversis coloribus & aliis necessariis ad picturas capse in qua reponitur corpus beati Edwardi & ad picturas Imaginum in prefata ecclesia & in magna camera Regis sicut continetur ibidem xxxij li. xvj sol. j d. ob. Et in stipendiis quorumdam cementariorum carpentariorum pictorum plumbariorum vitreariorum & aliorum minutorum operariorum & diversis operacionibus factis ad tascam & expensis quorumdam nunciorum missorum ad diversa loca pro negociis dictarum operacionum per predictum tempus sicut continetur ibidem DClxx li. v sol. x d. ob. Et habent de superplus xij sol. xj d. ob. quod annotatur in rotulo sequenti in compoto suo de eisdem operacionibus in rotulo compotorum. (E 372/114, rot. 19.)

Compotus operacionum ecclesie Westm' & domorum Regis ibidem a festo Purificacionis beate Marie virginis hoc anno per magistrum Robertum de Beverlaco cementarium & fratrem Ranulphum conversum abbacie de Cumbermere & per visum & testimonium Ade de Stratton' clerici & custodis earundem operacionum usque ad idem festum anno lvj.

Iidem reddunt compotum de CCvj li. xv sol. ix d. ob. receptis de thesauro Regis per manum Magistri Johannis de Chisull' & Philippi de Eya Thesaurariorum & camerariorum per predictum tempus. videlicet de tempore Magistri Johannis Cxlj li. x sol. iiij d. & de tempore predicti Philippi lxv li. v sol. v d. ob. Et de CCCClxviij li. vj sol. viij d. receptis de exitibus sigilli Regis per manum Johannis le Fauconer per idem tempus. Et de CCClv li. x sol. iiij d. receptis

of Tamworth. And of 3*s.* 10*d.* received from John of Sutton, sacrist of Westminster, from the offerings at the altar of the blessed Edward.

Total, £1,361. 3*s.* 1½*d.* Paid in cash, nothing.

And in marble, freestone both from Caen and from Reigate, ragstone, plaster, chalk, [and in] carriage of all the aforesaid, in windage, and in several things necessary for the same works during the aforesaid time, as is contained in a roll of particulars which the aforesaid have delivered into the Treasury, £459. 12*s.* 9*d.* And in heavy timber, boards, beams of both oak and alder, laths, hurdles, withies, grease, glue, and certain small necessaries for the same works with carriage of the aforesaid, as is contained in a roll of the same particulars, £53. 15*s.* 11½*d.* And in lead, iron, steel, charcoal, [and] firewood for making ironwork; in locks, ropes, glass, wax, pitch, and other things necessary for glass windows, and for making cement, in canvas for closing the windows of the aforesaid church, with carriage of all the aforesaid, as is contained there, £140. 14*s.* And in tiles, tile-pins, litter, [and] straw for covering the walls of the same church, as is contained there, £4. 11*s.* 4½*d.* And in gold leaf, enamels, various colours, and other things necessary for painting the reliquary in which the body of the blessed Edward is laid and for painting the images in the said church and in the king's great chamber as is contained there, £32. 16*s.* 1½*d.* And in the wages of certain masons, carpenters, painters, plumbers, glaziers, and labourers, and in various works done at task, and in the expenses of certain messengers sent to various places on business connected with the said works during the aforesaid time, as is contained there, £670. 5*s.* 10½*d.* And they have a balance of 12*s.* 11½*d.*, which is noted in the following roll in their account of the same works in the Roll of Accounts.

Account of the works at the church of Westminster and the king's buildings there, from the feast of the Purification of the Blessed Virgin this year [*2 February 1271*], *by Master Robert of Beverley, mason, and brother Ranulf, lay-brother of the abbey of Combermere, and by the view and witness of Adam of Stratton, clerk and keeper of the same works, until the same feast in the 56th year* [*2 February 1272*].

The same render account of £206. 15*s.* 9½*d.* received from the king's Treasury by the hand of Master John of Chishall and Philip of Eye, Treasurers, and of the chamberlains during the aforesaid time, that is to say: in the time of Master John, £141. 10*s.* 4*d.* and in the time of the aforesaid Philip, £65. 5*s.* 5½*d.* And of £468. 6*s.* 8*d.* received from the issues of the king's seal by the hand of John Le Fauconer during the same time. And of £355. 10*s.* 4*d.* received from Alice, Countess

de Alesia comitissa Lincolnie de fine pro habenda custodia. Et de xxv marcis receptis de magistro Johanne de Chisull' pro habenda custodia terre & heredis Johannis de Berneval. Et de C marcis receptis de executoribus Bonefacii quondam Cantuariensis archiepiscopi Regi legatis per eundem archiepiscopum per manus magistri Ricardi de Clifford. Et de v marcis receptis de Thoma Box cive London' de fine pro habenda carta. Et de xl marcis receptis de predicto magistro Ricardo de Clifford de exitibus archiepiscopatus Cantuariensis. Et de l marcis receptis de Hawisia de London' pro habenda custodia terre & heredis Patricii de Chawurc'. Et de v marcis receptis de Priore de Neketon' pro habenda confirmacione. Et de viij li. receptis de hominibus de Dorcestr' de firma sua de termino Sancti Michaelis hoc anno. Et de C sol. receptis de hominibus de Grimesby pro rehabenda villa sua. Et de v marcis receptis de Priore de Bermundes' pro receptamento.

Summa MCiiij^{xx}xvj li. xix sol. v d. ob. In thesauro nichil.

Et in marmore. libera petra tam de Cadamo quam de Reigate. grisa petra plastro. creta & cariagio omnium predictorum windagio. utensilibus diversis ad easdem operaciones per predictum tempus. sicut continetur in rotulo de particulis quem predicti liberaverunt in thesauro; CCCxlviij li. xiiij sol. vj d. Et in grosso maeremio. bordis tignis tam de quercu quam de alneto. latis. cleiis. virgis. uncto. visco & quibusdam parvis utensilibus ad easdem operaciones cum cariagio predictorum sicut continetur in rotulo de eisdem particulis xxv li. xj sol. iii d. ob. Et in plumbo. ferro. acero. carbone. busca ad ferramenta facienda. serruris & aliis necessariis. cordis. vitro. cera. pice. & aliis necessariis ad fenestras vitreas & ad cementum faciendum. canabo ad quasdam fenestras predicte ecclesie claudendas cum cariagio omnium predictorum sicut continetur in rotulo de eisdem particulis; Ciiij^{xx}xvij li. x sol. iiij d. ob. Et in tegulis cavillis litera stipula ad cooperiendum muros ecclesie predicte sicut continetur ibidem vij li. xv sol. iiij d. ob. Et in auro in folio & diversis coloribus & aliis minutis necessariis ad picturas imaginum in prefata ecclesia & in magna camera Regis sicut continetur ibidem; xvij li. xvij sol. iij d. ob. Et in stipendiis quorumdam cementariorum carpentariorum pictorum plumbariorum & vitreariorum & aliorum minutorum operariorum & diversis operacionibus factis ad tascam & expensis quorumdam nunciorum missorum ad diversa loca pro negociis dictarum operacionum per predictum tempus sicut continetur ibidem DCiiij^{xx}xviij li. x d. ob.

of Lincoln, from a fine for having wardship. And of £16. 13*s*. 4*d*. received from Master John of Chishall for having wardship of the land and heir of John de Berneval. And of £66. 13*s*. 4*d*. received from the executors of Boniface, formerly archbishop of Canterbury, left to the king by the same archbishop by the hands of Master Richard of Clifford. And of £3. 6*s*. 8*d*. received from Thomas Box, citizen of London, from a fine for having a charter. And of £26. 13*s*. 4*d*. received from the aforesaid Master Richard of Clifford from the revenues of the archbishopric of Canterbury. And of £33. 6*s*. 8*d*. received from Hawise of London for having wardship of the land and heir of Patrick of Chaworth. And of £3. 6*s*. 8*d*. received from the prior of Nocton for having confirmation. And of £8 received from the men of Dorchester from their farm for the term of Michaelmas this year. And of 100*s*. received from the men of Grimsby for regaining [the farm of] their town. And of £3. 6*s*. 8*d*. from the prior of Bermondsey for 'resetting'.[1]

Total, £1,196. 19*s*. 5½*d*. Paid in cash, nothing.

And in marble, freestone both from Caen and from Reigate, ragstone, plaster, chalk, and carriage of all the aforesaid, in windage [and] in certain necessaries for the same works during the aforesaid time, as is contained in a roll of particulars which the aforesaid have delivered in the Treasury, £348. 14*s*. 6*d*. And in heavy timber, boards, beams of both oak and alder, laths, hurdles, withies, grease, glue, and in certain small necessaries for the same works, with carriage of the aforesaid, as is contained in the roll of the same particulars, £25. 11*s*. 3½*d*. And in lead, iron, steel, charcoal, [and] firewood for making ironwork; locks and other necessaries, ropes, glass, wax, pitch, and other things necessary for glass windows and for making cement, in canvas for closing certain windows of the aforesaid church, with carriage of all the aforesaid, as is contained in the roll of the same particulars, £197. 10*s*. 4½*d*. And in tiles, tile-pins, litter, [and] straw for covering the walls of the aforesaid church, as is contained there, £7. 15*s*. 4½*d*. And in gold leaf and various colours and other small things necessary for painting images in the said church and in the king's great chamber, as is contained there, £17. 17*s*. 3½*d*. And in the wages of certain masons, carpenters, painters, plumbers and glaziers and labourers, and in several works done at task, and in the expenses of certain messengers sent to various places on business connected with the said works throughout the aforesaid time, as is contained there, £698. 0*s*. 10½*d*.

[1] 'Resetting' was a fine for receiving stolen goods or for harbouring criminals.

Summa misarum MCCiiij^{xx}xv li. ix sol. viij d. ob. Et habent de superplus iiij^{xx}xviij li. x sol. iij d. & xij sol. xj d. ob. de alio superplusagio quod habent in rotulo precedenti in compoto suo in rotulo compotorum. Summa utriusque superplusagii iiij^{xx}xix li. iij sol. ij d. ob. qui allocantur eis in rotulo sequenti in compoto suo de eisdem operacionibus in rotulo compotorum.

(E 372/115, rot. 1^{d}.)

Compotus operacionum ecclesie Westm' & domorum Regis ibidem a festo Purificacionis beate Marie Virginis hoc anno usque ad festum Sancti Edmundi Regis & martiris proximo sequens antequam Rex traderetur sepulture per Magistrum Robertum de Beverlaco cementarium & visum Ade de Stratton' clerici de Scaccario.

Idem reddit compotum de CCClxx li. xv sol. iiij d. ob. receptis de Thesauro Regis per manus Philippi de Eya Thesaurarii & camerariorum per predictum tempus. Et de CCClxx li. j marca de exitu sigilli Regis per manus Johannis la Falconer per idem tempus. Et de x marcis receptis de Ricardo de Middelton' tunc cancellario Regis pro toto comitatu Cumb' ut homines eiusdem comitatus quieti sint de turno vicecomitis. Et de xvj li. receptis de hominibus de Dorcestr' de firma sua de terminis Pasche & Sancti Michaelis. Et de xxv sol. viij d. receptis de Fulcone Paiforer & Radulfo de Sancta Ositha tunc Justiciariis Judeorum de xj bisanciis ab eis receptis & venditis. Et de CCC marcis receptis de Hawisia de London' de fine suo pro habenda custodia terrarum & heredum Patricii de Chaworc'. Et de lx marcis receptis de Priore de Northt' pro Willelmo de Fovile quondam priore de Northt' & postea priore de Lewes quia non habuit quos manucepit. Et de CC li. receptis de Isabella de Fortibus de fine pro relevio suo. Et de x marcis de Amicia Comitissa Devon' pro terra.

Summa MCCxij li. xij d. ob. In thesauro nichil.

Et in marmore, libera petra tam de Cadamo quam de Reigate, grisea petra. creta. plastr'. calce. windagio & cariagio omnium predictorum usque Westmonasterium ad operaciones predictas per predictum tempus CCv li. vj sol. x d. ob. quorum omnium particulas liberavit in Thesauro. Et in grosso maeremio. bordis. tignis tam de quercu quam de alneto. cleiis. lathis. virgis. uncto. visco. & quibusdam parvis utensilibus ad easdem operaciones & cariagio eorundem per idem tempus xiij li. xiiij sol. vij d. Et in plumbo. ferro. acero. carbone. busca ad ferramenta facienda. seruris. cordis. vitro. cera. pice & aliis necessariis ad fenestras vitreas tam ad domos predictas quam ad

Total expenditure, £1,295. 9s. 8½d. And they have a balance in their favour of £98. 10s. 3d. and 12s. 11½d. for another balance, which they have in the preceding roll in their account in the Roll of Accounts. Total of both balances, £99. 3s. 2½d., which is allowed to them in the following roll in their account for the same works in the Roll of Accounts.

Account of the works at the church of Westminster, and the king's buildings there, from the feast of the Purification of the Blessed Virgin Mary this year [*2 February 1272*] *until the feast of St. Edmund, King and Martyr, next following* [*20 November*], *before the king was committed to burial, by Master Robert of Beverley, mason, and by the view of Adam of Stratton, clerk of the Exchequer.*

The same renders account of £370. 15s. 4½d. received from the king's Treasury by the hands of Philip of Eye, Treasurer, and of the chamberlains during the aforesaid time. And of £370. 13s. 4d. from the issues of the king's seal by the hands of John le Falconer during the same time. And of £6. 13s. 4d. received from Richard of Middleton, the king's chancellor, on behalf of the whole county of Cumberland, so that the men of the same county shall be quit of the sheriff's tourn. And of £16 received from the men of Dorchester from their farm for the terms of Easter and Michaelmas. And of 25s. 8d. received from Fulk Paiforer and Ralph of St. Osyth, then Justices of the Jews, for 11 bezants received from them and sold. And of £200 received from Hawise of London from her fine for having wardship of the lands and heirs of Patrick of Chaworth. And of £40 received from the prior of Northampton on behalf of William de Fovile, formerly prior of Northampton and afterwards prior of Lewes, because he did not produce those whom he bailed. And of £200 received from Isabella de Forz from a fine for her relief. And of £6. 13s. 4d. from Amice, Countess of Devon, for land.

Total, £1,212. 1s. 0½d. Paid in cash, nothing.

And in marble, freestone both from Caen and from Reigate, ragstone, chalk, plaster, lime, windage, and carriage of all the aforesaid to Westminster for the aforesaid works during the aforesaid time £205. 6s. 10½d. the particulars of all of which he has delivered into the Treasury. And in heavy timber, boards, beams of both oak and alder, hurdles, laths, withies, grease, and glue, and certain small necessaries for the same works and carriage of the same during the same time, £13. 14s. 7d. And in lead, iron, steel, charcoal, [and] firewood for making ironwork; locks, ropes, glass, wax, pitch, and other things necessary for glass windows, both for the aforesaid

ecclesiam predictam & ad cementum faciendum cum cariagio eorundem per idem tempus xx li. xiiij sol. iij d. ob. Et in tegulis. cavillis. littera. arundine ad diversas domos cooperiendas & muros earundem operacionum cooperiendos viij li. v sol. per idem tempus. Et in tribus angelis ligneis factis ad tascham & positis in predicta ecclesia xx sol. Et in auro in folio aymall'. diversis coloribus & aliis necessariis ad picturam camere Regis per idem tempus vij li. xix sol. xj d. Et in stipendiis quorundam cementariorum. pavetariorum faciencium pavimenta coram diversis altaribus in eadem ecclesia. carpentariorum pictorum. plumbariorum. vitreariorum. minutorum operariorum & operacionum traditarum ad tascham & cuiusdam operarii facientis orlogium ad tascham per idem tempus. DCxlviij li. xij sol. viij d.

Summa misarum DCCCCv li. xiij sol. iiij d. Et debet CCCvj li. vij sol. viij d. ob.

Idem reddit compotum de eodem debito. In thesauro nichil. Et in superplusagio quod idem Magister Robertus & alii custodes earundem operacionum habent in Rotulo L° in compoto suo de eisdem operacionibus in Rotulo compotorum CC viij li. iiij d. ob. Et in alio superplusagio quod idem Magister & alii custodes earundem habent in Rotulo precedenti in predicto compoto suo in Rotulo compotorum iiij^{xx} xix li. iij sol. ij d. ob. Et habet de superplus xv sol. x d. ob.

(E 372/116, rot. 1^{d}.)

buildings and for the aforesaid church and for making cement, with carriage of the same during the same time, £20. 14*s.* 3½*d.* And in tiles, tile-pins, litter, [and] reeds for covering several buildings, and for covering the walls of the same works, £8. 5*s.* during the same time. And in three wooden angels, made at task, and placed in the aforesaid church, 20*s.* And in gold leaf, enamels, various colours, and in other things necessary for painting the king's chamber during the same time, £7. 19*s.* 11*d.* And in the wages of certain masons, paviors making pavements in front of various altars in the same church, carpenters, painters, plumbers, glaziers, labourers, and in works put out at task, and of a certain workman making a clock at task during the same time, £648. 12*s.* 8*d.*

Total of expenses, £905. 13*s.* 4*d.* And he owes £306. 7*s.* 8½*d.*

The same renders account of the same debt. Paid in cash, nothing. And in the balance, which the same Master Robert and the other keepers of the same works have in Roll 50 in their account of the same works in the Roll of Accounts, £208. 0*s.* 4½*d.* And in another balance which the same Master and the other keepers of the same works have in the preceding roll in their account aforesaid in the Rolls of Accounts, £99. 3*s.* 2½*d.* And he has a balance of 15*s.* 10½*d.*

16. Correspondence relating to the works at Westminster

(i) Suo speciali domino Edwardo de Westmonasterio suus R. de Shotendon' salutem quam sibi. Rogo uos quatinus sicut de uobis confido metallum ereum de quo uos rogaui tradatis domino H. capellano meo latori presencium & ego uobis inde satisfaciam quandocumque uolueritis. Et sic pro me faciatis ad presens quod uobis debeam ad grates speciales teneri. Valete. (Sewn on to E 101/466/29.)

(ii) Magistro Johanni de Oxonia suus R. de Bremel' salutem. Mitto vobis unam navatam marmoris per Osmundum latorem presencium cui habere faciatis quatuor li. & iij sol. & dim. marcam quam mihi acomodavit ad navem honerandam; et inde faciatis versus illos marenarios quod alias ad servicium nostrum fiant promtiores: et quam cicius poteritis michi denarios habere faciatis.

(Sewn on to E 101/467/1.)

(iii) Magistro Johanni de Oxonia suus Robertus de Bremele eandem quam sibi salutem & se totum. Mitto vobis unam marmoris navatam per Willelmum Justise cui habere faciatis pro frecto quinque marcas & dim. & decem solidos. & mittam vobis deo favente unam navatam ante Pentecost' & terciam si navim possim ad dictam petram deducendam invenire. Sciatis adventum meum in septimana Pentecost' & non ante quia temppus nunc instat in quo me absente negocia vestra non bene possunt expediri. (Sewn on to E 101/467/1.)

(iv) Amico suo karissimo magistro Johanni le Mazun suus W. de Engelby vicecomes Linc' salutem. cum dileccione scincera. Sciatis quod die sancte Margarete misi de Sancto Botulfo usque London' per preceptum domini Regis CCC.iiij^{xx}. vij pecias plumbi in quibus continentur xliij carrate per Simonem Mauger de Eylesford & postea misi per Stephanum Morice de Brigtlingee xj^{xx} & v pecias in quibus continentur xx carrate ad perfornandum lxiij carratas. Quod quidem plumbum tronatum fuit fideliter & plenarie per Nicholaum filium Jocei de London & coram ipso tradidi dictis Simoni & Stephano rectum pondus sicuti ipsi respondere voluerunt per duas tallias quas vobis mitto per latorem presencium. Unde beneplacitum vestrum & responsionem super hiis & aliis per eundem latorem litteratorie si placet michi significetis. Valete.

(Westminster Abbey Muniments, 16000(f).)

16. Correspondence relating to the works at Westminster

(i) R[obert] of Shottenden[1] sends warm greetings to his particular friend Sir Edward of Westminster. I ask you to justify my trust in you by handing over to Sir H. my chaplain the bearer of this letter the brass metal about which I asked you, and I will settle with you whenever you like. And if you do this for me now I shall be particularly grateful to you. Farewell. [1249]

(ii) To Master John of Oxford his [friend] Robert of Bromley sends greeting. I am sending you a shipload of marble by Osmund the bearer of these present (letters). Please let him have £4. 3*s*. and 6*s*. 8*d*. which he lent to me for the loading of the ship, and in this matter I beg you to behave towards those sailors so that at other times they may be the more ready for our service; and to let me have some money as quickly as you can. [1253]

(iii) To Master John of Oxford his [friend] R[obert] of Bromley sends the warmest greetings. I am sending you a shipload of marble by William Justise, who should be paid £4. 3*s*. 4*d*. for the freight; and, God willing, I may send you one shipload before Whitsun and a third if I can find a ship to carry the said stone. Know that I shall arrive during Whitsun week and not before, because this is a time when your business cannot be satisfactorily conducted in my absence. [1253]

(iv) To his dearest friend Master John the Mason, William of Ingelby, sheriff of Lincolnshire, sends greetings with sincere affection. Know that on the day of (the feast of) St. Margaret [either 8 or 20 July] I sent you from Boston to London by order of the lord king by Simon Mauger of Aylesford 387 pieces of lead which contain 43 chars, and afterwards I sent by Stephen Morice of Brightlingsea 225 pieces of lead containing 20 chars, in total 63 chars. This lead was faithfully and fully weighed by Nicholas FitzJoce of London and in his presence I delivered to the said Simon and Stephen the correct weight, as they themselves are prepared to answer, by two tallies which I am sending you by the bearer of this letter. Wherefore make known to me in writing your pleasure and answer on these and other matters by the same bearer if it please you. Farewell. [1259][2]

[1] A clerk in the king's service and later Dean of Chester.

[2] Cf. *Cal. Liberate Rolls 1251–60*, p. 458.

(v) Viro venerabili & discreto magistro Roberto de Beverle Ricardus le Wyte de quareria de Purbyke salutem in domino. Noverit discrescio vestra quod Petrus de Sartesye lator presencium in quantum potuit opus domini Regis penes nos in quareria expedivit emendo & cariando duas navatas petrarum ad opus domini Regis, ita scilicet quod omnibus computatis expensis exceptis stipendiis suis propriis custus dicti operis est xiij li. iij s. ob. In cuius rei testimonium litteras nostras patentes eidem habere fecimus.

Hiis testibus Petro de Clavile Willelmo de Clavile.

(Westminster Abbey Muniments, 16000(g).)

(v) To the respected and prudent Master Robert of Beverley Richard le Wyte of Purbeck quarry sends greeting in the Lord. Be it known to your prudence that Peter of Chertsey the bearer of these present (letters) did as much as he could to forward the work of the lord king in the quarry here by buying and carrying two shiploads of stone for the lord king's work, on such terms that all expenses included, except his own wages, the cost of the said work is £13. 3*s.* 0½*d.* In testimony of which we have given him our letters patent.

Witnesses: Peter of Clavile, William of Clavile.

[undated: between 1260 and 1272]

GLOSSARY OF TECHNICAL TERMS, ETC.

allocate	a writ crediting an accountant with a payment made by royal order.
ashlar	stone worked to a smooth face.
assise	shaped stones, here possibly forming a segment of a column (Salzman, p. 114).
bailey	a fortified enclosure forming part of a castle.
bailiwick	any administrative area (e.g. a county).
barbican	an outer fortification protecting a gateway.
bezant	a Byzantine gold coin worth between 10*s.* and 20*s.* sterling.
bosol'	segmental stones, e.g. forming sections of a column.
bos(s)eus	the plural of *bos(s)el*, a French term for a rounded moulding such as a roll or bowtell.
ceiling	the internal finish of a room, often panelling, but sometimes plaster.
cerches	see p. 251.
chapement bowe	probably a form of coping (Salzman, p. 109).
char	a measure of lead (literally 'a cart-load'). weighing about 2,184 lb.
coin	quoin, the stones forming the angles of a building.
ell	a measure of textiles equivalent to 45 inches.
fother	a weight of lead equivalent to $19\frac{1}{2}$ cwt.
gerb	a measure of iron (see sheaf).
hawk	a hod.
hes	a measure of iron (cf. Salzman, p. 287).
imprest	an advance of money to an accountant.
jamb	the vertical side of any opening.
liberate	a writ to the Treasury ordering the issue of money.
mark	the sum of 13*s.* 4*d.*
maul	a mason's hammer.
mullion	the perpendicular member dividing the lights of a window.
orbilon	perhaps stones cut in a circular or globular form.
orpiment	a yellow pigment.
parpent stone	a stone occupying the full thickness of a wall, so that it has two faces.
perch	a measure of length, now $5\frac{1}{2}$ yards.
pesage	a duty paid for the weighing of goods.
pott	a measure of sand.
prig-nail	a type of small nail.
puncheon	a short structural timber placed vertically.
quarter	a fourth part of a hundredweight (i.e. 28 lb.).

ragstone	a durable rough stone (in these accounts, from Kent).
sea-coal	coal brought by sea (usually from the Tyne).
seam	a weight equivalent to a quarter.
serches	see *cerches*.
sester	a measure equivalent to a quarter or 8 bushels.
sheaf	a weight of glass equivalent to 120 lb.; a weight of iron discussed by Salzman, p. 288.
sheriff's tourn	a biennial inspection of hundreds by the sheriff, usually productive of fines.
sinople	red ochre used as a pigment.
somer	a timber girder.
tablement	string-courses or the like.
tallage	a form of seigneurial taxation.
tally	a wooden stick marked so as to serve as a record of a financial transaction.
tingelnaill	a type of small nail.
verderer	a forest official responsible for preserving timber etc.
voussoir	one of the wedge-shaped stones forming an arch.
wey, weigh	a weight of glass equivalent to 5 lb. (Salzman, p. 175); a weight of lead equivalent to 182 lb. (Salzman, p. 263).
white cutter	a freemason.

GENERAL INDEX

Note. For the contents of the documents the references are to pages of the Latin text but proper names are in the forms adopted in the translation. A page-reference may imply more than one mention on the page in question.

Subjects not found in their alphabetical place in the index as a whole may be sought under one of the following chief subject-headings:

building operations, techniques and processes
building workers
furnishings, furniture
materials, building materials and components
tools, implements, equipment, utensils, etc.
trades and occupations
transport
weights and measures.

'The Building of the Tower of Babel': a drawing by an English artist of about 1300, showing the use of hurdles for ladders and scaffolding

PLATE 2

Dover Castle: an aerial view showing the twelfth-century keep and Inner Ward surrounded by the outer curtain, much of which was built during the reign of Henry III

Dover Castle: the curtain south of Peverell's Gate, showing masonry of Henry III's reign

PLATE 4

Dover Castle: The Constable's Tower

Dover Castle: The Fitzwilliam Gate

PLATE 6

Winchester Castle: interior of the Great Hall

Westminster Abbey: south side of the nave

PLATE 8

Westminster Abbey: the choir, looking east

Westminster Abbey: view from south transept

Westminster Abbey: the north transept

Westminster Abbey: the triforium of the north transept

PLATE 12

Westminster Abbey: the south wall of the south transept

Westminster Abbey: the triforium of the south transept

PLATE 14

Westminster Abbey: the entrance to the Chapter House

Westminster Abbey: the Chapter House

PLATE 16

Westminster Abbey: vaulting boss in south choir aisle